FEMINIST JUDGMENTS: FAMILY LAW OPINIONS REWRITTEN

This book provides new, feminist perspectives on famous family law cases that span generations. The chapters take court decisions and rewrite them with feminist ideas in mind. Each author of a rewritten opinion relied only on materials available at the time of the original decision. The decisions address topics such as the criminalization of polygamy, intimate partner violence as a ground for asylum, the enforcement of gestational surrogacy contracts, the rights of cohabitants, discrimination against transgender parents, immigration rules governing non-citizen parents, and child welfare and child support systems, among others. Each opinion is accompanied by a commentary that explains the original opinion as well as the case's contemporary relevance. The combination of a rewritten opinion and its commentary provides an in-depth examination of the most important topics in family law.

RACHEL REBOUCHÉ is Associate Dean for Research and Professor of Law at Temple University Beasley School of Law. She is an author of casebooks in family law and gender and the law. She has also co-authored *Governance Feminism: An Introduction* and co-edited *Governance Feminism: Notes from the Field*. She has published on family law, comparative law, relational contracts, and reproductive health in various journals and is currently working on a book on reproductive justice.

Feminist Judgments Series Editors

Bridget J. Crawford
Elisabeth Haub School of Law at Pace University

Kathryn M. Stanchi
University of Nevada, Las Vegas William S. Boyd School of Law

Linda L. Berger
University of Nevada, Las Vegas William S. Boyd School of Law

Advisory Panel for Feminist Judgments Series

Dean Spade, *Associate Professor of Law, Seattle University School of Law*

Robin L. West, *Frederick J. Haas Professor of Law and Philosophy, Georgetown University Law Center*

Verna L. Williams, *Dean and Nippert Professor of Law, University of Cincinnati College of Law*

Feminist Judgments: Family Law Opinions Rewritten

Edited by

RACHEL REBOUCHÉ
Temple University Beasley School of Law

CAMBRIDGE
UNIVERSITY PRESS

CAMBRIDGE
UNIVERSITY PRESS

University Printing House, Cambridge CB2 8BS, United Kingdom

One Liberty Plaza, 20th Floor, New York, NY 10006, USA

477 Williamstown Road, Port Melbourne, VIC 3207, Australia

314–321, 3rd Floor, Plot 3, Splendor Forum, Jasola District Centre, New Delhi – 110025, India

79 Anson Road, #06–04/06, Singapore 079906

Cambridge University Press is part of the University of Cambridge.

It furthers the University's mission by disseminating knowledge in the pursuit of education, learning, and research at the highest international levels of excellence.

www.cambridge.org
Information on this title: www.cambridge.org/9781108471701
DOI: 10.1017/9781108556989

First published 2020

A catalogue record for this publication is available from the British Library.

Library of Congress Cataloging-in-Publication Data
NAMES: Rebouché, Rachel, editor.
TITLE: Feminist judgments : family law opinions rewritten / edited by Rachel Rebouché, Temple University, Philadelphia.
OTHER TITLES: Feminist judgments (Family law)
DESCRIPTION: Cambridge, United Kingdom ; New York, NY, USA : Cambridge University Press, 2020. | Series: Feminist judgment series | Includes bibliographical references and index.
IDENTIFIERS: LCCN 2019042607 (print) | LCCN 2019042608 (ebook) | ISBN 9781108471701 (hardback) | ISBN 9781108458337 (paperback) | ISBN 9781108556989 (epub)
SUBJECTS: LCSH: Domestic relations–United States–Cases. | Feminist jurisprudence–United States.
CLASSIFICATION: LCC KF505 .F46 2020 (print) | LCC KF505 (ebook) | DDC 346.7301/5–dc23
LC record available at https://lccn.loc.gov/2019042607
LC ebook record available at https://lccn.loc.gov/2019042608

ISBN 978-1-108-47170-1 Hardback
ISBN 978-1-108-45833-7 Paperback

Contents

Advisory Panel for Feminist Judgments: Family Law Opinions Rewritten

Professor Naomi Cahn, George Washington Law School

Naomi Cahn is the Harold H. Greene Professor of Law at GW Law. She has written numerous law review articles on family law, feminist jurisprudence, and trusts and estates. She is the author of several books, including *The New Kinship* (2012); and *Test Tube Families: Why the Fertility Market Needs Legal Regulation* (2009); she has coauthored *On the Frontlines: Women, Gender, and the Post-Conflict Process* (2011; with Professors Fionnuala Ni Aoláin and Dina Haynes); *Marriage Markets* (2014) and *Red Families v. Blue Families* (2010), both with Professor June Carbone; and she has co-written casebooks in the fields of family law and trusts and estates. Her work has been featured in *The New York Times, The Washington Post, The Christian Science Monitor*, and *The New Yorker*, and she has appeared on numerous other media outlets.

Professor Cahn is a member of the American Law Institute and the American College of Trust and Estate Counsel. In 2017, she was awarded the Harry Krause Lifetime Achievement in Family Law by the University of Illinois College of Law. Prior to joining the faculty at GW Law in 1993, Professor Cahn worked in a domestic violence clinic at Georgetown University Law Center, and practiced with Hogan Lovells in Washington, DC, and with Community Legal Services in Philadelphia. At GW Law, she teaches courses on family law, trusts and estates, elder law, feminist jurisprudence, and child, family, and state.

Professor Nancy Dowd, University of Florida Law School

Professor Dowd is the David H. Levin Chair in Family Law and the Emeritus Director of the Center on Children and Families. She was the 2017

Fulbright-Lund University Distinguished Chair in Public International Law at the Raoul Wallenberg Institute of Human Rights and Humanitarian Law and Lund University. In 2018 and 2019, Professor Dowd was the Distinguished Guest Professor at Aalborg University. Her current work is in the areas of children's constitutional equality rights, and a general theory of children's rights, as well as making the case for children's specific right to equal education based on developmental equality. In addition, she writes about a developmental model of equality and focusing on the life course of African American boys from birth to age eighteen. Professor Dowd's most recent book is *Reimagining Equality: A New Deal for Children of Color* (2018). Two of her previous books focus on the radical reform needed in the juvenile justice system. *Justice for Kids* (2011) brings together activists and scholars to articulate ways to keep kids out of the juvenile justice system by diversion into other more helpful and supportive resolutions. *A New Juvenile Justice System* (2015) articulates the vision of a new youth justice system focused on child well-being and public safety. Her book, *The Man Question: Male Privilege and Subordination* (2010), explores masculinities theories as a means to expand gender analysis and incorporate hierarchies that affect gender, particularly race and class.

Professor Dowd served as the Director of the Center on Children and Families until 2015, and in that role focused on issues of juvenile justice, social justice, nontraditional families, gay and lesbian rights, and collaboration with the Center for the Study of Race and Race Relations on issues of race and families. While director, she was also involved with successful grants that established the Intimate Partner Violence Assistance Clinic, a groundbreaking collaboration between law and medicine to establish a cutting-edge clinic.

Professor Theresa Glennon, Temple University Beasley School of Law

Theresa Glennon is a professor of law at Temple University Beasley School of Law. Her teaching and scholarship focuses on the legal rights of children and families, with particular emphasis on family law, education, race, and disability. Prior to joining the Temple faculty in 1993, she was an assistant professor at the University of Maryland School of Law, where she taught in the Legal Theory and Practice Program. She was a staff attorney at the Education Law Center in Philadelphia from 1985 to 1989. Professor Glennon's courses at Temple include family law; torts; theory, policy and practice in family law; international and comparative perspectives on family law; and child custody law. Her family law publications cover a wide range of topics, including assisted reproductive technologies, child custody and custody relocation disputes, the effort to harmonize family law in Europe, paternity disputes, second parent adoptions, and the rights of mothers with mental illnesses in the child welfare system. Her publications in the area of education law have focused primarily on the issues of race and disability in education.

Professor Glennon is trained as a mediator in divorce and child custody matters and served as a volunteer mediator for the custody mediation project of the Good Shepherd Mediation Program. She is a member of the Family Law Sections of the American Bar Association, the Pennsylvania Bar Association and the Philadelphia Bar Association. She served as Chair of the Family and Juvenile Law Section of the American Association of Law Schools in 2012–2013 and continues to serve on its Executive Committee. She served for five years on the Board of Trustees of the Education Law Center, ten years on the Institutional Review Board for Public/Private Ventures, a nonprofit that conducts demonstration projects and research on programs for children, and four years on the Board of Trustees of Community Legal Services.

Professor Emerita Leslie Harris, University of Oregon School of Law

Leslie Harris is the Dorothy Kliks Fones Professor of Law Emerita at the University of Oregon, where she taught Family Law and other courses and directed the Oregon Child Advocacy Project, which provides education and assistance to attorneys advocating for the interests of children. She has written law review articles about the child welfare system, nontraditional families, family support duties, and property rights at divorce and is the coauthor of textbooks on family law and children and the law, which are widely used throughout the United States. She is an elected member of the American Law Institute and serves on advisory boards for the Oregon Juvenile Court Improvement Project and several other organizations. She was one of the first recipients of the law school's Orlando John Hollis Faculty Teaching Award.

Professor Solangel Maldonado, Seton Hall University School of Law

Professor Maldonado is the Eleanor Bontecou Professor of Law at Seton Hall Law. She teaches courses on family law, torts, wills and trusts, gender and the law, race and the law, and bioethics. Her scholarship has focused on the intersection of race and family law and the law's influence on social norms of post-separation parenthood. Her current work examines how the law shapes romantic preferences that perpetuate racial, economic, and social inequality.

Professor Maldonado is one of the reporters of the American Law Institute's Restatement of the Law, Children and the Law (in progress). She is a co-editor of *Family Law: Cases and Materials* (7th ed. 2019; with Judith Areen, Marc Spindelman, and Philomila Tsoukala) and *Family Law in the World Community* (3rd ed. 2015; with D. Marianne Blair, Merle H. Weiner, and Barbara Stark). She also serves on the editorial board of the *Family Court Review*.

Prior to joining the Seton Hall Law faculty, Professor Maldonado was a litigation associate with Kaye, Scholer, Fierman, Hays & Handler, LLP (now Arnold & Porter, LLP) and with Sidley, Austin, Brown & Wood in New York. She also clerked for then District Court Judge Joseph A. Greenaway, Jr., now on the United States Court of Appeals. She received her BA from Columbia College and her JD from Columbia Law School, where she was a Harlan Fiske Stone Scholar and the Managing Editor of the *Columbia Journal of Gender and Law*. In 2015–2016, she was a visiting scholar at the Center for the Study of Law and Culture at Columbia Law School. She has taught at Columbia Law School, Cardozo Law School, and the University of Illinois College of Law.

Professor Linda McClain, Boston University School of Law

Linda C. McClain is the Robert Kent Professor of Law at Boston University School of Law and is also affiliated faculty in the Women's Gender & Sexuality Studies Program. In addition to teaching family law, gender and law, and feminist jurisprudence, she teaches a seminar on Marriage, Families, and Gender in BU's Kilachand Honors College. She has authored or co-authored several books, most recently *Who's the Bigot? Learning from Conflicts over Marriage and Civil Rights Law* (2020). Her other books include *The Place of Families: Fostering Capacity, Equality, and Responsibility* (2006); *Ordered Liberty: Rights, Responsibilities, and Virtues* (2013; with James E. Fleming); two edited volumes, *Gender Equality: Dimensions of Women's Equal Citizenship* (2009; paperback ed., 2012; with Joanna L. Grossman; mentioned in the credits of the film, *On the Basis of Sex*), and *What Is Parenthood?: Contemporary Debates about the Family* (2013; with Daniel Cere); the co-authored casebook, *Contemporary Family Law* (5th ed. 2020), and the co-authored textbook, *Gay Rights and the Constitution* (2016). Professor McClain has also published numerous articles and book chapters.

Professor McClain has been a Laurence S. Rockefeller Visiting Faculty Fellow at Princeton University Center for Human Value and a faculty fellow at Harvard University's Edmond J. Safra Center for Ethics. She has taught as a visiting faculty at Harvard Law School, Penn Law, and the University of Virginia. A past chair of the Family and Juvenile Law Section of the Association of American Law Schools, she currently serves on the Executive Committee of that Section and the Section on Women in Legal Education. She is a member of the American Law Institute and the Council on Contemporary Families.

Co-Dean and Professor Kimberly Mutcherson, Rutgers Law School

Kimberly Mutcherson is Co-Dean and Professor of Law at Rutgers Law School. Her scholarly work is at the intersection of family law, health law, and bioethics, and she writes on issues related to reproductive justice, with a focus on assisted reproduction and abortion.

Dean Mutcherson teaches Family Law, Torts, South African Constitutional Law, and Bioethics, Babies, & Babymaking. She has served as a senior fellow/ sabbatical visitor at the Center for Gender and Sexuality Law at Columbia Law School, a visiting scholar at the Center for Bioethics at the University of Pennsylvania, and as a fellow at the Institute for Research on Women at Rutgers University. She won the Center for Reproductive Rights Innovation in Scholarship Award in 2013 and a Chancellor's Teaching Excellence Award in 2011.

Dean Mutcherson received her BA in history from the University of Pennsylvania and her JD from Columbia Law School, where she was a Stone Scholar. At Columbia, she received the Samuel I. Rosenman Prize for excellence in public law courses and outstanding qualities of citizenship and leadership at the law school. She also received the Kirkland and Ellis Fellowship for postgraduate public interest work. Prior to joining the faculty at Rutgers Law School in 2002, Dean Mutcherson was an acting assistant professor of lawyering at the New York University School of Law, a consulting attorney at the Center for Reproductive Law and Policy (now the Center for Reproductive Rights), and a staff attorney at the HIV Law Project.

Contributors

Jamie R. Abrams is Assistant Dean for Intellectual Life and Professor of Law at the University of Louisville Brandeis School of Law.

Mary Anne Case is Arnold I. Shure Professor of Law at the University of Chicago Law School.

Albertina Antognini is Associate Professor at the University of Arizona James E. Rogers College of Law.

Susan Frelich Appleton is Lemma Barkeloo and Phoebe Couzins Professor of Law at the Washington University School of Law.

Warren Binford is Professor of Law at Willamette University.

June Carbone is Robina Chair of Law, Science and Technology at the University of Minnesota School of Law.

Jo Carrillo is Professor of Law at University of California, Hastings, College of Law.

John Culhane is Distinguished Professor of Law at the Delaware Law School, Widener University.

Raff Donelson is Assistant Professor of Law at Penn State Dickinson School of Law.

Kate Sablosky Elengold is Clinical Associate Professor at the University of North Carolina School of Law.

Martha Ertman is Carole and Hanan Sibel Research Professor at the University of Maryland Law School.

Marie A. Failinger is Judge Edward J. Devitt Professor of Law at Mitchell Hamline School of Law.

Cynthia Godsoe is Professor of Law at Brooklyn Law School.

Melanie B. Jacobs is Senior Associate Dean for Academic Affairs and Professor of Law at the Michigan State University College of Law.

Lisa Fishbayn Joffe is Director of the Hadassah-Brandeis Institute at Brandeis University.

Alicia Kelly is Associate Dean for Faculty Development and Strategic Initiatives and Professor of Law at the Delaware Law School, Widener University.

Laura Kessler is Professor of Law at the University of Utah School of Law.

Suzanne A. Kim is Judge Denny Chin Scholar and Professor of Law at Rutgers Law School.

Aníbal Rosario-Lebrón is Assistant Professor of Lawyering Skills at Howard University School of Law.

Elizabeth L. MacDowell is Professor of Law at the William S. Boyd School of Law, University of Nevada, Las Vegas.

Katherine Macfarlane is Associate Professor of Law at the University of Idaho College of Law.

Maya Manian is Professor of Law at the University of San Francisco School of Law.

Seema Mohapatra is Associate Professor of Law at Indiana University Robert H. McKinney School of Law, Indianapolis.

Mary-Beth Moylan is Associate Dean for Academic Affairs and Experiential Learning and Professor of Lawyering Skills at the University of the Pacific, McGeorge School of Law.

Kristen Murray is Professor of Law at Temple University Beasley School of Law.

Natalie Nanasi is Assistant Professor of Law and Director of the Judge Elmo B. Hunter Legal Center for Victims of Crimes Against Women at Southern Methodist University School of Law.

Nancy Polikoff is Professor of Law Emerita at American University Washington College of Law.

Suzan M. Pritchett is Director of Clinics & Experiential Education and Associate Professor of Law at Drake University Law School.

Rachel Rebouché is Associate Dean for Research and Professor of Law at Temple University Beasley School of Law.

Macarena Saez is Director of the International Human Rights Clinic and Practitioner in Residence at American University Washington College of Law.

Tracy Thomas is John F. Seiberling Chair of Constitutional Law and Professor of Law at the University of Akron Law School of Law.

Zvi Triger is Associate Professor at The Haim Striks School of Law in Israel.

Jessica Dixon Weaver is Associate Professor of Law at Southern Methodist University School of Law.

Acknowledgments

This book is the product of feminist collaboration – feminist legal scholars collaborating with each other to publish rewritten judgments and commentaries. And my collaboration with those authors has been the best part about editing this collection. I thank each of them for their dedication and care in writing this book. I also thank the Feminist Judgment editors, who have provided consistent support and whose vision has generated this important series. In particular, Kathy Stanchi recruited me to edit this volume and has been helpful at every turn. I also gained insight from Kim Mutcherson, who shared her materials and advice from editing the Reproductive Justice volume in the series.

This book benefited from numerous conferences and workshops at which various chapters were presented. A participant in those conversations has been Dara Purvis, who was an early contributor to the development of this project. Likewise, the Advisory Committee, whose distinguished biographies are described above, offered guidance about which cases to select and how to organize the book.

Finally, I had generous support from my home institution, the Temple University Beasley School of Law. Foremost in offering assistance was senior legal assistant, Erica Maier. She provided invaluable help in preparing the manuscript for copyediting and drafted the first version of the index.

Acknowledgments

1

Introduction

RACHEL REBOUCHÉ

WHAT IS FAMILY LAW?

There is a canon of family law.[1] Those of us who teach family law know the cases that appear in almost every family law casebook, and that are the stand-out examples of core family law doctrines. Even though there are numerous cases from which to choose, picking iconic cases to rewrite was one of the easier tasks of my job in editing a *Feminist Judgments* volume on family law.

Editing a volume of rewritten cases from a feminist perspective, however, is a project that I approached with some trepidation. So much of family law has been influenced by feminist theory and feminist thought. Decades of scholarly writings map the intersection of feminism and gender rights and the laws governing, for example, marriage, divorce, cohabitation, parentage, child custody, and child support. The chapters in this book describe the history of feminist engagement in family law and the major shifts that have occurred (and continue to occur) in the field. Authors canvass the demise of legally enshrined coverture, the introduction of no-fault divorce and the equitable distribution of property, changing custody presumptions, standards for enforcing pre- or post-marital contracts, the increasing reliance on assisted reproductive technologies, recognition of various sexual identities, and the extension of relationship rights to couples of the same sex and to nonmarried partners. Given the earliest case in this book was decided in 1879 (on polygamy) and the most recent in 2018 (on asylum law), there is a lot of ground to cover.

The strength of this volume is not just its relationship to traditionally defined family law topics; it is also the authors' expertise in the family law issues that suffuse other legal fields. In cases that span welfare law, criminal

[1] Jill Hasday, *The Canon of Family Law*, 57 Stan. L. Rev. 825 (2004); Shani King, *The Family Law Canon in a (Post?) Racial Era*, 72 Ohio St. L. Rev. 575 (2011).

justice, immigration, education, and civil procedure, this book pushes the boundaries of how family law is defined. In this vein, the volume resists "family law exceptionalism," or the tendency to conceive of the field in narrow terms, which too often has discounted how various laws across disciplines govern and shape intimacy, sexuality, dependency, and relational exchange.[2] The regulation of the family and definitions of family are important in almost every legal area, even those which are not, unfortunately, captured in this volume. Were it not for the limitations of space, rewritten decisions in tax, employment, corporations, and torts could have easily captured how family law and feminism inform each other.[3] As it stands, I selected the cases for this book after consulting with an Advisory Panel, which suggested dozens of decisions from various courts and jurisdictions.[4] The Advisory Panel, composed of leading family law scholars and thanked in the acknowledgments, provided invaluable guidance in choosing the fifteen decisions that comprise the chapters of this book.[5]

Each chapter reflects longstanding and important feminist debates in the field of family law. For instance, chapters implicitly and explicitly push at the so-called divide between public and private regulation, drawing on an ongoing conversation about public and private spheres in family law.[6] Commentaries and rewritten opinions draw in other debates at the intersection of family law and feminist legal theory. How and why should intimacy be treated distinctly from, say, commercial, relationships, and what legal status should express that intimacy? When and why do feminists pull the legal levers of state punishment, such as in child support enforcement or in criminal consequences for domestic violence, and what are the lived effects that result? How does feminist legal theory embrace agendas for racial justice and aid in resisting old and new forms of discrimination? What theories of

2 For an ongoing conversation about "family law exceptionalism" among family law scholars, see Harvard Law School, *Up against Family Law Exceptionalism*, http://www.law.harvard.edu/faculty/jhalley/plst/Halley.pdf.

3 See the other volumes of the Feminist Judgment series in these areas.

4 I did not consider cases that were rewritten for the *Feminist Judgments: Rewritten Opinions of the United States Supreme Court* volume or that will be rewritten for other volumes in this series, such as on Reproductive Justice. I also avoided, to a significant extent, cases that have been the subject of projects like *Family Law Stories* (West Academic 2007).

5 Authors responded to a call for papers that I issued nationally and ranked their top three case choices; some judgments received a lot of interest and others were selected by only one or two applicants.

6 *See, e.g.*, Frances Olsen, *The Family and the Market: A Study of Ideology and Legal Reform*, 96 HARV. L. REV. 1497, 1498 (1983); Maxine Eichner, *The Privatized American Family*, 93 NOTRE DAME L. REV. 213 (2017).

masculinity emerge in feminist accounts? This introduction can only set forth an incomplete list of complicated questions, and responses to these queries depend on what one means by "feminism." The chapters of this book offer a range of answers.

WHAT IS A FEMINIST JUDGMENT?

Each chapter begins with a short commentary that provides context for the original case and introduces the approach of the rewritten decision. The new version of the iconic or important opinion follows, as a reimagined majority, concurring, or dissenting opinion, and relies only on materials available at the time of the original decision.

Although feminism and family law are a seemingly natural fit, taking family law's important cases and rewriting them is an exercise in creativity. Of course, some decisions lend themselves to a feminist rewrite. Judicial decisions spurred feminist activism because a court's interpretation of law – or the law itself – disadvantaged women or entrenched sexism. In these decisions, authors chose to rewrite majority opinions and reach opposite conclusions. Other original opinions track closely the feminist thinking of the era and could be called then, as they are likely thought of now, feminist judgments. Contributors to this book embraced that time period's thinking but wrote concurrences or differently styled majority opinions to reach a different result or to offer a different remedy. And then some rewritten opinions, because of the era or the arguments of the court, take the form of strong dissents, expressing feminist reasoning through disagreements with the majority's decision at that time.

In incorporating an array of feminist ideas, authors performed innovative and original research for their chapters. They searched the archives at the Library of Congress; retrieved original trial transcripts in litigation that occurred decades ago; interviewed the attorneys and, in one instance, a party of cases. Contributors dug into the facts of decisions, spotlighting details that showed the litigants in very different lights. They uncovered writings from scholars and advocates that reveal the early roots of feminist thinking – all materials available at the time of the original opinion's writing, but sources that were overlooked or ignored. Again, each author of a rewritten opinion was bound to the rules that govern the Feminist Judgments series: authors could only rely on the record of the original case and the precedent at the time of original writing. In tackling this endeavor, the process for each chapter varied based on the writer, but each chapter benefited from collaboration and dialogue between judgment and commentary authors. And as will be apparent in chapters that follow, some commentators and opinion authors disagreed, highlighting the diversity of feminist approaches.

A judgment can be feminist in numerous ways. The reader familiar with feminist legal writings readily will identify explicit and implicit invocation of prominent strands of feminist thought. These most frequently include liberal feminism, dominance feminism, cultural feminism, intersectional feminism, and sex-positive feminism.[7] This introduction will not affix definitions to these categories of feminisms; many of the commentaries that follow explain what they mean by these terms. Moreover, employing labels like "liberal feminism" risks ignoring divisions and contestations within feminist theory and can fail to recognize how feminisms overlap, inform each other, and conflict.[8] Instead, this volume tries to capture the timelessness and timeliness of feminist debates, bridging generations of feminist thinking and advocacy. This is an important moment for feminist legal theory to affirm its contemporary relevance and to map its future trajectories. Feminist theory must interrogate the deepening inequalities that characterize the distribution of resources. Racial justice and gender identity demand more attention. Feminist theory historically marginalized race and sexuality (as well as other sources of vulnerability) in its analysis of the harms that most affect its traditional subject – women.

Thus, perhaps the more interesting aspect of this book answers the question, why rewrite decisions in the first place? Is this project self-indulgent? It is no doubt a privilege and a luxury to imagine yourself a judge and pass judgment in your own voice. But what emerged from the process of writing this book – discussed among contributors at a number of conferences and workshops – is how generative reimagining the law can be. Among the reasons for writing these chapters and editing this book are to see more clearly the paths not taken: ideas, facts, and sources that could have supported alternative justifications or outcomes. Many commentators and opinion authors found a source of empowerment in rediscovering feminist ideas that were alive all along. Had their visions been made real, law and law reform strategies could have taken different courses. Imagine a U.S. Supreme Court that interpreted the Constitution to require the state to ensure people's basic

7 See Martha Chamallas, Introduction to Feminist Legal Theory (3d ed., Aspen 2013); Bridget J. Crawford & Anthony C. Infanti, *Introduction*, *in* Feminist Judgments: Rewritten Tax Opinions (Bridget J. Crawford & Anthony C. Infanti eds., 2018).

8 Janet Halley, *What Forms of Feminism Have Gained Inclusion in the Legal Order?*, in Governance Feminism: An Introduction (Janet Halley et al. eds., 2018).

needs were met, as Professor Susan Appleton writes in her reimagined *Dandridge v. Williams* opinion (Chapter 4). Seeing the Constitution as a source of positive rights to minimum welfare would change people's entitlements to food, security, and shelter.

In this vein, envisioning new directions and other possibilities for family law in 2019 is a politically salient project. Taking a feminist perspective can be a complicated endeavor, but it can also help transform law, to which the field of family law is a testament.

A ROADMAP FOR THE BOOK

The following roadmap provides a brief guide to what the chapters offer and suggests what themes circulate throughout the book. The cases appear in order of their date of original decision.

Professor Laura Kessler writes a dissent in the case of *Reynolds v. United States*, 98 U.S. 145 (1879). Contrary to original majority opinion, in which the U.S. Supreme Court upheld the convictions of Mormon polygamists, Kessler would have found a violation of polygamists' First Amendment right to free exercise of religion. Her reasoning is not only grounded in First Amendment principles, but also shines a light on the Court's contradictory jurisprudence on women's rights in marriage. She questions the majority's reflexive defense of monogamy as liberating for women and probes how the decision of the Court undercut the agency of Utah women in polygamous unions – wives who refused to testify against their husbands, who protested the federal government's treatment of Mormon communities, and who were the among the first to vote. Professor Marie Failinger's commentary contributes to the rich history in which Utah men and women were prosecuted for their marital arrangements. Rather than universally hurting women, both the imagined dissent and the commentary ask what happened to the women that the Supreme Court purportedly tried to save.

Professors Martha Ertman and Zvi Triger rewrite the majority opinion in the Nebraska Supreme Court case, *McGuire v. McGuire*, 59 N.W.2d 336 (Neb. 1953). In the original decision, the court held that spouses cannot sue each other for financial support while the parties remain living together in a marriage. Professor Ertman with Professor Triger, who joined as a concurring judge, would have allowed Mrs. McGuire to assert an equitable claim against Mr. McGuire for reasonable support, having received the bare minimum of support during the marriage. They note the then-recent changes in property distribution and spousal support that, though only relevant in divorce, recognize the rights of both spouses as partners to share in marital wealth. A claim for restitution or unjust enrichment would help Mrs. McGuire receive a return on what she invested over the course of the relationship without requiring her to seek a divorce. Writing the commentary, Professor Mary Anne Case disagrees with the premise of the rewritten judgment and focuses on Mrs. McGuire's agency. In Professor Case's view, Mrs. McGuire received what she bargained for in marrying an extraordinarily frugal man (to paraphrase the original decision) and by keeping separate her property (both by her labor and from a first marriage). Professor Case argues that the original decision allows couples to arrange their financial affairs and living arrangements in ways that suit their individual and potentially idiosyncratic needs.

Professor Susan Frelich Appleton rewrites the majority opinion in *Dandridge v. Williams*, 397 U.S. 471 (1970), a case upholding Maryland's limits on public assistance based on the number of dependents in a household. In the original opinion, the U.S. Supreme Court concluded that the law violated neither the Social Security Act nor the Constitution's Equal Protection and Due Process Clauses. Professor Appleton would have reached the opposite conclusion. Relying on then contemporary case law and writings on equal protection, she holds that distinctions affecting procreation based on income are subject to strict scrutiny analysis. Perhaps Professor Appleton's most robust justification for striking down welfare caps is a positive right to minimum welfare. That is, the Constitution guarantees "a right to the basic necessities of life, in turn imposing on society, that is, the state, an obligation to provide such basic necessities." As this introduction has already asked, how different would U.S. law and policy be if there was a right to minimum welfare? Professor Maya Manian takes up that question and reflects on how the rewritten *Dandridge* could have shaped the Court's reproductive rights jurisprudence, assessing a line of cases allowing states and the federal government to limit government funding of abortion. If alleviating the conditions of poverty is the responsibility of the state, then denying medically necessary abortion care under a state Medicaid program is difficult to justify.

The rewritten *Wisconsin v. Yoder*, 406 U.S. 205 (1972), by Professor Kristen Murray, would have upheld a Wisconsin law compelling Amish parents to send children to public school after the eighth grade – a law the Supreme Court held violated parents' rights under the Due Process Clause and the First Amendment. Professor Murray gives compelling reasons why the state's interest in education outweighs the Amish parents' desire to shield children from worldly influences after a certain age. Like the dissent offered by Justice Douglas in the original decision, Professor Murray considers the hardships imposed on youth who are deprived of a high school education. But unlike Justice Douglas, Murray's feminist account focuses on the role of daughters in Amish societies, who may have limited freedom to exit communities without education, having devoted themselves to skills that may not be rewarded – rightly or wrongly – outside Amish society. Professor Lisa Fishbayn Joffe brings an important historical and feminist perspective to the "right of exit" for Amish youth once they become adults. Professor Fishbayn Joffe demonstrates how the freedom to leave, as a safety valve for withdrawing from school, is illusory at best. Seldom are those leaving Amish communities, particularly women leaving marriages, financially or socially equipped to enter non-Amish society.

Professor Kate Sablosky Elengold writes a concurrence to the majority opinion in *Marvin v. Marvin*, 557 P.2d 106 (Cal. 1976), which recognized that cohabiting partners in nonmarital relationships may bring claims for property and support against each other based on express and implied contracts. Professor Sablosky Elengold writes a concurrence in order to emphasize the different treatment of married and unmarried partners and to provide guidance to lower courts for hearing the contract claims of unmarried partners. To the last point, she argues that future courts should rely on theories of trust. Theories of constructive or resulting trust sidestep questions of contribution, focusing on intent rather than the earnings invested in the accumulation of property jointly enjoyed. Professor Aníbal Rosario Lebrón supports the rewritten opinion's approach, explaining how and why, on remand, Michelle Marvin received nothing from her oral agreement with Lee Marvin. Professor Rosario Lebrón champions the feminist argument that courts recognize the financial value of nonwage domestic labor. And he explores how the rewritten decision could confer recognition on contracts made during the course of a range of relationships, not just those relationships that look like a contemporary marriage.

In the rewritten *Kulko v. Superior Court*, 436 U.S. 84 (1978), Professor Katherine Macfarlane dissents from the original Supreme Court opinion, which held that a father was not subject to personal jurisdiction in the state in which his children, to whom he owed child support, lived with their mother. Professor Macfarlane emphasizes the subtle bias against the mother's choices: the implication that her decision to divorce and then move to another state (with children who elected to voluntarily relocate there) was what severed the relationship between the father and the children, and created an impediment to forming ties with the new state. As Professor Macfarlane notes, the majority decision ignored the many ways in which a noncustodial father avails himself of the benefits provided by the state where the custodial parent resides; for example, relying on tax, education, transportation, and other systems, all publicly funded. Professor Mary-Beth Moylan highlights the salient gender critiques that followed *Kulko*.[9] She puts the case in its modern context by explaining the federal legislation that addressed the jurisdictional problems of child support and custody enforcement highlighted by *Kulko*.

In perhaps one of the most moving cases in the book, Professor Nancy Polikoff rewrites the majority decision of the Nevada Supreme Court in *Daly v. Daly*, 715 P.2d 56 (Nev. 1986). In *Daly*, the court upheld the termination of parental rights of Suzanne Daly, a father who had sex-reassignment surgery. Relying on Nevada's criteria for the termination of parental rights, Professor Polikoff holds that the lower courts misapplied the state statute. She demonstrates how the trial court's decision relied on discriminatory stereotypes about transgender parents and embraced the bias that motivated the mother's obstruction of visitation with Suzanne. In his commentary, Professor Raff Donelson probes how anti-trans tropes continue to exist in family law and circulate in popular opinion. In this vein, he tracks the still-current debate among feminists about how to recognize and to represent the rights of the trans community.

The original *Michael H. v. Gerald D.*, 491 U.S. 110 (1989) upheld California's statutory provision that a husband is conclusively presumed to be the parent of a child born during marriage, even in the face of genetic proof that he is not the biological father. Professor Albertina Antognini's rewritten majority opinion holds that the California presumption violates the Constitution on two grounds. Professor Antognini writes that the statute violates the Equal Protection Clause by discriminating on the basis of sex and the Due Process Clause by refusing to acknowledge the parent-child relationship that had developed between the nonmarital biological father and the child. In short, Professor Antognini recognizes legal rights for more than two parents, testing both marriage and biology as definitions of parentage. In doing so, she expands both our legal and cultural notions of what constitutes a family. Professor Suzanne Kim's commentary notes the implications of a decision that confers parental rights on married as well as unmarried fathers and explains what that recognition would mean for parents who have children within same-sex relationships. She notes how contemporary approaches to parentage, such as those contemplated by the 2017 Uniform Parentage Act, move away from gendered language and from the status-driven distinctions of marriage or biology.

DeShaney v. Winnebago County Department of Social Services, 489 U.S. 189 (1989), is a case infamous for its tragic facts. A child's mother, the

[9] Judith Resnik, *"Naturally" without Gender: Women, Jurisdiction, and the Federal Courts*, 66 N.Y.U. L. Rev. 1682 (1991).

noncustodial parent, sued Wisconsin social workers after the father's abuse resulted in the child's severe brain damage and a lifelong coma. The Supreme Court held that the failure of the state agency to protect the child did not violate the child's Fourteenth Amendment right to liberty. Professor Jessica Dixon Weaver rewrites the majority opinion and holds the agency accountable under the Constitution – both because the agency had established a special relationship by previously investigating child abuse and, under Section 1983, because of the state's "deliberate indifference." She shows how the ratification of the Fourteenth Amendment was a response to states' indifference to African Americans' suffering after slavery and connects that history to the state's historic treatment of children as property. The result is a judgment that obligates the state to protect the populations subject to historic discrimination. In her commentary, Professor Macarena Saez notes how Professor Dixon Weaver's opinion would have set the application of Section 1983 on a different jurisprudential course, specifically strengthening protections for survivors of intimate partner violence whose state protective orders had been ignored or unenforced.

Professors Alicia Kelly and John Culhane address the fairness of premarital agreements and reimagine the pro-contract case, *Simeone v. Simeone*, 581 A.2d 162 (Pa. 1990). The Supreme Court of Pennsylvania held that courts should enforce premarital contracts so long as couples signed them voluntarily and with full disclosure, meeting the requirements of any contract. Professor Kelly, writing for the majority, struck down the contract in *Simeone* for failing tests for procedural and substantive fairness. The premarital agreement at issue would have left the wife, who had almost nothing in the way of assets and limited earning capacity, with far less than she would have received at divorce. Professor Culhane's concurrence emphasizes the power imbalances that continue to characterize marital relationships, especially when one spouse performs the bulk of unremunerated labor in the home and one spouse is a high-income earner. He challenges the conclusion of the original majority, which justified the decision to uphold a lopsided bargain on the purported basis of sex equality in bargaining power. Professor Jamie Abrams notes the introduction of no-fault divorce as well as reform in property division and spousal support laws, which signal the state's recognition that marriage is a partnership. However, she concludes, as Professor Kelly does, that even though many of wives' previous legal incapacities have been removed from statute books, gendered scripts in marriage remain and can produce unfair bargaining between spouses.

Distinct from premarital agreements, *Borelli v. Brusseau*, 12 Cal. App. 4th 647 (1st Div. 1993), concerned a contract between spouses made during marriage. A wife entered into a contract with her late husband to provide nursing care for him at home in exchange for property at his death. A California appellate court held that contracts between spouses to provide care for compensation violate public policy and provide no consideration because spouses have a preexisting duty to deliver care. Writing for the court, Professor Jo Carrillo rejects the doctrines of consideration and public policy as reasons to deny Mrs. Borelli relief. In an innovative twist, she holds that the spouses' oral contract was a modification of the couple's premarital agreement, and enforcement of the contract is the obligation of the estate based on the fiduciary duty established during the marriage. Professor June Carbone's commentary addresses the feminist ambivalence about during-marriage contracts and about bargaining generally. At the heart of this ambivalence is a desire for some measure of autonomy, so that couples can negotiate in relationships, in tension with protections for spouses who might face financial and emotional coercion, particularly if that spouse has exchanged unpaid or domestic care for property.

The rewritten *Turner v. Rogers*, 564 U.S. 431 (2011), brings to the fore the intersection of feminism, racial justice, and poverty. In *Turner*, the Supreme Court held that the state need not provide an attorney to an indigent father who had been repeatedly imprisoned for child support arrears. Professor Elizabeth MacDowell writes a concurrence, agreeing that parents have no categorical constitutional right to counsel in child support enforcement cases. She holds, however, that the Due Process Clause requires procedural safeguards that balance "the interests at stake in child support enforcement." Describing a punitive system that disproportionately targets fathers of color and penalizes the poor, she outlines a robust screening and evaluation process to determine the noncustodial parent's ability to pay prior to incarceration. Professor Warren Binford, in her commentary, largely agrees with Professor MacDowell's approach, but concentrates on the connection between failure to pay child support and child poverty. In this regard, she finds unlikely common ground with the original opinion's dissent by Justice Clarence Thomas. Binford diverges from Justice Thomas's dissent, however, in introducing comparative examples of modern constitutions that recognize children's rights.

The enforceability of surrogacy arrangements – the subject of *In the Matter of the Parentage of a Child by T.J.S. and A.L.S.*, 54 A.3d 263 (N.J. 2012) – provides a snapshot of family law's dynamism. The Supreme Court of New Jersey held that gestational surrogacy agreements were unenforceable in the state. The court dismissed a couple's claim that law's different treatment of infertile men and infertile women was gender discrimination. Professor Seema Mohapatra, rewriting the majority opinion, reverses course and recognizes, under state equal protection principles, the parentage rights of a married woman to a child conceived with her husband's sperm and a donor egg implanted in a gestational surrogate. Her judgment tracks the trend across the country to permit gestational surrogacy contracts, as evidenced by the New Jersey Gestational Carrier Agreement Act, which permits gestational surrogacy and that the state passed while Professor Mohapatra was writing the reimagined decision. Professor Melanie Jacobs's commentary provides the needed background to this shifting approach to surrogacy contracts as well as information about the increasing use of assisted reproductive technologies in the United States. Both the rewritten opinion and commentary note that, even with greater legal permission for surrogacy, feminist disagreement remains about whether surrogacy exploits women or is an essential component of people's procreative rights.

As with surrogacy, the treatment of intimate partner abuse as a ground for asylum is an ever-evolving area of law. Originally, Professor Suzan Pritchett rewrote a Board of Immigration Appeals opinion, *Matter of A-R-C-G-*, 26 I&N Dec. 388 (B.I.A. 2014), which clarified the right to asylum for survivors of intimate partner violence. As the commentary authored by Professor Natalie Nanasi explains, in 2018, Attorney General Jeff Sessions overturned *A-R-C-G-* and issued an opinion declaring that domestic violence could not be the basis for an asylum claim. Professor Pritchett took the opportunity, writing as the Attorney General, to issue radically different guidance to immigration courts in the *Matter of A-B-*, 27 I&N Dec. 316 (A.G. 2018). She writes that not only is intimate partner violence a ground for asylum under current case law and international law, but also that women can constitute a "particular social group" under U.S. asylum law. Professor Nanasi explores the nuances of Pritchett's test for asylum in, for example, the nexus between particular social group and persecution. But more importantly, her commentary details the difficulties women overcome in fleeing violent spouses and the persistent misunderstanding of the prevalence and nature of intimate abuse.

A crucial decision for constitutional analysis of gender discrimination concludes the book. Professor Tracy Thomas rewrites the majority opinion in *Sessions v. Morales-Santana*, 582 U.S. 137 S. Ct. 1678 (2017). In that case, the U.S. Supreme Court held that a statute requiring a shorter period of time for establishing citizenship for children born overseas to unmarried U.S. citizen mothers than unmarried U.S. citizen fathers violated the Equal

Protection Clause. Professor Thomas's rewritten opinion, as Justice Ginsburg's original majority opinion did, focuses on the impermissibility of gender stereotypes about mothers' and fathers' relationships to their children. Departing from the original decision, Professor Thomas applies the shorter timeframe for citizenship (previously available only to mothers) to all children born overseas to unmarried U.S. citizens. Professor Cynthia Godsoe, in her commentary, emphasizes how family restrictions have discriminated against and excluded people of targeted races or ethnicities. And drawing on a theme that appears throughout the volume, she adds that the original opinion missed an opportunity to de-privilege marriage as the most significant means for acquiring citizenship.

***

Taken together, the chapters of this book – though engaging with dissimilar decisions across eras – express common themes. Several chapters wrestle with how to value domestic labor, still primarily done in greater proportion by women than by men, and how to upend heteronormative stereotypes. Those chapters ask how law should envision the role of mothers as providing special care for children (as in *Morales*) or in expressing one's gender identity (as related to trans-parents in *Daly*).

Many of the chapters claim new rights and protections for groups subject to longstanding discrimination, such as nonmarital families, same-sex partners and parents, and low-income families. In other instances, rewritten cases hint at future statutes and policies that would address an issue the original decision did not resolve. For example, successive iterations of the Uniform Parentage Act undermine the holding of *Michael H.* and the Uniform Interstate Family Support Act tackles the personal jurisdiction problem for child support in *Kulko*.

Chapters take up questions about how well-meaning decisions on women's behalf can work against a specific population's interests and needs. How does a feminist thinker, in *Reynolds* for example, discern the difference between laws that seek fairness or justice and laws that reinscribe paternalism or coercion? Feminist ideas remain contested and continue to evolve in areas of law like polygamy, religious education, contracts in relationships, and immigration. As noted, laws changed, in surrogacy and in asylum for instance, as this book was being written.

And as cases like *Dandridge*, *DeShaney*, and *Turner* make clear, had various family formations and constitutional rights been recognized in earlier eras, our family law jurisprudence might look very different today. Our Constitution might guarantee positive rights to basic state services, state statutes might incorporate more fluid definitions of family that respond to people's lived experiences, our immigration and asylum laws would build from compassion rather than punishment or exclusion. Perhaps this is the core ambition of this book and the *Feminist Judgment* series – to test what feminism and law reform can mean for advancing social justice, and to seek out opportunities to influence present debates.

2

Commentary on *Reynolds v. United States*

MARIE A. FAILINGER

INTRODUCTION

Reynolds v. United States is a struggle by men against men, reflecting men's fears, described in men's terms. In 1879, the Supreme Court ruled unanimously that a law criminalizing bigamy did not infringe upon individuals' First Amendment right to free exercise of religion – the Constitution protects religious beliefs but not necessarily religious practices like polygamy. Women – the ostensible subjects and victims of polygamy, then known as one of the "twin relics of barbarism" along with slavery – are barely seen or heard in the case as it progresses to the Supreme Court, as Justice Kessler's dissent makes clear. Yet, in *Reynolds*, the tropes of women's place in the world as men imagine it are very much present, even today.

The opening arguments of George Biddle, Reynolds's lawyer, appear to be standard legal disputes, suggesting that the Free Exercise Clause is a jurisdictional limitation on the power of the federal government to superintend local governments on religious issues.[1] But as perhaps everyone who kept up with "the Mormon question" of that time well knew, this framing of the Free Exercise claim primarily as a jurisdictional question was not simply a prelude to the main argument, but a shot across the bow to federal threats to the whole structure of the Mormon-led[2] territorial government and society in Utah. Historians Edward Firmage and Sarah Barringer Gordon have described the decades-long struggle by national governmental and social forces to sap the

[1] Sarah Barringer Gordon, The Mormon Question: Polygamy and Constitutional Conflict in Nineteenth Century America 77–79, 122–25 (2001).

[2] In 2018, the President of the Church of Jesus Christ of the Latter Day Saints, Russell M. Nelson, requested that the church not be referred to as "LDS" or "Mormons." This commentary uses those terms since they were commonly used from the time of *Reynolds* until recently.

strength of Mormon political power and wrest control of Utah's legal institutions away from Mormons – the persecution Mormons referred to as "The Raid."

According to Gordon and Firmage, the key centerpieces of the Mormon persecution were attacks on two Mormon-dominated legal institutions – local courts and their juries and the Mormon family. The 1862 Morrill Act targeted both institutions: the law annulled the Church of Jesus Christ of the Latter Day Saints (LDS) corporate charter granted by the territorial legislature, limited the real estate holdings of charitable organizations, and punished bigamy with a five-year prison sentence and a fine.[3] The unsuccessful 1870 Cullom bill would have excluded anyone who believed in polygamy from jury service, denied criminal jurisdiction to the local probate courts, and stripped wives of the privilege not to testify against their husbands. The bill also would have de-established Mormon political institutions by barring polygamists from voting and holding public office if they refused to take a "test oath" forswearing polygamy, which was similar to an oath required of Southern officeholders to forswear the Confederacy.[4] The 1874 Poland Act transferred jurisdiction of territorial probate courts to the federal court system for all but estate and guardianship cases, putting criminal polygamy and other cases in the hands of anti-Mormon federal judges, prosecutors, and marshals.[5]

The Court in *Reynolds* ultimately held that the federal government could pass a law preventing polygamy in the territories and that the Free Exercise Clause did not provide Mormons a religious exemption from the law, because "laws are made for the government of actions, and while they cannot interfere with mere religious belief and opinions, they may with practices."[6] However, a feminist reading of *Reynolds* cannot fail to notice two social concerns embedded in the text: claims that Mormons were a social contagion and the rush to treat Mormon women as passive victims of their fate, ignoring women's autonomy and responsibility.

[3] Edwin Brown Firmage & Richard Collin Mangrum, Zion in the Courts: A Legal History of the Church of Jesus Christ of Latter-day Saints, 1830–1900 131 (1988).

[4] Firmage & Mangrum, *supra* note 3, at 147; Kelly Elizabeth Phipps, *Marriage and Redemption: Mormon Polygamy in the Congressional Imagination, 1862–1887*, 95 Va. L. Rev. 435, 459–64 (2009) (noting that the bill likely faltered over the provision confiscating the property of convicted polygamists or those who fled the jurisdiction to provide for their plural wives, a Reconstruction-style remedy that both Democrats and some Republicans thought was a bridge too far).

[5] Gordon, *supra* note 1, at 148.

[6] *Reynolds v. United States*, 98 S.Ct. 145, 166 (1878).

CONTAGION

In American culture, because it is inflected with patriarchal values, those who present profound and potentially powerful differences have been portrayed as a threat to the social order. Indeed, often this threat is posed through the metaphors of armed attack and contagion – invading "hordes"[7] who bring disease – literally and socially – to the American body politic, threatening its very life. In the nineteenth century, roughly contemporaneously with the Mormon controversy, Chinese immigrants to the United States were described as a "plague of locusts," "moral lepers," their communities a "moral cancer on the city… [and a] Mongolian vampire" sapping the community's vitality.[8] Current popular narratives similarly depict Mexican and Central American undocumented workers as bringing infection to the body politic.[9] Muslims are described as a stealthy army of conspirators who sneak into our country and threaten our common civic and political life.[10] All of these tropes have been used to justify containment and repression with violence – physical or social violence, or the violence of the law.

So, too, the *Reynolds* Court subscribed to this claim that Mormons are foreign carriers of social contagion: polygamy, the Court noted, has always been "odious" among European peoples, and "almost exclusively a feature of the life of Asiatic and of African people."[11] As Gordon notes, the *Reynolds* Court embraced the references by government lawyer, Charles Devens, to "Hindu widows hurl[ing] on funeral pyres of their husbands" and "East Islanders . . . expos[ing] their new-born babes," claiming that religious exemptions meant unchecked chaos and violence.[12] The original *Reynolds* opinion echoed these analogies:

> Suppose one believed that human sacrifices were a necessary part of religious worship; would it be seriously contended that the civil government under which he lived could not interfere to prevent a sacrifice? Or if a wife religiously believed it was her duty to burn herself upon the funeral pile of

7 Keith Aoki, *"Foreign-Ness" & Asian American Identities: Yellowface, World War II Propaganda, and Bifurcated Racial Stereotypes*, 4 ASIAN PAC. AM. L.J. 1, 25–26 (1996).

8 *Id.* at 30–31, 33 n. 141.

9 *See* Marie A. Failinger, *Recovering the Face-to-Face in American Immigration Law*, 16 S. CAL. REV. L. & SOC. JUST. 319, 319–22, 328–34 (2007).

10 *See, e.g.*, Rene Sotolongo, *Terrorist Training Grounds Right Here in the U.S.*, OPLENS (July 2, 2018), https://www.opslens.com/2018/07/terrorist-training-grounds-right-here-in-the-united-states/ (claiming that since 1992, "stealth jihadis" have made their way to the United States and are creating terrorist training grounds) (last visited July 2, 2018).

11 *Reynolds*, 98 S.Ct. at 164.

12 GORDON, *supra* note 1, at 126 (quoting Charles Devens).

> her dead husband, would it be beyond the power of government to prevent her carrying her belief into practice? . . . To permit [polygamy by Mormons] would be to make the professed doctrines of religious beliefs superior to the law of the land, and in effect permit every citizen to become a law unto himself. Government could exist only in name under such circumstances.[13]

Eschewing all of the evidence Justice Kessler ably presents about the Founders' intentions for the Free Exercise Clause in her imagined dissent, the Court dealt a final blow to the possibility of Free Exercise tolerance by accepting the government's argument that monogamous marriage is the foundation of American social life and democratic security.[14] As Justice Kessler's dissent shows, the majority projects the personal onto the political by citing a political scientist's claim that polygamy "leads to the patriarchal principle and which, when applied to large communities, fetters the people in stationary despotism, while that principle cannot long exist in connection with monogamy."[15]

Thus, instead of providing some social catharsis over the conflict about polygamy, *Reynolds* added fuel to the fire, justifying even more repression of Mormons. Emboldened by the *Reynolds* decision, Congress passed the 1882 Edmunds Act, creating the offense of unlawful cohabitation, which permitted prosecution of men who had only one legal wife but additional spiritual wives, thus easing prosecutors' burdens of proof against Mormons.[16] (Indeed, under Congressional law, a polygamous husband who attempted to comply with federal law by avoiding sexual intercourse with his spiritual wives and even moving them to their own homes could still be convicted of "cohabitation" if he "appeared to be" or was reputed to be in relationship to those wives, as established by any contact he had with them.[17]) In the Edmunds Act, Congress also solidified the holdings of the *Reynolds* Court, permitting prosecutors to question and excuse jurors for their former or current practices of, or beliefs about, polygamy or their refusal to answer the questions.[18]

The Edmunds Act also succeeded where the Cullom bill failed, placing polygamists' rights to vote, hold office, or serve on juries in the hands of an

[13] *Reynolds*, 98 S.Ct. at 166–67.
[14] GORDON, *supra* note 1, at 142–44.
[15] *Id.* at 140; *Reynolds*, 98 S.Ct. at 165.
[16] GORDON, *supra* note 1, at 144–45, 151–53.
[17] FIRMAGE & MANGRUM, *supra* note 3, at 170–72. The contemporary Utah statute, 76-7-101, which punishes a married person who "purports to marry another person or cohabits with another person" was upheld by the Utah Supreme Court in *State v. Holm*, 137 P.2d 726, 744 (Utah 2006), but its cohabitation section was recently held unconstitutional in *Brown v. Buhman*, 947 F. Supp. 1120 (D. Utah 2013).
[18] *Id.* at 161.

unelected elections commission, and emptying all existing elected offices to be filled in future elections.[19] The 1887 Edmunds-Tucker Act provided that even legal wives could testify against their husbands in polygamy trials, albeit some limited aspects of the marital privilege were retained.[20] Meanwhile, federal judges refused to naturalize eligible foreign-born Mormons.[21] Eventually, an estimated 1,000 Mormons were convicted of polygamy, though authorities were likely aware that only about 2,500 Mormon husbands had taken multiple wives.[22]

As the Mormon persecution dramatically shows, national appeals to moral contagion from minority groups like those the *Reynolds* Court accepted have always come out badly. Fears of Japanese and Chinese immigrants not only resulted in pervasive discrimination and exclusion from entering the country, but also contributed to the Japanese internment in World War II.[23] Fears of Central American and Muslim immigration have resulted in repressive crackdowns, with government officials engaging in repressive acts not dissimilar to those that characterized the Mormon persecution.[24] As a result, vulnerable populations go underground, hiding from U.S. Immigration and Customs Enforcement officials.[25]

Indeed, the *Reynolds* Court's failure to welcome these others and its repression of family diversity due to fear of moral chaos has reaped disastrous consequences for many nonimmigrant families even today. As just one example, social fears about sexually diverse families have resulted in a long battle, fought on religious freedom grounds, between those who welcome the diversity of same-sex families and those who claim that anything but male-female monogamy portends the fall of American society.[26]

19 *Id.* at 161–62, 164–66.

20 *Id.* at 198.

21 *Id.* at 242–44.

22 *Id.* at 130, 166.

23 *See* Natsu Taylor Saito, *Symbolism under Siege: Japanese American Redress and the "Racing" of Arab Americans*, 8 Asian L.J. 1, 8–9 (2001) (describing how the internment was a "logical extension" of previous federal immigration laws excluding Asians, labor exploitation, lynching and Jim Crow laws, and alien land laws).

24 *See, e.g.*, Jeremy B. White, *"Everyone Is Fair Game.' It's Very Aggressive": Inside Donald Trump's Immigration Crackdown*, The Independent (Nov. 8, 2017), https://www.independent.co.uk/news/world/americas/us-politics/donald-trump-immigration-crackdown-one-year-election-ice-detain-drugs-crime-family-a8042266.html (visited Feb. 27, 2019).

25 *See, e.g.*, Kyung Lah, Alberto Moya, & Mallory Simon, *An Underground Network Is Readying Homes to Hide Undocumented Immigrants*, CNN (Feb. 26, 2017), https://www.cnn.com/2017/02/23/us/california-immigrant-safe-houses/index.html (last visited Feb. 25, 2019).

26 *See, e.g.*, *Obergefell v. Hodges*, 576 U.S. 135 S. Ct. 2584 (2015); *Masterpiece Cakeshop v. Colo. Civ. Rts. Comm'n*, 584 U.S. __, 138 S. Ct. 1719 (2018).

Yet attempts to "protect the victims" of minority groups' family practices like the Mormons' rarely result in progress for the victims. As with the fundamentalist Mormon-origin sects, as Elizabeth Harmer-Dionne has shown, these religious communities often "double down" on the religious ideology that majorities attack and close their religious society even more tightly to outsiders, exacerbating oppression against women. Or religious communities suffer the Mormon fate: responding to the cognitive dissonance caused by relentless government persecution, Mormons were forced to capitulate by abjuring their doctrines built on polygamy.[27]

WOMEN, RELIGION, AND HARD CHOICES

Feminists should also be chagrined at how the *Reynolds* Court ultimately chose to simplify and trivialize the difficult and paradoxical situation of women in Mormon families. Even today, feminists debate over whether sexually or physically abused women, sex workers, or sexually harassed workers should be portrayed as "innocent" and passive victims of a brutal and selfish patriarchal culture, or as survivors of such evils. When these women decide to stay in their relationships, should feminists understand them as victims of false consciousness or as autonomous and responsible adults who freely make choices for themselves that other women might regard as demeaning or self-destructive?[28]

As Justice Kessler's opinion properly shows, the *Reynolds* Court echoes the feminist debate about women and their roles when it accepts the government's portrayal of Mormon women as helpless victims of polygamy. Even female novelists of the time aided and abetted this narrative, writing almost a hundred novels and numerous anti-polygamy magazine stories in the mid-1850s, with "[s]tories of blushing brides whose hopes were dashed by a husband's self-indulgence [in marrying additional wives] ... challenging them to suffer with sanctity."[29]

Yet, as described in Justice Kessler's dissent, Mormon women did not play the passive role assigned to them by the federal courts. For example, they called a large public meeting to defend polygamy against "a corrupt press, and an equally corrupt priest craft leagued ... against us," arguing that Mormon

[27] Elizabeth Harmer-Dionne, *Once a Peculiar People: Cognitive Dissonance and the Suppression of Mormon Polygamy as a Case Study Negating the Belief-Action Distinction*, 50 Stan. L. Rev. 1295, 1300–1301, 1313–14, 1318, 1334–36 (1998).

[28] For discussions of these debates, *see, e.g.*, Martha Chamallas, Introduction to Feminist Legal Theory 28–30, 56–59, 72–73, 93–94, 100–102 (3d ed. 2013).

[29] Gordon, *supra* note 1, at 29–30.

women have the "right . . . to be granted the opportunity to participate in [the] 'honorable and sacred callings'" of marriage and motherhood that lead to eternal salvation.[30]

And, as George Reynolds's second wife Mary Jane Schofield did, they resisted federal power: when the federal marshal came to serve her with a subpoena in her husband's second polygamy trial, Mary Jane was nowhere to be found, a disappearance that the unwitting judge blamed on her husband's coercion.[31] Mormon wives' resistance against "The Raid" was underscored in numerous polygamy prosecutions in which wives also lied under oath, or "forgot" whether they or other women were married to their husbands, or where those women were.[32]

Ultimately, the federal government turned on Mormon women when they did not play the innocent, passive roles assigned to them, once the barriers against wives testifying against their husbands were removed by federal law. Anti-Mormon prosecutors, judges, and politicians became so incensed with Mormon wives' failure to play the cooperative victim that they started prosecuting the wives for perjury or obstruction of justice. Women were "taken from their beds" in their nightclothes by federal marshals, causing trauma and serious injury.[33] Women who refused to testify after the Edmunds-Tucker Act abrogated their marital privilege were imprisoned for contempt, even with their babies. Mormon wives petitioned Congress:

> [Under] the suspicion that any woman or young lady is some man's plural wife she is liable at any time to be arrested, not merely subpoenaed, and examined and browbeaten and insulted by the prosecuting attorney or his minions. But this is not all. In defiance of law and the usages of courts for ages, the legal wife is now compelled to submit to the same indignities.[34]

Yet Representative Dougherty replied to Congressman James Burnes about the women imprisoned with their babies for failing to name the children's fathers: "Sir, in this matter I have no sympathy except for the children" because these women knew they were violating "the laws of the land" when they agreed to a polygamous marriage.[35]

These attempts to portray Mormon women as either passive victims or conniving co-conspirators belie the more complicated story of their lives.

[30] *Id.* at 98.
[31] *Id.* at 115–16.
[32] *Id.* at 156, 161–63.
[33] Firmage & Mangrum, *supra* note 3, at 172–74.
[34] *Id.* at 206–207.
[35] *Id.* at 208.

The Church of the Latter-Day Saints has had an ambivalent theology when it comes to gender. On one hand, women play a central role in the salvific theology of traditional Mormonism. Even today, the (non-polygamous) LDS Church teaches

> that all human beings, male and female, are beloved spirit children of heavenly parents, a Heavenly Father and a Heavenly Mother. This understanding is rooted in scriptural and prophetic teachings about the nature of God, our relationship to Deity, and the godly potential of men and women. The doctrine of a Heavenly Mother is a cherished and distinctive belief among Latter-day Saints.[36]

Indeed, it is through marriage to women that Mormon men reach godhood, not through their own sacrifices, or their heroic efforts, or personal virtue, as in some other theological traditions.

At the same time, Mormon theology of this period clearly centered on men, who achieved personal salvation and increased their political power and social standing by marrying multiple wives and bearing numerous children. Indeed, the essence of LDS theology of the time was known as the "patriarchal principle," the idea that in taking multiple wives, LDS men gave "evidence of obedience to God's law of celestial marriage and the hope of eternal progression through stages of heaven to eventual godhood."[37] Women's salvation was adjunct to their husbands: "[f]or wives the reflected glory of their husbands' accomplishment was the gauge of their own future reward."[38]

Likewise, the social and political situation of Mormon women was deeply conflicted. As Justice Kessler notes, Mormon women were some of the first in the nation to gain the right to vote.[39] Yet outsiders were chagrined that they voted with, and politically protected, the very men and institutions that were said to oppress them.[40] Indeed, federal authorities became so frustrated with the political alignments of wives with their husbands that the government ultimately stripped Mormon women of the vote in the Edmunds-Tucker Act.[41]

Mormon women also played central roles in public economic life in LDS society, roles not open to their monogamous peers in other states. Many pursued careers in business, politics, medicine, and journalism; the heavy

[36] *Mother in Heaven*, CHURCH OF LATTER-DAY SAINTS, https://www.lds.org/topics/mother-in-heaven?lang=eng (last visited May 3, 2018).

[37] GORDON, *supra* note 1, at 23, 103–105.

[38] *Id.* at 92.

[39] *See* ELEANOR FLEXNER, CENTURY OF STRUGGLE 159–63 (3d ed. 1972).

[40] GORDON, *supra* note 1, at 97–98.

[41] *Id.* at 164, 171, 180.

constraints of domestic labor and attention to their husbands' and children's wants and needs were alleviated by having sister-wives to share these burdens. Elizabeth Harmer-Dionne quotes Emmeline B. Wells's declaration that polygamy "gives women the highest opportunities for self-development, exercise of judgment, and arouses latent faculties, making them more truly cultivated in the actual realities of life, more independent in thought and mind, noble and unselfish."[42]

In terms of family choice, on one hand, many Mormon women expressed dismay at having to share a husband with other women, and understood it as a "cross they had to bear" under the tenets of their faith.[43] In their religious courts, Mormon women who complained of their husbands' bad behavior were often charged with responsibility for the conflicts that had occurred. In one case, an "uncooperative wife" was told to "humble herself before God and her brethren and undo the evil she has done as much as possible, and not do so anymore, but seek to do good, be a wife in every deed unto her husband."[44]

On the other hand, unlike most states at this time, divorce was much more freely permitted to Mormon wives who wanted it; women were even permitted to divorce husbands to whom they were "sealed for time and eternity" after the husbands had died.[45] And Mormon religious courts ensured that husbands provided adequate support for their families and expedited uncontested divorces.[46] There were those who found in polygamous families sisterhood, and a respite from the onerous demands and constraints placed on wives and mothers in monogamous homes.[47]

Justice Kessler brings into sharp relief the hypocrisy of which Mormon wives accused the majority monogamous social culture, which often turned a blind eye to married men who had extramarital sex or engaged in serial monogamy. Particularly in Western communities where social norms were looser, these men would simply desert their wives, move to another town, and marry another wife, leaving first wives without any means to support themselves.[48]

[42] Harmer-Dionne, *supra* note 27, at 1331.
[43] *Id.* at 1330–31.
[44] Firmage & Mangrum, *supra* note 3, at 323.
[45] *Id.* at 324–29, 331–32; Gordon, *supra* note 1, at 175–76 (both noting that Utah permitted divorce for what we now call "irreconcilable differences" as well as grounds such as abuse and desertion.)
[46] Firmage & Mangrum, *supra* note 3, at 324.5.
[47] Harmer-Dionne, *supra* note 27, at 1330–31.
[48] Gordon, *supra* note 1, at 129.

We must also note the anti-polygamy claim, repeated in same-sex marriage debates, that banning polygamy would protect not only the women and children of polygamous marriages, but also the stability of other monogamous families.[49] That claim apparently rests on the notion that accepting a plurality of marriage forms will encourage those in monogamous, male-female marriages to engage in licentious and irresponsible behavior that portends familial, social, and political chaos. Yet nineteenth-century Mormons disputed that husbands entered polygamous marriage in order to indulge in outsized passions (though men's "gratification by plurality" was recognized in Mormon theology as a fact of life), and denied that they had any influence on the sexual practices of their non-Mormon neighbors.[50]

In weighing whether Mormon women and children were helped by the government's repression of Mormon theology and social structure, we should not forget that many Mormon men had to hide out for months from federal authorities seeking to imprison them for polygamous and other offenses, making it difficult for them to serve as breadwinners or parents to their children. Other families went without the economic and social contributions of fathers as they lay in prison for marrying multiple wives.[51]

CONCLUSION

The Mormon experience, and the American response to it represented in *Reynolds*, exposes the continuing failure of American law and social life to recognize that women universally live complicated and even paradoxical lives. Governments and communities try to simplify and stereotype women's lives. Too often social and political solutions either deny women's autonomy and trivialize their dignity or deny the social and political constraints that affect their choices.

The moral failure of attempting to stereotype women as either passive victims or autonomous Amazons harms women in many communities, not just in closed religious communities. The law has too often aided and abetted these harmful assumptions.[52] Obviously, in some societies and socioeconomic classes, constraints on women's choices are more profoundly unjust and harmful than in others. At the same time, women are capable of assessing

49 *Id.* at 31, 39–40.

50 *Id.* at 88–89, 92–93, 103–104.

51 Firmage & Mangrum, *supra* note 3, at 130; Gordon, supra note 1, at 156.

52 *See generally* Cary Franklin, *The History of the Anti-Stereotyping Principle in Constitutional Sex Discrimination Law*, 85 N.Y.U. L. Rev. 83 (2010) (describing the history of the work of feminist lawyers like Justice Ginsburg to identify and respond to sex stereotyping in the law).

the difficult choices imposed on them by the limitations and expectations of their communities and interpersonal commitments. And women are capable of making a sensible "least damaging" choice, given their circumstances, their interpersonal commitments to others and sometimes to the Divine, as well as their own sense of purpose and meaning, while retaining the ability to see clearly the constraints that bind them.

Sometimes that means that women side with their religious or ethnic or social communities or families against the insistent demands of some feminists that they are oppressed because of their religious, social, and moral commitments to those communities. Sometimes, as Harmer-Dionne proposes, they will resolve the cognitive dissonance by accepting, and even justifying, a course for their lives that may be unjust, but allows them to live without cognitively self-destructing. And sometimes they will resist domination in their own subcultures – and, through that resistance, change the situation of women in their community, even if that change is incremental and never complete. A robust reading of the Free Exercise Clause, which Justice Kessler's opinion comes closer to, is the most respectful way to give them these alternatives, and thus, the dignity they deserve.

REYNOLDS v. UNITED STATES, 98 U.S. 145 (1879)

JUSTICE KESSLER, DISSENTING

I do not propose to go into the subject of all of the evidentiary and procedural objections, as they involve mainly technicalities, but rather will make such observations as appear to me proper for consideration on the heart of this controversy: to wit, the general question of the scope and nature of the first amendment's protections of polygamy from the power of Congress.[1]

The opinion in this case proceeds, as it seems to me, upon grounds entirely too narrow. The substance and spirit of the first amendment of the Constitution have been sacrificed by an altogether crude distinction: "Laws are made for the government of actions, and while they cannot interfere with mere religious belief and opinions, they may with practices." I agree with the majority opinion that the first amendment cannot be read so broadly that any conduct asserted to be religion should be immune from regulation. I have

[1] In order to remain true to the period in which *Reynolds* was decided, this opinion substantially adopts the style, grammar, punctuation, and citation conventions of nineteenth-century judicial opinions and, in some places, borrows phraseology from nineteenth-century Supreme Court opinions and legal sources.

no doubt of the power of the Congress to provide for general criminal laws and to protect public peace and safety. A believer has no right to invade the private rights of others or to disturb public peace and order, no matter how conscientious the belief or how trivial the private right on the other side. The majority opinion appears to me to go altogether too far, however, in concluding that, because not all religious conduct is exempted from civil control, no religious practice is protected by the first amendment. A constitutional provision, adopted in the interest of religious freedom, and for the purpose of securing rights inhering in a state of freedom, and belonging to American citizenship, has been so construed by the majority as to defeat the ends the provision is apparently intended to accomplish. By this I do not mean that the determination of this case should be controlled by considerations of mere expediency or policy. I mean only to express an earnest conviction that the court has, in the interpretation of the constitutional provision, misread the history of the provision and thereby the intent with which it was adopted.

I

The Constitution of the United States (Amend. I) declares that "Congress shall make no law prohibiting the free exercise of religion." The majority quite rightly looks to the history of the times in the midst of which the provision was adopted to ascertain its meaning. Yet with all the light shed upon the history of the first amendment by the elaborate opinion of the majority, I am not persuaded that its narrow construction is evident in the provision's history.

Both Mr. Jefferson and Mr. Madison played vital roles in formulating the first amendment of the federal Constitution, and Mr. Madison's views can be distinguished from those of his fellow Virginian.

I shall begin with the Virginia religious freedom bill, for this bill is central to the history of the federal provision's formation. Precisely, the first amendment has the same objective and was intended to provide the same protection against government intrusion on religious liberty as this bill. The Bill for Establishing Religious Freedom was introduced in Virginia in 1779, whereupon it faced great opposition by religious officials, and was not adopted. The cause was reinvigorated in 1784, when Patrick Henry proposed a general tax in Virginia called the Bill Establishing a Provision for Teachers [Ministers] of the Christian Religion. Citizens would choose which Christian church received their support, or the money could go to a general fund to be distributed by the state legislature. Mr. Madison was a vocal opponent of the bill, publishing his "Memorial and Remonstrance against Religious Assessments," which asserted:

> The Religion then of every man must be left to the conviction and conscience of every man; and it is the right of every man to exercise it as these may dictate ... It is the duty of every man to render to the Creator such homage, and such only, as he believes to be acceptable to him. This duty is precedent, both in order of time and in degree of obligation, to the claims of Civil Society ... [I]n matters of Religion, no man's right is abridged by the institution of Civil Society and that Religion is wholly exempt from its cognizance.

It is to be observed, from this statement, that Mr. Madison felt it necessary, to the harmonious equality of all the contending sects, that some denominations receive exemption from previous legal duties and the benefit of some degree of forbearance. Coming as this does from the drafter of the first amendment, one year before the first Congress met to prepare the Constitution, it may be accepted as a more authoritative declaration of the intended scope and effect of the amendment thus secured than a single letter written by Mr. Jefferson in 1820, twenty years after the provision's enactment. Mr. Madison's pamphlet, with its arguments against even the weak form of establishment proposed in the Henry bill, was circulated throughout the state of Virginia and garnered thousands of signatures. With the overwhelming opposition of the people, the proposed plan for general assessment was crushed under it, and advantage taken of the crisis to carry through Virginia's religious freedom bill. The resulting law, An Act for Establishing Religious Freedom (12 Hening's 84–86), as the majority opinion concedes, is the original foundation of the first amendment.

Subsequently, at the first session of the first Congress, significant debate ensued, during which several versions of the amendment containing the words "rights of conscience" were considered and rejected. I Annals Cong. 451, 757–59, 796 (1789); S. Leg. J., Sept. 3, 1789; Aug. 25, 1789; H. Leg. J., Aug. 21, 1789. The substitution of the words "free exercise" for "rights of conscience" is to me a persuasive argument that those who framed it, and the legislatures of the states which adopted it, contemplated that the provision was to be construed more broadly than a mere protection of religious belief, especially in view of the distinctly plain meaning of the words "free exercise" in the period when the amendment was debated, adopted, and ratified. Samuel Johnson's dictionary defined "exercise" as "practice; outward performance." S. Johnson, *A Dictionary of the English Language* (London 1785). "Conscience" was understood as opinion or belief, which Johnson's dictionary defined as "knowledge or faculty by which we judge." *Id.* Noah Webster's American dictionary defined "exercise" as "employment." In contrast, Mr. Webster defined "conscience" as "natural knowledge, or the faculty that decides on the right or wrong of actions." N. Webster, A *Compendious Dictionary of the English Language* (New Haven 1806). It shall also be noted that several versions of the provision proposed, and ultimately rejected, contained protections for both "rights of conscience" and "free exercise," leaving the matter in no doubt, so far as it relates to the intentions of the founders, that the words "free exercise" are imbued with a distinct and broader meaning than mere belief.

Further, it is reasonable to infer that those who drafted and adopted the first amendment assumed the term "free exercise" meant what it had meant in their states; therefore, the wording of state constitutions, existing at the time, also provide evidence of the most satisfactory character of the original understanding of the scope of the provision. With the exception of Connecticut, every state had a constitutional provision protecting religious freedom by 1789. Although differing in their particulars, none of the provisions confined the protection to beliefs and opinions. Maryland's constitution, for example, prohibited punishment of any person "on account of his religious persuasion or profession, or for *his religious practice*." Md. Decl. Rts.1776, art. XXXIII. The Virginia Bill of Rights defined "religion" as "the duty which we owe to our Creator, and *the manner of discharging it*." Va. Bill Rts. 1776, § 16. Although several states confined their protections to "worship," it should be observed that this limitation was not carried over to the first amendment. The federal provision followed the most expansive models among the state constitutions.

A brief reference to actual free exercise controversies in the period before the adoption of the Constitution will also serve to place the provision's meaning in clearer light. In most colonies, Quakers and certain other Protestant sects, who conscientiously refused to take oaths, were excepted from oath requirements, for example, by permitting objectors to testify by affirmation in civil court or to vote by affirmation instead of oath. Mass. Acts & Res. 305. Jews, who held their own usages and rites, were exempted from Rhode Island's statute governing marriage ceremonies and from the operation of state incest law, "within the degrees of affinity or consanguinity allowed by their religion," and their marriages, solemnized according to Jewish forms and ceremonies, were treated as binding as if actually celebrated *in facie ecclesiae*, in the face of the church, because Jewish law was understood to recommend marriage between uncle and niece, a relationship otherwise illegal under Rhode Island law and subject to severe penalties. *An Act Regulating Marriage and Divorce*, 1798 R.I. Pub. Laws § 7. Quakers in some colonies were exempted from the requirement of removing their hats in court, which they considered a form of obeisance to secular authority forbidden by their religion. *An Act to prescribe the Affirmation of Allegiance and Fidelity to this State to be taken by the People called Quakers, and for granting them certain indulgences therein mentioned*, 1784 N.C. Laws ch. 209, at 488. These examples show that religion-specific exemptions from civil law, accommodating otherwise loyal and law-abiding citizens who were bound by religious duty not to comply with civil law, should have been familiar to the framers and ratifiers of the free exercise clause. It would have been strange for them to have imbued the Constitution with a narrower protection than provided in the states, when the very purpose of the provision was to ensure that Congress would not go outside its legitimate domain, and encroach upon freedom of exercise of religion, as they understood this right to exist at the time.

The assertion by the majority that, in the western and northern nations of Europe, polygamy has always been recognized as an offence against society and punished as a crime with more or less severity, is, I think, also not strictly accurate. Though it be true that no person, while married, may marry another person, such second marriage being absolutely null and void according to the common law, as found in *Riddelsen v. Wogen*, Cro. Eliz. 858 and many other cases, bigamy was not a criminal offence in England before the Bigamy Act of 1604. 1 Jac. ch. 11. The main purpose of the criminal statute in England was to protect a spouse from harm, especially the wife, for in most cases, the two wives of the bigamist were unaware of each other, and the husband was deserting or failing to support his prior wife as well as defrauding his new one. And so, it is to be noted without surprise, given this purpose, that bigamy is placed in eighteenth-century treatises in chapters on offences against women, alongside offences such as underage marriage without a father's consent and rape. *Baron and Feme. A Treatise of the Common Law Concerning Husbands and Wives* 383–94 (2nd ed. 1719). In a great number of cases in which the Bigamy Act was invoked, moreover, it was adjudged that the bigamous marriage was not in violation of the Act, on the ground that the first wife had not been abandoned, or deceived without her knowledge. For example, a husband and wife who were legally separated (divorced *a mensa et thoro*) were not within the criminal statute; a subsequent bigamous marriage in this circumstance would be void, but not a crime. *Id.* at 384; 3 Chitty, ch. 8, at 719; 2 Starkie, at 895. Similarly, when the first marriage had been formed many years earlier or far away, the parties separated by circumstance or a spouse having vanished, the accused was more often than not given the benefit of the doubt and acquitted. *G.D.*, Old Bailey (1691). These cases make it difficult to conclude, as do my brethren in the majority, that England approved of a general rigorous and systematic criminal punishment of polygamy. Provided the first wife was not deceived and left destitute, the courts were often quite lenient. Further, Chancellor Kent, on whom the majority relies, states in his treatise that the civil code of

France, adopted in 1804, did not criminalize polygamy, only rendering the second marriage unlawful, without annexing any penalty for the offence. 2 Kent, Com. 81, note (*e*).

In summary, the historical grounds relied upon in the majority opinion are more complex than indicated. The singular reference by the majority opinion to the views of Mr. Jefferson – whose position on free exercise was extraordinarily restrictive for his day, unsupported by the express terms of the Constitution, and out of step with the views of the drafter of the first amendment – and the majority's sweeping references to the general abhorrence of polygamy in the northern and western nations of Europe, do not take account of other authorities pointing in the opposite direction. Indeed, a careful examination of the relevant history of the first amendment throws serious doubt upon the majority's narrow construction of the provision, and the majority's application of it, in this case.

It would be unjust to the memory of the distinguished individuals who framed the Constitution to suppose that it was designed to protect a mere barren and abstract right of religious belief, without any practical operation upon the actual business of religious practice. The first amendment was undoubtedly adopted as part of the Constitution's great and useful purpose. It was to maintain the full freedom of religion, in all its forms and operations, by placing religion under the protection of the Constitution. And it would but ill become this Court, under any circumstances, to depart from the plain meaning of the words used, and to sanction a distinction between belief and practice, which would render the provision illusive and nugatory, mere words in form, to those who are most in need of its protections, for it is the religious practice of unpopular sects that are most likely to be restricted and persecuted. There can be no such thing as freedom of conscience without freedom to act.

II

Because I am convinced that the first amendment was intended to protect more than mere belief, and that polygamous marriages were not universally defined or adjudged as criminal at common law, I am compelled to consider whether the religious belief of the accused can be accepted as a justification of his polygamous marriage, an act made criminal by Congress. I emphasize, again, that I am in full agreement with the majority opinion that Congress has the power to prescribe criminal laws. *McCulloch v. Maryland*, 4 Wheat. 428–29. This power extends to the Territories. *Loughborough v. Blake*, 5 Wheat. 319. The claim of the accused for general invalidation of Section 5352 of the Revised Statutes is without any legal validity; the weakness of this claim may explain Mr. Biddle's abbreviated and undeveloped statement of it in his brief for the plaintiff in error. The request by the accused for exemption from the statute, however, requires our consideration in light of the proper construction of the constitutional provision protecting free exercise of religion. In order to undertake this inquiry, a fuller evaluation of the personal circumstances of the accused and the situation of his wives, as well as the conditions prevailing in the Territory of Utah in relation to the practice of polygamy, including any injury or outward disturbance of others caused by polygamy, is required.

The accused is personal secretary to Brigham Young, the former editor of the *Millennial Star*, and, except for his polygamous inclinations, otherwise the most upstanding kind of citizen. Based on these circumstances, there is reason to suspect that the indictment was founded on his association with the leader of the Mormon Church, who openly espouses and promotes the practice of polygamy among its members, rather than due to any injury or outward disturbance of others. The record shows only that his second wife, having been subpoenaed by the marshal, admitted her marriage to him. That is all. No wife of the accused was complaining to the federal marshals about her miserable life; no evidence of despotic behavior by the accused is before this court. The government has utterly failed to present evidence that the polygamous acts in question caused any physical harm or psychological injury to the wives of the accused, any physical or psychological harm to his children, or any physical or economic harm to other people. Further, much confusion is perpetuated by the majority opinion's comparison of polygamy to human sacrifice and suttee. Polygamy does not pose a physical threat to the participants, much less involve a termination of a human life.

Yet it is asserted in the majority opinion that polygamy is inherently despotic and, on this basis, that religious belief cannot be accepted as a justification of the peculiar marriage of the accused, which has been determined to be a crime by Congress. In support of this theory, the majority opinion relies on Professor Lieber, who asserts in his treatise that polygamy almost irresistibly leads to despotism. 2 Lieber, *Manual of Political Ethics*, bk. iii, ch. 1, at 9 (1839). It is worth pausing here to examine Professor Lieber's theory more closely, for it is the foundation upon which the majority's whole reasoning seems to rest, rather than any evidence in the record as to the immediate effects of the acts of the accused.

According to Mr. Lieber, marriage is the foundation of society, the family the first school of moral cultivation. It is in the family, through the strong affections of husband and wife, mother and child, where the vital regard of man to man, social duty, and love of country are born and nourished, and it is the family that creates social relations and abilities essential for the existence of a society larger than the family. 1 Lieber, *Man. Pol. Ethics*, bk. ii, ch. 3, at 147 (1st ed. 1838). So has this Court observed, *Randall v. Kreiger*, 23 Wall. 137, 147, and Mr. Story also says, in his 1834 treatise, *Commentaries on the Conflict of Laws* (§ 109), that "the contract of marriage is the most important of all human transactions. It is the very basis of the whole fabric of civilized society." Without for a moment doubting the correctness of these observations, neither Mr. Lieber nor the majority opinion explain precisely how polygamy inevitably leads to a state of despotism. The theory seems to rest on a chain of reasoning that, there being more adults and children in polygamous marriages, they are more prone to conflict and competition than monogamous marriages; that a longstanding, unselfish interest in another person and in shared children are less likely to develop in such families; and that because of these conditions, affection and altruistic family relationships are less likely to flourish in polygamous families. It is said that this, in turn, stunts the development of moral capacity for sympathy and thereby leads to a less civilized society. Perhaps there is truth in these ideas about social and political relations; they are at least plausible. Yet with all due respect for Professor Lieber's theory, it has no place in this Court's consideration of the precise question presented here – which is not whether Congress had the power to make polygamous marriage a crime – but having done so, whether the law must be applied without exception to an individual who practices polygamy because it is an accepted doctrine of his church and a duty he believes of divine origin. And to this question, the answer must be no, for the constitutional provision protecting free exercise of religion, which the founders intended to be given a liberal construction, must take precedence over a political theory on the connections between polygamy and historically despotic structures. It would be a perversion of justice to hold that the acts of the accused are unjustified as a matter of law on the basis of such a general proposition.

Further, I cannot agree that polygamy leads to despotism, any more or less than monogamy leads to despotism. Professor Lieber admitted as much when he observed in his treatise that the essential characteristic of monogamous marriage is the discarding of mutual right. By custom and law, monogamous marriage encourages forgetfulness of separate individual interest, and is based on kindness and forbearance of the husband. The authority of the father, too, is neither motivated nor legitimated by ideals of equality and justice; it is restricted only by personal attachment. Unlike the state, whose essential ideas are consent and the equal right which exists between person and person, monogamous marriage demands one-sided obligation, and knows not mutuality. *Id.* at 152. These principles of monogamy, if applied to the state, would also inevitably lead to absolutism and tyranny. The observation is echoed by Mr. Mill in his 1869 essay on marriage as it stood in England at the common law, which authorities everywhere agree is the basis of our country's marriage law. He said, "The family is a school of despotism, in which the virtues of despotism, but all its vices, are nourished." Mill, 81. Indeed, in monogamy, the wife is the bond servant of her husband: no less so, as far as her legal status, than the polygamous wife. The monogamous wife owes lifelong obedience to the husband. *Id.* at 55. Marriage allows men, without labor, to live on the labor and property of women. After marriage, the man is entitled to all of his wife's property of every kind, her moral existence is merged in his, and his will is her rule of action. E. P. Hurlbut, 1848 *Ess. Hum. Rts.*, 115. If she proves refractory, he has the power of moderate correction and chastisement. She is presumed by the law to be so much under his dominion as to be incapable of free moral action, insomuch that she is excused for any crime committed in his presence. No degree of drunkenness or low brutality on his part frees her from the yoke of marriage to him. *Id.* On the theory that, through marriage, her interests are represented, women are excluded from all active participation in government, notwithstanding their ability for clear intellectual perceptions and their consequent ability to perceive the wisdom and expediency of the laws. *Id.* at 120–22. As observed by Mr. Mill,

> She vows a livelong obedience to him at the altar, and is held to it all through her life by law. [T]he obligation of obedience stops short of participation in crime, but it certainly extends to everything else. She can do no act whatever but by his permission, at least tacit. She can acquire no property but for him; the instant it becomes hers, even if by inheritance, it becomes ipso facto his.
>
> Mill, 55.

It is relevant, also, to the majority's conclusion that polygamy threatens the freedom of those around it, while monogamy inhibits such evils, that the monogamous wife's position in most states is worse than the polygamous wife in Territorial Utah, where, at least, women have been included in the elective franchise since 1870. And it must also not be forgotten that enslaved persons were formally prohibited from marrying in Southern states before the Civil War, even though it is suggested by the majority that, because monogamy is so integral to the best interests of society, no state has ever departed from its ideal model of social life. From this examination of the law governing monogamous marriage both past and present, I am constrained to conclude, notwithstanding some recent modifications of the civil law in a different direction in some states, that monogamy, no less than polygamy, is a great engine of despotism.

And how have the presumably enslaved women of Utah responded to their condition? However the polygamous wife might seek to maintain her social status, however religious convictions might impel her, or iron circumstances restrain her, however ignorant or poor she might be, sooner or later, if the majority is right about her condition, one should expect that the assaulted, imprisoned, outraged instincts of human nature would arise and vindicate themselves, and that Mormon women would exercise the ballot to overturn the practice of polygamy. But this has not occurred. Enfranchised and exercising their political equality, and having the greatest rights of all citizens – the ballot – they have demonstrated determined opposition to Section 5352. Not without substantial pressure from federal marshals who subpoena them and compel them to testify against their husbands in violation of the law of unity; from prosecutors and judges who invade their privacy with all manner of questions about the intimate details of their home life, including sleeping arrangements and dates and times of the last sexual intercourse with their husbands; from federal officials who have brought indictments against them for sexual crimes such as fornication, transforming them into the legal equivalent of prostitutes; and from East Coast suffragist activists who visit their territory to admonish them to "wake up," establish "their own constitutions, creeds, and codes, and customs" unmediated by man, and to advise them that they would not be in their current state of dependence and degradation "but by man's free and fraudulent use of the authoritative 'Thus saith the Lord'" (Stanton, *Revolution*, July 13, 1871), the polygamous wives in the Utah Territories, and Mormon women more generally, have employed their recently elevated political position in support of polygamy, not against it. For, like the accused in this case, they believe that its justification lies in theological doctrine, despite its hardships.

Indeed, one may attribute the unusual equality of rights that women in Utah enjoy to their desire to stand up and defend polygamy. When Congress attempted, in 1870, to further facilitate its decade-long purpose to stamp out polygamy in the Territory of Utah by a proposed federal statute that would have denied citizenship, public office, the franchise, or any homestead benefit to anyone practicing polygamy (Cullum Bill), Mormon women were at the forefront of organized efforts to defeat it. They held a mass meeting, gathering some 3,000–4,000 women, to advocate the claims of polygamy and defend the men who practice it. Great Indignation Meeting, *Deseret Evening News*, Jan. 14, 1870, at 2 & Jan. 15, 1870, at 2. They also held meetings in fifty-eight towns, large and small, at which as many as 25,000 women attacked the proposed legislation and defended polygamy. *Deseret News*, Mar. 9, 1870, at 49. Shortly thereafter, the legislature of the Utah Territory granted women there the right to vote, in recognition of their confidence in their wives and sisters, and in response to the women's demand for the right of franchise. From this history, it is apparent that Utah has a more thoroughgoing structure of consent to their peculiar domestic form of marriage than all the states and territories that embrace monogamous marriage, except the Wyoming Territory, which enfranchised women in 1869.

It is undoubtedly true that many polygamous wives, like many monogamous wives, are victims of husbands who, without being in a legal sense malefactors in any other respect, indulge the utmost habitual excesses of bodily violence toward their unhappy wives, or toward whom the excesses of their wives' dependence inspires mean and savage natures, or who do not practice the consideration toward their wives which is required of them toward everybody else. The extensive record of women's political empowerment in the Utah Territories, however, and their unwavering defense of polygamy, may be accepted as authoritative evidence that the constitutional guarantee of religious freedom, while not prohibiting federal legislation making polygamy a crime, requires an exception from the operation of Section 5352 in this case, there not being any evidence in the record of specific harm to wives or children of the accused, injury of the equal rights of others, or evidence of disturbance of the general public order in the Territory of Utah; there being evidence, rather, that the practice is generally consensual and supported by polygamous wives. Such a disposition in this case would not only properly reflect the founders' intentions with respect to the scope of the Constitution's protections of religion, but would also, by its effect, further the parallel interests in religious freedom and equality of female citizens in the Territory of Utah.

III

Finally, in order that there may be no misapprehension of the views which I entertain in regard to the power of Congress to govern the Territory of Utah, I wish to be clear that my reasoning does not rest on the general proposition, promoted by the Southern states in defense of slavery, and rejected explicitly by the thirteenth and fourteenth amendments to the Constitution, that a state or territory has a right to regulate its own domestic affairs, and to mold the law of domestic relations to their own customs and usages, even if in conflict with federal law or the inherent rights of others. As Justice Curtis reasoned in his dissent in *Dred Scott v. Sandford*, 19 How. 693, 611 (Curtis, J., dissenting), it would be absurd to assert that the United States has the power to acquire a territory, and no power to govern it when acquired. I am in agreement with the majority opinion on this point. Yet how such a proposition is so elementary and self-evident as to require no argument by the majority of this Court to support it utterly confounds me, especially when delivering an opinion so pregnant with vital consequences for citizens of African descent and persons of color. Just three years ago, the majority of this court was faced with a very similar question in *United States v. Cruikshank et al.*, 92 U.S. 542, which concerned the constitutionality of the convictions of several white men under the federal Enforcement Act of 1870, for conspiring to falsely imprison and murder an estimated 105 citizens of African descent in a dispute over the results of the 1872 gubernatorial election in Louisiana, *id.* at 548–49, much graver offences than polygamy. Overturning the convictions of the white men, the majority opinion reasoned on the rights of the negro persons conspired against: "The Government of the United States, although it is, within the scope of its powers, supreme and beyond the states, can neither grant nor secure to its citizens rights or privileges which are not expressly or by implication placed under its jurisdiction," for the Constitution "adds nothing to the rights of one citizen as against another." *Id.* at 550, 542. The Constitution, said the Court, "secures the individual from the arbitrary exercise of the powers of government," *id.* at 554, but not from private action. Therefore, citizens of African descent must look to "municipal legislation" for protection from violence when other citizens deprive them of their inherent rights of peaceable assembly for lawful purposes, and of life and personal liberty. *Id.* at 553. Nor, according to recent decisions, does the fourteenth amendment of the Constitution apply to a woman in Illinois who wanted to practice law but was disabled by coverture, *Bradwell v. State*, 16 Wall. 130, or immunize from criminal prosecution a suffragist woman in Missouri who voted knowing that the local law restricted the franchise to men. *Minor v. Happersett*, 88 21 Wall. 162. Were today's majority to endeavor to reconcile its reasoning with these decisions, the effort would be involved in great difficulty.

It is heartening that my brethren are starting to think of the Constitution as entailing a positive vision of moral limits in our federal system. Yet I cannot help but observe that the majority has arrived at this sea change in its understanding of the Constitution, and the humanitarian precepts embedded in it, only upon consideration of a form of marriage that they propose sacrifices the sensibilities of women who are members of the white race. Are not men and women of African descent equally included in the Constitution's protections? In our system of government, is not a woman's right to pursue her true and substantial happiness as her own conscience shall dictate, as sacred a right guaranteed by the Constitution as her right, implicitly protected by the court's decision today, to maintain a specific station in the domestic sphere and society? Although these questions go beyond what is required for this decision, I can only hope that the majority opinion's expansive view of the constitutionally implied powers of Congress to legislate for the greater good, which I share, will be maintained going forward when presented with questions of Congress's power to secure individuals' right to personal security, personal liberty, and private property, whether such rights are threatened by hostile state legislation or personal prejudice, and whether the individuals be men or women, of African or European descent.

I dissent, therefore – First, because I think the first amendment protects religious practice from the dictates of general law, so long as the practice does not invade the private rights of others or disturb public peace and order, and, secondly, because no such invasion or disturbance has been shown in this case. I am of the opinion that the judgment of the Supreme Court of the Territory of Utah should be reversed.

3

Commentary on *McGuire v. McGuire*

MARY ANNE CASE

INTRODUCTION

Although cited in fewer than half a dozen other cases since it was decided in 1953, *McGuire v. McGuire* is discussed in well over one hundred law review articles and featured prominently in the overwhelming majority of family law casebooks published for the U.S. market.[1] The proposition for which it is generally thought to stand is that a wife "could not enforce any claims against her spouse during the course of the ongoing marriage."[2] As this commentary will argue, however, to cite the opinion reprinted in the casebooks for this proposition is to misunderstand it.[3]

THE FACTS OF *MCGUIRE* AND THE FEMINIST JUDGMENT

The striking facts of the case, undisputed by the parties and detailed in both the Nebraska Supreme Court opinion reversing the trial court's judgment and in Martha Ertman and Zvi Triger's rewritten feminist judgment may have contributed to making the case a classic. The defendant in the case, eighty-year-old Charles McGuire, despite having in his name bank deposits and government bonds totaling more than $100,000 as well as nearly four hundred

[1] *McGuire v. McGuire*, 59 N.W.2d 336 (Neb. 1953); Mary Anne Case, *Enforcing Bargains in an Ongoing Marriage*, 35 WASH. U. J. L. & PUB. POL'Y 225, 228 (2011).

[2] Ellen Wright Clayton & Jay Clayton, *Afterword: Voices and Violence – A Dialogue*, 43 VAND. L. REV. 1807, 1815 (1990).

[3] The argument on this point below is an extremely abbreviated version of that previously appearing in Case, *supra* note 1, at 228–36. Much of the information about the McGuires in that article and in the commentary below was acquired through the generosity of Dirk Hartog, who included an important chapter on McGuire in HENDRIK HARTOG, MAN & WIFE IN AMERICA: A HISTORY 6–39 (2000).

acres of farmland,[4] lived with sixty-six-year-old Lydia, his wife of more than thirty years, in a house lacking modern conveniences such as running water, an indoor toilet, a refrigerator freezer, or an automatic heating system. Among the things she alleged he declined to pay for were not only new furnishings and upgrades for their home and car, but new clothes for her, long-distance phone calls, excursions to a movie theater, charitable contributions, and the cost for her to travel to visit the two adult daughters of her first marriage.[5] Without separating from Charles or seeking to divorce him, Lydia sued "to require him to provide reasonable maintenance and necessaries of life."[6] She alleged that her advanced age and physical disabilities prevented her from continuing with the business of raising chickens from which she had in the earlier years of her marriage earned money to maintain herself.[7] The trial court entered a detailed order specifying exactly what improvements to the house and car were to be made at Charles's expense and additionally ordered him to pay Lydia the costs of an annual trip to visit each of her daughters and "a monthly allowance of $50 for spending money for wearing apparel and personal items for her beauty, comfort and pleasure."[8]

The Nebraska Supreme Court reversed the trial court's decree in its entirety, holding:

> The living standards of a family are a matter of concern to the household, and not for the courts to determine, even though the husband's attitude toward his wife, according to his wealth and circumstances, leaves little to be said in his behalf. As long as the home is maintained and the parties are living as husband and wife it may be said that the husband is legally supporting his wife and the purpose of the marriage relation is being carried out.[9]

A central question the *Feminist Judgments* project seeks to answer is whether the arguments made and conclusions reached by twenty-first-century feminists could also have been arrived at by judges at the time a leading case was originally decided, using materials and concepts available at that time. It is therefore worth highlighting that the feminist judgment of Professors Ertman and Triger not only affirms unaltered the judgment of the trial court in *McGuire*, but also in substantial measure tracks its operative reasoning.

[4] Case, *supra* note 1, at 338.

[5] *McGuire*, 59 N.W.2d at 337.

[6] Dist. Ct. Memorandum at 19, *McGuire*, 59 N.W.2d (No. 33305) [hereinafter "Dist. Ct. Memo"].

[7] Complaint at para. 6., *McGuire*, 59 N.W.2d (No. 33305).

[8] Dist. Ct. Memo, *supra* note 6, at 28, para. 4.

[9] *McGuire*, 59 N.W.2d at 342.

Apparently agreeing with the trial court that "[c]ourts should not encourage litigation between spouses, and should be reluctant to fix standards of living in an American home,"[10] Ertman and Triger endorse what they call the trial court's "narrowly tailored test"[11] of whether "the support and maintenance provided is so unreasonably inadequate under the circumstances that it shocks the conscience."[12] They not only agree that Lydia asks for no more than "what a deserving wife justifiably desires,"[13] but also confirm that, as the trial court held, "the wife has helped to earn and accumulate most of the worldly wealth held in the name of her husband, and she is entitled to share in its enjoyment."[14]

AN ALTERNATIVE VIEW OF THE MCGUIRES' MARRIAGE

Ertman and Triger contrast this feminist notion of marriage as a partnership in "which husband and wife can together make decisions and contribute to family life as equal partners" with the system of coverture which put all property and all decision-making authority in a marriage solely in the hands of the husband, a system they stress Nebraska had been well on the way toward dismantling by the 1950s. They see Charles McGuire as having the "old-fashioned ... view of marriage" associated with coverture, of behaving like a "despo[t] in the home"[15] contrary to modern American values and of exercising "coercive control ... over Lydia McGuire's everyday life." But are Ertman and Triger necessarily correct in their characterization of Charles McGuire and his marriage?[16]

There is a very different way to characterize the underlying facts in the *McGuire* case, one that might lead to a very different, but equally feminist, judgment as to how the case should be approached. The remainder of this commentary will set forth that alternative view of the facts, arguing that neither Ertman and Triger's analysis nor the legal academy's general approach to the case do those facts justice.

[10] Ertman-Triger Rewritten Opinion.

[11] *Id.*

[12] Dist. Ct. Memo., *supra* note 6, at 26.

[13] *Id.*

[14] Dist. Ct. Memo., *supra* note 6, at 27. This is also the view put forward by Lydia in her complaint, which alleged, that "a considerable amount of the assets of the defendant have been accumulated since their marriage through the joint efforts of both." *Id.*

[15] Ertman-Triger Rewritten Opinion, *supra* note 10.

[16] Ertman and Triger's characterization is not that of the trial court, and therefore not necessary to reach the bottom-line result that court reached and Ertman and Triger's opinion affirms.

Ertman and Triger describe the McGuires as "pool[ing] their efforts," with "Lydia's part of the traditional marital exchange" including "cooking, cleaning, washing, and other tasks that make a house a home," as well as "farm labor." She was, as they see it, now entitled to "judicial enforcement of Charles's complementary obligations to financially provide." These complementary obligations – a wife's to care for husband and home, a husband's to provide financial support – were indeed part of the sexed and gendered, not-yet reciprocal obligations of marriage that survived long past the abolition of formal coverture.[17] There was little a husband could legally do to force his wife to clean the house,[18] but, at common law, there was a well-established mechanism for a wife to force a solvent husband to provide for her financially. The doctrine of necessaries made a husband liable for things such as food, clothing, household items, and essential services furnished to his wife, who, while under coverture, had limited ability to contract in her own name. The trial court opinion affirmed by Ertman and Triger describes Lydia McGuire as suing for "reasonable maintenance and necessaries of life," each of which the trial court's order granted her. The sole dissenting judge on the Nebraska Supreme Court, who would have upheld only those portions of the trial court order awarding a monthly maintenance amount to Lydia and fees to her attorneys, correctly observed that "no award of a court of equity was necessary to establish" Lydia McGuire's "right to charge her husband with her necessaries of life."[19] Why then did Lydia McGuire not simply do as the dissenting judge implicitly suggested she could have and as wives as late as the early 1980s successfully did[20] – go out into the marketplace and buy what she thought she needed, sending the bill to her husband, who, to the extent what she purchased were indeed necessaries, would be obliged to pay?[21] After all, what constituted necessaries for a given married couple had always been a function of a husband's "means, position, and station in life,"[22] and what Lydia wanted to acquire were conveniences even her poorer neighbors had been able to afford.

[17] *See* June Carbone, *Borelli v. Brusseau*: Commentary, *in* Chapter 12 of this volume.

[18] *See* Ertman-Triger Rewritten Opinion, *supra* note 10 (discussion).

[19] *McGuire*, 59 N.W.2d at 245 (Yeager, J., dissenting).

[20] *See, e.g.*, *Sharpe Furniture, Inc. v. Buckstaff*, 299 N.W.2d 219, 224 (Wis. 1980) (requiring Mr. Buckstaff to pay, over his objections, for a sofa specially ordered by his wife because the "Buckstaffs are a prominent family and their socio-economic standing justifies a finding that the sofa at issue here was a suitable and proper item for their household").

[21] *Earle v. Earle*, 27 Neb. 277 (1889). As the leading Nebraska case discussed in both the original and feminist judgment of *McGuire* put it: "[i]t is a well established rule of law that it is the duty of the husband to provide his family with support and means of living . . . and for this purpose the wife has generally the right to use his credit for the purchase of necessaries." *Id.* at 281.

[22] *See Earle v. Earle*, 27 Neb.

Contrary to Ertman and Triger's assumption, Lydia McGuire most likely sought a court "order to take out credit in her husband's name," not "because she could not get credit on her own,"[23] rather because she had assets of her own creditors could look to for payment. She was not a wife under coverture, whose income and assets were as a matter of law fully under her husband's control, nor was she as a matter of fact totally financially dependent on her husband. Instead, she had entered the marriage with Charles, whose "reputation for more than ordinary frugality" and whose home life were known to her before marriage, as a widow with not only two young daughters, but an equal share with each of those daughters in eighty acres of real property inherited from her deceased husband and a business of her own she ran independently of her husband. Charles McGuire, who supported the daughters while they were in his home and contributed financially to their college education,[24] signed off on his wife's transfer of her interest in this land to the daughters in 1939, more than a dozen years before she sued him.[25] Even after the transfer, Lydia McGuire remained able "to use all of the rent money" from the transferred land and had indeed used some of it to visit her daughters.[26] At the time of trial in 1952, she had nearly $6,000 in a checking account,[27] including accumulated income from the eighty acres, money given her by her father, and some savings from the chicken and egg business she had managed on her own from the beginning of the marriage until very shortly before the trial.

Ertman and Triger claim that Charles McGuire "insists on exercising exclusive control over the property accumulated during their marriage, and relegates Lydia to living in impoverished conditions." The Nebraska Supreme Court was, however, correct when it found "that the plaintiff is not devoid of money in her own right. She has a fair-sized bank account and is entitled to use the rent from the 80 acres of land left by her first husband, if she so chooses."[28] In fact, there was no evidence Charles sought to exercise any control at all over either the assets Lydia brought to the marriage or those she accumulated in her

[23] Ertman-Triger Rewritten Opinion, *supra* note 10.

[24] Transcript of Record at 20, *McGuire*, 59 N.W.2d (No. 33305). *See also McGuire*, 59 N.W.2d at 227.

[25] *McGuire*, 59 N.W.2d at 227. Because he might have been much less willing to accede to the transfer had he known his wife would later ask for a such a substantial increase in household expenditures, Ertman and Triger seem wrong in their categorical assertion that "Charles McGuire has not suffered any detriment," but instead "benefit[ed]" from his wife's waiting so long to make her financial demands of him. Ertman-Triger Rewritten Opinion, *supra* note 10

[26] *McGuire*, 59 N.W.2d at 229.

[27] *Id.* at 230; Transcript of Record, *supra* note 24, at 20. This amount, reported to the court by her bank, was nearly four times the amount she had estimated to the court she had in the bank. *Id.*

[28] *McGuire*, 59 N.W.2d at 238.

own name during it. He may not have "inform[ed her] as to his finances or business,"[29] but she similarly "made no accounting to her husband."[30] And he lived in precisely the same "impoverished conditions" she did, with the same lack of modern conveniences, the same antiquated and dilapidated household furnishings, the same lack of diversions such as trips to the movie theater. According to Ertman and Triger, "[i]nstead of according his dutiful spouse with the respect due to a marriage partner, Charles McGuire treats her like an untrustworthy servant." But Charles is not like the husband of the patient Griselda of folklore,[31] who lived in regal splendor in his castle, while keeping his wife as a servant in rags, slavishly obedient to his whims. Charles treated his wife just as well as he treated himself, simply disagreeing with her about what was necessary. For him, new household furnishings were an unnecessary luxury, and there was evidence to back up his contention that he did support his wife. As the Nebraska Supreme Court observed, for example, he not only paid for groceries, but had paid for his wife's three abdominal operations, placing "no restrictions" on her choice of doctor.[32]

Ertman and Triger make reference to two "[a]lternative views of marriage" beyond the "traditionalist" view, one view that would "focus on women's autonomy" and another that would "pu[t] a proper value on their caretaking role." Their opinion rests on the latter approach, which also underlies many feminist arguments about what should constitute equitable division of assets at divorce as well as status-based proposals for approaches to the nonmarital family, such as the American Law Institute's Domestic Partners proposal, which, it must be stressed, has gained no traction under American law.[33] Instead of imposing, as some other countries do, a default status (and a default norm of asset sharing) on cohabiting couples, the laws in the United States generally give such couples only such rights and duties as they affirmatively agree to,[34] either by marrying or by entering into an express or implied, oral or written contract.[35]

[29] *Id.* at 228.

[30] Transcript of Record, *supra* note 24, at 20.

[31] *See, e.g.*, Giovanni Boccaccio, *Book 10, Tale 10, in* THE DECAMERON (John Payne trans., London, 1906) *available at* http://sites.fas.harvard.edu/~chaucer/special/authors/boccaccio/boc10-10.html

[32] *McGuire*, 59 N.W.2d at 230.

[33] *See* American Law Institute, *Domestics Partners, in* PRINCIPLES OF THE LAW OF FAMILY DISSOLUTION: ANALYSIS AND RECOMMENDATIONS (2002). Cynthia Grant Bowman similarly would reward women's caretaking labor in a status-based regime. Cynthia Grant Bowman, *A Feminist Proposal to Bring Back Common Law Marriage*, 75 OR. L. REV. 709 (1996).

[34] For further discussion *see* American Law Institute, *Domestics Partners*, *supra* note 33, n. 50.

[35] *See, e.g.*, *Marvin v. Marvin*, 557 P.2d 106, 110 (Cal. 1976), which is the subject of commentary in Chapter 6 of this book. In this case, whose general approach has since become widespread

American law no longer imposes a one-size-fits-all model even on married couples; they are by and large free to structure their lives and their finances as they please,[36] commingling them or keeping them separate without having their relationship legally questioned as a result.[37]

While there are good feminist reasons to value caretaking and encourage spousal interdependence, it is no less feminist to "focus on women's autonomy." As Ertman and Triger's opinion acknowledges, "[a]ll wives need not behave alike" and the law since the abolition of coverture has had the desirable effect of "reaffirming wives' independent legal existence." It therefore seems odd for Ertman and Triger to insist that it would be categorically wrong were Charles McGuire "to see each spouse within the marriage union as 'an island entire of itself.'" It was clear from the undisputed findings of fact that the pattern and practice of both McGuires from the very beginning of their marriage was not only to live frugally, but to seek to accumulate money, each in his or "her own name."[38] Feminism does not require disrespecting the McGuires' longstanding lifestyle choices simply because they do not meet some imagined ideal of marital unity. To force the couple closer together might be as perverse as demanding that she leave him and seek a divorce,[39] given their longstanding behavior and attitudes.[40]

in the United States, the California Supreme Court held that "courts should enforce express contracts between nonmarital partners except to the extent that the contract is explicitly founded on the consideration of meretricious sexual services. ... In the absence of an express contract, the courts should inquire into the conduct of the parties to determine whether that conduct demonstrates an implied contract, agreement of partnership or joint venture, or some other tacit understanding between the parties." *Id.* at 110.

36 For further discussion, *see* Mary Anne Case, *Marriage Licenses*, 89 MINN. L. REV. 1758, 1772–75 (2005) (describing the great flexibility afforded under twenty-first-century American law to married couples, as compared with couples seeking to obtain legal recognition for a domestic partnership, who were typically forced into a more rigid model requiring cohabitation, commingled finances, even specified affects such as living in "an intimate and committed relationship of mutual caring").

37 As the Massachusetts Supreme Judicial Court correctly observed in the pioneering same-sex marriage opinion in *Goodridge*: "benefits are available to married couples regardless of whether they mingle their finances or actually depend on each other for support." *Goodridge v. Dept. of Pub. Health*, 798 N.E.2d 941, 946 (Mass. 2003).

38 Dist. Ct. Memo, *supra* note 6, at 24.

39 They never did separate or divorce, perhaps because, while their case had been pending on appeal, Charles had, albeit "resent[fully]," complied with the District Court's order and modernized their home, made some payments to Lydia, and bought a used car with a heater to replace the one in which they had traveled together to court every day. *See* Letter from Charles McDermott, Attorney for Mr. McGuire (Apr. 18, 1977), *reprinted in* JUDITH AREEN & MILTON C. REGAN, JR., FAMILY LAW: CASES AND MATERIALS 150–51 (5th ed. 2006).

40 Their parallel lives continued to the end of their days. When he died in 1961, he left her $50,000, each of her daughters $1,000, and the bulk of his estate to members of his natal family,

ENFORCING MARITAL BARGAINS

The casebooks and commentators who continue to cite *McGuire* for the proposition that a court will not enforce a bargain between spouses in an ongoing marriage should look much more closely at the holding of the case in both its specific factual context and its general legal context. There was no suggestion in the Nebraska Supreme Court opinion, in the trial court, or in the complaint that the McGuires ever had any kind of bargain or contract between them, other than the contract for their entry into the status of marriage as it was then defined by the law of Nebraska. Therefore, when the Nebraska Supreme Court insisted that "[t]he living standards of a family are a matter of concern to the household, and not for the courts to determine,"[41] it was repudiating enforcement of a thick vision of status and had not necessarily repudiated the enforceability of any explicit, or even implied, agreement between spouses.

On the facts as presented, such evidence as a court might use to find an implied agreement does not favor Lydia McGuire's claim. As the Nebraska Supreme Court noted, "the marital relation has continued for more than 33 years, and the wife has been supported in the same manner during this time without complaint."[42] She had acquiesced in the household's prior level of expenditures and her practice from the beginning of the marriage had been to use her own money (of which admittedly there was less in recent years due to the cessation of her poultry business) to purchase items she now claimed her husband should be ordered to furnish her.[43] Even when she had more of it, she did not spend this money anywhere near as lavishly as the court ordered her husband to do. Precisely in the absence of an express contractual understanding between the McGuires as to their standard of living or level of expenditure and in the face of their longstanding contrary pattern and practice, for the court to choose Lydia's over Charles's view as to household living standards would be for a court to dictate living standards to them, rather than leaving this to the McGuires themselves to determine.

including his surviving brothers and the children of his predeceased siblings. When she died ten years later in 1971, Lydia was buried alongside her first husband, Charles Sellers, who had died in 1914. It might therefore be useful to view the McGuires as belonging to a class of couples who marry late in life, who do not have children together, who have already accumulated assets in their own names, and who have plans for those assets involving blood relatives. *See* Carbone, *supra* note 17.

[41] *Id.*

[42] *Id.* at 342.

[43] *Id.* at 338–42.

The lower court order affirmed by Ertman and Triger dictated living standards for the household in considerable detail. Especially in a world in which comparatively few judges can be relied on to apply feminist principles, this is a dangerous power to put in the hands of judges constrained only by what might "shock their conscience," a test which, Ertman and Triger's assumption to the contrary notwithstanding, cannot readily yield "narrowly tailored . . . limits [to] a court's discretion." As a glance at the relative percentages of assets spouses receive as "equitable distribution" in divorce cases would suggest,[44] the average family court judge is still likely to be shocked at the prospect of dividing assets fifty-fifty between an extremely successful businessman husband and his homemaker wife, and many judges see it as equitable to award a much more substantial share to him so long as she is left with what the court views as ample funds.[45]

There is a third alternative to either leaving the living standards of spouses in a marriage to a judge's conscience or leaving the spouses without a legal remedy short of separation or divorce.[46] That alternative would be to allow what the Nebraska Supreme Court's holding in *McGuire* has generally, but inaccurately, been thought to prevent – the enforcement by a court, even in an ongoing marriage, of marital bargains.[47] A court using this option might not have awarded Lydia McGuire a fully renovated and newly furnished home, given that she seems neither explicitly nor implicitly to have bargained for anything like this either before entry into or during the course of her long marriage to Charles McGuire. And few spouses might ever follow Lydia McGuire's lead and go to court while in an intact marriage. But leaving open the possibility may be the best way of vindicating the feminist

[44] Equitable distribution is what Lydia McGuire would likely have received had she successfully sued for divorce. *See Hoffmeyer v. Hoffmeyer*, 157 Neb. 842, 844 (1954).

[45] For further discussion of judges' tendencies disproportionately to favor income-earning husbands over homemaking wives, *see, e.g.*, Joan C. Williams, *Is Coverture Dead? Beyond a New Theory of Alimony*, 82 Geo. L.J. 2227 (1994) (coining the term "he who earns it, owns it" to describe the attitude of many judges).

[46] Saul Levmore has dubbed the latter approach "love it or leave it" and has correctly pointed out that this approach, still thought to apply to marriage, no longer applies in most other areas of law it formerly governed, such as business partnership. *See* Saul Levmore, *Love It or Leave It: Property Rules, Liability Rules, and Exclusivity of Remedies in Partnership and Marriage*, 58 Law & Contemp. Probs. 221, 226 (1995).

[47] In theory current law is open to this, *see* Unif. Premarital Agreement Act § 3, 9C U.L.A. 373 (1983) ("an agreement may provide for such matters as the choice of abode, the freedom to pursue career opportunities, the upbringing of children, and so on"). In practice, however "[s]tates that have adopted the Uniform Act . . . do not seem to enforce such contracts, and some have seemingly inconsistent statutory provisions." Elizabeth S. Scott & Robert E. Scott, *Marriage as Relational Contract*, 84 Va. L. Rev. 1225, 1303 n. 177 (1998).

value of allowing members of a couple to pursue happiness in ways that best suit them, however far from conventional gender roles and norms their approach might be.[48]

McGUIRE v. McGUIRE, 59 N.W.2D 336 (NEB. 1953)

JUSTICE ERTMAN, WITH JUSTICE TRIGER CONCURRING, DELIVERED THE OPINION OF THE COURT

Plaintiff Lydia Giese Sellers McGuire ("Lydia") brought this action in equity to recover suitable maintenance money from her husband, Charles McGuire ("Charles"). After trial the District Court of Wayne County rendered a judgment in favor of Lydia McGuire. It decreed that she was legally entitled to purchase necessaries on her husband's credit and obligate him for the following purchases: (1) improvements to their home or purchase of a modern home that has features such as indoor plumbing with hot and cold running water via a kitchen sink, bathroom sink, and bathtub, an indoor toilet, a refrigerator with the capacity to freeze ice and food, and a furnace; (2) a new automobile with working heating within thirty days; (3) a $50 personal allowance for her, payable on the first of each month; and (4) travel expenses for Lydia to visit each of her daughters at least once a year. We AFFIRM the District Court Judgment.

I RECITATION OF FACTS

When Lydia and Charles McGuire married in 1919, she was a widowed mother of two young daughters and he was a bachelor in his forties. The District Court found that Lydia knew that Charles "had reputation for more than ordinary frugality" when they married. It also found that both spouses "have worked hard and have been very frugal. The wife, in addition to the performance of ordinary housewife duties, helped with the chores, corn picking, harvest, and did much hard labor." Dist. Ct. Memo at 20. They started working the 160 acres that Charles had farmed since 1905, and over

[48] In prior work, I have argued, using, inter alia, game theory, that it is precisely those whose marital bargains diverge most from conventional gender roles who might benefit most from the possibility of enforcement of those bargains by a court bound by U.S. constitutional norms of sex equality, rather than being dependent for recourse only on the social pressure brought to bear by their neighbors, their clergy, or their marriage counselor. *See* Case, *supra* note 1, at 250–60.

time also farmed 238 additional acres of land that Charles purchased. At trial he was eighty and she was sixty-six years old. They had both retired from farming and hog raising – he rented out the land – and she also from raising 300 chickens each year for the chicken and egg money. He did not disclose to her the rent he received for the land, or income on government bonds that he purchased, some perhaps payable to Lydia but never delivered to her. The trial court found his net worth to exceed $200,000 and that she had only about $6,000 in a bank account.

When they married Lydia had two daughters – aged nine and eleven – from her prior marriage. Like many farming spouses, the McGuires pooled their efforts to finish raising those girls and work the land. Lydia's part of the traditional marital exchange included cooking, cleaning, washing, and other tasks that make a house a home, all on top of farm labor. Today those daughters are grown, educated by teaching and business colleges, married, and living with their own families in other states.

Having done her part of the traditional marital bargain for over three decades, Lydia McGuire seeks judicial enforcement of Charles's complementary obligations to financially provide. Few wives are driven to the extreme of litigation, but Charles McGuire refuses to share the substantial assets accumulated through their frugality and joint efforts.

Charles insists on exercising exclusive control over the property accumulated during their marriage, and relegates Lydia to living in impoverished conditions. Their house has no indoor plumbing, or a water heater, which requires Lydia to cook and clean without a kitchen sink, having to boil in a teakettle any hot water for cooking, clean-up, or bathing. The house does not have a bathtub, bathroom sink, or even an indoor toilet. Their transportation is likewise outdated: a 1929 Model A Ford with inadequate heating and a 1927 Chevrolet pickup. Lydia, now sixty-six years old, has weathered the last five or six Nebraska winters burdened by having to haul coal and ashes because Charles refused to purchase reliable indoor heat. Though he did buy her a coat four years ago, she has mostly had to pay for her own clothing, groceries, and both personal and household necessaries out of money earned from her chickens. His restrictions extend to their social, spiritual, and community lives. They have not gone to a motion picture show for the past twelve years, do not belong to any organizations or charities, and while he is a member of the church on his own farmland, at the time of trial that church had no minister and held no services.

Instead of according his dutiful spouse with the respect due to a marriage partner, Charles McGuire treats her like an untrustworthy servant. He refuses to tell her anything about his finances, and doles out money to her in tiny amounts – often 25¢ or 50¢ – to buy groceries, though none at all for the last three or four years. She cannot even take refuge in the love of her daughters, because he threatens to disconnect the phone if she makes a long-distance telephone call.

In sum, Lydia McGuire lives like Tantalus of Greek legend, sentenced by her husband to stand in a pool of water that recedes each time she tries to drink, shaded by a tree whose fruit is forever out of her grasp. Having toiled decades to build up family wealth, she is denied the fruits of comfort, convenience, and social community that grace twentieth-century America. Charles McGuire sees essentials of modern American life such as indoor plumbing as "luxuries," and insists that he alone has the power to decide what is a luxury in their household. Charles would have us treat each spouse within the marriage union as "an island entire of itself," contrary to John Donne's famous assertion in that same poem that "no man is an island." Leonard Unger, *Donne's Poetry and Modern Criticism* (1950).

But to be fully human is to be enmeshed in relationships, one of which is marriage. The marriage relationship, in turn, is enmeshed with the state. While our Constitution and other statutes recognize certain realms of privacy within the marriage, that laissez-faire approach does not extend so far as to support Charles's peculiar view of marriage as a relationship of master and servant, in which the servant must pay for her own as well as household expenses. We cannot accept this isolationist vision of the marital relationship.

In the words of the District Court, "[i]t is the duty of the court to determine whether the defendant is adequately and sufficiently maintaining and providing for his wife under their circumstances." Dist. Ct. Memo at 24. In short, Nebraska law does not treat a spouse as an island entire to oneself, or an island isolated from judicial relief when one spouse requires reminding of the obligations of relationship.

Having cast her lot with her husband, Lydia McGuire has few assets in her own name. For reasons not disclosed in the record, twenty years into the marriage, she transferred to her daughters her own interest in the eighty-acre parcel of land that she had inherited from her first husband, Charles Sellers. She is so at the mercy of Charles McGuire's headstrong nature that in her initial petition she asked for and received a temporary restraining order to protect her from him "in any manner imposing any restraint upon [her] personal liberty … or molesting her in any manner" while her suit was pending.

Regarding her main claim for a say in how marital assets are spent, the District Court granted her relief by ordering Charles McGuire to equip their home with running water, a water heater, kitchen sink, bathtub, toilet, and other relief as described above. It did not impose a uniform standard for all married couples, nor did it empower chagrined spouses to seek relief for every short-changing in married life. Instead, the District Court fashioned a "shock the conscience test" that balances the equity of granting relief to spouses like Lydia McGuire against interests in marital privacy:

> when it appears ... that the support and maintenance provided is so unreasonably inadequate under the circumstances that it shocks the conscience, is far below the common standards of any home under similar circumstances, and actually denies affordable facilities and conveniences when a deserving wife justifiably desires, then ... equity should grant relief.
>
> Dist. Ct. Memo. at 26.

This narrowly tailored test limits a court's discretion, allowing us to reject – as the District Court did – Charles McGuire's argument on appeal that the court lacked equitable jurisdiction "to determine whether or not a husband is reasonably providing his wife with necessaries of life."

We conclude that the District Court did not err in holding that the McGuire household provisions – no running water, no kitchen sink, no bathtub, etc. – are unreasonably inadequate in light of Charles McGuire's holdings as one of the ten richest farm families in this state. It falls below the standards of other homes in the neighborhood, even though some of those residents are poor. Lydia McGuire deserves to share in the family wealth she contributed to over three decades of farm work and household maintenance.

Because Charles McGuire's view of marriage is as old-fashioned as his resistance to indoor plumbing and other basic conveniences, a brief review of the changes in the legal treatment of husbands and wives shows why equity requires this result.

Eight decades ago Nebraska, like many other states, began to dismantle the common law doctrine of marital unity, under which "the husband and wife are one person in law: that is, the very being or legal existence of the woman is suspended during the marriage, or at least is incorporated and consolidated into that of the husband." William Blackstone, 1 Commentaries 442 (1765); Neb. Rev. Stat. 42-201 (1945) (married women's property act).

Though coverture deprived wives of contractual capacity, it also protected wives by requiring husbands to provide them with "necessaries." That duty required a husband to pay debts incurred by his wife for necessaries purchased on credit. Outside of the necessaries context, this court recently held that a wife was not bound by a non-competition contract that a husband entered with his business partner, hence reaffirming wives' independent legal existence, in sharp contrast to Blackstone's traditional view of the marriage. *Adams v. Adams*, 58 N.W.2d 172 (Neb. 1953). Nebraska never exempted husbands from rape claims regarding their wives, unlike other states that defined forcible rape as sexual intercourse with "a woman not the defendant's wife." *See, e.g.*, Neb. Rev. Stat. §§ 25-1203 (wife competent to testify against husband in rape prosecution) and 28-408 (1948) (rape definition not exclude spousal rape).

This favorable climate for Nebraska women helped produce people for whom the Cornhusker State is rightly famous. Consider the strong, talented women made famous in novels by Willa Cather, who grew up in Red Cloud, Nebraska and graduated from our state university in 1894. A dozen years earlier, Ada Bittenbender became the first woman admitted to the Nebraska Bar, was nominated to sit on this court a decade later, and was the third woman in the entire country to be admitted to practice before the U.S. Supreme Court. Likewise, Susan LaFlesche Picotte went from the Omaha Reservation to graduate at the top of her medical school class in 1889, reputedly the first Native American to earn a medical degree, and Mildred Brown and her husband S. E. Gilbert founded and published the Omaha *Star* in 1938 to serve the African-American community. Both Mrs. Brown and her paper helped Nebraska extend equality to Negroes by supporting the Omaha Bus Boycott in 1952, which continues to this writing. If it leads the bus company to hire black drivers, the boycott, and the Browns' support for it, could spur progress in the country's pursuit of race equality.

Finally, Nebraska-born Naomi Parker Fraley inspired the Rosie the Riveter war effort poster, representing the many women who left behind traditional household work and worked in factories to help the United States prevail in World War II. Heartland farmwives – and their husbands – also contributed to the war effort by producing meat, grain, and vegetables to feed troops and Allies whose farm economies lay dormant during the war. (Indeed, great increases in farm income during the war may well have contributed to the McGuires' considerable wealth.) Millions of American women volunteered to support our troops through canning, knitting, saving fats, and making household goods last longer. Wartime rations of gasoline, automobiles, and automobile tires required ingenuity in planning each trip to the doctor or grocery store. Rationing of essential grocery items – meat, dairy, sugar, coffee, oils, and canned foods – required a housewife to stretch supplies farther than usual. In the words of a 1942 Public Affairs Pamphlet, housewives must be "militant consumers . . . Their weapons are intelligent buying, conservation, and cooperation . . . Their budget is their battle plan." Helen Dallas, *How to Win on the Home Front*, Public Affairs Pamphlet No. 72 (NY Public Affairs Cmtee 1942). A good number did all of that on top of wage labor in factories support the war effort.

Equity does justice regarding the facts at hand, and here we must be mindful of the country as well as couples. The war efforts of American housewives helped keep European and Japanese despotism at bay. Today American housewives constitute the front lines of a new battle, this time against communism. Primary caretakers tutor children in American values alongside essential skills from tying shoes to earning their allowance. Private support within families is a dominant feature of American law and culture. If a family member such as Charles McGuire shirks this duty then the government must step in. Here, a court sitting in equity has exercised the modest intervention of granting Lydia McGuire a remedy to her husband's refusal to share household wealth with her. While the Soviet Union may dictate all aspects of family life, Nebraska law merely allows a branch of a branch – equity within the judiciary – to ensure a floor under which a husband cannot go. Households form the backbone of our nation, and a tolerance for despotism in the home may well breed a tolerance among those household members for despotism in the public square. *See, e.g.*, *Meyer v. Nebraska*, 262 U.S. 390 (1923); *Pierce v. Soc'y of Sisters*, 268 U.S. 510 (1925).

Still, our law and social norms sometimes fall short of American ideals of equality. Remnants of coverture remain in Nebraska as well as other states. No statute – federal or state – forbids lenders from declining to extend credit to married women. Women still need a male co-signer to get credit. In some jurisdictions, women still need a husband or father even to get a library card.

Lydia McGuire apparently sought an order to take out credit in her husband's name because she could not get credit on her own. Moreover, Charles signed the deed transferring to Lydia's daughters the eighty acres of real property that Lydia apparently held in her individual capacity. This fact suggests that practice, if not formal law, may well continue to hamper wives' economic independence. If Lydia cannot get credit in her own name, and her husband refuses to provide the household with necessaries such as heat, running water, clothing, and long-distance telephone service, she is saddled with the duty to provide housewifely services of cooking, cleaning, and otherwise maintaining the health, safety, welfare of the family without the suitable means to perform those duties.

II DOCTRINES OF LAW AND EQUITY

We first evaluate Lydia McGuire's claims under the rule of law. If law does not afford a remedy, then we must determine whether equitable recovery is necessary to prevent injustice. The standard of our review in equity cases such as this one accords great deference to the trial court's findings and conclusions.

A *Law*

Counsel for Charles McGuire contends that Nebraska law requires Lydia McGuire to divorce her husband before a court can order the husband to meet his obligations of support and maintenance. Yet this argument could place aggrieved spouses in a "no-exit" situation in which all doors are closed, not unlike the acrimonious characters stuck in a room together for eternity in Jean-Paul Sartre's play *No Exit* (1944). Its original French title, *Huis Clos*, is especially telling. It is the legal term *in camera*, i.e. private issues that belong behind closed doors. Marriage ought not to be reduced to an intolerable situation in which, as one character famously says in the play, "Hell is other people." Law and equity, which have designated marriage as the cornerstone of family and thus social life, must instead provide rights and remedies that make it a livable and indeed hospitable institution.

Nebraska law would only grant Lydia McGuire a divorce if she could prove "grounds" such as adultery, physical incompetence, imprisonment, willful abandonment for at least two years, habitual drunkenness, or incurable insanity. Neb. Rev. Stat. 42-301 (1952). Alternatively, she could plead "extreme cruelty" as ground for complete divorce or divorce from bed and board, if she could show that "the husband, being of sufficient ability to provide suitable maintenance for her, shall grossly or wantonly and cruelly refuse or neglect to do so." Neb. Rev. Stat. 42-302 (1952). To meet her burden of proof she would have to present "satisfactory evidence" from third parties to corroborate her claims. Neb. Rev. Stat. 42-335 (1952). Our state statute also prevents her from traveling to another state where divorce is easier to obtain, and then returning home enforce the judgment. 42 Neb. Rev. Stat. 905 (1952).

A court could conclude that the evidence described above – which Charles McGuire does not contest – establishes grounds for divorce. But the high bar for establishing those grounds makes that outcome far from certain. Under our precedent a husband forcing his wife to live in a smokehouse in the field instead of in the house and failing to provide necessaries did not constitute "extreme cruelty" by "grossly or wantonly and cruelly" refusing or neglecting to provide suitable maintenance. *Faller v. Faller*, 4 N.W. 1036 (Neb. 1880). Likewise, a husband moving from the couple's home in Ohio to Nebraska without telling his wife did not constitute "desertion" under the statute, because he invited his wife to join him in Nebraska. *Isaacs v. Isaacs*, 99 N.W. 268 (Neb. 1904).

Lydia McGuire initially pled cruelty and the District Court of Wayne County issued a temporary restraining order during the pendency of her proceeding. But she withdrew those allegations, perhaps because of the law's stringent standards. In the future, law could and perhaps should evolve to allow divorce for incompatibility instead of requiring "grounds," and also to better provide refuge from the coercive control that Charles McGuire exercised over Lydia McGuire's everyday life.

One statutory provision holds greater promise of granting Lydia McGuire a remedy if she were unable to meet the stringent burden of proof imposed on spouses seeking divorce. If a court declined to grant her a divorce from bed and board, Neb. Rev. Stat. 42-337 nevertheless authorizes a court to order a husband to provide support and maintenance to his wife and children during the course of marriage. Yet that provision's discretionary language – "the court may make such an order" – suggests that even if Lydia McGuire were to file for divorce from bed and board, and lost her case, any order of support would remain a matter of judicial discretion instead of entitlement.

Equity, in contrast, helps wives navigate the legal and practical barriers to controlling their finances so that they can share in the marital wealth to which they contributed.

B *Equity*

Principles of equity as well as Nebraska decisions support the District Court's judgment in favor Lydia.

Equity exists to fill justice gaps left by law's rigidity. Here, Nebraska law would simultaneously require Lydia to divorce to enforce Charles's support obligations, and prevent her from divorcing if she cannot establish grounds such as extreme cruelty. Nebraska statutes may codify husbands' marital duties, but they do not exhaust them. Equity provides a remedy when law does not, a righting of wrongs that this case illustrates.

Equity delivers justice via flexible principles where law's rigidity would otherwise perpetrate injustice. Judges sitting in equity exercise considerable discretion because the facts before them can differ greatly and the aim of justice can be a matter of art rather than mathematical precision. While the admirable goals of certainty and predictability shape law, the lived complexity of the human experience constantly produces new, surprising, and unpredictable facts and issues. Equity steps in to resolve any discrepancy between the benefits of certainty and the imperatives of justice, looking to substance and not merely to form.

Moreover, equity supports marriage instead of pushing people toward divorce. Logically, therefore, equitable precedents in Nebraska and elsewhere support Lydia's claim, and equitable defenses do not undercut it. Finally, the potential inequity of judicial meddling in miniscule matters of marital home maintenance is prevented by the District Court's narrowly tailored and precise test for when a court can order one spouse to properly provide for the other.

1 Equity Does Not Force Divorce

Even if the facts at hand sufficiently establish grounds for divorce such as "extreme cruelty" or constructive "desertion," equity does not require Lydia McGuire to take the extreme step of seeking separation or divorce as a condition precedent for her to get the maintenance and support that is her due. A traditionalist view of Nebraska and other states' barriers to divorce insists that they protect society's foundational institutions of marriage and family. Alternative views of marriage, which focus on women's autonomy or putting a proper value on their caretaking roles, might likewise refuse to force Lydia McGuire to file for divorce. In any case, our observation in *Brewer v. Brewer*, 113 N.W. 161 (Neb. 1907) remains true today: families deserve protection as "the unit of the social organism . . . [and are] absolutely necessary to continued social existence." *Id.* at 162.

To require Lydia to divorce or separate is to undermine every marriage by demoting marital obligations to legal nullities that spouses can perform or not at their whim. That outcome runs afoul of Nebr. Rev. Stat. 42-101, which declares that "marriage is considered a civil contract." Contracts require reciprocal obligations, or they are illusory. Shutting the courthouse doors to Lydia McGuire would demote the marital contract to a one-sided arrangement in which Charles could take Lydia's farm labor and homemaking services while giving virtually nothing himself in return. Courts have jurisdiction in equity to prevent this outcome, "doing what ought to be done." John Norton Pomeroy, Vol. II A *Treatise on Equity Jurisprudence* § 363 (p. 8) (1941).

Moreover, we find it inconsistent to argue in the same breath that the court should not interfere with the living standards of a family and also that the law may interfere with marriage by requiring Lydia to divorce Charles to enforce the most basic elements of the marriage contract. By asking us to penalize Lydia for her decision not to file for a divorce, Charles McGuire would have this court take away from spouses the decision whether to separate or divorce.

Instead of asking whether Lydia McGuire must petition for divorce, we could ask why Charles McGuire is only held to his half of the marital contract upon separation or divorce. If it seems strange that Lydia wanted to stay married, it is no less strange that a man whose wife must sue to obtain support and maintenance – opening up his finances and behavior to public discussion and record – did not himself file for divorce. His continued presence in the marriage – driving her to court for the trial, just as she cooked meals for him throughout the dispute – supports our view that he intends to continue to benefit from her services. The District Court's judgment accords with equity's abhorrence for unjust enrichment, also expressed in the maxim that equity "will not suffer a wrong without a remedy." In short, equity requires that Charles McGuire perform his side of the marital bargain.

When spouses prefer to continue as such, equity honors that decision. We find no logic in forcing Lydia McGuire to separate from or divorce her husband to receive adequate financial support. As we said in *Earle v. Earle*, 43 N.W. 118, 119 (Neb. 1889):

> While the statute books of this and other states amply provide for the granting of divorces in meritorious cases, yet we do not apprehend that it is the purpose of the law to compel a wife, when the aggrieved party, to resort to this proceeding, and thus liberate her husband from all obligations to her, in order that the rights which the law gives her, by reason of her marital relation with her husband, may be enforced. Such a conclusion would not generally strike the conscience of a court of equity as being entirely equitable.

The next question is whether other equitable principles justify the lower court's holding.

2 Equity Precedent Supports Claim

Nebraska courts sitting in equity have long recognized the type of claim that Lydia McGuire asserts. *See, e.g., Earle v. Earle*, 43 N.W. 118 (Neb. 1889). While precedent influences equity just as it shapes judicial opinions at law, we must also keep in mind that facts in equitable cases almost inevitably differ, since equity exists to address extraordinary circumstances that the law fails to account for. Accordingly, courts sitting in equity have wide discretion to award remedies to those unhappy wives and husbands in their different circumstances, meting out justice where law would let it slip through the cracks. All wives need not behave alike, and some wives might not insist on indoor plumbing or long-distance phone calls when a family's resources could provide these amenities. In her robust youth Lydia McGuire performed her half of the marital exchange despite primitive conditions imposed by her husband. Yet now, as she enters her older years, she seeks a say in marital spending to which she has long been entitled. Equity grants her the prerogative to change along with those circumstances.

Reported cases of wives obtaining financial maintenance from recalcitrant husbands support this result. The cases reveal the seemingly infinite possibilities marital misery. *See, e.g., Cochran v. Cochran*, 60 N.W. 942;

Chapman v. Chapman, 104 N.W. 880; *Price v. Price*, 106 N.W. 657; *Brewer v. Brewer*, 113 N.W. 161, 13 L.R.A.; *Rhoades v. Rhoades*, 111 N.W. 122, 126 Am. St.Rep. 611; and *Sinn v. Sinn*, 294 N.W. 381. The case of *Earle v. Earle*, 43 N.W. 118, is most analogous to the case before us. It matters not that *Earle* was decided prior to the enactment of the Nebraska statutes on wives' entitlement to maintenance and support during an ongoing marriage, 42 Neb. Rev. Stat. 337. Equity supplements those laws by protecting ever-present obligations of courts to administer justice rather than ministerially apply statutory formulae.

In *Earle* we held that "the authority to grant alimony grows out of the equity powers of the court." *Earle*, 294 N.W. at 119. Mrs. Earle obtained maintenance and support from her husband without seeking a divorce after her husband sent her away from him and ceased to provide for her. The court noted the "well-established rule of law" enforces a "marriage contract" that imposes on a husband the duty to "provide his family with support and the means of living" such as "lodging, food, clothing, etc. . . . as fits his means and station in life." *Id.* Common law deemed his heedless or wanton dereliction of that duty to be a crime. *Id.* The court in *Earle* departed from the approach of other states, which refused aggrieved wives that equitable remedy, justifying its course as "most in consonance with the spirit of the present civilization, and of our law." *Id.* It defended its minority view as necessary to protect wives' equitable claims for support during marriage and prevent "plac[ing] within the power of every man, who, unrestrained by conscience, seeks to be freed from his obligations to his wife and family, by withholding the necessary comforts and support due them." *Id.* at 120. Other cases confirm the wisdom of our approach.

A wife deprived of decision-making in her own home by an overbearing mother-in-law obtained equitable relief because, the court reasoned, "[e]very wife is entitled to a home corresponding with the circumstances and condition of her husband, over which she shall be permitted to preside as mistress." *Brewer v. Brewer*, 113 N.W. 161, 162 (Neb. 1907).

Most cases feature spouses living apart, often due to desertion by the husband without any fault by the wife. *See, e.g.*, *Cochran v. Cochran*, 60 N.W. 942; *Chapman v. Chapman*, 104 N.W. 880; *Price v. Price*, 106 N.W. 657; *Rhoades v. Rhoades*, 111 N.W. 122; and *Sinn v. Sinn*, 294 N.W. 381. But equity does not require a wife to decamp to recover.

A time-honored equitable maxim holds that "equity looks to the intent rather than to the form." Pomeroy, *supra*, at 8. A spouse may desert his or her marriage in every way other than physical removal, which equity may regard as constructive desertion. In *Brewer v. Brewer*, 113 N.W. 161, 162

(Neb. 1907), a young husband constructively drove his wife out of the marital home by allowing his mother to fence his wife out from "management of the household affairs." Yet the wife recovered, in part because she remained willing to live with her husband and even with his mother so long as the wife "could have control over her part of the house." *Id.* In one Massachusetts case, a wife similarly deprived of clothing, medicine, and other suitable support, obtained recovery despite continuing to cohabit with her husband. *Bucknam v. Bucknam*, 57 N.E. 343 (Mass. 1900). Equity may recognize constructive desertion when requiring a spouse to satisfy the statutory level of proof for desertion would produce injustice.

Lydia McGuire's petition is analogous to the situation of other wives who obtained relief in similar circumstances. To deny recovery in the present case would result in injustice by imposing inequality between Lydia and Charles McGuire, and also between Lydia McGuire and other women who are married to men financially capable of providing support, yet unwilling to do so. Equity delivers a remedy in that situation without requiring the wronged wives to move out, separate, or divorce.

3 Equitable Defenses Do Not Bar Recovery

The equitable defenses of clean hands and laches do not bar Lydia McGuire's recovery.

Lydia comes to equity with clean hands. The record details her unnecessarily harsh life conditions, her efforts to support herself and maintain the household in the face of her husband's refusal to share the benefits of wealth accrued by both of their labor. The District Court found that she "keeps house and cooks the meals, apparently without any complaint" and that she presents as "an attractive, refined, and mild mannered lady." Dist. Ct. Memo. at 23–24. Moreover, Lydia McGuire did not seek maintenance payments from her husband without first demonstrating her devotion to the household and to her husband, despite his behavior and treatment of her.

Nor does her delay pose an impediment via the doctrine of laches, which can preclude recovery. While "equity favors the vigilant, not those who slumber on their rights," Pomeroy, *supra*, § 418, at 169, that rule only requires "reasonable diligence," *Id.* § 419 a standard determined by the circumstances of each case. *Id.* § 419c, at 175. Laches is not measured only in time, but also asks whether allowing the delayed claim would be inequitable in light of changed conditions. *Id.* § 419(d), at 177. Delay does not operate as a waiver of the right to bring the claim unless the delay harmed the other party. *Id.* at 178.

Far from harming Charles, Lydia McGuire's delay in bringing her claim benefitted him. For three decades, she apparently managed to keep the family fed and cleaned, and the house clean, seemingly without complaint, all without basic conveniences that her peer homemakers took for granted, such as a kitchen sink, bathtub, and water heater. She did her best to be self-sufficient, though self-sufficiency defeats a main purpose of many marriages. Consequently, Charles McGuire has not suffered any detriment because of his wife's patience. To the contrary, Lydia's diligent patience facilitated the increase of the wealth that he has apparently titled in his own name. Equity will not silence her plea when advancing age and health concerns preclude that self-sufficiency and bring her forward to claim what has long been her due.

Nor can Charles McGuire persuasively assert reliance on those long years of suffering silence. Granted, Lydia entered her marriage to Charles fully aware of his extreme parsimony. But that was 1919. The ensuing three decades have replaced silent movies with "talkies," horses with automobiles, ice houses with electric refrigerators, and washboards with plug-in washing machines. The year the McGuires were married, telephone service was so new that AT&T was measuring 4,000 people's heads to gage the best dimensions for headsets so that callers' lips would be near the microphone while holding the handset to their ears. Nebraska women obtained full suffrage in 1920, a year after the McGuires married. Because progress requires that conditions of marriage change along with the times, Lydia McGuire need not be mired in 1919 technologies merely because she was married that year.

For some couples, delay could defeat a claim. Equity recognizes the importance of personal circumstances, here that people get married and stay married for various reasons. People, technologies, and politics change, and these dynamic conditions shape us. But the case before us does not present detrimental reliance on any delay.

Any reliance was manifestly unreasonable, so Charles cannot defeat Lydia's equitable claim by arguing that he relied on her many years of toil under nineteenth-century conditions. Instead, he should have reasonably expected that as family circumstances improved, his wife would share the wealth accumulated by their joint efforts. A couple may jointly decide to live in penury. But if Lydia opts not to, Charles cannot force her to languish in primitive conditions. Instead, equity recognizes Lydia's right to spend some of the funds she helped accumulate to acquire the basic comforts and conveniences of modern life. Any other view mires modern American marriage in long-abandoned rules of coverture that deprived women of a vote in their families even as law has evolved to allow them access to the voting booth in public life.

Finally, another equitable principle – restitution – justifies Lydia McGuire's recovery. Equity would disgorge Charles McGuire of those unjustly accumulated gains achieved by hoarding for his sole use wealth and income that justly belonged to the household. Nearly every dollar accrued during the marriage came directly or indirectly from their joint effort. Frugality joined forces with industry to produce impressive gains. Charles McGuire's "every man for himself" view of marital life conveniently overlooks his attempt to share the work of marriage but keep all the benefit to himself. The time has long passed when the household was the husband. Recognizing Lydia McGuire's claims merely reflects the trend in American family law and family life toward recognizing that husband and wife can together make decisions and contribute to family life as equal partners.

4 Recovery Is Not Interference in Marriage

Affirming the District Court's judgment does not impermissibly meddle in the parties' marriage. Generally speaking, a court sitting in equity may presume that parties to a marriage are best left to make decisions about the conditions of their lives together. That rule applies to most marriages, in which spouses get support from one another and need not sue to obtain their due. But in extraordinary circumstances, equity allows a person in Lydia McGuire's position to rebut that presumption to obtain specific performance of the support provision of the marriage contract. To rule otherwise treats the party seeking relief in these unusual circumstances as a mere servant without agency or voice in her own home. Indeed, Charles McGuire's argument for nonintervention essentially asks for judicial approval for his position that he alone determines the household's standard of living.

This case presents those unusual circumstances. Applying the District Court's "shock the conscience test," we conclude that granting Lydia McGuire equitable relief balances the equities of justice and marital privacy. Husbands do not have the exclusive power, as Charles McGuire's appeal put it, "to determine whether or not a husband is reasonably providing his wife with necessaries of life." Instead, consistent with the District Court's narrowly tailored test, "it appears . . . that the support and maintenance provided is so unreasonably inadequate under the circumstances that it shocks the conscience, is far below the common standards of any home under similar circumstances, and actually denies affordable facilities and conveniences when a deserving wife justifiably desires, then . . . equity should grant relief." Dist. Ct. Memo. at 26. The test does not empower spouses to obtain a court order directing the purchase of marble bathtubs with solid gold fixtures.

The complete absence of a bathtub in a modern American home, let alone hot water running from faucets, is so "far below the common standards of any home in similar circumstances" that it shocks the conscience.

Few spouses would meet this stringent standard for equitable recovery in an ongoing marriage. But this unusual case shows that Nebraska husbands, particularly those with the wealth of Charles McGuire, must treat their wives as partners, not as Cinderellas relegated to the corner of domestic life.

One crucial caveat remains. The essentials of the marriage contract – sexual relations, homemaking labor, and financial support – may get different treatment in the courts. Consummation in particular is unsuitable for specific performance for two reasons. First, contract law denies the remedy of specific performance in executory contracts for personal services. *Teske v. Dittberner*, 98 N.W. 57 (Neb. 1903); 3 Pomeroy, *Equity Jurisprudence* (2d ed.), § 1405. Second, as already noted, Nebraska does not treat consent to marry as a wife's blanket consent to any and all sexual incursions of her husband.

Homemaking labor presents a closer case. Because executory personal service contracts are not subject to specific performance, Charles McGuire could not obtain a court order forcing Lydia McGuire to scrub the kitchen floor just so. But were she to abandon those homemaking tasks, he might be able to seek maintenance payments from her that reflect the value of the services that she had deprived him of.

Courts routinely determine monetary obligations and award monetary damages, so they are equipped to do this work. Deferring to the discretion of the trial court as we must, we conclude that Lydia McGuire amply rebutted any presumption against judicial interference in an ongoing marriage. While the living standards of a family are generally a matter of concern to the household, and not for the courts to determine, extreme circumstances such as those before the court constitute an exception to that general rule.

We must note, however, that courts should be wary of claims of marital meddling. Existing case law allows court intervention within the household. A strict policy of nonintervention actually abandons family law's role in family life. Courts evaluate whether the husband's support has been "reasonable" or "suitable." Based on that evidence, a court will decide whether to accept or reject a wife's claims. When a court finds that the money that husbands gave to their wives was sufficient, it has evaluated the family's household economy. Without such relief, couples only have separation and divorce as options. As noted above, family law may evolve to relax the stringent standards of "fault" and allow couples to end a marriage for irreconcilable differences. But until then, family privacy as a shield to court review dramatically reduces the during-marriage options available to couples.

III CONCLUSION

Lydia McGuire came to court seeking justice and the District Court granted the remedy she sought. We affirm that judgment on the grounds that marriage is a two-way street, not merely a formal status, and a marital partnership gives both spouses a voice just as business partnerships do.

To rule otherwise would treat marriage as a one-person affair, designating the marital home as the powerful partner's castle and relegating the other to a servant in it even though she spent the better part of her life contributing to the family and its fortunes. Often spouses make their contributions to the household through a traditional household exchange in which one person focuses on the hearth and the other on income-generating activities.

Because marriage is not servitude, courts in equity will enforce a provider's marital duties if that provider refuses to share available resources with the other spouse. No zone of privacy allows a provider to hoard assets to himself and impose on other household members hardships of body, social life, and spirit so harsh that they shock the conscience.

The Judgment of the District Court is AFFIRMED.

4

Commentary on *Dandridge v. Williams*

MAYA MANIAN

INTRODUCTION

Junius and Jeanette Gary were married in Baltimore, Maryland in 1952. During the early years of their marriage, Jeanette suffered several miscarriages and was told that she could not have children. Much to their surprise, Jeanette eventually gave birth to eight children. The pregnancies took a toll on Jeanette's health and an automobile accident left Junius also unable to work any longer. The Gary family survived on public assistance through the federal welfare program, Aid to Families with Dependent Children (AFDC). However, Maryland's maximum grant regulation – a provision that placed an upper limit on welfare payments regardless of the number of children in the family – made it difficult for the Gary family to live under one roof. Yet Junius and Jeanette "shared one overriding goal: to keep the family together at any cost."[1] As their son Junius Jr. later explained: "Life was a constant struggle to make ends meet. There were hungry days. We had to ration. We sometimes only ate once or twice a day."[2] The Gary family sued to enjoin Maryland's welfare scheme as violating both federal statutory law and the Equal Protection Clause. The case ultimately reached the U.S. Supreme Court, which upheld "family caps" on subsistence payments to poor families in *Dandridge v. Williams*.[3]

1 Julie A. Nice, *A Sweeping Refusal of Equal Protection:* Dandridge v. Williams, *in* The Poverty Law Canon: Exploring the Major Cases 130–34 (Marie A. Failinger & Ezra Rosser eds., 2016) (telling the Gary family's story).

2 *Id.* at 131 (internal quotation marks omitted).

3 397 U.S. 471 (1970). The term "family cap" has been used to describe maximum grant regulations like that imposed in *Dandridge*, as well as laws that prohibit additional funds for children born to families already receiving welfare payments. *See C.K. v. Shalala*, 883 F.Supp. 991 (D.N.J. 1995). Critics argue that laws denying welfare benefits based on a parent's AFDC status at childbirth are more accurately termed "child exclusion" laws. *See* Susan

Although welfare law has traditionally been excluded from the family law canon, *Dandridge v. Williams* illustrates how deeply welfare rights – and the lack thereof – slice into family life.[4] *Dandridge*'s significance also cuts across a number of important domains in constitutional law, including poverty law and reproductive rights and justice. *Dandridge* signaled not only the end of the "welfare rights thesis" – the theory that the Constitution provides a "guarantee that every person's basic needs for food, shelter, medical care, and perhaps education will be met" – but also the beginning of an era of eroding governmental support for poor families.[5]

THE ORIGINAL OPINION

Justice Stewart delivered the opinion of the Court, framing the case from the outset not as a clash involving the human rights to make procreative decisions and to obtain basic subsistence for one's children, but merely as a matter of fiscal policy. Describing the crux of the case as about Maryland's efforts, "in the administration of an aspect of its public welfare program, to reconcile the demands of its needy citizens with the finite resources available to meet those demands," Justice Stewart rejected both the statutory and Equal Protection Clause challenges to family cap regulations.[6]

The AFDC program originated with the Social Security Act of 1935. Utilizing a "scheme of cooperative federalism," the jointly financed federal-state program allowed states the authority to compute a "standard of need" for each eligible family unit within its jurisdiction.[7] States had taken a variety of approaches to fulfilling family needs, including (i) providing every family with grants sufficient to meet the state-determined standard of need; (ii) providing all families with a reduced percentage of the standard of need; or (iii) providing most families with the standard of need but placing a maximum amount

Frelich Appleton, *Standards for Constitutional Review of Privacy-Invading Welfare Reforms: Distinguishing the Abortion-Funding Cases and Redeeming the Undue-Burden Test*, 49 VAND. L. REV. 1, 39–43 (1996).

4 *See* JILL ELAINE HASDAY, FAMILY LAW REIMAGINED 196 (2014) ("Legislators and jurists routinely take family law and welfare law to be entirely separate categories ... [y]et much of welfare law is family law as well"); *see also* Appleton, *supra* note 3, at 11–12 (describing what Jacobus tenBroek termed "the dual system of family law" in which different legal regimes and doctrines govern poor families versus wealthier families).

5 Susan Frelich Appleton, *Beyond the Limits of Reproductive Choice: The Contributions of the Abortion-Funding Cases to Fundamental-Rights Analysis and to the Welfare-Rights Thesis*, 81 COLUM. L. REV. 721, 754 (1981).

6 *Dandridge*, 397 U.S. at 472.

7 *King v. Smith*, 392 U.S. 309, 316 (1968).

or "family cap" on the total amount any one family unit may receive.[8] Maryland had followed this last option, adopting a "maximum grant regulation" per household.[9]

With regard to plaintiffs' claim that Maryland's maximum grant regulation violated the Social Security Act, Justice Stewart rejected the plaintiffs' assertion that the family cap contravenes the primary purpose of the federal statute – to ensure that children's basic needs are met within their family unit. The majority declared that "[s]o long as some aid is provided to all eligible families and all eligible children, the statute itself is not violated."[10] In addition, Justice Stewart dismissed the plaintiffs' concern that, unlike a scheme using an overall percentage reduction in the standard of need for all families, the family cap causes the breakup of larger families and punishes poor people's procreation. Justice Stewart acknowledged that "the lot of the entire family is diminished because of the presence of additional children without any increase in payments," and recognized that parents could increase their per capita family income by placing their children with other relatives who would be eligible for AFDC payments.[11] The majority brushed aside the distress of parents who felt coerced into sending their children away in order to receive enough cash to subsist. Justice Stewart reasoned that "the kinship tie may be attenuated but it cannot be destroyed."[12]

While whether state family cap regulations violated the federal statute is debatable,[13] the majority's narrow interpretation of the Equal Protection Clause has had a long-lasting and devastating impact on poor families. Justice Stewart rejected the notion that welfare regulations affecting the subsistence of poor children and their caregivers should be subjected to heightened scrutiny. Instead, the majority sanctioned the lowest possible standard of judicial review for social welfare programs, even where such programs impinge upon procreative decisions and family togetherness. Citing a string of cases addressing business regulations, the majority adopted a rational basis test that only requires some "reasonable basis" to support the statutory classification.[14] The majority

[8] *Dandridge*, 397 U.S. at 473.

[9] *Id.* at 473–74.

[10] *Id.* at 481.

[11] *Id.* at 480.

[12] *Id.*

[13] *See Rosado v. Wyman*, 397 U.S. 397, 408 (1970) (holding that states have wide discretion "to pay as little or as much as they choose" under the federal AFDC statute). The Court decided *Rosado* and *Dandridge* on the same day; the feminist revision of *Dandridge* treats April 6, 1970 as a clean slate and does not address the specific statutory issues raised in *Rosado*.

[14] *Dandridge*, 397 U.S. at 485–86.

opinion emphasized that "[i]n the area of economics and social welfare, a State does not violate the Equal Protection Clause merely because the classifications made by its laws are imperfect."[15] Although acknowledging that *Dandridge* dealt with a "dramatically real factual difference" from the business regulation cases because family caps involve "the most basic economic needs of impoverished human beings," Justice Stewart nevertheless approved a nominal level of judicial review.

Applying this minimal level of rational basis review, Justice Stewart concluded that Maryland's maximum grant regulation satisfied constitutional requirements. Maryland offered four "rationally supportable" grounds in defense of its family cap: that the state had legitimate interests "in encouraging gainful employment, in maintaining an equitable balance in economic status as between welfare families and those supported by a wage-earner, in providing incentives for family planning, and in allocating available public funds in such a way as fully to meet the needs of the largest possible number of families."[16] Ignoring the eugenic implications of the state's "incentive" for poor parents to limit their procreation by denying larger families sufficient welfare benefits,[17] the majority opinion found two state interests valid: "It is enough that a solid foundation for the regulation can be found in the State's legitimate interest in encouraging employment and in avoiding discrimination between welfare families and the families of the working poor."[18] Even though Justice Stewart acknowledged that physical disabilities prevented each of the named plaintiffs from working, the majority opinion's support of Maryland's state interests endorsed popular stereotypes about the indolence of the poor and the need for state-sponsored "encouragement" into the labor force. The majority did not address the potential for coercion in reproductive and parenting choices through denials of subsistence funds.

Finally, Justice Stewart concluded by emphasizing the limited role that courts should play in reviewing laws designed to provide for basic human needs. The majority opinion washed the judiciary's hands of any responsibility for constraining fiscal policies impacting poor children's well-being and their parents' reproductive rights, declaring: "But the Constitution does not empower this Court to second-guess state officials charged with the difficult responsibility of allocating limited public welfare funds among the myriad of

[15] *Id.* at 485.

[16] *Id.* at 483–84.

[17] *See* Michele Goodwin & Erwin Chemerinsky, *Pregnancy, Poverty and the State*, 127 Yale L.J. 1270, 1315–18 (2018) (describing the history of eugenics in the United States in the context of analyzing a lack of reproductive privacy for poor women of color in particular).

[18] *Dandridge*, 397 U.S. at 486.

potential recipients."[19] Pronouncing that "the intractable economic, social, and even philosophical problems presented by public welfare assistance programs are not the business of this Court," the majority left the government with seemingly unlimited discretion in how to distribute subsistence payments to poor families.

When the *Dandridge* decision issued, welfare rights advocates swiftly criticized its reasoning and result. Critics recognized that *Dandridge* would have wide-reaching consequences for the rights of the poor, arguing that its impact "goes well beyond its immediate effect on the benefits available to welfare recipients" because the case "had been considered by many active in welfare law as a vital first step towards the recognition of a legally enforceable 'right' of a citizen to the basic means of subsistence."[20] Unfortunately, the original opinion failed to bring this vision of welfare rights to fruition.

THE FEMINIST JUDGMENT

Justice Appleton's revised judgment departs from the original opinion both rhetorically and substantively in distinctly feminist ways. First, Justice Appleton grounds her analysis in the plaintiffs' social context and individual experiences living under the yoke of poverty. Feminist legal theorists have long advocated for using the particulars of narrative to render the lived experiences of marginalized individuals visible in legal discourse.[21] Unlike the original opinion, Justice Appleton tells the stories of the named plaintiffs in detail, highlighting how their stories reflect larger structural inequalities. The feminist judgment also situates the legal analysis within the social and historical context of the "war on poverty" and the governmental interventions generated by that "war" on the poor. Unlike the original opinion, which tacitly condones discriminatory attitudes towards the poor as lazy hyper-breeders and thus the cause of their own suffering, the feminist judgment relies upon empirical evidence to set forth a more sympathetic picture that exposes the interplay of structural forces trapping people in poverty.[22] Furthermore, the feminist judgment rejects the original opinion's assertion that government did not create poverty and thus bears no responsibility for rectifying the circumstances

[19] *Id.* at 487.

[20] *See* C. Thomas Dienes, *To Feed the Hungry: Judicial Retrenchment in Welfare Adjudication*, 58 Cal. L. Rev. 555, 562 (1970).

[21] *See* Martha Chamallas, Introduction to Feminist Legal Theory 4–6 (2003).

[22] *See* Khiara M. Bridges, The Poverty of Privacy Rights (2017) (examining the racialized stereotype of the "welfare queen" and how constitutional rights to family privacy remain out of reach for the poor).

of the poor. Rather, Justice Appleton shows how the government actively participated in creating economic inequality, particularly for African-Americans and for women.

Second, Justice Appleton uses an intersectional lens in analyzing the impact of the family cap. The feminist judgment addresses not only class, but also how systematic discrimination based on race, disability, gender, and age can intersect and operate together as interlocking systems of oppression, leading to indigence for the most vulnerable groups in society.[23] Rather than blaming the poor for their predicament – and particularly blaming those who "choose" to have larger families (especially in a pre-*Roe v. Wade* era when abortion was a crime) – Justice Appleton lays bare how stereotypical assumptions about welfare recipients reinforce structural inequalities along multiple axes of discrimination.

Third, not only does Justice Appleton demand heightened scrutiny of legislative classifications burdening the indigent, but she also brings within judicial purview poor people's fundamental rights of procreation and family togetherness that the original opinion undermines. The revised opinion rejects the "farming out" of children to relatives as a solution to the state's fiscal concerns. Presaging the Supreme Court's later decision in *Moore v. City of East Cleveland*, Justice Appleton recognizes that keeping one's family together is an essential aspect of the fundamental right to family privacy long recognized by the Supreme Court.[24] Furthermore, Justice Appleton's feminist judgment recognizes that the family cap operates as a coercive family planning measure with implications not only for the right of the poor to procreate, but also for access to abortion.[25]

[23] *See* Sumi Cho, Kimberlé Williams Crenshaw, & Leslie McCall, *Toward a Field of Intersectionality Studies: Theory, Applications, and Praxis*, 38 Signs 785 (2013) (explaining theory of intersectionality).

[24] In 1977, in *Moore v. City of East Cleveland,* the Supreme Court struck down a housing ordinance limiting occupancy to members of a single family and defining family in narrow and formalistic terms. *See Moore v. City of East Cleveland*, 431 U.S. 494, 504–506 (1977); Peggy Cooper Davis, Moore v. East Cleveland: *Constructing the Suburban Family, in* Family Law Stories (Carol Sanger ed., 2008) (describing how poverty, race, and family structures intersected in the *Moore* case). The feminist judgment also foreshadows later Supreme Court cases, including *Boddie v. Connecticut*, 401 U.S. 371 (1971); *Eisenstadt v. Baird,* 405 U.S. 438 (1972); *Weber v. Aetna Casualty & Surety Co.*, 406 U.S. 164 (1972); and *Plyler v. Doe*, 457 U.S. 202 (1982). These cases are not cited in the revised opinion since they were decided after 1970, but Professor Appleton included language from the cases, without citation, to remind the reader of paths taken after a reimagined *Dandridge*.

[25] *See also* Susan Frelich Appleton, *When Welfare Reforms Promote Abortion: "Personal Responsibility," "Family Values," and the Right to Choose*, 85 Geo. L.J. 155, 166–72 (1996) (describing how family caps and other welfare reform measures create incentives for poor women to seek abortion care rather than continue a pregnancy).

Finally, the revised judgment departs most dramatically from the original opinion in its approach to the Equal Protection Clause and the welfare rights thesis. While it seems an implausible reading of the Constitution in the era of the Roberts Court, at the time of the *Dandridge* decision a string of Supreme Court cases had suggested that the Court might recognize a "right to minimum welfare" under the Equal Protection Clause.[26] Scholarly literature of the era also proposed such a trajectory, from a thoroughly "negative" Constitution to one that provided a "positive" right "to the basic necessities of life."[27] The feminist judgment illustrates how welfare reform is a feminist, family law, and reproductive justice issue.

IMPLICATIONS OF THE FEMINIST JUDGMENT

Justice Appleton's robust reading of the Equal Protection Clause would have charted a new path for constitutional law. Shifting from a "negative" to a "positive" reading of constitutional rights would have dramatically altered poverty law, and would have allowed the Constitution to address structural inequalities at the intersection of poverty, race, disability, and gender. Although not all progressive scholars agree that the Constitution protects a "positive" right to minimum welfare, Justice Appleton's ambitious revision of *Dandridge* unmasks the "government's role in creating and perpetuating structures of society that account for poverty."[28]

Furthermore, the feminist judgment would have laid the foundation for a constitutional approach that protects not only reproductive rights, but also reproductive justice. The reproductive justice framework incorporates "not only a woman's right not to have a child, but also the right to have children and to raise them with dignity in safe, healthy, and supportive environments," and takes into account "a political context of intersecting race, gender, and class oppressions."[29] The Supreme Court decided *Dandridge* three years

[26] *See* Appleton Rewritten Opinion *infra*.

[27] *See* Appleton, *supra* note 5, at 734–37 (explaining constitutional debate between "negative" rights – which only immunize protected activity from governmental interference – versus "positive" rights – which compel affirmative government support for being able to engage in the protected activity). Although interpreting the Constitution to guarantee basic human needs can certainly be understood as feminist, not all feminist groups were necessarily in favor of such a bold approach. *See* Elizabeth Bussiere, (Dis)Entitling the Poor: The Warren Court, Welfare Rights, and the American Political Tradition 94–98 (1997).

[28] *See* Appleton Rewritten Opinion, *infra*.

[29] Dorothy Roberts, *Reproductive Justice, Not Just Rights*, Dissent Mag. (Fall 2015), *available at* https://www.dissentmagazine.org/article/reproductive-justice-not-just-rights; *see also* Dorothy Roberts, Killing the Black Body: Race, Reproduction and the Meaning of Liberty 57–103 (1999).

before *Roe v. Wade* established abortion care as a constitutionally protected right.[30] Justice Appleton's feminist judgment could have provided the framework for understanding the Constitution's protection of reproductive liberties as encompassing both the right to give birth and to keep one's family intact, as well as the right to choose not to give birth.

In line with a reproductive justice approach, Justice Appleton's feminist judgment could also have led the Court to a different resolution in the abortion funding cases. In 1977, in *Maher v. Roe*, the Supreme Court – despite *Roe*'s assertion that abortion is a fundamental right subject to strict scrutiny – applied rational basis review to the government's refusal to fund nontherapeutic abortion care for indigent women.[31] In 1980, in *Harris v. McRae*, the Court extended *Maher*'s logic even further, holding that the government may deny funding for medically necessary abortion care for poor women.[32] In both cases, the Supreme Court relied on the logic that selective funding by the government does not impinge upon fundamental rights, because the Constitution exclusively protects negative rights.[33] Poverty, the Court asserted, is not a state-imposed obstacle.[34] In contrast, the reproductive justice lens employed by Justice Appleton's feminist judgment uncovers the government's role in creating conditions of poverty – particularly for racial minorities and women – and holds the government to account by ensuring that poor people can meaningfully exercise reproductive choices.

The original opinion's approval of family caps also intersects with federal policy on family planning. It is notable that the *Dandridge* decision upheld family caps during an era of skyrocketing sterilization abuse of the poor. In the 1960s, a huge influx of federal family planning funding for sterilization coalesced with post-World War II fears about population growth, immigration, and welfare costs. This ushered in a new, although differently named, era of eugenics – the population control movement. The U.S. Department of Health, Education, and Welfare (HEW) paid for approximately 100,000 to 150,000 sterilizations of low-income women per year during the 1960s and 1970s.[35] Throughout the United States, medical personnel deployed coercive

[30] *Roe v. Wade*, 410 U.S. 113 (1973).

[31] *Maher v. Roe*, 432 U.S. 464 (1977). The Court ignored the argument that at the same time the government refuses to fund abortion care, it provides assistance for indigent women seeking care for pregnancy and childbirth.

[32] *Harris v. McRae*, 448 U.S. 297 (1980).

[33] *See Maher*, 432 U.S. at 471–75 (citing *Dandridge*); *Harris*, 448 U.S. at 314–18; *see also* Appleton, *supra* note 5, at 734–36.

[34] *See Maher*, 432 U.S. at 479–80 (citing *Dandridge*); *Harris*, 448 U.S. at 315–18.

[35] *See Relf v. Weinberger*, 372 F.Supp. 1196 (D.D.C. 1974).

tactics aimed at sterilizing poor patients, such as by threatening to withhold medical care from laboring pregnant women needing Cesarean surgery if they did not consent to sterilization.[36] Women of color were particularly at risk for sterilization abuse, with each region having its own disfavored group.[37] A 1970 National Fertility Study found that 20 percent of all married Black women had been sterilized; about the same percentage of Chicana women had been sterilized; and over 35 percent of women of childbearing age in Puerto Rico had been sterilized.[38] Activists organizing against sterilization abuse emphasized the links between coerced sterilization and funding cuts to social welfare programs. For example, in 1979 the Committee for Abortion Rights and Against Sterilization Abuse (CARASA) argued that, "The abortion cutbacks will mean increased sterilization abuse because federally funded abortions are no longer an option for poor women. Since birth control is never 100% effective, sterilizations become the only funded alternative to bearing unwanted children."[39] Taking into account the combined effects of *Dandridge* and *Harris v. McRae*, federal and state social welfare policies favoring funding for sterilization, while at the same time denying funding for abortion care and capping welfare funds for poor families, operate in concert to pressure poor people to undergo sterilization, echoing the long history in the United States of eugenic sterilization of the poor, the disabled, and racial minorities.[40]

CONCLUSION

The landscape of poverty law has only become harsher in the intervening decades since the *Dandridge* decision. The AFDC program – even with states'

[36] *See* Maya Manian, *Coerced Sterilization of Mexican-American Women: The Story of* Madrigal v. Quilligan, *in* Reproductive Rights and Justice Stories (Melissa Murray, Kate Shaw & Reva Siegel eds., 2019).

[37] *See* Lisa C. Ikemoto, *Infertile by Force and Federal Complicity: The Story of* Relf v. Weinberger, *in* Women and the Law Stories 196 (Elizabeth M. Schneider & Stephanie M. Wildman eds., 2011) (noting that sterilization abuse was occurring around the country in the 1960s and 1970s, with African-American, Chicana, Native American, Puerto Rican, and poor white women all targeted depending on the region).

[38] *See* Angela Davis, Women, Race, and Class 219 (1983).

[39] *See* Jennifer Nelson, Women of Color and the Reproductive Rights Movement 155 (2003); *see also* Khiara M. Bridges, *The Story of* Harris v. McRae, *in* Reproductive Rights and Justice Stories, *supra* note 36 (describing antisterilization abuse activism of CARASA in the context of legal challenges to the Hyde Amendment, which restricts federal funding for abortion care).

[40] *See, e.g.*, Paul A. Lombardo, Three Generations, No Imbeciles: Eugenics, the Supreme Court, and *Buck v. Bell* (2008); Alexandra Minna Stern, Eugenic Nation: Faults and Frontiers of Better Breeding in Modern America 99–110 (2005).

widespread adoption of family cap regulations – seems positively generous compared to the rules promulgated after "welfare reform."[41] Responding to popular racialized stereotypes of the "welfare queen" who refuses to seek employment and bears children in order to increase her cash assistance, in 1996 Congress replaced AFDC with Temporary Assistance to Needy Families (TANF).[42] TANF imposes a five-year lifetime limit for federal assistance to a family and, unlike AFDC, is not an entitlement under federal law.[43] After welfare reform, the "vast majority of poor children live in families that do not receive TANF."[44] State family cap regulations continue to remain popular under TANF, while wealthier families routinely receive government tax credits and healthcare subsidization for their children that popularly do not count as "welfare."[45]

Dandridge's legacy persists: "[C]ourts now routinely invoke *Dandridge* to justify reflexive rubber-stamp review, which has effectively immunized social welfare regulation from review and deconstitutionalized poverty law."[46] Without meaningful judicial review, equal constitutional protection of poor people's fundamental rights to reproductive choice and family togetherness remains illusory.

DANDRIDGE v. WILLIAMS, 397 U.S. 471 (1970)

JUSTICE APPLETON DELIVERED THE OPINION OF THE COURT

In 1964, our country initiated a war on poverty. All three branches of our federal government joined the fight, with President Johnson's declaration of unconditional war and issuance of executive orders, Congress's enactment of

[41] *See* Dienes, *supra* note 20, at 558 (estimating that approximately 40 percent of states had some type of family cap restriction as of 1970); Kelly J. Gastley, *Note, Why Family Cap Laws Just Aren't Getting It Done*, 46 Wm. & Mary L. Rev. 373 (2004) (explaining the history of welfare reform, adoption of TANF, and impact of family cap and child exclusion regulations).

[42] *See* Risa E. Kaufman, Note, *The Cultural Meaning of the "Welfare Queen": Using State Constitutions to Challenge Child Exclusion Provisions*, 23 N.Y.U. Rev. L. & Soc. Change 301, 301–12 (1997).

[43] Peter Edelman, Dandridge v. Williams *Redux: A Look Back from the Twenty-First Century*, 60 Drake L. Rev. 981, 982–86 (2012).

[44] *Id.* at 986.

[45] *See* Rebekah J. Smith, *Family Caps in Welfare Reform: Their Coercive Effects and Damaging Consequences*, 29 Harv. J.L. & Gender 151, 152–54 (2006). Government subsidization associated with the term "welfare" has acquired many negative connotations in the years since *Dandridge*. *See* Suzanne Mettler, *The Welfare Boogeyman*, N.Y. Times, July 23, 2018.

[46] Nice, *supra* note 1, at 130.

antipoverty legislation, and this Court's manifold opinions recognizing that our Constitution guarantees protection for the indigent among us.[1]

In the book that is often cited as inspiring our national war on poverty, *The Other America*, Michael Harrington defines the "American poor" as the "dispossessed in terms of what the rest of the nation enjoys, in terms of what the society could provide if it had the will." MICHAEL HARRINGTON, THE OTHER AMERICA: POVERTY IN THE UNITED STATES 178 (1963).[2] Of course, "the poor" do not constitute a monolithic swath of society. Rather, poverty and other characteristics often intersect, exacerbating vulnerability and disadvantage. Of the roughly 32 million people living below the government-identified poverty line, 8 million (or 25 percent) are sixty-five years or older and 11 million are under eighteen. Eight million (again 25 percent) live in consumer units headed by women. Although the majority are white, nonwhites are overrepresented, constituting 25 percent of the poor, double the percentage of nonwhites in the population as a whole. Poverty is

[1] The President launched the war on poverty in his State of the Union Address in 1964. President Lyndon B. Johnson, State of the Union Address (Jan. 8, 1964). He also signed several executive orders designed to improve employment prospects among the poor, including, for example, one establishing requirements for nondiscriminatory hiring and promotion of employees by government contractors. *See* Exec. Order No. 11246, 3 C.F.R. 167 (Supp. 1965). As part of the war on poverty, Congress authorized the development of federally directed local community action agencies and enacted permanent legislation to improve nutrition in low-income households. *See* Economic Opportunity Act of 1964, Pub. L. No. 88-452, 78 Stat. 508–34 (enacted "[t]o mobilize the human and financial resources of the Nation to combat poverty in the United States"); Food Stamp Act of 1964, Pub. L. 88-525, 78 Stat. 703–709 (enacted, inter alia, to "to provide for improved levels of nutrition among low-income households through a cooperative Federal-State program of food assistance"). In the meantime, several rulings by this Court also demonstrate special solicitude for the poor. *E.g.*, *Edwards v. California*, 314 U.S. 160 (1941); *Griffin v. Illinois*, 351 U.S. 12 (1956); *Gideon v. Wainwright*, 372 U.S. 335 (1963); *Douglas v. California*, 372 U.S. 353 (1963); *Shapiro v. Thompson*, 394 U.S. 618 (1969); *Goldberg v. Kelly*, 397 U.S. 254 (1970). For an analysis of many of these cases, Frank I. Michelman, *The Supreme Court – 1968 Term – Foreword: On Protecting the Poor through the Fourteenth Amendment*, 83 HARV. L. REV. 7 (1969).

[2] Harrington continues:

> Poverty should be defined in terms of those who are denied the minimal levels of health, housing, food, and education that our present stage of scientific knowledge specifies as necessary for life as it is now lived in the United States.
>
> Poverty should be defined psychologically in terms of those whose place in the society is such that they are internal exiles who, almost inevitably, develop attitudes of defeat and pessimism and who are therefore excluded from taking advantage of new opportunities.
>
> Poverty should be defined absolutely, in terms of what man and society could be. As long as America is less than its potential, the nation as a whole is impoverished by that fact. As long as there is the other America, we are, all of us, poorer because of it.
>
> MICHAEL HARRINGTON, THE OTHER AMERICA: POVERTY IN THE UNITED STATES 179 (1963)

also directly associated with ill health and disabilities as well as higher birth rates than average, in turn causing poor adults to suffer significantly more loss of work than others. *See id.* at 187–89 (noting disproportionate numbers of children in poverty and resulting loss of work for adults in poor families); PASCAL K. WHELPTON ET AL., FERTILITY AND FAMILY PLANNING IN THE UNITED STATES 243 (1966) (finding unwanted pregnancies are more prevalent in lower income and education groups studied).[3] Despite the recent enactment of Title VII of the Civil Rights Act of 1964 prohibiting discrimination in employment on the basis of sex and race, Pub. L. No. 88-352, 78 Stat. 241–68, § 703 (codified as 42 U.S.C. § 2000e-2), equality remains elusive and a significant pay gap separates Negro workers and women, on the one hand, and white male workers, on the other.[4] Americans with disabilities have no legal protection from discrimination in employment.

This case arises out of a particular antipoverty measure, the Federal Aid to Families with Dependent Children program (AFDC), which originated with

[3] Such higher than average birth rates and unwanted pregnancies stem largely from inadequate information about family planning methods among women living in poverty, according to a report issued by the Council of the Section of Family Law of the American Bar Association, under the leadership of New York Family Court Judge Nanette Dembitz. *See* Hon. Nanette Dembitz, *Law and Family Planning*, 1 FAM. L.Q. 103 (1967) (article based on report). Invoking Supreme Court cases ensuring equality for the poor, *see supra* note 1, and "the right to free choice in regard to family planning" derived from *Griswold v. Connecticut*, 381 U.S. 479 (1965), the report asserts: "[T]he first requirement for the effectuation of a right is the individual's knowledge that it exists; it can neither be exercised nor waived unless it is known. In terms of the right to family planning, equality for the poor therefore must mean, initially, equality with the affluent respecting information that methods of family planning and birth control are available." *Id.* at 105.

[4] Government data illuminate the racial disproportionality of poverty in the United States. For example, of over 25 million persons living below the poverty level in 1968, 31.5 percent are classified as "Negro and other races"; further, while 12.8 percent of all persons live below the poverty level, that figure is composed of 10 percent of the population classified as "white" and 33.5 percent of the population classified as "Negro and other races." U.S. Bureau of the Census, *Poverty in the United States: 1959 to 1968*, P-60 (No. 68) CURRENT POPULATION REPORTS 1, 1 (1969). This racial disproportionality prompted the following observation in a report for the Social Security Administration: "Poverty among white families merits concern because of the large number involved – 3.7 million families in 1967. Poverty among nonwhite families is of even greater concern in that it affects 1 family in 3 in this group." Carolyn Jackson & Terri Velten, *Residence, Race, and Age of Poor Families in 1966*, 32 SOC. SEC. BULL. 3, 11 (1969). *See also id.* at 4 ("In the United States as a whole, only 8 percent of the white families headed by a person under age 65, compared with 33 percent of the nonwhite families, were poor").

Even "[a]mong families above the poverty level, white men 'outearned' Negro men, no matter where they lived." *Id.* at 10. And, while the mean earnings for male workers in 1968 was $6,811, it was only $2,921 for female workers. U.S. Bureau of the Census, *Income in 1968 of Families and Persons in the United States*, P-60 (No. 66) CURRENT POPULATION REPORTS 1, 103–104 (1969).

the Social Security Act of 1935 to assist widowed mothers and later expanded to cover children of never-married mothers and, more recently, children of employable but unemployed fathers. Social Security Act of 1935, Pub. L. No. 74-271, 49 Stat. 620 (codified, as amended at 42 U.S.C. §§ 601–81 (1964 & Supp. V 1970)). In several parts of the United States, most of the children covered by AFDC are Black.[5]

As we have previously explained, AFDC operates on the basis of cooperative federalism, funded principally by the federal government but administered by the states. States may decline to participate in the program, but those wishing to take advantage of the substantial federal funds available for distribution to needy children must submit an AFDC plan for the approval of the Secretary of Health, Education, and Welfare (HEW), and such plans must conform to several requirements of the Social Security Act and HEW's rules and regulations. *King v. Smith*, 392 U.S. 309, 316–17 (1968).

Plaintiffs filed the instant class action challenging the State of Maryland's maximum family grant regulation, which caps the monthly sum any family may receive under AFDC at $250.00 in some counties and Baltimore City and at $240.00 elsewhere, regardless of family size and regardless of the sum indicated by the state's standard of need, as specified by a schedule that HEW approved. Plaintiffs sought to enjoin the application of the Maryland maximum family grant regulation on the ground that it conflicts with the Social Security Act and with the Equal Protection Clause of the Fourteenth Amendment. A three-judge District Court initially held the Maryland regulation invalid on both grounds; on a post-trial motion by defendants-state officials, the court subsequently modified its previous opinion by declining to decide the statutory issue, but it adhered to its earlier disposition of the equal protection claim. *Williams v. Dandridge*, 297 F. Supp. 450, 458–64 (D. Md. 1968 & 1969). This direct appeal followed, 28 U.S.C. § 1253 (1964), and we noted probable jurisdiction, 396 U.S. 811 (1969). Given the uncertainty left by the court below, we analyze the maximum family grant

5 For example, in Maryland, where this litigation arose, 77.5 percent of children receiving AFDC benefits are classified as Negro, while the figure for the South Atlantic region, which includes Maryland and eight other states, is 68.4 percent. *Social Security and Welfare Proposals: Hearings before the H. Comm. on Ways & Means*, 91st Cong. 473–74 (Pt. 2 1969) (materials requested by the Committee from the Department of HEW, Response Two, Table Six, showing AFDC families and recipient children by race). *See also* Office of Planning & Research, U.S. Dep't of Labor, The Negro Family: The Case for National Action 12 (Mar. 1965) (hereinafter Moynihan Report after its author, Daniel Patrick Moynihan) ("At present, 14 percent of Negro children are receiving AFDC assistance, as against 2 percent of white children").

regulation for its consistency with the Social Security Act and under the limitations imposed by the U.S. Constitution. We conclude that the regulation fails on both counts.

I

The named plaintiffs are Linda Williams, Junius Gary, and Jeanette Gary, who bring this class action individually on behalf of themselves and their minor children as well as on behalf of other similarly situated parents, relatives, and children. These plaintiffs and their situations reflect several attributes common among those living in poverty. The Williams family and the Gary family are Negro families; Linda Williams is a female head of household; individuals in each family suffer ill health; and each family includes eight members below the age of eighteen, in turn reflecting both high birth rates and overrepresentation of children.

Plaintiffs sue defendants Edmund P. Dandridge, Jr., who chairs the Maryland State Board of Public Welfare, and other welfare officials of the state and of the City of Baltimore, individually and in their official capacities. Based on the pleadings, the findings below, and the parties' stipulations (297 F. Supp. at 453–54; App. submitted with brs.), we have the following facts.

Maryland participates in the AFDC program. With regulations approved by HEW, Maryland has adopted a schedule setting forth standards of need. The schedule lists the monetary need for family units of one to ten persons, with decreasing additional amounts for each person over the original recipient but with a fixed additional amount for each person over ten persons. Maryland has also adopted a maximum family grant regulation, which provides that, irrespective of state-recognized family need, the state would not pay more than a fixed amount. The maximum grant permitted under AFDC in Baltimore City is $250.00 per month. The regulation's effect is to treat families with seven, eight, or more children as if, according to the standard of need, they had only six children. Further, the regulation applies only to members of a family unit who live together; it does not apply to an eligible recipient who resides in another household or a childcare institution.

Plaintiff Linda Williams lives in Baltimore City, Maryland, with her eight children, Dorothy (age sixteen), Linda Gayle (age fourteen), Mildred (age eleven), James (age ten), Anthony (age nine), Ronnie (age seven), Angela (age five), and Wanda (age four). This family has relied on AFDC since Linda Williams's husband, William Williams, abandoned the family over three years ago, soon after Wanda's birth. Now age thirty-three, Linda Williams cannot work outside the home because of a serious breast condition for which she has undergone multiple surgeries. Ronnie also has required hospital care and medical attention because of convulsions he has experienced since early childhood. With no relatives in the area to assist her, Linda Williams stays home at all times to care for the children.

Linda Williams's monthly expenses (shelter, subsistence for her family, school supplies for the children, and insurance), total $311.15, and she has no available resources of her own to apply to this sum. She must make many of her purchases on credit, and she faces significant debt. Sometimes, especially in the winter, the children cannot attend school because they lack the necessary clothing and shoes. She has begun buying food stamps, but she often has insufficient funds required for participation in the program and for other day-to-day needs. Despite the challenges that confront her, Linda Williams strives to keep all of her family together and to make up for the absence of the children's father.

Maryland's schedule places the standard of need for families the size of Linda Williams's at $296.15, a figure below the $311.15 she must spend monthly. Yet Maryland's maximum family grant regulation caps the amount of AFDC she may receive at $250.00. If Linda Williams did not value so highly keeping the family together, she could place two of her children with relatives; each child so placed would be eligible for $79.00 per month in assistance, and Linda Williams and her six remaining children would still be eligible to receive the maximum family grant of $250.00.

Plaintiffs Junius Gary and his wife Jeannette Gary married in 1952 and live together in Baltimore, Maryland, with their eight children, Junius (age eleven), Catherine (age ten), Anthony (age nine), James (age eight), Lynn Dora (age seven), Pamela (age six), Mark (age five), and Thelma (age four). Junius Gary received an honorable discharge after serving for two years in the U.S. Army. Following his active service, he worked as a chauffeur and truck driver, the type of duties he had in the Army, but severe neurological conditions suffered as the result of automobile accidents (including seizures, blackouts, and dizziness) required him to stop. Now age thirty-nine, he has disabilities that totally prevent him from working, although he has unsuccessfully tried to earn money in various jobs. Jeanette Gary, age thirty-eight, also suffers from medical problems, including high blood pressure and arthritis (in her arms and legs), for which she is receiving treatment at the Johns Hopkins clinic. She cares for the eight children at home. The Garys are totally without financial resources, a situation that arose only after the birth of their youngest child, when Junius Gary became too disabled to maintain employment.

The monthly expenses for the Gary family (shelter, subsistence, and school supplies) total $331.50. This is precisely the sum that Maryland's schedule calculates as their standard of need. Yet the Garys are limited to a monthly subsidy of $250.00 by reason of the maximum family grant regulation. Accordingly, they cannot buy food stamps, because they cannot afford to purchase the minimum required to participate in that program.

Despite the financial strain, the Garys want to keep the family together. Nonetheless, if Junius and Jeannette Gary placed two of their children with relatives, each child so placed would be eligible for assistance in the amount of $65.00 per month, and they and their six remaining children would still be eligible to receive the maximum grant of $250.00.

From the testimony in the case, the district court determined that "the maximum grant regulation had its genesis and rationale in the fact that the Governor and the General Assembly of Maryland failed to appropriate sufficient funds for Maryland's share of the cost of AFDC to satisfy the state-determined need of all persons entitled to benefit thereunder." 297 F. Supp. at 454. Thus, the court found that "[t]he purpose of the maximum grant regulation is solely to conserve state funds, by allocating state funds (less in amount than state-recognized need) among only some of the persons entitled thereto." *Id.* In their motion that resulted in the district court's supplemental opinion, as well as in their briefs to this Court, defendants offered additional justifications for the maximum family grant application. We review these assertions and the state interests that purportedly underlie them below, in our analysis of the constitutional issues. First, however, we turn to the question of Maryland's compliance with the Social Security Act and applicable federal rules and regulations.

II

Even though we have previously examined state regulations for consistency with the Social Security Act, we have never expressly decided the statutory question presented by this case: May a state provide benefits that fall short of its own stated standard of need? Although the present case poses an issue of first impression, the analysis in *King v. Smith*, 392 U.S. 309 (1968), offers instructive guideposts.

As *King* points out, Congress left certain matters to state discretion: "There is no question that States have considerable latitude in allocating their AFDC resources, since each State is free to set its own standard of need and to determine the level of benefits by the amount of funds it devotes to the program." 392 U.S. at 318–19 (footnotes omitted). Yet *King* also makes plain federal limitations on such state discretion because "any state law or regulation inconsistent with [the program's] federal terms and conditions is to that extent invalid." *Id.* at 333 n. 34.

For example, in *King* we struck down Alabama's "substitute father" regulation, which disqualified from AFDC benefits families in which the mother "cohabits" with any single or married man able to work. *Id.* at 311. The state asserted two interests in defending the regulation: First, it would discourage illicit sexual relations and, second, it would put families characterized by informal marriage-like relationships on a par with those characterized by a formal marriage because, at the relevant time, federal matching funds were not available for the latter. *Id.* at 319 n. 13. We found these justifications wanting in light of the federal statutory requirement that "aid to families with dependent children . . . shall be furnished with reasonable promptness to all eligible individuals." 42 U.S.C. § 602 (a) (9) (1964 & Supp. II) (as cited in 392 U.S. at 317). As we observed in that case, the state's asserted reasons bore no relation to need or the family's actual financial situation, the "substitute father" had no legal duty to support the children, and Congress rejected punishment for destitute children on the basis of their parents' personal choices. 392 U.S. at 326–27.

Here, as in *King*, we must test the state regulation against the federal statutory entitlement for "all eligible individuals." We also must take into account federal policies articulated in the statute, such as encouraging "care of dependent children in their own homes or in the homes of relatives" and "help[ing] maintain and strengthen family life." 42 U.S.C. § 601 (1964 & Supp. V 1970). Maryland's maximum family grant regulation cannot survive this analysis.

First, as shown by the situation of the Williams and Gary families, the regulation completely denies aid to individuals based solely on the fact that they were the last to be welcomed into an otherwise large family, contravening the statutory entitlement held by "all eligible individuals." *See also* Public Welfare Amendments of 1962, 42 U.S.C. § 602 (a) (14) (1964 & Supp. V 1970) (requiring program "for each child"); Social Security Amendments of 1967, 42 U.S.C. § 602 (a) (14) & (15) (1964 & Supp. V 1970) (requiring services for "each appropriate individual"). True, families might choose to spread the maximum amount, $250.00, among the entire family, but that approach – like the invalid measure in *King* – allocates sums that bear no relation to the standard of need identified in Maryland's schedule.[6]

[6] Of course, because of economies of scale, each successive child does not increase family expenses by an identical sum. Yet defendants have not made such arguments in support of the maximum family grant regulation nor have they asserted any relationship between the capped amount and actual need. Br. of Amici Curiae: Center on Social Welfare Policy and Law et al. at 52–53.

Second, the regulation encourages dissolution of nuclear family units by incentivizing large families to send some of the children to live with relatives' smaller families, in which these children will receive aid as determined by Maryland's standard of need. This perverse incentive not only undermines the federal goal of strengthening family life; it also undermines the state's cost-saving rationale for the maximum family grant because the children in question will in fact receive more generous assistance simply by living elsewhere.

Finally, we note that Maryland continues to receive a federal subsidy for every dependent child regardless of family size, although – because of the state regulation – large families receive none of this additional support. Thus, as the district court found, by capping the state's contribution of funds to large families, "the maximum grant regulation has the incidental effect of increasing the federal government's share of the cost of the total program beyond what would be the amount of that share had the maximum grant regulation not been adopted." *Williams v. Dandridge*, 297 F. Supp. 450, 454 (D. Md. 1968).

We remain unpersuaded by defendants' arguments, first lodged after the district court issued its initial opinion, that Congress and HEW must have authorized maximum family grants like Maryland's simply because they have used the term "maximum(s)." Based on our precedents, we do not draw the same inferences from this word usage as the defendants do. First, when Congress amended the Social Security Act to mandate state adjustments to AFDC cost of living standards and a proportional adjustment in any state imposed "maximums," Congress was referring to across-the-board percentage reductions. *See* Social Security Amendments of 1967, Pub. L. No. 90-248, § 213 (b), 81 Stat. 898 (1968) (codified as amended at 42 U.S.C. § 602 (a) (23) (Supp. V 1970)). Second and apart from this reading, we accord no more weight to the Social Security Act's reference to state "maximums" than we gave to the statutory references to state residency in *Shapiro v. Thompson*, 394 U.S. 618 (1969),[7] which we interpreted not to "approve, much less prescribe" the one-year residence requirement that we struck down in that case. *See id.* at 639. Likewise, we find determinative neither HEW's failure to cut off funds from the Maryland state plan and those of other states containing maximum grant provisions nor HEW regulations issued in the wake of the 1968 statutory amendments explicitly using the term "dollar maximum." 45 C.F.R. § 233.20 (a) (2) (ii) (1970). Indeed, the Secretary of HEW has condemned maximum

[7] We discuss this case in greater detail below in Part III.A.1.

family grant regulations as arbitrary and oppressive, so that HEW's position offers no support to defendants or at most remains equivocal.[8] Even beyond this weakness in defendants' arguments, we note that HEW's approval of "substitute father" provisions in state plans did not stand in the way of our conclusion in *King v. Smith*, as noted above, that such provisions contravene the Social Security Act.

III

Having determined that Maryland's maximum family grant contravenes the Social Security Act, we might end our opinion here. We proceed, however, to address the parties' equal protection arguments for several reasons. First, as shown by our precedents, we do not believe the statutory and constitutional questions can be so easily disaggregated. For example, in striking down state residency requirements for public assistance in *Shapiro v. Thompson*, 394 U.S. 618 (1969), we incorporated within our constitutional analysis why the Social Security Act cannot be read to authorize such requirements. *Id.* at 638–40. Second, the court below in the instant litigation and every lower court to consider the question has decided that maximum family grants violate the Equal Protection Clause. *See Kaiser v. Montgomery*, 319 F. Supp. 329 (N.D. Cal. 1969); *Dews v. Henry*, 297 F. Supp. 587 (D. Ariz. 1969); *Westberry v. Fisher*, 297 F. Supp. 1109 (D. Me. 1969); *Lindsey v. Smith*, 303 F.Supp. 1203 (W.D. Wash. 1969). *See also Collins v. State Bd. of Soc. Welfare*, 81 N.W.2d 4 (Iowa 1957) (finding equal protection violation under state constitution).

Finally, we reach the constitutional question posed in this case to solidify and clarify the trajectory that our earlier rulings have begun to sketch. We thus take this opportunity to announce definitively that the Equal Protection Clause mandates not only constitutional limitations on government's ability to use classifications that burden the poor, particularly when such invidious discrimination impairs the exercise of protected rights, but also a right to minimum welfare, that is, a right to the basic necessities of life.[9] Of course, this holding, while concluding our disposition of this case, leaves several questions to be resolved legislatively and in subsequent judicial proceedings.

8 In briefs submitted in analogous litigation, the Secretary of HEW has repudiated family maximum grant regulations. *See, e.g.*, Brief of Robert H. Finch, Secretary of Health, Education, and Welfare as Amicus Curiae, *Lampton v. Bonin*, 299 F. Supp. 336 (E.D. La. 1969) (No. 68-2092); Brief of Robert H. Finch, *Jefferson v. Hackney*, 304 F. Supp. 1332 (N.D. Tex. 1969) (Nos. 3-3012-B, 3-3126-B).

9 Observers have discerned that our precedents suggest this constitutional right even if we have previously stopped short of articulating it explicitly. *See, e.g.*, Michelman, *supra* note 1, at 9.

We do not, nor can we, prescribe a formula for Congress and the states to remedy the constitutional violation presented or to actualize the constitutional right that we recognize.

A *Identifying the Standard of Review: Strict Scrutiny*

In adjudicating challenges to classifications under the Equal Protection Clause, our cases have not adhered to a single standard of review. Although not without its critics,[10] our dominant method of analysis departs from deferential rational basis review to subject to strict judicial scrutiny laws that rest on suspect classifications or that implicate fundamental rights. Maryland's maximum family grant triggers such rigorous scrutiny on four different bases, as we explain below. Even if any one of these bases would not alone require heightened review, the co-occurrence and interaction of all four together certainly suffice.

1 Invidious Wealth-Based Discrimination

The Equal Protection Clause was intended to work nothing less than the abolition of all caste-based and invidious class-based legislation. Accordingly, we have previously treated classifications based on wealth as invidious discrimination, demanding the rigorous standard of review that we apply to race and other suspect categories. *See McDonald v. Bd. of Election Comm's*, 394 U.S. 802, 807 (1969) ("[A] careful examination on our part is especially warranted where lines are drawn on the basis of wealth or race."). *See also Loving v. Virginia*, 388 U.S. 1, 9 (1967) (noting "the very heavy burden of justification which the Fourteenth Amendment has traditionally required of state statutes drawn according to race"). Indeed, wealth-based classifications properly demand the same strict scrutiny that race-based discrimination evokes because nonwhite families and individuals face a substantially greater risk of living in poverty than their white counterparts.[11]

We have found invidious wealth-based discrimination at work in two types of cases. In the first type, we have invalidated government action that conditions access to a particular activity or institution on an individual's ability to

[10] For example, Justice Harlan has rejected a "dual-level test" for reviewing asserted violations of equal protection. *See Katzenbach v. Morgan*, 384 U.S. 641, 660–61 (1966) (Harlan, J., dissenting).

[11] For data showing the racial disproportionality of poverty in the United States, *see supra* note 4. *See also supra* note 5.

pay, thus causing a discriminatory effect. For example, in *Harper v. Virginia State Board of Elections*, 383 U.S. 663 (1966), we held that Virginia's poll tax violates the Equal Protection Clause because "as a condition of obtaining a ballot[,] the requirement of fee paying causes an 'invidious' discrimination." *Id.* at 668 (quoting *Skinner v. Oklahoma*, 316 U.S. 535, 541 (1942)).

Likewise, we held that Illinois could not require indigent persons convicted of a crime to pay for a trial transcript in order to exercise their state-granted right to an appeal. *Griffin v. Illinois*, 351 U.S. 12 (1956). Invoking the Equal Protection and Due Process Clauses, we wrote that "[t]here is no meaningful distinction between a rule which would deny the poor the right to defend themselves in a trial court and one which effectively denies the poor an adequate appellate review accorded to all who have money enough to pay the costs in advance." *Id.* at 18 (plurality opinion). Although the Constitution does not require states to provide appellate review, "at all stages of the proceedings [offered by a state] the Due Process and Equal Protection Clauses protect persons like petitioners from invidious discriminations." *Id.*

Last Term's case *Shapiro v. Thompson*, 394 U.S. 618 (1969), exemplifies a second type of situation in which we have found invidious wealth-based discrimination. In striking down one-year residency requirements for state public assistance, we emphasized that such laws violate equal protection by creating two classes of indigent state residents – those who are eligible for welfare because they have lived in the state for a year or more and new arrivals who are ineligible. *Id.* at 627 (expressing agreement with challengers' argument "that the statutory prohibition of benefits to residents of less than a year creates a classification which constitutes an invidious discrimination denying them equal protection of the laws").

The instant case resembles *Shapiro* more closely than it resembles *Harper* and *Griffin* because Maryland's maximum family grant regulation exacts no fee that the challengers cannot afford to pay. Instead, Maryland has created two classes of indigent citizens – those in families with six children or fewer who receive payments that meet the standard of need and those in larger families who receive less than the standard of need indicates.

Although both types of cases present discrimination that violates the Equal Protection Clause and thus provide support for our decision today, we deem the discrimination in the second type of case, including the instant case, to be especially invidious. Whereas in the first type of case the states' across-the-board fee requirement together with some individuals' lack of resources produce the discriminatory impact, in the second type the state, acting alone, refuses to supply support that by its own calculations members of the disfavored class need.

2 Fundamental Rights and Unconstitutional Conditions

We also use strict scrutiny to review Maryland's maximum family grant regulation because the classification that it creates impinges on constitutional rights that we have deemed fundamental. By penalizing large families, compared to families with fewer children, the regulation infringes the freedom to procreate, which we have described as "one of the basic civil rights of man . . . [that is] fundamental to the very existence and survival of the race." *Skinner v. Oklahoma*, 316 U.S. 535, 541 (1942). Thus, the regulation interferes with decisions that spouses like Junius and Jeanette Gary must be free to make in "the sacred precincts of marital bedrooms," *Griswold v. Connecticut*, 381 U.S. 479, 485 (1965), and that unmarried persons also must have the liberty to make in "the private realm of family life which the state cannot enter," *Prince v. Massachusetts*, 321 U.S. 158, 166 (1944). If the right of privacy means anything, it is the right of the individual, married or single, to be free from unwarranted governmental intrusion into matters so fundamentally affecting a person as the decision whether to bear or beget a child.

In addition to injecting the state into reproductive decisionmaking, the regulation "interferes with the liberty of parents . . . to direct the upbringing" of their children. *Pierce v. Soc'y of Sisters*, 268 U.S. 510, 534 (1925). Determining family size constitutes a significant facet of this liberty that parents may exercise without state intrusion and without fear of state efforts to standardize families. *See id.* at 535. Another facet of this liberty is the ability to keep one's family, including all the children, together, as Linda Williams and Junius and Jeanette Gary have struggled to do – rather than sending some of the children to live with relatives because of the financial exigency generated by the state's welfare scheme. *See Meyer v. Nebraska*, 262 U.S. 390, 399 (1923) (defining "liberty" in the Fourteenth Amendment to "denote[] not merely freedom from bodily restraint but also the right of the individual to contract, to engage in any of the common occupations of life, to acquire useful knowledge, to marry, establish a home and bring up children, to worship God according to the dictates of his own conscience, and generally to enjoy those privileges long recognized at common law as essential to the orderly pursuit of happiness by free men"). As applied to Negro families like those of the named plaintiffs, separation of children from parents recalls the heartless and pernicious practices of slavery, when traders and owners bought and sold their human chattel without regard to family bonds. *See, e.g.*, KENNETH M. STAMPP, THE PECULIAR INSTITUTION: SLAVERY IN THE ANTE-BELLUM SOUTH 252, 257–58, 266–67 (1961).

The fundamental character of autonomy in matters of procreation, family size, and household composition gains additional strength from the First Amendment. For some, the choice whether or not to limit conception rests on religion,[12] in turn raising questions under the Free Exercise Clause. *See Sherbert v. Verner*, 374 U.S. 398 (1963). Further, the interest in sharing a home with all of one's children – that is, occupying intimate, domestic space with family members – comes within the freedom of association protected by the First Amendment. *See Griswold*, 381 U.S. at 483.

We reject the defendants' arguments that, because public assistance constitutes a mere "privilege" that the state need not provide at all, the maximum family grant regulation represents a permissible limitation or condition. Our precedents establish that government may not condition the receipt of a benefit on the sacrifice of a constitutional right. *See Sherbert*, 374 U.S. at 404 ("It is too late in the day to doubt that ... [protected liberties] may be infringed by the denial of or placing of conditions upon a benefit or privilege"). Accordingly, in *Sherbert*, for example, we held that making an applicant for unemployment compensation ineligible because of her refusal to work on her Sabbath impermissibly forces her to choose between the benefit and the precepts of her religion. *Id.* Put differently, the limitation or conditions operated to deter, inhibit, and penalize the exercise of a constitutional right. *See also Speiser v. Randall*, 357 U.S. 513 (1958) (invalidating tax exemption conditioned on a loyalty oath). *See generally* Robert M. O'Neil, *Unconstitutional Conditions: Welfare Benefits with Strings Attached*, 54 CALIF. L. REV. 443 (1966).

The maximum family grant regulation challenged here functions in a similar manner. It operates to deter, inhibit, and penalize the exercise of constitutionally protected fundamental rights to make procreative decisions consistent with personal choices and/or religious beliefs, to keep one's family together, and to determine the composition of the household in which to rear one's children. As such, the classification established by the regulation warrants strict scrutiny. *See Sherbert*, 374 U.S. at 406.

3 Invidious Discrimination against Poor Children in Large Families

Although our Constitution guarantees parents the liberty to make decisions about procreation, childrearing, and household composition, we do not give children the authority to participate in such decisions. Children have

[12] For example, the Catholic Church opposes abortion, sterilization, and use of contraception. *See* POPE PAUL VI, HUMANAE VITAE (ON THE REGULATION OF BIRTH) (1968).

no say in who their parents are, much less whether their parents are able to work and how many children their parents decide to have. Hence, punishing children for parental conduct over which they have no control is illogical and unjust. We recognized such truisms when we invalidated, for invidious discrimination in violation of the Equal Protection Clause, Louisiana's exclusion of children born out of wedlock from recovery for their mother's wrongful death. *Levy v. Louisiana*, 391 U.S. 68 (1968). Among the questions we posed in that case, we asked: "Why should the illegitimate child be denied rights merely because of his birth out of wedlock?" *Id.* at 71.

The Maryland regulation results in a total denial of aid to individuals based solely on the fact that they were the last to be welcomed to an otherwise large family, although their situation is no fault of their own and their parents' decisions are constitutionally protected. In order to provide subsistence for all the members of these families, parents might choose to divide the $250.00 so that all of the children will get something, albeit less than the amount needed, or they might choose to send some of the children to live elsewhere in order to make available additional support. In either case, however, children who have no role in their parents' predicament and no say in their parents' response will endure the negative effect. Nor can these children participate in the democratic process to elect new representatives who might enact more humane welfare laws. If "the poor are politically invisible," HARRINGTON, *supra*, at 6, their children are all the more so. If ever there were a discrete and insular minority, lacking in political power and entitled to special solicitude under the Equal Protection Clause, these children indisputably constitute a paradigm example *See U.S. v. Carolene Prods.*, 304 U.S. 144, 152–53 n. 4 (1938).

4 A Right to Minimum Welfare

The established authorities on invidious discrimination and fundamental rights invoked above support the application of strict scrutiny in our review of the classification presented in this case. Yet we also arrive at this position on an additional basis that commentators, such as Professor Frank Michelman, have discerned in our past opinions.[13] We take the opportunity today expressly to recognize, explain, and elaborate even while leaving many details for another day: the U.S. Constitution's Equal Protection Clause guarantees a

[13] *See generally* Michelman, *supra* note 1.

right to the basic necessities of life, in turn imposing on society, that is, the state, an obligation to provide such basic necessities.[14]

This constitutional right to the basic necessities of life and the concomitant societal obligation rest on a firm infrastructure composed of several interlocking elements. One pillar in this infrastructure is the inescapable fact that, without the means of subsistence and the satisfaction of basic needs, other rights become meaningless. How can one exercise the right to vote, to travel, or to engage in free expression, for example, if one lacks food, shelter, and other requirements for survival? How can children enjoy the equal educational opportunities that we promised in *Brown v. Board of Education*, 347 U.S. 483 (1954), if they go to school hungry or cannot attend at all because they lack appropriate shoes and winter clothing? The point is obvious and has long been recognized. Philosopher John Stuart Mill, in making the case for security as the "most indispensable of all necessaries," concedes that it is nevertheless secondary to subsistence or "physical nutriment." JOHN STUART MILL, UTILITARIANISM, LIBERTY, AND REPRESENTATIVE GOVERNMENT 67 (A. D. Lindsay ed., Dutton 1951) (1861). Moreover, according to the United Nations' Universal Declaration of Human Rights:

> (1) Everyone has the right to a standard of living adequate for the health and well-being of himself and of his family, including food, clothing, housing and medical care and necessary social services, and the right to security in the event of unemployment, sickness, disability, widowhood, old age or other lack of livelihood in circumstances beyond his control.
>
> (2) Motherhood and childhood are entitled to special care and assistance. All children, whether born in or out of wedlock, shall enjoy the same social protection.
>
> G.A. Res. 217 (III) A, Universal Declaration of Human Rights, art. 25 (Dec. 10, 1948).

[14] The right that we expressly recognize today goes by various names in the literature. *See* Michelman, *supra* note 1, at 9 ("minimum welfare"); *id.* at 13 ("minimum protection against economic hazard" or satisfaction of one's "just wants"); *id.* at 35, 38 ("minimum protection"); Bernard Evans Harvith, *Federal Equal Protection and Welfare Assistance*, 31 ALB. L. REV. 210, 231 (1967) ("access to the basic necessities of life"). According to another way to articulate this right: "when individuals have insufficient resources to live under conditions of health and decency, society has obligations to provide support, and the individual is entitled to that support as of right." Charles A. Reich, *Individual Rights and Social Welfare: The Emerging Legal Issues*, 74 YALE L.J. 1245, 1256 (1965). Such societal obligations inhere in the generally accepted understanding of the Equal Protection Clause. *See* Joseph Tussman & Jacobus tenBroek, *The Equal Protection of the Laws*, 37 CALIF. L. REV. 341, 341 (1949) ("We now know that the equal protection clause was designed to impose upon the states a positive duty to supply protection to all persons in the enjoyment of their natural and inalienable rights – especially life, liberty, and property – and to do so equally").

A second pillar can be found in this society's hierarchy of values – made manifest in our Constitution and, more recently, in the war that our government is waging on poverty. Prioritizing economic values over human values or leaving an underclass without assistance to face "brutal need" would offend our American commitment to compassion as well as to equality. *See Goldberg v. Kelly*, 397 U.S. 254, 261 (1970); *see also Shapiro*, 394 U.S. at 633.

This hierarchy of values, in turn, brings into focus a third pillar of the equal protection right that we expressly recognize today. An affirmative right to the basic necessities of life, particularly for poor children like those in the instant case, follows directly from the constitutional principle of parental autonomy that we have found in the protection of "liberty" in the Due Process Clause. *See Meyer v. Nebraska*, 262 U.S. 390, 399 (1923); *Pierce v. Soc'y of Sisters*, 268 U.S. 510, 534 (1925). Without a guarantee of minimum welfare, a constitutional commitment to equality would be no more than an empty promise for children whose fate and future our law entrusts to parents, but who have no choice regarding those parents and no control over the family's financial and other circumstances. Put differently, the Equal Protection Clause would invalidate legal rules that assign children and their care to private families absent a guarantee that such families will be able to provide them with at least the bare essentials for survival. Equal protection might well require more for children, but certainly it can require no less.

For adults, we can arrive at a parallel conclusion upon close examination of a fourth pillar undergirding the right to minimum welfare, namely, government's role in creating and perpetuating structures of society that account for poverty, notwithstanding any declaration of war and other remedial gestures. We need not decide today whether intentional government action causing an inequality or a deprivation suffered by a particular class is always necessary to trigger a government obligation under the Equal Protection Clause.[15] This is so because, in the case at hand, we see ample evidence of purposeful government participation in the economic status quo, including the present distribution of both wealth and impoverishment in the United States.[16] Of course, we could

[15] Professor Michelman notes the absence of a proximate cause requirement for what he calls "minimum protection." Michelman, *supra* note 1, at 39. He explains: "The due process clause inveighs only against certain 'deprivations' by the 'state,' occurrences which seemingly cannot occur by mere default. On the other hand, the equal protection clause's injunction against 'denying' the 'equal protection of the laws' is not so clearly void of a requirement that the quiescent state must 'act' (*i.e.*, cease denying protection) in certain circumstances when it would choose not to." *Id.* at 17.

[16] Examples of government's role in shaping the economic status quo include "taxation, government expenditures, monetary policy, express and hidden subsidies, antitrust

begin with the deprivations inherent in Black enslavement and claims for reparations that remain unanswered, despite the enduring detriments borne by the descendants of enslaved men and women.[17] Yet more recent and even contemporary official actions deliberately seek to disadvantage one segment of society while advantaging another. In the 1930s, the Federal Housing Administration explicitly encouraged race-based deed restrictions and other means of maintaining residential segregation. FEDERAL HOUSING ADMIN., UNDERWRITING MANUAL §§ 228–29, 233, 284 (3) (g), 289 (1) (1936). Further, a report issued by the U.S. Department of Labor acknowledged the federal government's active role in the creation of residential racial apartheid after World War II by providing financial support for "vast white, middle- and lower-middle class suburbs around all of the Nation's cities," while purposely leaving the inner cities to Negroes. OFFICE OF PLANNING & RESEARCH, U.S. DEP'T OF LABOR, THE NEGRO FAMILY: THE CASE FOR NATIONAL ACTION 44 (March 1965). In other words, "[t]hree centuries of injustice have brought about deep-seated structural distortions in the life of the Negro American." *Id.* at 47 (tracing roots of such distortions to enslavement).

Sex provides another salient vector here, given how patriarchy and the laws of coverture have long prevented women from supporting themselves. *See, e.g., Bradwell v. State*, 83 U.S. 130 (1873) (upholding disqualification of women from practicing law). This Court allowed states to limit women's opportunities for full employment without imposing similar limitations on male workers. *See Muller v. Oregon*, 208 U.S. 412 (1908). Further, our legal system has chosen to assume that women should marry and to offer rewards for breadwinner-homemaker marriages. *See, e.g.*, I.R.C. § 6013 (1964 & Supp. 1970) (allowing married couples since 1948 to split income by filing

enforcement, banking laws, and other federal activities." *See* Harvith, *supra* note 14, at 242. Accordingly, it follows that:

> [O]nce the government begins to act affirmatively to influence the economy and to help the poor, it must carry through with programs effective enough to provide every American with access to the basic necessities. In short, if the government is going to be involved in the economy, and is going to wage a war on poverty, with all the attendant diversions of monies and energies from private sector groups which might otherwise seek to solve the same problems with more incentive and more adequate resources than they presently have, the government cannot do a sloppy job leaving millions of Americans in poverty.
>
> *Id.* at 243.

[17] Recently, James Forman, representing the National Black Economic Conference, interrupted services at the Riverside Church in New York City to demand reparations for slavery. Edward B. Fiske, *Churchmen Critical of Forman Tactics*, N.Y. TIMES, May 6, 1969, at 1, 36.

joint tax returns). While such laws subordinate all women, unmarried women confront compound disadvantages, which loom even larger for those who fall outside this country's white racial majority. Accordingly, it should come as no surprise that the National Welfare Rights Organization, which formed in 1966 to press for poverty relief, had a membership, including grassroots activists, that composed predominantly of Black female AFDC recipients.[18] Against this background, AFDC embodies conspicuous contradictions. On the one hand, since its inception, it has assumed traditional and distinctly different roles for women and men and written those into law. See S. REP. No. 74-628, at 17 (1935) (Report of the Senate Finance Committee building on state programs for "mothers' pensions"). On the other hand, a program like AFDC, corrected for violations of equal protection, has the potential to free women from their legally imposed economic dependence on men and to promise some modicum of dignity and citizenship for poor, minority mothers – who have had to endure the stigma of having their government use the term "pathology" to criticize how they live their lives and to denigrate the important role that they, as women, occupy in their families.[19]

Stepping back from such particulars, however, we acknowledge a more general proposition in order to emphasize government's deep engagement in today's economic inequality. Property ownership and our very understanding of relative wealth and its absence reflect legal conclusions, not natural "facts." *See* RESTATEMENT (FIRST) OF PROPERTY, chapter 1 (definitions) (1936). *See also* Robert L. Hale, *Coercion and Distribution in a Supposedly Non-coercive State*, 38 POL. SCI. Q. 470, 472 (1923) ("While there is no law against eating in the abstract, there is a law which forbids [one] to eat any of the food which actually exists in the community – and that is the law of property."); Charles A. Reich, *The New Property*, 73 YALE L.J. 733, 778 (1964) (noting how property "stems from government"). It follows that benefits like AFDC are properly considered rights because they "are based upon a recognition that misfortune and deprivation are often caused by forces far beyond

[18] In 1969, the National Welfare Rights Organization under the leadership of George Alvin Wiley "claim[ed] 30,000 members, most of them Negro women who [were] on welfare." *See* William Borders, *Welfare Militant on the Way Up: George Alvin Wiley*, N.Y. TIMES, May 27, 1969, at 32. *See also* Richard Cloward, *Poor Power: National Welfare Rights Movement*, THE NATION, Feb. 20, 1967, at 228 (noting how "Negroes dominate" the "welfare movement").

[19] The Moynihan Report contains an entire chapter entitled "The Tangle of Pathology" that emphasizes the matriarchal structure of many Black families. MOYNIHAN REPORT, *supra* note 5, at 29–45. Moreover, this report's observations about the "extraordinary growth in Negro population" suggests interest in curbing Black women's fertility. *See id.* at 25. *See also* Dembitz, *supra* note 3, at 109–10 (inquiring about the proper role of welfare workers in promoting family planning).

the control of the individual, such as technological change, variations in the demand for goods, depressions, or wars," and they promote the "goal of providing a secure minimum basis for individual well-being and dignity in a society where each man cannot be wholly the master of his own destiny." *Id.* at 785–86.

Accordingly, recognizing minimum welfare as a fundamental right under the Equal Protection Clause not only advances the human values that this country treasures; it also comports with the emerging understanding of "justice as fairness" in which mutually self-interested and rational persons would agree on two basic principles: "first, each person . . . has an equal right to the most extensive liberty compatible with a like liberty for all; and second, inequalities are arbitrary unless it is reasonable to expect that they will work out for everyone's advantage, and provided the positions and offices to which they attach, or from which they may be gained, are open to all." John Rawls, *Justice as Fairness*, 67 PHIL. REV. 164, 165 (1958).

B *Applying the Standard of Review*

The foregoing analysis plainly shows why the Maryland maximum family grant regulation is a far cry from the economic measures that we now routinely subject to deferential, rational basis review. *See Williamson v. Lee Optical of Oklahoma, Inc.*, 348 U.S. 483, 488 (1955). Instead, we have before us state action that affects the most intimate and personal human relationships and vital means of survival for some of our most vulnerable citizens. Such state action demands rigorous review.

Yet even if we used the rational-basis test, deferential review cannot mean abdication, precluding all inquiry about whether a law advances its purported purposes. Otherwise, "rationality" would be a toothless standard, so forgiving that it would tolerate even arbitrary state action, which the framers intended the Equal Protection Clause to avert. *See Levy v. Louisiana*, 391 U.S. 68, 71 (1968) (applying rationality review to invalidate illegitimacy-based classification); *Ry. Express Agency v. New York*, 336 U.S. 106, 112 (1949) (Jackson, J., concurring) (noting how the Equal Protection Clause requires "that cities, states and the Federal Government must exercise their powers so as not to discriminate between their inhabitants except upon some *reasonable differentiation fairly related to the object of regulation*") (emphasis added). Accordingly, we conclude that Maryland's four asserted justifications for the maximum family grant regulation, each of which we consider below, cannot survive judicial review, under the strict scrutiny that governs this case or even the rationality standard that defendants would have us apply.

1 Conserving State Funds and Maintaining Popular Support

At the original trial, defendants presented an exclusively economic justification for the maximum family grant regulation, based on evidence that the Governor and General Assembly of Maryland had failed to appropriate sufficient funds to finance fully the state's share of the AFDC program and that the regulation would provide the necessary reduction in expenditures. *See Williams v. Dandridge*, 297 F. Supp. 450, 467 (D. Md. 1968). As we wrote in *Shapiro v. Thompson*, 394 U.S. 618, 633 (1969): "The saving of welfare costs cannot justify an otherwise invidious classification." Indeed, singling out large families for disadvantageous treatment is an arbitrary way to save money.

We find no basis for altering this conclusion in the defendants' elaboration of the costs-saving argument presented in their brief to this Court. Here, they assert that the maximum family grant regulation is designed to maintain public confidence in the welfare program, which might otherwise face taxpayer resistance for providing overly generous assistance to large poor families. Appellants' Br. at 39–40.

We cannot countenance decisions by political actors to play fast and loose with the basic needs of impoverished human beings in order to curry favor with voters. The very purpose of our Bill of Rights is to protect constitutional rights and to safeguard minorities from invidious and discriminatory measures, even in the face of majoritarian opposition.

2 Encouraging Employment

In their post-trial motion and in their brief for this Court, defendants offer as an additional justification what they called the "principle of less benefit." *See* 297 F. Supp. at 467; Appellants' Br. at 33. They argue:

> The application of a maximum grant regulation was rational to avoid disincentives to employment on the part of families with employable members (including women eligible for work incentive referral under the 1967 amendments) and was also rational in its application to families with unemployed or disabled members, for whom benefit levels under state workmen's compensation and unemployment compensation laws have traditionally been set at a fraction of earnings in order to avoid disincentives arising from imperfect administration of eligibility requirements.
>
> Appellants' Br. at 34.

As we have noted, mere rationality will not suffice to save state action that invidiously discriminates against the poor. Even if it were, however, this regulation is not a rational way of providing a work incentive because it operates to "squeeze" financially only large poor families, like those of Linda Williams and of Junius and Jeanette Gary, without creating work incentives for other families receiving AFDC. In addition, the work-incentive rationale fails for families that include no employable adults, again like the named plaintiffs, who suffer from disabilities or cannot work outside the home because of care responsibilities inside the home – a fact that Maryland has recognized. Br. of Amici Curiae: Center on Social Welfare Policy and Law et al. at 38–39 (citing MD. DEP'T OF SOC. SERVS., PROFILE OF CASELOADS, RESEARCH REPORT NO. 5, at 6 (1969); STATE OF MD., MANUAL OF THE DEP'T OF PUB. WELFARE § 215.19 (superseded Nov. 1, 1968)). Regardless of the standard of review, the regulation is both too narrow and too broad.

3 Discouraging Desertion

Defendants also invoke the "principle of less benefit" to characterize the maximum family grant regulation as a means of discouraging desertion by employable fathers. *See* 297 F. Supp. at 467; Appellants' Br. at 34–35. The same flaws that defeat the work-incentive rationale also doom this asserted justification because they reveal its ineffectiveness and thus its irrationality. First, data fail to show that states with such caps have lower desertion rates than states without them. Br. of Amici Curiae: Center on Social Welfare Policy and Law et al. at 45 (citing DIV. OF PROGRAM STATISTICS & ANALYSIS, U.S. DEPT. OF HEALTH, EDUC., & WELFARE, CHARACTERISTICS OF FAMILIES RECEIVING AFDC, NOV.–DEC. 1961, TABLE 12 (Apr. 1963)). Second, the maximum family grant regulation is too narrow, given that the anti-desertion rationale would be equally relevant to small families. Third, as explained by the district court, the regulation is also too broad because it covers many families for whom this purpose has "no logical application," including Junius and Jeanette Gary's family. 297 F. Supp. at 468. Finally, to the extent the anti-desertion rationale is designed to discourage family dissolution, it is self-defeating because it creates financial incentives to send children away, as we have already pointed out. *See supra*. Thus, although we have no evidence that the regulation is inducing the father of Linda Williams's children to return home, the parties' stipulated facts show that the regulation impedes her efforts to keep all of her family together, given that "farming out" some of the children would improve the economic situation of all. *See* App. at 72–73.

4 Discouraging Childbearing

Defendants attempt to justify the maximum family grant regulation as a disincentive to childbearing. Appellants' Br. at 39–40. This is not only a family planning measure of dubious effectiveness but it also irrationally disadvantages children in an effort to shape the sexual and reproductive conduct of their parents, which our precedents have declared unconstitutional. *Levy*, 391 U.S. at 71. Further, Congress has emphasized that family planning must be voluntary, 42 U.S.C. § 602 (a) (15) (C) (Supp. V. 1970), while the Constitution prohibits coercive state action in such matters of personal privacy and, oftentimes, of religious faith, as we have explained above. *See supra*.

Indeed, if we were to allow the maximum family grant regulation to stand as a family planning measure, consider the additional scenarios that might follow. For example, states might limit eligibility for AFDC to families using birth control, in turn raising privacy-invading questions about the effectiveness of various methods, the responsibility of women versus men for contraception, and the enforceability of the condition, given that birth control sometimes fails. Perhaps welfare officials or physicians delivering babies in AFDC families would pressure or even require mothers to undergo sterilization – a scenario we can easily imagine, given that this Court has previously encountered involuntary sterilization measures targeting disfavored groups in society. *See Buck v. Bell*, 274 U.S. 200 (1927) (targeting "feeble-minded"); *Skinner v. Oklahoma*, 316 U.S. 535 (1942) (targeting certain felons). Further, what would this family planning rationale mean for abortion – which could soon be decriminalized, based on signs of possible law reform? *See United States v. Vuitch*, 305 F. Supp. 1032 (D.D.C. 1969), appeal docketed and Jurisdictional Statement filed in the U.S. Supreme Court by Erwin Griswold, Solicitor General of the United States, et al., No. 84, (Feb. 5, 1970) (requesting ruling by U.S. Supreme Court); N.Y. State S., S. 8556-A, 193rd Sess. (N.Y. 1970) (bill to legalize abortion pending in New York legislature). In a jurisdiction in which abortion is legal, could the state offer funding to poor women to cover the costs of terminating their pregnancies while withholding support for prenatal care and childbirth expenses for those choosing to carry to term? Certainly, our Constitution does not permit such unequal treatment, although placing our imprimatur on the maximum family grant regulation would strongly signal otherwise.

IV

As we have shown, poverty is a structural, societal problem that demands affirmative government correction. AFDC represents an intervention with as yet unrealized potential to effect positive change, but Maryland's imposition of a maximum family grant regulation without any acceptable justification violates the Equal Protection Clause.

This opinion represents the beginning, not the end, of the analysis. Like the district court below, we leave to legislators the development of an appropriate remedy for the constitutional violation that we find. 297 F. Supp. at 459. For example, law reformers have proposed innovations like a guaranteed annual income[20] or a negative income tax.[21] There will be time enough to examine such proposals and other alternatives once they have been enacted and suitable parties have presented a case or controversy for this Court to review.

[20] Under one theory, a "welfare crisis" could precipitate much needed legislative reform "for a guaranteed annual income and thus an end to poverty." Richard A. Cloward & Frances Fox Piven, *The Weight of the Poor: A Strategy to End Poverty*, THE NATION, May 2, 1966, at 510, 516.

[21] A negative income tax is, in effect, a subsidy for those earning below a certain level. According to its principal proponent, Professor Milton Friedman, its advantages include its direct aim at the problem of poverty and the useful form of help that it would provide, cash assistance. MILTON FRIEDMAN, WITH THE ASSISTANCE OF ROSE D. FRIEDMAN, CAPITALISM AND FREEDOM 192 (1962).

5

Commentary on *Wisconsin v. Yoder*

LISA FISHBAYN JOFFE

INTRODUCTION

I write this commentary from the perspective of a political philosopher rather than that of a constitutional lawyer. Political philosophers and legal theorists struggle with questions regarding the limits of multicultural toleration in the liberal state, questions that are worked out in practice in the context of legal disputes over constitutional principles. Questions about the competing interests of individuals, cultural minority groups and the state are put into sharp relief in controversies over the ways in which children are educated. The *Yoder* case has been taken up by many political theorists as an ideal lens through which to explore these issues. However, I will argue that some of the unique features of Amish culture, the location of the Amish in the American imagination, and the facts of this particular case may shape its relevance for a broader class of cases. One key factor that is often overlooked is the differentiated impact that gender norms in the Amish community have on the opportunities of boys and girls. Justice Murray provides a corrective to this lacuna in both the original judgment and philosophical consideration of it, delineating the limits of the reproduction of Amish patriarchy at the heart of her rewritten opinion.

THE ORIGINAL *YODER* DECISION AND CIVIC EDUCATION

Since the advent of public education, the state has sought to set minimum standards for curricula and school attendance in both public and private schools. Religious and cultural minority groups may establish schools and design curricula suited to needs and ideals of their community, subject to state regulations regarding minimal competencies that must be achieved through their programs. Among liberal philosophers, it is widely agreed that a minimally adequate education is one that creates competencies for gainful employment, capacities to understand and participate in democratic institutions, and an awareness that one is legally free, under the laws of the wider society, to cease to be a member of the minority community in which one is being raised and educated.[1] Controversy emerges, however, when these competencies are defined to include capacities to critically evaluate, revise and perhaps reject the practices of this religious or cultural community. Where is the line between inculcating in children the civic virtues that would make the exercise of autonomy possible but not explicitly training them to value or seek autonomy counter to religious tenets? For many theorists, the dispute at the heart of the *Yoder* case has been the lens through which they have examined this issue. This model is an imperfect one, not least because the form of life in the Amish community has significant differences from that of most other minority communities seeking to live in accordance with their own comprehensive doctrines.[2]

In *Wisconsin v. Yoder*, the Supreme Court heard a challenge to Wisconsin's compulsory school attendance law that requires children to attend school until age sixteen. The respondents, members of two Amish groups, viewed attendance at high school as contrary to their religious faith and refused to permit their children to attend. They believed that school attendance would put their children in danger of excommunication from the church and thus in danger of eternal damnation. The accused, fathers of two girls and one boy, were convicted at trial and fined. They appealed their conviction arguing that the law violated their First Amendment right to free exercise of their religion and their Fourteenth Amendment right to instruct their children in their faith. Their convictions were reversed on appeal before the Wisconsin Supreme Court and the reversal was upheld by the U.S. Supreme Court.

Writing for the majority, Justice Burger framed the issue as a conflict between the parents' genuine religious belief that withdrawal from school was required and the state's interest in ensuring that children received an adequate education.[3] He determined that the compulsory school attendance law indeed violated the First Amendment rights of parents to educate their

1 *See, e.g.*, Joseph Raz, The Morality of Freedom 410 (1988); M. Victoria Costa, Rawls, Citizenship and Education (2011).

2 Rawls defines a "comprehensive doctrine" as set of ideas that offers a coherent theoretical account of the religious, philosophical, and moral aspects of life rooted in a tradition and a set of practices. It includes ideals of personal virtue and character. John Rawls, Political Liberalism 13 (1993).

3 Interestingly, the Amish appellees do not argue that school attendance is itself a sin, but that it would expose one to the temptations to commit sin.

children in their faith and that the state did not present a sufficiently compelling case to justify violating this right. His analysis turned on the functions that education has served in American society: education should give children sufficient skills to find gainful employment and avoid becoming burdens on the public purse; it should instruct them in their duties to obey the laws of the United States and should educate them to "participate effectively and intelligently in our open political system."[4] Burger determined that Amish education met the first two criteria and that their religious commitment to "life in a church-oriented community, separated from the outside world and "worldly" influences, their attachment to nature, and the soil" entitled them to an exemption from the third.[5] Their training might not equip them to be active citizens in a liberal democracy, but it did equip them for participation, according to their status, in Amish society.

Burger's analysis is notable for the way in which the interests of children are treated. While parents may not make decisions that will jeopardize the health or safety of the child or impose significant social burdens on them, they are otherwise free to educate them as they see fit. Burger also accepts at face value the assertion by the Amish parents that their lifestyle would not survive if their children attended attend high school. He points to assertions that the practices of the group have remained unchanged for 300 years.[6] In fact, the many schisms in the Amish community reflect changing attitudes and practices.

In dissent, Justice Douglas cited the failure of the majority to treat the Amish children as individuals who might have their own religious and personal visions for their lives. He lamented that the Court did not hear from the children themselves. The children may have alternate visions for their lives – as an astronaut, pianist, or oceanographer.[7] The majority decision "forever barred from entry into the new and amazing world of diversity that we have today . . . If he is harnessed to the Amish way of life, by those in authority over him, and if his education is truncated, his entire life may be stunted and deformed."[8] Douglas would have affirmed the majority's decision in *Yoder*, but only in the case of Frieda Yoder, who had testified to her acceptance of Amish beliefs. He would have remanded the case for more evidence on the opinions of the other two children.

4 *Wisconsin v. Yoder*, 406 U.S. 205, 221 (1972).
5 *Id.* at 217.
6 *Yoder*, 406 U.S. at 219.
7 *Id.* at 244.
8 *Id.* at 246.

AMISH ADULT BAPTISM AND "RUMSPRINGA"

It is not surprising that a case involving the Amish occupies a central place in the discourse of the toleration of religious difference in American law and political philosophy. The Amish are an Anabaptist sect of Christianity that emerged with the Protestant Reformation in Europe. John Locke's notions of religious toleration, which have profoundly shaped American constitutional law, are a response, in part, to the religious persecution of these Anabaptist groups.[9]

The term "anabaptists" refers to the rejection of infant baptism and insistence that members must make a voluntary, informed commitment to religion as adults.[10] The Amish rejection of a Christian duty to engage with and support the state led to their persecution by European states during the sixteenth and seventeenth centuries and their immigration to the United States.[11] This understanding of their own history as one in which they have chosen to set themselves apart and have suffered because of it continues to shape the Amish self-perception and their engagement with the modern state.[12]

The Amish concerns with children's exposure to high school education and other forms of secular life is exacerbated by two unique features of Amish culture. The Amish do not accept converts, so the growth or decline of their numbers is based on reproduction and retention of children in the community.[13] Second, and more importantly, in preparation for their acceptance of the faith, usually between the ages of sixteen and twenty-one, Amish children are given an opportunity to experiment with other forms of life during a period of "rumspringa" ("running around").

Rumspringa is presented in popular media as an opportunity to engage in wild behavior.[14] However, it does not generally entail exposure to a broad or appealing alternate lifestyle. The adolescents usually remain at or near home

9 Geoffrey Dipple, *Anabaptists and 17th Century Arguments for Religious Toleration in Switzerland and the Netherlands*, *in* TOPOGRAPHIES OF TOLERANCE AND INTOLERANCE: RESPONSES TO RELIGIOUS PLURALISM IN REFORMATION EUROPE 171 (Marjorie Elizabeth Plummer & Victoria Christman eds., 2018).

10 STEVEN M. NOLT, THE AMISH: A CONCISE INTRODUCTION 14 (2016).

11 *Id.*

12 STEVEN M. NOLT & THOMAS J. MEYERS, PLAIN DIVERSITY: AMISH CULTURES AND IDENTITIES 5 (2007).

13 William A. Fischel, *Do Amish One-Room Schools Make the Grade? The Dubious Data of "Wisconsin v. Yoder,"* 79 U. CHI. L. REV. 107, 111 (2012) (citing a 2010 estimate of the Amish population of 250,000).

14 *See*, for example, reality television programs like *Breaking Amish* (2010–2014) and *Amish in the City* (2014).

and do not have the funds, education, or skills to travel, seek higher education, or get a job. Some may confine themselves to wholesome pursuits, while others may spend their time experimenting with alcohol, drugs, and promiscuity.[15] It is perhaps not surprising that this does not offer a tempting long-term vision for most of them and 85–90 percent return to take on the obligations of Amish faith.[16] Of those who leave, some join the "English" world, but most opt for communities like the Mennonites that practice a less onerous form of Anabaptism.[17]

Amish refusal to allow their children to attend high school is linked to concerns about shaping their dispositions and abilities during this exceptionally vulnerable period of their development. A curriculum that creates the inclination to think of oneself as an individual or to compete for success, and creates the competence to pursue education and employment outside the community, could turn the rumspringa period into a more direct path out of the faith.

AMISH EDUCATION BEFORE AND AFTER *YODER*

Until the mid-twentieth century, the Amish were content to send their children to public school with non-Amish children and to have them taught by non-Amish teachers. This began to change as school districts phased out one-room schoolhouses in Amish villages and replaced them with consolidated elementary schools for financial reasons. These new schools often were some distance away from home, both physically and ideologically. Instead of walking or biking to school, Amish children had to be bussed to a bigger town with a more diverse student population. Amish parents also felt a loss of control over what happened in school. Statewide changes in the curriculum included materials on science, sexual education, and patriotic values, all of which were viewed as threats to their way of life. Finally, conflict was created with Amish communities when states moved to fully enforce truancy laws rather than ignoring the frequent absences and gradual withdrawal of Amish children after the eighth grade.[18]

The *Yoder* case was not the first legal battle over compulsory education for Amish children. From the 1930s on, Amish parents and states struggled in

[15] Nolt, *supra* note 10, at 58. Groups like the Amish Youth Vision Project seek to address the prevalence drug and alcohol abuse among Amish youth during this period. *The Need for Alcohol & Drug Classes*, Amish Youth Vision Project, http://ayvp.org/?page_id=2 (last visited Mar. 2, 2019).

[16] Fischel, *supra* note 13, at 111–13.

[17] *Id.* at 111.

[18] Nolt, *supra* note 10, at 75.

various ways to resolve these controversies. Some fathers paid fines or were imprisoned rather than send their children to school. Other communities bought the abandoned one-room schoolhouses left behind by school consolidation and reopened them as private Amish schools.[19] In one notorious 1965 incident, Iowa school officials attempted to force Amish children onto a school bus to take them to a public elementary school. Photographs of terrified children fleeing into the wheat fields led the governor to overturn this policy and negotiate an exemption for the Amish from the obligation to attend school.[20] Wisconsin, however, was different in that the state was not inclined to accommodate or overlook truancy by children in the Amish community. This was perhaps because the Amish had only recently moved into the state in the 1960s and had no history of negotiated accommodation with it.[21]

Although the *Yoder* decision deals only with exemption from secondary school education, in its aftermath the Amish largely withdrew from public elementary education as well. As of 2016, there were more than two thousand Amish elementary schools. Teachers typically are unmarried young women who have studied only up to the eighth grade themselves.[22] The Amish school curriculum focuses only on developing math and literacy skills necessary for Amish life, somewhat equivalent to that offered by other rural American schools, but does not include science, social studies, or art.[23]

THE PHILOSOPHICAL AFTERLIFE OF *YODER*

Many political theorists have taken up a simplified version of the fact pattern in *Yoder* to explore the limits for tolerating educational practices that cut against the autonomy of children.[24] Misunderstanding *Yoder*'s facts has led scholars to identify the right of exit from a minority religious community as an essential element to a solution to such conflicts. If community members enjoy the formal right to leave rather than subject themselves to an alleged discriminatory practice, this is considered evidence to support the claim that a practice is not objectionable. Members may not experience it as discriminatory or, while viewing it as objectionable, determine on balance that it is

[19] *Id.*
[20] Fischel, *supra* note 13, at 117.
[21] *Id.*
[22] *Id.* at 115.
[23] *Id.* at 117.
[24] *See* Raz, *supra* note 1, at 410–11; Chandran Kukathas, *Is Feminism Bad for Multiculturalism?*, 15 Pub. Aff. Q. 83 (2001); Jeff Spinner-Halev, Surviving Diversity: Religion And Democratic Citizenship 111–24 (2001).

preferable to accept it rather than leave to face other, more unappealing challenges. Failure to exit is thus cited as evidence that the impugned practices are acceptable to those subjected to them, because members who really objected would exercise their right to leave.[25] It provides moral cover, absolving the liberal state of duties to intervene to provide justice to those subjected to the impugned practice, having put the onus for triggering these protections on those who fail to object to their oppression.

A simplified account of the Amish example of exit can be misleading. It has led to an exaggerated sense that children reared in communities organized around a comprehensive doctrine choose to remain part of them and that exit from such a community is easy. It is cited as an example of an autonomous choice to lead a life of restricted autonomy. Despite the fact that the Amish explicitly reject the value of autonomy, there appears to be one moment of personal choice (in the Amish case, rumspringa) in choosing to join the community and accept baptism as an adult. This moment of self-determination is expanded by some theorists into an assumption that all children in such communities have an occasion to choose, when in fact they do not.

Moreover, feminist critics have noted that the presence of an exit option does not take into account the ways in which the ability to exercise this option may be conditioned by the gender status of group members. This is particularly concerning when the women involved are in fact teenage girls, on the cusp of adulthood, who are negotiating their relationship to both their family and their community.[26]

Theorists who take account of gender have argued for moving from a focus on formal rights of exit to a conception of realistic rights of exit. This would take into account the special barriers to exit that may impair its use by women and the sorts of supports for exit that could be provided by the minority group, the state, or both.[27] Barriers to exit may be psychological, logistical, or economic. Women and girls may lack the ability to imagine life outside the community, may fear exclusion from the broader non-Amish community, and

[25] Kukathas, *supra* note 24, at 92–94.

[26] Carol Gilligan, *Exit-Voice Dilemmas in Adolescent Development*, *in* MAPPING THE MORAL DOMAIN 143 (Carol Gilligan et al. eds., 1988).

[27] *See* Susan Moller Okin, *Mistresses of Their Own Destiny: Group Rights, Gender, and Realistic Rights of Exit*, 112 ETHICS 205 (2002); ANNE PHILLIPS, MULTICULURALISM WITHOUT CULTURE (2007); Oonagh Reitman, *On Exit*, *in* MINORITIES WITHIN MINORITIES: EQUALITY, RIGHTS AND DIVERSITY 189–208 (Avigail Eisenberg & Jeff Spinner-Halev eds., 2005); AYELET SHACHAR, MULTICULTURAL JURISDICTIONS: CULTURAL DIFFERENCES AND WOMEN'S RIGHTS 117–43 (2001).

may lack the skills and economic resources to begin a new independent life. Addressing these challenges in a realistic way may require a model of resettlement similar to that made available to refugees seeking to build a new life in a new culture where they have to adopt the language, create new connections, and learn new marketable skills.[28]

In fact, exit may not be voluntary but rather a form of constructive expulsion from the community. Deployment of such forms of exit act as a safety valve that allows a community to decide whether or not to modify, over the long or short term, or preserve and protect inegalitarian practices.[29] Those who object to the way the minority culture operates are thrust out, unable to remain to try to transform it.[30]

THE REWRITTEN OPINION

Justice Murray faces the daunting challenge of unpacking the gendered nature of the barriers to exit that exist in the *Yoder* case. Her evaluation of the gender norms taught in Amish education is hampered by a lack of evidence in the record in the original *Yoder* case. There were no independent interviews of the children, or a cross-section of children in the community, and no analysis of gendered patterns of exit. Justice Murray, however, expertly teases out the ways in which these gender norms are communicated to boys and girls through all aspects of their religious instruction and socialization. Women and girls thus may be socialized to accept their situation and not to think of themselves as leaders of change or possessing the agency to act outside of the Amish community.

Justice Murray's judgment reframes the analysis to take gender into account and to interrogate the value of public education. Taking the latter, it identifies the essential question in the case as a controversy over whether the state's compulsory education law places an undue burden on religious freedom. The religious freedom interests of parents and children should not be elided but analyzed separately. While the actions and testimony of the fathers in the case make clear how the law impairs their desire to pass on their religious traditions to their children, the evidence regarding the religious beliefs and preferences of the children is thin. Justice Murray concludes that the brief affirmations of their fathers' views given in open court may not be accurate reflections of the

[28] *See* Andrew Wahlstrom, *Liberal Democracies and Encompassing Religious Communities: A Defense of Autonomy and Accommodation*, 36 J. Soc. Phil. 31, 43 (2005).

[29] Raz, *supra* note 1, at 410–24.

[30] *See infra*, note 27 (citing the work of Okin, Nussbaum, Reitman, Schachar).

children's views. Moreover, the mode of socialization described in her account suggests little opportunity for children to formulate their own religious conceptions. Discerning the true nature of children's religious beliefs could be difficult and disruptive to family harmony. Justice Murray concludes that rather than engage in such an inquiry, the Court may remain agnostic about the sincerity of the children's beliefs and accord them an equal education regardless of their religious affiliation.

Justice Murray's judgment argues that education should expose children to alternate forms of life and prepare children with the skills that might allow them to choose another life. This does not mean that the goal of education is rejection of the child's home life for something different or better. It simply means each child is guaranteed broader knowledge of the world, knowledge that enables children to fully participate in democracy. She notes the key roles performed by public education – to provide civic education necessary for children to be competent participants in America's democratic institutions and to provide training in the ethical values, practical skills, and academic competencies to enable them to live satisfying lives. She sees the connections between compulsory education and the prohibition on child labor. Children are doubly protected from exploitation as waged or unwaged workers by the duty upon their parents to ensure their attendance at school. An exemption from compulsory school attendance opens the door not only to informal apprenticeship in agrarian labors that underpin the Amish lifestyle, but also to other, less savory, forms of labor.

In terms of gender, Justice Murray draws a distinction between the impact of schooling decisions on the life chances of girls and women and those of boys and men. Boys and girls are educated together during elementary school and may do a range of similar chores. However, the distinct modes of practical education offered to male and female students after their withdrawal from formal education will provide gender-specific training for the lives they will be expected to lead within the Amish community. Petitioners' daughters, Frieda and Barbara, will be groomed to be mothers and housewives and perhaps to learn marketable skills like quilting. But as Justice Murray notes, wives are expected to live in "willing submission" to their husbands and many women have seven or more children. Vernon, a petitioner's son, will be trained to be a farmer and perhaps in some trade like woodworking or welding. Should any of the children wish at some point in the future to exit the Amish community, all may suffer from a lack of transferrable skills that might enable them to support themselves in the broader society.

But the disabilities inflicted on the girls may be more acute. Justice Murray notes that girls may be trained in domestic skills that may have little value in a gendered labor market. Reared in a society where their voices are not merely silenced because they are children, but also because they are women, they may find it even more difficult to formulate or implement an alternate plan for their life. The likelihood that they will be married in their teens and subject to the burdens of motherhood in their early twenties makes it even less likely that they might choose to exit. Divorce is not possible and permission to separate is rarely granted. More men than women choose to leave the community and spouses left behind are expected to avoid remarriage in the hope that their spouse will repent and return.[31]

Strangely, while withdrawal from school coincides with the onset of puberty, the original *Yoder* judgment fails to note the fact that high school also presents the opportunity for sexual temptation leading to love and marriage outside of the community. Is this a factor that might also have differential impacts on girls? Justice Murray, in her revised judgment, notes that Amish education aims to train men and women for their expected roles in marriage. The preservation of modesty and chastity and the avoidance of passionate attachments may be an unspoken aspect of this training.

Finally, Justice Murray's analysis points us to a set of factors that might provide realistic rights of exit for Amish girls and young women. Both boys and girls need to be educated about their rights and duties under American law. They need to be trained in intellectual and practical skills that will enable them to evaluate and take advantage of these opportunities if they choose.

CONCLUSION

Justice Murray's opinion is an important intervention in the balancing of the rights of children to a wide-open future of their own making and the rights of parents to convey their religious beliefs to their children so that their values are reproduced. While the state should be sympathetic to the fears of minority cultural communities that alteration of their traditional practices may jeopardize their continuity, evidence from Amish communities themselves suggests that they, like other cultural groups, have the capacity to reconstitute themselves after such changes in ways that continue to provide robust sources of meaning and connection for their members. Amish communities do change their ideology and practices frequently with regard to dress, attitudes towards rumspringa, buggy design, and use of technology. Justice Murray's

[31] Nolt, *supra* note 10, at 72.

judgment may have required them to demonstrate similar flexibility around gender norms and roles.[32]

WISCONSIN v. YODER, 406 U.S. 205 (1972)

JUSTICE MURRAY DELIVERED THE OPINION OF THE COURT

We granted review in this case to determine whether the Wisconsin Supreme Court correctly determined that respondents' convictions for violating Wisconsin's compulsory school attendance law were invalid under the Free Exercise Clause of the First Amendment to the U.S. Constitution. We find that it did not.

In this case, three Amish fathers – Respondents Jonas Yoder, Wallace Miller, and Adin Yutzy – were convicted of violating Wisconsin's compulsory education statute. The families are all residents of Green County, Wisconsin. Wisconsin's statute requires that children in Wisconsin attend school until they reach the age of sixteen. The three fathers refused to send their children to New Glarus High School after the children graduated from eighth grade; the fathers subsequently faced criminal charges for violating the compulsory education law.

The trial court denied the motion to dismiss the charges, finding that Wisconsin's compulsory school attendance law interfered with the Respondents' "freedom ... to act in accordance with their sincere religious belief" but that the requirement that their children attend high school until age sixteen was a "reasonable and constitutional" exercise of governmental power. App. at 153–75. The three fathers were convicted and fined five dollars each. App. at 175. The Wisconsin Circuit Court affirmed the convictions. App. at 175–83.

However, the Wisconsin Supreme Court overturned the lower courts' decisions. 49 Wis.2d 430, 182 N.W.2d 539 (1971). A majority of that court determined that the state had failed to demonstrate that its interest in "establishing and maintaining an educational system overrides the defendants' right to the free exercise of their religion." *Id.* This Court respectfully disagrees.

[32] Charles E. Hurst & David L. McConnell, An Amish Paradox: Diversity And Change In The World's Largest Amish Community 34–57 (2010). *See also* Rivka Neriyah & Ben Schahar, *Negotiating Agency: Amish and Ultra-Orthodox Women's Responses to the Internet*, 19 New Media & Soc. 81 (2017) (showing how Amish women engage with information technology as both gatekeepers and agents of change).

I

This case pits two important, deeply embedded cultural and constitutional concepts at odds: the religious upbringing of children and the state's responsibility to provide public education.

A *Amish Doctrine and Practices*

In order to understand the underlying issues, it is useful to consider accounts of Amish life provided by experts, one of whom provided testimony in the courts below. The three children involved in this case are Frieda Yoder, Barbara Miller, and Vernon Yutzy. All three children graduated from the eighth grade at Wisconsin public schools. Frieda and Barbara are both fifteen years old; they and their fathers belong to the Old Order Amish religious sect. Vernon, age fourteen, and his father are members of the Conservative Amish Mennonite Church.

Both sects follow what is called the *Ordnung*, the rules and customs of the Amish church. John A. Hostetler, *Amish Society* 58 (1968). All parts of Amish life are suffused by religion. Following the *Ordnung* means ceding to it the decisions of everyday life: what clothes one may wear, what tools one may use, what constitutes acceptable attitudes and positions about life. Note, *The Right Not to be Modern Men: The Amish and Compulsory Education*, 53 Va. L. Rev. 925, 934 (1967) [hereinafter *Modern Men*]. Life under the *Ordnung* requires discipline, long working hours, and rejection of modern conveniences. *Modern Men*, *supra* at 934.

The *Ordnung* also dictates the rules of family life. Amish society is patriarchal; the father always has the final word. *Modern Men*, *supra* at 934. Brothers are also dominant over sisters. At meals, fathers and sons sit down first at the table while mothers and daughters serve the food. Hostetler, *supra* at 156. Amish children do not question their elders and speak little in the presence of adults. *Modern Men*, *supra* at 934.

Most Amish families rely on farming to make a living. A large family is both economically desirable and necessary for Amish farming because the Amish use no tractors or electricity. *Modern Men*, *supra* at 935. The Amish family usually includes three or more generations living together. *Id.* at 934.

The *Ordnung* does not contain a specific rule banning Amish children from attending high school; however, the Amish object to the high school's "worldly influence," hence the fathers' objections in this case. App. at 110.

At whatever point they leave the New Glarus school system, Frieda, Barbara, and Vernon will begin their adult lives in this patriarchal society. Hostetler, *supra* at 148. In late adolescence, they will be urged to become members of the Amish church; baptism is viewed as a "rite of passage from youth to adulthood." Baptism is also a necessary prerequisite to marriage. *Id.* at 51–52.

Frieda and Barbara will likely be courted for marriage immediately after leaving the eighth grade, as the usual age for courtship among the Amish is fourteen to sixteen years old for young women. Hostetler, *supra* at 159. They will likely be married between the ages of twenty and twenty-two, *id.* at 83, following a wedding at which their families will present a dowry, id. at 161. They are likely to have upwards of seven children. Hostetler, *supra* at 82. Theirs will likely be marriages of "willing submission." *Id.* at 149. The young women will have primary responsibility for all household tasks, and cooking and washing dishes will be their sole provenance. *Id.* at 150. Women are expected to take care of their children, cook, clean, make clothes, preserve food, and garden, and will often help harvest crops *Id.* The young wives will attend church but will "learn in silence with all subjection." *Id.* at 151. Once eighteen, though entitled, they are unlikely to vote. *Id.* Their daughters will continue this pattern, beginning with their subordination to their brothers, and continuing on until they, too, leave school and begin their adult lives. *Id.* at 156.

Vernon, meanwhile, will begin courting around the age of sixteen. Hostetler, *supra* at 159. He likely will marry when he is twenty-two to twenty-four. *Id.* at 83. As patriarch, he will have final word in "domestic matters" and will handle all his family's banking and other financial tasks. *Id.* at 149. He may occasionally help his wife with household tasks on "special occasions" such as butchering and making apple butter, but his wife will aid him with his non-household work more than he will help with household tasks. *Id.* at 150. Once he turns twenty-one, if he has not yet married, he will be paid a monthly wage for work he does at home. *Id.* at 155–56.

In the case before us, the Amish argue that strict adherence to Amish beliefs is necessary to maintain Amish identity and community, and that the ability of the Amish to maintain this way of life depends entirely on the preservation of these principles in the next generation of Amish.

B *Public Education in Wisconsin*

The Wisconsin Constitution provides that "the legislature shall provide by law for the establishment of district schools which shall be free to all children between the ages of four and twenty years." Wisc. Const. Art. X. Its inclusion in the constitution suggests support for "the fundamental idea that public education supported by public taxation is essential to the well-being, progress, and perpetuity of the state." Conrad E. Patzer, *Public Education in Wisconsin* 87 (1924).

Compulsory education laws have been part of the fabric of our education system since the nation's inception. Massachusetts was the first state to pass a compulsory education law, in 1852, having enacted a similar law as a colony in 1647. Today, all but two states (Mississippi and South Carolina) have compulsory attendance laws.

The Wisconsin legislature first passed a compulsory education law in 1879. Patzer, *supra* at 76. It has since been amended several times; the current version requires that children in the state attend public or private school through the age of sixteen. Wis. Stat. § 118.15 (1969). Specifically, the statute provides:

> (1)(a) Except as provided under pars. (b) to (d) and (g) and sub. (4), unless the child is excused under sub. (3) or has graduated from high school, any person having under control a child who is between the ages of 6 and 18 years shall cause the child to attend school regularly during the full period and hours, religious holidays excepted, that the public, private, or tribal school in which the child should be enrolled is in session until the end of the school term, quarter or semester of the school year in which the child becomes 18 years of age.

Public education has long been a foundational part of American democracy. As far back as 1787, the Northwest Ordinance noted that "Religion, morality, and knowledge being necessary to good government and the happiness of mankind, schools and the means of education shall forever be encouraged." This Court has often affirmed such principles; for example, in *Meyer v. Nebraska* we stated that "[t]he American people have always regarded education and the acquisition of knowledge as matters of supreme importance which should be diligently promoted." 262 U.S. 390, 400 (1923). Compulsory education laws ensure that this promotion occurs. As one Wisconsin historian has noted, "[T]he history of education the world over demonstrates that unless some compulsion is exercised by the state, parents are apt to be derelict in sending their children to school and keeping them in school long enough to assure them a good education." Patzer, *supra* at 74.

In this case, the state advances two primary arguments in support of its system of compulsory education. First, it notes the long-held principle that some degree of education is a necessary prerequisite to effective participation in democracy. Here, the state quotes Thomas Jefferson: "Every government degenerates when trusted to the rulers of the people alone. The people themselves therefore are its only safe depositories. And to render even them safe, their minds must be improved to a certain degree . . . the influence over government must be shared among all people." Pet. Brief 11.

Second, the state notes that education plays a critical role in preparing society's children to fully participate in society; it is "vital to the perpetuation of society," "provides the intelligent electorate with leadership necessary to successfully run our government," and "helps to prevent crime and provide for the well-being and contentment of members of society." Pet. Brief 11.

We accept both of these propositions, and so it is that a clash exists. We now move to analyze the rights at issue: the freedom of religion of the Amish children and the parents' fundamental right to guide their children's upbringing. We then answer question at the heart of this case: whether the burden the law places on the Amish children and their parents is justified. As we have previously acknowledged when considering cases in which state laws burden fundamental rights such as these, this is a question that must be handled delicately. *Prince v. Massachusetts*, 321 U.S. 158 (1944).

II

As a threshold matter, our previous holding in *Prince* is instructive. In *Prince*, we affirmed that an aunt's religious freedom was not unduly burdened by Massachusetts' child labor laws that prohibited her niece from distributing religious literature alongside her. As in this case, the aunt rested her claim on First Amendment religious freedom, "buttress[ed]" by a claim of parental right under the Due Process clause. *Prince*, 321 U.S. at 164. As we then noted of these two claims, "One is the parent's, to bring up the child in the way he should go, which for appellant means to teach him the tenets and the practices of their faith. The other freedom is the child's, to observe these." *Id.* We further noted that "the family itself is not beyond regulation in the public interest" in the face of a claim of religious freedom and "neither rights of religion nor rights of parenthood are beyond limitation." *Id.* at 166.

Thus, proceeding delicately requires us to decouple the views and interests of children and their parents in order to adequately address the underlying constitutional burdens. The effect of upholding the Wisconsin Supreme Court's decision would be to treat the views and interests of children and their fathers as one and the same. To do so is to ignore the children's own personhood and constitutional interests. *See, e.g., Tinker v. Des Moines*, 393 U.S. 503, 511 (1969) ("Students in school as well as out of school are 'persons' under our Constitution. They are possessed of fundamental rights which the State must respect, just as they themselves must respect their obligations to the State"); *West Virginia State Board of Educ. v. Barnette*, 319 U.S. 624, 637 (1943) ("That they are educating the young for citizenship is reason for scrupulous protection of Constitutional freedoms of the individual, if we are not to strangle the free mind at its source and teach youth to discount important principles of our government as mere platitudes").

First, we accept that the Wisconsin compulsory education law infringes upon the sincere religious belief of those who follow the *Ordnung*, which counsels that the "worldly influence" of the traditional public high school is to be avoided. However, in certain circumstances, such an infringement may be justified. The Wisconsin statute can only withstand constitutional challenge if the incidental burden on the free exercise of religion is justified by a compelling state interest within the state's constitutional power to regulate. *See, e.g., Sherbert v. Verner*, 374 U.S. 398 (1963) (holding that South Carolina could not deny a Seventh Day Adventist her unemployment compensation benefits because she refused to work on her Sabbath day, Saturday); *Reynolds v. United States*, 98 U.S. 145 (1878) (upholding statute prohibiting polygamy despite claim that polygamy was part of the Mormons' religious practice).

Second, the right the Respondent fathers lay claim to is their right as parents to raise their children as they see fit. This right to parental autonomy, rooted in the Due Process clause, is not absolute. The state has "a wide range of power for limiting parental freedom and authority in things affecting the child's welfare; and this includes, to some extent, matters of conscience and religious conviction." *Prince*, 321 U.S. at 167.

It is without question that parents and guardians have the right to guide their children's education, including their religious education. *See, e.g., Meyer*, 262 U.S. 390 (1923) (striking down state statute prohibiting teaching of any foreign language in any school prior to eighth grade); *Pierce v. Society of Sisters*, 268 U.S. 510 (1925) (striking down Oregon law requiring attendance at public schools). However, parents' rights are circumscribed by the state's interest in equipping the next generation with the understanding and knowledge they need to participate fully in our democracy and our society. Thus, following *Meyer*, *Pierce*, and *Prince*, parents have a general right to ensure their children's educational upbringing, but interference with such a right is permissible when the state has a compelling interest that justifies its regulatory authority.

Here, despite the infringement on the rights of both the parents and the children, the compulsory education law is a clear exercise of the state's constitutional authority to regulate education.

III

A healthy system of state-regulated public education is necessary to allow a democracy to be fully functioning and to prepare its citizens to participate in it. *Meyer*, 262 U.S. at 400. ("The American people have always regarded education and acquisition of knowledge as matters of supreme importance which should be diligently promoted."); *Prince*, 321 U.S. at 168. ("A democratic society rests, for its continuance, upon the healthy, well-rounded growth of young people into full maturity as citizens, with all that implies.") Not so long ago, this Court itself noted that:

> [T]oday, education is perhaps the *most important* function of state and local governments. Compulsory school attendance laws and the great expenditures for education both demonstrate our recognition of the importance of education to our democratic society. It is required in the performance of our most basic public responsibilities, even service in the armed forces. It is the very foundation of good citizenship. Today it is a principal instrument in awakening the child to cultural values, in preparing him for later professional training, and in helping him to adjust normally to his environment. In these days, it is doubtful that any child may reasonably be expected to succeed in life if he is denied the opportunity of an education. Such an opportunity, where the state has undertaken to provide it, is a right which must be made available to all on equal terms.
>
> *Brown v. Board of Education*, 347 U.S. 483, 493 (1954) (emphasis added).

Education involves both the transfer of knowledge and hard skills such as reading and mathematical computation, and the introduction of social values and norms. Through education, all children are exposed to a world beyond their home and family lives. They learn the values and traditions of cultures other than their own. They also learn critical thinking skills that allow them to evaluate and critique their own lives and those of others they encounter, be they fictional characters in literature or classmates they would not otherwise know.

This does not mean the goal of education is rejection of the child's home life for something different or better. It simply means each child is guaranteed broader knowledge of the world, knowledge that enables the children to fully participate in democracy.

Compulsory education laws ensure that children receive some type of either public or private education up to a certain age; stated differently, they *promise* the children of the state some minimum amount of education. Is sixteen the "right" age to end this mandate or guarantee? Not necessarily – it may be more than enough for some children and not nearly enough for others. But states have the power to draw – and redraw – these lines as necessary, without interference from this Court, in order to provide a baseline level of education to each of their young citizens.

This baseline level of education can be an equalizing force, providing opportunity when there was none. This includes the opportunity to spend time with those different from oneself – to engage with other students across races, religions, and socioeconomic statuses.

Education, in essence, provides students with choices. Students who finish even the minimum amount of compulsory education can take a meaningful next step, whatever that might be. Students who do not finish lack options. A sixteen-year-old is not perfectly equipped to exercise that choice, but she is better equipped than an eighth grader.

In *Meyer* and *Pierce*, this Court struck down education-related state laws that, in some ways, *limited* children's educational choices. *Meyer* involved laws that prohibited the teaching of foreign languages prior to the eighth grade. The issue in *Pierce* was an Oregon law that mandated that children between ages eight and sixteen attend public schools. Both cases thus involved restricting, rather than expanding, children's educational options – they would have provided *less*, not *more*, education for students. Following *Meyer* and *Pierce*, the states retained the right to reasonably regulate schools, including control over curricular decisions and compulsory attendance, *Meyer*, 262 U.S. at 402; *Pierce*, 268 U.S. at 534, while parents retained the right to supplement the children's education at home and to opt out of certain elements of the school curriculum. *See, e.g., Barnette*, 319 U.S. 624.

Exempting the Amish children from the Wisconsin law would limit those children's educational options. After leaving the New Glarus public schools, Frieda, Barbara, and Vernon will receive informal vocational training to prepare them for – and only for – life in Amish society. Frieda and Barbara will be housewives. Vernon will likely be a farmer. To exempt them from compliance with the compulsory education law is to presume that they plan to stay in their communities and to adhere to Amish beliefs. Respondents would have this Court believe that the children's commitment to Amish society is unquestionable. However, there is a nonzero number of defectors from Amish communities; in some districts there are very few, and in others the number is "considerable." Hostetler, *supra* at 226. Most defectors leave between the ages of sixteen and twenty-three, which is also the typical time when Amish children are baptized and then married. *Id.* at 271, 83.

Respondents' expert witness Mr. Hostetler's own account of Amish society introduces us to three former Amish, one who "loved school from the day [he] started," Hostetler, *supra* at 215, a young woman who "read a great many books and anything [she] could get [her] hands on," *id.* at 216, and a third who "wanted to go to high school so badly that [he] remember[s] crying about it, trying to persuade [his] parents," *id.* at 217.

As the state notes, children who leave the Amish community with only an eighth-grade education will be ill-equipped to function in modern society.

The state's compulsory education laws work in tandem with laws prohibiting child labor to push back against this potential harm and guarantee an equal amount of minimum education for all. Failure to enforce these laws will thus have a deleterious effect on Amish children, particularly on Amish daughters. Earlier this term, this Court held for the first time that a state statute that discriminates on the basis of sex is subject to more searching constitutional scrutiny. *Reed v. Reed*, 404 U.S. 71 (1971). This Court is increasingly mindful – and skeptical – of laws that limit women's ability to participate in and contribute to society.

Respondents state that the harm of the long-term enforcement of the compulsory education law will be the undoing of Amish society. They suggest that two additional years of exposure to public education will result in "disturbance and alienation" of the Amish children. Resp. Brief at 26. Respondents argue that an eighth-grade education is sufficient, and Frieda, Barbara, and Vernon will gain no more pertinent knowledge in the final two years. Yet the opposite could be argued as well: why is the children's vocational training incompatible with their attendance at school? The children already participate in the life of the house and the farm even during their early educational years. Why could similar participation not continue until the children turn sixteen?

Applying the compulsory education law to all children, no matter their religious beliefs, allows states to sidestep the difficult issue of ascertaining what the children's religious beliefs and educational preferences actually are. Neither the parents nor the state nor this Court can read the minds of children to determine what these views might be, and neither the parents nor the children are necessarily reliable narrators on the topic of the child's authentic religious views. In fact, any child whose views divert from her parents' religious beliefs may not be comfortable voicing those views.

This is particularly true of Amish children, for whom an expression of doubt may be accompanied by shame and expulsion. The consequences of expressing such doubt and potentially leaving Amish society will be borne by both the child and the family, which may well be shunned by association. The record in this case indicates that to determine her religious beliefs, Frieda Yoder was asked a series of leading questions by counsel for both Appellant and the state. App. at 123. We express reservations that Frieda's testimony, given in open court and through primarily "yes" or "no" questions from counsel, is an accurate statement of what she actually believes.

Our decision today eliminates this thorny problem. No child must assert her desire to continue to attend high school, risking consequences for herself and her family; nor can a child whose religious beliefs counsel against attending school opt out in contravention of her parents' own beliefs and values. The law should be enforced as to all children.

The goal of education is to prepare society's children to live in that society. Amish children with an eighth-grade education may be well prepared to fulfill the social and political responsibilities of their own society, but not of society at large. Students who leave the church later on, when they have the fullness of adulthood about them, will be severely disadvantaged without the minimum high school education. This is true despite alternative avenues of educational credentialing that might be available to them as adults; any such avenues are second-best solutions that will not overcome the difficulties that result from stunted educational development.

Thus, an exemption from the compulsory education law would create both societal harm and harm to the children's welfare. The state's interest in avoiding such harm justifies the burden it places on the religious beliefs of the Amish children.

Likewise, the particular burdens – or lack thereof – on parental authority attendant to Wisconsin's compulsory education law are also justified. First, the law does not (and cannot) mandate that Frieda, Barbara, and Vernon attend any particular school, including New Glarus High School. The parents retain the right to exercise educational choices for their children within parameters that meet the state's educational standards. The informal, vocational training promised by the Amish does not suffice by state standards. This is perhaps not surprising, given the particular paths that Frieda, Barbara, and Vernon will find themselves on should their parents be exempted from the law. The parents' unwillingness to seek out an alternative is a matter of preference, not state mandate.

Second, there is no restriction on the amount of religious or vocational education the children can receive outside of any formal schooling. As we noted in *Pierce*, "[T]he child is not the mere creature of the state; those who nurture him and direct his destiny have the right, coupled with the high duty, to recognize and prepare him for additional obligations." 268 U.S. at 510.

Finally, our holding today does not mean that parents cannot request that their children be exempt from certain portions of the whole of what public education encompasses, be they social or curricular. *See, e.g.*, *Barnette*, 319 U.S. 624 (finding that students cannot be compelled to state the Pledge of Allegiance at school).

The exercise of state authority here is, as it was for the prohibition of child labor in *Prince*, an act of *parens patriae*, in which the state provides for the general well-being of the child. As Petitioners note in their brief, child labor laws and compulsory education laws work in tandem to provide for the children's welfare. For example, the Wisconsin child labor law prohibits the employment of a minor under the age of sixteen during compulsory school hours. The symbiotic relationship between school and labor laws makes clear that our rationale in *Prince* – that the child labor law was a permissible exercise of the state's authority to provide for the child's well-being – is relevant in this case as well. And here, as in *Prince*, that rationale is "not nullified merely because the parent grounds his claim to control the child's course of conduct on religion or conscience." 321 U.S. at 166.

To allow a broad exercise of parental autonomy in contravention of a compulsory education law would be to cut the teeth out of the law itself. Without the limitation we uphold today, parenting concerns could then be used by any parent or guardian to challenge compulsory education laws even if they had secular reasons for doing so.

To grant the Amish the exception they seek requires us to proceed in one of two ways. We could find an exception so narrow that only Amish fathers (for it is they who exercise this right) can claim to be exempt from state compulsory education laws. Or we could find that parental authority includes the right to claim any religious objection. The former requires that we find something exceptional about the Amish. The latter is so broad as to basically mean nothing about the law is compulsory.

The compulsory education statute interferes with fundamental rights, but the state intervention is justified. The provision of public education is among a state's most important functions. This Court cannot and should not favor the Amish children and parents and their religion over others, especially when the Amish could comply with the statute in ways other than sending the children to New Glarus High School. The statute does not mandate that the students attend any school in particular or even that they attend *public* school. The statute does not prohibit extracurricular religious education outside of school. The children and parents can pursue alternative models of primary education, but the purpose of education and the harms avoided by the state's reasonable regulation of education are compelling, even in the face of the right claimed by the Amish.

IV

Public education is a right and a privilege, and the compulsory school laws are a manifestation of that right. The state has committed to preparing its youth for full participation in society as adults. The Amish children may well choose to remain in their insular community, but the purpose of public education is to prepare them for that choice. Neither the Amish children nor their parents have the right to opt out of this primary level of education.

Parents cannot "make martyrs of their children before they have reached the age of full and legal discretion where they can make that choice for themselves." *Prince*, 321 U.S. at 170. Certainly, the parents have the right to provide children with the religious education they desire. But they do not have the right to do it in contravention of compulsory education laws.

The philosopher James Baldwin, speaking to a group of teachers in 1963, said the following:

> The paradox of education is precisely this – that as one begins to become conscious one begins to examine the society in which he is being educated. The purpose of education, finally, is to create in a person the ability to look at the world for himself, to make his own decisions, to say to himself this is black or this is white, to decide for himself whether there is a God in heaven or not. To ask questions of the universe, and then learn to live with those questions, is the way he achieves his own identity.
>
> James Baldwin, A *Talk to Teachers*, Saturday Rev., Dec. 21, 1963, at 42.

The state's interest in ensuring this consciousness for all its citizens is justified because of the importance of education, which acts as a safeguard for the welfare of the citizenry and of society writ large. Thus, no exemption can stand.

6

Commentary on *Marvin v. Marvin*

ANÍBAL ROSARIO-LEBRÓN

INTRODUCTION

"I got the subject of people living together out of the closet and right down at your dinner table. Women and men now talk about it openly. They discuss what they want out of a relationship."[1] Perhaps no other case in family law has been so intertwined with popular culture as *Marvin v. Marvin*.[2] The decision that had as protagonists Hollywood's star Lee Marvin, performer Michelle Triola Marvin,[3] and celebrity lawyer Marvin M. Mitchelson, has been, for the past four decades, the subject of popular shows,[4] news outlets,[5] and songs.[6] It introduced a neologism into our legal and lay dictionaries, the concept of *palimony* (an acronym of pal and alimony).[7] But more importantly, *Marvin*

[1] Michelle Triola Marvin's words about *Marvin v. Marvin's* legacy. Elaine Woo, *Michelle Triola Marvin Dies at 75; Her Legal Fight with Ex-Lover Lee Marvin Added "Palimony" to the Language*, L.A. TIMES, Oct. 31, 2009, http://www.latimes.com/local/obituaries/la-me-michelle-triola-marvin31-2009oct31-story.html

[2] 557 P.2d 106 (Cal. 1976).

[3] Michelle obtained a court order changing her surname to Marvin three days before her relationship with Lee ended. Herma Hill Kay & Carol Amyx, Marvin v. Marvin: *Preserving the Options*, 65 CAL. L. REV. 937, 955 (1977).

[4] *See, e.g.*, *Saturday Night Live: Point Counterpoint – Lee Marvin & Michelle Triola* (NBC televised broadcast Mar. 17, 1979), https://www.hulu.com/watch/2306; *The Tonight Show Starring Johnny Carson: Adam and Eve Skit* (Carson Entertainment Group televised broadcast Feb. 9, 1979), https://www.youtube.com/watch?v=Ih6LxwdwvlA

[5] *See, e.g.*, Sue Ellen Jares, *"Divorce without Marriage" Suits Today's Life-Style*, PEOPLE, Apr. 24, 1978, http://people.com/archive/divorce-without-marriage-suits-todays-life-style-argues-attorney-marvin-mitchelson-vol-9-no-16/; Anahad O'Connor, *Michelle Triola Marvin, of Landmark Palimony Suit, Dies at 76*, N.Y. TIMES, Oct. 30, 2009, https://www.nytimes.com/2004/09/20/obituaries/marvin-mitchelson-76-father-of-palimony-is-dead.html

[6] LEON RAUSCH, *Palimony*, *on* PALIMONY (Single, Derrick Records 1979), https://www.youtube.com/watch?v=DN1X3-g2Ozg

[7] Barbara Hunt Lazerson, *Marvinizing Can Lead to Palimony*, 63 AM. SPEECH 188, 189 (Summer 1988).

holds a seminal place in family law regarding the rights of nonmarital cohabiting couples.

As Marvin Mitchelson predicted, "[t]his decision … open[ed] the courthouse['s] door to everyone living together."[8] A basic search in any legal database will show that courts in almost forty jurisdictions have cited *Marvin*.[9] The importance of the decision lies in the way the Supreme Court of California *in bank* fashioned a remedy for the division of property between nonmarital cohabiting couples after their relationship ended without modifying the state's marital property law. By doing so, the decision in *Marvin* provided a blueprint that courts across the nation could use to provide appropriate remedies for nonmarital couples regardless of the states' underlying marital property law.[10] It also offered a wide range of options that could be adopted by the states without legislative action, irrespective of their public policies regarding marriage, adultery, cohabitation, or same-sex families.[11]

This development came at a pivotal moment in the history of familial organization in the United States. According to the data from the Census Bureau, the number of opposite-sex nonmarital couples cohabiting more than doubled from 523,000 in 1970 to 1,137,000 in 1978.[12] This shift brought new challenges to a judicial system that had long ignored and criminalized these families[13] and was thus ill-equipped to deal with the issues that sprang from such a living arrangement.

THE DECISION IN *MARVIN*

Michelle Triola Marvin endured firsthand the shortcomings of the legal system. After almost six years of cohabitation with Lee,[14] Michelle sued her former partner for one-half of the property acquired during their

8 Jares, *supra* note 5.

9 Brad Reid, *Property and Palimony Law for Unmarried Cohabitating Partners*, HUFFINGTON POST, May 12, 2015, https://www.huffingtonpost.com/brad-reid/property-and-palimony-law_b_7269314.html

10 *Id.*

11 Commentators on Marvin stated that the decision could be "viewed as a flexible approach representative of … [an] overt phase of reconciling legal doctrine with the existence of alternative family styles." *Case Comments, Property Rights upon Termination of Unmarried Cohabitation:* Marvin v. Marvin, 90 HARV. L. REV. 1708, 1711 (1977).

12 Lazerson, *supra* note 7, at 188–89.

13 Alexander C. Morey & Dixie Grossman, *Property Rights of Unmarried Cohabitants – Nothing New under the Sun*, 25 J. AM. ACAD. MATRIM. LAW. 87, 88 (2012).

14 Three of which Lee remained married to Betty Marvin. Kay & Amyx, *supra* note 3, at 955; *Marvin*, 557 P.2d at 111.

relationship,[15] based on an alleged agreement to combine efforts and earnings and share equally in all property accumulated during their time together.[16] When her case was called for trial, Lee presented a motion to dismiss.[17] The trial court treated his motion as one for judgment on the pleadings and denied Michelle the opportunity to amend the complaint.[18] Based on the facts averred and further stipulations, the lower court granted Lee's motion and entered judgment in his favor.[19]

When the case came to the Supreme Court of California, its task was to decide whether there was a cause of action under California law for the distribution of nonmarital property. This presented a challenge for the Supreme Court as the California Court of Appeals had conflicting precedent regarding the property rights of nonmarital couples.[20]

One position of the Court of Appeals was that California's Family Law Act[21] required the division of property according to community property principles (i.e. equal distribution of property acquired during the relationship).[22] In order to come within the scope of this rule as sketched in *In re Cary*,[23] the parties must have conducted themselves like a *traditional marriage*.[24] The Supreme Court of California discarded this option.[25] The other option, not fully embraced by the court either, was to follow *Beckman v. Mayhew*,[26] which rejected *Cary*'s interpretation of the Family Law Act and left nonmarital couples without remedy.[27]

The court considered the changing social mores regarding familial organization and the unfairness of allowing the advantaged partner to keep the full amount of the property acquired during the relationship and concluded that it was necessary to craft a remedy in line with the changing times and basic notions of fairness.[28] Accordingly, the court held that a nonmarital partner could bring a breach of contract claim for the division of the property acquired

[15] *Marvin*, 557 P.2d at 110.

[16] Kay & Amyx, *supra* note 3, at 955.

[17] *Marvin*, 557 P.2d at 111.

[18] *Id.*

[19] *Id.*

[20] *Id.* at 110.

[21] The Family Law Act was the first no-fault divorce law in the United States. Kay & Amyx, *supra* note 3, at 948.

[22] *Marvin*, 557 P.2d at 111.

[23] 34 Cal.App.3d 345 (1973).

[24] Kay & Amyx, *supra* note 3, at 951–52.

[25] *Marvin*, 557 P.2d at 120–21

[26] 49 Cal.App.3d 529 (1975).

[27] *Marvin*, 557 P.2d at 120–21.

[28] *Id.* at 110, 120–21.

during the relationship, provided that the parties had an express contract to pool resources not founded in a meretricious relationship (i.e. consideration based on sex).[29] That pooling of resources includes, in theory, not only the contribution of funds but also the rendering of domestic services.[30] In addition, the court held that in the absence of such an express contract, judges should inquire into the conduct of the parties to determine whether the parties had created an implied contract,[31] a partnership agreement, or a joint venture.[32] Furthermore, the court stated that a nonmarital partner could base the recovery claim upon some equitable remedies such as constructive or resulting trust,[33] or *quantum meruit*.[34]

Lastly, before remanding the case to allow Michelle to amend her complaint in accordance with the causes of actions discussed in the opinion,[35] the court added that its decision did not answer whether in the absence of a contractual obligation a nonmarital partner is entitled to support payments (i.e. palimony).[36] Despite leaving unaddressed the question of support, *Marvin* stands in the popular conscience as granting support rights to cohabiting couples. The truth, however, is that Michelle never recovered a penny.

MARVIN ON REMAND

When the case went back to the trial court, Professor Elengold's cautionary omen in her feminist judgment about the efficacy of equitable remedies came true. After the case was tried, the lower court found that there was no agreement – express or implied – between the parties to pool their resources.[37]

[29] *Id.* at 116.

[30] *Id.* at 119, 123.

[31] An implied contract is created when the parties have agreed to an obligation based on their actions but have not distilled their intentions in written or orally. *Silva v. Providence Hosp. of Oakland*, 97 P.2d 798, 804 (Cal. 1939).

[32] *Marvin*, 557 P.2d at 123.

[33] A constructive trust is typically used to transfer ownership of property to a person who has been deprived of it through fraud. A resulting trust, on the other hand, is used when the transferee does not intend to benefit from the transfer of property (e.g. paying for a property in someone else's name). *Martin v. Kehl*, 145 Cal. App. 3d 228, 238 (1983).

[34] *Marvin*, 557 P.2d at 122. *Quantum meruit* is based on "the well-established principle that 'the law implies a promise to pay for services performed under circumstances disclosing that they were not gratuitously rendered.'" *Huskinson & Brown v. Wolf*, 84 P.3d 379, 381 (Cal. 2004) (citations omitted).

[35] *Marvin*, 557 P.2d at 110, 123.

[36] *Id.* at n. 26.

[37] *Marvin*, 122 Cal. App. 3d 873–74.

However, it ruled that Michelle deserved rehabilitative support[38] in the amount of $104,000 for two years.[39] Yet the California Courts of Appeal found no grounds for the rehabilitative award.[40]

Both the majority and the dissent opinions of the Court of Appeal struggled to figure out the lower court's reasoning for the support award.[41] As the majority noted, the trial court found that Michelle benefited economically and socially from the relationship without suffering any damage therefrom.[42] In other words, the lower court understood that Michelle's domestic services were justly compensated by the support she received while in the relationship. Furthermore, the majority highlighted the lower court's finding that Lee had not been unjustly enriched by the relationship and had never acquired anything of value attributable to Michelle's funds or property. Thus, an obligation to pay for Michelle's maintenance was not supported by law or equity but, as the Majority indicated, it seems to have been predicated exclusively on Lee's capacity to respond to Michelle's need.[43] Similarly, the dissent, which agreed with the majority in the lack of findings to support the award, noted that the alimony was a contradictory reinstatement of the pooling of resources agreement that the trial court itself ruled nonexistent.[44] As Professor Elengold predicted in her concurrence, the reason for the incoherent trial court's decision lies on the court's reading of the complaint from a patriarchal and family normative lens that did not allow Michelle to share the wealth generated during the relationship.

A FEMINIST VIEW ON *MARVIN*

Rather than helping Michelle return to paid employment (as is the purpose of a rehabilitative award) or fairly divide the property resulting from the couple's joint efforts, the trial court tried to compensate Michelle for her domestic services. As her services aligned with the traditional gender roles of a *housewife*, the trial court could not fathom the couple explicitly or implicitly

[38] Rehabilitative support is a type of alimony for a finite period to allow a disadvantaged partner who did not pursue a career or a job while in the relationship to adjust and reinsert her/himself in the workforce. Daniel Jones, *Rehabilitative Alimony – The Goal of Self Support*, 20 J. CONTEMP. LEGAL ISSUES 25 (2012).

[39] *Marvin*, 122 CAL. APP. 3d at 874.

[40] *Id.* at 876–77.

[41] *Id.* at 876–78.

[42] *Id.* at 876.

[43] *Id.* at 876–77.

[44] *Id.* at 879. The dissent would have remanded the case for further determinations of facts to establish whether the alimony award was justified. *Id.*

contracting to share in the property acquired based on the rendering of domestic labor.[45] Even though on remand the lower and appellate court did not consider those services as ones that a woman in a cohabiting relationship is expected to provide gratuitously, the courts disregarded them as a contribution to the couple's capital. Contrary to the Supreme Court's admonition about employing a presumption of fair dealing[46] that absent acts affirming a separate property regime would make providing domestic services a *buy-in* to the property, the lower courts looked at Michelle's domestic services as something that was compensated by the support provided by Lee during their relationship.

This reading of *Marvin* evidences the costs of focusing reform efforts on formal equality without attending to substantive equality.[47] It presumes that equal distribution of property rests on giving back to each partner what they brought to the relationship without considering how those contributions impacted the pooling of resources. As such, it treats housework like any other job, comparable to employment in the paid sector. However, such a comparison is flawed, as courts consistently undervalue domestic contributions resting on an income-generating metric.[48] As a result, the role of homemaking (still predominantly performed by women) is not counted as an investment or a contribution to the couple's assets, minimizing the partners' mutual dependence on each other and their individual contributions to their capital.

Such an approach not only makes enforcing a contract to build and share wealth difficult but also, as Elengold predicts, makes equitable remedies based on resulting trust or *quantum meruit* almost impossible. If domestic services are not seen as valuable contributions, then they cannot be used to pay for the price of consideration for property as required by the doctrine of resulting trust. Similarly, they cannot be the basis for a *quantum meruit* action as the amount of services rendered needs to be higher than the value of support received.[49] As market price, even today, is not a good indicator of the value of domestic services in most cases (especially when women have forgone work

45 For a thoughtful discussion on how contract and not altruism should underpin the judicial assessment of household services *see* MARTHA M. ERTMAN, LOVE'S PROMISES: HOW FORMAL AND INFORMAL CONTRACTS SHAPE ALL KINDS OF FAMILIES (2015).

46 *Marvin*, 557 P.2d at 121.

47 For a deeper discussion on the limits of formal equality *see* Martha Albertson Fineman, *The Vulnerable Subject: Anchoring Equality in the Human Condition*, 20 YALE J.L. & FEMINISM 1, 2–5 (2008).

48 *See* Rachel Rebouché, *A Case against Collaboration*, 76 MD. L. REV. 547, 576 (2017).

49 *Marvin*, 557 P.2d at 122–23.

outside the home), the financial support received by one partner will be found to be higher than the undervalued domestic labor received by the other.

This approach undermines gender equality, as it leaves the disadvantaged partner, usually the woman, in a worse position than when the relationship started.[50] After leaving the workforce, women will have reduced marketable job skills and will be underpaid in comparison to what they could have been earned had they never left the labor force.[51] At the same time, it fails to recognize the stay-at-home partner's work and to fairly compensate her for it.

Furthermore, even though marriage has been heavily criticized in feminist scholarship for serving to extract labor from women without compensation at divorce,[52] the Supreme Court of California in *Marvin* did not challenge the institution. To the contrary, in a way, the court tried to reinscribe marriage's norms onto nonmarital relationships; undercutting the ability of those relationships to challenge marital expectations.[53] By enshrining marriage, at the end of its opinion, as the "most socially productive"[54] institution, the Supreme Court made marriage the stick by which nonmarital relationships should be measured. As Elengold worried in her concurrence, this aspect of *Marvin* has been used to justify the granting or denying of rights to nonmarital partners while unequivocally, and irrespective of the result, enforcing hegemonic notions about gender, family, and sexuality that perpetuate oppression.

As Professor Albertina Antognini poignantly observes,

> [t]he survey of the case law reveals that courts approach nonmarital relationships in one of two ways: either by looking to marriage as a requirement for what a nonmarital relationship should be, or by distinguishing the nonmarital relationship from anything approaching marriage. In the process, the cases reinforce particular conceptions of what individuals in relationships across the board ought to do, and how their contributions are valued.

50 *See* Albertina Antognini, *The Law of Nonmarriage*, 58 B.C. L. Rev. 1, 2 (2017) (citations omitted).

51 *See* Michael Selmi, *Family Leave and the Gender Wage Gap*, 78 N.C. L. Rev. 707, 712 (2000) (explaining how "women have less of an attachment to the labor force than men ... [which] contribute[s] to a cumulative workplace disadvantage that exacts a heavy price in terms of salary, promotions, and responsibility").

52 Reva Siegel has described how courts have imposed a regime of *enforced altruism* in the sphere of the family and marital property, in opposition to the ideology of material gain that controls the marketplace. Reva B. Siegel, *The Modernization of Marital Status Law: Adjudicating Wives' Rights to Earnings, 1860–1930*, 82 Geo. L.J. 2127, 2201–03 (1994).

53 This is not only the case in *Marvin*. "The cases that address nonmarital couples all assume, and many explicitly state, that the ultimate goal of their nonmarital jurisprudence is to promote marriage." Antognini, *supra* note 50, at 52.

54 *Marvin*, 557 P.2d at 122.

> By defining each nonmarital relationship differently, courts value the contributions made by each party to the relationship differently, but with a remarkably consistent result: the individual seeking property – which in nearly all cases is a woman – has a difficult time receiving anything outside of marriage.[55]

Consequently, even though under *Marvin* many nonmarital couples (including same-sex ones) have been able to ascertain recovery claims,[56] many have been left with no remedy.[57] Moreover, a large group of the litigants who have secured rights (mostly women)[58] have done so in a limited capacity, not equally sharing in the property acquired during the relationship.[59]

REIMAGINING *MARVIN*

As Professor Elengold reasons in her opinion, after continuous legal reforms of the more oppressive and discriminatory aspects of marriage, such an inegalitarian approach to cohabitants' rights is incoherent. Consequently, Elengold rejects a reading of *Marvin*'s majority that would predicate the distribution of nonmarital property on couples' status (i.e. likeness to marriage). She cautions lower courts and other jurisdictions against engaging in such a reading and offers one that is more consistent with the feminist pursuit of gender equality.

To point out the problems and contradictions of relying on marriage-like status rather than on the couple's intention, Elengold traces the history of gender equality within marriage in California. The culmination of that struggle was the enactment of a marital community property regime rather than a sex-neutral separate property system. By doing so, California recognized the domestic labor of women as a contribution to the couple's capital rather than as a gratuitous service. Yet *Cary* subverted that accomplishment in trying to protect women in nonmarital relationships by making the granting of property rights dependent upon proving a marriage-like relationship.

Even though the Supreme Court of California in *Marvin* rejected *Cary*, the Court adopted its underlying rationale as shown, inter alia, by its

55 Antognini, *supra* note 50, at 8.

56 *See, e.g.*, *Dee v. Rokower*, 976 N.Y.S.2d 470 (2013); *Malek v. Malek*, 768 P.2d 243 (Haw. Ct. App. 1989); *Kozlowski v. Kozlowski*, 403 A.2d 902 (N.J. 1979), superseded by statute, N.J. Stat. Ann. § 25:1–5 (2013).

57 *See, e.g.*, *Bergen v. Wood*, 18 Cal.Rptr.2d 75 (Ct. App. 1993); *Thomas v. LaRosa*, 400 S.E.2d 809 (W. Va. 1990); *Morone v. Morone*, 413 N.E.2d 1154 (N.Y. 1980).

58 Antognini, *supra* note 50, at 8.

59 *See, e.g.*, *Turner v. Freed*, 792 N.E.2d 947 (Ind. Ct. App. 2003); *Gazvoda v. Wright*, No. 07A01-0607-CV-288, 2007 WL 2284722 (Ind. Ct. App. Aug. 10, 2007).

characterization of Michelle's relationship as marital even though that language was never employed in the complaint.[60] Elengold's opinion discusses *Cary* in detail to show precisely how courts and prospective litigants could understand the status approach to be the controlling one; as the lower courts in *Marvin* did on remand.

As an alternative, Elengold offers intent as the overriding principle. As she explains when discussing the pitfalls of remedies such as *quantum meruit* or resulting trust, which can devalue women's contributions, courts should opt instead for a partnership model that is not dependent on assessing the value of housework in the same terms as paid employment. Accordingly, Elengold advocates for remedies in constructive trust, which focus the distribution of property on intent.[61] That approach, as Professor Antognini has argued too, leads to a more egalitarian division of assets while turning the relationship between the affective and the economic on its head.[62]

THE FUTURE OF *MARVIN*

However, other remedies beyond constructive trusts could express an intent approach. As later decisions from courts across the United States have shown, the intent approach can be grounds for awards predicated on contract[63] or other equitable remedies.[64] Interestingly, a year before *Marvin* was decided, another jurisdiction under U.S. power granted rights to nonmarital couples based on property law as well as on equity grounds, relying on an intent perspective.[65]

60 Kay & Amyx, *supra* note 3, at 955 (explaining how the Court rephrased the allegations to state that Michelle and Lee held themselves to the public as husband and wife).

61 One drawback to the intent approach is that it could decontextualize where these obligations originate from and make courts less willing to look at the relationships in their totality. This could create unfair results in cases such as where a nonmarital relationship followed a divorce, as the postdivorce relationship would not lead to a property distribution because the intent to have separate property is rendered clear by the prior divorce. Antognini, *supra* note 50, at 48–52.

62 *Id.* at 46.

63 *See Dutton v. Laine*, No. 93,934, 2006 WL 851389 (Kan. Ct. App. Mar. 31, 2006) (holding that furniture and other items bought during a period of cohabitation were jointly owned property based on the parties' intent of dividing the property as reduced in an agreement titled "Prenuptial/Cohabitation Agreement" and their conduct).

64 *See Wilbur v. DeLapp*, 850 P.2d 1151 (Or. Ct. App. 1993) (granting a distribution of nonmarital property in an equitable proceeding of which its primary determination was whether there was an intent to share equally).

65 *Caraballo Ramírez v. Acosta*, 104 D.P.R. 474 (1975). The precursors of this decision could be traced back a decade back when the Supreme Court recognized *in dicta* the possibility of such a cause of action. *Cruz v. Sucn. Landrau Díaz*, 97 D.P.R. 578 (1969); *Reyes v. Merlo*, 91 D.P.R. 136 (1964).

In 1975, the Supreme Court of Puerto Rico held that a woman had a claim to an equal division of property with her cohabitating partner, even though her partner was married to another woman while they cohabitated.[66] The court determined that, under Puerto Rico's property law, joint property was created between the woman and the marital community property of her cohabitating partner and his wife by reason of her contributions to his wealth (and thus the community estate of his marriage).[67] The court further held that the contribution need not be in funds but could be the rendering of domestic services.[68] The essential component of the analysis was the intent of the nonmarital couple – not the marriage-like conduct of the parties.[69]

This decision was later interpreted by the Puerto Rico Appellate Court to extend beyond cohabiting couples (i.e. nonsexual/romantic relationships).[70] Similar to Elengold's argument about how the constructive trust theory should operate under *Marvin* (i.e. making no distinctions between marital, nonmarital, or businesses relationships), the Supreme Court of Puerto Rico crafted a remedy that transcended the parameters of traditionally defined relationships.

This is, perhaps, the greatest contribution of Elengold's feminist judgment. Her opinion provides a reading of *Marvin* that could transcend the gendered tendency to adjudicate nonmarital distribution of property cases based on status and socially acceptable familial organizations,[71] providing not only rights to same-sex or opposite-sex unmarried couples but also to other family units that are not part of the mainstream.[72]

Certainly, modern developments should make Michelle Triola Marvin proud that her case took the subject of people living together, regardless of the arrangement, out of the closet and right down at our dinner tables, forcing us to expand our notions of family and discuss what we really want out of our relationships.

66 *Caraballo Ramírez*, 104 D.P.R. at 484.

67 *Id.* at 480–81.

68 *Id.* at 484–86.

69 *See id.* at 481–82.

70 *Cintrón Benítez v. Cordero Benítez*, No. KLAN0501519, 2006 WL 3032408 (P.R. Cir. Aug. 9, 2006) (stating that, even though, in the case the intent to jointly own was not proven, a daughter could do so with the former marital community property of her parents).

71 Albertina Antognini, *Against Nonmarital Exceptionalism*, 51 U.C. Davis L. Rev. 1891, 1892 (2018).

72 Some of these non-mainstream families include polygamous and polyamorous arrangements. Researchers estimate that 4–5 percent of Americans participate in some form of polyamory. Brenden Shucart, *Polyamory by the Numbers*, The Advocate, Jan. 8, 2016, https://www.advocate.com/current-issue/2016/1/08/polyamory-numbers. Other non-mainstream families include family units not based on reproductive or sexual relationships like a group of elderly people or siblings living together.

MARVIN v. MARVIN, 557 P.2D 106 (CAL. 1976)

JUSTICE ELENGOLD, CONCURRING

This is a case about the dissolution of an intimate relationship between two individuals, Michelle Marvin and Lee Marvin. The parties were never married. According to the plaintiff, in October of 1964, the parties moved in together. They "entered into an oral agreement" that while "the parties lived together they would combine their efforts and earnings and would share equally any and all property accumulated as a result of their efforts whether individual or combined." For seven years, the parties lived together as partners, holding themselves out as husband and wife. During that time, Ms. Marvin agreed to "give up her lucrative career as an entertainer (and) singer" to "devote her full time to defendant … as a companion, homemaker, housekeeper and cook." In return for her professional and financial sacrifice, Lee Marvin agreed to "provide for all of plaintiff's financial support and needs for the rest of her life."

During the time they lived together, defendant Lee Marvin found great success in his acting career. He won an Academy Award in 1965 for his role in the film *Cat Ballou* and found great commercial success in the film *The Dirty Dozen*, amassing property that included motion picture rights worth over $1 million. All of the property was acquired in his name. In May of 1970, the relationship soured and Mr. Marvin asked Ms. Marvin to leave the couple's shared home. He continued to support Ms. Marvin until November of 1971, but thereafter refused to provide her financial support or share the financial success that he had found during the course of their relationship.

Based on these facts, as alleged, Michelle Marvin requests this court to (1) declare plaintiff's contract and property rights under the agreement(s) alleged herein; and (2) impose a constructive trust on one-half of the property acquired during the course of the relationship.

The lower court granted defendant's motion on the pleadings and denied plaintiff's motion to amend her complaint. The majority reversed and remanded. In its decision, the majority held that (1) express contracts between nonmarital partners should be enforced unless the contract is explicitly founded on the consideration of meretricious sexual services; and (2) equitable remedies may be available to nonmarital partners in the absence of a contract. In the course of its analysis, the majority determined that California's Family Law Act does not govern the distribution of property acquired during a nonmarital relationship.

I concur in the majority's decision. I write separately for two primary reasons. First, I believe that this case forces us to consider the state's historic treatment of marriage and the gender roles inherent in those relationships. More specifically, I believe that this case compels a reckoning with the differential treatment that has been applied to married and unmarried partners. Second, I write to offer additional guidance to lower courts and parties on how to implement the majority's charge to remove the judicial barriers placed in front of unmarried partners in the face of dissolution of the relationship.

I

A

California's law with respect to married women's property and contract rights has evolved in an effort to put married women on more equal footing with married men. Professor Susan Westerberg Prager has recently published a careful and thorough accounting of California's property laws. She details how California was unable to rid itself of the vestiges of the separate property philosophy underlying its family law statutes until very recently. *See* Susan Westerberg Prager, *The Persistence of Separate Property Concepts in California's Property System*, 24 U.C.L.A. L. Rev. 1 (1976). Relying heavily on Professor Prager's extensive analysis, I set forth the salient history below.

In 1849, when California's constitution was originally drafted, common law supported the notion that, upon marriage, a woman's property became her husband's property. California rejected that notion and instead adopted a provision that read:

> All property, both real and personal, of the wife, owned or claimed by her before marriage, and that acquired afterwards by gift, devise or descent, shall be her separate property; and laws shall be passed more clearly defining the rights of the wife, in relation as well to her separate property, as to that held in common with her husband. Laws shall also be passed providing for the registration of the wife's separate property.
>
> Cal. Const. art. XI, § 14 (1849).

This language tracked reforms across the states known as "Married Women's Property Acts," which sought to bring some equity into the property rights of husbands and wives. California's constitutional language, like parallel Married Women's Property Acts, rejected the notion that a woman lost her independent rights in her property upon marriage. California's constitutional language, however, did not further define a married woman's property rights; the constitution left the details, including property and support rights in divorce, to be decided by the legislature.

The first California state legislature in 1850 legislated on marital property rights, granting property management and control to the husband for both the parties' common property and the wife's separate property and requiring a husband's consent prior to assigning validity to a will. *See* Act of April 17, 1850, ch. 103 §§ 6, 8, 9, Cal. Stat. 254. So, while California was technically a community property jurisdiction, separate property still ruled the day. The 1861 California state legislature amended the common property succession statute to require that a surviving husband would own all of the common property, but that a surviving wife would share the common property equally with any descendants. Act of May 8, 1861, ch. 323, § 1,Cal. Stat. 310–11. Although embedded in the state constitution, it wasn't until implementation of the Civil Code in 1872 and legislative action thereafter that a married woman was truly given full managerial power over her own separate property. Cal. Civ. Code § 162. And that reform did not, of course, apply to common property acquired during the marriage. Other statutes afforded a married woman increased access to "separate" property acquired during the marriage. *See* Act of March 4, 1870, ch. 138, § 2, Cal. Stat. 132 (applying a presumption of separate property for property conveyed in the wife's name); Act of March 9, 1870, ch. 161, § 1, Cal. Stat. 226 (exempting a wife's earnings from her husband's debts).

Between 1891 and 1927, the California legislature loosened a husband's hold on the married couple's property. It did that via two main routes: restricting the husband's management authority over community property and amending the husband's exclusive ownership of community property. Finally, in 1927, the California legislature explicitly stated that "[t]he respective interests of husband and wife in community property during continuance of the marriage relation are present, existing and equal interests under the management and control of the husband." Act of April 28, 1927, ch. 265, § 1, Cal. Stat. 484. Although it took another forty-six years for the California legislature to remove the notation to the husband's management and control (*see* Cal. Civ. Code § 5105), changes were made along the way to amend intestate succession and wills law to place husbands and wives on more equal footing. In the 1950s, the California legislature granted married women the right to manage and control their earnings, subject to certain limitations. Act of June 16, 1951, ch. 1102, Cal. Stat. 2860–61.

It was not until the 1970s, however, that the California legislature fully endorsed the concept of community property, whereby the husband and wife share equally in the common property acquired during marriage. Reacting to the sex discrimination challenges of the time, the California legislature chose a community property structure rather than perfecting a sex-neutral separate property philosophy. Today, the community property philosophy is codified: "Community property is property acquired by husband and wife, or either, during marriage." Cal. Civ. Code 687. The Civil Code further states that, "either spouse has the management and control of the community personal property . . . with like absolute power of disposition, other than testamentary, as the spouse has of the separate estate of the spouse." Cal. Civ. Code § 5125(a). And it eliminates the special presumption that property titled in a wife's name (as relative to a husband's name) is separate, rather than common, property. Cal. Civ. Code § 5110.

On its face, the relevance of this recitation appears limited. What, one might ask, does this have to do with Michelle Marvin's property rights today? How is the recitation of married women's evolving property rights relevant to Michelle Marvin, who was never married to Lee Marvin? History, of course, provides this court insight into the legislature's often difficult and often confusing choices. This particular history tells a story of a series of successive California state legislatures grappling with the changing nature of marriage and gender roles that sit at the heart of the state's community property laws. The legislatures, over time, recognized that property law, as it relates to familial relationships, can operate to enforce gender roles. The community property law changes were made in the midst of an increasingly vocal struggle for women's rights. And while they came in fits and starts, successive California legislatures' evolving view of married women's property rights reflected an attempt to create equity in property rights between married men and married women.[1] That history is thus relevant to a broader understanding of the legislature's approach to the relationship between gender and property.

It is in the latter part of that story, as the California legislature sought to break down traditional barriers to gender equality inside of a marriage, that the Family Law Act of 1969, Cal. Civ. Code § 4000 *et seq.*, was passed.

[1] California courts have long understood community property law to reflect the ideals of equality upon dissolution of marriage. As far back as 1859 in *Meyer v. Kinzer*, the California Supreme Court noted that "[t]he [community property law] proceeds upon the theory that the marriage, in respect to property acquired during its existence, is a community of which each spouse is a member, equally contributing by his or her industry to its prosperity, and possessing an equal right to succeed to the property after dissolution, in case of surviving the other. . . ." 12 Cal. 247, 251–52 (1859). Such a proposition has since been endorsed by modern California courts (*see In re Cary*, 34 Cal.App.3d 345, 348 (1973)) and the Civil Code as it currently exists. *See* Cal. Civ. Code § 687.

Through the Family Law Act, the California legislature restored mandatory equal division of community property as part of California's adoption of no-fault divorce. It also applied such rights to putative spouses, or those individuals who have an erroneous, but good-faith belief that they were legally married. *See* Cal. Civ. Code § 4452; *In re Cary*, 34 Cal.App.3d 345, 349 (1973) (cataloguing the application of the community property principle to putative spouses).

B

Around the same time that the California legislature passed the Family Law Act, the California Court of Appeals decided *In re Cary*, which has become a central case in analysis of the case at hand. To the extent that *Cary* applied the Family Law Act to nonmarital partners, the majority overrules it. I agree with the majority that the Family Law Act is not applicable in this case, but that does not mean that the *Cary* decision is irrelevant to the case at hand. The defendant, Lee Marvin, would have us view this case only from the lens of traditional marriage; he urges this court to draw a bright line – divorcing spouses receive a share in property and cohabitants do not. Because *Cary* offers a glimpse of the dangers that might arise if we viewed this case only from that frame, *Cary* is, indeed, worth a careful review.

By 1973, when *Cary* was decided, there had been a social and legislative movement in this state to break down the gender roles inside of a marriage as they related to property ownership and management. With that understanding, the *Cary* court determined that the property allocation principles of the Family Law Act must apply to unmarried partners as well as married partners. The *Cary* court noted that it would be inconsistent to understand the Family Law Act to "presume a legislative intent that a person, who by deceit leads another to believe a valid marriage exists between them, shall be legally guaranteed half of the property they acquire even though most, or all, may have resulted from the earnings of the blameless partner" while at the same time denying judicial aid to the "two persons who, candidly with each other, enter upon an unmarried family relationship." 34 Cal.App.3d at 352.

The *Cary* court, however, limited application of the Family Law Act to unmarried partners who "establish[ ] not only an ostensible marital relationship but also an actual family relationship, with cohabitation and mutual recognition and assumption of the usual rights, duties, and obligations attending marriage." 34 Cal.App.3d at 353. In other words, unmarried partners needed to appear to the external world as married partners. For the *Cary* court, the following facts created such an impression:

> Paul Cary and Janet Forbes, never married to each other, lived together for more than eight years. During that time they held themselves out to their friends and parents, and to the world generally, as a married couple; she always used the name of Cary. They purchased a home and other property, borrowed money, obtained credit, filed joint income tax returns and otherwise conducted all business as husband and wife . . . Four children were born to Paul and Janet; they were supported by Paul who always acknowledged them as his own. Their birth certificates and school registration recorded the parents as Paul and Janet Cary. While Paul worked Janet generally stayed at home taking care of the children and the house.
>
> Id. at 348.

It appears that the *Cary* court was swayed by the facts that made Paul Cary and Janet Forbes *look* like a married couple, facts which included (1) children in common; (2) surname in common; (3) a male breadwinner; and (4) a female homemaker. In other words, Paul Cary and Janet Forbes performed their relationship to look like a "traditional" married couple.

If we followed *Cary*'s lead, Michelle Marvin and Lee Marvin, whose relationship parallels that of Janet Forbes and Paul Cary, might pass the "marriage-like" test. Michelle Marvin adopted Lee Marvin's surname and gave up her career to support his. But the method by which the *Cary* court applied the Family Law Act to unmarried partners operates to reinscribe the traditional gender roles and property rights that the California legislature has attempted to shed through its evolution on marital property rights. The *Cary* court's opinion implies that the couple's "traditional" gender roles were, at least in part, what qualified them to take advantage of the state's protections designed for married couples. Had Janet not taken Paul's last name, would that have removed them from the same protections? Had Janet worked outside the home, would that have removed them from the same protections? What if the couple only had one child, or none?

The problem is that the *Cary* court's analysis of the reasons *why* Paul Cary and Janet Forbes were entitled to equal access to community property is at odds with the state's concerted effort to break down traditional gender roles inside of a marriage, as set forth above. Rather than assessing the strength of the partnership or even the parties' intentions with respect to the partnership, the *Cary* court looked to the presentation of the relationship, and looked for a presentation that reinscribed traditional gender roles. Therefore, this Court must be careful not to judge the current parties' relationship against the traditional and rigid views on marriage and gender roles. No couple (married or unmarried) should be required to prove "marriage-like" credentials to seek state protections. The California legislature – in fits and starts and perhaps insufficiently – has sought to remove such rigid requirements from married women; I see no reason to subject unmarried partners to such requirements. Feminist reformers have made the connection between divorce reform and the women's rights movement. Recognizing the ways that marriage and the laws of marriage have limited a woman's rights and independence, divorce reform has attempted to break some of those gender-based barriers. In other words, it is not logical that the legislature has tried to provide women with independent property rights and equality inside of a marriage but would seek to limit those same rights of women outside of a marriage.

Rather I agree with the majority's conclusion, at footnote 11, that our analysis should begin in contract analysis, by exposing the parties' intentions for the relationship. The parties' intentions should be considered regardless of how they performed their relationship, and can only be "ascertained by a more searching inquiry into the nature of their relationship." And rather than ask whether the parties have sufficiently achieved a traditional "marriage-like" presentation entitled to the protections of the Family Law Act (as *Cary* would have us do), I offer an alternative frame. I suggest that we consider Michelle Marvin and Lee Marvin's relationship as akin to a business partnership. It is, after all, what underlies *Cary*'s reliance on the Family Law Act to achieve its result in the first place. *See* 34 Cal.App.3d at 351 (citing ATTORNEY'S GUIDE TO FAMILY LAW ACT PRACTICE 250 (Cont.Ed.Bar. 2d ed. 1972):

> The basic theory of the [Family Law Act] is that, in disposing of the property, a dissolution of marriage should be treated much like the dissolution of a business partnership. Regardless of the economic circumstances of business partners or of their moral conduct during the existence of the partnership, on dissolution the partners receive a portion of the assets commensurate with their respective partnership interests.

Like a business partner dissolving her partnership, Michelle Marvin is entitled to plead and prove the existence of an express or implied contract. Should she make that proof, she is entitled to full effectuation of that contract. Although the parties' contract was oral and not written, the substantive law of contracts suggests that we give contracting parties the right to determine the terms of their own dealings, without looking behind those terms. *See Jenkins v. Valley Oil Co.*, 226 Cal.App.2d 41, 45 ("If no ambiguity or uncertainty is manifest in the language of a contract, where the words used are common ones, plain in their definition, import and connotation and free from enlargement or restriction to be implied from their use in any specialty field, the contract must be construed without reference to explanatory parol evidence"). Therefore, should Michelle Marvin prove the existence of the contract she alleges, the terms of that contract should prevail. And absent clear and express terms, the intention of the parties shall prevail. *See Swarthout v. Gentry*, 62 Cal.App.2d 68, 80–81 (1943) (plaintiff's uncontradicted testimony showed that, when he purchased the property in question, it was "acquired by the partners for the benefit of the partnership and for use by it and not for use by the individuals"). Any public policy interests attendant to the construct of marriage (of which I am wary) do not change the rights of individuals to contract, including a right to pool their work and earnings and share equally in the property accumulated in relation to that pooling. The majority's ten-case string cite clearly sets out that proposition. Ms. Marvin asserts that she was a party to an oral contract with Mr. Marvin under which they agreed to equally share all of the property the partners individually and collectively accumulated during their seven-year relationship. Should she prove the terms of the contract as alleged, Ms. Marvin would be entitled to half of the real and personal property the couple accumulated, including motion picture rights exceeding $1 million.

If we follow the *Cary* court's decision to assess "marriage-like" by searching for the traditional gender roles that have historically been bound up in the concept and construct of marriage, we risk reinscribing outmoded ideas of gender roles and separate spheres. If, instead, we seek out the partnership interests of the parties dissolving a relationship, we can more clearly hew to the parties' intentions. This approach is consistent with the outcome of *Cary*, California courts' treatment of partnership dissolution, and the access to judicial intervention that sits at the heart of the majority opinion.

II

And so I move to the central goal of this concurrence – to offer guidance to lower courts and parties on how to implement the majority's charge to remove the "judicial barriers that may stand in the way of a policy based upon the fulfillment of the reasonable expectations of the parties to a nonmarital relationship."

In the absence of an express or implied contract, as the majority notes, Ms. Marvin is entitled to plead and prove an action in equity. The majority sets forth several theories for recovery – resulting trust, in quantum meruit, and constructive trust. While contract law looks to the parties' stated terms and intentions, an action in equity is more concerned with the effects of the parties' agreement. I turn now to such an analysis.

A resulting trust, in the ordinary case, forms when a property is purchased by one person and titled in the name of another. *See Viner v. Untrecht*, 26

Cal.2d 261, 269 (1945). A resulting trust "arise[s] where the legal estate in property is transferred or conveyed, but the interest appears, or it is inferred from the terms of the disposition, or from the accompanying facts and circumstances, that the beneficial interest is not to pass to, or be enjoyed with, the legal title." *Fulton v. Jansen*, 99 Cal. 587, 590 (1893). The most obvious example is where a piece of property is conveyed to person A, but the price or consideration is paid by person B. In equity, person A holds the title in trust for the benefit of person B. *Id.* Resulting trusts can apply to either personal property or real property. *See Norman v. Burks*, 93 Cal.App.2d 687, 691 (1949). That quintessential situation, however, did not arise here. It is not as if Ms. Marvin purchased the property, but the property was titled in Mr. Marvin's name; rather, Mr. Marvin purchased and now owns property in his own name. Because consideration for property might be made in the performance of service (*Laing v. Laubach*, 233 Cal.App.2d 511, 540 (1965)), Ms. Marvin might argue that she has purchased part of Mr. Marvin's property and, because it is titled only in his name, she is the rightful beneficiary of half of his property. However, "[a] resulting trust cannot be enforced in favor of a person who has paid part of the consideration for the transfer of property unless it is possible to clearly establish the amount of money contributed by him or the proportion of his contribution to the whole purchase price." *Id.* at 517. *See also Woodside v. Hewel*, 109 Cal. 481, 485 (1895).

Recovery in quantum meruit permits the plaintiff to recover "the reasonable value of the services rendered, provided they were of direct benefit to the defendant." *Palmer v. Gregg*, 65 Cal.2d 657, 661 (1967) (*en banc*). The *Palmer* court explains that, in an action in quantum meruit,

> the defendant is regarded as a debtor to the extent of the value of something received by him and he is said to be under a legal duty sometimes called 'quasi contractual,' to make restitution of this value. In determining the amount of this value, expenditures made by the injured party are not included unless they (i.e., their benefits) were received by the defendant.
>
> Id. (citing *Corbin on Contracts* § 996, 17 (1964 ed.)).

While resulting trusts and recovery in quantum meruit might work in some intimate partner dissolutions, there is reason to be cautious. Both methods of equitable recovery rely on the valuation of the labor or contribution of the party claiming to be the rightful beneficiary.

Thus, these theories of recovery may be problematic because they create a situation that risks undervaluing the kind of domestic labor in which Michelle Marvin engaged. In essence, they give her a property right in her "wages," presumably as determined by like paid work and the court. According to her brief, Michelle Marvin provided "full time" services to Lee Marvin, "as a companion, homemaker, housekeeper, and cook" while simultaneously "giv [ing] up her lucrative career as an entertainer [and] singer." Appellant's Reply Brief at 10. It is hard to believe that Ms. Marvin will be fully compensated for her services under a quantum meruit or resulting trust formula. Domestic labor has historically been undervalued and left unprotected from unscrupulous conduct, including exploitation, wage theft, and even assault. For example, domestic workers were denied a household workers code under the National Recovery Administration and excluded from the protections of the Fair Labor Standards Act in the 1930s. Just two years ago, Congress amended the Fair Labor Standards Act to include domestic workers in minimum wage and overtime pay protections. Fair Labor Standards Amendments of 1974, Pub. L. No. 93-259, 88 Stat. 55 (1974) (codified at 29 U.S.C. §§ 201–19). Even then, however, the Amendments exempted persons "employed in domestic service employment to provide companionship services for individuals ... unable to care for themselves." 29 U.S.C. § 213(a)(15).

This historic unwillingness to value the work of a companion, homemaker, housekeeper, and cook was on display in this court's opinion in *Vallera v. Vallera*, where this court reversed the trial court's finding that an unmarried partner was entitled to one-half of the property accumulated during the relationship. The *Vallera* court held instead that, absent an express agreement to share accumulated assets between the unmarried couple, an action in equity would permit the woman "to share in the property jointly accumulated," but only "in the proportion that her funds contributed toward its acquisition." *Vallera v. Vallera*, 21 Cal.2d 681, 685 (1943). The majority in this case cited Justice Curtis's dissent positively, calling attention to the impropriety of this court's earlier determination that the value of Ms. Vallera's services as housekeeper, cook, and homemaker amounted to no more than "the cost of maintenance of herself and her two children." *Id.* at 686 (Curtis, J., dissenting in part). I find it inconsistent to recognize the undervaluation of homemaker services in *Vallera* without acknowledging that the same outcome – undervaluation of domestic labor – is likely should a court analyze this case under an action in quantum meruit or pursuant to a resulting trust.

Even if Ms. Marvin worked outside the home, for wages, a recovery in quantum meruit or resulting trust undoubtedly undervalues a woman's work because it is drawn from the value of the woman's work on the open market. We know, of course, that women are paid less on the open market than men. In fact, the Supreme Court of the United States has recently expressly recognized the real differences in access to property and wealth accumulation between men and women:

> There can be no dispute that the financial difficulties confronting the lone woman in Florida or in any other State exceed those facing the man. Whether from overt discrimination or from the socialization process of a male-dominated culture, the job market is inhospitable to the woman seeking any but the lowest paid jobs. There are, of course, efforts under way to remedy this situation. On the federal level, Title VII of the Civil Rights Act of 1964 prohibits covered employers and labor unions from discrimination on the basis of sex, 78 Stat. 253, 42 U.S.C. s 2000e – 2(a), (c), as does the Equal Pay Act of 1963, 77 Stat. 56, 29 U.S.C. § 206(d). But firmly entrenched practices are resistant to such pressures, and, indeed, data compiled by the Women's Bureau of the United States Department of Labor show that in 1972 a woman working full time had a median income which was only 57.9% of the median for males – a figure actually six points lower than had been achieved in 1955. Other date [sic] point in the same direction.
>
> Kahn v. Shevin, 416 U.S. 351, 353–54 (1974) (internal citations omitted) (upholding the constitutionality of a state statute allowing widows a $500 annual property tax exemption).

For all of these reasons, Ms. Marvin's work is likely to be undervalued and undercompensated under an in quantum meruit formula or pursuant to a resulting trust.

An action in quantum meruit is also problematic because it would permit and encourage a reversion to separate property as the key factor in property distribution. In other words, under in quantum meruit, Michelle Marvin retains a property right in her own earnings, rather than using her labor to "buy in" to the common property she assisted Lee Marvin in amassing. The California legislature has (finally) rejected the concept of separate property in favor of community property. For the reasons set forth above, I do not believe that a return to a separate property theory is consistent with this state's evolving concepts of forced gender roles inherent in married and unmarried relationships. I urge caution in returning to such a theory in this case. Rather, a community property approach is appropriate when a cohabitant can prove creation of a constructive trust.

I turn then to constructive trust, to which Michelle Marvin believes she is entitled. "The theory of a constructive trust was adopted by equity as a remedy to compel one to restore property to which he is not justly entitled, to another. The person holding the property may have acquired it through fraud, undue influence, breach of trust, or in any other improper manner." *Fowler v. Fowler*, 227 Cal. App.2d 741, 744 (Ct. App. 1964) (citing *Bainbridge v. Stoner*, 16 Cal.2d 423, 428). A constructive trust arises based on the "relation of the parties" and is generally imposed "to prevent unjust enrichment and accomplish an equitable purpose." *Ornbaum v. Main*, 198 Cal.App.2d 92, 98 (Ct. App. 1961). A constructive trust "may be imposed in practically any case where there is wrongful acquisition or detention of property to which another is entitled" (*Weiss v. Marcus*, 51 Cal.App.3d 590, 600 (Ct. App. 1975).

A constructive trust is a remedy for a finding of constructive fraud. Constructive fraud arises "(1) In any breach of duty which, without an actually fraudulent intent, gains an advantage to the person in fault, or any one claiming under him, by misleading another to his prejudice, or to the prejudice of any one claims under him." Ca. Civ. Code § 1573. "Constructive fraud arises on a breach of duty by one in a confidential or fiduciary relationship to another which induces justifiable reliance by the latter to his prejudice." *Odorizzi v. Bloomfield School Dist.*, 246 Cal.App.2d 123, 129 (1966). A confidential relationship exists "whenever a person with justification places trust and confidence in the integrity and fidelity of another." *Id.* This concept has been applied by California courts in family law matters, without limiting the protection to married couples. *See Vai v. Bank of American National Trust & Savings Assn*, 56 Cal.2d 329, 337–38 (1961) (recognizing that a fiduciary relationship exists between husband and wife under the community property system and that a confidential relationship "may exist although there is no fiduciary relation; it is particularly likely to exist where there is a family relationship or one of friendship") (citing RESTATEMENT OF TRUSTS 2d § 2 *Comment* b); *Schotte v. Schotte*, 203 Cal.App.2d 28, 32–33 (4th District 1962) ("Where a husband invests his separate funds in improving the property of his wife relying upon her oral promise to convey to him an interest therein if he would do so, in the event she refuses to convey as promised her agreement will be enforced by imposing a constructive trust on that property in favor of the husband, because the breach of her oral promise constitutes a violation of the confidential relationship between them ... Furthermore, the evidence herein establishes that, regardless of their marital status, an actual confidential relationship existed between the subject parties, and this fact supports an application of the foregoing constructive trust rule").

Why is this helpful? It is helpful because (1) it creates a scaffolding for a court to determine whether Ms. Marvin is entitled to a finding in equity and (2) it offers principles for recovery. It is useful, then, to separate the liability finding from the remedy. I begin with the former. A court considering whether a party has made out a case for constructive fraud might ask the following questions: Was there a fiduciary or confidential relationship between the parties? In the context of that relationship, did one party mislead the other with respect to a current or future financial interest? Did one party justifiably rely on that representation? Was the party who relied on the representation injured or prejudiced? In this case, Ms. Marvin and Mr. Marvin were arguably in a confidential relationship. Ms. Marvin has alleged that Mr. Marvin misled her by promising her financial support in exchange for her service to him as a companion, homemaker, and cook. Ms. Marvin has also alleged that she justifiably relied on that promise and she was prejudiced by her reliance. Therefore, she is – according to proof at trial – entitled to equitable relief under the theory of constructive fraud and the remedy of constructive trust.

I move now to the question of remedy. This is a more difficult and more fact-intensive question. In the case of a romantic relationship, it is hard to separate out promises, representations, and aspirations related to long-term commitment and future interests. There is a danger of a slippery slope here. Imagine, for example, a situation where a man and woman enter into a romantic relationship. Two weeks later, the woman wins a multimillion-dollar lottery and subsequently determines that she is uninterested in the romantic relationship. It does not follow that her partner of two weeks should be entitled to half of her multimillion-dollar lottery payout. And yet it seems unfair and unjust to permit one partner to change his or her mind about promises of financial support after the other partner has sacrificed past and future earnings in reliance on those promises, representations, and aspirations. Therefore, there must be some legal frame that cabins the recovery. That principle should be borne out of the justifiable reliance element identified above. In other words, courts should apply a reasonable person standard when assessing whether there was justifiable reliance and when determining the scope of the recovery. *See Gold v. Los Angeles Democratic League*, 49 Cal.App.3d 365, 374–75 (1975) (plaintiff did not reasonably rely on alleged misrepresentation and therefore could not have justifiably relied on it). So how might a court determine that Ms. Marvin reasonably relied on Mr. Marvin's promises?

Because (the amount of) her recovery may rise and fall on the reasonableness of that recovery, courts will search for guidance in determining whether a plaintiff like Ms. Marvin reasonably relied on her intimate partner's promises. One way to assess the reasonableness of the reliance is by comparing the presentation of the Marvins' relationship to a traditional marriage, marked by traditional gender roles. This is what the *Cary* court did, looking to the parties' performance of their relationship to identify markers of reasonable reliance. For the reasons set forth above, I reject that approach. Drawing once again on the option of treating intimate relationships more like business relationships, another path is to borrow from gender-neutral elements of justifiable reliance as they arise outside of intimate relationships. Upon review of California case law analyzing justifiable reliance in principal-agent, business, and family relationships, I offer the following factors as a starting place for determining reasonable reliance in a case like the one at hand today. First, courts might consider whether the plaintiff's actions were consistent with the allegation that she relied on the defendant's representation. *See Occidental Land, Inc. v. Superior Court*, 18 Cal. 3d 355, 363, 556 P.2d 750, 754 (1976) ("[A]n inference of reliance arises if a material false representation was made to persons whose acts thereafter were consistent with reliance upon the representation"). Second, courts might consider if the defendant's statements and actions were consistent (or inconsistent) with the alleged representation. *See Dickens v. Bunker*, 169 Cal.App.2d 383, 388 (1959) (plaintiff could not establish ostensible authority in reliance only on agent's – rather than principal's – assertion of the relationship). Finally, defendants may counter with evidence that the representation was explicitly conditioned or restricted. *See Pacesetter Homes, Inc. v. Brodkin*, 5 Cal.App.3d 206, 213 (1970) (plaintiff did not establish justifiable reliance where the record established that the defendant's promise was "hedged with significant qualifications"). This is not an exhaustive list, but rather a starting place for courts to consider relief and remedy under a constructive trust theory.[2]

I believe that this frame and its principles would be validly and usefully applied to any case in equity in which (1) one party relied on the assurance of another during the relationship and (2) dissolution of the relationship caused injury to the relying party. This approach is applicable across relationships and does not require a relationship to appear "marriage-like" and thus subject to the gender stereotypes of the decisionmaker. It does not fall prey to the dangers of assessing the value of domestic labor or risk undervaluing a woman's work inside or outside of the home. It is in keeping with the California legislature's evolution in legislating property rights, and is consistent with the majority's desire to break down "the judicial barriers that may stand in the way of a policy based upon the fulfillment of the reasonable expectations of the parties to a nonmarital relationship."

[2] It is worth noting that, under a constructive fraud theory, a plaintiff can sue for damages under a tort or quasi-contract theory or can pursue a suit in equity to impose a constructive trust. *Davies v. Krasna*, 35 Cal.App.3d 662, 662 (1973), vacated on other grounds by *Davies v. Krasna*, 14 Cal.3d 502 (1975). In a case like the one at hand, the damages would be financial; other equitable relief might risk infringing on one party's constitutional rights.

7

Commentary on *Kulko v. Superior Court of California*

MARY-BETH MOYLAN

INTRODUCTION

The case of *Kulko v. Superior Court*[1] has a place in both family law and civil procedure jurisprudence. In *Kulko*, the Supreme Court declined to find that California had personal jurisdiction over a father after his children relocated to live with their mother in California and the mother sued to modify custody and support in a state court. In the family law context, it underscored the need for uniform legislation to address child support orders and modifications. In the civil procedure context, it recognized distinctions between cases in the public commercial sphere and in the private family sphere for the purpose of establishing personal jurisdiction, but reiterated the applicability of the minimum contacts test as the measure of due process under the Fourteenth Amendment in all spheres. While the California courts that heard the motion to quash service presented by petitioner, Ezra Kulko, all determined that the long-arm statute of California appropriately reached him, the U.S. Supreme Court disagreed.

The majority opinion, written by Justice Marshall, mechanically employed the minimum contacts test established by *International Shoe Co. v. Washington*,[2] and held that a nonresident parent cannot be subject to a child support judgment in a state where his children reside without having established additional minimum contacts with the state. His consent to allow his children to live there was insufficient. The use of the *International Shoe* test in the family law context was a difficult fit, and the majority opinion did not choose to view the agreement between the Kulkos as an interstate legal relationship with ongoing force. The "purposeful availment" test that was

[1] *Kulko v. Super. Ct. Cal.*, City and County of S.F., 436 U.S. 84 (1978).
[2] *Int'l Shoe Co. v. Washington*, 326 U.S. 310 (1945).

the developing standard for asserting jurisdiction over nonresident defendants was created for business interactions, not personal ones. The role of a father as the nonresident parent, rather than the mother, may also have colored the view of the majority of justices. Minor children's needs were, and to some extent still are, more closely associated with the maternal parent. For all these reasons, the decision was one that was unsatisfactory from a feminist perspective.

BACKGROUND AND SOCIAL CONTEXT IN THE 1970S

While the Kulkos' marriage took place in the 1960s, and their divorce was granted in 1972, the litigation of the Kulko child custody issues spanned the 1970s. This decade was a robust one for issues involving women at work and in the home. The political and social climate of the late 1970s saw an increase in women entering the workforce,[3] as well as a demand for childcare programs for children of working mothers,[4] and the imminent failure of the Equal Rights Amendment as it stalled in efforts at ratification late in the decade.[5] This was a period of "women's liberation," of emerging movements for gay rights, farm worker rights, and immigrant rights, as well as an increased awareness of cultural identity and politics. Significantly also, most American workers were employed by a single employer during their work lives until the 1970s.[6] The change to a mobile workforce starting in the 1970s was not a favorable one for many families.[7] All of these changes offer the context in which the *Kulko* decision was reached.

Kulko was decided in 1978 against the backdrop of a decade of rising divorce rates across the United States.[8] At the time the litigants in *Kulko*

[3] Dhara Shah, 1954–1980 *Women in the Workforce*, The Evolution of Women in the Workforce (1865–2015) (Mar. 31, 2015), https://perma.cc/NYQ6-7R6Y

[4] President Nixon vetoed a bill that was passed by Congress that would have provided for universal childcare in 1971. Jennifer Ludden, *How Politics Killed Universal Child Care in the 1970s*, NPR (Oct. 13, 2016), https://www.npr.org/2016/10/13/497850292/how-politics-killed-universal-childcare-in-the-1970s

[5] The Learning Network, *March 22, 1972: Equal Rights Amendment for Women Passed by Congress*, N.Y. Times (Mar. 22, 2012), https://learning.blogs.nytimes.com/2012/03/22/march-22-1972-equal-right-amendment-for-women-passed-by-congress/

[6] Naomi Schoenbaum, *Mobility Measures*, 2012 B.Y.U. L. Rev. 1169, 1179 (2012).

[7] *Id.*

[8] AP, *U.S. Divorce Rate Falls to Lowest Level Since 1970*, NBC News (May 10, 2007), http://www.nbcnews.com/id/18600304/ns/us_news-life/t/us-divorce-rate-falls-lowest-level/. *See also*, Ana Swanson, *144 Years of Marriage and Divorce in the U.S. in One Chart*, Wash. Post (June 23, 2015), https://www.washingtonpost.com/news/wonk/wp/2015/06/23/144-years-of-marriage-and-divorce-in-the-united-states-in-one-chart/?noredirect=on&utm_term=.b4bocceefb67

obtained their divorce decree in Haiti in 1972, California had passed pioneering legislation allowing for no-fault divorce.[9] Other states followed California's lead, but it would not be until the end of the decade that most states granted divorces without fault attributed to one party or the other.[10] The emergence of no fault laws and the increased mobility of American society in the 1970s and 1980s meant that people started new lives in new states with divorce, custody, and child support decrees in tow. The realities of these judgments crossing borders and increased domestic relations litigation in states with no jurisdiction over some of the parties led to the passage of several uniform and cooperative statutes to ease the burden on families residing in different forums, as well as on the courts.[11] The uniform laws and the liberalization of custody relocation orders in most states also enabled more women who had entered the workforce to take advantage of employment-related moves to locations out of their home state.[12] Enforcement of child support orders across state lines was and is vitally important to women entering the workforce and moving with children.

BACKGROUND OF THE *IN PERSONAM* JURISDICTION TEST

Traditionally for a court to have jurisdiction over a person both to adjudicate her rights and to enforce a judgment, the court needed to have physical presence of the person or the person's property in the jurisdiction. Physical presence established *in personam* jurisdiction and *in rem* was the term used to attach a piece of property and gain jurisdiction over "the thing" that was subject to suit.[13] Increasingly, however, states passed long-arm statutes intended to extend the reach of state court jurisdiction over people residing outside of the jurisdiction, but engaging in activities that impacted people or businesses within the state. California was one of the first states to extend its long-arm statute to enforce marital obligations, and has been a leader in expanding the reach of jurisdiction to the fullest extent of the U.S.

[9] The Family Law Act of 1969 established no-fault divorce in California. *In re Marriage of McKim*, 6 Cal.3d 673 (1972).

[10] *See* Shah, *supra* note 3. In fact, New York, where the family primarily resided, did not adopt "no fault divorce" until 2010. N.Y. Domestic Relations Law § 170 (7). This might help explain the mother's decision to obtain a divorce in Haiti.

[11] *See* Uniform Child Custody Jurisdiction Act, Cal. Family Code §§ 3400 *et seq.*; Uniform Interstate Family Support Act, Cal. Family Code §§ 5700.101 *et seq.*; Uniform Divorce Recognition Act, Cal. Family Code §§ 2090 *et seq.*

[12] Schoenbaum, *supra* note 6, at 1192.

[13] Stephen N. Subrin et al., Civil Procedure: Doctrine, Practice, and Context 651 (5th ed. 2016).

Constitution.[14] In 1945, the Supreme Court in *International Shoe Co. v. Washington*[15] laid the foundation for modern personal jurisdiction jurisprudence and explained what the U.S. Constitutional limits would be.

While the Supreme Court recognized that the due process clause of the Fourteenth Amendment would not permit a court to exercise jurisdiction over an individual or a corporation with "no contacts, ties, or relations" in the state, it held that courts should measure the "quality and nature of the activity [in the state] in relation to the fair and orderly administration of the laws which it was the purpose of the due process clause to insure."[16] The Court focused its holding that the shoe company could be subject to personal jurisdiction in Washington on the "systematic and continuous" activities and obligations that the company engaged in over the course of a period of years and the "benefits and protections" of the law that were enjoyed by the company.[17]

Through the 1950s, courts expanded the reach of long-arm statutes using the *International Shoe* minimum contacts framework. However, in the late 1950s, a pair of cases created conflicts about the application of personal jurisdiction. Contradicting results in *McGee v. International Life Insurance Co.* and *Hanson v. Denkla* left lower courts walking a fine line when determining how far long-arm statutes could reach.[18] In *McGee*, the Supreme Court reversed the refusal of a Texas court to enforce a California judgment against an insurer who had engaged in a continuing relationship with an insured in California. The Supreme Court held that the delivery of the insurance contract in California and the acceptance of premiums mailed from the state were sufficient minimum contacts to meet the constitutional requirement, and that jurisdiction over the insurance company was reasonable.[19] In contrast, in *Hanson*, a Delaware trustee had established a relationship with the settlor of a trust before she moved to Florida. Even though the relationship continued after the settlor moved to Florida and communications flowed across state lines, the *Hanson* court distinguished *McGee* by finding that the Delaware trustee did not have minimum contacts with a person in Florida because the contact had been initiated by the settlor and not the

[14] *See, e.g.*, Cal L. Raup, *State Court Jurisdiction: The Long-Arm Reaches Domestic Relations Cases*, 6 Tex. Tech L. Rev. 1021, 1030–34 (1975); Cal. Code of Civ. Proc. § 410.10 (allowing the exercise of jurisdiction on "any basis not inconsistent with the Constitution of this state or the United States").

[15] *Int'l Shoe Co.* 326 U.S.

[16] *Id.* at 319.

[17] *Id.* at 319–20.

[18] *McGee v. Int'l Life Ins. Co.*, 355 U.S. 220, 223 (1957); *Hanson v. Denckla*, 357 U.S. 235 (1958).

[19] McGee, 355 U.S. at 223.

trustee.[20] The fine line resting on the initiator of the contact perplexed many academics and litigators.

The pendulum for expanding and contracting the reach of personal jurisdiction, especially in the commercial context, has continued to swing for decades. In 1977, the Supreme Court in *Shaffer v. Heitner* expanded the application of the minimum contacts test to *quasi in rem* proceedings.[21] In 1985, the Supreme Court in *Burger King Corp. v. Rudzewicz* stressed that the minimum contacts test of *International Shoe* should not be applied with any "talismanic jurisdictional formulas" but rather that each case needed to be considered on its facts to ensure that the exercise of personal jurisdiction would "comport with notions of fair play and substantial justice."[22] In 1987, the Supreme Court made clear that placing a product "in the stream of commerce" alone was not enough to satisfy the minimum contacts test.[23] The most recent cases from the Supreme Court seem to underscore that there must be "something more" than generalized business practices or incidental relationships with the forum to allow for personal jurisdiction to be properly exercised.[24]

DEVELOPMENT OF THE UNIFORM CHILD CUSTODY JURISDICTION ACT

As mentioned above, the issue of moving families and the need for transportable custody decrees gave rise to several uniform family law acts. By 1980, forty-four states had adopted the Uniform Child Custody Jurisdiction Act (UCCJA).[25] The jurisdiction requirements of the UCCJA focus on the contacts that the child has with the forum state, rather than personal jurisdiction

[20] *Hanson*, 357 U.S. at 251–53.

[21] *Shaffer v. Heitner*, 433 U.S. 186, 213–16 (1977).

[22] *Burger King Corp. v. Rudzewicz*, 471 U.S. 462, 486 (1985).

[23] *Asahi Metal Indus. Co. v. Super. Ct. Cal.*, 480 U.S. 102, 112 (1987). Many lower federal courts have adopted a clear nexus requirement, such that the claims sued upon must "arise from" the activities that the individual or corporation engages in within the forum. *See, e.g.*, *Crocker v. Hilton Int'l Barbados, Ltd.*, 976 F.2d 797 (1st Cir. 1992). However, some states have not required a strict "arising out of" prong when exercising jurisdiction through their long-arm statutes and will allow for the exercise of jurisdiction as long as there is a relationship between the contacts and the claim. *See, e.g.*, *Snowney v. Harrah's Ent., Inc.*, 35 Cal.4th 1054 (2005).

[24] *See J. McIntyre Machinery, Ltd. v. Nicastro*, 564 U.S. 873, 889 (2011) (Breyer, J., concurring in judgment)("the relevant facts found by the New Jersey Supreme Court show no 'regular … flow' or 'regular course' of sales in New Jersey and there is no 'something more,' such as a special state-related design, advertising, advice, marketing, or anything else").

[25] *In re Marriage of Leonard*, 122 Cal.App.3d 443, 450 (1st Dist. 1981).

over the parties.[26] Similarly, the Uniform Interstate Family Support Act (UIFSA) provides that a court may establish personal jurisdiction over nonresidents to establish, enforce, or modify a support order or determine parentage if a disjunctive list of eight criteria are satisfied.[27]

As a complement of UIFSA, Congress enacted the Full Faith and Credit for Child Support Orders Act (FFCCSOA), 28 U.S.C. § 1738B, which implements the full faith and credit clause and requires states to recognize, enforce, and not modify child support orders from other states.

The UCCJA, as well as the UIFSA, the FFCCSOA, and the Uniform Divorce Recognition Act,[28] are the kind of specific statutes conferring jurisdiction that the *Kulko* majority contemplated in the original opinion.

THE ORIGINAL OPINION

The U.S. Supreme Court posed the issue as "whether, in this action for child support, the California state courts may exercise *in personam* jurisdiction over a nonresident, nondomiciliary parent of minor children domiciled within the state."[29] The California Supreme Court, as well as the California trial and appellate courts, had determined that personal jurisdiction was proper because the defendant, Ezra Kulko, had caused an effect in the state and the exercise of jurisdiction over him for a cause of action resulting from that effect would be reasonable.[30] The California courts focused on the benefits that inure to a parent who gives consent for their children to live in the state. Specifically, the California Supreme Court explained that permitting a child to live in a state was a full invocation of the benefits and protections of a state. The California Court specified: "The parent

26 *Id.*

27 Uniform Interstate Family Support Act § 201(a) states that jurisdiction over a nonresident is proper if: (1) the individual is personally served with [citation, summons, notice] within this state; (2) the individual submits to the jurisdiction of this state by consent in a record, by entering a general appearance, or by filing a responsive document having the effect of waiving any contest to personal jurisdiction; (3) the individual resided with the child in this state; (4) the individual resided in this state and provided prenatal expenses or support for the child; (5) the child resides in this state as a result of the acts or directives of the individual; (6) the individual engaged in sexual intercourse in this state and the child may have been conceived by that act of intercourse; (7) the individual asserted parentage of a child in the [putative father registry] maintained in this state by the [appropriate agency]; or (8) there is any other basis consistent with the constitutions of this state and the United States for the exercise of personal jurisdiction.

28 *See* Schoenbaum, *supra* note 6.

29 *Kulko*, 436 U.S. at 86.

30 *Kulko v. Super. Ct.*, 19 Cal.3d 514, 521 (1977).

thereby avails himself to the total panoply of the state's laws, institutions and resources – its police and fire protection, its school system, its hospital services, its recreational facilities, its libraries and museums, to mention only a few."[31] The court concluded that a nonresident parent should be considered to have purposefully availed himself of the benefits and protections of the laws of California, unless there are unusual circumstances that would cause a court to diverge from that general rule.[32]

The U.S. Supreme Court rejected the California Court's reasoning for several reasons. First, it held that Ezra Kulko's acquiescence to his daughter's wish to live with her mother was not a purposeful availment of the sort contemplated by *International Shoe* and *Shaffer v. Heitner*.[33] Second, the Court concluded that Ezra Kulko did not financially benefit by his daughter's absence from his care for nine months of the year.[34] Third, the Court stressed that the effects test derived from the Restatement (Second) Conflicts of Laws § 37 (1971) "was intended to reach wrongful activity outside of the State causing injury within the State, … or commercial activity affecting state residents."[35] Because Ezra Kulko was not engaged in business activity, but rather was trying to keep harmony in his family by allowing an exception to a familial agreement that was made out of state, the effects test of the Restatement was not appropriately applied to his case. The U.S. Supreme Court indicated that the *Kulko* case was more akin to *Hanson v. Denkla*, in which one party to a contract unilaterally moved to another state and continued to conduct business from there, than to *McGee v. International Life Insurance Co.*, in which an insurance company solicited a renewal of the contract and sent premium notices to the insured who moved out of state.[36]

Finally, the Court acknowledged that California had interests in ensuring protection for the child resident, and conceded that California law might be the appropriate choice to govern the substance of the case. Justice Marshall also mentioned that thanks to California's participation in the Revised Uniform Reciprocal Enforcement Support Act of 1968, a California resident can claim support from a nonresident through his or her own state court without having to leave California.[37] However, the Court determined that there was

[31] *Id.* at 522.
[32] *Id.*
[33] *Kulko*, 436 U.S. at 94.
[34] *Id.* at 95.
[35] *Id.* at 96.
[36] *Id.* at 97.
[37] *Id.* at 98–99.

no permissible extension of the constitutional limits of the Fourteenth Amendment Due Process Clause to allow for a court to exercise jurisdiction over a nonresident parent who did nothing more than send a child to live with a resident parent.[38]

In the course of this opinion, Justice Marshall, joined by Chief Justice Burger, Justice Blackmun, Justice Stevens, Justice Stewart, and Justice Rehnquist, included an assortment of factual details that were unnecessary to the reasoning, but seemed to allude to extramarital relations by Sharon Kulko. For example, the opinion mentions that Sharon Kulko, upon execution of the separation agreement, flew immediately to Haiti to seek divorce, and "then returned to California, where she remarried and took the name Horn."[39] This detail about her remarriage in California suggests, without directly saying, that she is well-situated and somehow more at fault for the failure of the marriage. Absent from the opinion are details about Ezra Kulko's financial situation, present marital status, or reasons why both children sought to move to California in contravention of the original custody arrangement. Of course, since the controversy was about Ezra Kulko's contacts with the forum, the legally relevant facts would be the ones about his relationships with his ex-wife, his children, and the state of California. One can imagine that if the roles were reversed in this case, facts about the Sharon Horn's interactions with her children would have been a focus of the court's inquiry. Associating women with their role as mother within a family is endemic in both federal and state courts.[40]

Some explanation for the struggle to focus on the relevant facts may be attributed to the federal court's foray into to the unfamiliar terrain of domestic relations litigation. Federal courts have a long history of attempting to avoid domestic relations cases.[41] As Judith Resnik explained in her iconic article, *"Naturally" without Gender: Women, Jurisdiction, and the Federal Courts*, the "domestic relations" exception in federal court dates back to an 1859 case, *Barber v. Barber*.[42] In 1992, the U.S. Supreme Court clarified that the "domestic relations" exception does not exclude domestic relations cases from federal court based on any constitutional language, but the exception may be one that applies to divorce, alimony, and child custody cases brought to federal court

[38] *Id.* at 101.

[39] *Id.* at 87.

[40] Judith Resnik, *"Naturally" without Gender: Women, Jurisdiction, and the Federal Courts*, 66 N.Y.U. L. Rev. 1682, 1760–65 (1991).

[41] *Id.* at 1739–50.

[42] *Id.* at 1740.

through diversity jurisdiction or through other abstention doctrines.[43] The persistent nature of the debate about domestic relations cases in federal courts for over 150 years suggests that this is not a legal subject matter over which federal judges have, or wish to acquire, much expertise.

Justice Brennan, joined by Justice Powell and Justice White, wrote a very brief dissent. The dissent agreed that the *International Shoe* test required minimum contacts with the forum state to avoid offending traditional notions of fair play and substantial justice. Yet Justice Brennan would have found that the "appellant's connection with the State of California was not too attenuated under the standards of reasonableness and fairness implicit in the Due Process Clause, to require him to conduct his defense in the California courts."[44] The dissenting justices did not really grapple with the unique nature of the legal relationships in the domestic relations setting, but simply would have placed more focus on the reasonableness factors than the majority.

Several cases in California following *Kulko* made clear that the U.S. Supreme Court's message about personal jurisdiction had been heard.[45] Still, the courts in California and elsewhere have made a distinction between cases involving support and those involving custody.[46] The role and benefit of the UCCJA and UIFSA are intended to ensure that at least for custody and support purposes, the impact of *Kulko*'s stringent personal jurisdiction requirement does not prevent clear decrees supporting children's safety and security.

KULKO REWRITTEN

In the rewritten *Kulko* dissent that follows, Justice Katherine Macfarlane picks up with Justice Brennan's final words about standards of reasonableness and fairness being the benchmarks of the Fourteenth Amendment. The rewritten opinion focuses on the continuing relationships that establish minimum contacts and the reasonableness factors that later emerged in the *Burger King* case that was also authored by Justice Brennan. She reasons first and foremost that the agreement between the parties should have been viewed as any other interstate contract between two parties. She criticizes the majority for

[43] *Ankenbrandt v. Richards*, 504 U.S. 689, 695–99 (1992).

[44] *Id.* at 102.

[45] *Kumar v. Super. Ct.*, 32 Cal.3d 689, 703 (1982) (*en banc*); *McArthur v. Super. Ct.*, 235 Cal. App.3d 1287, 1293–94 (6th Dist. 1991).

[46] *In re* Marriage of Leonard, 122 Cal.App.3d at 459.

characterizing the dispute as something other than contractual, and notes that "paternalism has consequences here, serving to convert a contract into a benevolent decision stripped of legal meaning."[47] Justice Macfarlane appropriately sees purposeful acts that invoke the benefits and protections of California law in the form of the relationship between the nonresident father and his children, and the ongoing negotiations about care and support of the children between the parties. She concludes that the balance of the economic factors and inconveniences establish both the necessary minimum contacts and meet the fairness threshold for holding the nonresident accountable in California.

Supporting the existence of minimum contacts sufficient to meet the *International Shoe* standard, the rewritten opinion focuses on the benefits and protections available to the parent through the services rendered by the state to the child. It also points to the purchase of tickets to send a child to the state, and the child's continued contact with her nonresident parent from the state during the school year. Undoubtedly, Ezra Kulko initiated contact with his daughter in the state on a regular and continuous basis while she resided in California. Additionally, the rewritten dissent points to key facts that were omitted from the California Supreme Court opinion or the U.S. Supreme Court opinion, but appeared in the Court of Appeal decision, and should have been included in the later opinions. Namely, that the nonresident father proposed a new agreement to the resident mother after his daughter moved to California.[48] This outreach to a resident of California to renegotiate an existing agreement would be the kind of contact that was recognized as sufficient in *McGee v. International Life Insurance Co.*[49] Similar to *McGee*, the active solicitation of a continued contract with a resident of California should be a sufficient ongoing contact, especially in light of the subject matter of the contract – the care of a child. If there is any ongoing contract between two parents, it is the agreement that helps enforce care and support obligations to children.

In applying the reasonableness factors, the rewritten opinion focuses on the choice that appellant made to allow his children to reside in California, as well as the responsibility of the father to provide for his children. Importantly, the new opinion addresses the practical reality of child support determinations and what a lack of support would mean for the children residing in the state. The new opinion quotes a portion of the appellee's brief that cautions that

[47] Macfarlane Rewritten Opinion, *infra*.
[48] *Kulko v. Super. Ct.*, 63 Cal.App.3d 417 (1976).
[49] *McGee*, 355 U.S. at 223.

"if appellant prevails, 'a custodial father will be able to relieve himself of the day-to-day responsibilities of raising children and, by the same acts, avoid his support duties.'"[50] Changes in parenting over the decades, and in expectations of strong relationships with nonresident parents, make this caution even more pronounced now than when the appellee's brief was written in 1977. The age of social media and text messaging has made continuous contact and parental oversight a matter that does not require physical presence as much as constant electronic vigilance. It is abundantly reasonable to think and to expect that a nonresident parent will be present in his child's life regardless of his physical absence from the state where the child resides.

Justice Macfarlane in the rewritten opinion also takes into consideration the unequal economic power of the parties as it relates to their respective ability to litigate outside of the forum where they reside. In the original opinion, Justice Marshall paints a picture of Sharon Kulko as a woman who is quick to seek more support from her ex-spouse who remained behind in New York. But the rewritten opinion references the timing of the court action in relation to the second child's permanent move to California. The opinion underscores that for several years one of the children resided with the mother without a request for additional support. The new opinion also indicates that Ezra Kulko is a doctor, a fact that appeared in briefing to the U.S. Supreme Court, but did not make it into the opinion. All of these economic factors should come into play when balancing the fairness of causing one or the other party to litigate at a distance. The consideration of such factors makes the rewritten opinion a much more complete examination of the full breadth of due process considerations.

CONCLUSION

The intersection of family law and civil procedure is not an easy one to navigate. There is considerable difficulty in threading the needle between family relationships and legal ones. In *Kulko*, the original opinion categorized the matter as one of maintaining family harmony and did not hold the father accountable for a legal agreement that stretched across state lines. The rewritten opinion recognizes the similarities to the line of cases involving ongoing interstate insurance agreements and acknowledges the legal relationship that both father and mother are engaged in postdivorce. Relying both on the interpersonal contacts of family members and the reasonableness factors

[50] Macfarlane Rewritten Opinion, *infra*.

that would emerge later in the *Burger King* case, the rewritten opinion comes to a more sensible conclusion that strikes a balance between support for children and the due process rights of noncustodial parents.

KULKO v. SUPERIOR COURT OF CALIFORNIA, 436 U.S. 84 (1978)

JUSTICE MACFARLANE, DISSENTING

The question presented is whether the nonresident appellant Ezra Kulko, the nondomiciliary parent of minor children domiciled in California, has "certain minimum contacts [with the forum state] such that the maintenance of the suit does not offend 'traditional conception[s] of fair play and substantial justice'" embodied in the Due Process Clause of the Fourteenth Amendment. *International Shoe Co. v. Washington*, 326 U.S. 310, 316 (1945). The majority holds that he does not. I respectfully disagree, with the Court's characterizations of the facts of this case, as well as with its application of established jurisdictional principles. Instead, I conclude, as the California Supreme Court did, that California's exercise of jurisdiction here was proper. Appellant should be subject to the jurisdiction of the California courts so that those courts may hear appellee Sharon Kulko's claim for child support.

California Code of Civil Procedure § 410.10 permits the exercise of *in personam* jurisdiction on bases consistent with the Constitution. In this matter, the California Supreme Court noted that where a nonresident defendant has caused an effect in the state by an act or omission outside the state, personal jurisdiction over the defendant in cases arising from that effect may be exercised whenever "reasonable." 19 Cal.3d 514, 521 (1977). An exercise of jurisdiction was reasonable here, according to the California courts, because appellant sent his minor daughter to live with her mother, the appellee, in California, and therefore "purposely availed himself of the benefits and protections of the laws of California." *Id.* at 521–22. I would have affirmed that sound judgment.

I

A

The Court begins its discussion of the facts by highlighting the parties' contacts with New York and minimizing their contacts with California. The Court's factual recitation begins with the reminder that appellant "married appellee Sharon Kulko in 1959, during appellee's three-day stopover in California from a military base in Texas to a tour of duty in Korea," and that at the time, "both parties were domiciled in New York." The three-day stopover is an irrelevant fact, and appellee does not rest her claim for jurisdiction on it. And as the Court itself acknowledges, "nor did the California court."

By mentioning that the parties once lived together in New York, and merely stopped over in California, the Court attempts to minimize the parties' connections to California and maximize their relationship to New York. But personal jurisdiction is not a contest with one clear winner. Domicile in one state does not preclude personal jurisdiction in another. Moreover, we have long since abandoned the notion that personal jurisdiction exists only in the place in which a defendant is present. *McGee v. Int'l Life Ins. Co.*, 355 U.S. 220, 222 (1957). Current or former residents of one state, such as New York, can be subject to personal jurisdiction in the courts of another state, such as California, regardless of where they were married, where they lived during their marriage, and where they live now. Appellant could be subject to personal jurisdiction in several states at once, so long as the minimum contacts test was met in each one.

The Court also connects the parties and their children to New York. We are told that the parties lived in New York during their marriage, and that both of their children were born in New York. New York City is where "[t]he Kulkos and their two children resided together as a family" until the Kulkos separated. Also of note to the Court is that the parties' separation agreement was drafted in and executed in New York. These facts do not affect the determination as to whether appellant, an individual, is subject to jurisdiction in another state; an individual nonetheless can avail himself of the resources of another state, creating the basis for jurisdiction.

The Court's choice to focus on New York facts is misleading. Focusing on connections to New York sweeps in irrelevant information about appellee's New York-related actions, treating them as relevant to determining whether her ex-husband should be subject to jurisdiction in California. It also frames the parties' marriage as the defining event surrounding the Court's determination as to whether appellant should be subject to jurisdiction in California. Yet the first question the Court must answer is whether *appellant* had sufficient minimum contacts in California.

In addition to the emphasis on New York facts, the majority appears to demonize the appellee. For example, the Court reminds us that "[f]ollowing the separation, Sharon Kulko moved to San Francisco, California" and that she "remarried and took the name Horn." Her new name is of no consequence to this decision, yet the Court suggests its distaste for appellee's choice to leave one husband and then marry another. With respect to appellant, the Court highlights equally irrelevant facts to paint him in a favorable light, noting that "[w]hile Sharon Kulko waived any claim for her own support or maintenance, Ezra Kulko agreed to pay his wife $3,000 per year in child support."

The relevant facts, which give rise to this dispute, are as follows.

On September 25, 1972, the Civil Court of Port-au-Prince in the Republic of Haiti granted appellee Sharon Kulko a divorce decree from appellant Ezra Kulko. The parties had two children during their thirteen-year marriage: Darwin, born in 1961, and Ilsa, born in 1962. Pursuant to the parties' separation agreement, the children would reside with appellant while attending school, and would reside with appellee during the summer and during their Christmas and Easter vacations. Appellant agreed to pay $3,000 in annual child support in connection with the time the children resided with appellee. The divorce decree incorporated the terms of the separation agreement.

Following the parties' separation, appellant remained in New York, and appellee moved to California.

In December 1973, before leaving New York to spend the Christmas holiday with appellant, Ilsa told appellant that she wished to reside full-time with appellee in California. In response, appellant bought Ilsa a one-way ticket to California, and Ilsa left New York. Appellant permitted Ilsa to take all of her clothing with her. In 1974 and 1975, Ilsa lived with appellee during the school year, and spent each summer with her father in New York. At the conclusion of both summers, appellant purchased Ilsa's return tickets to California.

In January 1976, Darwin told appellee that he too wished to live with appellee in California. Appellee sent Darwin a plane ticket to San Francisco, and he joined her there.

B

On February 5, 1976, shortly after Darwin's permanent move to California, appellee filed an action in California Superior Court seeking to establish the foreign divorce decree as a California judgment; to award her full custody of Ilsa and Darwin; and to increase appellant's child support payments as the children would spend the majority of each year with their mother.

The Court highlights that appellee filed this action "[l]ess than one month after Darwin's arrival in California," but does not mention that at the time this action was commenced, Ilsa had spent the majority of each year with appellee since 1974. A fair characterization of the timing of this action is that appellee did not rush to court, as the Court suggests she did.

I also find it relevant, though the Court does not, that appellant declined to contest California's jurisdiction with respect to the issue of custody on appeal. He contested jurisdiction, as the Court notes, "with respect to the claim for increased [child] support." As a result, this is a case about financial obligations, a topic familiar to the Court's personal jurisdiction jurisprudence, and not about the custody of the parties' children. The California appellate court affirmed the lower court's summary denial of the motion to quash, reasoning that appellant's assent to his children's decision to move to California "caused an effect in th[e] state" that justified the exercise of jurisdiction. 63 Cal. App. 3d 417, 417 (1976).

The California Supreme Court agreed with the courts below, finding that appellant's decision to send Ilsa to live in California with appellee caused him to purposefully avail himself of the benefits and protections of California law. 19 Cal.3d 514 (1977). Moreover, California courts found that assertion of personal jurisdiction over appellant was reasonable.

II

A

The Court begins its discussion of controlling rules by introducing the Due Process Clause as one that "operates as a limit on the jurisdiction of state court to enter judgments affecting rights or interests of nonresident defendants." The Due Process Clause may, but does not always, limit jurisdiction over nonresident defendants. It limits jurisdiction only when an individual would be subject to binding judgments in a forum with which he has established no meaningful "contacts, ties, or relations." *International Shoe Co. v. Washington*, 326 U.S., at 319. The imposition of jurisdiction over nonresidents is never a surprise because we require "fair warning that a particular activity may subject [nonresidents] to the jurisdiction of a foreign sovereign." *Shaffer v. Heitner*, 433 U.S. 186, 218 (1977) (Stevens, J., concurring in judgment). A potential defendant should "reasonably anticipate" out-of-state litigation when he commits "some act" by which he "purposefully avails [himself] of the privilege of conducting activities within the forum State, thus invoking the benefits and protections of its laws." *Hanson v. Denckla*, 357 U.S. 235, 253 (1958).

This is a case about an interstate contract between two parties who were once married. But the Court's application of legal principles is muddled by reference to decisions not at issue here. It holds that personal jurisdiction over appellant could be based on neither his decision to marry appellee in

California, nor on appellant's agreement, at the time the parties separated, that his children could live in California with appellee for three months. Neither of these issues are at the heart of the parties' dispute, which appellant himself has narrowed to the question of whether he should be required to litigate his child support agreement in California.

In the context of interstate contracts, we have endorsed the exercise of jurisdiction over nonresidents when their activities "reach out beyond one state and create continuing relationships and obligations with citizens of another state ... in the latter state." *Travelers Health Ass'n v. Virginia*, 339 U.S. 643, 647 (1950). A defendant's connections with a state in which he does not reside is what provides fair warning of the potential exercise of jurisdiction in that state. For twenty years, we have recognized that "modern transportation and communications have made it much less burdensome for a party sued to defend himself in a State where he engages in economic activity," and therefore litigating claims related to that economic activity in another forum is fair. *McGee v. International Life Insurance Co.*, 355 U.S. 220, 223 (1957). In *McGee*, we held that a state judgment entered against a nonresident insurance company complied with due process and noted that such a judgment is proper where the suit at issue is "based on a contract which ha[s] substantial connection with [the forum]." *Id.*

Once we have decided that a nonresident defendant deliberately established minimum contacts with the forum state, these contacts and other factors will establish whether personal jurisdiction comports with "fair play and substantial justice." *International Shoe Co. v. Washington*, 326 U.S. at 320. We have noted that when a forum state has an interest in protecting its residents with respect to the fulfillment of contractual obligations, jurisdiction is appropriate. *Travelers*, 339 U.S. at 648. We have also considered the ability of plaintiffs to litigate outside of their state of residence; where such litigation would be expensive and troublesome, fairness justifies the exercise of jurisdiction in the plaintiffs' forum state. *Id.* at 648–49. Just like an insurance contract, a child support agreement controls a commercial transaction involving set payments. That the child support is the result of a failed marriage is no reason to artificially distinguish the agreement in question here from past agreements we have considered in our personal jurisdiction jurisprudence.

B

The Court works hard to recharacterize the subject of the parties' dispute as something other than litigation over contractually mandated support payments. The Court labels appellant's actions as passive rather than contractual;

for example, he merely consented to Ilsa's wish to reside with appellee in California. And the actual party to the agreement that established where the children would live – appellee – is erased.

Appellant's decision was made not as a result of a contract, the Court informs us, but due to his interests in "family harmony." The record is silent as to why appellant consented to Ilsa's decision to live with appellee. To the extent it rewards appellant for magnanimous behavior we would otherwise take for granted had it been undertaken by the appellee, we must turn away from the use of "romantic paternalism" when it has the effect of reinforcing gender stereotypes. *Frontiero v. Richardson*, 411 U.S. 677, 684, 93 S. Ct. 1764, 1769, 36 L. Ed. 2d 583 (1973). Paternalism has consequences here, serving to convert a contract into a benevolent decision stripped of legal meaning. And the stereotypes relied upon to reach the conclusion that appellant was acting in the interest of family harmony only benefit the husband. Appellee, the wife, is denigrated for her choices to move, to remarry, to change her name. Yet those choices may have also been made in the interest of family harmony.

One reasonable interpretation of appellant's assent is that he presumed it would be less expensive for him if his children resided with appellee for the majority of the year. The Court concedes that there may have been a "diminution in appellant's household costs," but without explanation, states that this has nothing to do with the child's presence in California, but instead derives from Ilsa's absence from New York. But the child did not disappear into thin air; the child's financial needs are as pressing as they were in New York and they remain the appellant's responsibility, regardless of the state in which appellee lives.

Turning back to interstate contractual principles, and our relevant jurisdictional rules, I agree with the Supreme Court of California that the exercise of jurisdiction was constitutional.

First, I agree with the forum state's courts that appellant's purposeful acts invoked the benefits and protections of California's laws. Here, appellant permitted his daughter to leave his home state and reside in California. As the California Supreme Court noted,

> [P]robably no parental act more fully invokes the benefits and protections of California law than that by which a parent permits his minor child to live in California. The parent thereby avails himself of the total panoply of the state's laws, institutions and resources - its police and fire protection, its school system, its hospital services, its recreational facilities, its libraries and museums, to mention only a few.
>
> 19 Cal. 3d at 522.

I agree that "a nonresident parent who allows his minor child or children to reside in California has by that act purposely availed himself of the benefits and protections of the laws of California to such an extent that absent unusual circumstances or countervailing public policies such act would support personal jurisdiction over the nonresident parent for actions concerning the support of these children." *Id.*

Appellant purchased Ilsa a one-way ticket to California in December 1973. With his consent, she brought all of her clothing with her to California. At the conclusion of appellant's summer visitation with Ilsa in 1974, he again purchased her a ticket to California so that Ilsa might spend the school year with her mother in California. He did the same in 1975. Ilsa permanently resides in California, and as a result of appellant's purposeful acts, appellant benefits from California's care and protection of Ilsa.

The Court characterizes the benefits appellant's daughter received in California as services provided to his daughter, but not to him, and that, moreover, he did not purposefully seek them out. Until children reach the age of majority, states, either on their own or working in tandem with parents, provide for children's well-being. A concrete example is the provision of a public education. If the state failed to do so, in most instances parents would be responsible for the unprovided services. The benefits and services provided to Ilsa do directly benefit appellant. Moreover, if Ilsa resided with appellant in New York, appellant could reasonably anticipate that she would receive services there, whether he sought them out or not. That a state provides services to a child without affirmatively seeking a parent's consent to do so is not dispositive with respect to personal jurisdiction. Rather, it is a benefit that a parent can reasonably anticipate, and the type of foreseeable benefit that justifies the exercise of personal jurisdiction.

These acts alone establish substantial connections with the forum state. Moreover, the negotiations appellant entered into with appellee, a California resident, further support the exercise of jurisdiction. Following Ilsa's move to California, appellant wrote appellee asking her to propose a "fair & equitable arrangement" that would supersede their original support agreement. 133 Cal. Rptr. 627, 628. That is, he attempted to renegotiate a contract with a resident of California.

As in *McGee*, the support agreement is a transaction that involves parties "separated by the full continent." Similar to *McGee*, here, innovation has rendered such transactions easy to enter into and alter. Indeed, the child support was payable in six installments to be sent to appellee's California address. I find it relevant to our minimum contacts analysis that appellant has the ability to engage in economic activity – supporting his children – in California.

Though our jurisprudence alone supports the exercise of personal jurisdiction, such an outcome complies with the RESTATEMENT (SECOND) OF CONFLICT OF LAWS, which endorses the exercise of jurisdiction over an individual who "causes effects in the state by an act done elsewhere with respect to any cause of action arising from these effects." RESTATEMENT (SECOND) OF CONFLICT OF LAWS § 37 (1971). The Court acknowledges that the effects test speaks to "commercial activity affecting state residents." The Restatement does not carve out an exception for agreements related to child support, though the Court apparently does.

Though its holding rests independently on the conclusion that appellant had no minimum contacts with California, the Court additionally explains why the exercise of jurisdiction over appellant would be unreasonable. It rests this conclusion on the absence of any claim that "appellant has visited physical injury on either property or persons within the State of California," even though the absence of physical injury is not dispositive. The Court again characterizes this case as one regarding "personal, domestic relations" as opposed to "commercial transactions in interstate commerce." Yet the parties are divorced, and custody is not at issue. This case turns on appellant's financial obligations under a contract, albeit one that arose because of the termination of personal, domestic relations. But the divorce resulted in a contract nonetheless.

I would have found that the exercise of personal jurisdiction is reasonable. In *McGee*, we gave weight to the forum's "manifest interest in providing effective means of redress for its residents when their insurers refuse to pay claims." *McGee*, 355 U.S. at 223. Similarly, California has an interest in ensuring that child support, intended to support its residents, is adequate. It also has an interest that the child support payments are actually made. Appellee, a resident of California, must provide for the "food, shelter, clothing, schooling, and other needs" of her children, 133 Cal. Rptr. at 628, permanent residents of California. In the absence of adequate child support, or child support payments that are never made, appellee's financial burden may become untenable. Without the ability to exercise jurisdiction over appellant, and thereby ensure that he helps adequately support his children, California may be forced to provide financial assistance to appellee and her children even though that obligation is one that appellant and appellee share.[1]

[1] California was the first state to employ long-arm jurisdiction statutes to enforce marital obligations. Cal. L. Raup, *State Court Jurisdiction: The Long-Arm Reaches Domestic Relations Cases*, 6 TEX. TECH L. REV. 1021, 1030 (1975).

The record does not suggest that appellant would be inconvenienced by litigating the issue of his child support obligations in California. What is known, however, is that the payment of child support has always flowed from appellant to appellee, suggesting that appellant's income is greater than appellee's. Appellant is in fact a doctor. Even when the parties' children resided for the majority of the year with appellant, appellee was never liable to appellant for support. In *McGee*, we were persuaded to support the exercise of jurisdiction over a nonresident if resident plaintiffs "were forced to follow the [nonresident defendant] to a distant State in order to hold it legally accountable." *Id.* at 223. I refuse to ask appellee to hold appellant legally accountable in a distant state.

Still, the Court is adamant that child support issues can easily be litigated by appellee in New York. Yet it can be inferred that appellee's economic status might render out-of-state litigation in New York expensive and troublesome, which is relevant to assessing "fair play and substantial justice." Witnesses that may speak to the children's needs and the particularities of their care, factors which will influence the amount of child support awarded, reside in California. Moreover, it is no secret that women earn significantly less than men. *See, e.g., Sail'er Inn, Inc. v. Kirby*, 5 Cal. 3d 1, 19 n. 20 (1971) (citing the 1970 report issued by the President's Task Force on Women, which concluded that white women earn $4,279 for year-round full-time employment, whereas white men earn $7,396 and black women earn $3,194 while black men earn $4,777) (citing A MATTER OF SIMPLE JUSTICE: THE REPORT OF THE PRESIDENT'S TASK FORCE ON WOMEN'S RIGHTS AND RESPONSIBILITIES 18 (1970)).

As noted above, women have fewer economic opportunities than men do, a situation exacerbated by our nation's "long and unfortunate history of sex discrimination." *Frontiero*, 411 U.S. at 684. The Task Force data, along with common sense, suggest that it would be a burden on appellee to litigate child support obligations in New York, but that it would not be a burden for appellant to litigate the same in California. This acknowledges a truth faced by most women who decide to leave a marriage: their earning capacity will never equal that of their former spouse.

Nonetheless, not only is appellee presumed to have the means to litigate her child support action in New York, she is criticized for living somewhere other than New York. The Court treats appellee's decision to move to California as a "basic consideration of fairness" that "point[s] decisively in favor of appellant's State of domicile as the proper forum for adjudication of this case" because while appellant remained in New York, appellee "moved across the continent."

Perhaps New York was a state in which appellee could no longer reside. The facts are silent as to why appellee moved. At a minimum, appellee's decision to leave New York should not influence the outcome here. We have disclaimed assumptions that place preservation of the domestic sphere on the shoulders of women alone. *Id.* at 684–85. Appellee should not be penalized for leaving a relationship or leaving a state after divorce. The Court's holding unreasonably limits the ability of a parent to move following a separation and divorce because even if her children follow her, she may lose the ability to litigate the issue of child support. As appellee has argued, if appellant prevails, "a custodial father will be able to relieve himself of the day-to-day responsibilities of raising children and, by the same acts, avoid his support duties."

The exercise of our jurisdictional principles leads me to agree with the California courts' conclusions, and also help avoid injustice. I therefore dissent.

8

Commentary on *Daly v. Daly*

RAFF DONELSON

INTRODUCTION

In *Daly v. Daly*,[1] the Supreme Court of Nevada upheld a district court decision to terminate a transwoman's parental rights, largely because of her gender identity. The woman at the heart of the case was Suzanne Daly. Suzanne (then Tim Daly) had been married to Nan Daly. Together, they had raised a daughter, Mary. After the dissolution of their marriage, Nan was granted custody over Mary, while Suzanne (still as Tim) enjoyed visitation rights with the child. Once Tim transitioned to become Suzanne, Nan sought, through legal and illegal means, to separate Mary from Suzanne, eventually petitioning a Nevada district court to terminate Suzanne's parental rights. The district court granted the petition, and the Supreme Court of Nevada affirmed.

The decision to terminate was 3-2, but both the majority opinion and the dissent are unfortunate reminders of the discrimination against trans persons then and now. This perhaps should come as little surprise, for it was an unfortunate time for the LGBT community. At the time of the decision, many jurisdictions saw homosexuality "as cause to deny custody to a parent and severely to restrict visitation."[2] Also, *Bowers v. Hardwick*,[3] the U.S. Supreme Court decision upholding Georgia's anti-sodomy statute against a due process challenge, was decided just three months after *Daly*. Professor Nancy Polikoff, writing as Justice Polikoff, pens an eloquent new majority opinion that corrects the mistakes of the original opinions in *Daly* and envisions a more tolerant world.

[1] 715 P.2d 56 (Nev. 1986), *overruled by In re Termination of Parental Rights as to N.J.*, 8 P.3d 126 (Nev. 2000).

[2] Katheryn D. Katz, *Majoritarian Morality and Parental Rights*, 52 Alb. L. Rev. 405, 455 (1988).

[3] 478 U.S. 186 (1986).

THE ORIGINAL OPINIONS

Suzanne Daly's case was decided by a divided court. Numerically speaking, she was close to victory, but a careful look at the reasoning and rhetoric in both the majority opinion and the dissent reveals another story. Suzanne and the trans community as a whole had no friends on the bench that day.

Both the majority and the dissent began their legal analyses by interpreting the Nevada statute that governed terminations of parental rights, Nevada Revised Statutes § 128.105. As the court understood the statute, at the time,[4] in order to terminate parental rights, a court first had to find parental fault, defined by courts as "jurisdictional grounds for termination."[5] A finding of parental fault allowed courts to move to the second inquiry, whether "termination is in the child's best interests,"[6] or "dispositional grounds"[7] for termination. Only upon finding both jurisdictional and dispositional grounds could a court rightly enter a judgment to terminate someone's parental rights.

The majority opinion, written by Justice Steffen, found both jurisdictional and dispositional grounds for termination. Steffen, following the district court decision below, heavily relied on the claim that Suzanne's lifestyle risked "serious physical, mental or emotional injury" to Mary.[8] Such risk is among the factors NRS § 128.105 listed as proof of the requisite parental fault. To prove that visiting with Suzanne would not be in Mary's best interest, the majority cited this risk of injury along with three other factors: (1) "Mary's revulsion over Suzanne,"[9] (2) that Suzanne's friends included "lesbians, homosexuals and transsexuals"[10] that she would not hide from Mary, and (3) that Suzanne was a "selfish person."[11] Evidence for the supposed selfishness lay in Suzanne's belief that she still could enjoy her fundamental right to parent[12] after undergoing a medically recommended surgery.

4 The Nevada Supreme Court later changed its interpretation of these termination provisions. *In re Termination*, 8 P.3d 126. More on that below.

5 *Daly*, 715 P.2d 56, 57 (Nev. 1986).

6 *Id.* at 59.

7 *Id.*

8 *Id.* at 58.

9 *Id.*

10 *Id.*

11 *Id.*

12 *Troxel v. Granville*, 530 U.S. 57, 65 (2000) ("the interest of parents in the care, custody, and control of their children – is perhaps the oldest of the fundamental liberty interests recognized by this Court"). The *Troxel* Court went on to cite the storied line cases that recognize this fundamental right, *e.g.*, *Meyer v. Nebraska*, 262 U.S. 390 (1923); *Pierce v. Soc'y of Sisters*, 268 U.S. 510 (1925); *Prince v. Massachusetts*, 321 U.S. 158 (1944); *Stanley v. Illinois*, 405 U.S. 645 (1972); and *Wisconsin v. Yoder*, 406 U.S. 205 (1972).

By transitioning, said the majority, "Suzanne … has terminated her own parental rights as a father."[13]

These were harsh words from the majority, but the dissent, though finding for Suzanne, was not much kinder. In many ways, it was worse. Justice Gunderson's dissent argued that there were neither jurisdictional nor dispositional grounds for terminating Suzanne's parental rights. Nonetheless, this was no full-throated endorsement of Suzanne or her capacity to parent. Indeed, it was a troubling dissent for three reasons.

First, throughout the dissent, Gunderson refused to refer to Suzanne with feminine pronouns. This was an unhappy departure from the majority opinion. This rhetorical issue was not just a slight to Suzanne; instead, it suggests that the state itself, through one of its most important representatives, will not recognize and respect trans folk for who they are. Justice Gunderson should have used feminine pronouns to refer to a trans woman, just as the majority did and just as other courts had done when dealing with trans litigants.[14]

Second, Gunderson opined that gender reassignment surgery is a mistake. He suggested this twice in a rather short opinion, and, in doing so, Gunderson only underscored the same transphobic message alluded to above. In one passage, Gunderson wrote that the surgery "may well yet be condemned as quackery."[15] Not so, as it turns out. Thirty years after *Daly*, the medical profession still recommends gender reassignment surgery as an appropriate treatment option for those suffering from gender dysphoria.[16] In another passage, Gunderson suggests that Suzanne "has followed the possibly poor advice of eminent medical authorities"[17] by undergoing surgery. Here, Gunderson raised ungrounded doubt about respected medical opinion. One can only wonder why Gunderson saw fit to cast doubt on Suzanne's doctors and course of treatment, since he was no medical professional himself and did not cite any countervailing authority, but the effect of his skepticism was to insult to Suzanne and other trans folk.

[13] *Daly*, 715 P.2d at 59.

[14] In looking at other cases involving trans individuals from the time, several courts used gender-appropriate language, *e.g.*, *Pinneke v. Preisser*, 623 F.2d 546, *passim* (8th Cir. 1980); *Rush v. Parham*, 625 F.2d 1150, *passim* (5th Cir. 1980). Of course, some did not, *e.g.*, *Cisek v. Cisek*, No. 80 C.A. 113, 1982 WL 6161, at *1 (Ohio Ct. App. July 20, 1982) (early case terminating a trans woman's visitation rights).

[15] *Daly*, 715 P.2d at 64 (Gunderson, J., dissenting).

[16] Cynthia S. Osborne & Anne A. Lawrence, *Male Prison Inmates with Gender Dysphoria: When Is Sex Reassignment Surgery Appropriate?*, 45 Archives Sexual Behav. 1649, 1649 (2016) ("Cross-sex hormone treatment and sex reassignment surgery (SRS) are widely accepted treatments for GD [gender dysphoria] or transsexualism").

[17] *Daly*, 715 P.2d at 64 (Gunderson, J., dissenting).

Third and most problematic of all, Gunderson's arguments for Suzanne largely turn on a technicality, and an incorrect one at that, rather than a genuine finding that Suzanne was a proper parent. The dissent repeatedly claims that the risk of emotional harm, found by the lower court and emphasized by the majority, will not materialize for Mary because Suzanne was not pursuing visitation rights, just retention of her parental rights. As Gunderson put it in one place, "it seems inappropriate to bottom a ruling against him [Suzanne] on the supposition that visitation with him could injure Mary."[18] As the primary basis for ruling for Suzanne, this argument is worrisome for two reasons. First, Gunderson would have had Suzanne win but only on the condition that she never visit her daughter. This is not a triumph for Suzanne or trans folk more broadly. Second, what Gunderson found "inappropriate" is required by the statute's plain language. The statute in question provided that termination can be warranted if there is "[r]isk of serious physical, mental or emotional injury to the child *if he were returned to, or remains in, the home of his parent or parents*."[19] Based on its plain language, the statute does not ask a court to discuss whether the child *will* return to or remain in the parent's home; rather, it asks courts to assess the risks the child would face if the child *were* in the parent's home. Gunderson seemed to argue that visitation should be denied only when visitation is risky for the child, while parental rights should be terminated only when retention of such rights is risky for the child. The statute, on the other hand, provides that parental rights shall be terminated when visitation is risky for the child. Although disentangling visitation from other parental rights has some logic, Gunderson's view was at odds with the law. The Nevada legislature had a point: if a person runs the kind of home a child should never visit, given its dangers, that person is unfit to parent.

THE FEMINIST JUDGMENT

Both the majority and dissenting opinions from *Daly* traffic in painful anti-trans sentiment. This is why the refreshing, reimagined feminist opinion from Justice Polikoff shines so brightly. Polikoff's magisterial opinion largely speaks for itself; however, some context may prove helpful. There were later developments in the law that are worth noting, and it is worthwhile to situate the opinion within feminist theory and feminist debate.

[18] *Id.* at 60.

[19] Nev. Rev. Stat. § 128.105 (1985).

First, about the law: *Daly* was overruled fourteen years later.[20] The overruling had nothing to do with trans issues. The Nevada Supreme Court found that it had misinterpreted the parental rights termination provisions. As the court explains in *In re Termination of Parental Rights as to N.J.*, the Nevada legislature amended the statute multiple times in order to encourage courts to adjudicate these suits differently.[21] Whereas courts had required a finding of parental fault, a jurisdictional ground, before it could broach the question of whether retention or termination of parental rights would best serve a child's interests, the legislature chose to make consideration of the child's best interests paramount.[22] In other words, the two-step inquiry was to be jettisoned in favor of a one-step inquiry – a best interests approach. Parental fault is now one factor to weigh in determining a child's best interests. This later development is relevant to Polikoff's opinion given how she disposes of the case. Polikoff finds no jurisdictional grounds for termination and concludes the inquiry, ruling in favor of Suzanne. Though she makes a passing comment about Mary's best interests, that is not the focus of her opinion. By not discussing the so-called dispositional grounds, Polikoff's feminist judgment would be superseded today.

Though Polikoff's judgment would be overruled today, that decision would have been a landmark in its time both because of its author and its precedential value. In 1986, it would have been remarkable to have a woman on the Nevada Supreme Court at all, for the state did not elect a woman to its highest court until 1992.[23] Polikoff's fictional opinion is set more than six years before the real Justice Miriam Shearing took her seat on the bench.[24] Second and perhaps more important, Polikoff's opinion would have had great precedential value. It is hard to prove a counterfactual; nevertheless, it seems undeniable that a pro-trans message from a conservative state's Supreme Court would have been both astounding and resounding at the time. While the original *Daly* decision may well have had a chilling effect, Polikoff's decision may have worked just the opposite effect: such an opinion could have inspired trans folk in Nevada and beyond to feel more at liberty to be themselves without fear that courts could cut their familial ties. Specifically, Polikoff's decision is sure to have impacted one contemporary case in another state, *M.B. v. D.W.*[25]

[20] *In re Termination*, 8 P.3d at 132 n. 4.

[21] *Id.* at 130–31.

[22] *Id.* at 131.

[23] Philip Hager, *Nevada Elects First Woman to High Court*, L.A. TIMES, Nov. 5, 1992, at A12.

[24] For more about Justice Shearing, *see* Mary Berkheiser, *Justice Miriam Shearing: Nevada's Trailblazing Minimalist*, 6 NEV. L.J. 156 (2005).

[25] 236 S.W.3d 31 (Ky. Ct. App. 2007).

This 2007 case reached the Kentucky Court of Appeals and relied on *Daly* in terminating a trans woman's parental rights. The cases bear an uncanny resemblance. Twenty years of progress by the LGBT movement[26] made the Kentucky court somewhat more forgiving of a decision to transition,[27] but the result was no different. That court unanimously followed *Daly* in holding that a trans woman's openness about her identity can cause enough emotional distress for her daughter that terminating parental rights is appropriate. No doubt, the Kentucky court's citations to *Daly* would have been different and the decision in *M.B. v. D.W.* might have changed if the Kentucky judges had to grapple with an opinion from Justice Polikoff. Even if the Kentucky court still had ruled against the trans woman, the decision would have required a more searching form of analysis to distinguish itself from the affirming opinion handed down by Justice Polikoff, which treats a very similar parent in a similar situation but comes out the other way.[28]

Having offered some legal context for better appreciating Polikoff's opinion, I now turn, in the final portion of this Commentary, to considering her opinion as a feminist text. If one thinks of the opinion as a *feminist* opinion, written in 1986, its sensitivity toward the plight of trans women would be extraordinary. In the mid-1980s, Suzanne Daly and others like her were under siege, not just from the Right but also from some feminist quarters. Just a few years before the litigation began in *Daly*, Janice Raymond wrote *The*

[26] In the twenty years between *Daly* and *M.B.*, the LGBT movement made great strides in terms of legal victories and social acceptance. On the legal side, *see Romer v. Evans*, 517 U.S. 620 (1996) (striking down Colorado's anti-gay Amendment 2); *Lawrence v. Texas*, 539 U.S. 558 (2003) (legalizing sodomy); *Goodridge v. Dep't of Pub. Health*, 440 Mass. 309 (2003) (legalizing same-sex marriage). On the social acceptance side, Barney Frank came out in 1987, making him the first openly LGBT member of Congress; the 1990s featured primetime television shows with openly gay and lesbian lead characters, *e.g.*, *Ellen* and *Will and Grace*; eventually, Hollywood would give voice to trans characters in big-budget films like the 1999 docudrama *Boys Don't Cry* and the 2005 film *Transamerica*.

[27] "Neither do we hold that a parent's undergoing gender reassignment is, in itself, grounds for such termination." *M.B. v. D.W.*, 236 S.W.3d at 38.

[28] According to esteemed civil rights activist and litigator Shannon Price Minter, "[w]hile recent custody decisions about transgender parents are less likely to display overt bias, they often reflect more subtle forms of discrimination. One common theme is a tendency to subject a parent's transition process to extremely close scrutiny and to penalize the parent for any possible missteps or failures of judgment." Shannon Price Minter, *Transgender Family Law*, 56 FAM. CT. REV. 410, 417 (2018). This is certainly what happened in the Kentucky case because the court relied heavily on the fact that the trans parent transitioned and then appeared before her daughter without warning her of the changes. While this tendency is present today, modern courts would have to do some distinguishing work, for there is similarity with *Daly*. In Polikoff's opinion, she recognizes that Suzanne made a parenting mistake, yet Polikoff still found for her because the mistake was minor and does not justify terminating parental rights.

Transsexual Empire. Raymond's book argues that trans women are just men who perpetrate patriarchy by unusual means. Male-to-female transsexuality was, for Raymond, an "attempt to wrest from women the power inherent in female biology."[29] In another place, Raymond claimed that male-to-female gender reassignment surgery is an attempt "to make the biological woman obsolete by the creation of man-made 'she-males.'"[30]

Raymond's style of feminism will shock some contemporary readers. As Julia Serano notes, many feminists today "especially younger ones who came of age in the 1980s and 1990s ... recognize that trans women can be allies in the fight to eliminate gender stereotypes."[31] Nonetheless, as Serano continues, "other feminists – particularly those who embrace gender essentialism – believe that trans women foster sexism by mimicking patriarchal attitudes about femininity."[32] Gender-essentialist feminism, or what some characterize as "Second Wave feminism,"[33] was at its height in the late 1970s when Raymond was writing.[34] Polikoff's opinion, if we think of it as an intervention in mid-1980s feminist thought, would serve as a reminder that the Second Wave, revolutionary as it may have been, offers a limited vision of the emancipatory potential of feminism.[35] Indeed, Polikoff's opinion can be seen to anticipate later feminist thinkers who recognize "that most transgendered people are daily the victims of the most intense and public attempts to discipline gender in ways feminists have long criticized."[36]

[29] Janice G. Raymond, The Transsexual Empire xvi (1979).

[30] *Id.* at xvii.

[31] Julia Serano, *Skirt Chasers: Why the Media Depicts the Trans Revolution in Lipstick and Heels*, *in* The Transgender Studies Reader 2, 226, 231 (Susan Stryker & Aren Z. Aizura eds., 2013).

[32] *Id.*

[33] There is scholarly dispute about what unifies the Second Wave, when it begins, when it ends, and whether the periodization of feminism into "waves" is useful. For description of these disputes, *see* Linda Nicholson, *Introduction*, *in* The Second Wave: A Reader in Feminist Theory (Linda Nicholson ed., 1997). For the purposes of this text, I consider the Second Wave a loose movement in the academy and beyond, united behind the idea that women constitute a uniquely oppressed class. This uniting idea entails a kind of commonality among women and a deep difference between women and men. Theoretical commitment to this supposed commonality among women and the supposed difference from men is what I mean by *gender essentialism*.

[34] Other titles from the time include Mary Daly, Gyn/Ecology: The Metaethics of Radical Feminism (1978). Raymond was Daly's doctoral student. Michelle Goldberg, *What Is a Woman?*, New Yorker, Aug. 4, 2014, https://www.newyorker.com/magazine/2014/08/04/woman-2

[35] *See* Janet Halley, Split Decisions: How and Why to Take a Break from Feminism 260–73 (2008).

[36] Cressida Heyes, *Feminist Solidarity after Queer Theory: The Case of Transgender*, *in* Transgender Studies , *supra* note 31, at 201, 202.

Polikoff's pro-trans message is not just useful as a foil for feminists from forty years ago. While few speak with Raymond's ardor, there are more recent instances of feminist theory[37] and praxis[38] that remain unsympathetic to trans women. As Cressida Heyes points out, "much of what has been written about trans people by non-trans feminists has not only been hostile, but has also taken an explicit *dis*identification with transsexuals' experiences as its critical standpoint."[39] As such, "'trans liberation' and 'feminism' have often been cast as opposing movements."[40] This opposition has reared its head quite a few times. The Kimberly Nixon case and the Michfest affair stand out as two of the more notorious incidents in recent memory.

Kimberly Nixon, a trans woman and sexual assault survivor, sought to enter the Vancouver Rape Relief (VRR) volunteer training program in 1995.[41] In this program, volunteers would learn to provide assistance and counseling to women survivors of rape and other gender-based violence. During Nixon's first training session, someone from VRR suspected that Nixon was transgender.[42] Upon confirmation, VRR removed Nixon from the program on grounds that all volunteers had to be cis women. VRR reasoned that Nixon would not be able to empathize properly with survivors who came seeking help because Nixon had not lived her entire life as a woman. Of course, there was no rule that one live one's entire life as woman, just that one be a cis woman. VRR was apparently unpersuaded by the fact that Nixon's experience as a sexual assault survivor might make her particularly well-suited for connecting with some of the assistance-seekers. Nixon, in turn, sued VRR in the British Columbia Human Rights Tribunal, claiming that the British Columbia Human Rights Code forbade the anti-trans discrimination in which the group engaged. Nixon won at the Tribunal, only to lose when VRR successfully appealed to the Supreme Court of British Columbia.[43] Nixon then appealed

[37] *See, e.g.*, BERNICE HAUSMAN, CHANGING SEX: TRANSSEXUALISM, TECHNOLOGY, AND THE IDEA OF GENDER (1995); SHEILA JEFFREYS, GENDER HURTS: A FEMINIST ANALYSIS OF THE POLITICS OF TRANSGENDERISM (2014).

[38] Deep Green Resistance as well as Lisa Vogel, founder of Michfest, are examples of prominent, non-academic feminist activists who see themselves as aiming for a better world for women, while intentionally excluding and marginalizing trans women. *See* Goldberg, *supra* note 34.

[39] Heyes, *supra* note 36, at 203.

[40] *Id.* at 202.

[41] For the details of this case, I rely on Lori Chambers, *Unprincipled Exclusions: Feminist Theory, Transgender Jurisprudence, and Kimberly Nixon*, 19 CAN. J. WOMEN & L. 305 (2007).

[42] *Nixon v. Vancouver Rape Relief Society*, 2002 BCHRT 1, para. 26

[43] *Nixon v. Vancouver Rape Relief Society*, 2003 BCSC 1936, para. 120 ("I find the Tribunal failed to correctly interpret and apply the Supreme Court of Canada decision in Caldwell on of the application of s. 41 in this case and that its conclusion that s. 41 did not permit Rape Relief to exclude Ms. Nixon from its peer counselling training program was unreasonable").

to the highest court of British Columbia, only to lose again.[44] The litigation resolved twelve years after it began when Nixon appealed a final time, only to meet a denial of certiorari from the Canadian Supreme Court.[45]

Lest one think that contemporary cases of anti-trans feminism is a Canadian anomaly, it is useful to recall the more recent Michfest Affair. Michfest, or the Michigan Womyn's Music Festival, was a popular, outdoor festival for women to enjoy music, food, community, and safety in a space exclusively for women and girls.[46] The festival, founded in 1976, lasted for forty years. Its abrupt closure in 2015 may have stemmed from its trans-exclusionary policies.[47] The founder, Lisa Vogel, barred trans women from attendance, and this policy, as North American feminism has grown more inclusive, caused dissension, and various performers began to boycott the event.[48]

CONCLUSION

These incidents are not stories from long ago. They highlight that, even in the twenty-first century, there are cis-women feminists who cannot see trans-women feminists as foot soldiers in the same battle, fighting the same foe. These stories also demonstrate that gender essentialism, a root cause of the conflict between trans liberation and feminism, is not dead yet. This is just one reason why Justice Polikoff's opinion, which respects trans identity, calls out bigotry, and boldly champions the rights of a trans woman, is just as needed now as it would have been in 1986.

DALY *v.* DALY, 715 P.2D 56 (NEV. 1986)

CHIEF JUSTICE POLIKOFF DELIVERED THE OPINION OF THE COURT

Appellant, Suzanne Daly, appeals the lower court order terminating her parental rights. Because the district court failed to properly apply the statute authorizing such termination, we reverse.

The Supreme Court of British Columbia is an intermediate court, hearing both trials and appeals from within the province.

44 *Nixon v. Vancouver Rape Relief Society*, 2005 BCCA 601.

45 *Nixon v. Vancouver Rape Relief Society*, 2007 Carswell BC 222.

46 Goldberg, *supra* note 34.

47 Trudy Ring, *This Year's Michigan Womyn's Music Festival Will Be the Last*, THE ADVOCATE, Apr. 21, 2015, https://www.advocate.com/michfest/2015/04/21/years-michigan-womyns-music-festival-will-be-last

48 *Id.* ("The exclusion of transgender women from the fest has led performers such as the Indigo Girls, Antigone Rising, and Lea DeLaria to withdraw from the event").

Appellant was born Tim Daly and is the biological father of Mary Toews Daly, the child at issue in this case. Tim Daly's name was changed to Suzanne Daly by order of the court on December 9, 1982. Respondent Nan Daly is the biological mother of Mary Daly.[1] The parties were married on September 17, 1969, at Oakland, California. The minor child, Mary Toews Daly, was born on August 21, 1973, at Oakland. The parties are both employed full-time. Nan is a secretary at the Desert Research Library Institute in Reno, Nevada. Suzanne is a Scientific Research Specialist at the Berkeley Laboratory at the University of California at Berkeley.

The family lived in Oakland for the first five years of the child's life. In August, 1978, Nan, Mary, and Nan's mother moved into a home in Reno, Nevada. Nan testified that Tim did not live in the Reno home but visited there while maintaining the family home in Oakland. Tim saw Mary every four to six weeks, when he would come to Reno and stay for three to four days. In May 1979, Tim informed Nan that he wanted a divorce. A final decree of divorce was entered on February 17, 1981, at Reno, Nevada, in the Second Judicial District Court. Nan was awarded custody and control of Mary, subject to the visitation rights of Tim. Initially, Tim regularly exercised visitation rights under the decree, including the entire month of August 1981, and again in October 1981 and January 1982. The parties' relationship during this period was not cordial. Each testified to disputes about finalizing the property matters contained in the divorce decree, payment of child support, and visitation.

Nan testified that Tim had been a violent alcoholic. Her accusations were serious and would have been accorded great weight in a proceeding to restrict Tim's visitation rights had they been established at the time of the divorce. Because the issues were not raised at that time; because the present action was filed entirely on the basis that Tim is a transsexual; and because the lower court's order did not mention or make findings about these accusations, this court will not address them.

The matters leading to the present action began in August 1981 when Mary was visiting Suzanne in Oakland. During that visitation, father and child engaged in their usual activities, including reading, playing, talking, and going to museums. Suzanne sometimes took Mary to work with him, where she would show her a variety of things in the laboratory and the Hall

[1] For ease of reference, this opinion refers to the appellant as Tim (and the male pronoun) during the period of the marriage and subsequent contact with Nan and Mary through August 1981, and as Suzanne (and the female pronoun) from the period of her transition in California beginning in 1981, including the time Mary visited her there. The record contains neither the exact date Tim began using the name Suzanne nor when, or whether, he began using the name in Mary's presence.

of Science. The parties agree that Mary is a highly intelligent, thoughtful, and verbal child.

During this month of visitation, Suzanne discussed with Mary that she was changing. In the context of discussing a blouse that Suzanne bought for Mary as a birthday present, Suzanne told Mary that she was wearing women's clothing. A few days later, Suzanne was removing the male underwear from her dresser and told Mary she was getting rid of "guy stuff." Mary responded to this by saying that he was a guy, and Suzanne responded that it was true but that she did not want to be and that she did not need to be and so she would not be in the future. She had other similar conversations with Mary, including about pretty clothes that they both liked and about hairstyles. At the end of this month-long visit, as Suzanne was preparing to return Mary to Reno, she told Mary that she did not think she should tell her mother and grandmother about the changes she was making as they would probably try to use it against her.

At Suzanne's subsequent visitation with Mary in October 1981, she took Mary to a rap group session for transsexuals at the Pacific Center for Human Growth Awareness (hereinafter "Center"), where Suzanne was also a volunteer. The Executive Director of the Center, Andrea Canaan, a social worker, testified that she observed Suzanne and Mary together and that their relationship appeared to be "fun," "calm," and "well-balanced." Mary visited Suzanne again in January 1982.

In February 1982, Mary told her mother that her father was a transsexual. Nan described Mary as calm and mature during the conversation, but said that Mary ended up in tears. Mary told her mother of the meetings she attended with other transsexuals. Nan testified that Mary told her of her father saying she should not tell her mother or grandmother.

Nan testified that two days later, on February 16, 1982, she took Mary to a child psychologist named Dr. Towle. Dr. Towle was not a witness at the hearing in the court below. From that time until the present, Nan has not permitted Suzanne to exercise the visitation rights provided for in the divorce decree. Nan did not file a petition in the district court to modify that decree. She admitted that she made a decision to cut off visitation, acting on her own authority as Mary's mother. When Suzanne arrived for scheduled February visitation with Mary, Nan called the Sheriff and reported Suzanne as violent, and on Nan's direction the Sheriff told Suzanne that she could not visit with Mary and should talk to her lawyer. On May 12, 1982, Nan filed the instant petition to terminate parental rights.

We summarize the trial testimony in this case as follows, to permit the proper application of the law to the ruling below.

Nan Daly testified to the matters above. In addition, she described Mary as a changed child when she returned from visiting her father in August 1981. Nan described Mary as hyper; going from being wide awake to very sluggish; sitting at the kitchen counter for hours cutting paper into small pieces; spending hours tracing the grain of the oak floors; wetting the bed; having a very short attention span; being unable to follow instructions or perform simple tasks; acting like an infant; being inattentive; having scrawled handwriting; not getting along with her classmates; and being withdrawn. On cross-examination, Nan confirmed that she did not discuss her concerns about Mary with anyone during this time and that she did not seek professional counseling for her. Nan did not call any witness, including her mother who lived in the home with her and Mary, to corroborate her allegations that Mary behaved differently when she returned from her August 1981 visit with her father.

Nan testified that it was in her daughter's best interests that her father's parental rights be terminated. She stated that she could not accept the person sitting in the courtroom as her ex-husband; that by definition a father is a male figure; and that she and Mary were being asked to accept something bizarre and abnormal. She speculated that Mary would be unable to form a relationship with the other sex or even with other girls because of the secret about her father. She stated that it was not in Mary's best interests to be in the company of transsexuals, transvestites, and homosexuals.

On cross-examination, Nan admitted that she failed to pick up a package for her daughter from Suzanne that was sent for Mary's birthday in August 1982. Nan had a conversation with Mary about the package and asked her to think about whether she wanted to receive it. She stated that Mary did not respond to her. Nan also admitted to a conversation with the principal of Mary's school on January 31, 1983, when Suzanne, in the company of her attorney, approached the principal about seeing Mary. Nan told the principal that it would be contempt of court to permit Suzanne to see Mary, although the only court order in effect at the time was the divorce decree which did authorize visitation. Nan testified that her justification was that the divorce decree gave her full legal custody and that she had filed the termination petition. Later that day, when Suzanne and her attorney approached the home where Mary resides with her mother and grandmother, the grandmother came out of the home with a rifle and pointed it at their car. In February 1983, Nan filed for and obtained a court order restraining Suzanne from attempting to contact Mary. Nan stated categorically of the period in question that, "I have refused to allow Mary to see her father." Transcript of Trial Court Proceedings, Record on Appeal at 299, *Daly v. Daly*, 102 Nev. 66 (1986) (No. 15423).

Nan testified that she had told Mary that the hearing before the court concerned termination of her father's parental rights and that she was doing it for Mary's protection. When asked on cross-examination what she was protecting Mary from, she testified as follows: "that the person her father has become is not representative of the type of people she goes to school with. It's not representative of the parents of her classmates. It's not representative of the community in which we live. It's not representative of the County of Washoe or of this State." Transcript of Trial Court Proceedings, Record on Appeal at 265–66. She also testified that she was unwilling to help Mary deal with the fact that her father was now a woman; that it was not healthy for Mary to have to deal with that; and that "Mary's father doesn't exist anymore." Transcript of Trial Court Proceedings, Record on Appeal at 263.

Dr. Richard Weiher testified in support of Nan's petition. He interviewed both Nan and Mary on February 7, 1983, approximately two weeks before the hearing below. He spent one hour with Mary. He found Mary to be a happy and well-adjusted child who was anxious about the court hearing. On the basis of his hour with Mary he concluded that she was not prepared to adjust emotionally to her father's transition and he recommended that Suzanne not be permitted to visit with Mary. When questioned whether there was a serious risk or emotional or mental injury to Mary if she were allowed to be in her father's presence, he said, "Yes." Transcript of Trial Court Proceedings, Record on Appeal at 56.

Dr. Weiher also testified that Mary was "still coping with her own gender identity and that has yet to gel." Transcript of Trial Court Proceedings, Record on Appeal at 61. He elaborated that "she still has some questions about how she is likely to be . . . she is far from having made all the decisions about how she is going to conduct herself as a young lady or as a woman." Transcript of Trial Court Proceedings, Record on Appeal at 63. He also testified that Nan Daly was unwilling to go to the lengths required to affect a reconciliation between Suzanne and Mary and that Nan's disapproval of Suzanne contributed to Mary's confusion.

Nan called two additional witnesses. Carol Mueller, a program assistant in the Academically Talented Program in which Mary had been enrolled for two and a half years, testified that Mary was gifted and well-adjusted and also stated that she was not aware of any particular positive or negative change in Mary over those two and a half years. Margaret Ann Weien, a neighbor and friend, testified that her son and Mary have been in school together since kindergarten and saw each other frequently. She described Mary as a very quiet child who was normal and polite and played and did "kid things." Transcript of Trial Court Proceedings, Record on Appeal at 91. She had never heard Mary speak about her father. On cross-examination she stated that Mary had not appeared outwardly bothered in the previous year or two.

Appellant Suzanne Daly called as a witness Dr. Ira Pauly, a psychiatrist with an expertise in gender dysphoria, otherwise known as transsexualism. Dr. Pauly did not interview any of the parties in this case and testified solely as an expert witness. Dr. Pauly has treated approximately 200 transsexuals, and he published the first large review of the literature on male-to-female transsexuals over twenty years ago, in 1965. Ira B. Pauly, *Male Psychosexual Inversion: Transsexualism: A Review of 100 Cases*, 12 ARCHIVES OF GENERAL PSYCHIATRY 172 (1965).[2] He testified that transsexuals are as fixed in their gender identity as those who, in his words, are "fortunate enough to be born into a body which coincides with [their] psychological gender identity." Transcript of Trial Court Proceedings, Record on Appeal at 100, *Daly v. Daly*, 102 Nev. 66 (1986) (No. 15423). He also distinguished transsexualism from homosexuality, clarifying that homosexuals do not think of themselves as born into the wrong body.

Dr. Pauly testified to the standard of care for individuals undergoing sex reassignment, including the Real Life Test, which consists of a year of living in the individual's choice of gender. For a biological male, this involves living full-time, changing one's name, and assuming a female identity.

On the subject of parenting, Dr. Pauly testified that there is very little data on this subject in the literature because it is a relatively new phenomenon. He personally had experience with between five and ten patients who were parents, and two or three whose children he had contact with. He had experience with children and stepchildren working through the parent's transition well and also with some who were not able to accept the situation and it did not work out well. In his opinion, there was nothing about transsexualism that determined whether it would work out. Rather, he testified, who the people were and what kind of human beings they were would determine the outcome. He also testified that children have generally seen cross-gender behavior or cross-dressing and that the revelation of gender transition is not always as big a surprise as the non-transsexual parent had feared.

[2] Dr. Pauly's impressive body of work includes over a dozen articles. In a recent article, he and co-author Milton Edgerton note that approximately fifty articles on the subject of transsexualism, which they deem "a new medical subspecialty," have been published every year since 1970. Ira B. Pauly & Milton T. Edgerton, *The Gender Identity Movement: A Growing Surgical-Psychiatric Liaison*, 15 ARCHIVES OF SEXUAL BEHAVIOR 315, 319 (1986). They further note that standards of care for those with gender dysphoria were published in 1979, and that over 150 researchers meet every other year to share their work at the Harry Benjamin Internal Gender Dysphoria Symposium. *Id.* at 318.

With respect to the wishes of the child, Dr. Pauly testified that the child's wishes should be taken into account but that the child's desires are usually shaped by the custodial parent. He said it would be necessary to carefully evaluate whether the child's opinion is truly his or her own or has been biased by the parent with whom they have been living.

Dr. Robert Kenney, a physicist at Berkeley Laboratory who knew Suzanne Daly for sixteen or seventeen years, testified that he had observed Suzanne and Mary together before Suzanne's transition, that he had seen love between them, and that "Mary was the apple of Tim's eye," something he described as "quite obvious." Transcript of Trial Court Proceedings, Record on Appeal at 127. When Suzanne brought Mary to work or to lunch with co-workers, Dr. Kenney saw her as very bright and able to engage in conversations among adults. He said he personally enjoyed having Mary along, as did other fellow-employees. During Mary's month-long visit with Suzanne in 1981, Dr. Kenney saw Mary frequently at the lab with her father. They would have a short chat each time. He testified that Mary did not seem any different during her August 1981 time with her father than she had seemed on earlier occasions. He described Suzanne as a loving and caring parent and said that he would strive to be like Suzanne as a parent.

Appellant called Lynn Frazier, a licensed Marriage, Family and Child Counselor in San Francisco with a certificate in Human Sexuality from the University of California Medical Center and an expertise in counseling transsexuals. Ms. Frazier evaluated Suzanne Daly over five sessions, following the requisite standards of care, and determined that she was an appropriate candidate for sex reassignment. She had also seen Suzanne on numerous occasions as the facilitator of a rap group for transsexuals at the Pacific Center.

Ms. Frazier testified that Suzanne Daly was slightly depressed upon initial evaluation and that she improved decidedly when she began cross-living. She has become a role model at the Pacific Center. She described Suzanne's adjustment to the Real Life Test as being very good, probably better than transsexuals as a whole.

Ms. Frazier has counseled about ten transsexuals who were parents and testified that it is important for the parents to work out an amicable solution. She testified that Suzanne talks about Mary with great caring and is very concerned about her welfare. She cries when she reports being unable to see Mary. Ms. Frazier did not believe that how Suzanne introduced Mary to her transsexualism showed poor judgment. She did not believe it was harmful for a nine-year-old to attend a rap session. She said that watching a parent go through a transition can be traumatic for a child but that counseling for the child is helpful in that regard. She testified that it was important for Mary to have a relationship with both her parents and that there was no stigma in having Mary attend therapy to help her understand that her father is now a woman.

When asked about possible stigma to Mary from her peers at school, Ms. Frazier testified that such stigma would pass if the child was supported at home. When asked what would happen if the natural mother could not accept the transition, Ms. Frazier stated that it would be like any situation where divorced parents cannot agree on something important. In that instance they should try to get together in the best interest of the child. She testified that she has seen acceptance and understanding over time with family members, especially when they receive some education about transsexuality. At one point in cross-examination, counsel for the Respondent asked Ms. Frazier if "homosexuals, transsexuals, and all the perverts" were more accepted in San Francisco than in Reno. Ms. Frazier resisted the term "perversion" and noted that sex roles were becoming less rigidly defined. Transcript of Trial Court Proceedings, Record on Appeal at 166.

Suzanne Daly testified that after Nan refused to let her see Mary she contacted her previous attorney, but that attorney refused to file an action to enforce visitation because she was a transsexual. The attorney also refused to turn over her case file. Suzanne testified about her efforts to see Mary and to contact her, all of which were thwarted by Nan.

When cross-examined about whether she had lesbians, homosexuals, and transsexuals in her home, Suzanne said she did. When asked if she considered those individuals normal, she said yes. She also testified that she had no hesitation about Mary spending time with her friends, including those who were lesbians, homosexuals, and transsexuals, because they are wonderful people. When asked whether it would impair Mary's mental health to guide her to accept a lifestyle with lesbians, transsexuals, and homosexuals, Suzanne answered, "Certainly not. It's hatred and bigotry that's [sic] a danger to her mental health." Transcript of Trial Court Proceedings, Record on Appeal at 333.

I THE RULING BELOW

There is surprisingly little dispute about the facts of this case. From those facts, however, the trial court below drew a number of unwarranted conclusions. These include the following: that if Suzanne has visitation there is a risk that Mary will be in "an environment of persons who prefer sexual minorities which are not normal or typical or are irregular and not generally accepted by society"; that Mary is under emotional distress over the current situation; that

Suzanne is selfish and is not thinking in a realistic way about Mary; that wanting Mary to accept her shows disregard for Mary's welfare; that Suzanne has very serious emotional problems; that "Mary doesn't need exposure to a person who has what Dr. Pauly calls a 'gender identity' problem or who is undergoing psychotherapy treatment for the same, which is dramatic and emotional." Decision in the Second Judicial District Court of the State of Nevada in and for the County of Washoe, In the Matter of the Parental Rights as to Mary Toews Daly, Minor Child at 4–5, No. 82-3979 (1983).

The court was also mindful of what it called the "distressing situation" between Mary's parents, which it found "permeated the entire proceedings." *Id.* at 5. The court continued that it was "mindful that hostility and alienation, originating with the custodial, nontranssexual parent, are common and frequently result in a poisoning of the relationship between the transsexual parent and the child." *Id.* The court concluded that failure to terminate Suzanne's parental rights would cause the Dalys to be faced with multiple problems and that "there is a serious risk of physical, mental and emotional harm to this child should we take this chance." *Id.*

Further findings of the court were that Mary stated generally in chambers that she did not want to be with her father and that he doesn't exist anymore; that the situation impairs the child's emotional development; and that "the anxiety and confusion created over this termination proceeding is not to the advantage of the child." Decision in the Second Judicial District Court of the State of Nevada in and for the County of Washoe, In the Matter of the Parental Rights as to Mary Toews Daly, Minor Child at 6, No. 82-3979 (1983).

II DISCUSSION

The court below skated around the most pertinent facts in this case. Respondent Nan Daly was understandably confused and distressed about her ex-husband's transsexual status. In response, however, she took it upon herself to violate the terms of the divorce decree and withhold visitation from the appellant, Suzanne Daly. She also embarked on a systematic campaign to alienate Mary from her father, a campaign that for all appearances was effective. She then sought a coup de grace – the severance of Suzanne's parental rights – and she has the temerity to base her claim on the lack of contact between Suzanne and Mary for seventeen months, a lack of contact she orchestrated and enforced, all without approval from the courts of this state.

The proceedings below were infused with insinuations and bigotry, none of which concerned the core issue in this case – Mary's relationship with her father. Suzanne is a transsexual. She has friends who are transsexual and also friends who are gay and lesbian. The lower court referred to such individuals as "not normal or typical," but there was no evidence whatsoever that any of these individuals had or would harm Mary in any way. Decision in the Second Judicial District Court of the State of Nevada in and for the County of Washoe, In the Matter of the Parental Rights as to Mary Toews Daly, Minor Child at 4, No. 82-3979 (1983).

This court discounts entirely the testimony of Dr. Weiher who, in preparation for the hearing below, spent one hour with Mary. He spoke with Nan before meeting Mary and relied on the facts provided by Nan. He was unaware, for example, that Mary had willingly visited her father in Oakland twice after the visit during which Mary learned of her father's transition and before she spoke with her mother about it.

By the time Dr. Weiher spoke with Mary she had been victimized by her mother's antipathy towards her father for more than a year. Dr. Weiher also testified there was no risk of emotional harm to Mary from being permanently deprived of all contact with her father. While such a conclusion may be accurate in some instances, it strains credulity to reach such a conclusion on the basis of such scant evidence and without observing Mary and her father together. In *Chapman v. Chapman*, 607 P.2d 1141 (Nev. 1980), we noted that

> the record does not contain any [psychological] evidence . . . as to the child's relationship with her mother . . . While there may be cases which are so clear that such evidence is not necessary, because the "best interests" of the child require the severance of all ties with the natural parent despite a "due regard . . . to any and all ties of blood and affection," this case is not one of them.
>
> *Id.* at 1145.

That reasoning equally applies to the lack of evidence below concerning Mary's relationship with her father.

We note that Nan did not call as a witness Dr. Towle, who examined Mary immediately after Mary told Nan about her father's transition. The trial court therefore lacked any credible, contemporaneous expert evidence of the impact on Mary of her father's transition or her visits with her father in 1981 and 1982.

This court is aware that Suzanne's decision to tell Mary of his transition and to tell her not to discuss this with her mother placed Mary in an awkward position. Instructing a child to keep a secret from her other parent is not in the child's best interests. Suzanne's poor judgment in this matter, however, pales in comparison with Nan's active hostility toward Suzanne. In conveying that hostility to Mary, Nan has acted against Mary's best interests.

III THE LAW

This is not a dispute over custody or visitation rights. It is a proceeding to permanently sever Suzanne's status as Mary's legal father. Termination of parental rights requires a two-step process. First, there must be jurisdictional grounds authorizing termination, proven by clear and convincing evidence. Nevada Revised Statutes 128.105 recognizes the following jurisdictional grounds:

1. Abandonment of the child;
2. Neglect of the child;
3. Unfitness of the parent;
4. Risk of serious physical, mental or emotional injury to the child if he were returned to, or remains in, the home of his parent or parents;
5. Only token efforts by the parent or parents:
   (a) To support or communicate with the child;
   (b) To prevent neglect of the child;
   (c) To avoid being an unfit parent;
   (d) To eliminate the risk of serious physical, mental or emotional injury to the child, or
6. With respect to termination of parental rights of one parent, the abandonment by that parent.

If jurisdictional grounds are proven, the court then determines if termination is in the child's best interests. If jurisdictional grounds are not proven, the analysis ends and termination is denied. The party seeking termination has the burden of proving the requisite elements by clear and convincing evidence. *Santosky v. Kramer*, 455 U.S. 745 (1982); *Champagne v. Welfare Div. of Nev. State Dept. of Human Resources*, 691 P.2d (Nev. 1984). We apply the statute in light of the evidence adduced at trial, mindful to reverse findings of fact by the trial court only when they are clearly erroneous.

Suzanne has not abandoned her daughter. The trial court found that Suzanne was denied contact with Mary after Mary revealed to Nan that her father was a transsexual. The trial court also found that Suzanne's efforts to exercise visitation were frustrated. In *In re Adoption of Doe*, 101 N.M. 34, 677 P.2d 1070 (N.M. 1984), termination of parental rights was unjustified where the petitioning grandparents had prevented the mother from having any meaningful contact with her children: "Petition … should not be granted because [the grandparents] by their own conduct have been instrumental in helping to destroy the parent-child relationship." *Id.* at 1072. We adopt such reasoning.

Suzanne has not neglected her daughter. Witnesses to the most recent visitation between Suzanne and Mary testified to a warm and loving parent-child relationship.

Suzanne is not an unfit parent. The court below said the following about Suzanne's fitness:

> If the natural father is not capable for whatever reason to be a father for the child within minimal acceptable standards, he is deemed to be unfit . . . The record and testimony fairly reflects that there is a risk [that the child will be] put in an environment of persons who prefer sexual minorities which are not normal or typical or are irregular and not generally accepted by society.
>
> Decision in the Second Judicial District Court of the State of Nevada in and for the County of Washoe, In the Matter of the Parental Rights as to Mary Toews Daly, Minor Child at 4, No. 82-3979 (1983).

The court's reasoning establishes not Suzanne's unfitness but its own inability to properly apply the law.

The evidence reflected no harm to Mary from her visitation with her father in August or October 1981 or January 1982, during which time she associated with friends of her father, including those who were gay, lesbian, and transsexual. The presence of such persons in Suzanne's life is not evidence of unfitness. *See Chapman v. Chapman*, 607 P.2d 1141, 1144 (Nev. 1980) ("While [the] facts indicate that appellant's mode of life is clearly more bohemian than respondents' . . . we cannot say that this evidence justifies the permanent and irrevocable termination of the relationship between parent and child"). The court's reference to Suzanne's moral character and the moral environment she would create for Mary was a blatant reference to Suzanne's status as a transsexual and the presence in her life of other transsexuals and of lesbians and gay men. Such facts do not reflect lack of moral character or the creation of an immoral environment.

The trial court also found that "Suzanne has some very serious emotional problems." Decision in the Second Judicial District Court of the State of Nevada in and for the County of Washoe, In the Matter of the Parental Rights as to Mary Toews Daly, Minor Child at 5, No. 82-3979 (1983). This finding is clearly erroneous. Suzanne was diagnosed with gender dysphoria and is undergoing sex reassignment as recommended by the medical standards of care and the psychotherapist who examined her. That psychotherapist, Lynn Frazier, testified below that Suzanne is well-adjusted and a role model to others.

The majority of the trial court's reasoning addressed the risk of serious physical, mental, or emotional injury to Mary. The court found that Mary was experiencing emotional distress, anxiety, and confusion. This court has no doubt that such a finding is correct. When evaluating the risk of serious emotional injury to Mary, however, we must carefully examine the source of such possible injury. We do so in light of the record below.

Suzanne revealed to Mary that she was a transsexual and told her not to tell her mother and grandmother. As noted above, asking a child to keep a secret from her custodial parent is not in a child's best interests. Suzanne understandably – and correctly – feared that Mary's mother would restrict her contact with Mary based on her transition. Nonetheless, requiring a child to keep any secret on a matter of importance burdens a child and should be avoided. Such an error in judgment by itself, however, is not substantial enough to justify termination of parental rights.

We appreciate Nan's shock at learning that Mary's father was undergoing gender reassignment. The general public knows little about transsexuals, and we do not fault her for any ignorance on the matter. As Mary's mother, however, Nan had an obligation to act in Mary's best interests. She could have made an effort to learn about the subject from any number of sources.[3] She made no such efforts. If she had sought out a professional with expertise on the subject, she might have found Dr. Ira Pauly, a witness for Suzanne below, right here in Reno. Dr. Pauly is the Chair of the Department of Psychiatry at the University of Nevada School of Medicine and has made his career as an expert on transsexualism. This suggests that the Reno community is not as uniformly hostile to transsexuals as Nan and her counsel have asserted, an argument we address below.

If Nan believed that visitation was no longer in Mary's best interests, her available course of action was to petition the court to restrict Suzanne's visitation rights and to offer proof sufficient to justify such restriction. Nan's own unwillingness to assist her daughter in adjusting to her father's unusual trajectory is not such evidence.

Instead of petitioning the court, Nan took it upon herself to cut off all contact between Suzanne and Mary, lied to Mary's principal in January 1983 by stating there was a court order prohibiting visitation, and embarked upon a campaign of vilification. These actions were contrary to Mary's best interests and show Nan's inability to place her child ahead of her own emotions. Even the court below referred to Nan's hostility, which resulted in

[3] Through her local library, for example, she might have found a number of "Dear Abby" columns, including one that included the name and address of a California doctor who could provide up-to-date literature about transsexualism. Abigail Van Buren, *Ease the Mind and Cure the Body*, The Paris News (Paris, Texas), Feb. 4, 1981 at 23. *See also* Abigail Van Buren, *Help Can Be Found for Transsexuals*, Del Rio News Herald (Del Rio, Texas), Dec. 20, 1982 at 3.

poisoning the relationship between Suzanne and Mary. The court below was willing to allow Nan to reap the benefit of her intransigence. We are not.

Both Suzanne and Nan have engaged in behavior that could be emotionally damaging to Mary. Suzanne's error in judgment took place at one moment in time, however, and is no longer the dominant feature in this dispute. "All parents are guilty of failure to provide proper care on occasion; and a parent does not deserve to forfeit the sacred liberty right of parenthood unless such unfitness is shown to be severe and persistent and such as to render the parent unsuitable to maintain the parental relationship." *Champagne v. Welfare Div. of Nev. State Dept. of Human Resources*, 691 P.2d 849, 855 (1984). The trial court heard no evidence that would support such a finding as to Suzanne.

Nan's error in judgment, on the other hand, is of a continuing nature. She created the present circumstances before us in which Mary now does not wish to see her father and appears unable to accept his transition. In reality, it is Nan who cannot accept the transition, and it is her attitude that is currently the greatest threat to Mary's emotional well-being.

We note that this is the first dispute in this state arising from a parent's post-divorce gender reassignment, but it is not the first case in the country. In *Christian v. Randall*, 516 P. 2d 132 (Colo. App. 1973), a Colorado appeals court reversed a trial court order switching custody of four children from their mother, who had transitioned to become a man, to their father. The appeals court noted that the children were happy, healthy, and well-adjusted and that there was no evidence that anything in their home impaired their emotional development.

Mary is also a happy and well-adjusted child, albeit a child experiencing some anxiety, as is common, because of the dispute between her parents. Like the Colorado court, we hold that living with or visiting a transsexual parent is not inherently harmful to a child's emotional development, and it cannot therefore be the basis for terminating parental rights.

Much was made by the mother below, and by her witnesses, about the possible reaction of Mary's peers to the knowledge of her father's gender reassignment. This court first notes that Nan did not afford Suzanne or Mary the opportunity to discuss any concerns Mary might have on this subject and to accommodate those concerns. We note that Suzanne does not live in this state, that visitation generally takes place at Suzanne's home in Oakland, and that, if Mary wished, Suzanne could have picked her up at home rather than at school for some period of time during Mary's adjustment to her father's new status. Nan determined on her own to eradicate Suzanne from Mary's life. This reflected Nan's reaction to her ex-husband's transition, not Mary's concerns at all.

We are guided by a ruling by a New Jersey appeals court in *M.P. v. S.P.*, 404 A.2d 1256 (N.J. Super 1979), reversing a lower court decision to change custody of two children from the mother to the father because the mother was a lesbian. The eleven-year-old daughter expressed embarrassment about her mother's same-sex partner and wanted to live with her father. The court acknowledged the possibility of anxiety flowing from community disapproval of the mother. It noted, however, that "the law governing grants of custody does not yield to such narrow considerations. Of overriding importance is that within the context of a loving and supportive relationship there is no reason to think that the girls will be unable to manage whatever anxieties may flow from the community's disapproval of their mother." *Id.* at 1262.

We quote at length the remainder of the New Jersey court's reasoning:

> If defendant [mother] retains custody, it may be that because the community is intolerant of her differences these girls may sometimes have to bear themselves with greater than ordinary fortitude. But this does not necessarily portend that their moral welfare or safety will be jeopardized. It is just as reasonable to expect that they will emerge better equipped to search out their own standards of right and wrong, better able to perceive that the majority is not always correct in its moral judgments, and better able to understand the importance of conforming their beliefs to the requirements of reason and tested knowledge, not the constraints of currently popular sentiment or prejudice.
>
> Taking the children from defendant can be done only at the cost of sacrificing those very qualities they will find most sustaining in meeting the challenges inevitably ahead. Instead of forbearance and feelings of protectiveness, it will foster in them a sense of shame for their mother. Instead of courage and the precept that people of integrity do not shrink from bigots, it counsels the easy option of shirking difficult problems and following the course of expedience. Lastly, it diminishes their regard for the rule of human behavior, everywhere accepted, that we do not forsake those to whom we are indebted for love and nurture merely because they are held in low esteem by others.
>
> We conclude that the children's best interests will be disserved by undermining in this way their growth as mature and principled adults. Extensive evidence in the record upon which we have not commented amply confirms the trial judge's finding that defendant is a worthy mother. Nothing suggests that her homosexual preference in itself presents any threat of harm to her daughters or that in the ordinary course of their development they will be unable to deal with whatever vexation may be caused to their spirits by the community.
>
> *Id.* at 1263.

In *Doe v. Doe*, 284 S.E.2d 799 (Va. 1981), the Virginia Supreme Court refused to terminate the parental rights of a noncustodial mother solely on the grounds that she was a lesbian. The father of the child sought the termination in the context of a petition to permit his new wife to adopt the eight-year-old son. The mother, who lived in Ohio, had visitation rights for eight weeks of summer vacation and alternate Christmas and Easter holidays.

The father's concerns included the child's difficulty coping with the difference between his rural heterosexual lifestyle and the mother's more bohemian and alternative lifestyle in the college town of Yellow Springs, Ohio. A witness for the mother acknowledged the possibility that the child would receive cruel comments from peers, but testified that being deprived of his mother would inflict more harm on him than any peer reaction. Another witness, who had known the mother and child for six years and who was also a professional counselor, testified that it was possible the child would receive cruel comments but that he was self-assured and would talk the situation out with either of his parents and handle it as well as any well-adjusted child could.

The trial court granted the adoption, thereby terminating the mother's parental rights, on the grounds that her lesbian relationship would have a detrimental effect on the child and would result in serious emotional and mental harm to him. The Virginia Supreme Court reversed, holding that the evidence did not support such a conclusion. Rather, the mother was capable and devoted and her status as a lesbian had not harmed her child and was not a basis for terminating her parental rights. *Id.* at 805.

We find the reasoning of the Virginia court instructive. We look beyond that reasoning, however, to note that emotional harm to Mary is more likely to spring from her mother's continued hostility towards her father than from her father's status as a transsexual. This cannot under any circumstances be a basis for terminating the father's parental rights.

Nan has already fostered a sense of shame for Suzanne in Mary's eyes. This court does not countenance that behavior and will not compound it. We note that the U.S. Supreme Court has refused to allow a trial court to base a child custody determination on the private prejudices of one parent or of a community. *See Palmore v. Sidoti*, 466 U.S. 429, 104 S. Ct. 1879, 80 L. Ed 2d 421 (1984) (overturning a Florida court ruling transferring custody of a White child from her White mother on the sole basis that she married a Black man). We adopt that reasoning here.

This court also has had occasion to address the legal significance of possible reactions to a child's living situation in the context of a custody dispute arising from an interracial marriage. In *Beazley v. Davis*, 545 P.2d 206 (Nev. 1976), we reversed a trial court custody award to a Black father that was based upon the fact that the children looked Black. The trial court believed the children would suffer trauma living with their White mother when she had additional children with her new husband, who was White. We reversed because the trial court failed to focus on what custody arrangement would best serve the children's interests. We noted that children raised in a happy home would be able to cope with inevitable racial prejudice and tension and that they would "learn that people were unique individuals who had to be judged as such." *Id.* at 208 (citation omitted). Similarly, we believe that Mary, who is a bright and well-adjusted child, will learn to cope with prejudice against her father as potentially expressed by her peers.

In *Beazley*, we noted that Nevada judicial officers must abide by the equality requirements of the Fourteenth Amendment to the Constitution. Therefore, "in the absence of a showing that race in custody proceedings is necessary to the accomplishment of a permissible State policy, such a consideration would constitute impermissible discrimination." *Id.* The decision of the U.S. Supreme Court in *Palmore v. Sidoti*, quoted above, further confirms that we were correct in that view. *Supra*. While no discrimination on the basis of race is present in the instant case, the reasoning of the court below, based solely on Suzanne's status as a transsexual and the presence in her life of other transsexuals and lesbians and gay men, approaches irrational prejudice that the Fourteenth Amendment cannot tolerate. Just as the children in *Beazley* were "denied the benefit of an unprejudiced hearing focused solely on an inquiry into what custody order would be in their best interest and welfare," *id.*, so Mary was denied the benefit of an unprejudiced hearing focused on the legal standard for termination of parental rights.

Mary's participation in the rap group at the Pacific Center has already taught her that her father is not unique. We are not so naïve as to believe that the damage caused by her mother's intolerance, exacerbated by the trial court ruling below, will be quickly undone. But renewed contact with her father will restore a positive parent-child relationship between Suzanne and Mary. Such a relationship is in Mary's best interests.

In light of the above, we find that Respondent did not prove by clear and convincing evidence a jurisdictional ground for termination under Nevada Revised Statutes 128.105. That concludes the requisite legal analysis. Although not necessary, we also conclude that the termination of parental rights requested here is not in Mary's best interests. We reverse the judgment of the court below and remand for proceedings expeditiously reinstating visitation in a manner consistent with Mary's best interests and this opinion.

9

Commentary on *Michael H. v. Gerald D.*

SUZANNE A. KIM

INTRODUCTION

In *Michael H. v. Gerald D.*, the U.S. Supreme Court addressed a "marital presumption,"[1] which established parental rights for the husband of a mother even if the husband is not the biological father. Writing for a plurality of the Court, Justice Scalia concluded that an evidentiary presumption that precludes a biological father from asserting parental rights does not violate the Due Process and Equal Protection Clauses of the Fourteenth Amendment. The case raised overarching but underacknowledged questions about how we define family, parenthood, motherhood, fatherhood, and children's interests.

[1] Marital presumptions remain on the books: "All fifty states have some version of a marital presumption pursuant to which a husband is presumed to be the legal parent of a child born to his wife. Under the 2002 Uniform Parentage Act ('UPA'), this marital presumption applies in all circumstances, even when the husband is and knows he is impotent or sterile. Section 204(a)(1) of the 2002 UPA provides that '[a] man is presumed to be the father of a child if he and the mother of the child are married to each other and the child is born during the marriage.' Thus, under this provision, if a wife becomes pregnant as a result of sexual intercourse with a man not her husband, her husband is presumed to be the legal parent of the resulting child. Under Section 607 of the 2002 UPA, this presumption generally becomes conclusive on the child's second birthday." Memorandum from Courtney Joslin on Marital Presumption to the Drafting Comm., UPA Revisions (Jan. 31, 2016) (on file with author). The 2017 amendments to the UPA make five major changes. *See generally*, Uniform Parentage Act (2017) Summary, Uniform Law Commission. https://www.uniformlaws.org/HigherLogic/System/DownloadDocumentFile.ashx?DocumentFileKey=4bdb2267-4880-1669-72da-fc059caba3f5&forceDialog=0. First, it aims to "ensure equal treatment" of children of same-sex couples. *Id.* Second, it provides for the "establishment of a de facto parent as a legal parent." *Id.* Third, it provides for the preclusion of a legal parent-child relationship "by the perpetrator of a sexual assault that resulted in the conception of the child." *Id.* Fourth, the UPA updates surrogacy provisions to reflect the current surrogacy practices. *Id.* Finally, the UPA includes a new article that addresses the right of children born through assisted reproductive technology to access information regarding gamete providers. *Id.*

The Antognini rewritten opinion elegantly grapples with these questions by uncovering the detrimental impacts on parents and children because of the marital presumption's application in this case. Had an opinion like this prevailed, the legal regulation of the family would likely have progressed more quickly toward recognizing functional relationships over formal ones rooted solely in marriage. The opinion would also have ushered in deeper consideration of the role of gender and biology in legal determinations of parentage.

THE ORIGINAL OPINION IN *MICHAEL H. V. GERALD D.*

Michael H., the biological father of the child Victoria, filed a filiation action in state court to establish paternity and a right to visitation.[2] In the action, however, Gerald D., the husband of Victoria's mother, Carole, moved for summary judgment, based on the California statute creating a presumption that a child born to a married woman living with her husband (who is not impotent or sterile) is the child of that marriage. In other words, although Michael H. held Victoria out as his daughter and sought to establish legal paternity, Gerald D. was presumed to be Victoria's father. Based on the statute, the marital presumption could be rebutted by blood tests, but only if a motion was made either by the husband (Gerald) or the wife (Carole), and the wife can only do so if the child's biological father has filed an affidavit acknowledging paternity. Neither Carole nor Gerald sought to rebut the presumption. The statute derived from the longstanding aversion in common law toward designating children as "illegitimate,"[3] with the significant legal impairments such status brought.[4]

Michael H. asserted that the marital presumption violated his procedural due process rights by terminating his liberty interest in his relationship with

[2] Michael H.'s biological connection to Victoria was not contested. Five months after Victoria was born, Carole and Michael had blood tests conducted, "which showed a 98.07% probability that Michael H. is Victoria's father." *Michael H. v. Gerald D.*, 491 U.S. 110, 114 (1989).

[3] *Id.* at 125.

[4] *See, e.g.*, Solangel Maldonado, *Illegitimate Harm: Law, Stigma, and Discrimination against Nonmarital Children*, 63 Fla. L. Rev. 345, 346–47 (2011) ("Under the common law, nonmarital children had no right to parental support and no right to inherit from or through a parent. They faced legal and societal barriers when they sought public office, entry into professional associations, or to transfer their own property at death"). Along with these impairments came virtual control by fathers over their children historically. *See* Mary Ann Mason, From Father's Property to Children's Rights: The History of Child Custody in the United States 92–93 (1994); *see also* Erin Bajackson, *Best Interests of the Child – A Legislative Journey Still in Motion*, 25 J. Am. Acad. Matrim. Law 311, 312–13 (2013) (describing the history of the presumption to award custody to fathers).

Victoria without giving him an opportunity to prove paternity in an evidentiary hearing. Moreover, Michael asserted that the marital presumption violated his substantive due process rights, based again on his liberty interest in his relationship with Victoria,[5] which proceeded from both his biological fatherhood and his established parental relationship.[6] Victoria asserted her own due process challenge, seeking to preserve her relationships with both Michael H. and Gerald D. Victoria also argued that her equal protection rights were violated by the marital presumption statute because parents, but not children, could rebut the presumption.

THE REWRITTEN OPINION

The rewritten opinion departs from the original opinion dramatically by making the equal protection arguments central to its analysis, thus highlighting the gendered operation of the marital presumption statute. It also embraces a substantive due process analysis, focusing on caregiving functions as a basis for protecting a range of parents.

The focus on equal protection allows the Antognini Rewritten Opinion to highlight the gender asymmetry in the marital presumption. As Justice Antognini reasons, "if Michael had been Michelle, and Carole had been Carl, under the laws of California there is no doubt that Michelle would have been considered the mother … To generalize: the law recognizes the woman, wed or unwed, to always be the mother of the child."[7] In other words, "marriage dictates rights and responsibilities only where the parent is a man." While the

[5] *Michael H.*, 491 U.S. at 121.

[6] *Id.* at 123.

[7] Antognini Rewritten Opinion. By engaging the gendered nature of the marital presumption, the rewritten opinion foreshadows cases like *Sessions v. Morales-Santana*, 137 S. Ct. 1678 (2017), and *Nguyen v. INS*, 533 U.S. 53 (2001), both of which address gender-differentiated conceptions of parental roles. *See Morales-Santana* (holding unconstitutional a statute that provided for derivative citizenship where only one year of continuous physical presence was required before unwed mothers could pass citizenship to their children, but five years of continuous presence was required for unwed fathers). In *Morales-Santana*, the Court noted the harmful effects of gender-based stereotypes in parenting: "Laws according or denying benefits in reliance on '[s]tereotypes about women's domestic roles,' … may 'creat[e] a self-fulfilling cycle of discrimination that force[s] women to continue to assume the role of primary caregiver.'" *Morales-Santana*, 136 S. Ct. at 1693 (citing *Nevada Dept. of Human Resources v. Hibbs*, 538 U.S. 721, 736 (2003)). *See also Nguyen* (holding that a statute making it more difficult for a child born abroad and out of wedlock to one citizen parent to claim citizenship through that parent if the citizen parent was the father did not violate the equal protection guarantee of the Fifth Amendment, because, *inter alia*, fathers and mothers are not similarly situated with regard to proof of biological parenthood).

rules reflect a "gender asymmetry" in how marital status converges with parental status, it also reinforces gendered social outcomes. This mutually constitutive dynamic operated at the heart of the Supreme Court's early gender equality cases. Such legal rules lock parents into these gendered roles – like them or not: "dictating that maternal marital status does not matter for purposes of establishing parentage, while paternal marital status does, helps create this lopsided state of affairs by allowing fathers to choose whether to parent, while denying mothers that very same choice."[8]

In bringing front and center the problems of fit between the government's stated objectives and its selected means of achieving them, Antognini illuminates the "patchy" and "perverse" effects of the statute's attempt to "protect an intact marital family." The rewritten opinion also reveals the original opinion's neglect of the deep parental and children's relational interests at stake.

The rewritten opinion enquires into how much marital unity we can presume in cases in which the marital presumption comes into play – when a wife has a sexual relationship outside of the marriage.[9] And, as Antognini writes, even if "Carole were to divorce Gerald and marry Michael, [the statute] would prevent Michael from being recognized as Victoria's father." To the extent that the statute aims to bolster family unity, the statute "work[s] to preclude the formal family stability it aims to promote." Such an outcome is indeed perverse, demonstrating hyper-formalism at its best (or worst).

In evaluating both Michael's and Victoria's equal protection claims, the rewritten opinion pursues the significance of parents' and children's biological connection and functional relationships. Failing to vindicate the state's asserted objective of marital unity, the statute also falters in protecting the welfare of children because it undervalues unwed fathers.[10] The focus on the marital

[8] Antognini Rewritten Opinion. The Antognini rewritten opinion also addresses Justice Scalia's indictment of Carole's sexual behavior. Scalia's approach resonates with the Florida court's harsh view in *Palmore v. Sidoti*, 466 U.S. 429 (1984), a race-based equal protection case, who cohabitated with and then married an African American man. *See* Katharine T. Bartlett, *Comparing Race and Sex Discrimination in Custody Cases*, 28 Hofstra L. Rev. 877, 880 (2000). In contrast, the Antognini Rewritten Opinion observes that adultery is no longer a crime. Moreover, in contrast to Justice Scalia's description of the set of facts as "extraordinary," the Antognini Rewritten Opinion cites Alfred Kinsey, demonstrating the commonplace nature of extramarital relationships for both men and women.

[9] This argument is reminiscent of those favoring enforcement of marital status-based obligations. *See McGuire v. McGuire*, 59 N.W.2d 336 (1953). One can assume an already "weakened marital bond" in a situation in which a wife sues to enforce a marital duty of support, thus vitiating the argument against enforcement based on the need to protect marital unity. Antognini rewritten opinion.

[10] Citing *Stanley v. Illinois*, 405 U.S. 645, 650 (1972); *Caban v. Mohammed*, 441 U.S. 380 (1979); *Lehr v. Robertson*, 463 U.S. 248 (1983).

status of Michael H., or lack thereof, reinforces a formalism detached from actual caregiving. In recognizing Victoria's equal protection claim, the rewritten opinion lays a predicate for increasingly robust recognition of de facto parenthood, rooted in caregiving relationships, by highlighting the inequality of drawing formalist distinctions between a marital and nonmarital parent.

The rewritten opinion's due process analysis also proceeds from a deep commitment to functional understandings of parenthood and to children's, as opposed merely to adults', interests. In deciding whether the equal protection analysis dictates extending the marital presumption to mothers too, or to no parents, Antognini focuses on the interest of the child, Victoria, in "preserving a relationship with the adults in her life." As Antognini writes, "This parent-child relationship does not, however, point in only one direction. To state the obvious, the child is an integral part of that relationship and, like the parent, is cloaked by the constitutional protection the relation itself receives ... Stated otherwise, the interests of the parent and the child in the preservation of their relationship are two sides of the same coin."

This framing contrasts with that in the original opinion, which centered solely on Michael H.'s interests. The attention to Victoria, for whom formalistic distinctions mean little, permits greater attention to the function of parenting. In analyzing whether the state had violated Michael H.'s substantive due process rights, Justice Scalia pursued a narrow approach for determining what fundamental interests may be at stake. Justice Scalia sought to answer the question of whether a fundamental interest was at stake by asking "whether the relationship between persons in the situation of Michael and Victoria has been treated as a protected family unit under the historic practices of our society."[11] He described the situation of the litigants as "a married woman, her lover, and their child, during a three-month sojourn in St. Thomas, or during a subsequent 8-month period when if he happened to be in Los Angeles, he stayed with her and the child."[12] Differing dramatically from Justice Brennan's broader substantive due process analysis in dissent, Justice Scalia's approach foreclosed consideration of the relational interests Michael H. and Victoria had toward one another.[13]

[11] *Michael H.*, 491 U.S. at 124.

[12] *Id.* at 123 n. 3. Justice Scalia similarly described the issue as one of whether Michael as "adulterous natural father" has parental rights regarding "a child born into an extant marital union." *Id.* at 120, 127.

[13] Antognini Rewritten Opinion. The methodological difference between Justices Scalia and Brennan, writing in dissent, on how broadly or narrowly to construe the fundamental interests at stake for Michael H. determined the outcome of the due process analysis in the original decision. The degree of specificity with which Justice Scalia framed the rights Michael

Antognini's focus on preserving a child's relationship with the adults in her life paves the way for greater attention to who engages in caregiving. This contrasts with line-drawing like "[d]ifferentiating between classes of children on the basis of their parents' behavior" as occurred in illegitimacy cases. Instead, "[f]ailing to recognize the real relationship that has developed between Victoria and Michael would disadvantage Victoria because of the decisions undertaken by Michael and Carole – namely, to have sexual relations outside of marriage. No similar impediment would be placed, for example, on a child's relationship with parents who had sex only within marriage."

Once a child's interests in preserving care relationships comes into view, a limit to two parents makes less sense. As Antognini states, "Liberty requires that we acknowledge the existence of an established parent-child relationship, even if that means we recognize more than two fathers, or more than two mothers ... [W]e have interpreted our Constitution to refuse to dictate the form a family ought to take, and instead to protect an individual's right to choose how that family is constituted." In protecting relational interests, Antognini seeks to preserve the work of care, rather than the particular form in which it takes.

CONTEMPORARY SIGNIFICANCE OF THE REWRITTEN OPINION

Viewed through a contemporary lens, the original *Michael H.* decision and the rewritten opinion highlight a host of tensions between functional and formalist impulses in family law. The Antognini opinion would undoubtedly have reshaped dramatically the law of parenthood by eliminating the marital presumption and introducing a function-based approach focused on caregiving.[14] The focus on caregiving functions and on children's interests in the rewritten opinion would also have laid a foundation for treating parent-child relationships more expansively than through the zero-sum approach evinced by Justice Scalia's opinion.

Anchored in a narrow historical reading of past precedent, Justice Scalia's substantive due process analysis viewed the question of parentage, between

H. asserted, relying on a limited historic account of the recognition of unmarried fathers, predetermined the outcome of the case. *Id.* at 127 n. 6. Justice Scalia "refer[red] to the most specific level at which a relevant tradition protecting, or denying protection to, the asserted right can be identified," while Brennan determined that the fundamental right implicated was "parenthood." Jack M. Balkin, *Tradition, Betrayal, and the Politics of Deconstruction*, 11 Cardozo L. Rev. 1613, 1614 (1990) (citing *Michael H.*, 491 U.S. at 127 n. 6).

[14] *See generally* Martha Albertson Fineman, The Neutered Mother, the Sexual Family, and Other Twentieth Century Tragedies (1995) (arguing for recognition of dependency and caregiving in family law and policy).

Michael H. and Gerald D., as requiring one to be the "winner" and the other the "loser."[15] Antognini's exploration of the possibility of more than two parents flows from an underlying commitment to functionalism in family law.[16] Antognini explores the possibility of more than two parents: "Nothing in our laws has expressly restricted the parent-child relationship to only *two* parents."[17] The rewritten opinion would have hastened the possibility of such outcomes for families that depart from the one- or two-parent mold.[18] This approach resonates with recent cases supporting recognition of more than two parents at a time. For instance, in *D.G. v. K.S.*, a New Jersey state court determined that, pursuant to a "tri-parenting" arrangement between a same-sex couple and the longtime friend, who was the biological mother, all three adults were entitled to joint legal and joint physical custody.[19] While two of the parents were biological parents, the third (the same-sex spouse of the biological father) was deemed a psychological parent based on his involvement in the care, education, and development of the child.[20]

By sweeping away the marital presumption, Antognini steers clear of the continuing hold that gender and biology have on assessments of parental roles. For instance, in *Nguyen v. I.N.S.*, the Court determined that a statute placing

15 "Here, to provide protection to an adulterous natural father is to deny protection to a marital father, and vice versa. If Michael has a 'freedom not to conform' (whatever that means), Gerald must equivalently have a 'freedom to conform.'" *Michael H.*, 491 U.S. at 130.

16 *See, e.g., Moore v. City of East Cleveland*, 431 U.S. 494, 506 (1977) ("By the same token the Constitution prevents East Cleveland from standardizing its children and its adults by forcing all to live in certain narrowly defined family patterns"); *Pierce v. Soc'y of the Sisters*, 268 U.S. 510, 535 (1925) (striking down an Oregon law requiring all children to attend the state's public schools, holding that the Constitution "excludes any general power of the State to standardize its children by forcing them to accept instruction from public teachers only").

17 This approach connects squarely with the avowed commitment to pluralism in constitutional family law. *See, e.g., Moore*; *Pierce*; and *Meyer v. Nebraska*, 262 U.S. 390 (1923).

18 Contemporary cases have permitted legal recognition of more than two parents. *See D.G. v. K.S.*, 133 A.3d 703, 706 (Ch. Div. 2015) (holding that the biological father and his same-sex spouse and biological mother were entitled to joint legal and joint physical custody); *K.A.F. v. D.L.M.* 96 A.3d 975, 982–83 (N.J. App. Div. 2014) (holding that "the consent of both legal parents is not required to create a psychological parent relationship between their child and a third party … it is sufficient if only one of the legal custodial parents has consented to the parental role of the third party. In that circumstance, a legal custodial parent has voluntarily created the relationship and thus has permitted the third party to enter the zone of privacy between her and her child"). *See also* Matthew M. Kavanagh, *Rewriting the Legal Family: Beyond Exclusivity to a Care-Based Standard*, 16 Yale J.L. & Feminism 83 (2004).

19 444 N.J. Super. 423, 429, 133 A.3d 703, 706 (Ch. Div. 2015) ("O.S.H. is a female minor child born in 2009. Plaintiff, D.G., is the biological father of O.S.H., and K.S. is the child's biological mother. Plaintiff, S.H., is D.G.'s same-sex spouse, who has bonded with and has become a psychological parent of O.S.H.").

20 *Id.* at 435.

greater barriers to citizenship for a child born abroad and out of wedlock to a citizen-father, as compared to a citizen-mother, did not violate the equal protection guarantee of the Fifth Amendment, because, *inter alia*, fathers and mothers are not similarly situated with regard to proof of biological parenthood.[21] Moreover, efforts to apply the marital presumption when the gender of parties is reversed from those in Michael H. meet resistance due to gendered and biologically based understandings of parental relationships. In the 2006 case of *Amy G. v. M.W.*, a wife and her husband (the biological father of the child at issue) sought to assert the marital presumption against the parental claims of the child's biological mother. The California appellate court rejected the due process and equal protection claims of the married woman, on the ground that mothers and fathers are not equally situated because of differences in reproductive roles. According to the court,

> While a biological father's genetic contribution to his child may arise from nothing more than a fleeting encounter, the biological mother carries the child for the nine-month gestational period. Because of this inherent difference between men and women with respect to reproduction, the wife of a man who fathered a child with another woman is not similarly situated to a man whose wife was impregnated by another man.[22]

Biology also prevailed over the couple's substantive due process claim to family and marital integrity. The court deemed that any interest in protecting the marital family unit was insufficient to "displace the biological mother."[23]

The rewritten opinion portends important developments in law's treatment of diverse families, especially if gender, function, and biology do not have the same salience as they had in *Michael H.* The opinion's focus on functional relationships is a persuasive choice, given the experience that same-sex parents have had with the marital presumption. While the presumption is considered to be a benefit of same-sex couples' access to marriage, obtained twenty-six years after *Michael H.*, state courts grapple with its application to same-sex families in which couples are not biologically related to children.

The situation is more complex when marital presumptions are based on gendered assumptions about parenthood layered on top of biological ones. In other words, merely extending marital presumptions to same-sex couples does not support parent-child relationships across the range of families. In the context of today's nationwide marriage equality, "even if the wording of state

[21] 533 U.S. 53 (2001).
[22] *Amy G. v. M.W.*, 142 Cal. App. 4th 1 (2006).
[23] *Id.*

law marital presumptions is altered to apply to a 'spouse' instead of just to a 'husband,' this revision does nothing to assist fathers in same-sex couples,"[24] and same-sex mothers in some states continue to face resistance to the presumption applied to non-gestational mothers.[25] As I write elsewhere, "The marital presumption fails to assist these parents, as the presumption is doctrinally inapt in the absence of a contemporaneously birthing mother and marital spouse. Similarly, for couples raising children of prior (heterosexual) relationships, which characterizes a large number of families of color,[26] marriage would have no effect on securing greater parentage status for spouses – either female or male."[27]

If adopted, the 2017 version of the Uniform Parentage Act would significantly address gender and biologically based inequities in parentage law.[28] These changes include a robust focus on functional parent-child relationships and elimination of gendered language in recognition of parentage.[29] Even with these changes, however, the revised UPA's focus on privileging of genetics and gestation will continue to disadvantage nonbiological parents and children.[30] These ongoing developments – and challenges – highlight the wisdom of Antognini's approach in eschewing marital-based approaches to parentage and focusing intently on functional parenthood.

MICHAEL H. v. GERALD D., 491 U.S. 110 (1989)

JUSTICE ANTOGNINI DELIVERED THE OPINION OF THE COURT

The specific issue this case raises is whether Section 621 of California's Evidence Code is constitutional. The provision conclusively presumes that a child born to a married woman living with her neither impotent nor sterile husband is the child of the marriage.[1] The analysis we must undertake forces

[24] Suzanne Kim, *Transitional Equality*, 53 U. Rich. L. Rev. 1149 (2019); Nancy Polikoff, *Marriage as Blindspot, in* After Marriage Equality: The Future of LGBT Rights (Carlos A. Ball ed., 2016); Douglas NeJaime, *The Nature of Parenthood*, 126 Yale L.J. 2260, 2308 (2017).

[25] Kim, *supra* note 24 at 1173; Polikoff, *supra* note 24, at 23–25.

[26] Polikoff, *supra* note 24, at 12–13.

[27] Kim, *supra* note 24, at 1173; Polikoff, *supra* note 24, at 12–13.

[28] Kim, supra note 24 (citing Courtney G. Joslin, *Nurturing Parenthood through the UPA (2017)*, 127 Yale L.J.F. 589, 602 (2018); NeJaime, *supra* note 24, at 2308 (revealing prioritization of biological and different-sex parents).

[29] Joslin, *supra* note 28, at 602.

[30] *Id.*

[1] The presumption is subject to challenge only by the husband or the mother and biological father together. Cal. Evid. Code § 621 (West Supp. 1989).

us to confront a fundamental question: how does California law define who is a parent to a child? Formulating a response raises a corollary concern: is there a limit on how many legal parents a child can have? We now hold that California's provision violates Equal Protection given the sex-based distinctions it relies on. We also conclude that Due Process requires the legal recognition of a parent-child relationship developed between an adult and a child, even if it means there may be more than one father, or more than one mother, and thereby more than two parents. The Constitution nowhere imposes a cap on the number of parents the law can acknowledge. It does, however, demand the protection of a parent-child relationship where established.

The facts before us are uncontested. Michael H. had sexual relations with Carole D. while she was married to Gerald D. During her marriage to Gerald, Carole had a child, Victoria D. Blood tests show there is a 98.07 percent probability that Victoria is biologically related to Michael, not Gerald. Gerald was, and continues to be, Carole's husband. Both Michael and Gerald claim the status of father to Victoria. Needless to say, this is not the first time a child is born to a married woman from a relationship that took place outside of marriage.[2] Nor, dare we predict, will it be the last.

Michael argues that Section 621 violates his rights under the Equal Protection and Due Process clauses of the Fourteenth Amendment of the Constitution.[3] He does not come before us alone. Victoria also argues that Section 621 violates her rights under the Due Process and Equal Protection clauses. We agree, to a certain extent, with both Michael and Victoria. We hold that

2 Adultery has long been a subject of human interest and experience – for both men and women. *See* ALFRED C. KINSEY, WARDELL B. POMEROY, CLYDE E. MARTIN, & PAUL A. GEBHARD, SEXUAL BEHAVIOR IN THE HUMAN FEMALE 416–45 (1953) ("the preoccupation of the world's biography and fiction, through all ages and in all human cultures, with the non-marital sexual activities of married females and males, is evidence of the universality of human desires in these matters, and of the universal failure of the existent social regulations to resolve the basic issues which are involved"); ALFRED C. KINSEY, WARDELL B. POMEROY, & CLYDE E. MARTIN, SEXUAL BEHAVIOR IN THE HUMAN MALE 583–94 (1948) ("social attitudes are particularly interesting in view of the fact that a considerable proportion of those who react most violently against the known instances of extra-marital relations, may have similar experience in their own histories").

3 Michael raises the Equal Protection claim for the first time before this Court. Michael's failure to raise the claim below does not, however, deprive us of the ability to resolve it. The decision to address it is prudential, rather than jurisdictional. *See Bankers Life & Cas. Co. v. Crenshaw*, 486 U.S. 71, 79 (1988) (assuming the "not passed or pressed upon below" rule is prudential rather than jurisdictional). Because these issues are of a constitutional magnitude, we believe it is important to provide guidance rather than remain silent on what equal treatment under the Constitution entails, and so we take up Michael's arguments here.

Section 621 violates Equal Protection by relying on impermissible sex-based distinctions. Our conclusion that it violates Equal Protection does not, however, provide guidance on how to resolve the discrepancy – whether the statute can be amended to apply to all parents or to none.[4] Turning to Victoria's claims furnishes a resolution: we hold that Section 621 violates Victoria's due process rights by imposing a conclusive presumption of parentage and depriving her of the ability to demonstrate the existence of a parent-child relationship with an adult other than her mother's husband.[5] Accordingly, resolving the Equal Protection issue merely by extending the statute to apply to all parents, regardless of their sex, would still be unconstitutional, given the due process concerns the statute raises.

I FACTUAL AND PROCEDURAL BACKGROUND

Carole married Gerald in 1976. They attempted to have children twice during their marriage, but were unable to do so due to a miscarriage the first time, and a therapeutic abortion the second time.[6] Brief for Appellee 4. In 1978, Carole and her neighbor, Michael, began an affair. Two years later, Carole informed Michael that she was pregnant with his child.[7] At this time, Carole also informed Michael that she was planning on having an abortion. Because Carole had been pregnant with twins, the abortion terminated only one of the fetuses she was carrying. On May 11, 1981, Carole gave birth to a daughter. Brief for Appellant Michael H. 3.

Gerald was in the delivery room with Carole at the Cedars-Sinai Hospital in Los Angeles when she gave birth. One month after Victoria was born, Gerald's parents traveled from their home in France to Los Angeles to meet Victoria. Brief for Appellee 4. Shortly thereafter, Gerald had to travel for work. At some point after Carole gave birth, she called Michael to inform him of the event. A few months later, Carole and Michael visited a clinic at the University of California at Los Angeles to determine Victoria's paternity. The Human Leukocyte Antigen ("HLA") test showed a 98.07 percent probability that Michael is related to Victoria.

[4] While the question could be resolved on Due Process grounds alone, doing so would ignore the gender inequities imposed by California's statutory scheme.

[5] As the due process analysis will demonstrate, Victoria's rights are intimately linked to Michael's. We focus on her claims, however, to place the child and her interests at the center of the constitutional analysis. *See* Section III.

[6] Carole had one child from a prior marriage. J.A. 43, No. 87-746.

[7] Michael had a child from a prior marriage, who was born with severe mental and physical disabilities. J.A. 59.

Carole and Michael continued their relationship. In 1982, Carole and Victoria moved to St. Thomas to live with Michael. During a two-month period, Carole held Michael out as Victoria's father and the three of them lived together as a family unit. Brief for Appellant Michael H. 3-4. Carole then returned to Los Angeles, where she began a relationship with another man, Scott K. Eventually, Carole reconnected with Gerald. Thereafter, Carole attempted to restrict Michael's visits with Victoria. In response, Michael filed a filiation suit, which initiated the instant case. *Id.* at 4.

Sometime after the commencement of the suit, Carole reconciled with Michael. Carole continued to hold Michael out as Victoria's father, and Victoria called him "Daddy." *Id.* Michael shared a bank account with Carole and financially supported Carole and Victoria. According to Michael, he "developed a warm, close and loving parent-child relationship" with Victoria. *Id.* In 1984, Carole signed a Stipulation to resolve the pending filiation suit, acknowledging Michael's paternity. *Id.*

The following month, however, Carole ended her relationship with Michael, and resumed her relationship with Gerald. Brief for Appellee 8. After Carole separated from Michael, she accused him of refusing to leave the apartment where Victoria and Carole lived, and of exhibiting worrisome behavior towards Victoria. *Id.* at 6–7.

In the wake of Carole's split with Michael, and while his paternity was being adjudicated, Victoria's court-appointed guardian ad litem, along with Michael himself, sought visitation *pendente lite*. Brief for Appellant Michael H. 5. The Los Angeles County Superior Court appointed an independent psychologist to evaluate all of the parties and to submit a recommendation. *Id.* The psychologist's report found that Carole had "difficulty with intimacy" which would "have consequences in her day-to-day parenting as well as her short-term relationships with peers." J.A. 55. The report identified Michael "as the single adult in Victoria D.'s life most committed to caring for her needs on a long-term basis" and acknowledged the importance of Michael remaining a part of Victoria's family. J.A. 51. The report also found that Gerald had an "attachment to both Carole and Victoria" and that he "demonstrates the capacity to be a fine parent and role model." J.A. 45, 58. The report predicted that "[t]he probability that Carole and Gerald will maintain a joint household is low." J.A. 45.

Carole and Gerald remain married: they live together with Victoria and a son, whose biological relationship to Gerald is not contested. Brief for Appellee 8; *Michael H. v. Gerald D.*, 191 Cal. App. 3d 995, 1002 (1987).

The Superior Court granted Gerald's request for summary judgment by applying the conclusive presumption of Section 621 to find that Gerald is

Victoria's father, given that he was married to, and living with, Carole when Victoria was born. *Michael H.*, 191 Cal. App. 3d at 1000. The California Court of Appeal affirmed the grant of summary judgment, holding that Section 621 controlled the outcome of the case. The court further reasoned that the application of the statute did not violate the Due Process rights of Michael or Victoria, based on the state's substantial interests in protecting the marital family and the welfare of the child. *Id.* at 1009–10. It also summarily denied Victoria's Equal Protection claim.[8]

We take up each of these issues in detail below, and identify the constitutional infirmities in California's statutory scheme.

II SECTION 621 VIOLATES EQUAL PROTECTION

A *Background*

California Evidence Code Section 621 sets out that "the issue of a wife cohabiting with her husband, who is not impotent or sterile, is conclusively presumed to be a child of the marriage." Cal. Evid. Code § 621 (West Supp. 1989). The presumption may be rebutted in only one of two circumstances: when the husband is impotent or sterile; or when the husband, or the wife along with the natural father, petition for blood tests within two years of the child's birth. *Id.*

The statute's most recent amendment occurred in 1981, although it has remained mostly intact since its original enactment in 1872. Cal. Civ. Proc. § 1962(5) (Olney 1872); 1981 Cal. Stat. 4760–61. The revisions made over the years were mainly to modernize the statute to comport with current mores and technological advances, including updating the use of "legitimate" to "child of a marriage," and allowing the introduction of blood-test evidence to rebut the presumption of the husband's biological connection to the child. 1981 Cal. Stat. 4760–61.

As written, Section 621 applies to prevent men, but not women, who may have a biological connection to a child, from being recognized as parents. That is, the statute's presumption applies to preclude men from being acknowledged as fathers if they have a child with a woman who is married to someone else. The statute does not, by its terms, preclude a woman from being acknowledged as a mother in the same situation. The statute addresses only

[8] The court dismissed Victoria's claim that the statute violated equal protection because it prevented her from challenging the presumption of paternity while allowing mothers and fathers to do so. *Michael H.*, 191 Cal. App. 3d at 1010.

"the issue of a wife." Clearly then, if a married woman has any issue, it is hers under the statute. But what of the issue of a married man? The statute is silent on this question. Interpreting this omission leads to an answer: given that the statute does not address the issue of a husband, if a man married to someone else were to have a sexual relationship with an unmarried woman, any issue born to her would also be considered hers, instead of his. As such, "the right of a biological mother to remain a parent is *never* open to question . . . whereas a biological father may be deprived of parental rights." Brief for Appellant Michael H. 10.

To crystallize this fundamental point, let us reverse the sex of the parties before us: if Michael had been Michelle, Carole had been Carl, and Gerald had been Jane, under the laws of California, nothing prevents Michelle from being considered the mother. Yet Michael is not considered the father. The law recognizes the woman, wed or unwed, as the mother of the child. The law recognizes the man as the father only sometimes – generally when it accords with his role of husband, as the statute suggests.

This state of affairs is, of course, understood to follow from what is patently obvious: the woman who gives birth is visibly related to the child, while the father, who does not, may not be. *Mater semper certa est, pater semper incertus est.*[9] Yet maternity too is revealing itself to be an open question. Consider the recent case of *In re Baby M*, decided by the New Jersey Supreme Court last year, which addressed the legality of a surrogacy contract. *In re Baby M*, 109 N.J. 396 (N.J. 1988). The intended mother in that case, who was married to the intended father, was not the woman who was pregnant with, and genetically related to, the child.[10] The fact pattern underlying *Baby M* illustrates how bearing a genetically related child can be divorced from the intent to be the mother of that child. While the surrogate in *Baby M* shared both a gestational and genetic link with the child, scientific advances suggest that even bearing a child can be divorced from having a genetic connection with the child. Clifford Grobstein et al., *Frozen Embryos: Policy Issues*, 1985 New Eng. J. of Med. 505 (1985). As such, intent, genetics, and gestation may each be located in three different women. California, whose Civil Code codified the Uniform

[9] This principle is followed by most countries around the world. *See* HARRY D. KRAUSE, 4 INTERNATIONAL ENCYCLOPEDIA OF COMPARATIVE LAW 28–29 (Aleck Chloros ed., 1976) (noting that the first part of this Latin maxim "resolves the question of the child's relationship with his mother in most systems," identifying French family law as the sole exception that "does not consider maternity a matter of course").

[10] The New Jersey Supreme Court ultimately invalidated the surrogacy contract entered into by the married couple and the surrogate, reasoning that it conflicted with specific statutory provisions and the public policy of the state. *In re Baby M*, 109 N.J. at 423–44.

Parentage Act in 1975, contains some of these different definitions of motherhood by recognizing either blood test evidence or giving birth as alternative ways of proving maternity. Cal. Civ. Code §§ 7003, 7015 (West 1991); Cal. Evid. Code § 892 (West 1991). These examples establish that motherhood, like fatherhood, is a contested terrain, which Section 621 fails to address in its simple use of the phrase "issue of wife."

What remains clear, however, is that the statute differentiates between parents based on sex:[11] Michelle would be considered the parent of the child, but Michael is not. The question we must then answer is the following: does this distinction offend constitutional principles? We hold that it does.

B *Gender-Based Distinctions*

Given the gender-based distinction at the core of Section 621 – applying different rules to men and women – it must survive heightened scrutiny to withstand a challenge under the Equal Protection Clause. Specifically, the gender-based distinction "must serve important governmental objectives and must be substantially related to achievement of those objectives." *Craig v. Boren*, 429 U.S. 190, 197 (1976). Of course, we have not struck down every gender-based classification that has come before us: "When men and women are not in fact similarly situated in the area covered by the legislation in question, the Equal Protection Clause is not violated." *Caban v. Mohammed*, 441 U.S. 380, 398 (1979) (Stewart, J., dissenting).

At first blush, having a statute apply only to men and not to women in their roles as fathers and mothers may appear preordained by virtue of a woman's ability to bear children (especially where the rule, as here, originated in the mid-nineteenth century). Peering beneath the veneer of biology, however, reveals a series of laws regulating, and in the process defining, the relationship that men and women have vis-à-vis their children. Turning to the history of how our legal rules allocate parentage uncovers the importance not of biology, but of *marriage*, to that determination. In particular, it discloses the importance of preserving the ability of children born to a marriage to receive recognition and support from their father. 1 William Blackstone, *Commentaries on the Laws of England* 435 (1st ed. 1975) ("establishment of marriage in

[11] Section 621 further distinguishes between who can challenge the marital presumption. The statute identifies two possibilities: the husband, of his own accord, and biological unwed father, if joined by the mother. Cal. Evid. Code § 621(c), (d) (West Supp. 1989). Because we find that the statute violates equal protection by preventing men, but not women, from being acknowledged as parents, we do not address the additional question of whether differentiating between who can challenge the presumption also violates a constitutional principle.

all civilized states is built on this natural obligation of the father to provide for his children; for that ascertains and makes known the person who is bound to fulfill this obligation"). Outside of marriage, the man was for the most part absolved of responsibility.[12] If he was not married to the woman with whom he had a child, the law placed the duty of care onto the mother. It was she who was "bound to maintain [the child] as its natural guardian." 2 James Kent, *Commentaries on American Law* 216 (O. W. Holmes, Jr., ed. 1896).[13] The difference that emerges between men and women in whether they were recognized as parents is therefore not established by who gives birth, or even by who has a genetic connection to the child, but rather by whether the legal tie of marriage exists.

Considering our case law up until now proves this point neatly. In *Quilloin v. Walcott*, we reviewed an Equal Protection challenge to a statute that required the consent of wed parents and unwed mothers, but not of unwed fathers, to place a child for adoption. 434 U.S. 246 (1978). Our analysis focused on the differences between fathers – wed and unwed – rather than between unwed fathers and unwed mothers. *Id.* at 256. Because "legal custody is, of course, a central aspect of the marital relationship," we reasoned that unlike an unwed father, "even a father whose marriage has broken apart will have borne full responsibility for the rearing of his children during the period of the marriage." *Id.* In the absence of marriage, states impose other affirmative legal requirements prior to acknowledging a relationship between parent and child. In *Parham v. Hughes*, we held that a law in Georgia allowing mothers but not fathers to bring a wrongful death action for a child born outside of marriage did not violate Equal Protection. 441 U.S. 347 (1979). We relied on "[t]he fact [] that mothers and fathers of illegitimate children are not similarly situated." *Id.* at 355. They were not similarly situated, we reasoned, on account of a legal

[12] This is not to imply that unwed fathers never had fiscal responsibility over children born outside of marriage. The English common law imposed financial obligations on unwed fathers, which some American states codified. *See* 2 JAMES KENT, COMMENTARIES ON AMERICAN LAW 216 (O. W. Holmes, Jr., ed. 1896) (noting that in Ohio, for instance, "the courts of common pleas ascertain[ed] and enforce[d] the duty of putative father to maintain his bastard child"). *But see* Jacobus tenBroek, *California's Dual System of Family Law: Its Origin, Development, and Present Status: Part I*, 16 STAN. L. REV. 257, 313–14 (1964) (noting that in New York and California "[t]he poor law imposition of support liability on both parents of illegitimate children was not similarly transferred to the Civil Code" and instead "the Civil Code seems to place liability exclusively on the mother").

[13] In the absence of "any compulsory order being made upon him," the father would be liable for the child only if "he has adopted the child as his own," which required "the consent of the mother, for the putative father has no legal right to the custody of a bastard child, in opposition to the claim of the mother." *See* Kent, *supra* note 12, at 215–16.

distinction, not a biological one – under Georgia law "only a father can by voluntary unilateral action make an illegitimate child legitimate." *Id.* These differences the law acknowledges between parents are based on whether the parent has taken relevant *legal* action – either to marry or to legitimate a child – rather than any biological difference between men and women in their ability to bear or rear children.

What these cases leave unsaid, of course, is that the sex of the parties still matters in the following way: marriage dictates rights and responsibilities only when the parent is a man. The gender asymmetry is patent, as the legal tie of marriage affects only fathers, not mothers. The rules in these cases work in tandem to ensure that men are viewed as fathers only within marriage while women are viewed as mothers regardless of marriage. Fatherhood coincides nearly perfectly with husbandhood.

Unwed fathers are not, however, without rights. In fact, when the distinctions have not been created by law, we have held that differentiating between unwed mothers and unwed fathers violates Equal Protection. We have resisted the suggestion that mothers and fathers are somehow inherently different when it comes to recognizing their status as parents. Indeed, in *Caban v. Mohammed*, we roundly rejected a statute that required only the consent of the unwed mother, and not the unwed father, prior to placing a child for adoption, given the lack of "any universal difference between maternal and paternal relations." 441 U.S. 380, 389 (1979). Instead, we have made sure to emphasize that "maternal and paternal roles are not invariably different in importance." *Id.*; *see also Stanley v. Illinois*, 405 U.S. 645 (1972) (finding unconstitutional a statute that presumed that unwed fathers, but not unwed mothers, were unfit parents).

C *State's Interests*

Before us today, the state has two potential justifications for its decision to differentiate on the basis of sex. The first is its interest in preserving the integrity of the marital family; the second is protecting the welfare of the child. *See Michael H.*, 191 Cal. App. 3d at 1008–10; *see also Michelle W. v. Ronald W.*, 39 Cal. 3d 354, 363 (1985) (in bank).

Let us begin with the state's first justification for upholding the statute's gender-specific operation. We cannot but agree that the preservation of the marital family is a substantial state interest and our jurisprudence has long protected the marital union: "The institution of marriage has played a critical role both in defining the legal entitlements of family members and in developing the decentralized structure of our democratic society." *Lehr v. Robertson*,

463 U.S. 248, 261 (1983). Accordingly, "state laws almost universally express an appropriate preference for the formal family." *Id.* at 256–57.

Unfortunately, Section 621's protection of the marital family is woefully incomplete. It succeeds in protecting the marital family only in situations where a wife has an affair with a man, but not when a husband has an affair with a woman. The state is hard-pressed to provide reasons justifying this asymmetry. If anything, it should operate in a sex-neutral way to protect the marital families of both men *and* women. Now, it is true that only a wife having an affair will bear the visible consequences in the event that she becomes pregnant. As such, the rule protects the wife's marriage when her pregnancy results from someone other than her husband. A husband having an affair may not need this same "protection," given that he does not bear the physical consequences of the sexual act. Acknowledging the fact that pregnancy affects women rather than men does not, however, justify the statute's protection of wives over husbands. In fact, it perpetuates a state of affairs in which women rear children who have some biological connection to them, while men do not. Section 621 assumes and thereby ensures that women will always take on the role of mother, whereas men may only sometimes take on the role of father. Holding that maternal marital status does not matter for purposes of establishing parentage, while paternal marital status does, helps create this lopsided state of affairs in the first instance.[14]

We have already warned of "classifications which distribute benefits and burdens on the basis of gender," as they "carry the inherent risk of reinforcing the stereotype about the 'proper place' of women." *Orr v. Orr*, 440 U.S. 268, 283 (1979). Women are not solely destined for the "benign offices of wife and mother," *Bradwell v. State*, 83 U.S. 130, 141 (1972) (Bradley, J., concurring), and so our laws should neither presume nor reinforce these roles as determinative for women, and not men.

Even bracketing the gendered operation of the statute, the protection it provides the marital family is still patchy at best. The conclusive presumption is meant to safeguard an intact marital family. Yet the presumption only becomes relevant when the wife has, or is suspected of having, a sexual relationship outside of marriage, which may evince an already weakened marital bond. Moreover, the husband can, within two years of a child's birth,

[14] In the process, it allows fathers to choose whether to parent, while denying mothers that very same choice. Of course, some women who bear a child may eventually choose to place the child for adoption. The question before us, however, addresses an antecedent matter, which is to consider how the presumption defines the relationship between women and children differently than between men and children in establishing who is a parent to a child, a legal connection either parent may later renounce.

unilaterally request a paternity determination – another action that reveals a debilitated bond, or that could result in debilitating the marital bond, regardless of the results of said test. Finally, if the test were to show there is no genetic connection between husband and child, that revelation would lead to the termination of the legal connection between father and child, insofar as the husband would no longer be required to financially support the child. *See McGillis v. Hofeditz*, 101 Cal. App. 2d 760 (1951) (holding the marital presumption had been overcome and that the biological father was instead responsible for providing child support).

The statute further has the perverse effect of preventing a family that desires to be together from legally coming together. For instance, if Carole were to divorce Gerald and marry Michael more than two years after Victoria's birth, Section 621 would prevent Michael from being recognized as Victoria's father. This is precisely what followed from the Supreme Court of California's application of the provision to a similar set of facts. In *Michelle W. v. Ronald W.*, the adult parties before the court were the mother, the mother's ex-husband, and the biological father of the child, who was the mother's current husband. 39 Cal. 3d 354, 358–59 (1985) (in bank). The ex-husband, who had no biological connection to the child, was declared to be the father under the statute. The biological father, who had subsequently married the mother, was thus prevented from asserting parentage. *Id.* We do not mean to critique the outcome of *Michelle W.*, which adeptly recognized the caretaking provided by the mother's first husband and preserved the relationship formed with the child. Rather, we wish to highlight the way in which the statute can work to preclude the establishment of the formal family stability it aims – and claims – to promote. In fact, until the instant case, California's presumption had been applied only in the context of divorced parents, and its implementation in every case had led to the declaration that the mother's ex-husband was the child's father.[15] These examples all question whether the statute's aim of promoting family stability is in fact fulfilled, and they appropriately complicate the relevant inquiry given the existence of more than one family unit in each case.[16]

[15] Until now, the statute has been applied only to protect existing father-child relationships. In *Michelle W.*, the Supreme Court of California "left open the validity of section 621 as applied to a situation where the state is preventing the establishment of a relationship between a putative father and child." 39 Cal. 3d at 362. *See also Vincent B. v. Joan R.*, 126 Cal. App. 3d 619 (1981) (defeating the putative father's interest even where the mother was no longer married to the husband who had conclusively been established as the child's father under the presumption).

[16] By recognizing only one family, and one father-child relationship, the law creates a zero-sum game. *See* discussion *infra* Section III.

The second justification the state offers for the statute is to protect the welfare of the child. The California Appellate Court reasoned that Victoria's welfare "would be harmed, not protected if she were permitted to rebut the conclusive presumption of legitimacy." *Michael H.*, 191 Cal. App. 3d at 1010. In so doing, the court articulated the statute's central concern as preventing a child from being considered "illegitimate," which once had severe consequences at law. Kent, *Commentaries on American Law* 314–15 (under the common law the child was considered to have no legal parent). We have, however, long ago struck down as unconstitutional laws that disadvantage a child based on his or her parents' marital status. *See Levy v. Louisiana*, 391 U.S. 68, 71 (1968) ("Why should the illegitimate child be denied rights merely because of his birth out of wedlock?"). Because such a distinction is no longer tenable, neither is the state's interest. The State of California, despite the Court of Appeal's language to the contrary, has also eliminated any distinction between children based on whether their parents are married: California, as we have noted, has adopted the Uniform Parentage Act, which officially "abolish[ed] the incidents of illegitimacy and establish[ed] the legal equality of children." *Michelle W.*, 39 Cal. 3d at 362, n. 5 (quoting 6 B. E. Witkin, *Summary of California Law* 217–18 (8th ed. 1984)). As California no longer impermissibly differentiates between "legitimate" and "illegitimate" children, ensuring legitimacy can no longer be a valid state interest.

Yet the statute, by conclusively presuming the husband is the father, expresses a judgment that ensuring that a child is born into a marriage will always promote the welfare of the child.[17] In this way, the statute prioritizes marriage over any potential biological connection, or any functional relationship that may have developed. Marriage, however, is not coterminous with the Constitution. Looking to our case law addressing unwed fathers is instructive. We have, time and again, identified values worth preserving other than marriage, and have specifically provided constitutional protection to "those family relationships unlegitimized by a marriage ceremony." *Stanley v. Illinois*, 405 U.S. 645, 651 (1972).

In *Stanley v. Illinois*, we held that an unwed father has a fundamental liberty interest in the relationship developed with his children. 405 U.S. at 658. We had occasion in that case to address the constitutionality of an Illinois statute that excluded unwed fathers from the list of parents entitled to a hearing prior to having their children taken away from them. *Id.* at 650.

[17] If establishing genetic paternity were the real concern, there would be a mechanism by which a man could prove his biological connection to the child and have that connection recognized – which is precisely what the statute prevents.

In holding that such a statute violated due process and equal protection, we defined the father's constitutional interest as "the companionship, care, custody, and management of his . . . children." *Id.* at 651. We were likewise intent on protecting the relationship that developed between an unwed father and his children in *Caban v. Mohammed*. 441 U.S. 380 (1979). In *Caban*, we struck down a New York statute that allowed an unwed mother, but not an unwed father, to veto placing a child for adoption. *Id.* at 394. We reasoned that "maternal and paternal roles are not invariably different in importance" and acknowledged that "an unwed father may have a relationship with his children fully comparable to that of the mother." *Id.* at 389.[18]

To be clear, then, our jurisprudence has identified at least two facets of parenthood, separate and apart from marriage, that lead to constitutional rights: a biological connection, given that these unwed fathers were all genetically related to the child, and the existence of a developed relationship between the father and child. A hierarchy of values still emerges, with the latter – establishing a relationship between parent and child – holding a particularly privileged position in our law. As we have said before, and repeat anew, "biological relationships are not exclusive determination of the existence of a family." *Smith v. Org. of Foster Families for Equal. & Reform*, 431 U.S. 816, 843 (1977). Justice Stewart echoed that same conclusion a few years later and declared: "Parental rights do not spring full-blown from the biological connection between parent and child. They require relationships more enduring." *Caban*, 441 U.S. at 397 (Stewart, J., dissenting). Our decision in *Lehr v. Robertson* expanded on this very point, clarifying that "the mere existence of a biological link does not merit equivalent constitutional protection." 463 U.S. 248, 261 (1983).[19] In *Lehr*, we found no fault in a statutory scheme that did not provide an unwed father with notice of the pending adoption proceeding of his biological child. *Id.* at 250. In the process, we identified the crux of what warrants constitutional protection – the development of "a relationship." *Id.* at 261. Robert Lehr, the biological father of the

[18] In that case, we noted that the unwed father, Abdiel Caban, and the unwed mother, Maria Mohammed, "lived together as a natural family for several years" with their two children. *Caban*, 441 U.S. at 389. Moreover, "both mother and father participated in the care and support of their children." *Id.* As such, "[t]here is no reason to believe that the Caban children – aged 4 and 6 at the time of the adoption proceedings – had a relationship with their mother unrivaled by the affection and concern of their father." *Id.*

[19] Biology is also decreasing in importance in other legal fields. *See, e.g.*, Jan Ellen Rein, *Relatives by Blood, Adoption, and Association: Who Should Get What and Why*, 37 VAND. L. REV. 711, 713 (1984) ("the traditional preoccupation with blood ties is now on the wane" in inheritance laws regulating adopted children).

child who had been placed for adoption, had not lived with the child, had not provided any financial support to the child, and had failed to enter his own name into a putative father registry.[20] *Id.* at 252. In the absence of a "developed parent-child relationship," Lehr had no rights to claim. *Id.* at 261. The Constitution extends its panoply of protections only to "an unwed father [who] demonstrates a full commitment to the responsibilities of parenthood." *Id.*

Given this context, it bears mention again that until the lower court's decision in *Michael H.*, Section 621's conclusive presumption had been applied exclusively to allow, rather than to prevent, the recognition of a developed father-child relationship. *See Michelle W.*, 39 Cal. 3d at 361, n. 4. ("We leave open the question of the validity of section 621 as applied . . . to termination situations for a case in which the issue is squarely presented.") Moreover, the two-year limit set forth in the statute itself represents California's preference for the existence of an actual relationship, over and above a genetic link. In upholding the two-year limit imposed on requests for paternity determinations, the Court of Appeal explained the importance of the relationship already established by age two, which outweighs any possible biological connection or lack thereof: "This social relationship is much more important, to the child at least, than a biological relationship of actual paternity." *In re Marriage of B.*, 124 Cal. App. 3d 524, 530–31 (1981) (quoting William P. Hoffman, Jr., *California's Tangled Web: Blood Tests and the Conclusive Presumption of Legitimacy*, 20 Stan. L. Rev. 754 (1968)).

The case before us exposes the insurmountable holes in the statute's ability to adequately preserve the relationship that has developed between a parent and child where that relationship is between an unwed father and child. As such, the statute fails to carry out the state's interest in promoting the child's welfare.

Because the statute does not bear a substantial relationship to either of the state's asserted interests, neither our Constitution nor our case law supports Section 621's differentiation between parents on the basis of sex.

III SECTION 621 VIOLATES DUE PROCESS

Our conclusion that California's scheme violates Equal Protection does not provide legislatures with guidance on how to resolve the discrepancy – whether

[20] We suspend, for the purpose of this analysis, any assessment of whether the unwed mother in these cases took part in preventing the unwed father from developing a relationship with the child. *But see Lehr*, 463 U.S. at 271 (White, J., dissenting) (noting that accepting appellant's allegations as true means that "but for the actions of the child's mother there would have been the kind of significant relationship that the majority concedes is entitled to the full panoply of procedural due process protections").

the presumption of parentage ought to extend to mothers too, or to no parents at all. Looking to the child's interest in preserving a relationship with the adults in her life helps furnish a resolution. We now address Victoria's separate pleas to provide constitutional protection to the relationship she has developed with Michael. Notably, the guardian ad litem appointed by the court to ensure that Victoria's interests would be represented concluded that a de facto parent-child relationship exists between Michael and Victoria, and that it is in Victoria's best interests to preserve such a relationship. Brief for Appellant Victoria D. 32, n. 4. While the guardian ad litem's assessment by no means controls the constitutional question at hand, it helps underscore the import of the issue for Victoria. We consider here Victoria's challenge based on the Due Process clause of the Fourteenth Amendment, which sounds in both substantive and procedural notes.

We have already set forth our uninterrupted history of recognizing the parent-child relationship as deserving of constitutional protection: "the interest of a parent in the companionship, care, [and] custody" is paramount and "undeniably warrants deference and, absent a powerful countervailing interest, protection." *Stanley*, 405 U.S. at 651. This parent-child relationship does not, however, point in only one direction. To state the obvious, the child is an integral part of that relationship and, like the parent, is cloaked by the constitutional protection the relation itself receives.[21] In *Stanley*, we found that the Due Process clause safeguarded the father's interest "when at stake was the dismemberment of his family." *Id.* at 658. That concern is at stake here for Victoria too – Victoria's family relationship is under threat of being terminated by the conclusive presumption set forth in Section 621. Stated otherwise, the interests of the parent and the child in the preservation of their relationship are two sides of the same coin.

We now find that Section 621 is unconstitutional: it interferes with the fundamental right we have identified inheres in such a relationship and it provides no mechanism for Victoria to prove the existence of that relationship. Accordingly, we hold that it is impermissible to prevent a child from seeking recognition of an established parent-child relationship by conclusive presumption.

Our treatment of illegitimacy is edifying. The relevant relationship before us is between parent and child, not between parents: children should not be

[21] Webster's New Collegiate Dictionary defines the term "relationship" in the following manner: "the state or character of being related or interrelated; CONNECTION <show the ~ between two things>." WEBSTER'S NEW COLLEGIATE DICTIONARY (150th ed. 1981).

discriminated against based on their parents' choices.[22] Differentiating between classes of children due to their parents' behavior runs exactly contrary to the wisdom espoused by our case law, which makes clear that a parent's decision ought not to inflict harm on the child. "[A] state may not invidiously discriminate against illegitimate children by denying them substantial benefits accorded to children generally." *Gomez v. Perez*, 409 U.S. 535, 538 (1973). Failing to recognize the real relationship that has developed between Victoria and Michael would disadvantage Victoria *because of* the decisions undertaken by Michael and Carole – namely, to have sexual relations while Carole was still married. No similar impediment would, for example, be placed on a child's relationship with parents who had sex only with each other during their marriage. But here, where adults biologically related to Victoria freely chose to enter into a sexual relationship while not married to each other, it is Victoria who suffers the consequences.[23] This is so even though Carole and Michael would not be subject to any legal sanctions for their actions, as California has abolished the crime of adultery.[24]

Recognizing the plurality of relationships children establish with adults is especially important in the context of families who may have experienced rupture through death, divorce, or change by other means.[25] The blended family form is increasingly common, as families undergo multiple marriages and divorces.[26] Rather than hinder this movement, states have recognized and enabled such mobility, evinced by the near-nationwide recognition of no-fault

[22] California defines the parent and child relationship to apply "equally to every child and to every parent, regardless of the marital status of the parents." Cal. Civ. Code § 7002 (West 1983); *see also* Unif. Parentage Act (Unif. Law Comm'n 1973) (rendering the parents' marital status irrelevant); Brief for Appellant Victoria D. 31.

[23] "[T]here is no constitutionally sufficient justification for denying such an essential right to a child simply because its natural father has not married its mother. For a state to do so is 'illogical and unjust.'" *Gomez*, 409 U.S. at 538.

[24] Since 1955, the Model Penal Code has recommended that all states abolish laws against adultery. Model Penal Code § 213.6 (Am. Law Inst. 1955). California followed suit in 1975, and adultery is no longer a crime in that state. 1975 Cal. Stat. 133.

[25] "Today, the nuclear family consisting of a husband wage earner, a wife homemaker, and two or more dependent children, that was once held up as typical and normal, accounts for less than 10 percent of all households." Family Service America, The State of Families: 1984–1985 8 (1984).

[26] "Only 67% of the children under 18 were living with their own father and mother who were still in their first marriage." Paul C. Glick, Marriage, Divorce, Widowhood, and Remarriage by Family Characteristics: June 1975 16 (U.S. Dep't of Commerce, Bureau of the Census, ed. 1977). Moreover, women with children who divorce, can and do remarry. *Id.* at 8–10.

divorce.[27] In practice then, children of a divorced couple often have two sets of parents; not recognizing the reality of these many relationships would be detrimental to those children, and to the integrity of their families. Given the growing percentage of children who experience the divorce of their parents, or who are born to unmarried parents, we must ensure that the relations they form are treated with the same respect as the relations of children born into an intact marriage. It is not our role to hamper the development or recognition of real family ties between children and the adults who raise them – be they biological parents, divorced parents, unwed parents, adoptive parents, stepparents, or any other type of parent.

Our Constitution does not force families into a straitjacket. Quite the opposite: it protects the rights of families to define for themselves how they are composed and what shape they wish to take. Families are dynamic entities that adapt and change; how families are formed varies, depending on custom, culture, or need, which the law ought to facilitate rather than frustrate.[28] As Justice Stevens set forth in one critical line in *Lehr*: "The intangible fibers that connect parent and child have infinite variety." 463 U.S. at 256.

While we have never explicitly held that there can be more than one legal father, or more than two legal parents, we do so now. Liberty requires that we acknowledge the existence of an established parent-child relationship, even if it means that we recognize more than two fathers, or more than two mothers. Significantly, we see no reason to limit recognition to one father or one mother. Nothing in our laws expressly restricts the parent-child relationship to only *two* parents. Rather, we have refused to interpret our Constitution to dictate the configuration a family ought to take, and instead have understood it to protect an individual's right to choose how his or her family is constituted. *See, e.g., Pierce v. Soc'y of Sisters*, 268 U.S. 510, 534–35 (1925) (striking down a statute that "unreasonably interfere[d] with the liberty of parents and guardians to direct the upbringing and education of children under their control").

[27] Divorce, which used to only be available on the basis of fault, is now available to married couples everywhere. *See* Herma Hill Kay, *Equality and Difference: A Perspective on No-Fault Divorce and Its Aftermath*, 56 U. CIN. L. REV. 1, 1, 5–7 (1987) (identifying California's recognition of no-fault divorce in 1963, and then noting that all fifty states have a no-fault option, with some variation).

[28] Justice Brennan's concurrence in *Moore v. City of East Cleveland* explains the multiple forms and functions families may take on: "[t]he 'extended family' that provided generations of early Americans with social services and economic and emotional support in times of hardship, and was the beachhead for successive waves of immigrants who populated our cities, remains not merely still a pervasive living pattern, but under the goal of brutal economic necessity, a prominent pattern virtually a means of survival for large numbers of the poor and deprived minorities of our society." 431 U.S. at 508 (Brennan, J., concurring).

That freedom of choice begins with the constitutional protections we provide the decision of whether to even begin a family, as in the decision of whether to bear and beget a child. *Eisenstadt v. Baird*, 405 U.S. 438, 453 (1972); *see also Roe v. Wade*, 410 U.S. 113, 152–53 (1973). Importantly, "[W]hen the government intrudes on choices concerning family living arrangements, this Court must examine carefully the importance of the governmental interests advanced and the extent to which they are served by the challenged regulation." *Moore v. City of E. Cleveland*, 431 U.S. 494, 499 (1977).

Imposing an arbitrary number on how many relationships the law recognizes is misguided for another important reason: it does not take into account the child's interests. The child's well-being should be squarely at the center of any decision involving the protection of the parent-child relationship. It is always instructive in this quickly developing area of law and human relations to look to the expertise of states, and the directions they have taken in response to evolutions in family structure. One trend that is particularly pertinent to the question before us is the rise in the use of a "best interests" analysis in custody determinations.[29] As the name of the analysis suggests, the focus of these cases is on the promotion and protection of the best interests of the child. California is one of the many states that has adopted the "best interests" analysis by statute; it is coupled with a declared public policy to "assure minor children of frequent and continuing contact with both parents after the parents have separated or dissolved their marriage." Cal. Civ. Code § 4600(a), (b) (West 1983); Brief for Appellant Victoria D. 23–24.

The interests of the child are central not only to questions of custody, but also to questions of who can function as a parent in certain situations. California has given due consideration to an individual who may become a "de facto" parent, such as a foster parent, and recognizes that he or she can claim proper standing in a dependency proceeding. *Christina K. v. Superior Court*, 184 Cal. App. 3d 1463, 1469 (Cal. Ct. App. 1986). In particular, the Supreme Court of California has defined a de facto parent for purposes of standing to include whether the person "on a day-to-day basis, assumes the role of parent, seeking to fulfill both the child's physical needs and his psychological need for affection and care." *In re B.G.*, 11 Cal. 3d. 679, 692 n. 18 (1974) (in bank). Significantly, the court's analysis does not rely on either biology or marriage. Where a de facto parent is recognized, the court has held

[29] *See* David L. Chambers, *Rethinking the Substantive Rules for Custody Disputes in Divorce*, 83 MICH. L. REV. 477, 478 (1984) (identifying the movement of states to "replace[] the maternal presumption with a rule directing courts to be guided solely by the child's 'welfare' or 'best interests'").

that those individuals "should be permitted to appear as parties to assert and protect their own interest in the companionship, care, custody and management of the child." *Id.* at 693.

Given the importance of the relationship between a parent and child, and the due process protections we have bestowed upon it, we are mindful that we may have a number of relationships worthy of protection. Here, Victoria has established relationships with Michael and Gerald. Both were present in her life in crucial and substantial ways. Both have functioned as important figures in Victoria's development. And both, at different times in Victoria's infancy, have lived with Victoria, held Victoria out as their own, and had a relationship with Carole, Victoria's mother. The report ordered by the Los Angeles County Superior Court found Michael to be "the single adult in Victoria D.'s life most committed to caring for her needs on a long-term basis." J.A. 51. Gerald has also been integral to Victoria's early life and maturation: he was by all accounts "a lovingly responsible father to Victoria, and was, in fact, most oftentimes Victoria's sole caretaker." Brief for Appellee 5. At various points in Victoria's life, Michael was "Daddy" and Gerald was "Poppa." Brief for Appellant Victoria D. 28. As such, it appears that both Michael and Gerald have demonstrated a "developed parent-child relationship" with Victoria. *Lehr*, 463 U.S. at 261. It would be arbitrary and artificial to hold that only *one* of these men can be deemed her father. Neither marriage nor biology trumps the importance of the "companionship [and] care," *Stanley*, 405 U.S. at 651, that arises in the connection between parent and child.[30]

Victoria has a fundamental right in the relationship she develops with Michael. Section 621 fails to provide her with any avenue to protect it. Only Gerald, or Michael if accompanied by Carole, are afforded that recourse. Cal. Evid. Code § 621(c), (d) (West Supp. 1989). While "[p]rocedure by presumption is always cheaper and easier," we have struck it down "when … the procedure forecloses the determinative issues of competence and care, when it explicitly disdains present realities in deference to past formalities" and when, as here, "it needlessly risks running roughshod over the important interests of *both parent and child*." *Stanley*, 405 U.S. at 656–57 (emphasis added).

We have already held that Section 621 violates the Equal Protection clause by unjustifiably differentiating between parents on the basis of sex. We now hold that where there is more than one stable parent-child relationship; where

[30] It is crucial to note that this problem of constitutional dimensions would also arise if the statute were amended to apply to a *woman*'s marital family – the conclusive presumption would still terminate the relationship between mother and child regardless of any functional relationship, and regardless of any biological connection.

the adult has undertaken responsibility in the rearing of and caring for the child; and where the child considers that adult to be a parent, then that relationship merits the constitutional protections we have granted others in that same situation, without imposing a numerical limit. That limit will emerge naturally, by the lived constraints of establishing relationships between children and adults as well as by the relations formed between parents. Because we have a factual record restricted to a motion for summary judgment, we remand to the trial court to determine the extent of Victoria's relationship with Michael. Deciding otherwise, and conclusively depriving Victoria of her right to establish a relationship with Michael, would divest her of the due process rights she holds in the relationship with her father – or fathers, as the case may be.

Reversed and remanded.

10

Commentary on *DeShaney v. Winnebago County Department of Social Services*

MACARENA SAEZ

INTRODUCTION

In 1980, after the divorce of Randy and Melody DeShaney, a court granted Randy DeShaney custody of his one-year-old son, Joshua.[1] In 1982, Winnebago County Department of Social Services (DSS) received the first report that Joshua may have been subject to abuse by Randy. DSS, however, took no action until 1983, when hospital authorities notified DSS that Joshua had been admitted with injuries consistent with child abuse. DSS ordered Joshua's temporary removal from the parental home and formed an ad hoc team to review Joshua's situation. The team decided that there was no conclusive evidence of abuse and returned Joshua to Randy, issuing several recommendations agreed to by Randy, including that he obtain counseling services, enroll Joshua in a preschool program, and that his girlfriend move out of the home (on suspicion that she may be abusing Joshua).

For the next six months, the same caseworker made monthly visits to the home and consistently took notes of Randy's failure to comply with the agreement.[2] Joshua was not enrolled in a school program, the girlfriend had not moved out, and Joshua showed signs of further abuse. During that period, Joshua was admitted two more times to the hospital with injuries consistent with abuse, and the social worker again recorded the incidents in her files but took no further action. After these incidents, Randy did not allow the social worker to see Joshua, stating he was too sick to have visitors. Even then, the social worker took no further action. In March 1984, when Joshua was four years old, he was admitted in the hospital with injuries so severe that he

[1] *DeShaney v. Winnebago Cty. Dep't of Soc. Servs.*, 489 U.S. 189, 192 (1989).
[2] *Id.* at 193.

suffered from permanent brain damage. Joshua would spend the rest of his life in an institution for people with severe mental disabilities.[3]

THE HISTORY OF THE *DESHANEY* CASE

The Fourteenth Amendment of the U.S. Constitution prohibits any state from depriving "any person of life, liberty, or property, without due process of law." The federal civil rights statute, 42 U.S.C. § 1983, enacted by Congress in 1871, has been the instrument to seek redress for the deprivation of constitutional rights. Early on, the Supreme Court limited the scope of Section 1983, and finding a violation of the Due Process Clause has not been an easy road.[4] Section 1983 claims require two basic elements: "(1) the conduct that harms the plaintiff must be committed under color of state law (i.e., state action), and (2) the conduct must deprive the plaintiff of a constitutional right."[5] Courts have been hesitant to interpret the Fourteenth Amendment as imposing on states an affirmative duty to protect.[6] There are, however, cases in which the Supreme Court has established that states have positive obligations, particularly when individuals have been deprived of liberty by the state and cannot, for that reason, care for themselves. For example, in the case of inmates and, in some circumstances, individuals institutionalized in mental health facilities, states can create a "special relationship" with the plaintiff because the individual was under custody or care of the state.[7]

Joshua and his mother brought a Section 1983 action against Winnebago County, the DSS and several DSS employees for deprivation of Joshua's "liberty without due process of law, in violation of his rights under the Fourteenth Amendment, by failing to intervene to protect him against a risk

3 Crocker Stephenson, *Boy at Center of Famous "Poor Joshua!" Supreme Court Dissent Dies*, J. SENTINEL (Nov. 11, 2015), http://archive.jsonline.com/news/obituaries/joshua12-b99614381z1-346259422.html/ (Joshua DeShaney passed away in 2016, at the age of thirty-six).

4 For an analysis of Section 1983 *see* Roberta M. Saielli, DeShaney v. Winnebago County Department of Social Services: *The Future of Section 1983 Actions for State Inaction*, 21 LOY. U. CHI. L. J. 169 (1989).

5 *Ketchum v. Alameda Cty.*, 811 F.2d 1243, 1245 (9th Cir. 1987), citing *Haygood v. Younger*, 769 F.2d 1350, 1354 (9th Cir. 1985).

6 *DeShaney*, 489 U.S. at 194 (stating that the Due Process Clause of the Fourteenth Amendment does not require a state or local government entity to protect its citizens from private violence).

7 *DeShaney*, 489 U.S. at 198 (citing *Robinson v. California*, 342 U.S. 165, 172 (1952)) (obligation to provide medical care to incarcerated individuals); *Youngberg v. Romeo*, 457 U.S. 307 (1982) (regarding the state obligation to provide some services to individuals who are institutionalized). *Estelle v. Gamble*, 429 U.S. 97, 106 (1976) (referring to individuals in custody as having a special relationship with the state).

of violence at his father's hands of which they knew or should have known."[8] The District Court granted summary judgment for respondents, and the U.S. Court of Appeals for the Seventh Circuit affirmed, holding that a state's inaction is not a violation of the Due Process Clause of the Fourteenth Amendment.[9] Judge Posner, writing the majority opinion for the Seventh Circuit, made a distinction between individuals deprived of liberty and Joshua's situation.[10] DSS had not deprived Joshua of his liberty and there was no direct causation between his injuries and the role played by DSS.[11] On February 21, 1989, the U.S. Supreme Court affirmed.[12] It held that states have no affirmative duty under the Constitution to protect an individual from actions by private individuals.[13]

The main issue before the Supreme Court was whether the Fourteenth Amendment imposed on states a positive obligation to protect life, liberty, and property when private individuals put those interests at risk. The Rehnquist Court, in a six to three opinion, stated: "The [Due Process] Clause is phrased as a limitation on the State's power to act, not as a guarantee of certain minimal levels of safety and security."[14] According to the Court, the Fourteenth Amendment is limited to protecting individuals from state abuse of power, but it does not extend a positive obligation of protection, not even when such protection may be necessary for the realization of those rights.[15] Prior to this case, the Supreme Court had established that the Due Process Clause did not impose an obligation on states to provide government aid.[16] *DeShaney* confirmed this doctrine.[17]

Plaintiffs argued that when Joshua was referred to DSS, he had been placed in a special relationship with the state that had triggered a positive obligation of protection that DSS had failed to fulfill.[18] The majority in *DeShaney*

[8] *DeShaney*, 489 U.S. at 194.

[9] *Id.* at 194.

[10] *DeShaney v. Winnebago Cty Dep't Soc. Servs.*, 812 F.2d 298, 301 (7th Cir. 1987).

[11] *Id.* at 302.

[12] *DeShaney*, 489 U.S. at 203.

[13] *Id.* at 191.

[14] *Id.* at 195.

[15] *Id.* at 196.

[16] *DeShaney*, 489 U.S. at 196 (citing *Harris v. McRae*, 448 U.S. 297, 317–18 (1980)) (discussing the Due Process Clause of Fifth Amendment and finding no obligation to fund abortions or other medical services); *Lindsey v. Normet*, 405 U.S. 56, 74, 92 (1972) (discussing the Due Process Clause of the Fourteenth Amendment and finding no obligation to provide adequate housing). *See also Youngberg*, 457 U.S. at 317 ("As a general matter, a State is under no constitutional duty to provide substantive services for those within its border").

[17] *DeShaney*, 489 U.S. at 197.

[18] *Id.* at 197.

disagreed.[19] Joshua was not, the Court stated, under the care of the state like individuals who are deprived of liberty.[20] According to the Court, once DSS returned Joshua to his father, he was not in a worse-off position than before.[21] As stated by Chief Justice, "the State does not become the permanent guarantor of an individual's safety by having once offered him shelter."[22] The majority decision contemplated that there could be other mechanisms to redress the harm, such as through tort law, but not connected to a constitutional right.[23] In a final reflection, Justice Rehnquist observed that just as the inaction of the social worker was criticized, so too would the premature removal of Joshua by the government, which would have improperly affected the father's constitutional parental right.[24]

In his dissenting opinion, Justice Brennan starts by analyzing what DSS actually did and not what it failed to do. In his opinion, the state obligation does not derive from an omission but, just as in the case of inmates, from the actions of the government that put Joshua into the protection of the state.[25] Every person who tried to intervene on Joshua's behalf hit the same wall: DSS was ultimately in charge, even though doctors, neighbors, the father's ex-wife, and the police tried to intervene. For Justice Brennan, the lack of effective actions by DSS once it had opened a file on Joshua amounted to abuse of power.[26] Justice Brennan explained at length the connection between institutionalization cases (*Youngberg v. Romeo* in particular) and Joshua's situation.[27] What triggered the duty to protect inmates and institutionalized individuals was not the deprivation of liberty. The common denominator between *Youngberg* and Joshua's claim is that the state actions prevented the help of others: "If a State cuts off private sources of aid and then refuses aid itself, it cannot wash its hands of the harm that results from its inaction."[28] There is not a bright line between state action and omission.

Justice Blackmun, criticized by some scholars for his appeal to emotions,[29] wrote a short dissenting opinion stating that "compassion need not be exiled

[19] *Id.* at 198.
[20] *Id.* at 199.
[21] *Id.* at 201.
[22] *Id.* at 201.
[23] *Id.* at 202.
[24] *Id.* at 203.
[25] *Id.* at 205.
[26] *Id.* at 212.
[27] *Id.* at 206–208, 212. *See also Youngberg v. Romeo*, 457 U.S. at 324 (holding a state has a duty to provide reasonable safety for all residents and personnel in an institution).
[28] *Id.* at 207.
[29] Laura Krugman Ray, *Judicial Personality: Rhetoric and Emotion in Supreme Court Opinions*, 59 Wash. & Lee L. Rev. 193, 231 (2002).

from the province of judging,"[30] and added what became one of the most quoted paragraphs of this case:

> Poor Joshua! Victim of repeated attacks by an irresponsible, bullying, cowardly, and intemperate father, and abandoned by respondents who placed him in a dangerous predicament and who knew or learned what was going on, and yet did essentially nothing except, as the Court revealingly observes, … "dutifully recorded these incidents in [their] files."[31]

THE IMPACT OF *DESHANEY*

Across the country several news outlets reported on Joshua's case. This interest, however, did not translate into legal interventions of third parties or civil rights groups supporting an expanded reading of the duty to protect. Only two amicus briefs were filed on behalf of plaintiffs and none came from women's organizations.[32] However, *DeShaney*'s impact was soon visible in cases such as *Balistreri v. Pacifica Police Department* and *Town of Castle Rock v. Gonzales.* In *Balistreri* a woman sued the police department for failing to enforce a protection order against her husband.[33] The Ninth Circuit, relying on *DeShaney*, stated that "[t]he affirmative duty to protect arises not from the State's knowledge of the individual's predicament or from its expressions of intent to help him, but from the limitation which it has imposed on his freedom to act on his own behalf."[34] In *Town of Castle Rock v. Gonzales*, the Supreme Court used the same reasoning when Jessica Gonzales alleged that police officers violated the Due Process Clause of the Fourteenth Amendment by failing to properly respond to her request for assistance after her former husband had violated a restraining order by abducting their three daughters from the front yard of her house. After hours of inaction by the police, the husband drove a truck to the police station, opened fire and was killed. The police found the bodies of Gonzales' three daughters, killed by the husband, in the back of the truck.[35] The Supreme Court, citing *DeShaney*, stated that "[i]t is perfectly clear, on the one hand, that neither the Federal Constitution itself, nor any federal statute, granted respondent or her children any individual entitlement to police protection."[36]

[30] *DeShaney*, 489 U.S. at 213.
[31] *Id.* at 213.
[32] *Id.* at 190.
[33] 901 F.2d 696, 698 (9th Cir. 1988).
[34] *Id.* at 700.
[35] *Town of Castle Rock v. Gonzales*, 545 U.S. 748, 750 (2005).
[36] *Id.* at 773.

DeShaney reinforced the idea that the Constitution protects citizens from state interventions and not from private citizens even when the state was aware of the risk.[37] After *DeShaney*, a state only has a duty to protect its citizens' constitutional rights when it creates a special relationship with an individual.[38] A relationship between the state and a person, however, only becomes "special" when the state strips the individual of autonomy such that only the state can provide the necessary protection of an individual's constitutional rights. These cases show tragic outcomes in situations in which individuals thought that the state was protecting them or others. Can doctors or neighbors denouncing a situation of child abuse trust that their complaints will save a life? Can domestic violence survivors obtaining a temporary protection order trust that such document will truly enhance their safety? *DeShaney* weakened the trust of citizens in state institutions and left vulnerable individuals with diminished constitutional rights.

A FEMINIST *DESHANEY* DECISION

Professor Weaver's opinion changes the course of Section 1983 litigation by broadening the protection offered by states to vulnerable individuals. In her opinion, Winnebago County had an affirmative duty under Section 1983 to protect Joshua, derived from the special relationship formed the first time that DSS received information of Joshua's abuse by his father. From the outset of her opinion, Professor Weaver identifies DSS as "reckless" in its failure to protect Joshua, triggering a violation of Joshua's life and liberty without due process.

In the first section of her opinion, Professor Weaver analyzes the history of the Fourteenth Amendment, passed to protect freed black slaves not only from state actions but also from the actions of private citizens. Professor Weaver illustrates this point by referring to the Rosewood massacre in 1923 – six days of killing and terrorizing of a prosperous black neighborhood in Florida abetted by the total indifference of the state. Professor Weaver's opinion argues that the Fourteenth Amendment was called on to protect individuals from situations like the Rosewood massacre. The state's indifference towards individuals it should have protected, Weaver states, enables private perpetrators to inflict harm.

Professor Weaver's opinion holds that all the requirements, established by prior case law, for forming a special relationship were met by DSS in Joshua's case. Based on *Jensen v. Conrad*, Weaver finds three elements that create a

37 *DeShaney*, 489 U.S. at 194.

38 *Id.* at 196.

special relationship between the state and an individual: (1) the victim or perpetrator was in state custody at the time of or prior to the incident; (2) the state had expressly stated its desire to provide affirmative protection to a class of individuals; and (3) the state knew of the danger to the victim.[39] According to Professor Weaver, Joshua's case met all three elements. Even if he was not in the custody of the state at the moment of the last beating, he had been in the custody of the state before, triggering at that moment a special relationship that continued because the state expressed its desire to provide affirmative protection to Joshua by assigning a social worker to his case. The third element cannot be denied since the notes of the social worker and medical reports were very clear about Joshua's state of danger.

Professor Weaver's analysis of the "special relationship" between Joshua and the state relies on two cases rejected by the Court of Appeals for the Seventh Circuit when it decided against Joshua and his mother.[40] In one of these cases, decided by the Third Circuit, the court held that "once the State learns that a particular child is in danger of abuse from third parties and actually undertakes to protect him from that danger, a 'special relationship' arises between it and the child which imposes an affirmative constitutional duty to provide adequate protection."[41]

In addition to the "special relationship," constitutional tort law establishes that state responsibility under Section 1983 is triggered by the state's "deliberate indifference," as when "supervisory personnel 'exhibited deliberate indifference to a known injury, a known risk, or a specific duty.'"[42] Professor Weaver notes that the same indifference placed Joshua in a worse-off position than if DSS had not intervened in the first place. Similar to Justice Brennan's dissenting opinion in *DeShaney*, Professor Weaver emphasizes that the DSS's inaction had dire consequences by allowing Joshua's father to continue the beatings without anyone, other than DSS, being able to stop him.

Professor Weaver also rejects the idea that the social worker assigned to Joshua was protected by qualified immunity. Wisconsin legislation states, "The immunity provided under this subsection [referring to Wis. Stat. § 48.981(4)] does not apply to liability for abusing or neglecting a child."[43] The social worker's responsibility was not to describe Joshua's abuse, but to

[39] 747 F. 2d. 185, 190–94 (1984).

[40] *Estate of Bailey by Oare v. York County*, 470 U.S. 1052, 105, S.Ct. 1754, 84 L.Ed.2d 818 (1985), *Jensen v. Conrad*, 747 F.2d at 190–94 (in dicta), *cert. denied*, 470 U.S. 1052, 105 S.Ct. 1754, 84 L.Ed.2d 818 (1985).

[41] *Estate of Bailey by Oare*, 470 U.S. at 194.

[42] *Doe v. N.Y. City Dep't of Soc. Servs.*, 649 F.2d 134, 145 (2d Cir. 1982).

[43] Wis. Stat. § 48.981(4) (2018).

protect him from it. Professor Weaver challenges the reader to find a good explanation for the social worker's inaction, when she knew, as stated during trial, that the phone would ring one day with the news of Joshua's death.

Finally, Professor Weaver adds two elements to her opinion that were absent from the original one. She adds an analysis of the responsibility of states under the Child Abuse and Prevention Treatment Act (CAPTA) of 1974. Professor Weaver also bases her decision in Wisconsin's interpretation of the doctrine of *parens patriae*.[44] The basic tenet of *parens patriae* is that the state has the right to step in as the guardian of children when parents do not fulfill their parental obligations.[45] This allows the state to act on behalf of the child in cases of abuse or neglect, and it supports the proposition that the state takes seriously the protection of children in both private and public realms.[46] In theory, the doctrine suggests that what matters are the needs of the most vulnerable members of society. This doctrine, however, has often been invoked by states to remove children disproportionately from poor families and families of color. This was the case for generations of Native Americans who were removed from their families without due process.[47] Rather than protecting the most vulnerable members of society, the government has used this doctrine as a tool to oppress them.

The dark past of the *parens patriae* doctrine makes it hard to see its potential positive interpretation. Professor Weaver's use of the doctrine in *DeShaney*, however, can be viewed as feminist, with the state having an obligation to intervene based on an ethic of care. As such, the duty to protect children is not a prerogative but an obligation. As Martha Fineman has proposed, family law should revolve around dependent relationships.[48] In this vein, this duty applies across public/private spheres, challenging the insulation of private life that has been so detrimental to gender equality.[49] If the state has an obligation to

[44] The doctrine of *parens patriae* came to the colonies from England. Judith Areen, *Intervention between the Parent and Child: A Reappraisal of the State's Role in Child Neglect and Abuse Cases*, 63 GEO. L.J. 887, 898 (1975).

[45] *Id.* at 893.

[46] JOAN C. TRONTO, CARING DEMOCRACY: MARKETS, EQUALITY, AND JUSTICE 139, 140 (2013).

[47] For the history of the Indian Adoption Project and the use of the *parens patriae* to justify forced adoptions of Indigenous children in the United States, *see* MARGARET D. JACOBS, WHITE MOTHER TO A DARK RACE: SETTLER COLONIALISM, MATERNALISM, AND THE REMOVAL OF INDIGENOUS CHILDREN IN THE AMERICAN WEST AND AUSTRALIA, 1880–1940 55 (2009).

[48] Martha Albertson Fineman, *Care and Gender*, *in* REASSEMBLING MOTHERHOOD: PROCREATION AND CARE IN A GLOBALIZED WORLD 6 (Yasmine Ergas et al. eds., 2017).

[49] For instance, the family as a sphere of nonintervention was once the justification for not protecting women and children from domestic violence. *See* Reva B. Siegel, *"The Rule of Love": Wife Beating as Prerogative and Privacy*, 105 YALE L.J. 2117 (1996).

protect children in vulnerable situations, there is no private sphere the state cannot penetrate. Under a *parens patriae* doctrine based on an ethic of care, it would be unacceptable to justify state inaction because of a risk that intervening too soon could violate the constitutional parental rights, as the majority worried in *DeShaney*. At the same time, any intervention by the state would take into consideration the context of how intervention would affect other members of the family. As Professor Weaver's opinion points out, with a duty to intervene effectively, DSS might not have waited until the last episode of abuse to call Joshua's mother. It might have also ensured that the actions required by Joshua's father had been met or remove Joshua from his care when they were not. Potential liability under Section 1983 could have resulted in DSS agencies being more proactive in protecting children from parental abuse, if at least to avoid liability. Given this interpretation of *parens patriae*, the social worker's inaction could not be deemed reasonable, and therefore conferred no qualified immunity. In fact, the interpretation of qualified immunity in place in 1989 was that "in light of the discretion and responsibilities of [her] office, and under all of the circumstances as they appeared at the time, the officer acted reasonably and in good faith."[50] Under Professor Weaver's approach, it is difficult to see any level of reasonableness or good faith in the social worker's actions.

CONCLUSION

There is no single way of deciding cases with a feminist perspective.[51] There are, however, some characteristics of legal reasoning that make a decision arguably "feminist." As Professor Bartlett spotted more than twenty years ago, methodology may matter more than the outcome of a decision. Bartlett's feminist legal method had, among others, two distinctive features.[52] First, a feminist legal method asks "the woman question," which requires the author to place women at the center of the decision.[53] We can expand the woman question to ask the question of the "powerless person." This requires understanding the situation from the perspectives of those who do not see the legal system as their protector but as the cause of harm. Joshua could not seek help from the social worker; he was too young and he was completely dependent

[50] *Wood v. Strickland*, 420 U.S. 308, 330 (1975).

[51] Cynthia Grant Bowman & Elizabeth M. Schneider, *Feminist Legal Theory, Feminist Lawmaking, and the Legal Profession*, 67 FORDHAM L. REV. 249, 251 (1998).

[52] Katherine T. Bartlett, *Feminist Legal Methods*, 103 HARV. L. REV. 829, 831 (1990).

[53] *Id.* at 831.

on others for his protection. A second feature of a feminist legal method is to focus on the context in which a conflict takes place.[54] A powerless person is not "essentially" powerless but lacks agency in the specific context that triggers the harm. Joshua was surrounded by adults who abused him, who repeatedly treated his physical injuries, who observed and recorded his injuries. Professor Weaver's opinion places Joshua and his constitutional right to substantive due process at the center of the decision.

This opinion would have not changed the life of Joshua, but it may have brought a sense of justice to Joshua's mother and would have helped avoid other tragic outcomes by emphasizing state accountability in similar situations. Perhaps a more robust constitutional torts system would have changed the behavior of the police force at Castle Rock, preventing the death of Jessica Gonzales's three daughters. Professor Weaver's opinion would have strengthened the concept of the special relationship between the state and individuals and would have forced states to take the duty to care more seriously. Professor Weaver's *DeShaney* could have contributed to states taking citizens' protection from abuse more seriously.

DeSHANEY v. WINNEBAGO COUNTY DEPARTMENT OF SOCIAL SERVICES, 489 U.S. 189 (1989)

JUSTICE WEAVER DELIVERED THE OPINION OF THE COURT

The question presented in this case is whether state authorities have a federal constitutional duty to protect a child from a known risk of physical abuse by his parent or guardian.

Petitioners are a mother and her male toddler who was physically abused and permanently injured by his father, who had custody of him. Respondents are state agents, social workers, and local officials, who learned that the petitioner was being harmed by his father through complaints made through a federally mandated reporting system. Although respondents had reason to believe the father was beating the petitioner, they did not take action to help or remove him from his father's home. Petitioner sued respondents claiming that their failure to act deprived him of his liberty and life in violation of the Due Process Clause of the Fourteenth Amendment to the U.S. Constitution. We hold that the state had an affirmative duty under 42 U.S.C. § 1983 to protect

[54] *Id.* at 831.

Joshua from harm because there was a "special relationship" established by the state child welfare services unit. This special relationship was established because the state had prior temporary custody of Joshua, affirmatively demonstrated its intent to protect Joshua from harm, and had knowledge of the specific danger to Joshua in his father's care. We further hold that the state welfare authorities' repeated failure to protect Joshua from a known danger, his physically abusive father, constitutes a deprivation of liberty within the meaning of the Fourteenth Amendment Due Process Clause.

I FACTUAL AND LEGAL BACKGROUND

The facts of this case are horrendous. Petitioner Joshua DeShaney was born in 1979 to married parents, Randy and Melody DeShaney. In 1980, the DeShaneys divorced, and custody of Joshua was awarded to his father. Randy DeShaney then moved to Nennah, Wisconsin and took baby Joshua with him. He married again, but subsequently divorced. His second wife was the first person to report to police that Joshua DeShaney was a victim of child abuse in January 1982, at the time of their divorce.

Neenah, Wisconsin is a city located in Winnebago County, Wisconsin. The Winnebago County Department of Social Services (DSS) authorities received the complaint from Randy DeShaney's second wife that he had previously "hit the boy causing marks and [was] a prime case for child abuse." App. 152–53. DSS interviewed the father, who denied the accusations. DSS did not pursue them further. A year later, in January 1983, Joshua was admitted to a local hospital with multiple bruises and abrasions. Suspicious of child abuse, the examining physician notified DSS. The hospital immediately obtained an order from a Wisconsin juvenile court to place Joshua in the temporary custody of the hospital. The county convened an ad hoc "Child Protection Team" three days later, which was comprised of a pediatrician, psychologist, police detective, the county's lawyer, several DSS caseworkers, and various hospital personnel. Even though the entire Team acknowledged that Joshua had probably been abused, the county's civil attorney was unwilling to pursue the case in court. Randy DeShaney suggested that his girlfriend might have been responsible for Joshua's injuries. App. 154. Therefore, the Team recommended several protective measures for Joshua, including enrolling him in a preschool program, providing certain counseling services for his father, and encouraging his father's girlfriend to move out of the home. Randy DeShaney promised to cooperate with DSS in accomplishing these actions and entered into a voluntary agreement with the county.

The juvenile court dismissed the child protection case and returned Joshua to his father's custody, based on the recommendation of the Team. Only one month later, DSS was called by emergency room personnel to report that Joshua had been treated for suspicious injuries. Once again the DSS caseworker concluded that there was no basis for action. The caseworker made monthly visits for the next six months to the DeShaney home. During that time, she observed several suspicious injuries on Joshua's head, and noticed that he had not been enrolled in school, and that the girlfriend had not moved out. Randy DeShaney did not uphold his end of the agreement with DSS. The caseworker recorded the incidents in her files. Even though the caseworker had continuing suspicions that Joshua was being physically abused by someone in the household, she did not seek another emergency order to obtain temporary custody of him. In November 1983, Joshua was treated once again for injuries in the emergency room that were believed to be caused by child abuse. When the caseworker made two more visits to the DeShaney home, she was told that Joshua was too ill to see her, and she still took no protective action.

It appears that DSS was unsurprised that Joshua eventually suffered a catastrophic injury. In fact, the DSS caseworker's response to Joshua's last and most debilitating injury was, "I just knew the phone would ring some day and Joshua would be dead." 812 F.2d 298, 300 (7th Cir. 1987). While Joshua did not die in March 1984, his father beat him so severely that he fell into a life-threatening coma. He underwent emergency brain surgery, which revealed a series of hemorrhages caused by traumatic injuries to the head inflicted over a long period of time. Joshua suffered acute brain damage and will spend the rest of his life confined to an institution for the severely mentally disabled. His father was subsequently tried and convicted of child abuse.

Joshua and his mother, Melody DeShaney, brought this suit under 42 U.S.C. § 1983 against respondents Winnebago County, DSS, and various individual employees of DSS. They alleged that respondents had failed to intervene to protect Joshua against the known risk of violence in his home. The complaint further set forth that respondents had violated his rights under the Fourteenth Amendment by depriving Joshua of his liberty without due process of law. The U.S. District Court for the Eastern District of Wisconsin granted summary judgment for respondents.

The Court of Appeals for the Seventh Circuit affirmed. *DeShaney v. Winnebago County Dep't of Soc. Servs.*, 812 F. 2d 298 (7th Cir. 1987). It held that petitioners did not bring forth an actionable § 1983 claim for two distinct reasons. First, the court held that the Fourteenth Amendment Due Process Clause does not require a state or local governmental entity to protect its citizens from "private violence, or other mishaps not attributable to the conduct of its employees." *Id.* at 301. The court specifically rejected the position held by two Circuit Courts that a "special relationship" arises between the state and a child when the state learns that a particular child is in danger of abuse from third parties and takes action to protect him from that danger. *Estate of Bailey by Oare v. County of York*, 768 F. 2d 503, 510–11 (3d Cir. 1985); *Jensen v. Conrad*, 747 F.2d 185, 190–94 (4th Cir. 1984), cert. denied, 470 U.S. 1052, 105 S.Ct. 1754, 84 L.Ed.2d 818 (1985). The court denied that this "special relationship" imposes an affirmative constitutional duty to provide adequate protection. 812 F.2d, at 303–304. Second, the appellate court held that the causal connection between respondents' conduct and Joshua's injuries was too attenuated to establish a deprivation of constitutional rights actionable under § 1983. 812 F.2d, at 301–303.

We now reverse.

II LEGAL AUTHORITY

A *42 U.S.C. § 1983*

42 U.S.C. § 1983 is a federal act that provides a civil action for the deprivation of rights, privileges, and immunities set forth by the Constitution. It states:

> Every person, who under color of any statute, ordinance, regulation, custom or usage, of any State or Territory, or District of Columbia, subjects, or causes to be subjected, any citizen of the United States or other person within the jurisdiction thereof to the deprivation of any rights, privileges, or any immunities secured by the Constitution and laws, shall be liable to the party injured in an action at law, suit in equity, or other proper proceeding for redress, except that in any action brought against a judicial officer for an act or omission taken in such officer's judicial capacity injunctive relief shall not be granted unless a declaratory decree was violated or declaratory relief was unavailable.

From a historical perspective, this law was passed to enforce the provisions of the Fourteenth Amendment. *Monroe v. Pape*, 365 U.S. 167 (1961). The pertinent part of the Fourteenth Amendment law reads: "No State shall make or enforce any law which shall abridge the privileges or immunities of citizens of the United States; nor shall any State deprive any person of life, liberty, or property, without due process of law." It was originally enacted as Section 1 of the Ku Klux Klan Act of 1871. The bill was intended to protect the rights of freed black slaves. It was also used as a means of legal redress against a state representative who was unable or unwilling to enforce a state law. In order to prevail in a 1983 action, a plaintiff must prove two essential elements: (1) that the alleged conduct occurred under color of state law, and (2) that the alleged conduct deprived plaintiff of rights, privileges, and immunities secured by the U.S. Constitution or a federal statute.

This case hinges on whether the conduct that petitioners complain of occurred under the color of law. If the answer to that question is yes, it is clear that the state-sponsored conduct denied Joshua of his right to life and liberty under the Fourteenth Amendment, as well as the federal statute, the Child Abuse Treatment and Protection Act, Pub. L. No. 93-247 (1974). While Joshua is an Anglo-American child who is not the descendant of slaves (that we know of), he has rights of life and liberty that fall under the umbrella of the Fourteenth Amendment. In the literal sense, liberty means freedom. By law, parents have the right of care, custody, and control over their children; therefore, a child's freedom is dependent on his or her parents. The privacy rights of parents to raise their children as they see fit, without interference from the state or third parties, are well-established. *Stanley v. Illinois*, 405 U.S. 645, 651 (1977); *Wisconsin v. Yoder*, 406 U.S. 205, 232–33 (1972); *Prince v. Massachusetts*, 321 U.S. 158, 166 (1944). When a parent does not provide adequate care for a child or exerts violent, harmful control over the child, it is an act of neglect or abuse. This type of abuse is a deprivation of liberty because the parents are the only persons legally responsible for the child's well-being. It is well-established law that the state has authority that supersedes the rights of a parent or guardian who is endangering the safety of a child. *Prince*, 321 U.S. 158, 167, 169–70 (1944).

B *The Fourteenth Amendment*

In discussing the history of Section 1983, it is important to note also the evolution of the Fourteenth Amendment and its protection of rights established within the American family. As noted above, the Fourteenth Amendment has long been established as a means by which this Court has set forth the constitutional rights of parents and children within the family unit. Parents have the right to direct the upbringing and education of children under their control. *Meyer v. Nebraska*, 262 U.S. 390 (1923); *Pierce v. Society of Sisters*, 268 U.S. 510 (1925); *Wisconsin v. Yoder*, 406 U.S. 205 (1972). The right to marry, establish a home, and rear one's children as one deems fit are civil rights guaranteed by the Fourteenth Amendment. *Skinner v. Oklahoma*, 316 U.S. 535 (1942). Along with protecting a family's fundamental right to exercise parental autonomy, the Court also has recognized a fundamental right to familial privacy. *Griswold v. Connecticut*, 381 U.S. 479 (1965). In *Moore v. City of Cleveland*, the Court emphasized that "freedom of personal choice in matters of . . . family life is one of the liberties protected by the Due Process Clause of the Fourteenth Amendment." 431 U.S. 494, 499 (1977).

While parents' rights to family autonomy and privacy are fundamental, they are not absolute. *Prince v. Massachusetts*, 321 U.S. 158, 166–67 (1944); *Darryl H. v. Coler*, 801 F.2d 893 (7th Cir. 1986). The state may invade upon these constitutionally protected areas if a compelling interest existed and the means of doing so is narrowly tailored. *Carey v. Population Servs. Int'l*, 431 U.S. 678, 686 (1977). In fact, the state has a duty under the *parens patriae* doctrine to protect children who are vulnerable to harm. *Prince v. Massachusetts*, 321 U.S. 158, 166 (1944). Even though this Court has held that the Constitution protects children's rights, their rights are not synonymous with those of adults because of "the peculiar vulnerability of children, their inability to make critical decisions in an informed, mature manner; and the importance of the parental role in child rearing." *Bellotti v. Baird*, 443 U.S. 622, 634 (1979). The Court has allowed the state to place limitations on children's constitutional right to account for their vulnerability and afford them necessary protections. *New Jersey v. T.L.O.*, 469 U.S. 325 (1985); *H.L. v. Matheson*, 450 U.S. 398 (1981). Beyond having a duty to protect children, the state has an interest in safeguarding children from harm.

Shamefully, the state has not always carried out this obligation. In the early history of our country, children were treated like property.[1] Specifically, children were deemed to be the property of the father.[2] With the right of ownership came the right of chastisement. Physical abuse within the family was not treated as a crime because children, similar to wives, did not have the same rights and legal protections as men.[3] As the head of the household, the law allowed for fathers to have ownership of their children "as assets of their estate, and any services or earnings of the child became the property of their

[1] 1 William Blackstone, Commentaries *451 (Cooley, 3d ed. 1884) (noting that although the right of life or death of the father over the child was abolished, he still maintained a very large and absolute authority over the child).

[2] Michael Grossberg, Governing the Hearth 237 (1985) (noting that American courts followed the system of English law inherited by the colonies, whereby the father had an absolute right to the custody of his children).

[3] *Bradley v. State*, 1 Walker 156 (Miss. 1824) (holding that a man has a right to beat his wife and moderate chastisement would be allowed); *State v. Black* 60 N.C. 162 (N.C. 1864) (noting that wife beating is a private family matter); *Gorman v. State*, 42 Tex. 221 (1875) (noting that a stepfather is *in loco parentis* of his wife's children by a former husband, so long as they are supported and maintained by him, and he has the same right of reasonable chastisement to enforce his authority).

paternal masters in exchange for life and maintenance."[4] Paternal dominance over children continued until the mid-1800s, when some courts began to assert that parental rule was not absolute power conferred by God, but a civic duty conferred and regulated by the state, in the interest of children and the public. *Mercein v. People*, 25 Wend. 65, 102–103 (N.Y. 1840). When a father attempted to use the Fourteenth Amendment to affirm his right to regain custody of his children, claiming his rights had been violated by state action, a California court rejected this argument. *Wadleigh v. Newhall*, 136 F. 941 (N.D. Cal. 1905). The court stated that "there is no parental authority independent of the power of the state." *Id.* at 947–48; *Prince*, 321 U.S. 158, 166–67 (noting that the state has a "wide range of power for limiting parental freedom and authority in things affecting the child's welfare" including a duty to protect children from ill-health or death because of parental exposure of the child to communicable diseases).

The Fourteenth Amendment was originally intended to protect the rights of humans who were legally deemed property. It follows the Thirteenth Amendment that abolished slavery and involuntary servitude, except as punishment for a crime. The Fourteenth Amendment was just as vital to the freedom of slaves as the Thirteenth Amendment. It was intended to protect the rights of emancipated slaves as citizens and to ensure that the government would not take their lives, property, or freedom without a fair trial or legal process. It was designed to guarantee protection for them as vulnerable citizens. Without it, the state could continue to do what it had always done throughout two and a half centuries of slavery – make and enforce laws that violated the humanity of formerly enslaved people, and allow violation of laws by private citizens who sought to deprive emancipated people of their lives, freedom and property based on discrimination. History is ripe with cases in which private citizens maimed and killed black citizens who were former slaves while police officers, governing officials, and other state civil employees who knew about the violence stepped aside, did nothing, or even assisted in the slaughter. While these incidents may not be widely known, they were reported in newspapers of their time.[5]

[4] *Meyer* and *Pierce* confirmed this traditional right of the parent as owner by expanding the Fourteenth Amendment to cover parental control of the child. The Supreme Court in *Meyer* and *Pierce* set forth that parents have natural rights to prepare their children for citizenship by giving them suitable education for their station in life, nurturing them, and directing their destiny. *Meyer v. Nebraska*, 262 U.S. 390, 400 (1923); *Pierce v. Society of Sisters*, 268 U.S. 510, 534–35 (1925).

[5] *Atlanta Mob Kills Ten Negroes*, N.Y. TIMES, Sept. 23, 1906 (reporting that 10,000 to 15,000 whites roamed the streets of Atlanta to attack blacks, destroying businesses and homes based on four white women's allegations of rape by black men); *Evidence in Riot Case Shows Police*

When this Court handed down its decision in *Meyer* in 1923, earlier that same year, there were reports of racial violence resulting in numerous deaths in Rosewood, Florida. This horrifying event, known as the Rosewood Massacre, is an example of why the Fourteenth Amendment was enacted. A community of prosperous blacks who owned their property and homes was destroyed by mobs of white men, who set fire to all of the black homes, the school, and the church in the town. Over a period of six days, mobs of white vigilantes terrorized the black people of Rosewood and engaged in random acts of violence against local blacks.[6] There were at least six documented deaths, but the estimates are that over forty people were killed. The torch was lit by an allegation of a married white woman who claimed she had been attacked and beaten by a black man. Rape was later inferred by the sheriff and the white men who set out to find the assailant. Without due process of the law, several black men and women were killed based on the word of one woman, who had been known in the black community as having a secret white boyfriend.[7]

The police force, mayor, and even the governor were made aware of the burning of property, torture, maiming, and killing of black men, women, and children over a six-day period, but nothing was done to protect these citizens. In fact, there were no indictments or charges brought by the state of Florida against any state officials or private citizens.[8] While the Fourteenth Amendment was intended to hold accountable state actors like those in Rosewood, it did not stop similar situations from occurring across the country. Tulsa, Oklahoma experienced similar "race riots" that called into question whether the county and state officials played a vital role in the death of black citizens and the destruction of their property.[9] While the state may not have been able to change the moral compass of white mobs, county and state officials were obligated to attempt to control them and provide protection and due process for the black citizens of Rosewood. When the state has a duty to

Brutality, DECATUR HERALD, Sept. 23, 1908 (regarding the Springfield Race Riot of 1908 where mobs of whites murdered blacks and destroyed black businesses and homes based on allegations by two white women of rape and murder by black men; *Rosewood Race Riot Resulted in Killing 2 White and 4 Black*, JACKSONVILLE TIMES-UNION, Jan. 6, 1923; Associated Press, *Last Negro Homes Razed in Rosewood*, N.Y. TIMES, Jan. 8, 1923; *Tulsa Race Riot Jury Indicts Police Chief*, N.Y. TIMES, June 26, 1921.

6 *Rosewood Race Riot Resulted in Killing 2 White and 4 Black*, JACKSONVILLE TIMES-UNION, Jan. 6, 1923; *Many Die in Florida Race War*, MIAMI DAILY METROPOLIS, Jan. 6, 1923.

7 Gary Moore, *Rosewood Massacre*, FLORIDIAN, July 25, 1982.

8 *Rosewood Probe May Continue Through Weekend at Levy County Seat*, GAINESVILLE DAILY SUN, Feb. 13, 1923; *Not Justifiable*, GAINESVILLE DAILY SUN, Jan. 8, 1923.

9 *Tulsa Race Riot Jury Indicts Police Chief*, N.Y. TIMES, June 26, 1921.

protect the general public through its police power, yet makes a distinct decision not to do so even when put on notice of the harms committed, it acts in violation of the Fourteenth Amendment.

While it may seem that the Rosewood Massacre has no bearing on Joshua's situation, inaction on the part of the state was the reason that the black community in Rosewood was destroyed and citizens lost their lives. Once state officials became aware of what was happening, it was incumbent on them to provide protection to the black citizens and their property. However, they did nothing at all, even though they were the only persons legally authorized to protect the citizens of Rosewood through their police power. The Due Process Clause forbids the state from depriving an individual of life, liberty, or property without due process of law. While this clause has been interpreted as a negative right in certain cases, its language can be extended to impose an affirmative obligation on the state to ensure that certain classes of people who are vulnerable to specific foreseeable harm are protected. The state claims that because Joshua's physical harm was perpetrated by a private actor, his father, there is no tort committed by a state actor that would present liability under the 42 U.S.C. 1983 and the Fourteenth Amendment. We reject this argument. As a young child, Joshua was vulnerable to specific, known physical harm in his father's home. Because the state was aware of the harm and was the only entity legally authorized to protect Joshua, it violated his due process rights by its failure to protect him.

III ANALYSIS

A *The Special Relationship Created by the State*

This case is one of first impression in that the victim, a child at risk of abuse and neglect, was in the custody of his parent, a private party, when he sustained a severe head injury. Between 1982 until his near-fatal beating in March of 1984, the state had received at least eleven reports that Joshua's father was beating him. On nine occasions, the state personally saw or was advised of specific injuries including cigarette burns, lacerations, and bruises on Joshua. Four of these incidents, prior to Joshua's final injury, were so serious that he was taken to the hospital. Though DSS released Joshua from temporary state custody to his father's home, it had the authority and obligation under Wisconsin law to monitor Joshua in his home to ensure that he was safe. The question at hand is what type of state action creates a special relationship such that there is an affirmative duty of protection under the Fourteenth Amendment Due Process Clause.

When individuals are placed in custody or in the care of the government, state custodians are sometimes charged with affirmative duties, the nonfeasance of which may violate the Constitution. *Doe v. New York City Dept. of Social Services*, 649 F.2d 134, 141 (1981). In *Youngberg v. Romeo*, 457 U.S. 307 (1982), state officials violated the Fourteenth Amendment when they failed to protect a patient in a psychiatric institution from physical harm. As stated above, Joshua was not in state care when he was injured. Had he been injured in state foster care, the state would easily be found to have deprived him of his right to substantive due process. *Taylor v. Ledbetter*, 791 F. 2d 881(11th Cir. 1986), aff'd in part, rev'd in part on reh'g, 818 F.2d 791 (11th Cir. 1987) (*en banc*). The child victim in the *Taylor* case was severely injured by her foster mother's physical abuse. Because the child was involuntarily placed in a foster home, the situation is analogous to that of a prisoner or involuntarily committed mental patient, and the Due Process Clause imposes upon the state an affirmative duty to provide adequate protection. *Estelle v. Gamble*, 429 U.S. 97, 103 (1976).

In *Stoneking v. Bradford Area School District*, 856 F.2d 594 (3d Cir. 1988), the court held that under applicable state law, a special relationship arose between the school officials and the students entrusted to their care, and that the state child abuse reporting and *in loco parentis* statutes, coupled with a common law duty of officials to students, evidenced a desire on the part of the state to provide affirmative protection for the students. *Stoneking* involved the sexual assault of a high school student by a teacher on school property and on school-sponsored trips where the school administration was aware of other student complaints of the teacher's sexual abuse for a long period of time. The court further stated that government officials could be held liable under the due process clause for failing to protect individuals against physical harm at the hands of third parties where a "special relationship" between the state and the individual existed. This case is different than the case at hand because the harm occurred on state property and when the child was under the supervision of the state.

Estate of Bailey by Oare v. York County, 768 F.2d 503 (3d Cir. 1985) and *Jensen v. Conrad*, 747 F. 2d. 185, 190–94 (4th Cir. 1984), cert. denied, 470 U.S. 1052 (1985), provide more similar fact scenarios to Joshua's situation. In *Estate of Bailey*, a five-year-old girl died after being returned to the custody of her mother by the state. Prior to her death, family members reported that they found severe bruises and evidence of abuse on the child's body. A hospital physician determined that the mother's boyfriend's excessive striking caused the injuries. The state agreed to return the child to the mother if she made arrangements for her boyfriend to move out. Without an independent investigation to determine the whereabouts of the boyfriend, the child was returned to her mother. A month later, the child died from physical injuries inflicted by the boyfriend and the mother. They were both convicted of murder, and the child's father brought suit under 42 U.S.C. § 1983.

The court rejected the argument that the challenged state conduct of mere omissions would be actionable only if the child had been in the legal custody of the state when the incident occurred. The *Bailey* court held that the state and local entities owed a duty of protection to persons who were not in [state] custody. *Estate of Bailey*, 768 F.2d 503, 510 (1985); *White v. Rochford*, 592 F.2d 381, 385 (7th Cir. 1979) (reversing the dismissal of a complaint alleging that police, who had arrested the driver of a car, subjected the three passenger children to a "health-endangering situation" by abandoning them, causing the three children to be subjected to cold weather and danger from traffic). The state was aware that the five-year-old girl faced a special danger. When the agency knows that a child has been beaten, this strengthens the argument that some sort of special relationship had been established. *Jensen v. Conrad*, 747 F.2d 185, 195 n. 11 (1984).

In *Jensen*, the court found that state officials have a constitutional duty to protect a child from a known threat of physical abuse. 747 F. 2d. at 190–94. The facts in this case involved a minor who had died from abuse inflicted by her mother. The district court held that the state and county officials had no legal duty to protect a child not in their legal custody. Although the Fourth Circuit affirmed the dismissal of the complaint, it did so on the basis of qualified immunity. The court actually rejected the argument that a right of protection can never exist in the absence of a custodial relationship. The Fourth Circuit set forth three factors to determine if a special relationship exists between the state and a third party. *Id.* The first factor is whether the victim or perpetrator was in state custody at the time of the incident or prior to the incident. The second factor is whether the state directly expressed a desire to provide affirmative protection to a particular class of individuals. The third factor is whether the state knew of the danger to the victim.

The facts of this case provide evidence that all three of these factors were met, and therefore there was a special relationship between the state of Wisconsin and Joshua. The first factor was satisfied because Joshua had been in state custody for a period of time prior to the incident. The state had removed him from his father's care several months before his father permanently injured him. The reason for the removal was because Joshua had bruises that were identified by a doctor as being consistent with intentional physical abuse by his father. There was active intervention in Joshua's life by the state, which triggered a fundamental duty to provide aid to him once it learned of the severe danger to which he was exposed. In *Davidson v. Cannon*, 474 U.S. 344, 354 and n. 3 (1986) (dissenting opinion), the dissenting opinion asserted that certain forms of state action can lead to a subsequent duty to act. When police officers stood by while a man was beaten in a club (who subsequently died), the city was held liable for his death under the Due Process Clause because the police officers had knowledge that the deceased was in danger but failed to act to protect him. *City of New Kensington v. Horton*, 857 F.2d 1463 (3d Cir. 1988). The city had an official "policy" of not interfering in violent incidents which occurred in private clubs. The fact that the police officer's knowledge gave rise to an affirmative duty to protect relied on the special relationship doctrine set forth in *Estate of Bailey*.

The state continued to monitor Joshua by sending a social worker out to the home once a month to check on his well-being. The state set forth conditions by which the father could obtain custody of Joshua. A document was generated by DSS to set out the safety measures the state required of Joshua's father in order for him to regain and to keep the custody he had temporarily lost due to his violent actions. In fact, by surveilling Joshua in his home, the state effectively removed any other remedy or protection that could have helped Joshua maintain his safety. Once the state affirmatively undertakes to oversee the safety and well-being of a child, mandatory reporters presume that any help Joshua needs will be afforded to him through the social worker on his case. Joshua's noncustodial parent also had the expectation that she would be contacted if the state were to notice any signs of abuse or neglect of Joshua while in his father's care. The social worker collected important facts that demonstrated that Joshua was being abused. By continuing to visit Joshua and document his father's actions and inactions, as well as Joshua's health and subsequent injuries after his return to his father's care, the state met the second factor. Applicable state law, coupled with the state's decision to actively monitor Joshua demonstrates the express state desire and obligation to Joshua.

The third factor can unfortunately be shown many times over. The state knew of the danger to Joshua because every time the social worker visited Joshua, she had reason to believe that his father was abusing him. A constitutional violation under 1983 occurred when the social worker came to realize the consequences of returning Joshua to his father's custody. This realization occurred in February 1983, when she learned that Randy DeShaney had not held up his end of the agreement with DSS. Joshua's liberty interests were violated again once the social worker saw visible marks of child abuse, with no valid explanation by his father. As explained earlier, the social worker's knowledge gave rise to an affirmative duty to protect Joshua. She was assigned to protect him from a specific danger, and in fact protecting Joshua from that danger was precisely the task for which she was employed. The state policy – established by statute – required DSS to conduct an investigation of any indication of abuse and submit a report. DSS failed to conduct new investigations after it returned Joshua to his father, even though it learned of indications of abuse. DSS, as the only agency authorized to investigate abuse and neglect of children, effectively disabled others from coming to the aid of an endangered child. The state's exclusive power to remove children from abusive homes, as established by law, creates a state responsibility to protect those children's liberty rights when there is a known danger.

B *The Child Abuse and Prevention Treatment Act*

Beyond the state's interest in safeguarding children from harm, the U.S. Congress enacted a federal law, the Child Abuse and Prevention Treatment Act (CAPTA), 42 U.S.C. §§ 5101 *et seq.*, in 1974 that requires each state to provide protective mechanisms for abused and neglected children. CAPTA provides that each state must have an emergency response system for reporting child abuse and neglect, and it further designates certain professionals as mandatory reporters. Mandatory reporters are typically government professionals who are licensed by individual states to provide services to children or families. They also include employees of agencies, organizations, or companies that are licensed by the state to provide services to children or families. States require mandatory reporters to immediately report any reasonable suspicion of child abuse and neglect to the police or child protective services through the emergency response system.[10] Once the mandatory reporter makes the report, he or she is not required to do anything else to help the child who is suspected to be in danger. The emergency response system is set up to quickly determine, based on the level of risk to the child, if and how the child can be protected. There are no other nonprofit organizations or third parties that are obligated by law or have standing under the law to affect the parental rights of children who are being neglected or abused. In other words, the federal government holds states responsible for a system where the only entity that has legal authority to intervene in the private home of a family to protect a child from abuse is the state.

In the case at hand, Joshua initially came to the attention of the state because of the second ex-wife of Joshua's father. She was not a mandatory

[10] Pub. L.No. 93-247; 42 U.S.C. § 5106a.

reporter, but she reported her knowledge of Joshua's abuse to the state and nothing was done. There was little else she could do besides report the suspected abuse because she was not a parent. When Joshua was brought to the hospital with suspicious injuries, every person that saw him in the hospital was a mandatory reporter. The state held him in the temporary custody of the hospital while it determined whether his father's home was a safe place to which he could return. Arguably the hospital was *in loco parentis* while a team of professionals made this determination. Joshua was five years old at the time, unable to protect himself. The vulnerability of abused children and their dependence on outside assistance is recognized in the Brief of Amici Curiae of American Civil Liberties Union Children's Rights Project et al.[11] Similar to a state-institutionalized patient, a foster care child, and a child in school, Joshua was rendered helpless by virtue of his status at the time the state first encountered him in the hospital. When the decision was made by the state to return Joshua to his father using a specific safety plan that included regular monitoring of his status and well-being, the state affirmatively asserted its intention to protect him using applicable federal and state law.

Mandatory reporting is taken very seriously. A report is required for each incident of suspected child abuse, and each incident should be investigated. Even where a prior report of abuse has been made, if subsequent new abuse comes to light, that new abuse should be documented and investigated. It is a crime in most states for a mandatory reporter to fail to report any suspicion of child abuse. If the state has knowledge of a failure to report, it can prosecute the individual failing to report child abuse with a felony. Beyond reporting requirements, state noncompliance with CAPTA also has major consequences. If states do not comply with CAPTA requirements, they risk losing federal funds that support foster care programs. This hierarchal relationship between the federal government and states regarding the regulation of child abuse and neglect establishes an affirmative duty on the part of the state to investigate and substantiate reports of child abuse and neglect. Once abuse or neglect is substantiated, there is a subsequent state duty to remove the child from that environment and place the child in a safe temporary home. When a child becomes a part of the state child protective system, CAPTA effectively removes any obligation of a private citizen to take individual protective action to address child abuse and neglect. Once a citizen or mandatory reporter makes a report to the state emergency response system, they rely upon the state

[11] Brief for American Civil Liberties Union Children's Rights Project, et al. as Amici Curiae Supporting Petitioner, No. 87-154 (June 10, 1988).

to take appropriate action to provide the necessary intervention to protect the child's safety and well-being.

It defies logic to explain how a mandatory reporter with direct knowledge of the physical abuse of a child, employed by the state and tasked with protecting children from abuse, could sit idly by without taking any affirmative step to protect a child from future harm. Ann Kemmeter, as the ongoing case worker, should have submitted her reports of Joshua's new injuries to DSS so that a new investigation could have been initiated. The Seventh Circuit's conclusion that DSS and the caseworker were not responsible for Joshua's welfare and did not contribute to Joshua's injuries was wrong. The Wisconsin Children's Code, § 48.981, requires the Department to respond to reports of child abuse with an immediate investigation when there is reason to suspect that a child's health or safety is in immediate danger. A determination must be made whether a child is in need of protective services, and if those services are needed, they are to be provided. Instead of meeting the needs of Joshua and providing him the protective services he needed, the case worker grossly neglected her basic duties and violated the standards of practice for social workers. The red flags she documented in her case record reflect numerous indicators of abuse, including head scars and bruises that were inconsistent with his father's explanation of the injuries, cigarette burns on his body, a second hospitalization for traumatic injury (along with a second hospital report of child abuse), a battered girlfriend, and a report that Joshua had fainted and was brought to the hospital unconscious. App. 119–21, 132. She was supposed to report these new incidents of abuse to the investigative division so that they could have initiated new inquiries regarding the cause of these new injuries.

The dissent argues that the state would have been subject to a suit if it had removed Joshua. Parents who believe their child was temporarily removed from their custody without reason have the opportunity to appear in court and present evidence or testimony to rebut the state's complaint. Indeed, the Due Process Clause protects the rights of parents whose children have been removed from their custody by the state. *Stanley v. Illinois*, 405 U.S. 645 1972; *Doe v. Staples*, 706 F.2d 985 (6th Cir. 1983). The Sixth Circuit in *Doe v. Staples* clearly established that "in the context of child removal," due process requires advance notice and a hearing regardless of whether there was probable cause to believe the children have already been abused. *Doe*, 706 F.2d at 986–87. The question this court must answer, then, is what due process the Constitution accords Joshua? There were only two ways that Joshua's life could have been protected given the gross negligence of the social worker. First, his mother, if she had been aware of the abuse, could have filed a suit to request a temporary restraining order and/or a change of custody for Joshua. This option was removed from Joshua because his mother was not contacted by the social worker over the period of time when the social worker, acting on behalf of DSS, observed continuous physical abuse. Without knowledge of the harm being meted out in the father's home, Joshua's mother was not in a position to protect him.

Second, the state could initiate a suit to protect Joshua as it should have back in 1982 when the father's second wife reported that he was being abused. If the county attorney had filed a suit and brought the matter before a judge, Joshua would have been appointed an attorney or a guardian ad litem (GAL), whose legal responsibility would have included interviewing the child and other persons with knowledge of his well-being. CAPTA requires the appointment of a GAL for every child involved in judicial proceedings. 42 U.S.C. § 5106a(b)(2)(A)(xiii). Even though Joshua was a toddler at the time of the first reporting and interviewing him may have been difficult, CAPTA provided money to states to train GALs who represent children. This training would include how to obtain a first-hand, clear understanding of the situation and the needs of a young child. *Id.* Ultimately the child's GAL would have made a recommendation to the court about what action would be in Joshua's best interest.

Instead of following the laws and policies set forth by the federal and state government, the social worker instead denied Joshua his due process and literally deprived him of a normal life. Rather than just documenting the harm that Joshua was clearly suffering, the social worker should have reported new incidents of abuse to state investigators, consulted with a supervisor, and contacted the county attorney on Joshua's behalf. She failed miserably, violating the state law and CAPTA. As a result of her gross negligence, the evidence and reports of continuous, serious child abuse were not investigated properly, and therefore appropriate protective measures were not taken to prevent Joshua's irreversible, life-altering injuries.

C DSS Liability: *The Establishment of Deliberate Indifference*

When an official is charged with fault in exercising an affirmative responsibility, there are two fundamental requisites for 1983 liability. The first is that the omission must have been a substantial factor leading to the denial of a constitutionally protected liberty or property interest. *Rizzo v. Goode*, 423 U.S. 362 (1976). The second is that the officials in charge of the agency being sued must have displayed a mental state of "deliberate indifference" to "meaningfully be termed culpable." *Doe v. New York City of Dept. of Soc.*

Servs., 649 F.2d 134, 141 (2d. Cir. 1981). In *Doe*, the U.S. Court of Appeals for the Second Circuit held that deliberate indifference should not be inferred from a failure to act in a foster care situation, as compared to a prison context. *Id.* at 142. Repeated acts of negligence could be evidence of indifference. However, negligence (gross or otherwise) is a type of conduct, while deliberate indifference is a state of mind. The two are closely related in that grossly negligent conduct can create a strong presumption of deliberate indifference. The Court defines "deliberate indifference" as key to the analysis of whether Winnebago County was grossly negligent in its treatment of Joshua.

In *Doe*, the court emphasized that deliberate indifference cannot exist absent some knowledge triggering an affirmative duty to act on the plaintiff's behalf. *Id.* at 145. However, actual knowledge is not the only type of knowledge that would suffice. The state could be held liable under 42 U.S.C. 1983 if it, or its top supervisory personnel, exhibited deliberate indifference to a known injury, a known risk, or a specific duty, and their failure to perform the duty or act to ameliorate the risk or injury was a proximate cause of plaintiff's deprivation of rights under the Constitution. The social worker knew of the subsequent injuries to Joshua, and while she documented them, it is not clear whether she reported them to a supervisor and a supervisor made the decision not to contact the investigative unit regarding these additional injuries. What is clear is that DSS's inaction was a substantial factor leading to Joshua's final, near-fatal abuse. She was an agent of DSS, and thus DSS was responsible for safeguarding Joshua from the injuries that occurred between February 1983 and March 1984.

The state significantly increased the danger to Joshua by returning him to the custody of the father. When a state statute creates a duty of child protection and sets forth guidelines to ensure appropriate protection, the child is entitled to this protection under *Board of Regents v. Roth*, 408 U.S. 564, 576 (1972) (setting forth that statutory and administrative standards can create an entitlement to a benefit protected as a right to procedural due process of law). In this case, the state was very aware of the injuries that Joshua had already received at the hands of his father. It was monitoring Joshua in his father's home because it knew the level of risk to him was high. Despite visible signs and multiple reports of physical abuse by mandatory reporters, state agents left Joshua in his father's care. Joshua was eventually beaten so badly that he suffered severe head trauma, leaving him mentally disabled for the rest of his life. The state's repeated failure to act left Joshua in a position of danger, thus violating his due process rights. The social worker assigned to Joshua exhibited "deliberate indifference" to a risk of harm to a child under the supervision of the state. *Doe v. N.Y. City Dep't of Soc. Servs.*, 649 F.2d 134 (1981).

D *Qualified Immunity for Social Workers*

Government officials performing discretionary functions generally are shielded from liability for civil damages insofar as their conduct does not violate clearly established statutory or constitutional rights of which a reasonable person would have known. *Harlow v. Fitzgerald*, 457 U.S. 800, 818 (1982). Qualified immunity also is only available if the state official acts in good faith. See Wis. Stat. 48.981(4) (1987–1988). While good faith is presumed, it can be rebutted, and the presumption removed. This court is aghast with the complete lack of diligence the state had in pursuing safety for Joshua. The entire situation could have been avoided, and while it is not the place of this Court to stand in judgment of the moral obligations of individuals, it is the placc of this Court to hold state actors liable for violation of "clearly established statutory or constitutional rights of which reasonable persons would have known."

An instructive case regarding qualified immunity is *Anderson v. Creighton*, 483 U.S. 635 (1987). Although this case dealt with a Fourth Amendment search, it addressed police officers' qualified immunity from civil action if the action the officer took "could reasonably have been thought consistent with the allegedly violated rights." In the case at hand, the social worker could not have reasonably thought that her actions were consistent with Joshua's rights under the Fourteenth Amendment. Only if the state had investigated the additional injuries of Joshua and removed him from his father's care would it have had qualified immunity because the action taken was reasonable and consistent with any alleged violation of parental rights.

It is unclear whether the social worker in this case acted in bad faith or in conformance with office policy, even if that policy was in contradiction to the statutory requirements of the state child protection laws. If the caseworker knew the phone would ring one day, and she would learn (from the same emergency personnel who had treated Joshua so many times for physical abuse in the past) that Joshua was dead, what exactly was her reasonable expectation of her duty to Joshua? She was not some scribe whose only role was to write down what she saw (or did not see) when she visited his home. She was tasked with making reports of abuse to the state so that the state could take appropriate action to protect Joshua from harm. Moreover, she was tasked with acting in a reasonable manner and notifying the county attorney that the father failed to fulfill his agreement with the state. It is unclear from the record whether the social worker's supervisors established certain lax customs within the department regarding the reporting of new injuries in an ongoing case, or were grossly negligent in their training.

Upper Darby Township et al. v. Colburn, 946 F.2d 1017 (1991), is instructive in the analysis of whether the social worker, her supervisors, and the state can use the state of mind defense set forth in *Daniel v. Williams*, 474 U.S. 327, 334 (1986). This defense basically states that mere negligence does not amount to intentional conduct sufficient to make out a deprivation under the Due Process clause.[12] *Colburn* is a Third Circuit case in which the court held that respondent's allegations were sufficient to show that a town had a "custom" of inadequate monitoring of suicidal detainees to support a § 1983 claim against the municipality. Two pre-trial detainees had committed suicide in the town's jail in the last three years. In *Colburn*, a pre-trial detainee committed suicide with a handgun that her jailors failed to find when they searched her prior to placing her in the cell. Respondent's estate alleged that a police officer, her supervisors, and the municipality violated the detainee's due process rights by failing to prevent her suicide. They acted negligently and recklessly in searching and supervising the detainee, and the town was liable for this misconduct because it had a "custom" of laxity in both searching of persons taken into police custody as well as monitoring of pre-trial detainees. The individual officer knew or should have known that the detainee was a suicidal risk because she had twice before tried to commit suicide in the presence of the police and had visible scars on her wrists from previous suicide attempts. Nonetheless, the officer did nothing to protect her. This was sufficient to state a due process claim against the officer.

This Court is not in a position to make a finding as to whether state officials' violated petitioner's liberty rights in a grossly negligent manner. This part of petitioner's claim is remanded to the lower court for review consistent with this opinion.

Reversed and remanded for damages to petitioners consistent with this opinion and a determination by the lower court regarding whether DSS has a custom or policy of not adequately investigating subsequent incidents of child abuse while monitoring children in private homes.

[12] The Court in *Daniel* ultimately overruled *Parratt v. Taylor*, 451 U.S. 527 (1981), holding that mere lack of care by a state official does not "deprive" an individual of life, liberty, or property under the Fourteenth Amendment. *Daniel v. Williams*, 474 U.S. 327, 330–31 (1986). While *Parratt* concluded that § 1983 contained no state of mind requirement independent of that necessary to state a violation of the underlying constitutional right, *Daniels* stated that the guarantee of due process has been applied to deliberate decisions of government officials to deprive a person of life, liberty or property. *Id.* at 331.

11

Commentary on *Simeone v. Simeone*

JAMIE R. ABRAMS

INTRODUCTION

Simeone v. Simeone is an ideal case for inclusion in this volume because of its breadth and its timing. The overarching question presented by *Simeone* was whether courts should treat signatories to prenuptial agreements (notably women) just like any other contracting parties or whether courts should scrutinize prenuptial agreements more carefully than ordinary contracts. In considering this question, the case addressed the intersections of women's relative rights and status within both private contracts and intimate relationships, and also public economic, social, and political systems.

It addressed these questions in a 1990 Pennsylvania Supreme Court decision, following notable second-wave feminist victories and on the brink of third-wave feminism's emergence in the early 1990s. Second-wave feminism brought women substantial advancements, but many of those achievements were siloed reforms within the family, employment, education, and other fields – reforms in no-fault divorce, the criminalization of domestic violence, and equitable property distribution. *Simeone* prompts rich dialogue on the breadth of feminist issues and the trajectory of feminist reforms.

This commentary begins by explaining how prenuptial agreements work generally and how they present unique problems of unequal bargaining power and timing. It then examines the history of the original opinion. It concludes by highlighting how Justice Kelly and Justice Culhane incorporate feminist perspectives into their opinions consistent with the overall *Feminist Judgments* project.

PRENUPTIAL AGREEMENTS: THE STAKES AND THE STATE

Prenuptial agreements seek to bypass the control of the state and the uncertainty that state intervention involves in resolving property and spousal support obligations. The state can play a powerful – and even paradoxical – role in marital dissolution. It is the power of the state to redistribute assets that motivates the more resourced party to seek a prenuptial agreement. Yet prenuptial agreements risk leaving the less well-resourced party (often women) vulnerable and disempowered financially or state-dependent for decades. In contrast, if a developer breaches its agreement to construct a house to certain specifications by a specified date, the state will intervene to remedy the harms of the breach, but the state itself will not face financial risk. The state thus has notable interests in intervening in the enforcement of premarital agreements that might leave one spouse dependent on state assistance. Indeed both the American Law Institute and the Uniform Premarital Agreement Act would set aside contracts that leave a spouse to seek state assistance.

The validity of prenuptial agreements is about fairness and the proper role of the state. It is also about timing. If the state intervenes and examines prenuptial contracts for fairness, at what time should fairness be relevant? If a wife signs a prenuptial agreement as an able-bodied, employed individual waiving her right to future spousal support, that might have been a fair and reasonable decision in the moment. What if, however, she becomes disabled or unemployable *after* executing the prenuptial agreement? Should courts look at the fairness only at the time the prenuptial agreement was executed, only at the time it is to be enforced, or both?[1]

Simeone thus presents questions of whether prenuptial agreements should be treated as a special form of contract warranting closer scrutiny or whether actualizing the agency and autonomy of women might demand that we treat both signatories as fully equal participants in prenuptial contract negotiations. The next section examines the facts and background of *Simeone*.

CASE BACKGROUND

Simeone v. Simeone involved a prenuptial agreement between an unemployed nurse, Catherine Simeone, and a physician, Frederick Simeone. At the time of their marriage, Frederick earned $90,000 a year and held existing assets worth approximately $300,000. The parties disagreed as to whether Catherine knew the agreement would be presented to her for signature. On the eve of the couple's wedding, Frederick's attorney presented Catherine with the

[1] Notably, each of these frameworks are viable competing modern legal rules adopted in jurisdictions today. *See, e.g.*, American Law Institute Principles of the Law of Family Dissolution §§ 7.04, 7.05 (2002); Uniform Premarital and Marriage Agreements Act §§ 9, 10 (2012).

prenuptial agreement to sign. Catherine signed the agreement without advice from an attorney. Frederick's attorney did not disclose the specific legal rights Catherine was signing away.

The prenuptial agreement limited support payments to Catherine to $200 a week and maxing out at a total payment of $25,000. The couple separated in 1982 and began divorce proceedings in 1984. Between separation and divorce, Frederick made payments pursuant to the prenuptial agreement and reached the $25,000 cap on support set forth in the agreement. In 1985, Catherine filed a claim for alimony *pendente lite*. The validity of the agreement was upheld and her claim for alimony denied because she had waived her right to petition for alimony of any kind in the prenuptial agreement. The Court of Common Pleas of Philadelphia County and the Superior Court agreed with the master's report supporting the validity of the prenuptial agreement.

Reading *only* the original Pennsylvania Supreme Court opinion reveals no facts beyond those presented above. We do not know why Mrs. Simeone is unemployed, what Mrs. Simeone's net worth was at marriage and at separation, what the parties' net worth is at the time of enforcing the prenuptial agreement, or any other details about their health, lifestyle, or division of labor during the almost decade-long marriage. The absence of these facts foreshadows the direction that the Pennsylvania Supreme Court went in its holding.

This case is often taught in family law courses quite early in the course material. Perhaps most telling to the dynamics of the case, when presented with a client counseling role-play based on the text of this prenuptial agreement, second- and third-year law students simply cannot adequately advise Mrs. Simeone on what is at stake for her. The entire recitation of the facts from the original opinion was provided in the above paragraphs. This reality highlights how individuals negotiate their rights in "the shadow of the law."[2] In order to advise Mrs. Simeone adequately, it would be critical for an attorney to know what she would likely have been entitled to had she gone to court in a divorce *without* a prenuptial agreement. Students at this early point in the semester do not know this information. In fact, at this point in the semester, students do not even know how to pronounce alimony pendente lite! In that sense, reading the original opinion, our family law students are all like Mrs. Simeone, aware abstractly that she was giving up rights, but unsure what those rights are exactly. That reality foreshadows the concerns Justices Kelly and Culhane seek to address.

[2] *See, e.g.*, Robert H. Mnookin & Lewis Kornhauser, *Bargaining in the Shadow of the Law: The Case of Divorce*, 88 YALE L.J. 950, 968 (1979).

The argument Mrs. Simeone made before the Supreme Court was that the contract was unenforceable because it did not explain, and she did not know, what the law would have given her if she did not sign. The Supreme Court granted Mrs. Simeone's appeal due to conflicting interpretations of a recent case, *Estate of Geyer*, 516 Pa. 492, 533 A.2d 423 (1987), on this point. The Supreme Court held in *Geyer* that a prenuptial agreement was valid if it "*either* made a reasonable provision for the spouse *or* was entered after a full and fair disclosure of the general financial positions of the parties and the statutory rights being relinquished."[3] Under one interpretation, if $25,000 made reasonable provision for Catherine, then the agreement would be valid, even if she did not know what rights or benefits she was actually relinquishing. However, if *Geyer* required instead that – in all cases – spouses understand what rights they were surrendering under the agreement, then the agreement would be invalid.

The Supreme Court interpreted *Geyer* as requiring only full and fair disclosure in the narrow sense and affirmed the decisions of the courts below, finding the Simeone prenuptial agreement to be a valid and enforceable contract. Justice John Flaherty explained in the majority opinion that only traditional contract law doctrines applied to prenuptial agreements because – to hold otherwise – "would constitute a paternalistic and unwarranted interference with the parties' freedom to enter contracts."[4] This reasoning, as Brian Bix has argued, is in its own right narrow for contracts generally, expressing "a view of contract law that is decades behind the developments in contractual doctrine and commentary."[5] Flaherty explained further that, "[i]f parties viewed an agreement as reasonable at the time of its inception, as evidenced by their having signed the agreement, they should be foreclosed from later trying to evade its terms by asserting that it was not in fact reasonable."[6]

Instead, the Pennsylvania Supreme Court held that prenuptial agreements should be governed only by "traditional principles of contract law."[7] Looking only to contract principles, the court found that the Simeone agreement was valid because there was no fraud, misrepresentation, or duress. Applying contract principles requiring that the agreement not be procured through

[3] *Simeone v. Simeone*, 525 Pa. 392, 397, 581 A.2d 162, 163 (1990) (analyzing Estate of Geyer, 516 Pa. 492, 533 A.2d 423 (1987)).

[4] *Id.* at 166.

[5] Brian Bix, *Bargaining in the Shadow of Love: The Enforcement of Premarital Agreements and How We Think about Marriage*, 40 Wm. & Mary L. Rev. 145, 182, 188 (1998).

[6] *Id.*

[7] *Id.*

fraud or misrepresentation, the court required financial disclosure. To be valid, an agreement must be based upon "a full and fair disclosure of the financial positions of the parties."[8]

Justice Flaherty reasoned that men and women are equal and, as such, the court should not paternalistically "protect" women by applying any special review to prenuptial agreements. Flaherty explained that previous decisions reviewing prenuptial agreements "rested upon a belief that spouses are of unequal status and that women are not knowledgeable enough to understand the nature of contracts that they enter. Society has advanced, however, to the point where women are no longer regarded as the 'weaker' party in marriage, or in society generally."[9]

This opinion is noteworthy compared to others in this volume for that reason. Here, the underlying jurisprudence purported to actually advance gender equality and support changing gender norms. However, this opinion is an example of formalism – a form of equality feminism launched just as feminisms moved in difference directions.

Even accepting the court's holding directing a limited review only to basic principles of contract validity (fraud, duress, etc.), the court's decision is noteworthy given the financial and social dynamics of weddings in this era.[10] Had the couple followed traditional wedding norms of the time, on the eve of her wedding, Catherine and her family would likely bear all of the risk of canceling the wedding the day before. She would also likely bear a disproportionate share of the social stigma that would come with canceling a wedding on the eve of its occurrence. Thus, while reasonable readers of the original opinion might conclude that the financial duress of canceling a wedding would bend the will of a signatory, the court did not see it that way. The court saw formal equality and ended its analysis at that. This analysis positioned Pennsylvania as a jurisdiction uniquely favoring freedom of contract so long as proper disclosure occurred, ultimately codifying, with revision, what the pro-contract Uniform Premarital Agreement Act required.[11]

[8] *Id.* at 167.

[9] *Id.* at 165.

[10] *See, e.g.*, Cele C. Otnes & Elizabeth Pleck, Cinderella Dreams, The Allure of the Lavish Wedding (2003) (chronicling the history of engagements, wedding rituals, and wedding ceremonies, particularly their commercial and consumerist underpinnings); Keith Bradsher, *Left at the Altar: Modern Tales of Woe*, N.Y. Times, Mar. 7, 1990, at C1 (noting that weddings can cost between $50,000 and $100,000 and the costs are less recoverable the closer to the wedding the cancellation occurs).

[11] 23 Pa. Con. Stat. Ann. § 3106 (incorporating the language of the UPAA without the requirement of unconscionability). *See, e.g.*, Barbara Ann Atwood, *Ten Years Later: Lingering Concerns about the Uniform Premarital Agreement Act*, 19 J. Legis. 127 (1993) (explaining that

Justice Papadakos concurred. The short concurrence agreed that the Simeone agreement was valid; however, he strongly disagreed with Flaherty's assessment of women's equality. Most poignantly, Papadakos wrote, speaking more to his fellow Justice than to the constituents of the case and the courts:

> I fear my colleague does not live in the real world. If I did not know him better, I would think that his statements smack of male chauvinism, an attitude that "you women asked for it, now live with it." If you want to know about equality of women, just ask them about comparable wages for comparable work. Just ask them about sexual harassment in the workplace.[12]

These points remind us of the law reform work underway at the time to which Justice Kelly will ultimately draw upon in her opinion. Papadakos concluded that prenuptial agreements involve two unequal parties in which one has greater authority over the other, and, as such, the law should protect the weaker party. His opinion criticized his colleague more than the law, suggesting that the facts of the case did not lead toward the points the majority wanted to believe were true. He concurred in the opinion, however, reasoning that – consistent with *Geyer* – the agreement was valid.

Dissenting, Justice McDermott also disagreed with the use of traditional contract law to govern prenuptial agreements because of the "solemnity of the matrimonial union."[13] Rather than contract law principles, McDermott would require that a party trying to invalidate a prenuptial agreement must "establish by clear and convincing evidence, that a full and fair disclosure of the worth of the intended spouse was not made at the time of the execution of the agreement."[14] Additionally, he would "find a pre-nuptial agreement voidable where it is established that the parties were not aware, at the time of contracting, of existing statutory rights which they were relinquishing."[15] His reasoning reinforced historic public policy considerations to preserve marriage and families that, in a previous era, invalidated premarital agreements in the state.[16] He was also concerned that the

the UPAA already departs dramatically from the common law in many states by requiring a spouse to prove that a premarital agreements was either not voluntary or unconscionable when executed to set aside its terms).

12 *Simeone*, 581 A.2d at 168 (Pa. 1990).

13 *Id.*

14 *Id.* at 169.

15 *Id.*

16 *See, e.g.*, Graham C. Woodward, *The Public Policy of the State of Pennsylvania*, 63 Penn L. Rev. 84, 85, 95–98, 104 (1914) ("The preservation of the marriage relation in its present status is a well established policy of the court of this Commonwealth. To this end provisions in contracts or wills in restraint of marriage or encouraging the dissolution of an existing marriage

majority's approach could lead to a spouse becoming a "ward of the state" unnecessarily.[17]

While the majority rejected a reasonableness test requiring an examination of the contract terms, McDermott listed five factors to consider when assessing the reasonableness of an agreement: "(a) the financial situation of each spouse; (b) the age of the parties; (c) the number of children each has; (d) the intelligence of the parties; (e) the standard of living each spouse had before marriage and could reasonably expect to have during marriage."[18] McDermott advocated for a case-by-case approach. McDermott would have remanded *Simeone* to allow Mrs. Simeone to challenge the agreement's validity by arguing that she was not advised of the rights she was relinquishing and that the support provisions provided were inequitable.

FEMINIST REWRITE

Justice Kelly approaches the decision more holistically, reframing both the role of the state and the interests at stake. Justice Kelly is clear and forceful that marriage is not just a contract, but also a status from which a larger set of societal considerations emerge. The state is rightly interested in the property and contract rights being negotiated between these two signatories, as well as in principles of fairness and equality between spouses.

Prenuptial agreements are special, in part, because spouses are fiduciaries owing a larger good faith duty to each other than transactional parties. Unlike commercial transactions where parties negotiate in their own self-interest at arm's length, here the parties are negotiating in a context of dependency, emotion, and intimacy. The parties have a tendency to trust each other. While Justice Kelly does not invoke gender directly in her analysis, she gestures strongly to the questions wrestled with by cultural feminism debates.[19] Do "parties" have a tendency to trust in the abstract or is it actually that *women* have a tendency to trust men in intimate settings? Justice Kelly's analysis implicitly suggests that this relational trust is a value that we should want in marital relationships and that the law should support. The opinion might nudge men closer toward trusting behaviors in intimate relationships while, at

are not enforceable, while settlements of connubial difficulties and transactions tending to preserve or foster marriages are encouraged").

17 *Id.*

18 *Id.* at 170.

19 *See, e.g.*, Linda Alcoff, *Cultural Feminism versus Post-Structuralism: The Identity Crisis in Feminist Theory*, 13 SIGNS 405 (1988).

the same time, revealing how law provides cover for men who abuse women's trust in an intimate relationship.

Justice Kelly squarely rejects the idea that a prenuptial agreement should be enforced, if unfair, just by complying with asset disclosure requirements. All agreements instead must pass both a procedural and a substantive fairness review. Unlike the original opinion, procedural fairness is not just met by full and fair disclosure of assets. Rather, procedural fairness also requires a deeper consideration of unconscionability, which pushes courts to examine power differentials and context. These power differentials reveal how the financially vulnerable spouse (the wife) may rely too heavily on assumptions that the other spouse (the husband) is being fair and reasonable.

The only way to ensure that power differentials do not make the agreement procedurally unenforceable is to give the agreement to the signatory at least thirty days before the wedding and require independent legal counsel (if need be at the drafting party's expense) or an informed waiver of the right to counsel. If the husband is paying for the lawyer and likely active in the selection of the lawyer, might that power differential replicate itself again in the attorney-client consult? Justice Kelly also reveals how power and markets are shaping negotiations and relationships.

While Justice Kelly would strike down the validity of the Simeone prenuptial agreement on procedural grounds alone, she nonetheless addresses substantive fairness concerns. The original majority and concurring opinions agreed that they would not have looked at substantive fairness at all; Justice Kelly would have found the contract unfair at enforcement. Justice Kelly, consistent with a holistic approach, looks beyond the two parties to the effect of similar premarital contracts on the community more broadly. When two parties enter private agreements related to their marital relationships, they negotiate within the "shadow of the law." Justice Kelly reminds us that the norms within which these parties are negotiating their private agreements are also norms that we value as a society and shape concepts of substantive fairness.

She focuses on economics and how the law heavily values men's contributions to marriage while undervaluing women's contributions. Justice Kelly notes how the state has worked hard in other law reforms to strengthen rights for women. A prenuptial agreement would tear down those protections, Justice Kelly explains. This analysis deploys feminist economics as a necessary tool to see "reasonableness" in the substantive fairness lens.[20]

[20] *See, e.g.*, Julie A. Nelson, *Feminism and Economics*, 9 J. ECON. PERSP. 131 (1995); Barbara Bergmann, *The Economic Risks of Being a Housewife*, 72 AM. ECON. REV. 81 (1981).

To presumptively disallow prenuptial agreements, though, because of these underlying policy concerns, would go too far.[21] Justice Kelly instead frames a separate substantive inquiry around reasonableness timed both at execution and enforcement. Justice Kelly introduces factors for determining reasonableness that expand on the factors offered in Justice McDermott's original dissent. Kelly would examine the totality of the circumstances, including a comparative look to the rights and remedies available under existing law as well as contributions of the spouses to the marriage and to childcare. Justice Kelly's opinion reveals the deficiencies in the underlying court record. Whereas the original opinion simply referred to Catherine Simeone as an unemployed nurse, Justice Kelly highlights that Simeone was the primary caregiver for the couple's daughter. This fact reveals how important this deeper inquiry might be to understanding fairness. Valuing marital contributions differently was not just *hypothetical*; it actually played out in the facts of the case when understood through the case transcript, not the original opinion.

These facts, and the factors Justice Kelly would have applied, are essential determinations of the equitable distribution of property at divorce. Indeed, the innovation of equitable distribution is to value domestic labor and caregiving, not just title and earned income. Family law reforms moved the state toward equitable distribution based on principles of fairness and contribution. Justice Kelly stops short of injecting a cultural feminism perspective that might critique the underlying culture that enables undervaluation of "women's work." Implicit in her reasoning though is the point that many of the gender differentials in economic contributions emerge *during* the marriage, thus necessitating a fairness review at *both* execution *and* enforcement.

Justice Culhane concurs and highlights candidly the limits of formal equality. He wrote separately to address the critique that drove the original opinion: that it was paternalistic of the state to intervene in these contracts otherwise. He reminds readers that there are larger shared values at stake than predictability. Shared values relating to fairness are not as present in a simple commercial transaction. While the original opinion believed that formal equality required a hands-off approach to reviewing prenuptial agreements, Culhane notes that – despite all the formal protections enacted for women – these protections are the starting point, not the ending point to equality analysis.

Justice Culhane also adds a dose of pragmatism. He argues that it is not just about power and economic differentials but also about the optimism that makes signatories to prenuptial agreements discount the possibility of

[21] Martha M. Ertman, Love's Promises: How Formal and Informal Contracts Shape All Kinds of Families (2015) (explaining how contracts positively shape and sustain families).

divorce. They frankly get the calculus wrong. They underestimate the benefits the state would give them and overestimate the durability of their marriages. He threads the needle carefully to avoid treating men and women differently, and instead looks at how expectations and assumptions often play out between couples.

CONCLUSION

Together, Justices Kelly and Culhane offer a new legal framework and critical economic and political context to prenuptial agreements. Their opinions foreshadow that women's equality required a look beyond institutions like the family, the military, and employment, to larger questions of state power and market forces.

SIMEONE v. SIMEONE, 581 A.2D 162 (PA. 1990)

JUSTICE KELLY DELIVERED THE OPINION OF THE COURT

This appeal raises important questions concerning the policies and legal standards for enforceability of marital agreements. We seek to clarify and eliminate confusion by stating more definitely the applicable standards and foundational principles in this field. These issues are in need of reevaluation, elucidation and modernization in light of the now prevalent view of marriage as an economic, social and emotional partnership of equals. This view, adopted in Pennsylvania and across the nation, has dramatically changed the former system that made title and market earnings the primary source of ownership rights between spouses. Our legislature rejected this approach because it was not consistent with conceptions of partnership marriage. In addition, the title regime systematically and sometimes severely disadvantaged women who often participate less in paid market work and perform more unpaid family care work. In the previous regime, the work women tend to specialize in, to benefit the family, did not confer ownership rights, even within the family. To redress this, contemporary law has committed to two core values. First, both spouses make contributions to the welfare of the family and do so as a team. Accordingly, the benefits and burdens of collaboration and joint labor should be shared. Second, like paid market work, unpaid work for the family must be accorded value in determining spousal economic rights. This is a critically important step toward gender equality.

Notably, standard form prenuptial agreements are designed to override these reforms and policies by returning to a title system that treats spouses as if they are solo actors, stripping away the sharing, joint contribution and equality principles of marriage law. We cannot ignore the terms and effects of such contracts on individuals and in our sociolegal system. As we explain in depth in this opinion, both procedural and substantive fairness must be evaluated in determining the enforceability of a marital agreement.

It is against this backdrop that we consider the agreement between Catherine Walsh Simeone, appellant, and Frederick Simeone, appellee.

I FACTUAL AND PROCEDURAL BACKGROUND

In this case the contract was presented to and signed by Mrs. Simeone the evening before the wedding. Mr. Simeone was represented by an attorney who drafted the contract and was present that evening. The terms of the agreement were not explained to Mrs. Simeone by Mr. Simeone's attorney. Mrs. Simeone did not have her own attorney. The meeting lasted five to ten minutes. The parties disagree about whether Mrs. Simeone knew in advance that she would be asked to sign a prenuptial agreement. She denies having such knowledge. At the time of their marriage in 1975, Mrs. Simeone was a twenty-three-year-old nurse who was unemployed due to injuries from a car accident. Mr. Simeone was thirty-nine years old and Chief of Neurosurgery at Pennsylvania Hospital. Mr. Simeone had an income of approximately $90,000 per year, and Mrs. Simeone had none. Mr. Simeone also had assets worth approximately $300,000, including a collection of antique cars. Mrs. Simeone's net worth was $3,000. Two years after they married, the couple welcomed a newborn daughter. Mrs. Simone has been the child's primary caregiver and a homemaker for the family throughout the nine-year marriage and did not work outside the home. R. 58a, 107a, 113a, 266, 840a.

Under the agreement Frederick Simeone is the sole owner of all property he owned before the marriage and also all property he acquired after marriage by any means. The agreement explicitly states that Mr. Simeone owns property "as if the marriage had not taken place and he had remained unmarried." R. 84a, Simeone Prenuptial Agreement, p. 5, paragraph 7. The contract waives Catherine Simeone's rights to any claims against Mr. Simeone's estate at death, other than $100,000 if Mrs. Simeone is his surviving widow. It also waives her rights to any property in his name at divorce. Further, the contract waives Mrs. Simeone's claims to alimony, including *alimony pendente lite*, except for $200 a month up to a maximum amount of $25,000. Every time there is a waiver stated for Mrs. Simeone for a right she would otherwise have by law, the agreement states that such is a fair and reasonable term. There are also waivers by Mr. Simeone of property claims he might have against

Mrs. Simeone, but these waivers did not include the same assertion about fairness. The implication is that Mr. Simeone's attorney was concerned about the contract being evaluated for lack of fairness to Mrs. Simeone, but not vice versa. A potential alimony claim for Mr. Simeone is also not mentioned and not waived. The contract focused on obtaining waivers from Mrs. Simeone. R. 84a–84a7, Simeone Prenuptial Agreement.

The parties separated in 1982, and divorce proceedings were commenced in 1984. Between 1982 and 1984 Mr. Simeone made payments up to the $25,000 limit. In 1985, Ms. Simeone filed a claim for *alimony pendente lite.* A master upheld the validity of the prenuptial agreement and denied this claim. Exceptions to the master's report were dismissed by the Court of Common Pleas of Philadelphia County. The Superior Court affirmed. *Simeone v. Simeone*, 551 A.2d 219 (Pa. Super. 1988).

Mrs. Simeone's appeal challenges the validity of the contract based on a lack of reasonableness. She also asserts that the bargaining and execution process for the contract was defective for a number of reasons including: duress; her lack of legal representation; lack of knowledge of her legal rights; lack of full disclosure of Mr. Simeone's financial resources; and a breach of the duty of good faith and fair dealing by Mr. Simeone. Mr. Simeone opposes these claims.

II LEGAL ANALYSIS AND POLICY FOUNDATIONS OF MARITAL AGREEMENTS

We hold that marital agreements in Pennsylvania must meet the standards of both procedural fairness and substantive fairness – or they will not be enforced. These core principles have long been an integral part of our laws and policies in this field. We clarify and expound on the meaning, foundations, and application of these rules in this opinion.

In summary, prenuptial agreements must comply with all the requirements for enforcing any contract, such as mutual assent, voluntariness, a lack of duress, mistake, and fraud, as well as conscionability and compliance with public policy. However, beyond this, we specify more exacting standards for enforcement of marital agreements, because of their special nature. The key requirements for a finding of procedural fairness are: that the agreement must be made with full and fair disclosure of the financial situation and the legal rights and obligations of the parties; that the party seeking to challenge the agreement is given at least thirty days before the wedding to review it, and is given an opportunity to consult with an independent attorney; and that the agreement is signed no later than seven days in advance of the wedding. The two key requirements for a finding of substantive fairness are that the agreement is reasonable at the time of formation and at the time of enforcement.

We take this approach to achieve balance among the important interests at stake in marital contracts. We recognize that such agreements may be an exercise of the parties' freedom to contract. Settling property rights with respect to marriage may serve the useful function of permitting the parties to arrange their financial affairs as they best see fit. On the other hand, contracts can be found unenforceable based on defects in the formation process and also for public policy reasons. Policing prenuptial agreements in this way not only protects the parties involved, but also serves important societal purposes, because enforcing such contracts poses broader risks of harm. When evaluating marital contracts, the state has an interest in protecting the financial interests of spouses during marriage, at divorce, and at the death of a spouse. Marriage is not an ordinary contract between two parties dealing at arm's length, but a legal status from which certain rights and obligations arise grounded on the values of fairness, intimate partnership, and sex equality. These interests and values must be taken into account in this unique context.

A *Background Law Governing Prenuptial Agreements*

It is important to draw a clear distinction between issues of procedural and substantive fairness. We must acknowledge, however, that our earlier decisions have been less than a model of clarity on the rules that apply to these agreements, and on the relationship between these two dimensions of fairness. The origin of the problem can be traced to *In Re Hillegass' Estate*, 244 A.2d 672 (Pa. 1968), where we connected procedure to substance, holding that the party seeking to nullify the agreement must present "clear and convincing evidence that the deceased spouse at the time of the Agreement made *neither* (a) A reasonable provision for the intended spouse [substance], nor (b) A full and fair disclosure of his (or her) worth [procedure]."[1] *Id.* at 675.

By the terms of this test, a party who made full disclosure of assets could command enforcement of a manifestly unfair and unreasonable contract, apparently on the (unstated) theory that, as long as full disclosure has been made, the party seeking to avoid the terms of the agreement has waived any claim to be treated fairly. Thus, a prenuptial agreement would potentially be

[1] The *Hillegass* court then set forth several considerations it deemed material in determining whether the agreement was reasonable. *Hillegass*, 244 A.2d at 675–76. These are discussed in the next section of this opinion. As we continue to explain next, we reject this view. Only marital contracts that are both procedurally and substantively fair will be enforceable.

enforced even if it were unfair to the party challenging it. We reject that approach today.

Matters were then made worse just three years ago. Our plurality decision in *In Re Estate of Geyer*, 533 A.2d 423 (Pa. 1987), appears to have added an *additional* hurdle for a party challenging a prenuptial agreement to clear. While purporting to apply the *Hillegass* test, the *Geyer* plurality stated that any contract entered into "knowingly and intentionally" would be enforceable. The court may simply have been stating the requirement of full and fair disclosure in different language, but the unfortunate effect has been to further conflate procedure and substance by implying that contracts voluntarily entered into are, by definition, reasonable. The *Geyer* plurality stated: "the Superior Court read *Hillegass* as requiring an antenuptial agreement to make reasonable provision *and* to be entered into after full and fair disclosure. This was a misreading of *Hillegass* which provides that an agreement can survive if *either* (but not necessarily both) of these requirements is satisfied." *Id.* at 427 n. 9. If anything, *Geyer* made it even more difficult to challenge prenuptial agreements, and the plurality made clear its view that those challenging these contracts would be looked upon unfavorably:

> Under *Hillegass* ... the question of what is reasonable in an antenuptial agreement ultimately becomes a question for the courts; a question that makes all antenuptial agreements potentially litigable, notwithstanding that the parties were aware of the terms of the agreement when they signed. Antenuptial agreements which are knowingly and intentionally executed should not be abrogated. Unreasonable conditions or consequences may prove that an agreement was not knowingly entered into; but absent that lack of knowledge the surviving party should be required to live with the bargain. Nonetheless, in order to enforce such an agreement a court should be convinced that the agreement in question was in fact made knowingly and intentionally.
>
> *Id.* at 429.

The parties' briefings in the case before us reflect the difficulty of resolving the complexities in our earlier decisions. It is incumbent on us, therefore, to set forth, in clear terms, the rules that apply in deciding whether to enforce prenuptial agreements. As we will explain in detail, to be enforceable, such agreements must be both procedurally *and* substantively fair.

1 Procedural Fairness

As is the case with all contracts, prenuptial agreements will not be enforced if they are unconscionable. The doctrine of unconscionability considers both procedural and substantive fairness. Thus, no prenuptial contract will be enforced unless it is procedurally fair. If this requirement is not met, the agreement will not be rescued by a judicial determination that the terms satisfy the requirements of substantive fairness by making reasonable provision for the spouse challenging the contract.[2] We follow *Hillegass* in holding that procedural fairness requires "full and fair disclosure" of assets, but find that, in the unique context of prenuptial agreements, procedural fairness imposes additional burdens on the party seeking enforcement. For reasons we will explain, the spouse initiating the agreement must present it to the other spouse at least thirty days before the wedding, and the contract must be signed and executed no later than seven days before the wedding. Each spouse must have an opportunity to consult with an independent attorney. Both sides must be represented by counsel unless the requirement is waived, in writing.

These requirements are a necessary consequence of our view that a contract between two people who are soon to marry is different from a standard commercial contract and raises distinct concerns. As we will explain more fully, in the prenuptial context, the parties do not bargain at arm's length, but are in a trusting, intimate relationship. In addition, they are entering into an agreement against the backdrop of planning a shared life together, with consequences that will follow them throughout the marriage and upon its dissolution.

We begin our discussion of procedural fairness by drawing on well-established principles of contract law. Any defect in the bargaining process that deprives one party of meaningful choice leads to a finding of procedural unfairness. *Williston on Contracts* § 18.10. Often, procedural defects in the bargaining process that result in one party's ability to take advantage of the other (procedural unconscionability) lead to unfairness in the terms and conditions that ultimately find their way into the agreement (substantive unconscionability). As stated in the Restatement (Second) of Contracts, "[o]rdinarily . . . an unconscionable contract involves other factors as well as overall imbalance." *Id.* § 208, Comment (c). It will be helpful, then, to describe unconscionability both in general terms and by considering it in more specific categories – not only those of procedure and substance, but also by comparing the unique, fiduciary context of prenuptial agreements to more standard, commercial contracts.

In *comment a* to section 208, the Second Restatement recognizes the value of this nuanced approach, and sets forth the necessity of carefully weighing the

[2] Unlike this case, both *Hillegass* and *Geyer* involved agreements waiving financial claims at the death of a spouse, rather than the dissolution of the marriage. The decision in this case is intended to apply to both contexts.

facts, circumstances, and broader context in which "the determination that a contract . . . is or is not unconscionable is made." Consideration is given to the "setting, purpose and effect" of the contract, and "[r]elevant factors include weaknesses in the contracting process like those involved in more specific rules as to contractual capacity, fraud, and other invalidating causes; the policy also overlaps with rules which render particular bargains or terms unenforceable on grounds of public policy." *Id.*

Parties to a marriage stand in a fiduciary relationship. "Agreements between spouses, unlike ordinary business contracts, involve a fiduciary relationship requiring the utmost of good faith." *Christian v. Christian*, 365 N.E.2d 849, 855 (N.Y. 1977). The law in some states has been less clear on whether the same is true of *future* spouses, but we have held that future spouses are in a relationship of trust. More than fifty years ago we said:

> As this Court has, on many occasions, pointed out, the relation of prospective spouses is one of extreme mutual confidence, requiring the exercise of the utmost good faith in all transactions between them, and when they enter into an antenuptial agreement determining property rights, a duty arises having no place in the ordinary contractual relationship to be frank and unreserved in the disclosure of all circumstances materially bearing upon the contemplated agreement.
>
> *In re* Groff's Estate, 341 Pa. 105, 110 (Pa. 1941).

We continue to believe this is the better-reasoned position. As future spouses, after all, the parties are creating an agreement that will affect their mutual lives mostly after the couple has married.

Our precedent has recognized the importance of context, so we have imposed the requirement of full and fair disclosure of assets as a condition of enforcement of the agreement. *Hillegass*, 244 A.2d at 675. In standard contracts, of course, no such obligation is imposed, unless the parties specifically bargain for it. But in the context of an impending, emotional, and long-term intimate relationship, such disclosure is a necessary bulwark against the possibility that the party in the less favorable financial situation will be less than fully aware of what is being given up. A specific comparison may help to illustrate the reason for the distinction. While a lumber company does not care about the assets of the home builder that has just purchased its product, potential spouses have good reason to discover each other's financial background – because that knowledge provides the backdrop against which significant concessions of *future* property rights are about to be made. In short, any analysis of the rules for interpreting unconscionability in the commercial context is of limited utility in the unique context of marriage – a dynamic, mutually dependent relationship. In an arm's length, business setting, the parties generally act as independent actors, both properly considering only whether a proposed transaction will be economically advantageous to themselves. The two may prosper; or one may prosper while the other loses; or both may lose – but the parties are not necessarily connected in any intrinsic way beyond the contract itself. Indeed, in the modern age of instantaneous electronic communications, the parties may never even meet face to face.

The two parties to a prenuptial agreement are situated quite differently, even before marriage. Once they are married, the divergence from parties in commercial transactions only increases. Typically, spouses plan and save for retirement jointly, commingle their assets, and – as in this case – often "invest" in children, both financially and emotionally. Their financial futures are braided; the expectation is that if one spouse succeeds or fails, so too does the other. Thus, an affirmative duty of disclosure arises in this unique context. Failure to make such disclosure is therefore a species of fraud, rendering the contract unconscionable, and therefore unenforceable.

Another defect in the bargaining process that can lead to a finding of unconscionability is duress. Again, context can be decisive in determining whether one party has acted under duress – that is, not truly voluntarily. In *Carrier v. William Penn Broadcasting Co.*, we defined duress in the commercial setting as:

> that degree of restraint or danger, either actually inflicted or threatened and impending, which is sufficient in severity or apprehension to overcome the mind of a person of ordinary firmness . . . The quality of firmness is assumed to exist in every person competent to contract, unless it appears that by reason of old age or other sufficient cause he is weak or infirm. Where persons deal with each other on equal terms and at arm's length, there is a presumption that the person alleging duress possesses ordinary firmness . . . [citations omitted in original]. Moreover, in the absence of threats of actual bodily harm there can be no duress where the contracting party is free to consult with counsel.
>
> 233 A.2d 519, 521 (Pa. 1967).

We affirm the holding in *Carrier*, which involved contractual dealings between two drug companies. But the meaning of such "quality of firmness" cannot be uncritically lifted from that context and applied to duress in the prenuptial context. Consider, specifically, whether a contract between two commercial parties would be set aside where the party resisting enforcement of the bargain had neglected to secure legal counsel. In the absence of extraordinary facts – such as threats of physical violence – we would let the consequences of that error lie, because both parties can fairly be presumed to understand the necessity of obtaining counsel. We would not assume that duress had contributed to the failure to do so.

But experience teaches that the situation and relationship of parties to a prenuptial agreement are quite different. While few would consider signing off on a substantial commercial contract without the advice of counsel, operating without an attorney is common in the prenuptial context. As noted above, the parties are in a relationship of trust and are planning a life together, so there is a natural tendency for the party adversely affected by the contract to engage in wishful thinking that the soon-to-be spouse is being fair and reasonable – and that the relationship will endure. Also, the party being asked to sign the contract will often be unschooled in the legal complexities and contingencies that the agreement typically entails. One court recently put it this way: "Candor compels us to raise to a conscious level the fact that … prenuptial agreements will almost always be entered into between people with property or an income potential to protect on one side and people who are impecunious on the other." *Gant v. Gant*, 329 S.E.2d 106, 114 (W. Va. 1985). We share the concerns family law scholar Judith Younger has recently emphasized, that prenuptial agreements are generated within "'a confidential relationship' involving parties who are usually not evenly matched in bargaining power. The possibility, therefore, that one party may overreach the other is greater than in the case of ordinary contracts." Judith Younger, *Perspectives on Antenuptial Agreements*, 40 RUTGERS L. REV. 1059, 1065 (1987–1988). In addition, as Younger observes,

> antenuptial agreements are to be performed in the future, in the context of a relationship which the parties have not yet begun and which may continue for many years after the agreement is executed and before it is enforced. The possibility that later events may make it unwise, unfair, or otherwise undesirable to enforce such agreements is also greater than in the case of ordinary contracts.
>
> Id.

Engaging an advocate is the surest way to combat this tendency to uncritically accept the agreement terms and the good faith of the other party – who, after all, the party being asked to sign is soon to *marry*. Accordingly, each party must have a reasonable opportunity to locate and consult with independent legal counsel. We therefore seek to preemptively avoid allegations of unconscionability when contract enforcement is sought by requiring that the party challenging enforcement be provided with the contract *at least thirty days* before the scheduled date of the wedding. That party may then choose to waive the right to counsel, but such waiver must be in writing, and must recite that, if that party is unable to afford counsel, the party drafting the agreement will pay the reasonable costs of retaining an attorney to review the agreement. This approach is consistent with that adopted in some of our sister states. *See, e.g.*, MINN. STAT. ANN. § 519.11(1)(b) (West Supp. 1988). *See also In re Estate of Crawford*, 730 P.2d 675 (Wa. 1986); *Bauer v. Bauer*, 464 P.2d 710, 712 (Or. Ct. App. 1970); *Gant v. Gant*, 329 S.E.2d 106, 116 (W. Va. 1985) (cited in Younger, 40 RUTGERS L. REV. at 1076).

The facts of the case before us suggest one additional requirement: the agreement must be signed and executed no later than seven full days before the scheduled date of the wedding.

This case dramatically illustrates the need for these requirements. Here, Mr. Simeone concedes that Mrs. Simeone did not have independent legal counsel, and further admits that the final contract was presented to her on the eve of the wedding. In his brief, Mr. Simeone dismissively emphasizes that Mrs. Simeone "just wanted to sign and go so she could get to the hairdresser." Brief for Appellee at 4. This observation was intended to support the view that Mrs. Simeone was untroubled by signing the agreement. We draw the opposite conclusion. The emotions attendant to an imminent wedding, and the daunting "to do" list – here including a visit to the hairdresser – make a rational assessment of the legal consequences of a prenuptial agreement exceedingly difficult. Thus, we hold that the prenuptial agreement in this case did not meet the requirements of procedural fairness. That is enough to resolve this case in Mrs. Simeone's favor, because a finding of procedural unfairness is sufficient to invalidate the prenuptial agreement.

Nonetheless, because the question whether prenuptial agreements must also be *substantively* fair has been a source of confusion to lower courts, we will now address that issue.

2 Substantive Fairness

In addition to procedural fairness, premarital agreements must be substantively fair to be valid.[3] This component of the legal standard is a continuation, revision, and expansion of our longstanding approach that prenuptial

[3] Some prenuptial agreements deal with other issues, and the concerns expressed here are not present in those other contexts. For instance, two people who come from strong, but different, religious traditions may wish to avoid difficult issues in the future by agreeing to raise their children as Christian, Jewish, Muslim, or in no religious tradition at all. Such an agreement is fundamentally different from the standard prenuptial agreement, because it is often a way for the marriage "community" to deal with a difficult issue affecting the entire family by

agreements be evaluated for reasonableness.[4] The factors to consider in a reasonableness analysis are explained this section. We adopt this standard because marital contracts are of great importance to individuals and to society.

As we have said, freedom of contract is an important value. Yet that freedom has always had its limits as a matter of contract law and it must be balanced with other state interests. As described earlier in the section on procedural fairness, the well-established contract doctrine of unconscionability operates as a tool for policing agreements. Again, that doctrine has a substantive as well as a process dimension. The content of an agreement may be found unenforceable because the terms are unacceptably unfair to one party or are unenforceable on grounds of public policy. Restatement (Second) of Contracts § 208 (1981), Comment (a).

However, as we have made clear, the special nature of marriage contracts calls for higher standards of fairness. A contract that shifts or eliminates a legal duty established in marriage law is distinct from an agreement between commercial actors who have no claims against each other absent the contract. A marital agreement may well set aside otherwise applicable public policies that are embodied in legal rules designed to facilitate fairness and economic justice between the parties, as well as other goals such as family partnerships and sex equality. For these reasons, careful review for substantive fairness is justified.

Consider the potential effects of the terms of a standard prenuptial contract that is in anticipation of a first marriage and devised to protect the interests of the more economically powerful spouse. Spouses who have wealth and income have attorneys who draft an agreement to protect their interests against the other spouse's claims. The way to do that is to obtain a waiver that eliminates or drastically reduces the financial claims that a spouse otherwise would have at divorce or death. The design and operation of such a contract is

anticipating and addressing a potential problem to the benefit of all. It may often further harmony rather than compromising it. In a recent Superior Court decision, the majority declined to enforce an oral agreement to raise the couple's children in the Jewish faith, but the court expressly reserved the question whether a *written* agreement would be enforceable. *Zummo v. Zummo*, 574 A.2d 1130, 1161 n. 22 (Pa. Super. 1990). We agree that a written agreement would be less likely to create problems when difficult issues arise during divorce and custody proceedings, but express no opinion as to whether an oral agreement would be enforceable under appropriate circumstances.

4 As we have explained, our previous legal standard was that premarital agreements are invalid (a) if there no reasonable provision for a spouse or (b) if there was no full and fair financial disclosure. *In re Hillegass' Estate*, 244 A.2d at 675. This standard is replaced by the requirement that marital agreements must be *both* procedurally fair and substantively fair to be valid. The justifications and rules for procedural fairness have already been explained.

to vitiate the legal impacts of marriage. This poses an acute risk to a spouse whose interests would have been protected by marriage law. At the same time, it may undermine the law's policy objectives. Indeed, the regime governing spousal economic relations at divorce and at death is designed to achieve some measure of fairness between the parties. Accordingly, if these rules are jettisoned in an agreement, that triggers a concern for fairness, as well as the state's interests in supporting family-centered policies.

The instant case presents a representative example to explore potential fairness and other policy concerns in prenuptial contracts. The Simeone contract specifically says that property ownership is to be "as if the marriage had not taken place." That means the market wage earner is the owner and more generally that title controls. In the Simeone contract there is also a waiver of Mrs. Simeone's alimony claims beyond a cap of $25,000. There was no waiver of Mr. Simeone's alimony claims. Pennsylvania law also gives a surviving spouse a right to inherit property of a spouse at death. This right was also waived, other than $100,000 for Mrs. Simeone if she were to be a surviving widow.

What is the potential effect of such waivers of marital legal rights? Compare two situations. First, imagine a situation in which each spouse was in fact a solo economic actor and was going to focus efforts on earning wages in the paid labor market, and had or would thereby acquire independent title to property. Such a contract could possibly serve the interests of both parties. Each spouse would own the product of their individual labor and have the benefit of human capital investments in themselves and the earning power that can produce. Importantly, however, the impacts are very different if one spouse engages in the paid labor market and the other spouse performs much of the unpaid family care work, such as caring for a child, and does not work or has only limited work for pay outside the home. This specialized organization of work is common in families, even today: "[H]usbands are likely to earn more than their working wives. For their part, women continue to assume a large share of the family's domestic responsibilities, a share compounded with the arrival of children." Margaret F. Brinig & June Carbone, *The Reliance Interest in Marriage and Divorce*, 62 TULANE L. REV. 855, 869 (1988) (internal citations omitted). When contract waivers are applied to a family with these behaviors, the market-focused spouse alone acquires the financial benefits of that work, while the spouse focused on family care does not. The caregiving spouse also receives no recompense for family work. In addition, the family caregiver is burdened with diminished earning power from having stepped back from the wage market. Under the contract, the more a couple integrates their lives by sharing and allocating market and unpaid family labor, the greater the skewing of benefits to the market spouse and burdens to the home-focused spouse.

The Simeone contract demonstrates the unfairness that predictably can occur when a contract extinguishes marital rights that are intended to provide fair outcomes for spouses who are economically interdependent and share paid and unpaid labor. Mrs. Simeone was twenty-three and unemployed at the time of the contract execution. The couple anticipated integrating their lives and labor, and then went on to live a shared life with intense role specialization. Mrs. Simeone was a full-time, at-home wife and mother for the couple's child, who was born within two years of the marriage. The evening before the wedding, Mrs. Simeone was asked to sign an agreement where she gave up *far more* than her soon-to-be husband. The terms make Mrs. Simeone extremely vulnerable to financial hardship by denying her legal claims to share in monetary benefits produced from her family caregiving work. In addition, Mrs. Simeone alone is assigned the burdens of having diminished attachment to the labor market resulting from the caregiving role she took on to benefit the family. Conversely, the contract secured for Mr. Simeone alone ownership of property and income that would be earned and accumulated with the support of shared work.

In sum, the contract generated profoundly unfair economic outcomes for Mrs. Simeone and negated the laws and policies intended to establish fairness especially for family caregivers like her. It was based on a pretense of individual and separate lives, when in fact the couple shared their lives as partners in marriage.

In addition to concerns of unfairness in an individual case, contracts such as the Simeones' that override marriage laws are a clear rejection of the recently modernized policy foundations of marriage. The previous system, in all but the nine community property states, was that property ownership for spouses followed title to that property. Thus, the wage-earning spouse (typically male) enjoyed an enormous advantage when it came to the distribution of marital assets at the time of divorce. That regime has now been abandoned by the Pennsylvania Legislature and across the country. It has been replaced with new rules for equitable division at divorce that provide that title and market earnings do *not* determine ownership. Instead, economic resources acquired during marriage are seen as the product of a shared life based on the understanding that marriage is a partnership of equal persons where both spouses make meaningful contributions to the family. Thus, nonmarket contributions of family care count alongside market earnings.

Our marriage dissolution statutes delineate this modern approach. The Pennsylvania legislature recently and clearly affirmed the policy foundations of marriage laws, stating "the family is the basic unit in society and the protection and preservation of the family is of paramount public concern." 23 Pa. C.S.A. 3102 (a). The court is to "give primary consideration to the welfare of the family," 23 Pa. C.S.A. 3102 (a)(3), to "mitigate the harm to the spouses and their children caused by the legal dissolution of the marriage," 23 Pa. C.S.A. 3102 (a)(4), and to "effectuate economic justice between parties who are divorced or separated and grant or withhold alimony according to the actual need and ability to pay of the parties and insure a fair and just determination and settlement of their property rights," 23 Pa. C.S.A. 3102 (a)(6).

More specifically, marital property is defined as "all property acquired by *either* party during the marriage." 23 Pa. C.S.A. 3501 (a) (emphasis added). The statute directs courts to "equitably divide, distribute or assign … the marital property between the parties without regard to marital misconduct in such percentages and in such manner as the court deems just after considering all relevant factors." 23 Pa. C.S.A. 3502 (a). The factors notably include "[t]he contribution or dissipation of each party in the acquisition, preservation, depreciation or appreciation of the marital property, *including the contribution of a party as homemaker.*" Pa. C.S.A. 3502 (a)(7) (emphasis added). The system is designed to recognize that spousal contributions may take different forms, as where one spouse is the primary marketplace wage-earner, while the other spouse's contribution may be characterized as "in-kind," unpaid labor.[5]

By valuing all contributions to the marriage – not just market wages, but household labor and childrearing, scheduling and planning, and so many other quotidian tasks – the legal system realizes the expectations of both spouses, and promotes reliance on a division of labor, broadly construed. This encourages collaboration that can benefit families and promote stability.

As the concurring opinion cogently explains in more detail, marital partnership laws also help advance sex equality. They recognize that family care work, still disproportionately done by women, makes essential contributions to the wealth and welfare of the family. Both family work and market work are

5 Although listed item (7) is the most directly applicable, the thrust of many of the factors constitutes a recognition that marriage is a partnership, where the spouses may take on unpaid labor in order to support the marital community. *See* (3) The age, health, station, amount and sources of income, vocational skills, employability, estate, liabilities and needs of each of the parties; (4) The contribution by one party to the education, training or increased earning power of the other party; (5) The opportunity of each party for future acquisitions of capital assets and income; (6) The sources of income of both parties, including, but not limited to, medical, retirement, insurance or other benefits; and (10) The economic circumstances of each party at the time the division of property is to become effective. 23 Pa. C.S.A. 3502.

valuable sources of labor that create an entitlement to share property and income streams produced during marriage.

The Simeones' prenuptial agreement upends all of this, valuing and sheltering market income (typically, the husband's), while *completely disregarding* all other contributions, including care work. Take, for example, Mrs. Simone's waivers, that can be understood to say this:

> I contract away to my right to have any economic reward from my labor and contributions to the family. I give up my right to monetary compensation for the work I do in the family even though I recognize I will likely make more contributions to the family than my spouse. Further, I recognize that I may sacrifice or significantly limit my own career development for the sake of the family and will forgo any compensation for those losses even when they are produced by a joint decision. At the same time, I will claim no ownership in the fruits of the labor done by my partner who will alone reap the economic rewards and human capital development that we generate together through our partnership.

As this restatement of the contract terms makes clear, this is substantively unfair to Ms. Simeone. Standard waivers like these in prenuptial agreements place the parties back into a title system, one that devalues and disregards what has typically been "women's work" of providing family care. That undermines the policies that are the foundation of recent law reforms that, belatedly, recognized both the value of unpaid care work and the reality that most marriages are complex partnerships. In addition, as should now be evident, basing ownership solely on title and market work can also produce profoundly unfair burdens on one spouse while the other prospers.

In some cases, of course, it may be that both parties have a more limited partnership in mind than the interconnected life described above. If the requirements of procedural fairness are met, our commitment to individual autonomy and to the equality of men and women should result in enforcing prenuptial agreements entered into by parties with more independent financial goals. Two high-earning spouses with grown children, for instance, might wish to protect their own earnings in order to provide for these children over a financially well-positioned spouse. Although many, perhaps most, marriages contain assumptions of interdependence and reliance, some do not. The law should be flexible enough to differentiate between different cases, and a rich, contextual evaluation of the substantive fairness of agreements is the way to accomplish that goal.

It is for these reasons that we adopt the requirement that marital agreements be substantively fair and so reasonableness must be evaluated both at the time of contract formation and at the time of enforcement. We overrule our earlier opinion in *In Re Estate of Gelb*, 228 A.2d 367 (Pa. 1967) that evaluated reasonableness only at the time of the agreement. Reasonableness will depend on the totality of the circumstances, including, but not limited to, (a) the extent to which the contract departs from rights and remedies available under existing law; (b) whether the contract creates an overall imbalance in the obligations and rights imposed by the bargain; (c) the contributions of a spouse to the marriage, including unpaid family care work; (d) whether there are children and, if so, the contributions of a spouse to caring for those children; (e) the financial situation of each spouse at the time of the marriage and the time of contract enforcement; and (f) the degree to which the contract complies with public policy (including recognition of partnership marriage, noneconomic contributions and gender equality). Contracts that are not reasonable to a spouse will not be enforceable.

As we have already explained, the contract in the instant case is not enforceable as it does not meet the standard of procedural fairness. Nor does it meet the standard of substantive fairness as the terms are unreasonable to Mrs. Simeone.

JUSTICE CULHANE, CONCURRING

I join Justice Kelly's opinion in full. I write separately for two reasons. First, to draw attention to an important distinction that is often overlooked; namely, the difference between formal, legal equality and what we might call "substantive" equality. While the law has made great strides toward recognizing and protecting the legal rights of women, the economic and social realities lag far behind. The reasons for this distinction are complex, and impossible to fully canvas in this opinion. A few observations are in order, however, on the limitations of a focus on formal legal equality. Second, today's decision to closely examine prenuptial contracts will predictably engender criticism. That criticism is, to an extent, understandable, because today's decision does not fully address the concern expressed in *Geyer* that permitting challenges to premarital agreements on the necessarily fact-specific ground of "fairness" will lead to much litigation. This concern requires a response.

I GENDER EQUALITY: AN UNFINISHED PROJECT

I begin by noting that there has been remarkable progress toward legal equality for women. Federal civil rights law protects women against some forms of discrimination in employment, housing, education, and public accommodations. *See* Civil Rights Act of 1964, Title VII, 42 U.S.C.A. §§ 2000e *et seq.*

(employment); Fair Housing Act (FHA) (42 U.S.C.A. §§ 3601 *et seq.*); Title IX of the Educational Amendments of 1972, 20 U.S.C.A. §§ 1681–88; Civil Rights Act of 1964, Title II, 42 U.S.C.A. § 2000a–b. Over the years, these protections have been expanded, especially in the area of employment. *See* Pregnancy Discrimination Act (PDA) of 1978 (Pub.L. 95–555), codified at 42 U.S.C. § 2000e(k) (defining discrimination "because of sex" to include "pregnancy, childbirth, or related medical conditions"). Although the proposed Equal Rights Amendment to the U.S. Constitution approved by Congress in 1972 was never ratified by the three-fourths supermajority of states required, since the 1970s the U.S. Supreme Court has applied heightened scrutiny to laws that discriminate overtly on the basis of sex. This approach has generally resulted in a declaration that such laws violate the Fourteenth Amendment's guarantee of equal protection under the law. *See, e.g.*, *Craig v. Boren*, 429 U.S. 190 (1976) (striking down an Oklahoma law that allowed women to purchase beer at a younger age than men).

Pennsylvania residents enjoy additional protections. Here in the Commonwealth, a parallel effort to secure a constitutional amendment did succeed, resulting in a guarantee of equality on the basis of sex being added to the state constitution: "Equality of rights under the law shall not be denied or abridged in the Commonwealth of Pennsylvania because of the sex of the individual." Pennsylvania Constitution, Article I, § 28 (1971). This law has been used for the benefit of men and women alike, because the constitution's guarantee of equality applies to both sexes. In *Conway v. Dana*, 318 A.2d 324 (Pa. 1974), for example, we held that the presumption that the male parent was primarily responsible for the support of a couple's minor children violated the state's equal protection law, and stated that this rule was "clearly a vestige of the past and incompatible with the present recognition of equality of the sexes." *Id.* at 326. The best interest of the child, we concluded, requires looking to all sources of support rather than beginning from the notion that the father should bear the greater share of responsibility.

Against this backdrop, it is tempting to conclude that this commitment to equality should lead this court to forgo policing of prenuptial agreements for basic fairness. If men and women are truly equal in the eyes of the law, we should simply allow them to structure their bargains in any way that seems sensible to them. To follow this line of reasoning a step further, one might conclude that taking a deeper look at these contracts is paternalistic, and draws on outmoded ways of thinking about the autonomy of men and (perhaps especially) women.

That conclusion, however, misses the point that formal, legal equality between men and women is the *starting point* for analysis rather than the conclusion. In *Conway*, shedding the presumption of primary paternal responsibility meant the court could look at the parents as having formally equal status, and could then proceed to evaluate the actual facts and circumstances of each couple. It might then turn out that, in most cases, the father will still end up paying the greater share of child support, but not simply because he is a man. According to the most recent data from the Bureau of Labor Statistics, men continue to earn more than women in virtually every job category. In 1989, women earned, on average 0.687 of every dollar men earned. *See* U.S. CENSUS BUREAU, CURRENT POPULATION SURVEY, 1961 THROUGH 1989 ANNUAL SOCIAL AND ECONOMIC SUPPLEMENTS, TABLE A-4.[6] Child support will be related to income and to custodial time, as is proper.

The situation is analogous here. We start by treating the husband and wife as legal equals, but we must not end there. While the facts in each case will differ, and in some cases the wife will have bargaining power superior to her husband's, we must not blind ourselves to the reality that in many cases the lived realities of men and women in many marriages are different – in ways that matter for the interpretation and enforcement of prenuptial agreements. Just as the constitutional guarantee of equality and federal and state laws protecting women against bias do not prevent, say, workplace discrimination (often including lower wages), neither does a recognition that men and women have equal legal capacity to enter into a prenuptial agreement foreclose the need to examine the facts of each case carefully. Often, the wife still has the responsibility for tending to the home – especially when, as here, the couple has one or more children – while the husband is earning market wages. As highlighted in the majority opinion, a prenuptial agreement that allows the husband to retain most of his earnings may result in systematically undervaluing (or even completely discounting) the wife's contribution to the family's financial situation. Of course, where the situation is reversed, the husband's domestic work also risks being undervalued. Formal legal equality takes us only so far, but by beginning from that perspective we can properly evaluate the facts and circumstances of each case.

[6] The gap appears to be closing: "The real median earnings of female workers increased between 1988 and 1989 by 1.8 percent to a level of $18,780. Real median earnings of men, on the other hand, declined by 1.8 percent to $27,430. This real increase in female earnings combined with two consecutive years of decline in men's earnings resulted in a male-female earnings ratio of .68, currently at an all-time high. This ratio has increased from 62 in 1982 and 60 in 1980, as women's median earnings have generally been increasing faster than men's median earnings throughout the 1980's." U.S. CENSUS BUREAU, MONEY INCOME AND POVERTY STATUS IN THE U.S.: 1989 (Advance Data). But men still far out-earn women, a fact that sheds the harsh light of reality on the promise of equality.

Premarital agreements demand close inspection because of their differences from other sorts of contracts. Parties entering into marriage have distinct expectations for their union, and these typically do not include serious consideration of the possibility that the relationship will not work out. Indeed, they may start with an unrealistically low estimate of the possibility of divorce (or the early death of the spouse), and then further discount the possibility to zero – and therefore not seriously weigh the wisdom of giving up valuable property rights.

This naivete is beneficial in some ways – as optimism is a good entry point into such a complex life arrangement – but it can also undermine, or even cripple, a person's ability to think critically about what is truly at stake in a prenuptial agreement like the one in question here. The standard model of an autonomous actor making rational choices in their own economic best interests has come under question even in commercial contract decision-making, but its deficiencies are even more acutely presented in the emotionally charged premarital setting. The natural tendency will be to give excessive weight to the looming, present benefit of marriage – a benefit that will often be seen, accurately or not, as contingent upon acceding to the financially more powerful party's demands – and to greatly discount the future benefits that will be lost if the agreement is signed, and then enforced. Less concretely, but no less importantly, there is a powerfully expressive component to marriage that is drawn down by painful discussions of cold economic realities, especially since these will, in any case, only be realized at divorce or death.

For these reasons, certain prenuptial agreements constitute an extreme departure not only from modern family law principles but from certain truths about human nature and the deep importance of marriage to many people. It is therefore appropriate for this court to police such agreements carefully. By training a critical eye on prenuptial agreements, the majority's requirements of both procedural and substantive fairness are an apt response to the continuing challenges of gender inequality.

II COMPETING VALUES: PREDICTABILITY V. FAIRNESS

The strongest argument for declining to peer too closely at prenuptial agreements revolves around the right of contracting parties to rely on them without resorting to costly litigation. The *Geyer* plurality criticized an earlier decision by this court, *In Re Hillegass Estate*, 244 A.2d 672 (Pa. 1968), in part because under the approach set out in that case "the question of what is reasonable in an antenuptial agreement ultimately becomes a question for the courts; a question that makes all antenuptial agreements potentially litigable, notwithstanding that the parties were aware of the terms of the agreement when they signed." *Geyer*, 533 A.2d at 428, citing *In Re Hillegass Estate*, 244 A.2d at 672. To avoid that uncertain, potentially vertiginous situation, the court continued, "[a]ntenuptial agreements which are knowingly and intentionally executed should not be abrogated." *Id.*

This is a valid concern, and it is certainly possible that policing prenuptial agreements for substantive fairness will result in a decline in the number of such contracts. Flexible standards, and the unusual approach of assessing the issue at the time enforcement is sought, might together reduce the predictability that the law so prizes and thereby lead to fewer such agreements being entered into. Against this possibility, though, a few competing considerations, which seem to me decisive, can be brought to bear.

First, a financially well-positioned future spouse who believes a prenuptial agreement is necessary is not likely to refuse to enter into such a contract even if the rules for evaluating it are less favorable than he or she might wish. It seems reasonable to expect that such a party, with the assistance of counsel, will instead strive to make the contract equitable to both parties, and to take into account the nonmarket contributions to family wealth that the majority opinion so eloquently explains. In other words, policing contracts for substantive fairness might lead to agreements that are closer to the couple's lived reality. And it might be that only the most oppressive potential agreements are the ones that don't get made in the first place.

Second, predictability and certainty are important values in law, but they are not the only values. Again, contracts dealing with the rights and liabilities of spouses call up considerations that are removed from the standard issues presented in the commercial context. The default rules for the division of property and support payments when marriages end are not only intended as a proxy for what most couples are assumed to want; they are also an expression of societal values of fairness between couples who make a commitment of this depth. It is reasonable for the law to insist that departures from that important baseline be clear (as determined by the procedural requirements set forth today) and that they be "fair enough" to justify their departure from the default rules that would otherwise apply. The loss of predictability and certainty, in other words, is the tribute that prenuptial agreements must pay to reasonable, fair dealing.

Some will find today's decision paternalistic, or perhaps inconsistent with the commitment of this Commonwealth to the equal treatment of the sexes. But two adults planning to marry are uniquely situated, and the law must not blind itself to the reality that, left unexamined, the standard prenuptial agreement rewinds the clock to an earlier era, when title controlled ownership of marital assets, and the nonwage earning spouse – usually a woman – was often left in a difficult financial situation when the marriage ended. If that is equality, it comes in a strange guise.

We have chosen an approach that reflects the parties' relationship, and their reasonable expectations that the contributions of both spouses will be valued. Today's decision marks a decisive step in the right direction, and I join it enthusiastically.

12

Commentary on *Borelli v. Brusseau*

JUNE CARBONE

INTRODUCTION

When it was decided in 1993, the decision in *Borelli v. Brusseau*[1] sent shockwaves through the legal community. *Borelli* involved the enforceability of an oral contract between a husband and wife in which the wife promised to care for her ill husband in return for his promise to "leave her" assets worth approximately $500,000 that would have otherwise been largely his pursuant to their premarital agreement.[2] The wife, Hildegard Borelli, quit her job, brought the husband, Michael Borelli, home and cared for him until his death a few months later. But the husband neither transferred the property to her nor changed his will, which left the property to his daughter from a prior union, Grace Brusseau. The California Supreme Court ruled that the oral agreement was unenforceable because it lacked consideration, given spouses' duty to support each other, and violated the public policy against such agreements.

The opinion stunned feminists. Insisting that spouses should care for each other without compensation, it seemed to resurrect what had once been a gendered assignment of marital obligations in which the wife owed the husband a duty of care in exchange for his financial support.[3] Moreover, the opinion also seemed to apply different standards to premarital agreements, which typically favor husbands, than to the later marital contract, which

[1] *Borelli v. Brusseau*, 12 Cal.App.4th 647, 651, 16 Cal.Rptr.2d 16, 18 (1993), *modified* (Jan. 22, 1993).

[2] *Id.* at 650 (the opinion uses quotation marks around the word "leave"). On the value of the property, *see* Wendy L. Hillger, Borelli v. Brusseau: *Must a Spouse also Be a Registered Nurse? A Feminist Critique*, 25 PAC. L.J. 1387, 1414–16 (1994). Hildegard did receive $100,000 pursuant to Michael's will and his interest in the property in which they resided.

[3] *See* Reva B. Siegel, *The Modernization of Marital Status Law: Adjudicating Wives' Rights to Earnings, 1860–1930*, 82 GEO. L.J. 2127 (1994).

favored the wife. And given that Hildegard had been employed full-time and gave up that employment to provide round-the-clock care for her husband, feminists were outraged at the court's failure to recognize the extraordinary nature of the services that she provided for Michael. Jo Carrillo has done a superb job of imaging an alternative outcome, one that would appropriately acknowledge that today's spouses, male or female, cannot be expected to drop all other obligations to provide around-the-clock care for a seriously ill spouse, and that calls on the courts to review the fairness and not just the form of marital agreements.[4]

Underlying the original case, however, are two additional considerations that the original California Supreme Court decision avoided by grounding the outcome in the doctrine of consideration. The first involves the question of how strictly the courts should police family bargains. Feminists have been critical of the neoliberal framework that defers excessively to contractual arrangements and fails to take into account contextual circumstances that go to the power dynamics that underlie private bargains.[5] The power dynamic in this case involves not just disparities in wealth, but disparities in health. A trial on remand would almost certainly have involved an inquiry into the strength of Hildegard's proof that that Michael in fact made the alleged promises, his capacity to have meaningfully agreed given his poor health, and the circumstances that surrounded and shaped their bargain. Technical doctrines like consideration and the statute of frauds have often been designed to block such potentially painful and contentious inquiries. Carrillo's opinion, which argues at length that neither consideration nor the statute of frauds should preclude modifications of a premarital contract on these facts, only partially addresses the tension between bright line rules versus fact-specific inquiries that underlie this case. The California Supreme Court's original judgment in the matter, in contrast, seemed determined to keep the courts out of such emotionally charged inquiries altogether.

The second issue goes to the substantive fairness of the transaction. Carrillo's opinion appropriately frames the issue not just as an arrangement for nursing care but as an amendment of the earlier premarital agreement,

[4] *See, e.g.*, Jill Elaine Hasday, Family Law Reimagined 69–70 (2014).

[5] *See, e.g.*, Margaret Jane Radin, *Market-Inalienability*, 100 Harv. L. Rev. 1849, 1861 (1987) (criticizing the commodification of intimate exchanges); Robin L. West, *Law's Nobility*, 17 Yale J.L. & Feminism 385, 398–99 (2005) (summarizing the critique that the preferences of the subordinated self will reflect the interests of those in the dominant position). *Cf.* Martha M. Ertman, *Exchange as a Cornerstone of Families*, 34 W. New Eng. L. Rev. 405, 407 (2012) (arguing that exchange characterizes transactions within families as much as transactions without and that such agreements should ordinarily be enforceable).

which deprived Hildegard of a community property interest in the property Michael brought into the marriage. Given that Michael was already in his seventies at the time of the marriage, the value of Michael's separate property may not have reflected efforts during the second marriage and thus may have remained largely separate even without the premarital agreement. The more difficult issue concerns Hildegard's finances. She was thirty-nine at the time of the marriage and almost fifty by the time of Michael's death.[6] Over the course of the marriage and particularly with her decision to quit her job to care for him, she may have become more dependent on his resources. The during-marriage agreement could accordingly be seen as an appropriate adjustment of their marital understandings rather than an isolated exchange of property for care. As with other factual determinations in the case, however, it is impossible to reach a final judgment on the basis of the complaint alone, leaving unanswered important questions that a trial court could have asked on remand. Carrillo's proposed opinion does a good job of focusing judicial attention on the relationship between the premarital agreement and the later proposed alteration, but cannot finally resolve the issues without more information.

This commentary will, first, discuss the significance of the original decision; second, explore Carrillo's reframing of the nature of the exchange between Michael and Hildegard; third, consider the reasons for judicial reluctance to interfere in family disputes and their relationship to feminist concerns about overreliance on contract; and fourth, consider the elements going into a substantive evaluation of the fairness of Michael and Hildegard's agreement.

THE BASIS FOR FEMINIST OUTRAGE

This decision provoked feminist dissent because of its seeming resurrection of older doctrines associated with women's subordination within marriage. Marriage historically linked men's superior financial resources and obligation to support their dependent wives and children with women's duty to obey and provide domestic services to their families.[7] Within this system, men were seen as family heads, and the doctrine of marital privacy, which insulated family decisions from legal redress, reaffirmed male authority within the household.[8] In England, Blackstone had declared that, within marriage, "the husband and wife are one person in law: that is, the very being or legal existence of the

6 *Borelli*, 16 Cal.Rptr.2d at 17.

7 *See* Siegel, *supra* note 3.

8 Martha Fineman, *What Place for Family Privacy?*, 67 GEO. WASH. L. REV. 1207 (1999).

woman is suspended during the marriage, or at least is incorporated and consolidated into that of the husband: under whose wing, protection, and cover, she performs everything."[9] American case law, though it began to recognize the wife's separate legal existence by the end of the nineteenth century, nonetheless used these notions of the marital bargain to restrict the ambit for during-marriage contract.[10] The Kentucky Supreme Court held in 1922, for example, that "an agreement by the husband to pay his wife for performing [her] ordinary household duties was not only without consideration, but against public policy."[11]

Hildegard argued that the earlier cases denied her equal protection "because husbands only have a financial obligation toward their wives, while wives have to provide actual nursing services for free."[12] Although the *Borelli* court acknowledged that early precedents, with their references to different obligations by husbands and wives, were gendered, it insisted that modern cases applied the same obligations to both spouses. The court maintained further that: "If the rule denying compensation for support originated from considerations peculiar to women, this has no bearing on the rule's gender-neutral application today. There is as much potential for fraud today as ever, and allegations like appellant's could be made every time any personal care is rendered."[13]

The court concluded that the issue was not whether such "sickbed bargaining" was "more useful than unseemly," but whether "such negotiations are antithetical to the institution of marriage as the Legislature has defined it," and concluded that they were.[14]

Borelli also produced a vigorous dissent. Justice Poché maintained that the earlier cases were outdated. He observed that "when the simple justice of redressing obvious wrongs is involved, the arguments for domestic harmony have been rejected and are now in full retreat"; husbands and wives can now be prosecuted for crimes against each other, and sue each other for torts and breach of contract.[15] Moreover, he ridiculed the idea that spouses owe each other a *personal* duty of care, suggesting that "in 1993 that such a contract is

[9] William Blackstone, Commentaries on the Laws of England *442 (citations omitted).

[10] Siegel, *supra* note 3, at 1239–41 (describing enactment of the Married Women's Property Acts, and how the idea of "marital service" restricted contract rights with respect to women's work within their own homes).

[11] *Lewis v. Lewis*, 245 S.W. 509, 511 (Ky. 1922).

[12] *Borelli*, 16 Cal.Rptr.2d at 19.

[13] *Id.* at 20.

[14] *Id.* at 20.

[15] *Id.* at 22 (Poché, J., dissenting).

without consideration means that if Mrs. Clinton becomes ill, President Clinton must drop everything and personally care for her."[16]

Carrillo's judgment addresses these concerns. She would overturn the trial court decision as upholding "an insidious social norm of male dominance." She emphasizes the valuable nature of the services Hildegard provided. Michael, who had been hospitalized for heart-related issues in March 1983, February 1984, and January 1987, suffered a stroke in August 1988.[17] Doctors transferred him to a rehabilitation center, and recommended that he be moved to a nursing home or convalescent center.[18] Michael, however, wanted to return home, and in October 1988, Hildegard agreed, despite the fact that he required "round-the-clock care, and rehabilitative modifications to the house, in order for him to live at home."[19] Carrillo observes that Hildegard did more than merely "support" Michael, and that for the trial court to require that Hildegard provide such care without compensation offers "a dystopian view of a society where a woman, Hildegard, is to marry, rely on her husband for economic support, see him through life threatening illnesses, provide him with full-time hospice care, and leave the marriage without a penny or a complaint."

In order to properly acknowledge Hildegard's contributions, Carrillo reframes the nature of the case. The California Supreme Court treated the alleged agreement as a discrete contract: Hildegard's nursing care in exchange for Michael's assets. Instead, Carrillo treats their agreement as a modification of the premarital agreement they entered into on the eve of their marriage in 1980. That agreement provided that the separate property Michael brought into the marriage would remain his separate property,[20] and that Hildegard would waive any right to challenge his estate after his death. A modification of a premarital agreement does not require consideration to be effective, and Carrillo therefore does not discuss the issue as such. But, in 1986, California adopted a statute that required alterations of premarital agreements be in writing, and this agreement was not. Carrillo argues, however, that the since the 1986 law did not apply retroactively to premarital agreements signed before the effective date of the new law, neither should it apply to alterations of such agreements. Her argument dramatically lowers the hurdle for enforcement.

[16] *Id.* at 24.

[17] *Id.* at 17.

[18] *Id.* at 17–18.

[19] *Id.*

[20] *Id.* at 23 n. 2 (Poche, J. dissenting) ("Although the record does not include a copy of this contract, it seems obvious from the context of this litigation that its general import was to segregate and preserve substantial assets as to Mr. Borelli's separate property").

From a feminist perspective, Carrillo's technical reframing of the legal issues in the case serves an important purpose. It emphasizes that the Borellis' agreement should not be treated as "sickbed bargaining" but rather as understandable adjustment of the parties' finances as the nature of their marriage changed. To care for Michael, Hildegard quit her job and became dependent on Michael in a way that their premarital agreement had not contemplated. And while Michael died less than four months after he moved back home, the commitment Hildegard made to him was an open-ended one, with potentially long-term consequences on her earning potential. Considering this agreement together with the premarital agreement emphasizes the one-sided nature of the Borellis' financial arrangements and the role of this agreement in correcting the resulting inequities.[21]

Is Carrillo's reimagining persuasive? That depends less on the technical analysis in Carrillo's proposed opinion than of the policy issues that drive the resolution of this case. The California Supreme Court's embrace of the doctrine of consideration to resolve the matter short-circuited discussion of the other potential issues in the case, and those issues can be quite complicated – as Carrillo's proposed opinion suggests. If these issues are resolved in Hildegard's favor, then on remand the trial court would be faced with the basic questions of whether Hildegard can prove the contract existed and whether Michael had the capacity to enter into an agreement at all. The Supreme Court decision almost certainly involved a desire to avoid having the courts enmeshed in these issues, and the policies underlying that desire merit consideration in their own right.

JUDICIAL DISTASTE FOR FAMILY LAW DISPUTES

When the California Supreme Court disdainfully referred to "sickbed bargaining," it may well have been expressing its distaste for the inquiry necessary to resolve such issues as much, if not more, than for the bargain itself. The courts have long developed doctrines to keep the judiciary out of family disputes, and feminists have long criticized these doctrines as upholding patriarchal authority and marginalizing women's ability to seek redress for

[21] As Brian H. Bix notes, "in the cases where one party is offering to 'return' rights waived in the premarital agreement, there is likely a strong intuition for enforcement – either as a matter of fairness, or because of a feeling of 'poetic justice.'" Brian H. Bix, *The ALI Principles and Agreements: Seeking a Balance between Status and Contract*, *in* Reconceiving the Family: Critique of the ALI's Principles of Family Law Dissolution 387 (Robin Frewell Wilson ed., 2006).

family conflicts.[22] Carrillo shifts the discussion away not only from the individual exchange in favor of the financial arrangements in the marriage as a whole, but also from procedural elements toward the overall fairness of the agreement. Nonetheless, had the court been willing to consider the validity of the agreement, the next step would have been a remand to address two critical – and difficult – issues:

- Could Hildegard establish that the alleged agreement in fact existed?
- Was Michael mentally competent to enter into such an agreement and did he do so voluntarily?

The *Borelli* court's reference to there being "as much potential for fraud today as ever"[23] expressed distaste for opening the judicial doors to these issues, whatever the merits of Hildegard's individual case.

The California legislature had tried to address the issue of proof by requiring that the agreement be in writing. We do not know how strong Hildegard's evidence about the existence of the agreement was, but such determinations always pose the possibility of unfairness where one of the parties to the agreement has died. Inevitably, the case would have involved Hildegard's testimony about Michael's intent without the possibility of a response from Michael.

If Hildegard established that the agreement existed, the trial court would also have dealt with Michael's capacity to enter into such an agreement and the voluntariness of his promises. Michael had suffered a stroke and the complaint stated that throughout Michael's "August, 1988 hospital stay and subsequent treatment at a rehabilitation center, he repeatedly told [Hildegard] that he was uncomfortable in the hospital and that he disliked being away from home."[24] The complaint also stated that he had become "concerned and frightened about his health and longevity." We do not have any further information about Michael's cognitive functioning or his mental state, but declining health often raises issues about capacity and "undue influence," even when the agreements are in writing.[25]

As noted above, the *Borelli* majority, in expressing its concerns about the case, observed that "allegations like appellant's could be made every time any

[22] *See, e.g.*, Ertman, *supra* note 5, at 440 (discussing the unfairness of refusing to enforce a bargain where one party's performance is complete).

[23] *Id.* at 20.

[24] *Borelli*, 16 Cal.Rptr.2d at 17.

[25] Indeed in the will context, "the doctrine of undue influence . . . is infamous among teachers of estates law for the elasticity with which it is applied by courts to ensure a 'just' distribution of testators' estates." Melanie B. Leslie, *The Myth of Testamentary Freedom*, 38 Ariz. L. Rev. 235, 243 (1996).

personal care is rendered."[26] Carrillo focuses less on Michael's health than on "whether Michael breached the statutory fiduciary duty he owed to Hildegard in the transaction between them." Taking the facts asserted in the complaint as true, Carrillo asserts that Michael breached these duties to the extent he promised to transfer property to Hildegard, encouraged her reliance on that promise, failed to transfer the property as promised, and did not tell her of his failure to do so. In this inquiry, Carrillo does not ask what fiduciary obligations a healthy spouse owes a sick spouse.

Ultimately, therefore, Carrillo's approach rejects doctrines that resolve these cases on bright line procedural grounds in favor of an examination of the substantive fairness in the case.

THE MARRIAGE BARGAIN

Much of the feminist critique of marriage has been a challenge to historic assumptions that marriage involves husbands' duty of support in return for dependent wives' duty to obey and serve. Replacing these gendered notions has been a partnership ideal that assumes that both spouses contribute equally to the accumulation of marital assets. California's community property regime rests on such principles. In the absence of a premarital agreement like the one in *Borelli*, the spouses would jointly own the assets produced by either party's efforts over the course of the marriage and they would jointly bear responsibility for marital debts, such as the husband's medical and nursing expenses.

The complication in this case occurs, however, because it addresses assets produced over the course of several relationships. At the time of the Borellis' marriage in 1980, Michael was in his seventies, Hildegard was thirty-nine, and each had a child from an earlier relationship.[27] It is also reasonable to assume that he entered into a premarital agreement at least in part to preserve the assets from his first marriage for Grace, the child of that marriage.[28]

The full details of the relationships in the *Borelli* case are not in the record. But the facts in the case suggest two alternative, not necessarily incompatible, scenarios. The first is that Michael acquired the bulk of his estate during his relationship with Grace's mother, and that the assets were the product of

[26] *Borelli*, 16 Cal.Rptr.2d at 20.

[27] *Id.* at 17.

[28] *See, e.g.*, Jennifer M. Riemer & Peter M. Walzer, *Premarital Agreements for Seniors*, FAM. ADVOC., Winter 2017, at 40, 42 (observing that "[m]arrying seniors often have children from prior marriages, and they typically want to make sure that these heirs, as well as spouses, are taken care of").

their joint efforts. If the first wife died, she would ordinarily have left her community interest in the assets of the marriage to Michael, trusting him to pass on a reasonable share of the estate to their daughter. When he married Hildegard, he was in his seventies, and almost certainly did not anticipate that this new marriage would produce additional children, or that Hildegard would make a contribution to his accumulation of assets comparable to that of the first wife. Second marriages of this kind are more likely to involve premarital agreements than first marriages and Michael's desire to keep his premarital assets as separate property would be consistent with community property principles as an expression of partnership norms – the partnership underlying the first marriage.[29]

The second scenario is that Michael set out to keep his greater assets separate from Hildegarde's, deliberately took advantage of her increasing contributions to their union over the course of his repeated hospitalizations, and then reneged on his promise to compensate her for the fact she gave up her own income to care for him. Carrillo embraces this second scenario, observing that "the likelihood that Michael set out as early as 1980 to take unfair advantage of Hildegard seems high." In accordance with this scenario, Michael's failing health could well have meant that Hildegard contributed not only to Michael's nursing care, but the management of his meat company or other assets. Even without ill-health, it would not be unusual that over the course of a marriage that lasted almost a decade, the parties increasingly comingled their financial affairs. In the absence of a premarital agreement, Hildegard would therefore have acquired an increasing community share in his assets. In this context, the premarital agreement becomes unfair, and the later agreement a corrective adjusting for the party's changed circumstances.

Which of these scenarios is true? We may never know. The *Borelli* opinion, like Carrillo's rewrite, takes the assertions in the complaint as true, and a full exploration of the facts never occurred. Nonetheless, the resolution of the case, whether on the pleadings or the merits, inevitably makes assumptions about the fairness of the underlying result. It is important to emphasize, however, that both of these scenarios view marriage as a partnership of equals. Instead, they differ in the balance they effect between first marriages and second ones. The first assumes that Michael can enter into a second marriage without assuming an obligation to share his superior assets

[29] *See* American Academy of Matrimonial Lawyers, *Prenuptial Agreements on the Rise Finds Survey*, AAML (Oct. 28, 2016) (finding that the incidence of prenuptial agreements had increased and that the increase reflected more higher order marriage at older ages).

with his second wife after his death. The second assumes that whatever assets Michael brought into the second marriage should be shared, and that he had no right to presume that his wife would care for him without an adjustment in their financial arrangements to protect her. A feminist perspective does not necessarily justify the second perspective over the first, but neither does the first perspective justify the original majority opinion's out-of-hand dismissal of the possibility of a marital bargain for care work as void as against public policy.

CONCLUSION

Feminists agree on the rejection of gendered stereotypes as the basis for the assignment of family obligations. And they tend to favor contextual judgments about the fairness of particular bargains rather than formal rules that preserve patriarchal advantages within marriage. That said, they provide neither an unequivocal embrace of family contracts nor a rejection of the possibility of family bargaining. Instead, feminists tend to favor the option that the California Supreme Court rejected: a fact-specific inquiry into the nature of the Borelli's marital bargain and a determination of fairness in the context of all of the circumstances.

BORELLI v. BRUSSEAU, 12 CAL. APP. 4TH 647 (1ST DIV. 1993)

JUDGE CARRILLO DELIVERED THE OPINION OF THE COURT

I INTRODUCTION

The matter before us arose in this way. Plaintiff filed a complaint that Defendant responded to with a demurrer and a motion to dismiss. Defendant did not also file an answer or cross-claim. There has been no discovery, no trial, and no verdict. We have before us (only) a complaint, a general demurrer, and the trial court judgment sustaining the demurrer and permanently dismissing the Plaintiff's complaint. Ordinarily Plaintiff would have a statutory right to amend her complaint once as a matter of course. Cal. Civ. Proc. Code § 472 (hereinafter Civ. Proc.). The trial court order, however, effectively bars Plaintiff from bringing her contract claim against the Borelli Estate.

Plaintiff appeals the trial court (referee's) order. On appeal, California uses these standards of review: the *de novo* standard, the substantial evidence standard, and the abuse of discretion standard. We apply the abuse of discretion standard in this case.[1]

An abuse of judicial discretion is a "manifest abuse exceeding the bounds of reason." *Kuhns v. California*, 8 Cal. App. 4th 982, 988 (1992). In the context of an appellate review of a trial court order to sustain a demurrer without leave to amend, an abuse of discretion is a judgment that permanently dismisses a complaint that states a viable cause of action or is curable. *Blank v. Kirwan*, 39 Cal. 3d 311, 318, 703 P. 2d 58, 61–62 (1985); *Aubry v. Tri-City Hospital District*, 2 Cal. 4th 962, 967, 831 P. 2d 317, 320 (1992) (in bank). In reviewing a trial court order for gender bias, we hold that an abuse of judicial discretion is a trial court judgment that, because of gender bias, ignores or subverts contract or property rights acquired by a person during marriage. Applying these standards, we find that the referee's judgment is an abuse of discretion because it exceeds the bounds of reason, dismisses Plaintiff Hildegard Borelli's viable complaint without giving her an opportunity to amend it, and relies on gender-biased stereotypes as the basis for disregarding and thus impairing contract and property rights that were or may have been acquired by Plaintiff Hildegard Borelli during her marriage to the late Michael Borelli.

II FACTUAL AND PROCEDURAL BACKGROUND

A *Grace Brusseau*

Grace Brusseau is the Defendant in this case. Grace is Michael Borelli's daughter from a prior marriage and the executor and primary beneficiary of the Michael J. Borelli Estate. Michael,[2] who died in 1989, devised to Grace the bulk of his estate, including the Borelli Meat Co., California properties, vacation condominiums, business partnerships, personal property, financial accounts, sums on deposit in bank accounts and the furniture in the residence he shared with Plaintiff Hildegard Borelli, who is his surviving spouse.

B *Hildegard Borelli's Complaint*

Hildegard is the surviving spouse of Michael Borelli. Following Michael's death, Hildegard submitted a contract obligation – a bill based on a contract – to Grace as executor of the Borelli Estate. The bill sought payment in the form

[1] David I. Levine et al., California Civil Procedure (1991).

[2] As is the practice of the California courts, we refer to the parties by their first names. No disrespect is intended.

of describable assets now listed in the complaint. Grace denied Hildegard's request for payment. Hildegard subsequently filed the complaint in the action before us.[3]

Hildegard's complaint alleges the following facts.

On April 24, 1980, Michael asked Hildegard to sign a premarital contract, which she did.

On April 25, 1980, Hildegard and Michael married.

In 1983, 1984, and 1987, when Michael experienced heart problems, he became concerned about his longevity. Michael told Hildegard that he intended to leave the following describable assets (hereinafter "the listed assets") to her.[4]

1 A lot in Sacramento.
2 A residence in Kensington, Contra Costa County.
3 A life estate in a condominium in Hawaii.
4 A 25 percent interest in the Borelli Meat Co.
5 Sums on deposit in all of Michael's bank accounts on the date of his death.
6 All furniture in the marital residence.
7 Michael's interest in an unidentified business partnership.
8 The cost of educating Michael's stepdaughter, Monique.
9 Health insurance for Hildegard and Monique.

In August 1988, Michael suffered a stroke that again required his hospitalization. Sometime in October 1988, Michael told Hildegard that he did not want to live in an assisted living facility. He wanted to live at home even if it meant that he would need twenty-four-hour care in a house modified for his physical limitations.

In October 1988, Hildegard and Michael entered into an oral agreement in which Michael promised to transfer to Hildegard the listed assets. The complaint alleges that Hildegard agreed to care for the decedent in his home, for the duration of his illness, thereby avoiding the need for him to move to an assisted living facility as his doctors recommended. The complaint also alleges that, due to their marriage, the parties were in a confidential relationship when they reached the October 1988 agreement.

[3] California fact pleading uses the term "cause of action" and relies on a primary right theory to focus on the injury to the plaintiff relative to the duty of the defendant.

[4] These assets are describable and thus particular enough to support an order to compel specific performance.

Hildegard cared for Michael until his death. Michael accepted her care.

On January 25, 1989, Michael died without having transferred the listed assets to Hildegard.

Michael's will devised $100,000 to Hildegard and the bulk of the Borelli Estate to Grace. The marital residence passed to Hildegard by right of survivorship.

The oral 1988 contract cause of action is the sole basis for the claimed remedy of specific performance.

C *Grace's Demurrer*

Except for the code sections it cites, Grace's demurrer is nearly unintelligible. Oral argument did not clarify matters. Therefore, in the interest of clarity, we restate and consolidate the specified objections made in the demurrer and in oral argument. If Grace objects, she may demur (again). *Priebe v. Sinclair*, 90 Cal. App. 2d 79, 87, 202 P. 2d 577, 582 (1949) (dispute over engagement ring).

Grace's demurrer challenges Hildegard's complaint for alleging a contract for personal services between spouses in violation of public policy. CAL. CIV. CODE. § 5100 (hereinafter CIV.).[5] Additionally, the demurrer challenges the complaint for failing to state facts sufficient to constitute the essential elements of an oral contract (CIV. § 1565), mutual consent and consideration (CIV. §§ 1638 and 1605), or the absence of Hildegard's coercion of Michael (CIV. §§ 1565 and 1567). We find that each specified objection attacks the complaint on the basis that it "does not state facts sufficient to constitute a cause of action." CIV. PROC. § 430.80(a). Accordingly, we rule that each specified objection is properly before us.

D *The Referee's Order to Sustain the Demurrer without Leave to Amend*

The referee sustained Grace's demurrer without leave to amend.

Hildegard subsequently appealed on the ground that the trial court abused its discretion when it dismissed her complaint with prejudice.

[5] CAL. FAM. CODE § 720. The California Family Code, enacted on January 1, 1992 and effective January 1, 1994, continues the Civil Code Sections hereinafter footnoted. The California Family Code is evidently the first and certainly the most comprehensive standalone family code enacted by any U.S. state to date. We decide this case within the legal transition from the Civil Code family law provisions (sometimes referred to as the Family Act) to the Family Code. Therefore, this court deems it necessary to footnote Family Code citations as descriptive materials where necessary.

The primary function of any appellate court is to review trial court judgments for legal error. This is a court of appeal charged with furthering the state's paramount interest in equitable dissolution. California community property law generates complexity, but code provisions presume a straightforward exercise of judicial discretion. Code provisions, however, are only as gender-fair as the judicial discretion used to interpret and enforce them.[6] Since gender is at once fluid, individual, relational, and institutional, a gender-biased exercise of discretion becomes a strong systemic negative that harms or can harm the disregarded individual and similarly situated individuals.

Spouses may contract between themselves to modify the default rules of community property. Moreover, whether a jurisdiction recognizes it or not, there are philosophical reasons for regulating private contracting in the context of marriage. Included among them are these. One, the community property sharing principle rejects the idea of marriage as a union between two atomized, self-interested persons who transact at arm's length. It does this by how it vests each spouse with a one-half community property interest on the date one or both acquire an asset. Two, the presumption of undue influence in a transaction between spouses operationalizes the ideal that a person can be simultaneously autonomous and vulnerable in a marriage. Three, disclosure requirements discourage the idea of marriage as taking place in a purely private sphere into which the parties can retreat by contract, especially if the retreat allows one spouse to take any unfair advantage of the other in a transaction between them over property. And, four, trial courts are entrusted with a broad grant of discretion to apply and develop the rules of the California community property system, but courts must exercise their discretion in a way that furthers the state's paramount interest in equitable dissolution and thus in the public well-being.

III DISCUSSION

A *The Standard of Review on Appeal*

California fact pleading requires that the complaint contain "a statement of facts constituting the cause of action, in ordinary and concise language" and "a demand for judgment for the relief to which the pleader claims to be entitled." CIV. PROC. § 425.10. Fact pleading also requires that the cause of

[6] CAROL SMART, THE TIES THAT BIND: LAW, MARRIAGE AND THE REPRODUCTION OF PATRIARCHAL RELATIONS 149–50 (1984) (presenting empirical findings on how locally powerful law enforcers (judges, referees, and lawyers) undermine gender-fair legislative changes by the exercise of gender-biased discretion in domestic court matters).

action be "in the language of the statute that is germane to the action." *Goss v. Fanoe*, 114 Cal. App. 2d 819, 823, 251 P.2d 337, 340 (1952). A failure to allege an essential statutory element in a complaint is a basis for sustaining a demurrer under *Blank*. Hildegard had the burden of proving the sufficiency of the complaint before the referee. *Cooper v. Leslie Salt Co.*, 70 Cal. 2d 627, 636, 451 P. 2d 406, 412 (1969) (in bank). The referee made her ruling by identifying general contracts law and the duty of support during marriage as the law germane to the oral contract cause of action in Hildegard's complaint. CIV. PROC. § 425.10.

In reviewing the referee's order to sustain the demurrer, we apply long-settled rules articulated in *Blank* and rearticulated in *Aubry*. These rules require that we treat the demurrer as admitting all material facts properly pleaded, and that we do not assume as true any contentions, deductions, or conclusions of fact or law stated in the demurrer. *Moore v. Regents of University of California*, 51 Cal. 3d 120, 125, 793 P.2d 479, 480 (1990) (in bank). The demurrer admits the facts in the complaint. Nevertheless, it attacks the complaint for pleading a void contract or, alternatively, a contract that does not meet statutory formalities, as set out above in Part I(C).

Since the case is before us on demurrer, we regard the allegations in the complaint as true. *Speegle v. Board of Fire Underwriters*, 29 Cal. 2d 34, 41, 42, 172 P. 2d 867, 871, 872 (1946) (in bank). The rules for reading the complaint are found in *Blank*; those rules require us to "give the complaint a reasonable interpretation, reading it as a whole and its parts in their context" with the goal of achieving "substantial justice between the parties." CIV. PROC. § 452. The complaint alleges two contracts between spouses, and a context defined as the spouses' acts and course of conduct in relation to the disputed property, or the general circumstances of the marriage. *Kenney v. Kenney*, 220 Cal. 134, 136, 30 P. 2d 398, 399 (1934) (in bank). Pleading circumstances may necessitate using a general set of facts. If so, according to Justice Traynor in *Speegle*, the plaintiff who pleads "the general set of facts upon which [the] cause of action is based" should be given an opportunity to amend and "should not be deprived of [her] right to maintain [her] action on the ground that [her] pleadings were defective for lack of particulars." Finally, for purposes of this appeal, *Cooper* places the burden of proof on Hildegard to prove that her complaint is sufficient to state a cause of action or that it is curable.

B *Reading the Complaint*

The rule in *Blank*, stated in full above, requires us to read the complaint with the goal of achieving substantial justice between the parties. We thus read count one, count two, and the circumstances of the marriage in conjunction with each other.

We organize our opinion according to the counts as alleged in the complaint.

Count one alleges a written 1980 contract presented by Michael to Hildegard for her signature on the day before their marriage.

Count two alleges an oral 1988 contract made during the marriage based on the confidential relationship that existed between Hildegard and Michael as spouses. The purpose of the oral contract was to allow Michael to provide for Hildegard outside of his will. The reciprocal terms of the contract convey Michael's reasonable intention to provide for Hildegard outside of his will. The contract terms obligated Michael to transfer the listed assets to Hildegard, and they obligated Hildegard to agree in the future to accept those assets in release of claims against the Borelli Estate. The benefit Hildegard conferred on Michael (the consideration) was her promise concerning property rights and obligations, not nursing care. At Michael's death, Hildegard learned that Michael had not transferred the listed assets to her or otherwise authorized Grace to satisfy the 1988 contract debt.

The circumstances of the marriage are these, at the very least. Michael reasonably relied on Hildegard's oral promise not to assert her rights as a surviving spouse because he did not revoke the will that left the bulk of his estate to Grace. Hildegard, for her part, reasonably relied on Michael's oral promise to convey the above listed asserts to her outside of his will because she approached the Borelli Estate as a contract creditor rather than as a disinherited spouse. Michael had legal capacity until his death because his legal capacity was not judicially determined during his lifetime. Michael withheld financial facts from Hildegard, which gave him an unfair advantage over her in the 1988 contract transaction. Grace took possession of sums on deposit in Michael's bank accounts on the date of his death.

Finally, *Blank* mandates that our ruling achieve substantial justice between the parties. The referee's order permanently barred Hildegard from bringing a contract cause of action against the Borelli Estate; however, it did not bar any other causes of action that may have accrued in her favor. *Estate of Katleman*, 13 Cal. App. 4th 51 (1993). After our ruling in this proceeding, in addition to her contract related causes of action, Hildegard continues to have a cause of action for unintentional disinheritance. Grace continues to have the option to fulfill the oral 1988 contract or else to defend the Borelli Estate against Hildegard's claim as an unintentionally disinherited spouse. Settling Hildegard's unintentional disinheritance claim against the Borelli Estate by reference to the oral 1988 contract could leave Michael's will intact. Litigating

Hildegard's unintentional disinheritance claim against the Borelli Estate could void Michael's will. Our ruling achieves substantial justice between the parties, therefore, by how it leaves open the option for each party to pursue an outcome that either honors or voids Michael's will.

C *Count One*

Before marriage to Hildegard, Michael owned the Borelli Meat Co., unidentified business partnerships, identifiable real properties, personal property financial investments, and sums on deposit in bank accounts. On April 24, 1980, one day before their marriage on April 25, 1980, Michael presented a contract to Hildegard concerning his property. The specialized law of premarital contracts governs an agreement between prospective spouses made in contemplation of marriage and concerning property, choice of law, or personal obligations. Civ. § 5310.[7] Prospective spouses are not in a confidential relationship with each other, but a premarital contract takes effect on the date of marriage when the parties assume general "obligations of mutual respect, fidelity, and support" to each other as spouses. Civ. § 5100. Michael and Hildegard signed a 1980 contract made in contemplation of marriage that concerned property and personal obligations. Hence, that contract meets the definition of a premarital contract. The 1980 premarital contract was in writing and signed by the parties. Although it meets formalities of both the former law (the law on premarital contracting through December 31, 1985) and the current law, Civ. § 5302,[8] it was executed on April 25, 1980, six years before the current law went into effect. Based on the date of contract execution alone the law germane to count one must be the specialized premarital contracting law through December 31, 1985.

The 1980 contract confirmed the duty of spousal support during marriage. A premarital contract provision that attempts to modify or waive spousal support rights during marriage or after dissolution is void as against public policy. *Marriage of Higgason*, 10 Cal. 3d 476, 479, 485, 487, 516 P. 2d 289, 290, 295, 296 (1973) (in bank). During marriage, spouses are in a confidential relationship when they transact with each other. Civ. § 5103.[9] In this case, Michael obligated himself to support Hildegard from his separate property in the 1980 premarital contract, but he did not otherwise protect his property

[7] Fam. § 1610.

[8] Civ. § 5302 et seq., known as the California Premarital Agreement Act (CPAA), was enacted in 1985 and will be continued as Fam. § 1601.

[9] Fam. § 721.

from commingling. Michael's promise was redundant because on the date of marriage Michael and Hildegard each became statutorily obligated to support one another with community property or, if none was available, with their respective separate property. Civ. §§ 5100 and 5120.140.[10] Also on the date of marriage, each spouse's individual property became separate property. Civ. §§ 5107 and 5108.[11] Since the explicit terms of the 1980 contract did no more than replicate the default rules of the California community property system as to support and property characterization, its terms are permissible subject matter for a premarital contract, meaning that the 1980 contract is potentially enforceable.

The complaint implicitly alleges consideration. Consideration is not required to plead a premarital contract under the premarital contracting law through December 31, 1985. Civ. § 5302. Neither is consideration required under the CPAA, which took effect on January 1, 1986. Civ. § 5311.[12] Reading the explicit non-mutual support term (Michael obligated himself to support Hildegard but Hildegard did not also obligate herself to support Michael) in conjunction with the explicit property term (Michael declared separate property but did not protect that property from commingling) reveals a gap concerning community property. That gap supports the inference that Michael (who prepared the contract) assumed the spouses would not work or otherwise acquire community property during the marriage. On the date of the marriage, Michael was seventy-two and in his retirement years. Hildegard was in her thirties. Although Michael was not lawfully entitled in his status as Hildegard's spouse to restrict her from earning an income during marriage, he appears to have negotiated from her an implicit promise to refrain from working during the marriage. Even if this promise was not legally enforceable, it benefited Michael by producing and reproducing Hildegard's financial dependence on him.[13]

Finally, count one does not state a remedy, but it does state facts sufficient to plead that Michael coerced Hildegard into signing the written 1980 contract. Those facts are that Michael presented the finalized contract to

[10] Fam. §§ 720 and 914.

[11] Fam. § 770.

[12] Fam. § 1611.

[13] Marilyn Frye, *Oppression*, *in* The Politics of Reality: Essays in Feminist Theory 8–10 (1983) (arguing that women, no matter their economic class, are molded and restricted in their financial choices by how, in home or work situations, they are brought into the service of men; and that the phrase "'[w]omen's sphere' may be understood as the 'service sector,' taking the latter expression much more widely and deeply than is usual in discussions of the economy." *Id.* at 10).

Hildegard for her signature on the day before the wedding thus effectively restricting and immobilizing her ability to review the contract alone or with independent counsel. These facts could be the basis for curing the complaint to add a challenge to the enforceability of the written 1980 contract.

D *Count Two*

In accordance with *Blank*, we treat the demurrer as admitting all material facts and we read the complaint as a whole and treat its allegations as true. Count two states an oral contract cause of action and the remedy of specific performance. The remedy of specific performance rests entirely on count two. If we read the counts as related, we could analyze the oral 1988 contract (the second contract) as amending the written 1980 premarital contract (the first contract). Under this theory of the case, the enforceability of the second contract becomes an issue if and only if the first contract is enforceable. If so, the premarital contracting law through December 31, 1985 would be germane to count two for reasons we discuss next.

1 Hildegard Has a Right to Plead the Oral 1988 Contract

Count two pleads an oral 1988 contract entered into two years after the current law known as the CPAA took effect. Civ. § 5314. There are similarities and differences between the former law and the CPAA. The similarities are that both apply to premarital contracts. One salient difference is that an oral contract can be pleaded under the former law but not under the CPAA, which positively mandates "a written document signed by the parties." Civ. §§ 5314 and 1622. The CPAA also extends this mandate to premarital contract amendments and revocations. Civ. § 5311. Count two does not state facts sufficient to plead a writing signed by both parties. Under the former law, this omission is not fatal to the complaint if the 1988 contract relates back to the 1980 premarital contract execution date. Under the CPAA, however, the failure to plead a written contract would be grounds for dismissing the complaint without leave to amend. *Blank* precludes us from assuming the truth of Grace's legal conclusion that the CPAA is the law germane to count two. Therefore, we take up the issue of retroactive application of the CPAA to the alleged 1988 oral contract.

Marriage of Bouquet, 16 Cal. 3d 583, 586, 592, 593, 546 P. 2d 1371, 1372, 1376, 1377 (1976) (in bank), held that a marital property rule can be retroactively applied even if it impairs a vested property interest. The rationale is that the state has a paramount interest in equitable dissolution that is part of the police power to protect "health, safety, morals, and general well being of the people." Thus, an impairment that furthers equitable dissolution is permissible under CAL. CONST. art. I, § 7. *Marriage of Buol*, 39 Cal. 3d 751, 762, 705 P. 2d 354, 361 (1985) (in bank), held, however, that a marital contract enhancement rule that impairs a separate property interest cannot be retroactively applied if to do so would violate CAL. CONST. art. I, § 7. And *Marriage of Fabian*, 41 Cal. 3d 440, 715 P. 2d 253 (1986) (in bank), held that a marital contract enhancement rule that impairs a community property interest cannot be retroactively applied if to do so would violate CAL. CONST. art. I, § 7.

The legislature has enacted a multitude of changes to effect the state's paramount interest in equitable dissolution. No-fault dissolution took effect in 1970. CIV. § 4506.[14] Gender-equal management took effect in 1975. CIV. § 5125. *See* Carol S. Bruch, *Management Powers and Duties under California's Community Property Law: Recommendations for Reform*, 34 HASTINGS L.J. 227 (1982). Enhanced formalities for transmutations and reimbursements became operative in 1984. CIV. § 5110.710. The CPAA took effect in 1986. CIV. § 5302. The legislature enacted a standalone Family Code in 1992, to take effect on January 1, 1994. Many former laws were obsolete because of explicit and implicit gender bias in favor of husbands (men) and to the detriment of wives (women). In no way do we note changes in the law to apologize or otherwise obscure the structure of gender dominance that existed in the past and continues through the present. There has been some legal progress in furtherance of the state's paramount interest in equitable dissolution. Obviously, we need more.

If the 1988 contract amends the 1980 premarital contract, the question becomes whether, for purposes of pleading the complaint, the former law through December 31, 1985 or the current CPAA, which took effect on January 1, 1986, is germane to the cause of action in count two. The CPAA is a new statute that bars retroactive application on its face. CIV. § 5203.[15] *Bouquet* involved a marital property characterization statute that did not bar retroactive application. *Buol* and *Fabian* involved marital contract enhancement statutes that did not bar retroactive application. By statutorily barring retroactive application of the CPAA, the legislature expressed its intent to have amendments relate back to the date of the original premarital contract. Therefore, if the 1988 contract amends the 1980 contract, then the premarital contracting law through December 31, 1985 must be the law germane to count two.

[14] FAM. § 2310.

[15] FAM. § 1503.

In oral argument, Grace countered that the retroactive application of the CPAA is irrelevant since Hildegard has no property rights in the Borelli Estate to impair. *Blank* requires that we disregard Grace's point as a conclusion of law. Community property acquired during marriage vests in undivided one-half shares. Civ. § 5110.[16] Sums on deposit in any bank account of a married person are presumptively community property unless the separate property proponent (Grace) proves otherwise with character-specific accounting records. Cal. Prob. Code § 5305. Hildegard's complaint asserts a vested community property interest in unknown items of property held by the Borelli Estate based on the default community property rules of acquisition, commingling, and bank deposits. Taking the facts stated in the complaint as true, Hildegard also asserts a vested separate property right in the assets listed in the complaint. Considering all of the above, it becomes apparent that retroactive application of the CPAA, with its mandate of a written contract signed by both spouses, would impair Hildegard's vested property rights without due process of law by requiring her to produce a written 1988 contract signed by both her and Michael. As in *Buol* and *Fabian*, this would hold Hildegard to an impossibly high standard, especially now that Michael is dead.

Accordingly, we find that the CPAA is not germane to the 1988 oral contract. In so ruling, we affirm Hildegard's right to allege an oral contract under the specialized premarital contracting law through December 31, 1985 and – assuming the oral 1988 contract does not amend the written 1980 contract – under general contracts law.

2 The Complaint States Facts Sufficient to Constitute Mutual Consent

The demurrer attacks the complaint for failing to state facts sufficient to constitute the essential statutory element of mutual consent that is free, mutual, and communicated by each party to the other. Civ. § 1565. Grace cites *Sackett v. Starr*, 95 Cal. App. 2d 128, 134, 212 P. 2d 535, 539 (1949) for the proposition that mutual consent for an oral contract must be pleaded with facts of a clear unequivocal offer, a written promise to convey, or performance in reliance on the contract. We distinguish *Sackett* because it involves an oral contract between strangers concerning real estate. We find instead that *Kenney* is germane to pleading mutual consent to an oral contract between spouses.

Kenney involved a contested dissolution. The wife moved for a new trial after the trial court found an oral contract based on the husband's testimony that the parties had agreed before and during the marriage that all property, no

[16] Fam. § 760.

matter when acquired, was community property. The court of appeal found substantial evidence of an oral agreement as confirmed by the spouses' acts and conduct in their property-related dealings and transactions, which included selling, purchasing, mortgaging, and improving properties.

Estate of Sehabiague, 47 Cal. App. 2d 793, 799, 119 P. 2d 30, 34 (1941), applied *Kenney* in a probate proceeding to find substantial evidence of an implied community property contract based on the spouses' acts and conduct of buying, selling, and exchanging properties. *Estate of Piatt*, 81 Cal. App. 2d 348, 351, 183 P. 2d 919, 921 (1947), applied *Kenney* in a probate proceeding to find substantial evidence of an implied contract from circumstances of the marriage showing the parties had not quarreled over the status of their respective property rights. *Handley v. Handley*, 113 Cal. App. 2d 280, 283, 248 P. 2d 59, 61 (1952) relied on *Kenney* to find that there was substantial evidence of an oral community property contract based on circumstances of the marriage. Those circumstances included statements in private letters, handwritten notations on tax documents, casual conversations about the applicability of California community property law, and purchases for and improvements to the disputed house.

Grace offers the legal conclusion that *Kenney* is not germane to count two because *Kenney* involved the acquisition of property, not the transmutation of property already owned. Because *Blank* precludes us from assuming as true Grace's legal conclusion on this point, the question we now address is whether the complaint alleges a transmutation. Starting in 1985, a transmutation requires "a writing by an express declaration that is made, joined in, consented to, or accepted by the spouse whose interest in the property is adversely affected." Civ. § 5110.710. *Blank* requires us to read the complaint in its parts and as a whole with the goal of achieving substantial justice between the parties. Hildegard does not purport to plead the essential elements of a transmutation because she cannot state facts sufficient to constitute a written express declaration made by Michael of his present intent to change the character of the listed assets from his separate property to her separate property. Additionally, it is unreasonable to assume that Michael intended the oral 1988 contract to effect an immediate transfer of assets, such as real estate and business interests, that would require compliance with the statute of frauds or with corporate or partnership bylaws. Consequently, we do not read the complaint to allege a transmutation.

Alternatively, Grace contends that *Kenney* applies in this case only to the marital residence because the spouses' acts and conduct of modifying the residence for Michael's illness only extend to that property. If so, Grace concludes, the complaint is insufficient to plead clear and explicit mutual consent as to the listed assets. Civ. §§ 1565, 1638. The law favors construing contracts "to carry into effect the reasonable intentions of the parties." *California Lettuce Growers v. Union Sugar Co.*, 45 Cal. 2d 474, 481, 289 P. 2d 785, 790 (1955) (in bank). An appellate court cannot write or rewrite a contract, but it can use context to fill in uncertainties about the parties' reasonable intentions. *Bettancourt v. Gilroy Theatre Co.*, 120 Cal. App. 2d 364, 367, 261 P. 2d 351, 353 (1953). "That is certain which can be made certain." Civ. § 3538. Hence, an attached note can become part of the complaint. *Ward v. Clay*, 82 Cal. 502, 23 P. 227 (1890) (in bank). Industry practice can be context under the rule in *California Lettuce Growers*. A pattern of contracting can be context under the rule in *Speegle*. Circumstances of the marriage can be context under the rule in *Kenney*. In this case, context makes it feasible to ascertain that in forming the oral 1988 contract Michael and Hildegard intended to provide for Hildegard outside of Michael's will in exchange for Hildegard's promise to effect a release (in the future) of her claims against the Borelli Estate as an unintentionally disinherited spouse. Once ascertained, intent and purpose allow the list of assets pleaded as facts in Hildegard's complaint to cast light on the reciprocal terms of the oral 1988 contract thus providing facts sufficient to constitute the essential statutory element of mutual consent as to those assets.

Grace argues that Michael did not disinherit Hildegard because he devised $100,000 to her. Despite Michael's devise, the presumption against unintentionally disinheriting a spouse continues to protect Hildegard. Prob. § 21630. Grace cannot rebut this presumption by merely pointing to the line in Hildegard's complaint that states there was a devise. Neither can she rebut the presumption without a character-specific equitable accounting to show that the $100,000 devise is a meaningful sum relative to the total value of the Borelli Estate. Prob. § 6560. Absent such an accounting, we take as true that the complaint pleads the $100,000 devise as the insubstantial testamentary gift that motivated Michael to enter into the oral 1988 contract to transfer the listed assets outside of his will.

To rebut this presumption, Grace would have to file an answer so as to introduce facts that Michael manifestly expressed a clear intention to disinherit Hildegard. *Estate of Turney*, 101 Cal. App. 2d 720, 226 P. 2d 80 (1951). *Blank* requires us to read the demurrer as admitting all material facts, which in this case would be that the devise was insubstantial relative to the total estate and hence a motive for the oral 1988 contract. Without filing an answer or a cross-claim, Grace cannot refer to the face of Michael's will as clear proof of his intention to disinherit Hildegard because the will is not before us. Prob. § 6561. Neither can Grace rely on any contract to rebut the presumption against disinheritance because the only written contract in this case is the 1980 premarital contract that Hildegard signed without the benefit of independent counsel. PROB. §§ 140–42.[17] Therefore, the law and policy against unintentional disinheritance continue to protect Hildegard for purposes of this proceeding.

As discussed above, Michael's testamentary pattern can be considered as the context that makes feasible the intent and purpose of the oral 1988 contract, its reciprocal terms, and the spouses' reasonable reliance on its reciprocal promises. The complaint states facts sufficient to constitute intent and purpose: Michael reasonably intended to transfer the listed assets to Hildegard outside the will; Hildegard reasonably intended to obtain a share of Michael's estate by a transfer outside his will. The complaint states facts sufficient to constitute reciprocal terms: Michael promised the listed assets as a provision in lieu of the will; Hildegard promised to agree in the future to accept the listed assets as a basis for releasing her support and property claims against the Borelli Estate. The complaint states facts sufficient to constitute reasonable reliance: Michael devised the bulk of his estate to Grace; Hildegard brought a contract cause of action against the Borelli Estate in the first instance, not a cause of action as an unintentionally omitted spouse. The complaint may be inartful, but it states facts sufficient to constitute the essential statutory element of mutual consent.

3 The Oral Contract Concerns Property Rights and Obligations, Not Personal Services

Grace attacks the complaint for pleading a void contract for personal nursing services by her reliance on this code section: "Except as otherwise provided by law, spouses cannot, by a contract with each other, alter their legal relationships, except as to property." CIV. § 4802; FAM. § 1620. *Higgason* enforces property terms but voids contract terms that seek to modify or waive the parties' obligations of "mutual respect, fidelity, and support." CIV. § 5100. Between persons who are not married to each other, mutual consent can be consideration for a promise of personal services. Between persons who are married to each other, by contrast, mutual consent cannot be consideration for a promise of personal services. CIV. § 5100. Grace cites multiple cases. We distinguish two and deem the others irrelevant.

In *Brooks v. Brooks*, 48 Cal. App. 2d 347, 350–51, 119 P. 2d 970, 972 (1941), parties executed an employment contract, not made in contemplation of

[17] Added by Cal. Stats. 1983, c. 842 § 22.

marriage, for live-in nursing services. Subsequently, nurse and patient married. The husband continued to pay the wife under the employment contract. The marriage did not produce community property. In time, the wife "voluntarily left [the husband] against his consent." The court voided the contract, citing the duty of support; it also ordered the wife to repay the husband for his consideration, meaning for the monthly payments he had made on the live-in nursing contract during marriage. CIV. § 4802. Grace relies on *Brooks* to argue that Hildegard was bound to render personal services to Michael incidental to her marital status, and that those services included housekeeping and nursing.

Grace's argument is so misguided and incorrect on this point that it lets slip her disdain for Hildegard and the California legislature, as well as her willingness to go a long distance to do whatever it takes to walk away with her father's estate and legally banish her same-age stepmother in the process. To accept *Brooks* as the law germane to the cause of action before us would be to return Hildegard, the institution of marriage, the state's paramount interest in equitable dissolution, the state's power to further public well-being, and this court's particular charge to address gender bias to a past where women are second-class citizens. In that past, married women were to endure by working in service to their husbands and by being grateful for whatever little financial crumb their husbands deigned to let drop their way.

Hildegard was not bound to provide personal services to Michael that included housekeeping and nursing, not by the ruling in *Brooks*, not by the premarital contract, and not by her marital status. Moreover, *Brooks* does not bind this court. *Auto Equity Sales v. Superior Court*, 57 Cal. 2d 450, 369 P. 2d 937 (1962) (in bank). Instead, we are free to understand the duty of support for what it is today, which is a tool that allows a spouse in need to obtain support from a spouse who is financially stable due to an income, savings, investments, or inherited wealth. The duty of support ensures third-party contractors that they will be able to reach community and separate property no matter which spouse incurs a contract debt for living expenses. During marriage, the duty of support marshals community property before separate property. After a date of separation, the duty of support obligates the owning spouse's separate property to pay for basic living expenses of the spouse in need. CIV. § 5120.140. Until 1975, the husband (because of his gender) was the exclusive legal manager of the community property estate. The wife (because of her gender) had no legal right to manage and control community property notwithstanding her partnership and property stake in the marriage. CIV. § 5125; FAM. § 1100. Male management unfairly burdened married women with multiple negative consequences, including the inability to obtain credit without a husband's signature.[18]

Higgason involved a contested dissolution proceeding in which the conservator and daughter of a wealthy older wife sought to enforce a premarital agreement against her mother's husband. Under former law the duty of support was nonmutual: a husband had the duty to support a wife even if she owned separate property, but a wife only had the duty to support a husband if he was in need. The trial court, exercising its discretion, enforced the premarital agreement, thus displacing the wife's duty to support the husband onto the public. The court of appeal reversed, holding that "[w]here the husband is unable, from infirmity, to support himself, and he has no [property], his [and the public's] right to have the wife support him from her separate property . . . is not a matter left to the discretion of the trial court; by the terms of Civ. § 5125."

We take from *Higgason* that there are circumstances in which the duty of support is too important to the public well-being to leave it to trial court discretion. Grace cites *Higgason* because it involves an age-gap marriage between an older wealthy wife and a younger husband, who at the time of the marriage "was a waiter, earning $2 an hour plus tips, and had little or no means." The wife's adult daughter successfully challenged her mother's capacity and filed a petition for annulment of the marriage. When that failed, the daughter filed a petition for dissolution on her mother's behalf because, as she implied, her mother's husband was entertaining one or more same-sex lovers in the marital home, thus making her mother fearful. Unless and until Grace files an answer to the complaint, we will not and cannot assume that Hildegard engaged in similar behavior or caused Michael to be afraid.

Legally, what Grace attempts to accomplish with the *Higgason* innuendo is to paint Hildegard as unduly influencing Michael, who, because of his illness was a person of unsound mind. We have addressed this issue above. We point out, again, that by her innuendo Grace attempts to distract our attention from the complaint. Notwithstanding Michael and Hildegard's age, wealth, and health differences, we take as fact the allegations in the complaint that Michael produced the conditions for Hildegard's financial dependence when he rushed her into signing a 1980 premarital contract that benefited him at her expense. As discussed above, Michael assumed no greater duty to support Hildegard by the written 1980 contract than the law already required of him, whereas Hildegard implicitly undertook to live in a marriage in which she

[18] Nat'l Comm'n on Consumer Finance, Report on Consumer Credit in the United States (1972). The Equal Credit Opportunity Act, 15 U.S.C. §§ 1691–93 (1974).

would not earn money, job experience, retirement benefits, or Social Security credits. Additionally, Hildegard was adversely affected by how the 1980 contract was silent about her (not Michael's) community and separate property rights. What Hildegard owned was of no consequence on April 24, 1980. Today, it is, because whatever Hildegard obtains from the Borelli Estate is statutorily reachable by those of Michael's creditors whom Grace leaves unpaid. Civ. § 5120.110.[19]

Based on the above, we find that the complaint states facts sufficient to constitute an oral contract cause of action for which there is mutual consent about terms that involve property rights, not nursing care.

4 The Complaint States Facts Sufficient to Constitute a Breach of Fiduciary Duty Cause of Action

Grace attacks the complaint for failing to state facts sufficient to constitute the essential statutory elements of Michael's voluntary consent. Civ. § 1567. A transaction between spouses is "subject to the general rules governing fiduciary relationships which control the actions of persons occupying confidential relations with each other." Civ. § 5103. Grace contends that the contract cause of action does not fall within the scope of the spouses' confidential duty because the spouses were contracting over Michael's separate property, not over community property. Civ. § 5103. Consequently, she argues, the general law of contracts, which Grace identifies as the law germane to the cause of action, requires that Hildegard plead freely given mutual consent on Michael's part, otherwise it insufficiently pleads apparent consent, which is voidable at Grace's option. *Blank* requires us to analyze Grace's contention that Hildegard bears the burden of alleging the absence of coercion.

Grace asserts that Hildegard took care of Michael when they were alone in the marital residence, thus making her care absolute, arbitrary, and entirely discretionary. She argues that the possibility of coercion places a burden on Hildegard to plead facts of Michael's voluntary consent to the oral contract. Civ. § 1567. *Perdue v. Crocker National Bank*, 38 Cal. 3d 913, 922, 702 P. 2d 503, 510 (1985) (in bank), held that if a contract includes "reciprocal promises" the fact that the contract permits one party to set or change a key term does not render the contract discretionary or illusory. The oral 1988 contract includes reciprocal promises made feasible by context, and those promises concern property, not personal services as discussed above.

[19] Continued in Fam. § 910 except that the term "community property" was replaced with the broader term "community estate."

Yet the complaint does state that Hildegard cared for Michael until his death and that she did so by herself. It also states that the oral 1988 contract is based on the spouses' confidential relationship because they were transacting over property and thus they were subject to "the general rules governing fiduciary relationships which control the actions of persons occupying confidential relations with each other." Civ. § 5103. The spousal fiduciary duty, because it protects the spouse who is adversely affected in a transaction between spouses, is more specialized than the general duty of support found in Civ. § 5100, which protects third-party creditors, as discussed above. The parameters of the spousal fiduciary duty are "the same rights and duties of nonmarital business partners"; and the mandate is that "neither [spouse] shall take any unfair advantage of the other [spouse]" in "any transaction" between them, not just in transactions involving community property. Civ. § 5103. In 1988, Michael and Hildegard were contracting over transfers that would occur outside of Michael's will. Therefore, we find that the complaint need not plead facts of Michael's voluntariness. It need only plead a transaction between the spouses, which it does.

When spouses transact with each other over property they do so from within their confidential relationship. For that reason, upon pleading that the benefited spouse (Michael in this case) obtained "any unfair advantage" in the transaction, an evidentiary presumption of undue influence arises to protect the adversely affected spouse (Hildegard, as alleged in the complaint). Civ. § 5103. The burden of rebuttal shifts to the advantaged spouse to prove voluntariness. Rebuttal would require evidence that the adversely affected spouse voluntarily decided to go through with the contract despite the absence or insufficiency of financial disclosure by the benefited spouse. Civ. § 5103.

What unfair advantage did Michael obtain in the transaction with Hildegard?
What information did Michael have the duty to disclose to Hildegard?
Does the complaint state facts sufficient to plead these essential statutory elements?

When spouses transact in a confidential relationship the absence of disclosure goes to the issue of consent. Civ. § 1565 *et seq.* Intentional concealment can deceive a trusting person into acting against her own interest, with the risk being a deprivation of property or legal rights, or some other actionable injury. Civ. § 3294. Michael was an experienced business owner with a successful business incorporated in 1950 in the state of California. Hildegard did not own a business.

As the complaint is silent about whether Michael disclosed financial facts to Hildegard, we take as true that Michael did not disclose information about the value of the inventoried assets or the value of his estate. By not disclosing this financial information to Hildegard, Michael obtained an unfair advantage over Hildegard in the 1988 transaction. In 1988, Hildegard did not have the benefit of independent counsel. In fact, Hildegard may not have even known that she had a statutory right to a share of Michael's estate. Michael's lack of financial disclosure adversely affected Hildegard by leading her to accept the listed assets in exchange for valuable legal rights without knowing (a) the net value of the listed assets in October 1988 as compared to (b) the net value of Michael's estate in October 1988. Without this information, Hildegard could not make an informed decision about a transaction designed to nullify her rights as a surviving spouse. To plead a cause of action for breach of the spousal fiduciary duty the complaint need only state facts sufficient to constitute the essential statutory elements of any transaction and any unfair advantage obtained by Michael in that transaction due to a breach of fiduciary duty. The complaint so states.

5 The Complaint States Facts Sufficient to Imply an Impairment to an Undivided Community Property Interest Cause of Action

Finally, breach of fiduciary duty is the factual basis for a cause of action for the impairment of the community property estate. CIV. § 5125.1. The following sentence is difficult to read, but it is critical to furthering the state's paramount interest in equitable dissolution. A community property impairment includes but is not limited to "a single transaction, or a pattern or series of transactions, which transaction or transactions have caused or will cause a detrimental impact to the claimant spouse's undivided one-half interest in the community estate." CIV. § 5125.1. The remedy for community property impairment is damages, plus the holding of any profits from the transaction in trust for the community, plus mandatorily assessed attorney fees, plus court costs. CIV. § 5125.1. At the very least, the complaint states facts sufficient to constitute a claim for an impairment of Hildegard's community property interest in the sums on deposit in all of Michael's bank accounts on the date of his death. PROB. § 5305. The remedy of specific performance covers only the listed assets. However, the complaint implicitly states a cause of action for the impairment of the community property estate. Therefore, the complaint is curable on this issue.

E *The Referee's Abuse of Judicial Discretion*

Grace relies on *Brooks, Higgason* and the duty of support found at CIV. § 5100 to paint the misogynistic caricature that was adopted by the referee to disqualify Hildegard's legal story of her own marriage.[20] We now address the trial court's bias against the younger spouse in an age-gap marriage.

Brooks is about a young nurse who married her paraplegic patient, separated from him, then became his surviving spouse to the disapproval of the decedent's sister. *Brooks* is followed by *Brooks v. Brooks*, 53 Cal. App. 2d 95, 127 P. 2d 296 (1942), and *Brooks Estate, Brooks v. Brooks*, 28 Cal. 2d 748, 171 P.2d 724 (1946) (in bank), all of which chronicle years of litigation between a surviving spouse and the decedent's sibling over his estate. *Higgason* is the story of a wealthy older woman, yes; but the court lets us know that it disqualifies the younger husband's argument, again pursued over years of litigation, because he was relatively poor compared to his wife and because he was rumored to have a same-sex lover. *Sonnicksen's Estate*, 23 Cal. App. 2d 475, 73 P. 2d 643 (1937), is the story of the nurse who became a wife and was later named executor of her deceased husband's estate to the ire of his adult child. That ire played itself out in the courts in the form of *Estate of Sonnicksen, Sonnicksen v. Sonnicksen*, 23 Cal. App. 2d 480, 73 P. 2d 646 (1937), and, years later, *Sonnicksen v. Sonnicksen*, 45 Cal. App. 2d 46, 113 P.2d 495 (1941). These stories are the legal Rorschach test that the referee reacted to by projecting her personal associations onto Hildegard rather than do the intellectual work of identifying the law germane to the cause of action. How do we know? The referee issued a final judgment to dismiss Hildegard's viable complaint with no reasonable rationale whatsoever.

One can acknowledge particular issues that arise in age-gap marriages, but to do so does not transform Michael into a starry-eyed innocent. Nor does it transform him into a generous actor. Michael received social applause for supporting Hildegard, but he did no more than the law already required of him as a spouse. The facts alleged in Hildegard's complaint for the 1980 contract indicate that it was not the product of Michael's accidental, occasional, or avoidable steps. The 1980 contract included Michael's implicit (unspoken) term that Hildegard acquiesce in her financial dependency so that Michael could begin to mold her into a suitable young wife for a man of his social class.[21]

Michael initiated the oral 1988 contract from his privileged position as a wealthy man who built at least one successful business in the San Francisco Bay Area. Through the 1980 contract, Michael reproduced his young wife's financial dependence on him first because of his need for a certain kind of stay-at-home wife and later because of his health issues. The oral 1988 contract was not naïve or generous. It was Michael's surreptitious way to pass off to his

[20] Carol Smart, Feminism and the Power of Law (1989).

[21] Frye, *supra* note 13, at 2.

daughter the task of defeating his spouse's legal rights to his estate after his death. To this end, Grace would like us to immobilize Hildegard by affirming the referee's order dismissing the complaint without leave to amend.[22]

Next, there is the issue of the $100,000 devise, which Hildegard's disclaimer of leads Grace to contend is proof of Hildegard's greed. Under *Blank*, we are unable to assume the truth of Grace's contention that Michael's devise to Hildegard was substantial. Only comparing the value of the devise to the total value of the estate, as discussed above, could assist in labeling the devise substantial or not for purposes of the pleadings, which is what we assess here. Michael could have disinherited Hildegard, but to do so legally he would have had to communicate that decision to her. Instead, he used his will to signal to Grace that Hildegard was his expendable younger wife.[23]

California law protects a spouse against unintentional disinheritance, yet Hildegard's legal vulnerability on this issue has receded into the background.[24] Caricatures of Hildegard as the problematic young wife have instead emerged to the foreground.[25] Had Hildegard divorced Michael, she would be financially better off today. Instead she stayed to care for Michael's most basic physical needs, on his terms, one of which was that Hildegard would take title to a house in Kensington by right of survivorship and (no more than) $100,000 of Michael's otherwise seemingly substantial estate, unless Michael changed his mind.

Experts try to explain the trope of age-gap marriage, but from the older man's point of view. Whom do these experts inform that the benefits can outweigh the risks if the young woman is not "looking for a meal ticket"? *See Should You Marry an Older Man? An Interview with Mel Krantzler*, HARPER'S BAZAAR, June 1980, at 30, 40. Benefits for whom? Benefits for the women, this particular expert explains, because older men "delight in the teacher role, in being able to expose their [younger] wives to the benefits of their wider range of experience." *Id.* All older men ask in return, again according to this particular expert, is that their young wives reinforce a certain type of "assertiveness and masculinity." *Id* at 30.

Like the above expert, popular media experts concern themselves with the older man's sexual issues, not with the younger woman's concerns about marrying an older man. For example, the experts do not discuss the

22 *Id.* at 2–7.

23 *Id.* at 2, 12.

24 *Id.* at 8.

25 MARIANA VALVERDE, SEX, POWER AND PLEASURE (1985) (analyzing sexuality from a woman-centered, non-expert perspective using romance novels as a tool for understanding how gold-digger stereotypes eroticize gender-based power differentials).

production or reproduction of the younger woman's financial dependence on the older man. Neither do they discuss the foreseeable conflict a younger spouse may have with the older man's adult children at his death. Instead, popularizers of academic discussion return to the touchstone of male dominance as a natural state in which it is the prerogative of the wealthy older man to have sexual access to young women – those he marries and those he does not. *Schwegmann v. Schwegmann*, 441 So. 2d 316 (1983), *Blackledge v. Schwegmann*. 443 So. 2d 1122 (1984).

As an omitted spouse, Hildegard is a member of a group, comprised almost entirely of women and dispersed geographically and demographically.[26] So concealed is this group that its members' individual situations offer little or no data to reveal "the unity of the structure bearing down on all members of the group."[27] We read about young omitted spouses in the case law that banishes them. Cases such as *In re King's Estate, King v. Wilson*, 63 Cal. App. 2d 365, 146 P. 2d 952 (1944), and *In re King's Estate, Brewer v. King*, 121 Cal. App. 2d 765, 770, 264 P. 2d 586, 589 (1953), two cases that record the ongoing legal banishment of Gladys, a thirty-four year old woman who married an eighty-five-year-old man. Gladys's husband ultimately left the bulk of his estate not to Gladys, but to a carpenter who had helped him with his properties. Following her husband's death Gladys spent years attempting to recover her statutory share of her husband's estate from the carpenter and, later, from the carpenter's heirs. Gladys's last complaint identified herself as her husband's "heir." The reviewing court affirmed a demurrer without leave to amend on the ground that heir is a legal conclusion not a fact. It then went on to deride Gladys for filing what it concluded was a vexatious, harassing, and abusive complaint, even though the complaint was curable.

Legal opinions malign and caricature these young women who survive their older male spouses. To paraphrase the artist Georgia O'Keeffe: the courts have hung all of their own and others' associations about femaleness onto these women who, like Hildegard, are treated as parasites on their husband's estate in the legal documents of their detractors. Rather than analyze the law, the lawyers, referees and judges feel justified in gossiping and tisk-tisking about young female plaintiffs whom they hold to a double standard relative to their older male counterparts.[28] None of this is within the bounds of reason, law, or

[26] Frye, *supra* note 13, at 8.

[27] *Id.*

[28] *See also* Sally Engle Merry, *Rethinking Gossip and Scandal*, *in* Toward a General Theory of Social Control: Fundamentals (Donald Black ed., 1984); Sally Engle Merry, *Anthropology and the Study of Law*, 34 J. Legal Educ. 277 (1984).

the state's paramount interest in equitable dissolution. Therefore, we find that the trial court abused its discretion in ordering the dismissal of Hildegard's complaint, which states causes of action and is curable, without leave to amend.

IV CONCLUSION

Hildegard's complaint tells of an age-gap marriage, illness, and the use of contracts as an instrument of gender control. *Brewer* stands for the general proposition that a court has the power to prevent an abuse of the legal process by disposing of complaints that are "sham, frivolous, or wholly vexatious." Grace cites *Sonnicksen* to sound the patriarchal clarion call to label Hildegard's attempt to recover the listed assets from Michael's estate vexatious as a matter of law. Why? Because Hildegard and Michael had sex? Because Hildegard cared for Michael? Because Hildegard's complaint seeks to hold the Borelli Estate accountable? Because Michael devised his estate to an adult child from a marriage that produced offspring? The patriarchal clarion call is vexatious. Hildegard's complaint is not.

Hildegard fully performed all aspects, delegable or not, of her support duty. In the last difficult months of his life, she took care of Michael's basic physical needs, provided him with company, coordinated his professional care, took care of the house and Monique, and engaged in all the other tasks of the householder whose family member is in hospice care. We stress that Hildegard's marriage ended by Michael's death, leaving Hildegard with the legal status of a surviving spouse. Therefore, until otherwise established, Hildegard holds the keys to Michael's estate, not Grace.

Whether the referee accepted Grace's version of events is irrelevant. Hildegard was married to Michael when he died. The state claims a paramount interest in equitable dissolution (partitioning property at the end of marriage), not in reproducing "the ideological underpinnings, of a particular dominant family structure and oppressive gender relationships."[29] Hildegard was not Michael's employee. She is not owed wages. Hildegard was a marital partner. Until Grace in her capacity as executor of the Borelli Estate establishes otherwise, Hildegard is entitled to and thus owed her partnership share of the Michael J. Borelli Estate and any property that she can ultimately prove Michael promised her in exchange for her release of claims against the Borelli Estate.

[29] SMART, *supra* note 20.

We rule that Hildegard has met her burden of demonstrating that the complaint is sufficient to state a cause of action and curable where it is lacking. If Grace seeks to continue a conversation in court about Hildegard's perceived faults, Grace must file an answer or a cross-claim. Otherwise, on demurrer to Hildegard's first complaint, Grace is not entitled to ask this court to restrict or penalize Hildegard in every direction.[30]

For the reasons stated above, we overrule the order sustaining the demurrer without leave to amend.

[30] FRYE, *supra* note 13, at 4–5.

13

Commentary on *Turner v. Rogers*

WARREN BINFORD

INTRODUCTION

In *Turner v. Rogers*,[1] Justice Clarence Thomas distinguished himself as arguably the most progressive Justice on the U.S. Supreme Court – at least with respect to children's rights. The case was brought by a noncustodial father who had accrued $13,814.72 in unpaid child support and was imprisoned for a year after being held in civil contempt for his failure to pay. It was just one of six times Mr. Turner had been held in contempt for failing to pay $51.73 per week to support his child between 2003 and 2010.[2]

Before he was held in contempt that sixth time, the family court judge presiding over the case in South Carolina asked Turner if he had anything to say for himself. Turner described years of drug addiction, including methamphetamine, marijuana, "and everything else." He explained he had not worked regularly, and claimed he had recently become disabled, and that he was now "off the dope." He acknowledged, "I know I done wrong, and I should have been helping her [the child's mother], and I'm sorry. I mean, dope had a hold on me."[3]

In response to Turner's explanation for his repeated delinquency, the family court judge sentenced him to twelve months' incarceration, placed a lien on his SSI and other benefits, and promised to make him eligible for work release if he had a job.[4] Turner appealed and the case wound its way to the U.S. Supreme Court where the Court held that Turner's incarceration violated the Due Process Clause because he received "neither legal counsel nor alternative

[1] *Turner v. Rogers*, 564 U.S. 431, 458–61 (2011).
[2] *Id.* at 431.
[3] *Id.* at 437.
[4] *Id.*

procedures" giving him clear notice that his ability to pay child support was the "critical question" in his civil contempt hearing.[5]

The story of Michael Turner is not unique. As of April 2017, 5.5 million noncustodial parents in the United States owed a total of $114 billion in unpaid child support.[6] Of the $33.7 billion owed annually, 40 percent ($13.6 billion) will never be received by the children whose lives may depend on that support.[7] The failure of parents to provide adequate support for their children has dire consequences for both children and their custodial parents, and since 80 percent of custodial parents who are owed child support are women,[8] the question of child support and its enforcement should be viewed not only as a children's issue, but as a feminist one as well.

THE MAJORITY OPINION

In writing for the majority, Justice Stephen Breyer's sixteen-page majority opinion focused almost exclusively on the constitutional claims presented by Turner and omitted any mention of the parties' child or children generally. Justice Breyer largely ignored the important role that child support is intended to play in preventing childhood poverty. Indeed, the majority opinion refers to the child of Mr. Turner and Ms. Rogers only twice – both times simply as "the child" – and to children generally only once.[9] Instead, the Court framed the obligation as one owed between the parents, even stating that the child support enforcement proceeding was for the mother's benefit (rather than the child's).[10] When poverty is mentioned, it is used to define a stereotypical poor, unemployed woman saddled with children.[11] Most of the Court's analysis is focused on the *father*'s constitutional rights under the Sixth and Fourteenth Amendments and *his* ability to pay the child support owed.

5 *Id.* at 449.

6 Dennis Putze, *Who Owes the Child Support Debt?* U.S. Dept. of Health and Human Services Office of Child Support Enforcement (Sep. 15, 2017), https://www.acf.hhs.gov/css/ocsedatablog/2017/09/who-owes-the-child-support-debt; *see also Turner*, 564 U.S. at 459 ("In South Carolina alone, more than 139,000 noncustodial parents defaulted on their child support obligations during 2008, and at year end parents owed $1.17 billion in total arrears").

7 Timothy Grall, *Custodial Mothers and Fathers and Their Child Support*: 2015, U.S. Dept. of Commerce, Econ. & Statistics Admin., U.S. Census Bureau, 1, 12 (Jan. 2018), https://www.census.gov/content/dam/Census/library/publications/2018/demo/P60-262.pdf

8 Grall, *supra* note 7, at 2.

9 *Turner*, 564 U.S. at 437, 443.

10 *Id.* at 447.

11 *Id.* ("The custodial parent, perhaps a woman with custody of one or more children, may be relatively poor, unemployed, and unable to afford counsel").

Specifically, the father argued that he was entitled to state-appointed counsel at his civil contempt hearing because of the risk of imprisonment. The majority held that although the Due Process Clause does not *automatically* require the appointment of legal counsel for indigent defendants in civil contempt proceedings, some safeguards must be in place to prevent the erroneous deprivation of liberty.[12] Specifically, the Court provided that such safeguards could include, for example: notice that the defendant's ability to pay the child support is highly important; the utilization of forms or another standardized method of ensuring that critical financial information was gathered from the defendant; an interactive hearing process that allowed defendants to answer relevant questions about their financial situation; and an express finding by the court that the defendant was able to pay the child support owed.[13] Although the Court rejected Turner's claim that he was entitled to state-appointed counsel, it held that the state court erred in finding him able to pay and thus in civil contempt because (1) he was not given "clear notice that his ability to pay would constitute the critical question in his civil contempt hearing"; (2) he was not provided with a form or the equivalent "designed to elicit information about his financial circumstances"; and (3) the court never held that he was able to pay.[14] Thus, Turner's incarceration violated his right to Due Process and the case was remanded for further proceedings, again, all with almost no mention of the child who was, or at least should have been, at the center of the case. It was the child's right to support that was violated for seven continuous years, and the entire proceeding was born from the need, and society's continuous failure, to provide a financial safety net for children. The fact that the case positioned the father against the court, rather than the child or even the mother, reflects the positions of power that society has created, which are reflected in our legal system generally and the U.S. Constitution specifically.

JUSTICE THOMAS'S DISSENT

Surprisingly, it is arguably the most conservative justice on the U.S. Supreme Court, Clarence Thomas, who in Parts I and II of his dissent swiftly and resolutely dismissed the constitutional arguments benefiting the father and then devoted Part III of his opinion to refocus the legal analysis on the child

[12] *Id.* at 448 (emphasis in original).

[13] *Id.*

[14] *Id.* at 449.

and the child's interests.[15] In that last section, Justice Thomas argues that the majority erred in engaging the balancing analysis under *Mathews v. Eldridge*, 424 U.S. 319 (1976) because it weighs the individual's interest against that of the government rather than the interests of the child and the custodial parent.[16] According to Justice Thomas, the interests of the child and custodial parent "are the very reason for the child support obligation and the civil proceedings that enforce it."[17] He then provides an overview of the research that existed at that time to suggest that nonpayment or inadequate payment of child support can play a significant role in determining whether a child experiences poverty.[18] Recognizing that the "interests of children and mothers who depend on child support are notoriously difficult to protect,"[19] Justice Thomas argued that many "deadbeats" game the system by working in the "underground economy," quitting jobs, becoming self-employed, or engaging in illegal activity in order to "shield their earnings from child support enforcement efforts."[20] In light of these maneuvers, Justice Thomas highlights the critical role that civil contempt proceedings play in coercing many parents to fulfill their support obligations, and highlights the "interests that children and mothers have in effective and flexible methods to secure payment."[21]

Thomas's focus on the child's interests in a case like this is similar to what is happening in other countries that have more modern constitutions in which children's rights and interests are expressly recognized and protected.[22] Indeed, the United Nations Convention on the Rights of the Child expressly requires state parties to ensure that "[i]n all actions concerning children, whether undertaken by public or private social welfare institutions, courts of law, administrative authorities or legislative bodies, the best interests of the child shall be a primary consideration."[23] Thus, for example, section 28 (2) of

15 *Id.* at 458–61 (Thomas, J., dissenting).

16 *Id.* at 458.

17 *Id.*

18 *Id.* at 458–59.

19 *Id.* at 459 (citing *Hicks v. Feiock*, 485 U.S. 624, 644 (1988) (O'Connor, J., dissenting) ("The failure of enforcement efforts in this area has become a national scandal" (internal quotation marks omitted)).

20 *Turner*, 564 U.S. at 459.

21 *Id.* at 461.

22 *See, e.g.*, Constitution of the Republic of South Africa, May 8, 1996, Art. 28(2); Constitution of the Republic of Angola, Jan. 21, 2010, Art. 80(2); Constitution of the Republic of Ecuador, Sep. 28, 2008, Art. 44; Constitution of the Federal Democratic Republic of Ethiopia, Dec. 8, 1994, Art. 36(2); Constitution of the Republic of Uganda, Sep. 22, 1995, Art. 34(1).

23 UN Convention on the Rights of the Child, opened for signature Nov. 20, 1989, 1577 U.N.T.S. 3 (entered into force Sep. 2, 1990).

South Africa's Constitution holds that "a child's best interests are of paramount importance in every matter concerning the child,"[24] and a recent case involving nonpayment of child maintenance obligations (child support) before the Constitutional Court of South Africa expressly relied on the best interests of the child principle in reaching its decision.[25] The Constitutional Court of South Africa had previously summarized the critical importance inherent in effective enforcement of payment of child maintenance obligations in words that closely resembled the concerns raised by Justice Thomas in the *Turner v. Rogers* dissent:

> The judiciary must endeavor to secure for vulnerable children and disempowered women their small but life-sustaining legal entitlements. If court orders are habitually evaded and defied with relative impunity ... the constitutional promise of human dignity and equality is seriously compromised for those most dependent on the law ... Our maintenance courts and the laws they implement are important mechanisms to give effect to the rights of children ... Failure to ensure their effective operation amounts to a failure to protect children against those who take advantage of the weaknesses of the system.[26]

Of course, the United States famously is the only recognized country in the world that has not ratified the U.N. Convention on the Rights of the Child, and nowhere in the U.S. Constitution is there any express mention of "children's rights." That is what makes Justice Thomas's dissent so surprising. Although Justice Thomas, whose dissent was joined by Justice Scalia in its entirety, did not go so far as to adopt the "best interests" language increasingly found in international instruments, other countries' constitutions, and state case law and statutes here in the United States, his dissent expressly refers to the "interests" of children four times and, similar to the Constitutional Court in South Africa, clearly recognizes that the interests of the child "are the very reason" for both child support and any proceedings needed to enforce those obligations.[27]

[24] S. Afr. Const., 1996, § 28(2).

[25] *SS v. V V-S*, 2018 ZACC 5 at paras. 23–25, 37, 41–43 (S. Afr.).

[26] *Bannatyne v. Bannatyne*, 2002 ZACC 31; 2003 (2) SA 363 (CC); 2003 (2) BCLR 111 (CC) at paras. 27–28 (S. Afr.).

[27] *Turner*, 564 U.S. at 458–61. In considering the dissent's significance, it is critical to be mindful of the fact that Chief Justice Roberts and Justice Alito only joined Parts I-B and II of the dissent, meaning that this more child-focused analysis only reflected the views of Justices Thomas and Scalia, the latter of whom has been replaced on the Court by Justice Gorsuch.

SOCIOECONOMIC IMPLICATIONS OF CHILD SUPPORT ARREARAGE

What is not radical about Justice Thomas's dissent in *Turner v. Rogers* is the argument that child support plays a critical role in preventing childhood poverty.[28] In many low-income families, child support is critical to the families' financial stability. Of those who received the full amount of child support owed, the amount of child support received represented 58 percent of the mean personal income of the custodial parent.[29] If all child support obligations were paid in full, it is estimated that 200,000 custodial parent families in the United States would rise out of poverty and the poverty rate of custodial families would be reduced from 26.7 to 24.1 percent.[30] Although neither of these figures is statistically significant, to the 200,000 families who are no longer living in poverty, the full payment of child support can make a world of difference, potentially saving the child's life.

The negative impact of child poverty has been well documented over the course of decades of research, as has the compelling need to prevent it. Children in the lowest socioeconomic quintile are 52 percent more likely to die of any cause, 76 percent more likely to be murdered, 69 percent more likely to be injured unintentionally, and 13 percent more likely to be born with a defect than children in the highest socioeconomic quintile.[31] Those children who do survive face a cluster of other health problems including chronic conditions and developmental problems such as "low cognitive achievement, poor social skills, and behavior problems,"[32] as well as obesity.[33] Children raised in poverty are also more likely to experience abuse.[34] Indeed, counties with higher concentrations of poverty have more than three times the rate of fatal child abuse than countries with the lowest poverty concentrations.[35] Children in chronically impoverished families also have lower cognitive and academic performance, higher school dropout rates, and more behavior problems than

[28] *Id.* at 458–59.

[29] Grall, *supra* note 7, at 13.

[30] *Id.*

[31] *See* Gopal K. Singh & Michael D. Kogan, *Widening Socioeconomic Disparities in US Childhood Mortality, 1969–2000*, 97 AM. J. PUB. HEALTH 1658, 1658 (2007).

[32] Marianne M. Hillemeier et al., *Measuring Early Childhood Health and Health Disparities: A New Approach*, 17 MATERNAL & CHILD HEALTH J. 1852, 1852 (2013).

[33] Hedwig Lee et al., *Longitudinal Associations between Poverty and Obesity from Birth through Adolescence*, 104 AM. J. PUB. HEALTH 70, 70–76 (2014).

[34] *See* Caitlin A. Farrell et al., *Community Poverty and Child Abuse Fatalities in the United States*, 139 PEDIATRICS 1, 1 (2017).

[35] *Id.* at 1.

children who do not experience poverty,[36] and it is well documented that educational success has a profound impact on an individual's trajectory for success as an adult.[37] It is critical that authorities invest in effective child support enforcement policies that are aimed at reducing child poverty, in addition to strategies that address the root causes of poverty. For every dollar spent reducing childhood poverty in the United States, seven dollars would be saved from avoidable costs such as loss of economic productivity, increased healthcare costs, crime-related costs, child abuse and neglect, and homelessness.[38] Clearly, the prevalence of childhood poverty in the United States is caused by much more than child support arrears, but the complexity and insidious nature of childhood poverty compels action on every front where society can have an impact in trying to ensure that each individual child receives the resources they need, especially when a legal entitlement has been established.

Since the 1970s, the United States has recognized that child support is a critical source of income for children of separated parents and has developed a program of enforcement at both the national and state levels to help ensure financial stability for families with children. While imperfect, when one looks at the cost-effectiveness of the child support enforcement system in the United States, one finds that the program has a fivefold return on investment, collecting $5.33 for every dollar spent.[39] South Carolina's use of civil contempt with threat of incarceration for nonpayment of child support is part of that program. Civil contempt is used by numerous other states as well, including Colorado, Connecticut, Florida, Illinois, Indiana, Kentucky, Massachusetts, Minnesota, Oklahoma, Oregon, Texas, Utah, and Virginia.[40] The approach is described as "highly effective at shaking money loose from non-custodial parents who otherwise would not pay a cent."[41]

[36] Patrice L. Engle & Maureen M. Black, *The Effect of Poverty on Child Development and Educational Outcomes*, 1136 Annals New York Acad. Sciences 243, 244 (2008); *see also* H. B. Ferguson & M. P. Mueller, *The Impact of Poverty on Educational Outcomes for Children*, 12 Paediatrics & Child Health 701, 702 (2007).

[37] Engle & Black, *supra* note 36, at 244.

[38] Michael McLaughlin & Mark Rank, *Estimating the Economic Cost of Childhood Poverty in the United States*, 42 Soc. Work Res. 73, 73–83 (2018).

[39] Melody Morales, *The Child Support Program Provides More Support to Families in 2016*, *in* U.S. Dept. of Health and Human Services Office of Child Support Enforcement (2017), https://www.acf.hhs.gov/css/ocsedatablog/2017/12/the-child-support-program-provides-more-support-to-families

[40] *See Turner*, 564 U.S. at 460 (citing Compendium of Responses Collected by the U.S. Dept. of Health and Human Services Office of Child Support Enforcement, Dec. 28, 2010, Reprinted in App. to Brief for Sen. DeMint et al. as Amici Curiae 7a).

[41] Brief of Sen. Demint et al. as Amici Curiae in Support of Respondents at 20, *Turner v. Rogers*, 564 U.S. 431 (2011) (No. 10-10).

Although it may be surprising to some that Justice Thomas authored a dissent with a significant focus on children's interests, what is not surprising is that the opinion repeatedly refers to mothers and children as a seemingly inseparable dyad, referring to children followed by "and mothers" four times (three times expressly and the fourth time referring to "the child and custodial parent, who is usually the child's mother"), as though the mother is an appendage to her child.[42] Certainly, Justice Thomas did not invent the dyadic relationship between mothers and their children that is born from biology and reinforced through social, political, and legal values and frameworks, and his recognition that their fates are largely intertwined in the circumstances described in *Turner v. Rogers* is supported by data. Custodial mothers have seen the percentage of custodial parent families with child support orders or agreements drop from 64.2 percent in 2004 to just 52.7 percent in 2015,[43] while the amount of child support obligations has remained statistically unchanged at approximately $5,760 per year since 1993.[44] Moreover, the amount of child support actually *received* has dropped on average and the number of custodial parents who have child support agreements but receive nothing at all from the other parent has increased from 24.2 percent in 1993 to 30.7 percent in 2015.[45] In short, custodial parents are receiving fewer child support entitlements, and when child support is ordered or agreed to, it is for the same amount as a quarter-century ago (controlled for today's dollars). In reality, the recipients, who are predominantly women and children, are paid less, or, more often than before, nothing at all.

Thus, it is not a surprise that children in these woman-led families have a poverty rate of 37.2 percent,[46] compared to a poverty rate of 14.4 percent for children not in custodial-parent families.[47] When one looks more closely, it appears that the connection between poverty and custodial-parent households is a distinctly gendered phenomenon, which is why child support was and continues to be viewed as a feminist issue.[48] Custodial mothers entitled to

[42] *Turner*, 564 U.S. at 458, 459, 461.

[43] Grall, *supra* note 7, at 15.

[44] *Id.* at 2.

[45] *Id.*

[46] *Id.* at 3, Table 1.

[47] *Id.*

[48] *See, e.g.*, Jocelyn Elise Crowley, The Politics of Child Support in America (2003); Paula Roberts, Ending Poverty As We Know It: The Case for Child Support Enforcement and Assurance 39–51 (1994); Ron Haskins, Work over Welfare: The Inside Story of the 1996 Welfare Reform Law (2006); Paul K. Legler, *The Coming Revolution in Child Support Policy: Implications of the 1996 Welfare Act*, 30 Fam. L. Q., 519 (1996).

child support have a far lower mean household income ($58,036) than custodial fathers ($73,308).[49] Moreover, custodial fathers have poverty rates that are almost 13 percentage points lower than custodial mothers.[50] Custodial mothers are much more likely than custodial fathers to participate in at least one public assistance program (48.5 percent compared to 30.5 percent, respectively), and custodial mothers have increased their families' reliance on SNAP (food stamps) in recent years.[51] Although the rate of poverty in custodial mother families has decreased overall since 1993, the improvement in their economic status appears to be attributable to an increase in the custodial mother's employment in full-time, year-round employment (from 40.9 percent in 1993 to 50.0 percent in 2015), rather than an increase either in the amount obligated or the far lesser amount actually received as child support.[52] This behooves policymakers to invest more resources in closing the gender and race wage gaps, developing affordable, high-quality childcare and afterschool programs, offering universal early childhood education programs, and creating more job protections for parents, including mandatory paid parental leave, breastfeeding protections, and flexible and shared work schedules. In the end, it appears that the most reliable way to ensure the economic stability of custodial parent families is to ensure the economic success of the custodial parent.

The truth is that child support is for the benefit of the child and the Court's failure to place the child at the center of its analysis in *Turner v. Rogers* is a reflection of 229 years of patriarchal jurisprudence in which children are seldom seen or heard and women have largely been assigned derivative existences. Indeed, even though child support is the progenitor of this case, the child who is the beneficiary of that support enjoys neither party status nor is given much acknowledgement let alone consideration by the Court. It is the woman's role to stand in and advocate for the parties' child, and it is the woman whose interests receive more consideration than the child's, although nowhere near as much consideration as the man's. Decisions like *Turner* are the direct progeny of patriarchy, subjugating women's interests and identities and largely "ghosting" children even though such cases are – or at least *should* be – for the child's direct benefit. Indeed, the legal system's ability to effectively enforce child support literally could determine the length and quality of the child's life.

49 Grall, *supra* note 7, at 13.

50 *Id.* at 4.

51 *Id.* at 10, 15.

52 *Id.* at 14.

THE FEMINIST JUDGMENT

In the feminist judgment, Professor Elizabeth MacDowell reframes and broadens the analysis in a concurring opinion. Like Justice Thomas's dissent, the concurring opinion recognizes that the case exists for the benefit of the parties' child. Writing as Justice MacDowell, she highlights the role that child support enforcement is intended to play in alleviating child poverty and recognizes the failures of the current system to do so effectively. For example, she emphasizes that when a noncustodial parent is incarcerated, it harms not only that parent, but the child and any other family members who rely on that parent for emotional and financial support. Justice MacDowell also outlines the harmful impact that the current system has on the larger community, especially as it relates to race and poverty.

Because of these high stakes, Justice MacDowell outlines the myriad benefits that the appointment of counsel would bring to complicated cases such as *Turner*, and emphasizes that the alternative safeguards that the majority identified are likely insufficient to ensure Due Process. She devotes considerable thought to additional steps, including a more robust screening and evaluation process to determine the noncustodial parent's ability to pay, that can be taken to ensure resolution of the conflict prior to incarceration of a parent. Justice MacDowell goes further and encourages a more "forward-thinking view" to prevent the conflict in the first place by taking a proactive approach early on by, for example, encouraging more contact between children and noncustodial parents and providing employment services.

Justice MacDowell envisions a justice system that takes a restorative or rehabilitative approach to child support enforcement rather than a punitive one, in order to create better outcomes for all members of the family in light of their "intertwining interests." For example, Justice MacDowell sees the potential of non-lawyer professionals such as social workers to serve on multidisciplinary teams to assist lawyers with fact-finding in family-centered cases and emphasizes the need for appointment of legal counsel in many cases, especially complex ones, explaining: "Lawyers can help their clients (and the courts) by encouraging actions in accordance with a better nature; by assisting clients in identifying resources, and providing guidance in solving problems." Additionally, Justice MacDowell mentions job training and drug treatment as alternatives to incarceration. Although she says that considering such programs is "not the purpose of today's decision," she recognizes that "greater use of such measures rather than civil contempt would be a positive result for many low-income families" and she is correct. Justice MacDowell reminds us that, by tying children so closely to a parent's economic circumstances in the current system, society is passing along the parents' economic vulnerabilities to their children, largely unmitigated, which in a complex society in which all of our interests are interrelated, benefits no one, especially the child. Moreover, her judgment recognizes that punishing people – mostly fathers – who cannot and potentially never could pay child support – hurts children and mothers. And a system that disproportionately punishes black men entrenches the racism that pervades the U.S. criminal justice system in ways antithetical to the feminist values of equality and dignity.

TURNER v. ROGERS, 564 U.S. 431 (2011)

JUSTICE MACDOWELL, CONCURRING

I join Parts I, II, and III-A of the lead opinion, which elaborate why this case is not moot, and set forth the applicable legal framework for determining the issue presented: whether the Due Process Clause of the Fourteenth Amendment requires appointment of counsel to an indigent defendant in a civil contempt case that results in his incarceration. I also agree with the conclusion reached by my colleagues that civil contemnors in child support cases have no categorical right to counsel, but that Petitioner's right to due process was nonetheless violated. Majority Opinion at 448, 449. However, I disagree with the lead opinion's analysis of the balancing test set forth in *Mathews v. Eldridge*, 424 U.S. 319, 96 S.Ct. 893, 47 L.Ed.2d 18 (1976), and its resulting conclusions regarding what procedures will satisfy due process. *See* Majority Opinion at 446–48.

The lead opinion misapprehends the nature and complexity of the interests involved in civil contempt cases in the child support context.[1] As set forth below, protecting the due process rights of indigent child support obligors serves many important government interests, including those associated with children and their custodians. All of these interests are deeply intertwined. Additionally, my colleagues disregard the utter failure of the very procedural safeguards they recommend to bring about a fair proceeding. *See id.*, at 447 (Petitioner was provided the opportunity to speak); 447–48 (the judge received a form with Petitioner's financial information – his recent application for disability); *id.* (the judge was prompted by a printed form to make an express finding of ability to pay but did not do so). These facts illustrate the problems for defendants in largely *pro se* courts, and the important role counsel play in

[1] The lead opinion also misstates the balancing of interests we set forth in *Mathews*, which are neither as broad nor as limited as those suggested by my colleagues. I address this, too, below.

these matters – one that goes well beyond their significant role in aiding with the resolution of legally complex matters.

In the absence of a categorical right to counsel, procedural safeguards must be designed and implemented taking into account the interdependent nature of the interests at stake in child support enforcement, and the uniquely challenging nature of due process rights protection in the courts where enforcement is adjudicated. I write separately to more fully analyze the important individual and governmental interests at stake in this case, and to provide guidance in accordance with this analysis on what alternative procedures will satisfy the Due Process Clause in this and similar cases.

I

A

As stated, this case requires us to untangle the complex interests involved in the enforcement of child support obligations. In this context, it is helpful to recall at the outset that the parties in the underlying case and cases like it are at least putative family members, as well as individuals with interests that may be distinct from one another or even in conflict. Further, while the parents in the case below are on opposite sides of a legal dispute, they are entangled in a legal process that neither one of them constructed, and which exists for the benefit of nonparties to the litigation: their child, and (as discussed further below) the state.

Nonpayment of child support contributes to the poverty of women and children, as described in some detail by the dissent. But nonpayment of support results not just because, in some instances, "deadbeat dads" fail to pay support, but because the economic fates of impoverished women and children are often tied to those of poor men. This is a result of the government's reliance on the child support enforcement system to deal with child poverty. This "elaborate procedural mechanism," Majority Opinion at 444, exists to collect payments from parents both to unburden the government from having to provide economic assistance itself, and to reimburse the government when it does provide aid. *See, e.g.*, 43 U.S.C. Sec. 608 (a)(3) (2009) (requiring states to assign themselves all child support benefits as a condition of received federal welfare monies); S.C. Code Ann. Sec. 43-5-65(a)(1) (2009) (requiring welfare applicants to assign their children's rights to the state). As discussed in more detail below, a parent who runs afoul of this system cannot be assumed a "deadbeat." Whether an indigent noncustodial parent with child support arrears can pay *something* is precisely the question the judge must determine at a civil contempt proceeding such as the one at issue here.

B

This case arises from the twelve-month incarceration of Petitioner, an unemployed father, possibly unable to work because of a disability, for contempt of an order to pay child support. The sentence was imposed without a finding that he could in fact purge his debt and thereby obtain his release from jail. Majority Opinion at 437–38. Our holding that this case is not moot – despite the end of Petitioner's initial period of confinement – rests on the likelihood that this scenario will repeat itself and evade review. *Id.* at 440. Indeed, it has already repeated, with Petitioner spending another six months in jail for contempt after the period of confinement giving rise to this appeal. *Id.* Thus, this Court's ability to hear Petitioner's case rests on the apparent fact that incarcerating low-income child support obligors with arrears – possibly, as in this case, without due process – is business as usual in South Carolina.

As reflected in the lead opinion's recitation of facts, Petitioner has been in arrears continuously since his support was first ordered in 2003. *Id.* at 436. Omitted is important context: when establishing the order at issue here, the court imputed income to Petitioner even though he was unemployed, and made the order retroactive to the date of a prior negotiation conference, set by the South Carolina Department of Social Services Child Support Enforcement Division, to establish Petitioner's support obligation. Brief for Petitioner 8; *see also* Brief for Respondent, Appendices, 1a. As a result, Petitioner was more than $200 in arrears before his first payment, Brief for Petitioner at 9, initiating a cycle of past due payments followed by threatened and then actual incarceration, Majority Opinion at 436–37. The first several Orders to Show Cause resulted in purged amounts. *Id.* But the record does not reflect whether the court ever found willful nonpayment at any of the enforcement hearings.

II

A

Determining what process is due in order to render this civil proceeding fair requires us to consider the relative weight of the interests at stake. *Mathews*, 424 U.S. at 335. Here, those include Petitioner's interest in avoiding further erroneous deprivation of his liberty, and the comparative value of "additional or substitute procedural safeguards" in preventing that deprivation. *Id.*

We must also consider the interests of the government in this particular procedural setting, including those in favor of greater protections, *Goldberg v. Kelly*, 397 U.S. 254, 264, 90 S.Ct. 1011, 25 L.Ed.2d 287 (1970), and any countervailing interests *Id.* at 266; *Mathews*, 424 U.S. at 335. As stated earlier, I agree with the judgment set forth in the lead opinion that these considerations do not result in a categorical right to counsel in civil contempt cases in the child support context. Therefore, my purpose is to provide a roadmap so that future courts can identify *what* procedures will be sufficient to satisfy due process when counsel is not appointed, *when* alternative procedures cannot satisfy the constitution and counsel must be appointed, and *how* that determination might be made in accordance with due process. To discuss these procedures in context, I first detail the interrelated private and public interests involved.

As set forth in the lead opinion, wrongful deprivation of liberty in a case like this one means that the child support obligor can be sentenced to jail for up to a year with no way to purge his or her debt. *See* Majority Opinion at 436 (describing South Carolina's civil contempt scheme). Thus, a wrongful deprivation transforms a civil sanction, wherein the defendant has no right to counsel in the underlying proceeding, into a criminal one, in which case the obligor would have a right to counsel in the first instance. *Id.* at 445. The threat of incarceration renders the need for accuracy in determining the obligor's ability to pay of paramount importance. *Id.* What the lead opinion underestimates is the level of importance of this determination to the governmental interests at stake. By focusing on the potential unfairness for a *pro se* custodial parent if the contemnor is provided a lawyer, or the possibility that a child for whom the support was ordered waits longer to receive the amount owed if defense counsel in involved, the lead opinion misses the larger picture. *Id.* at 446–47.

Specifically, the interests of poor custodial mothers and their children are aligned with those of the noncustodial parent who owes support, as well as the government. All have a strong interest in avoiding a wrongful deprivation of the noncustodial parents' liberty interests. Therefore, it is not only the defendant's liberty interest, but also the shared and public nature of this interest that weighs in favor of appointing defense counsel generally. The commonality of interests in this case derive from factors including the impact of incarceration on the defendant's ability to provide economic support, the changeable nature of parental custodial arrangements and support obligations, and the dignity interests of poor families.

First and most obviously, the defendant is unlikely to develop an ability to pay support from a jail cell if the determination of ability to pay is made incorrectly. Indeed, time spent in jail may compromise a child support obligor's future as well as current earning potential. *Argersinger v. Hamlin*, 407 U.S. 25, 37 n. 6; 92 S. Ct. 2006; 32 L. Ed. 2d 530 (1972) (observing that even short stints of incarceration "will usually result in loss of employment with a consequential substantial detriment to the defendant and his family") (internal quotation marks omitted). *See also* Brief for the Legal Aid Society of the District of Columbia *et al.*, as *Amicus Curiae* 20–21 n. 13–15 (citing studies). While civil contempt does not result in a criminal conviction, incarceration itself may have a significant detrimental impact on future earnings prospects, separate from a conviction. *See, e.g.*, The Pew Charitable Trusts, Collateral Costs: Incarceration's Effect on Economic Mobility 10 (2010) (Pew Study) (reporting that individuals who are incarcerated experience significantly more severe economic consequences than those who are placed on probation).

Second, the roles of custodial and noncustodial parent, and child support obligor and recipient, can change at any time. This fact is perfectly illustrated in the present case, where Respondent Rogers is no longer custodian of her and Petitioner's child. Brief for Respondent ii (explaining that Rogers's father is now the sole guardian of Rogers's child with Petitioner, and that the family court has redirected child support payments to him). As a noncustodial parent, Rogers could be ordered to pay support for her child and held accountable through contempt proceedings in the event of a failure to pay. In that instance, she would benefit from the protections that Petitioner seeks and that she and her father, the child's guardian, now oppose.

Here it is important to underscore how the interests of custodial parents are being considered: as public, not private interests. The lead opinion is vague on this point. But the Due Process Clause covers state action, and it is state interests that must be weighted and balanced against the Petitioner's liberty interest, not private ones. The government agencies responsible for child support collection and enforcement share this strong interest in an accurate determination of the key legal issue – the obligor's ability to pay. This is true in what we might call their *parens patriae* role, in which they work to obtain support on behalf of minor children, and to prevent child poverty, and in their role as creditor, seeking to minimize unreimbursed welfare payments made to custodial parents on behalf of their children. Both efforts involve the collection of child support payments from obligors, which incarceration for civil contempt without actual ability to pay inhibits.

This brings us to the third way in which the public interests at stake in this case are aligned with Petitioner's interest in avoiding a wrongful deprivation of liberty: consideration of the dignity of poor individuals and families. Precedent instructs us to consider government interests broadly, including those interests that may require implementation of additional due process protections. Goldberg, 397 U.S. at 264–65. These include more expressive government functions, such as protecting the dignity of the poor and the integrity of systems for preventing poverty. *Id.* (considering "the Nation's basic commitment . . . to foster[ing] the dignity and well-being of all persons within its borders"). The lead opinion acknowledges these important functions in its consideration of fairness to *pro se* custodians, but stops short of the full picture.

Also important is the obligor's perceptions of procedural due process. The obligor is less likely to comply with court orders, and make payments when they can, if they perceive the enforcement procedures have been unfair. More broadly, the dignity interests of poor families, who make up the vast majority of those with child support arrears, Majority Opinion at 446, counsel a more robust approach to due process protection in child support enforcement.

Families of indigent child support obligors have frequently endured government intrusion on the most intimate matters of family decision-making. With very limited exception, welfare recipients like Rogers are required to cooperate with the child support agency in determining paternity so that support orders can be established, whether or not the mother believes this is the best or safest option for her and the child. Additionally, whether the custodial parent will work, and how the noncustodial parent will contribute to a child's care, are matters determined not by parents of poor children alone, but also by the state. And both parents will be assigned financial roles that they will likely struggle to fill. In consequence, adult members of poor families are often pitted against one another to scrape by, losing dignity and autonomy while child poverty continues largely unabated.

Many of these dynamics are easy to perceive in this case. The transcript of the hearing on the Order to Show Cause records Petitioner's expressions of guilt and shame about his failure to pay support, and Rogers's desire for the judge to impose jail time. It is not hard to imagine Rogers's frustration. Her child's father is an addict who has provided only intermittent financial support, sometimes only after a threat of incarceration – whether through orders that were wrongfully imposed or not. Like her child's father, she is poor. Yet, as described earlier, none of this means that custodians like Rogers or their children will benefit from the noncustodial parent's incarceration, especially if the obligor cannot purge their child support arrears while in custody. Rather, the dignity interests of poor families – an important public interest – are further harmed by a wrongful deprivation of the obligor's liberty.

Children in particular suffer more than economic harms from proceedings that result in a parent's wrongful incarceration. They are deprived of parental contact, and exposed to the stigma resulting from having an incarcerated parent. These experiences may have lasting negative effects. It is not surprising that children with an incarcerated parent are found to have more behavior problems and worse outcomes at school. *See* Pew Study 21. The custodial parent may suffer from more than economic harm as well. Partners of prisoners, too, experience the stress of shame and isolation. *See* JEREMY TRAVIS, ELIZABETH CINCOTTA MCBRIDE & AMY L. SOLOMON, URBAN INST. JUSTICE POL'Y CTR., FAMILIES LEFT BEHIND: THE HIDDEN COSTS OF INCARCERATION AND REENTRY 2–4 (rev. 2005). Indeed, there may be unique harms that result when a custodial parent is perceived as having played a part in causing the incarceration when they have pursued child support arrears. A wrongful determination of ability to pay exacerbates and extends all of these harmful effects by greatly increasing the likelihood that the parent obligor will spend the maximum amount of time in custody.

Also important to note here are the differential racial impacts of these determinations, evidenced in some states. Studies in Wisconsin, for example, indicate that low-income minority parents are much more likely to be singled out for contempt proceedings than other parents. Brief of Center for Family Policy and Practice as *Amicus Curiae* 22 (reporting findings from Milwaukee and the Madison, Wisconsin area). A study in Dane County Wisconsin found that 48 percent of individuals booked for nonpayment of support, including for civil contempt, were African American, yet African Americans made up only 4 percent of the local population. *Id.* The disproportionate costs of punitive child support enforcement measures like civil contempt borne by low-income racial minorities threaten to further undermine the legitimacy of the child support system and the courts. Race thus weighs heavily in this analysis.

B

Accurate determination of the key legal issue, ability to pay, may also be more challenging than acknowledged by the lead opinion, rendering additional or alternative procedural protections of high value. The challenge of accurate determination relates to the nature of the proceeding as well as the legal issues, and to the role played by counsel in these cases. While not warranting appointment of counsel in every case, they must inform the procedural safeguards that the constitution requires.

To begin, child support enforcement is different in key respects from the other noncriminal proceedings where we have found no categorical right to counsel. Those include administrative proceedings that involve "predictive and discretionary" decision-making, and we reasoned that the introduction of counsel could significantly impede those proceedings' rehabilitative goals.

See Gagnon v. Scarpelli, 411 U.S. 778, 790, 93 S.Ct. 1756, 36 L.Ed.2d 656 (1973) (holding there is no categorical right to counsel at probation revocation hearings). In *Gagnon*, we followed *Morrissey v. Brewer*, 408 U.S. 471, 408, 92 S. Ct. 2593, 33 L. Ed. 2d 484 (1972), in finding that probation revocation hearings were not part of the criminal case. 411 U.S. at 781. We held that a requirement that indigent probationers be appointed counsel could change an informal proceeding into a more formal one and the role of the hearing body into that of a judge. *Id.* at 778–79. In contrast, the purpose of a civil contempt proceeding in a child support case is not rehabilitative but coercive, and involves traditional judicial fact-finding on the issue of the defendant's ability to comply with the child support order.

Two additional issues further distinguish this case from others in which we found no categorical right to council. First, the defendant does not, as a matter of course, receive assistance with the case from a non-lawyer professional. *See Vitek v. Jones*, 445 U.S. 480, 496–97, 499–500, 100 S.Ct. 1254, 63 L.Ed.2d 552 (1980) (Powell, J. concurring in part) (finding no categorical right to counsel for indigent convicts before transfer to mental health facilities because assistance from mental health professionals is available). Nor does the court have the type of assistance with fact-finding that we discerned in another family court setting, in *Lassiter*, where social workers played a significant role in developing the factual record. *See Lassiter v. Department of Social Servs. of Durham Cty.*, 452 U.S. 18, 22–23, 33, 101 S.Ct. 2153, 68 L.Ed.2d 640 (1981) (describing the pivotal role of social workers in investigating and providing evidence in a termination of parental rights case).

Second, also unlike *Lassiter*, where the state bore the burden to prove its case by "clear, cogent, and convincing evidence," *id.* at 29, 101 S.Ct. 2153, the defendant in a civil contempt case bears the burden of proof on the issue of inability to pay. *See Brasington v. Shannon*, 341 S.E.2d 130, 131 (S.C. 1986) (once the moving party establishes noncompliance with an existing court order, the burden is on the defendant to prove inability to comply); *Hicks v. Feiock*, 485 U.S. 624, 637–41, 108 S.Ct. 1423, 99 L.Ed.2d 721 (1988) (the burdens of proof and persuasion may rest on the defendant in a proceeding for civil contempt); accord Majority Opinion at 442. Therefore, it is the indigent defendant who must put forward sufficient, competent evidence in order to avoid the wrongful deprivation of liberty that we are concerned with preventing in this case. *Maggio v. Zuitz*, 333 U.S. 56, 75–76, 68 S.Ct. 401 (1948) (defendant who presents no evidence, or evidence the court does not find credible, has not met his burden).

Moreover, the nature of the legal issue to be determined may be more complex than assumed by the lead opinion, going beyond basic issues of income. Determination of willful nonpayment is subject to varying legal standards. *See* Brief for Petitioner 35–36 n. 20, 21 (detailing standards in various jurisdictions). Some jurisdictions require civil contemnors to show that funds to purge their debt cannot be obtained from a source other than income, such as a loan, in order to establish an inability to pay defense. *See, e.g., In re Gawerc*, 165 S.W.3d 314, 315 (Tex. 2005) (requiring the contemnor to show he has no alternative source of funds to purge his debt). Other courts have demanded "credible evidence" of necessity for expenses, *see In re Powers*, 653 N.E.2d 1154, 1158 (N.Y. 1995), and denied an inability to pay defense where lack of funds was believed to be self-induced or unreasonable. *See, e.g., Electric Works Pension Trust Fund of Local Union #58 v. Gary's Elec. Serv. Co.*, 340 F.3d 373, 383 (6th Cir. 2003); *In re Power Recovery Sys., Inc.*, 950 F.2d 798, 803 (1st Cir. 1991); *Combs v. Ryan's Coal Co.*, 785 F.2d 970, 984 (11th Cir. 1986). Similarly, in South Carolina, evidence of the contemnor's assets and lifestyle has been used to defeat a defense of inability to pay. *Thornton v. Thornton*, 492 S.E.2d 86, 90–91, 94–95 (S.C. 1997). These cases present complicated legal issues beyond what the average *pro se* litigant can be expected to handle.

Other issues concerning the underlying order may also complicate findings on the issue of willfulness. Common practices in setting the underlying order like imputing income, which we see in the present case, and prohibitions on retroactive modification of support awards leave many obligors with support obligations that are beyond their means. *See* Brief of Center for Family Policy and Practice as *Amicus Curiae* 10–16 (detailing routine practices and systemic issues in the child support system that disadvantage poor noncustodial parents). These are problems inherited by the judge tasked with making findings on the issue of willfulness, and heighten the stakes involved in making an accurate determination.

Yet the role of counsel in contexts such as these is not just about providing assistance with complex cases. Lawyers can help their clients (and the courts) by assisting them in understanding the law and encouraging compliance, identifying resources, and providing guidance in solving problems. Such assistance may even facilitate resolution of the matter without a hearing. The presence of counsel also helps to provide system accountability. Lawyers help to identify and address structural problems in legal systems such as recurrent legal issues or procedural abuses; their presence may work prophylactically to prevent abuses as well. *See In re Gault*, 387 U.S. 1, 386 n. 55, 87 S.Ct. 1428, 18 L.Ed.2d 527 (1967) (quoting with approval the National Crime Commission's report, which states that "with lawyers come records of proceedings; records make possible appeals which, even if they do not occur, impart by their possibility a healthy atmosphere of accountability").

The importance of this role is apparent in *pro se* cases, in which due process failures appear common. In this context, it is important to note that the state is not monolithic and its interests are not singular. While the court *enacts* governmental interests I have identified previously, including the *parens patriae* function, and has institutional interest in litigants' perceptions of procedural due process, these compete with another institutional imperative: the efficient processing of cases. This imperative can be in tension with the protection of contemnors' due process rights.

As we have acknowledged in previous cases, "the contempt power [is] uniquely liable to abuse." *Mine Workers v. Bagwell*, 512 U.S. 821, 831, 114 S.Ct. 2552, 129 L.Ed.2d 642 (1994) (citing *Bloom v. Illinois*, 391 U.S. 194, 202 (1968), quoting *Ex parte Terry*, 128 U.S. 289, 313 (1888) (internal quotation marks omitted). "Unlike most areas of law, where a legislature defines both the sanctionable conduct and the penalty to be imposed, civil contempt proceedings leave the offended judge solely responsible for identifying, prosecuting, adjudicating, and sanctioning the contumacious conduct." *Id.* Thus, civil contempt "strikes at the most vulnerable and human qualities of a judge's temperament[.]" *Id.* (citing *Bloom*, 391 U.S., at 202) (internal quotations omitted). Fact-finding for "contempts involving out-of-court disobedience" and disputed material facts are particularly susceptible to abuse without procedural protections. *Id.* at 833–34.

The South Carolina contempt statute provides minimal constraints on judicial fiat in light of these concerns. Judges retain responsibility for fact-finding related to the defendant's alleged noncompliance with their orders, and have discretion to impose coercive sanctions including imprisonment.[2] Moreover, as we have seen, proving inability to pay can raise complex issues of fact and law, for which the defendant has the burden of proof and persuasion.

In contrast, no significant government interest stands in the way of imposing more substantial procedural safeguards. "Financial cost alone is not a controlling weight." *Mathews*, 424 U.S. at 348. Nor is it a logical one given the costs (economic and otherwise) imposed by incarcerating contemnors who cannot pay their child support arrears. Neither can the government's interest in expediency outweigh the substantial countervailing public and private interest

2 *See* S.C. Code Ann. § 63-3-620 (Supp. 2010) (any adult who willfully violates a court order "may be punished by a fine, a public work sentence, or by imprisonment in a local detention facility, or by any combination of them, in the discretion of the court, but not to exceed detention in a local detention facility for one year, a fine of fifteen hundred dollars, or a public work sentence of more than three hundred hours, or any combination of them").

in accuracy and fairness. The question is whether these interests give rise to a categorical right to counsel.

Petitioner argues that the potential for an erroneous finding of willful nonpayment (and thus an erroneous deprivation of liberty) requires a categorical right to counsel. Even with the greater potential for deprivation that I have identified here, I disagree. Petitioner's argument bootstraps the right to counsel to a system failure, wherein the coercive function of civil contempt is transformed into a punitive one. But many contempt cases may be amenable to resolution without counsel because the ability to purge the debt is relatively straightforward. These may include cases identified by the lead opinion, where the question of ability to pay is closely tied to indigence. A subset of these cases will involve defendants who can, with proper preparation and tools, make their case in court. But there is an additional reason for broadening the options available for providing procedural due process.

To be abundantly clear, the issue here is that the court is routinely sending a poor man to jail for a year at a time with no evidence of ability to pay, thus aiding in the social marginalization of poor families, and contributing to the creation of a modern-day debtor's prison. Elizabeth G. Patterson, *Civil Contempt and the Indigent Child Support Obligor: The Silent Return of Debtor's Prison*, 18 CORNELL J. L. & PUB. POL'Y 95, 117 (2008) (cited Majority Opinion at 445–46). What this demonstrates is not the need for counsel in all civil contempt cases, but for robust procedural safeguards, including those that help replicate the broader role envisioned for counsel in ensuring court accountability. In this sense, by not establishing a categorical right to counsel we may well be requiring local governments to do more, not less.

While appointment of counsel has rightly been our gold standard for protecting procedural rights, rules requiring indigent contemnors to be appointed counsel may actually be ineffective due to structural limitations. Inadequate budgetary resources may inhibit the ability of appointed defense counsel to provide the requisite level of representation, or – in severely underfinanced jurisdictions – any representation at all. *See* Brief for Law Professors Benjamin Barton and Darryl Brown as *Amici Curiae* 14–20 (detailing problems associated with underfunding in public defender offices). For these reasons, appointment of counsel may paradoxically be necessary yet insufficient to protect due process rights and address system failures. That said, the alternatives to counsel I will set forth here are not the cheap version of access to justice. The point is to identify what it is that due process should actually achieve, by any means necessary.

III

The lead opinion identifies the following, minimal procedural safeguards that must be present in the absence of appointment of counsel to an indigent defendant:

> (1) [N]otice to the defendant that his "ability to pay" is a critical issue in the contempt proceeding; (2) the use of a form (or the equivalent) to elicit relevant financial information; (3) an opportunity at the hearing for the defendant to respond to statements and questions about his financial status (*e.g.*, those triggered by his responses on the form); and (4) an express finding by the court that the defendant has the ability to pay.
>
> Majority Opinion at 447–48.

Based on the foregoing, in the absence of automatic appointment of counsel for indigent defendants, I expand on these alternative procedural safeguards with three additional procedures that must be present: procedures to determine when appointment of counsel is constitutionally required, inform defendants of their rights in preparation for the hearing, and facilitate judicial accountability.

First, a process for screening and evaluating cases must be in place in order to determine which cases require the appointment of counsel, and which are appropriate for determination without counsel being appointed. As suggested in the lead opinion, appointment of counsel for indigent defendants may be necessary because the government is a party to the action and represented by counsel, or because the legal issues are complex. *Id.* at 449. Complex legal issues include those that cannot be resolved with the provision of basic financial information provided by the defendant. That might include cases where legal issues on the ability to pay should be briefed, such as whether the defendant can be made to sell personal assets or to borrow funds to pay owed support. Appointment of counsel may also be necessary when the legal or factual issues are not particularly complex, but defendants lack the capacity to represent themselves due to health or other reasons.

The availability of a form to elicit relevant information from the defendant (as proposed in the lead opinion) may be helpful. But it is unlikely that a form alone can capture all of the information necessary for evaluating the case and the capacity of the defendant to present it. An adequate screening process will likely require a more interpersonal effort, such as an interview of the defendant. The screening and evaluation process does not need to be conducted by a lawyer. However, it should be conducted (or, at a minimum, closely supervised) by someone with sufficient legal knowledge of the relevant issues to evaluate the issue of complexity. Because the evaluation will include an assessment of both legal issues and personal capacity for self-representation, a team approach involving lawyers and social workers may be ideal. Individuals in this evaluative role should also ideally be independent of the court hearing the case.

While, as noted above, it can benefit courts to have assistance from attorneys in educating the defendant and presenting the case, relying solely on judges to determine when counsel is needed may result in underutilization of attorney assistance. The lead opinion in this case reflects some of the biases about lawyers that judges hold, including that they will cause undue delay or prejudice unrepresented parties. A reluctance to appoint counsel may be stronger in a largely *pro se* court where the absence of counsel allows judicial authority and decision-making to go largely unchallenged. Examples of individuals better positioned to make the determination of whether counsel is needed are employees of legal aid or other civil society organizations that are structurally independent of the court, or an arm of the justice system not supervised by the judiciary.

Second, there must be a process in place for preparing defendants who are not appointed counsel for their hearings. As provided in the lead opinion, defendants have the right to be heard on the key legal issue of ability to pay, and an express finding that they have the ability to pay must be made before they can be found in contempt. The presence of these rights means little if defendants do not know about them. This information may be provided to defendants in printed form. However, some defendants may benefit more from a verbal presentation. The point is to prepare them to participate effectively in their case. Defendants should also have the opportunity to ask questions and get informed answers about their rights and the court process. This information need not be provided in a one-on-one session; group classes for litigants may be both efficient and effective.

Third, there must be mechanisms in place for assisting defendants after the court hearing and for monitoring the court process. As for the former, it is essential to have procedures in place to assist defendants after the hearing as well as beforehand. Such assistance need not include representation in formal appeals, but should include information about their rights after a hearing and referrals to any legal resources available in the community.

But many *pro se* defendants will not have the wherewithal to press their rights in court, preserve a record, or appeal. Indeed, the facts of this case make clear how difficult it is to challenge even egregious errors in cases like these and how long problems can continue without resolution. Thus, there should also be a process in place for independently accessing the procedural health of the courts hearing civil contempt cases, which are so often characterized by a dearth of attorneys. The assessments could take the form of courtroom observation, case file review, or a combination of both. What is essential is that the assessment be conducted using a methodology designed to effectively evaluate whether the requirements set forth here are being followed.

Questions to be considered include: Is an effective method for assessing cases in place? Are cases warranting appointment of counsel being identified and appointment made? Are self-represented defendants informed of the key legal and factual issues, and is the court receiving the information required to make its determination? Are defendants aware of, and granted the opportunity to exercise, their right to be heard? Is the judge making express findings, based on the evidence presented, on the defendant's ability to pay? Like initial case screenings and evaluations, these assessments should be made by an independent legal aid organization, or another civil society or government entity that operates independently of the courts hearing civil contempt cases.

To reiterate, these measures are only necessary in those jurisdictions lacking a policy of appointing counsel to all indigent defendants in civil contempt cases where a child support obligor may be incarcerated. Notably, however, some of these measures, such as the assessment process described above, may complement procedures for categorical appointment of counsel. Moreover, all of these measures can easily be crafted to accommodate and directly benefit *pro se* individuals who are seeking enforcement of support orders. Case screening and evaluation procedures can include collection of relevant information from custodial parents or guardians who wish to participate in the process; information about defendants' rights and court processes can be expanded to be inclusive of the rights of all parties. And all parties benefit from an accountable court system.

Finally, I will observe that the requirements set forth here might discourage some jurisdictions from relying as heavily on civil contempt as an enforcement mechanism. This would not be a bad outcome. Our government has taken the inherently precarious path of relying on child support paid by noncustodial parents as a primary method for child poverty prevention. This means that all of the economic vulnerabilities of low-income parents adhere, potentially unmitigated, to their children. These vulnerabilities include punitive child support enforcement policies such as civil sanctions, which expose child support obligors to the possibility, or even (as we found in South Carolina) the *likelihood*, of an unconstitutional deprivation of liberty, with all of its attendant harms for the entire family and the public. Yet the federal government now takes a more forward-thinking view, and encourages states to utilize what it has determined to be more cost-effective and productive measures in cases involving low-income parents. These include early intervention before substantial arrears accumulate and modification of orders; increased contact between children and noncustodial parents; and provision of employment services. *See* Brief for the United States as *Amicus Curiae* 21–23 (citing NATIONAL CHILD SUPPORT ENFORCEMENT, US. DEP'T OF HEALTH & HUMAN SERVS., STRATEGIC PLAN: FY 2005–2009). While not the purpose of today's decision, encouraging greater use of such measures rather than civil contempt would be a positive result for many low-income families.

IV

Petitioner received neither appointment of counsel nor the alternative procedural safeguards described above, and was nonetheless found in contempt and incarcerated. Therefore, his due process rights under the Fourteenth Amendment were violated. Moreover, there is indication in the record that he was eligible for appointment of counsel based on the criteria set forth above. In particular, his case presented potentially complex legal issues including admitted unlawful drug use. Whether that is an ongoing circumstance and raises legal questions regarding of willful nonpayment is one of the issues to be assessed in the screening and evaluation process to be conducted in the courts below.

14

Commentary on *In the Matter of the Parentage of a Child by T.J.S. and A.L.S.*

MELANIE B. JACOBS

INTRODUCTION

In 1988, the New Jersey Supreme Court case *In re Baby M.* gripped the nation.[1] A married couple contracted to pay $10,000 to a woman who agreed to be inseminated with the sperm of the husband and, following a successful pregnancy, surrender to their custody the resulting baby. Shortly after the baby's birth, however, the surrogate absconded with baby – for whom she was both the genetic and birth mother – and sued to declare the surrogacy contract void. The New Jersey Supreme Court held that the paid surrogacy contract was unenforceable and refused to terminate the surrogate's rights. The court vested custody in the husband-father and, by default, his wife, however.[2]

The *Baby M.* decision significantly impacted how couples proceed with surrogacy. While the surrogate in *Baby M.* was both the baby's gestational and genetic mother, most couples engaging in surrogacy thereafter use(d) a gestational surrogate and either an egg donor or the egg of the intended mother.[3] Such was the case in *In re T.J.S.*[4]

Nearly twenty-five years after *Baby M.*, the New Jersey Supreme Court heard *In re T.J.S.* A married husband and wife, T.J.S. and A.L.S., sought the services of a surrogate because A.L.S. was unable to carry a child to term. Through in vitro fertilization, the couple used T.J.S.'s sperm to fertilize an

[1] *In re Baby M*, 537 A.2d. 1227 (N.J. 1988).

[2] *Id.* at 1259–64.

[3] *See* Clyde Haberman, *Baby M and the Question of Surrogate Motherhood*, N.Y. Times (Mar. 23, 2014), www.nytimes.com/2014/03/24/us/baby-m-and-the-question-of-surrogate-motherhood.html ("What we have today, almost exclusively, is called gestational surrogacy. A couple thousand babies a year are believed to be born in the United States through this method").

[4] *In the Matter of the Parentage of a Child by T.J.S. and A.L.S.*, 54 A.3d 263 (N.J. 2012).

ovum of an anonymous donor. The resulting embryo was then transferred to a surrogate. Following a successful pregnancy, the surrogate delivered the baby and transferred custody to T.J.S. and A.L.S. The facts of *T.J.S.* are illustrative of the many couples and surrogates who have a positive surrogacy experience that is conflict-free. What, then, created the controversy that resulted in a hearing before the New Jersey Supreme Court?

In *T.J.S.*, all of the parties to the surrogacy contract – both intended parents and the surrogate – agreed that the wife should be named as the child's legal mother on the birth certificate. The Bureau of Vital Statistics, however, argued that it could not list the intended mother as the baby's mother on the birth certificate because she was not a parent under the New Jersey Parentage Act.[5] Parentage is ordinarily determined by the fact of having given birth, genetic connection, or through the marital presumption (the husband of a child's mother is presumed to be the child's father). Here, the Bureau of Vital Statistics argued, the intended mother was neither the birth mother nor genetic mother and had not adopted the baby so could not be recognized as the mother on the birth certificate. The Bureau's position was supported by the trial court and then upheld by both the appellate court and New Jersey Supreme Court.

Around the time *T.J.S.* was decided, the New Jersey legislature passed a bill whereby gestational surrogacy contracts would be enforceable, but the Governor vetoed the bill. Without that specific statutory guidance, the court in *T.J.S.* was required to review then current parentage and adoption laws. It was not until May 2018 that a statute governing surrogacy was enacted.[6] The Gestational Carrier Agreement Act specifically states that "gestational carrier agreements executed pursuant to this act are in accord with the public policy of this State"[7] and clearly repudiates further reliance on *Baby M.* to prohibit compensated surrogacy contracts. The Act sets forth specific eligibility requirements for the surrogate and intended parents and, assuming those are met, the intended parents are the legal parents of the child immediately upon the child's birth.[8] Had the Gestational Carrier Agreement Act been enacted, A.L.S. would have been considered the child's legal parent at birth and would have been placed on the birth certificate.

T.J.S. presents an interesting case for feminists because it addresses the legitimacy of surrogacy as well as equal reproductive rights for women and

5 *Id.* at 264.

6 New Jersey Gestational Carrier Agreement Act, Pub. L. 2018, c. 18 (codified in scattered sections of N.J. Rev. Stat. § 9:17).

7 *Id.* § 9:17–61.

8 *Id.* § 9:17–63.

men. Surrogacy divides feminists, as there is no one surrogacy law and there is also no single feminist position on surrogacy.

SURROGACY IN THE UNITED STATES

Each year, several thousand babies are born to gestational surrogates. The late 1980s and early 1990s heralded an increased use of in vitro fertilization ("IVF").[9] The increased availability of IVF made gestational surrogacy preferable to traditional surrogacy in which the surrogate has a genetic connection to the child and also births the child. In gestational surrogacy, the surrogate does not have a genetic connection to the child; rather, she has agreed to have transferred to her uterus embryos that may or may not contain the gametic material of the intended parents. Disaggregating the genetic and birthing functions appealed to many surrogacy supporters as a means by which to make legalizing the relationship between the intended mother and child easier and also to lessen the emotional connection a surrogate may develop with a child.

Whether an intended parent – someone who uses in vitro fertilization and gestational surrogacy to have a baby even if the individual does not have a genetic connection to the baby – must adopt a baby born through surrogacy or can be identified at birth or shortly thereafter as the child's legal parent varies among states. There is no single "surrogacy law" in the United States but instead a spectrum of regulation from prohibition to permission. While the current trend in the United States is to permit surrogacy contracts, that is far from universal. In some states, like New York and Michigan, paid surrogacy is criminalized.[10] Although bills to permit surrogacy parentage contracts were introduced in both states, they failed to advance.[11] In other states, like Illinois, paid gestational surrogacy is legal and governed by statute.[12] States like

[9] In IVF, the fertilization of an ovum by sperm occurs in a petri dish and, if the fertilization is successful, an embryo develops. That embryo could be transferred to the uterus of the intended and/or genetic mother or, in gestational surrogacy, the embryo is transferred to the gestational surrogate's uterus.

[10] *See* MICH. COMP. LAWS § 722.855 (2017) ("A Surrogate parentage contract is void and unenforceable as contrary to public policy"); MICH. COMP. LAWS § 722.859 (2017) (providing for criminal penalties, including imprisonment and fines, for a participating party and a person who arranges a surrogate parentage contract); N.Y. DOM. REL. LAW § 122 (McKinney, Westlaw through L. 2018, chapters 1 to 277) ("Surrogate parenting contracts are hereby declared contrary to the public policy of this state, and are void and unenforceable").

[11] Assemb. B. 6959, 2017–18 Leg., 240th Reg. Sess. (N.Y. 2017); S.B. 811, 2015–16 Leg. Sess. (Mich. 2016).

[12] 750 ILL. COMP. STAT. ANN. 47/25(d)(3) (West, Westlaw current through P.A. 100-585 of the 2018 Reg. Sess.); ILL. ADMIN. CODE tit. 77, § 500.25 (2018).

California, which also permits compensated surrogacy, have robust surrogacy markets.[13] While not all states have laws supportive of surrogacy, the trend is to enforce compensated gestational surrogacy contracts. In states in which surrogacy contracts are enforceable, the statutes or case law generally recognize enforceability of gestational surrogacy contracts and clarify that a gestational surrogate does not have legal rights to the child she delivers.[14] The 2017 Uniform Parentage Act supports compensated gestational surrogacy and, in some cases, traditional surrogacy.[15]

Even with a trend toward recognizing surrogacy contracts, surrogacy in the United States remains controversial. Feminists are divided over the propriety of surrogacy: "Scholars, especially feminist scholars, continue to raise serious concerns about the ways in which surrogacy has the potential to exploit and injure women, diminish family life, degrade the process of procreation and women's role in it, and devalue the worth of children."[16] Opponents of surrogacy – especially paid surrogacy – argue that women of lesser financial means will be exploited by the lure of financial gain. For instance, the *Baby M.* court referenced the "potential degradation some women may suffer"[17] through surrogacy and explicitly cautioned about the potential for surrogacy to "benefit ... the rich at the expense of the poor."[18] Some feminist theorists argue against compensated surrogacy because they seek to protect the emotional and physical well-being of the surrogate.[19]

Surrogacy supporters, though, see surrogacy as an extension of reproductive rights and potentially a source of empowerment for intended mothers, otherwise unable to have children, and for surrogates. Greater autonomy for some women, such as intended mothers, does not automatically come at the expense of other women – surrogates. As Professor Andrea Carroll writes,

[13] *Johnson v. Calvert*, 851 P.2d 776 (Cal. 1993); *In re Marriage of Buzzanca*, 72 Cal. Rptr. 2d 280 (Ct. App. 1998).

[14] *See, e.g.*, ME. REV. STAT. ANN. tit. 19-A, § 1928 (West, Westlaw current through Chapter 417 of the 2017 Second Regular Session and emergency legislation through Chapter 460 of the Second Special Session of the 128th Legislature) (providing that intended parents may apply for a pre-birth order vesting in them full legal parental rights immediately upon the birth of the child).

[15] UNIF. PARENTAGE ACT (UNIF. LAW COMM'N 2017).

[16] Kimberly M. Mutcherson, *How Parents Are Made: A Response to Discrimination in Baby Making: The Unconstitutional Treatment of Prospective Parents through Surrogacy*, 88 IND. L.J. 1201, 1209–10 (2013).

[17] *In re Baby M.*, 537 A.2d at 1250.

[18] *Id.* at 1249.

[19] Andrea B. Carroll, *Family Law and Female Empowerment*, 24 UCLA WOMEN'S L.J. 1, 6–7 (2017).

"[m]en are consistently empowered in the reproductive decision-making process [e.g., sperm donation] while women are not . . . Affording men and women differing levels of control over their procreative choices sends a startling message of female disempowerment of which all policymakers should be cognizant."[20] In fact, many surrogates report satisfaction, not exploitation, concerning their surrogacy experience.[21]

Two themes emerge from the differential legal treatment of surrogacy. First, some states, like New Jersey courts in the era of *Baby M.*, view surrogacy through an adoption lens. Courts that view surrogacy through an adoption lens require the nongenetic/nonbirth mother to adopt the child she intends to parent. These laws address potential parental rights of the surrogate, showing great concern for the potential vulnerability and exploitation of the surrogate. More recently, in a 2016 Idaho case, a gestational surrogate and her husband filed a petition for declaratory judgment that the intended father (who also contributed sperm) and the intended mother should be listed on the birth certificate as the child's legal parents.[22] Despite the fact that all the parties wanted the intended parents to be noted as the child's legal parents at birth, the court refused and stated that there was no legal basis by which to grant the relief sought. Rather, the court said that the current adoption regime was the parties' only recourse.[23]

Other courts, such as the California Supreme Court, perceive surrogacy as an extension of procreative liberty and have determined that an intended mother can be declared a legal parent at birth. In *Johnson v. Calvert*, an early iconic case, the court was required to decide which of two women was the child's legal mother: the woman who provided her ova and intended to raise the child with her husband (and the genetic father), or the woman who was the gestational surrogate.[24] Holding that it could declare only one woman the legal mother, the court used the doctrine of intentional parenthood to establish that the intended, genetic mother was, in fact, the legal mother.

[20] *Id.* at 8.

[21] Pamela Laufer-Ukeles, *Mothering for Money, Regulating Commercial Intimacy*, 88 Ind. L.J. 1223, 1224 (2012) ("Empirical studies of commercial surrogacy have largely concluded that surrogates and commissioning couples are satisfied and enriched by the process").

[22] *Doe v. Doe*, 372 P.3d 1106 (Idaho 2016).

[23] *Id.* ("The legislature has provided only the currently existing termination and adoption regimes, which give no special consideration to intended parents who have obtained the services of a surrogate. Unless and until the legislature chooses to enact legislation specifically addressing surrogacy, Intended Parents must proceed within the legal avenues available to them to establish legal parenthood").

[24] *Johnson v. Calvert*, 851 P.2d. 776 (1993).

The *Calvert* court further rejected the application of adoption laws to surrogacy[25] as well as the argument that surrogacy is *per se* exploitative of poor women.[26] Rather, *Calvert* focused on the surrogacy contract within the ambit of procreative liberty and emphasized the rights of intended parents. In a contemporary case evoking *Calvert*, the Iowa Supreme Court in 2018 upheld the validity and enforceability of a compensated gestational surrogacy contract after the surrogate sued to invalidate the contract and assert parental rights over the child with whom she had no genetic relationship.[27] The court noted the importance of surrogacy to infertile couples who wish to raise their own children and, further, stated the importance of recognizing the "personal autonomy of women willing to serve as surrogates."[28] The Court favorably cited *Johnson* and stated that compensated gestational surrogacy is not *per se* exploitative of surrogates and rejected the *Baby M.* case.[29] At least one scholar notes that intent theory "disregards both the biology and the caretaking relationship of pregnancy"[30] and that "the Constitution requires some recognition of parental rights as a consequence of gestational mothering."[31]

In terms of statutory guidance, Article 8 of the 2017 Revised Uniform Parentage Act regulates and permits compensated surrogacy agreements when certain conditions are met.[32] For instance, a gestational surrogate must be at least twenty-one years old; complete a medical and mental health evaluation; and have independent legal counsel. Further, the intended parents must also be twenty-one or older and complete medical and mental health evaluations.[33] A surrogate parentage contract that meets the statutory requirements is enforceable and, further, the intended parents are the legal parents of the child at birth.[34] Thus, while there is no single approach to surrogacy, the judicial and legislative trends suggest support for compensated surrogacy agreements and recognition of intentional parentage.

25 *Id.* at 784 ("Gestational surrogacy differs in crucial respects from adoption and so is not subject to the adoption statutes").

26 *Id.* at 785.

27 *P.M. v. T.B.*, 907 N.W.2d 522 (Iowa 2018).

28 *Id.* at 525.

29 *Id.* at 539 ("The argument that a woman cannot knowingly and intelligently agree to gestate and deliver a baby for intending parents carries overtones of the reasoning that for centuries prevented women from attaining equal economic rights and professional status under the law") (quoting *Johnson v. Calvert*, 851 P.2d at 785).

30 Jennifer S. Hendricks, *Essentially a Mother*, 13 Wm. & Mary J. Women & L. 429, 479 (2007).

31 *Id.* at 482.

32 Unif. Parentage Act Art. 8 (Unif. Law Comm'n 2017).

33 *Id.* § 803 (discussing eligibility).

34 *Id.* § 809 (discussing parentage).

THE ORIGINAL *T.J.S.* OPINION

New Jersey's Parentage Act recognizes the marital presumption and, further, includes a provision whereby a husband is treated as a child's father by operation of law if his wife is artificially inseminated with donor sperm.[35] Without the benefit of legislation authorizing gestational surrogacy and the legacy of *Baby M.*, the couple made an alternative argument: that just as T.J.S. would have been afforded parental status had A.L.S. been inseminated with donor sperm, A.L.S. should be afforded parental status because she consented to IVF, embryo transfer, and surrogacy using her husband's sperm. The couple further alleged that a failure to treat A.L.S. as the child's legal mother violated her rights to equal protection under the New Jersey and U.S. Constitutions.

The appellate court reviewed the Parentage Act and determined that the plain language of the Act does not include a presumption of parentage for a woman whose husband "fathers a child with another woman" and instead held that the only recourse under the Act is stepparent adoption.[36] Further, the appellate court determined that the statute does not violate an infertile married woman's equal protection rights. The court ruminated on the respective procreative efforts of a surrogate and sperm donor, finding that a surrogate's potential parental rights are much worthier of protection than those of a sperm donor.[37] Protecting the surrogate's rights lies at the heart of the court's opinion. Explicitly rejecting *Johnson*'s reasoning and the doctrine of intentional parenthood, the court affirmed that adoption was the intended mother's only recourse.[38]

The appellate court opinion was affirmed *per curiam* by the New Jersey Supreme Court, meaning that the court was divided in its decision, and, as a consequence, the lower court's ruling stands. The concurrence supported the appellate court decision. At the heart of its opinion, the concurrence voiced general disapproval of compensated surrogacy and emphasized the vitality of the *Baby M.* decision. Although other jurisdictions had upheld compensated surrogacy contracts, the concurrence rejected the trend in surrogacy law and adhered to a strict interpretation of *Baby M.*, in which all paid surrogacy contracts are illegal.

[35] N.J. STAT. ANN. § 9:17–43 (West, Westlaw current through L.2018, c. 104 and J.R. No. 9) (creating a rebuttable presumption that the husband of child's mother is the child's father).

[36] *In re T.J.S.*, 16 A.3d 386, 391 (N.J. Super. Ct. App. Div. 2011).

[37] *Id.* at 396.

[38] *Id.* at 398.

The dissent would have held in favor of the plaintiffs and flatly denied the applicability of *Baby M.* Without the benefit of the 2018 Gestational Carrier Agreement Act, the dissent focused its analysis on the couple's equal protection claim. Unlike the lower court and concurrence, the dissent focused on the comparison between infertile married men and women rather than a comparison of surrogates and sperm donors. The dissent framed the New Jersey Parentage Act broadly and determined that infertile married women should have the same parentage presumption as infertile married men.

FEMINIST JUDGMENT

Professor Mohapatra, writing as Justice Mohapatra, supports the national trend of enforcing compensated gestational surrogacy agreements and offers an inclusive and expansive vision of families. She anticipates the demise of *Baby M.*'s reach and the limits of the adoption approach to gestational surrogacy. Mohapatra laments the lack of legislative guidance concerning gestational surrogacy agreements but clearly and forcefully states that, "[t]here is nothing in the *Baby M.* case to suggest that this court should invalidate all surrogacy arrangements." Mohapatra acknowledges that in the absence of statutes governing surrogacy, the court may seek guidance from the adoption statute but clarifies that adoption is distinct from surrogacy. In fact, Mohapatra discusses how the court is forced to use an adoption statute that does not envision surrogacy – "a much different scenario" – and this lack of legislative guidance results in using "imprecise laws to make important determinations of how a surrogacy should proceed." For instance, Mohapatra goes further than the original dissent in questioning why the adoption statute's seventy-two-hour waiting period should be imported to the surrogacy context to ensure the gestational surrogate has relinquished parental rights.

Anticipating the passage of the Gestational Carrier Agreement Act (or something similar), she makes clear that the gestational surrogacy contract at issue is enforceable and suggests general support for compensated surrogacy claims. She writes that *Baby M.* has been misinterpreted by lower courts to be a broad rejection of surrogacy and that there are "good arguments to be made about why assisted reproduction and surrogacy is an acceptable method of becoming a parent" even in cases in which the surrogate is paid. Had her opinion been the majority opinion, it would have significantly advanced surrogacy discourse. Surrogacy opponents routinely rely on the *Baby M.* case to argue against surrogacy; an opinion diminishing the precedential value of *Baby M.* and affirming the rights of intended couples to contract with surrogates would have been a great leap forward for surrogacy advocates.

Clarifying the legality of the surrogacy contract, Mohapatra's opinion focuses on equal protection analysis to highlight why the wife-mother should enjoy a presumption of parenthood as the husband-father would in a similar situation. Mohapatra embraces a broad view of procreative liberty to establish a concomitant right for an infertile married woman to enjoy a presumption of parentage when her husband fertilizes an egg and the resulting embryo is transferred to a surrogate. Mohapatra endorses what Professor Carroll advocated: more robust and expansive reproductive rights for women. Mohapatra rejects the appellate court's emphasis on differences between surrogates and sperm donors and instead focuses her equal protection analysis on similarly situated husbands and wives.

This approach has significant equal protection benefits for women, beyond gestational surrogacy. As Mohapatra writes, the disparate treatment of infertile married men and women is not based on physiological differences but on "archaic stereotypes about men as breadwinners who can financially support the child and women as not adding to the financial security of the child." She condemns the use of stereotypes to permit continued disparity between an infertile married man and infertile married woman. Instead of a reductionist approach that creates a tautology requiring women to be treated differently from men, Mohapatra emphasizes the similarities of the parties. By formulating the question presented as whether a married infertile woman is entitled to the same rights as a married infertile man, Mohapatra is able to create parity for the parties and to justify a plain reading of the Parentage Act that provides a parentage presumption for a married woman as it does for a married man.

Mohapatra's approach opens the door to greater rights for women in all reproductive decisions and beyond. The historical foundations of family law rested on disparate treatment for wives and subordination of women to men. Perhaps the most well-known explanation for wives' legal incapacity was offered by Sir William Blackstone in 1765: "[b]y marriage, the husband and wife are one person in law: that is, the very being or legal existence of the woman is suspended during the marriage."[39] Starting with the Married Women's Property Acts in the late 1800s, women have slowly emerged from the oppressive version of family Blackstone opined.[40] Feminist advocacy has resulted in greater parity for women in the realms of divorce, spousal support, custody, and child support.[41] Extending the marital presumption of

[39] 1 William Blackstone, Commentaries *442.

[40] *See* Martha Minow, *"Forming Underneath Everything That Grows": Toward a History of Family Law*, 1985 Wis. L. Rev. 819, 828–32 (1985).

[41] *Id.* (arguing that the linear progression of rights for women is overly simplistic and offering a more robust and nuanced discussion of women's rights within the family sphere).

parenthood to wives who use surrogacy advances deeper spousal equality. She provides an important equal protection analysis that advances the rights of women and same-sex couples.

By readily embracing surrogacy and other assisted reproductive technologies along with intentional parenthood doctrine, Mohapatra supports the rights of infertile heterosexual and homosexual individuals and couples to create families. In her opinion, Mohapatra urges the legislature to make the Parentage Act gender-neutral to support same-sex parents. T.J.S. was decided two years before *Obergefell v. Hodges*,[42] in which the Supreme Court held that the U.S. Constitution requires marriage equality. Professor Douglas NeJaime has argued that marriage equality will actually foster greater acceptance of surrogacy; as more same-sex couples avail themselves of marriage and choose to start families, they will need ART to have families.[43] He points to the recent introduction of a surrogacy bill in New York to support his argument; while the bill failed to pass,[44] there is growing momentum to permit compensated gestational surrogacy contracts.[45] Mohapatra's opinion supports those efforts.

Although *T.J.S.* would have had a different outcome under the Gestational Carrier Agreement Act, it is important to recognize that compensated surrogacy is still far from universal and the law remains in flux. Mohapatra's opinion clarifies many of the legal and policy arguments in favor of compensated gestational surrogacy. Her rewritten opinion provides a refreshing counterpoint to the original opinion that relied on outdated gender stereotypes and a narrow view of assisted reproductive technologies and its impact on family formation.

IN THE MATTER OF THE PARENTAGE OF A CHILD BY T.J.S. AND A.L.S., 54 A.3D 263 (N.J. 2012)

JUSTICE MOHAPATRA DELIVERED THE OPINION OF THE COURT

This case is about the unequal treatment of similarly situated infertile married women and infertile married men under New Jersey law. Specifically, the

[42] *Obergefell v. Hodges*, 135 S.Ct. 2584 (2014).

[43] Douglas NeJaime, *Marriage Equality and the New Parenthood*, 129 Harv. L. Rev. 1185, 1253 (2016).

[44] *See supra* text accompanying note 9.

[45] *Id.*

New Jersey Parentage Act (Parentage Act) grants to an infertile married man the right to become the legal father of a child who is conceived when his wife is artificially inseminated with the sperm of another man. N.J. Stat. Ann. § 9:17–38, 44 (West 2012). Although the man has no genetic connection to the child, the law allows him to have his name placed on the birth certificate as the natural father and to avoid the cost, uncertainty, and delay involved in adoption. N.J. Stat. Ann. § 9:17–38, 44(a) (West 2012); N.J. Admin. Code § 8:2-1.5(b) (2005). However, the law does not provide a comparable right to an infertile married woman. N.J. Stat. Ann. § 9:17–38, 44(a) (West 2012); N.J. Admin. Code § 8:2-1.5(b) (2005). This court holds that the law violates equal protection under New Jersey law and reverses the Appellate Division's judgment.

I FACTUAL AND PROCEDURAL HISTORY

The facts are undisputed. Plaintiffs T.J.S. and A.L.S. are a married couple who had a strong desire to have a child. A.L.S.'s eggs were not viable, and she was unable to carry a child to term. In 2008, in their quest to have a child, the couple sought the aid of A.F., a woman unrelated to T.J.S and A.L.S. A.F. agreed to serve as T.J.S and A.L.S.'s gestational carrier. That is, she agreed to be implanted with an embryo that was not genetically related to her and carry the pregnancy to term. In 2008, with the aid of a fertility clinic and appropriate medical personnel, T.J.S.'s sperm was used to fertilize the ova of an anonymous donor. The anonymous donor had relinquished her legal rights to the eggs. Two embryos were then implanted into the uterus of A.F. A.F. has no genetic connection to the child and has never asserted any legal right to the child. A.F. noted in a certification that she intended only to carry the child to term for plaintiffs who would then become the sole parents of any child born.[1] Even with this certification, under the surrogacy agreement, A.F. retained certain rights. Seventy-two hours after the birth of the child, A.F. could surrender all parental rights to the child, allowing T.J.S. and A.L.S. to be listed as the child's birth parents; or, at any time after the birth of the child and before relinquishing parental rights, she could assert a claim to the child.[2]

[1] As discussed later in this opinion, there is no issue related to the competing rights of the gestational carrier A.F. in this case. Unlike the *Baby M.* case discussed by the trial and appellate court, this is not a situation where the gestational carrier has expressed any desire to claim parentage. *See supra*; *In re Baby M.*, 537 A.2d 1227, 1234–35 (N.J. 1988).

[2] A child can only be eligible for adoption if the mother surrenders her parental rights to the child. *See* N.J. Stat. Ann. § 9:3–41(a) (West 1994). Under New Jersey law, a surrender that occurs earlier than seventy-two hours after "the birth of the child" is not valid. N.J. Stat. Ann.

In keeping with the terms of the gestational carrier agreement, and with the consent of A.F., plaintiffs filed a pre-birth complaint in the Chancery Division, Family Part in Camden County seeking an order requiring that their names be printed on the child's birth certificate "as the biological parents of the child" after A.F. relinquished any parental rights. *In re T.J.S.*, 16 A.3d 386, 389 (App. Div. 2011). A few days later, the trial court entered the order, which was not opposed, in the form that plaintiffs had requested.

New Jersey's Adoption Statute does not permit a birth mother to surrender parental rights until the completion of a seventy-two-hour waiting period following the birth of the child. N.J. Stat. Ann. § 9:3–41(e) (West 1994). The trial court ordered that the birth certificate, which would reflect T.J.S. as the father and A.L.S. as the mother, would not become valid until A.F. surrendered her rights seventy-two hours after giving birth. The child, T.D.S., was born on July 7, 2009. T.D.S. was genetically related to T.J.S. and the anonymous egg donor. Three days later, the gestational carrier relinquished all parental rights to the child and a birth certificate was issued listing T.J.S. and A.L.S. as the child's parents.

After issuance of a birth certificate, the Department of Health and Human Services, Bureau of Vital Statistics ("the Department") filed a motion seeking to have the court vacate its order. The Department, which had not been afforded notice of plaintiffs' application, contended that there was no basis in the applicable statutes for the relief that plaintiffs had requested from the court. The trial court granted the Department's motion and vacated its previous order. While the trial court's motion was pending, the Department sealed the original birth certificate and issued a new one listing T.J.S. as the father but leaving blank the mother's name. The trial court concluded that: (1) the State Registrar has standing in the matter by virtue of her "vital statutory responsibilities" to record birth records correctly and legally; (2) the Parentage Act does not permit, either explicitly or implicitly, A.L.S. to be declared the parent through a pre-birth order adjudication; (3) the statute does not violate A.L.S.'s equal protection rights under Article I, paragraph 1 of the New Jersey Constitution; and (4) A.L.S.'s exclusive remedy is stepparent adoption pursuant to N.J. Stat. Ann. §9:3–48 (West 2004). The court recognized that the issuance of the pre-birth order in this case was not a novel procedure and had been approved by the Camden Vicinage, as followed in other counties, but it did not deem it

§ 9:3–41(e) (West 1994). A child can only be eligible for adoption if the mother surrenders her parental rights to the child. *See* N.J. Stat. Ann. § 9:3–41(a) (West 1994); *In re T.J.S.*, 16 A.3d 386, 391 (App. Div. 2011).

proper in this case where A.L.S. was not biologically or genetically related to T.D.S. *See A.H.W. v. G.H.B.*, 772 A.2d at 948.

The plaintiffs, A.L.S. and T.J.S, appealed the trial court's ruling. Plaintiffs argued that the provisions of the Parentage Act conferring paternity upon a husband either presumptively, in which the child is born to the wife during marriage, or by operation of law, in which the wife is artificially inseminated with donor sperm, should be read gender neutrally to apply to the infertile wife. Plaintiffs also argued that the law is facially unconstitutional because it treats differently similarly situated groups – infertile married men and women – without sufficient justification. N.J. Stat. Ann. § 9:17–43(a) (West 2018); N.J. Stat. Ann. § 9:17–44 (West 2018). The Appellate Division affirmed the trial court's judgment, rejecting both the statutory and constitutional arguments that plaintiffs advanced on appeal. A.L.S. and T.J.S have appealed to this court. *In re Parentage of T.J.S.*, 16 A.3d 386 (N.J. Super. Ct. App. Div. 2011).

For the reasons set forth below, we reverse the judgment of the Appellate Division and hold that equal protection requires the presumption of maternity to be afforded to A.L.S. under the facts of this case. Appellate Judge Parrillo's analysis of the plain language of the Parentage Act does not properly account for arrangements resulting from gestational surrogacy, and this court rejects the Appellate Division's reasoning, which concluded that "a presumption of paternity cannot be understood or interpreted to create a presumption of maternity." N.J. Stat. Ann. § 9:17–38–59. Gestational surrogacy was not in practice or available when the Parentage Act was enacted. This court cannot abdicate its responsibility to ensure that the spirit of the Parentage Act is followed even in novel situations. *See Chambers v. Chambers*, No. CN00–09493, 2002 Del. Fam. Ct. LEXIS 39, at *4, *10 (Del. Fam. Ct. Feb. 5, 2002) (finding that although lesbian partner was not an egg donor, she was still a legal parent).

II LEGAL ISSUES PRESENTED

This court must determine the following issues of law:

Is an infertile married woman who enters into an arrangement with a gestational carrier, impregnated with embryos created with donor eggs and her husband's sperm, in a similar position as an infertile married man who uses donor sperm to impregnate his wife?

If so, is the differential legal treatment of the infertile man for the purposes of determining parentage constitutionally permissible under New Jersey's equal protection jurisprudence?

We find that an infertile married woman who uses a gestational carrier to have a child is similarly situated to an infertile married man who uses a sperm donor to impregnate his wife. Therefore, we hold that treating an infertile married woman differently than an infertile married man violates equal protection guarantees of the New Jersey Constitution.

III ANALYSIS

There are numerous ways that a person can become a parent today compared with when the Parentage Act was enacted. This court will review the changing methods of parenthood and the lack of statutory guidance to demonstrate the context within which we must decide the legal issues of this case. Then, we will discuss why this court disagrees with the lower courts' reliance on the *Baby M.* case and equal protection analysis. We finally invite the New Jersey Legislature ("Legislature") and Governor to update the Parentage Act to reflect the realities of how citizens of New Jersey are becoming parents today.

A *Legal Background*

1 The Expanding History of Parentage

The history of the law of parentage and adoption is relevant to the adjudication of this case. Historically, parentage was seemingly straightforward. Under the common law, "a child's legal parents were the mother who gave birth to that child and the man to whom she was married." Nancy D. Polikoff, A *Mother Should Not Have to Adopt Her Own Child: Parentage Laws for Children of Lesbian Couples in the Twenty-First Century*, 5 STAN. J. CIV. RTS. & CIV. LIBERTIES 201, 208 (2009). Children born out of wedlock had only one legal parent, their birth mother. *Id.* Biological or genetic relationship was irrelevant in the absence of marriage. *Id.* However, in *Stanley v. Illinois*, the U.S. Supreme Court determined that an unmarried father had a right to rear his children, stating that "[t]he rights to conceive and to raise one's children have been deemed 'essential,' 'basic civil rights of man,' and 'rights far more precious than property rights.'" *Stanley v. Illinois*, 405 U.S. 645, 651 (1972). Legislatures began to recognize the many financial, emotional, and other advantages that children gained from having two parents, regardless of marriage or biological connection.

Thus, state statutes allowed paternity proceedings to confer legal parentage on nonmarital biological/genetic fathers, a status that came with both rights and responsibilities. Longstanding adoption statutes have allowed married couples who were not biologically or genetically related to a child to attain parental rights. More recently, adoption laws allowed an unrelated person who married a child's mother or father to become a legal parent, and not just a stepparent. For couples who chose not to marry or could not marry under previous restrictions on same-sex marriage, courts granted second-parent adoptions. These expansions of parenthood were based upon the best interests of the child and those interests included the financial and psychological benefits of having two parents.

Concurrent to law's evolving recognition of legal parentage was the increasing reliance on assisted reproduction. Assisted reproduction was not contemplated at common law, and the issues related to assisted reproduction were not considered by the 1973 Uniform Parentage Act, which our Parentage Act is based upon. Yet endless possibilities of parenthood and genetic connection are now possible due to assisted reproduction. In 1973, when the Uniform Parentage Act was enacted, in vitro fertilization was not being used to aid in childbearing. In fact, Louise Brown, the first person successfully conceived using in vitro fertilization, was born in England in 1978. Janet L. Dolgin, *The Law Debates the Family: Reproductive Transformations*, 7 Yale J.L. & Feminism 37, 86 (1995). In vitro fertilization allows an embryo to be created outside a woman's body with donor gametes that are unrelated to either the intended mother or father. Gestational surrogates carry and deliver a baby to which the surrogate is unrelated and, often, for unrelated intended parents. In other instances, such as in this case, one parent combines his or her genetic material with a donor egg or sperm. For instance, lesbian couples commonly elect to have one member of the couple provide her egg to be fertilized by donor sperm and implanted via in vitro fertilization into the other partner. Courts have struggled to define who is a parent in these types of situations. John L. Hill, *What Does It Mean to Be a "Parent"? The Claims of Biology as the Basis for Parental Rights*, 66 N.Y.U. L. Rev. 353, 372–73 (1991).

2 Lack of Statutory Guidance on Surrogacy in New Jersey

Like many states, New Jersey courts have struggled with how assisted reproduction should affect parental rights, and a confusing and often contradictory body of case law has emerged. This court was one of the earliest to deal with a conflict related to traditional surrogacy in *In re Baby M.*, 537 A.2d 1227

(N.J. 1988) ("Baby M.").[3] Although this court did not ban and has never banned gestational surrogacy, the New Jersey Legislature has failed to enact a law related to gestational surrogacy which would guide intended parents, gestational carriers, the general public, and this court. Because of the lack of statutory guidance, family lawyers who are involved in drafting surrogacy agreements, which set out the rights of gestational carriers and intended parents, are left guessing about what provisions might protect the interests of the state.

Although New Jersey has not previously determined intent as relevant in determinations of parentage, it is time to revisit that policy. Lower courts in New Jersey have been misinterpreting Baby M. and rejecting parties' intent even in cases of gestational surrogacy. For example, a New Jersey lower court case, *A.G.R. v. D.R.H. & S.H.*, No. FD-09-1838-07 (N.J. Super. Ct. Ch. Div., Dec. 23, 2009), mistakenly applied the holding of Baby M. to a gestational surrogacy arrangement. The case involved a married gay couple and a gestational surrogate, who happened to be the sister to one of the men. *Id.* at 2. The gestational surrogate was impregnated using in vitro fertilization with a donor egg and gave birth to twins who were not biologically related to her in October 2006. *Id.* Although she initially surrendered custody to the couple, five months later, the gestational surrogate demanded custody of the twins. *Id.* The New Jersey court lower court found that the gestational surrogate, who had agreed to carry the non-genetically related fetus to term to help her brother and his husband, to be the mother of the twins. *Id.* at 5. Thus, she was awarded her three days of visitation a week. *Id.* The lower court misapplied the Baby M. standard to a gestational surrogacy arrangement. Other states, like California, have explicitly allowed the intent of the parties to be the proper test for parenthood. *See Johnson v. Calvert*, 851 P.2d 776, 783–84 (Cal. 1993). Doing so allows for the autonomy of the parties to be respected, and it avoids the cost, uncertainty, and emotional struggle of adoption.

3 The Intent of the Surrogate and Parents Is the Crux of Our Analysis, not the *Baby M.* Case

Although trial and appellate courts relied on *Baby M.*, the public policy concerns about traditional surrogacy are not relevant to our adjudication

[3] In a traditional surrogacy arrangement, the surrogate is biologically related to the child she is carrying. As a result, the legal issues are much different than a situation involving a gestational surrogate, who agrees to be implanted with an embryo not genetically related to her. Joseph F. Morrissey, *Surrogacy: The Process, Law, and the Contracts*, 51 Willamette L. Rev. 459, 470 (2015).

today. In *Baby M.*, the surrogate agreed to carry a child using an intended father's sperm and her own egg in exchange for payment. The case at hand involves neither compensation for gestational services nor reliance on a traditional surrogate genetically related to the resulting child. A.F. has surrendered all legal claims to T.D.S. and has requested not to be placed on T.D.S.'s birth certificate.

Based on the facts of *Baby M.*, we deemed commercial surrogacy contracts in traditional surrogacy arrangements to be void against public policy. *In re Baby M.*, 537 A.2d 1227 (N.J. 1988). But this court did not disavow all surrogacy arrangements. *Id.* In fact, this court stated that "[w]e find no offense to our present laws where a woman voluntarily and without payment agrees to act as a 'surrogate' mother, provided that she is not subject to a binding agreement to surrender her child." *Id.* In *Baby M.*, this court was concerned that a paid surrogacy arrangement with a woman who was carrying her own child and agreed to give up parental rights prior to birth for money looked very similar to baby selling. *Id.*

The lower courts in this case have misinterpreted *Baby M.* to be a broad rejection of all surrogacy arrangements. At the time *Baby M.* was decided, in vitro fertilization and gestational surrogacy were not prevalent in surrogacy practices. *In re Baby M.*, 537 A.2d at 1227. In *Baby M.*, the surrogate was giving up a child that she was genetically related to. In gestational surrogacy, this genetic connection does not exist. The introduction of these technologies has changed many of the concerns we raised in *Baby M.* In fact, assisted reproduction and gestational surrogacy are increasingly common methods of becoming a parent, even in cases where a gestational carrier is paid to carry a fetus unrelated to her to term. In *Baby M.*, we were also concerned that a woman was being paid to give up her own child. We did not consider the propriety of commercial gestational surrogacy because it did not exist. Nor do we need to today. This is a job for the New Jersey Legislature. Rather, this court is only tasked with determining if infertile married men and infertile married women are similarly situated when they rely on donor gametes in an effort to become parents.

4 Review of Statutory Framework

The plaintiffs ask for A.L.S. to be named on T.D.S.'s birth certificate as T.D.S.'s legal mother after A.F., the gestational carrier gave up any parental rights to T.D.S. afforded to her by the Parentage Act. Birth certificates are issued by the Bureau of Vital Statistics and "memorialize, among other facts, information concerning the relationship of a child to his or her natural or adoptive parents." *In re Parentage of T.J.S.*, 16 A.3d at 389–90. As noted by Judge Parillo below, "a birth certificate simply records the fact of parentage as reported by others; it neither constitutes a legal finding of parentage nor independently creates or terminates parental rights." *Id.* In order for an individual's name to appear as a parent on a child's birth certificate, the Registration of Vital Statistics Act requires the existence of a legally cognizable parent-child relationship. N.J. Stat. Ann. § 26:8-1–69 (West 2007). This court holds today that such a relationship exists between A.L.S. and T.D.S. and that finding otherwise would violate equal protection guaranteed by our state constitution.

The Appellate Division notes that the Parentage Act was adopted in 1983 and was based upon the Uniform Parentage Act of 1973. *In re Parentage of T.J.S.*, 16 A.3d at 389–90. The Parentage Act "was created to ensure that children born out of wedlock are treated the same as those born to married parents and to provide a procedure to establish parentage in disputed cases." Assembly Judiciary, Law, Public Safety and Defense Committee, Statement to Senate Bill No. 888, 2 (1982). It was designed to "make the identification of a child's father easier and thereby reduce the number of children requiring public assistance." *Fazilat v. Feldstein*, 848 A.2d 761, 768 (N.J. 2004). Thus, the plain language reading by Judge Parillo does not comport with the reality of the facts facing A.L.S. and T.J.S here. *See In re T.J.S.*, 16 A.3d 386 (N.J. 2011). This court cannot bury its head in the sand until the New Jersey Legislature acts to update its laws to reflect the myriad ways that in vitro fertilization and gestational surrogacy have changed how children are born today.

The Parentage Act defines the "parent and child relationship" as "the legal relationship existing between a child and the child's natural or adoptive parents, incident to which the law confers or imposes rights, privileges, duties, and obligations. It includes the mother and child relationship and the father and child relationship." N.J. Stat. Ann. § 9:17–39 (West 2018). As noted by Judge Parillo, under the plain language of the Parentage Act, parenthood is established in the following ways: (1) genetic contribution; (2) gestational primacy, i.e., giving birth; or (3) adoption. *In re Parentage of T.J.S.*, 16 A.3d at 391 (citing N.J. Stat. Ann. § 9:17–41, 41(a), and 41(c)) (West 2018). In addition, "a rebuttable presumption of paternity derives from the parties' legal relationship, i.e., marriage or its equivalent, when a child is born during the course of a marriage or within 300 days of its termination." N.J. Stat. Ann. § 9:17–43(a)(1) (West 2018). This presumption, that a man is the father of a child born to his wife, extends to a husband who consents to his wife being inseminated with donor sperm under the supervision of a licensed physician. N.J. Stat. Ann. § 9:17–44(a) (West 2018); *In re Parentage of T.J.S.*, 16 A.3d at 391.

The parental presumption contained in Section 43(a) only applies to fathers, not mothers. N.J. Stat. Ann. § 9:17–43(a) (West 2018). Thus, when a married couple utilizes the services of a gestational surrogate due to the female's infertility, she is not presumed to be the mother. The intended mother's only recourse is adoption. N.J. Stat. Ann. § 9:3–37–56. Similarly, Section 44 only applies to an infertile husband. N.J. Stat. Ann. § 9:17–44 (West 2018). The Appellate Division suggests that this is proper because "as noted in the adoption context, any such provision would conflict with the express legislative enactment affording a birth mother seventy-two hours to decide whether to relinquish the child before a surrender of her parental rights is deemed valid." *In re Parentage of T.J.S.*, 16 A.3d at 391 (citing N.J. Stat. Ann. § 9:3–41(e) (West 1994)).

Although New Jersey does not ban noncommercial surrogacy or even commercial gestational surrogacy, the legislature has yet to enact a bill that appropriately governs surrogacy. Thus, this court is forced to use existing statutes that do not describe accurately the surrogacy situation. Our adoption statute is often the statute used to examine certain aspects of surrogacy in New Jersey, although surrogacy is distinct from adoption. Adoption is anticipated after a woman is pregnant, not before, as in the case of surrogacy, and is governed by a complicated set of laws and procedures.[4] This state's adoption statute contains a seventy-two-hour waiting requirement because it contemplates a birth mother struggling with whether or not to give up her biological child. N.J. Stat. Ann. § 9:17–41(c) (West 2018). One of the key purposes of adoption law is to ensure certainty and clarity for the birth mother and the adoptive parents. In the case of a woman who is carrying a child unrelated to her for another party per an agreement signed before pregnancy, the need for such a seventy-two-hour period is less important or meaningful. *See In re T.J.S.*, 16 A.3d 386 (N.J. 2011). This is just one of many examples of how New Jersey's lack of legislative guidance in the area of surrogacy results in courts using inapplicable laws to make important determinations of the rights of parties to surrogacy agreements.

[4] Through a carefully regulated court proceeding, the state creates the status of parent and child between individuals who are not genetically related and severs the child's relationship to the genetic parents and their families. N.J. Stat. Ann. § 9:3–39.1(West 2012). "Once an adoption decree has been issued, the adoptive family replaces and becomes the legal equivalent of the biogenetic family for all purposes under the law. The adoptee receives a new birth certificate with the names of her adoptive parents substituted for the names of the woman and man, if any, listed as her parents at birth." NAOMI CAHN & JOAN HEIFETZ HOLLINGER, FAMILIES BY LAW: AN ADOPTION READER 1 (2004).

Unlike adoption, in gestational surrogacy there is no severing of any existing legal relationship. The intended parents are those who have entered into the gestational surrogacy arrangement with the gestational carrier. Additionally, unlike a birth mother who decides after her pregnancy to relinquish the baby she delivers, a gestational carrier only becomes pregnant to deliver a child for the intended parents. The child would not exist were it not for the people who intended to become the child's parents. Additionally, the gestational carrier in this case, who is trying to help another couple, does not want to be on the birth certificate of a baby who is not related to her and should not be saddled with the duties of parenthood. Her intent should be relevant in determining parentage in New Jersey.

The New Jersey Legislature recently passed a bill that would have permitted, under prescribed conditions, pre-birth orders naming the intended parents as the sole legal parents of a child conceived through gestational surrogacy. *See* S. 1599, 215th Leg. (N.J. 2012); A. 2646, 215th Leg. (N.J. 2012). The New Jersey Gestational Carrier Agreement Act would have mandated various regulatory safeguards, including the requirements that gestational carriers "be at least 21 years of age, have given birth to at least one child, have completed medical and psychological evaluations[,] . . . and have retained an attorney independent of the intended parent." S. Health, Human Servs. & Senior Citizens Comm., Statement to S. Bill No. 1599 (May 17, 2012). Had such law been enacted, intended parents would be deemed legal parents prior to birth regardless of genetic connection. Additionally, a gestational carrier would have been required to "agree to surrender custody of the child to the intended parent immediately upon the child's birth" in the gestational carrier agreement. The Governor vetoed this bill because he believed that the legislature had not "sufficiently studied" "serious and significant issues" concerning gestational surrogacy. Governor's Veto Message to S. Bill No. 1599 (Aug. 9, 2012). Therefore, the courts in New Jersey are left without clear guidance about how the legislature intends its laws to be interpreted in cases of gestational surrogacy.[5] In spite of this, our review of the facts and applicable laws finds that the current law impermissibly treats infertile married women who use a willing surrogate to have a child differently from an infertile married man who uses a sperm donor to have child in violation of New Jersey's equal protection right.

[5] The New Jersey bill allowing gestational surrogacy is in keeping with the trend nationwide of legalizing surrogacy. *See, e.g.*, Ala. Code § 26-17-801 (West); Tex. Fam. Code Ann. § 160.754 (West 2003); Utah Code Ann. § 78B-15-801 (West 2008).

B *Equal Protection Claim of A.L.S. and T.J.S.*

What this court must determine is whether the state can justify the different treatment of infertile married men and infertile married women, both of whom rely on donated gametes, though women must seek the services of gestational carriers, under the Parentage Age.

The Equal Protection Clause of the U.S. Constitution mandates that no state shall "deny to any person within its jurisdiction the equal protection of the laws." U.S. Const. Amend. 14, § 1. Although the New Jersey Constitution does not contain an equal protection clause, this court has held that the concept of equal protection is implicit in the New Jersey State Constitution. *McKenney v. Byrne*, 412 A.2d 1041, 1046 (N.J. 1980). In fact, we have held that our state equal protection guarantee may in fact be even "broader than the right provided by the [federal] Equal Protection Clause." *Doe v. Poritz*, 662 A.2d 367, 414 (N.J. 1995); *State v. Chun*, 943 A.2d 114, 141–43 (N.J. 2008). Thus, New Jersey courts' analysis of equal protection does not begin by assessing the status of a particular protected class or the fundamental nature of the implicated right, which is the equal protection paradigm of the federal courts. *Id.* Instead, we apply a balancing test that weighs the "nature of the affected right, the extent to which the governmental restriction intrudes upon it, and the public need for the restriction." *Caviglia v. Royal Tours of Am.*, 842 A.2d 125, 132 (N.J. 2004). Thus, in New Jersey, the disparate treatment must "bear a real and substantial relationship to a permissible legislative purpose." *Taxpayers Ass'n of Weymouth Twp. v. Weymouth Twp.*, 364 A.2d 1016, 1037 (N.J. 1976).

Under our current law, unlike an infertile husband, an infertile wife has no right to have her name placed on the birth certificate as the natural mother under the Parentage Act and is burdened by the cost, legal uncertainty, and the delay of adoption. *In re T.J.S.*, 16 A.3d 386, 398 (N.J. 2011). We decide today, in light of the factual circumstances of this case, that the New Jersey Constitution requires an infertile wife to be treated equally – that her name be placed on the birth certificate as the natural mother as would happen if she were an infertile husband under N.J. Stat. Ann. § 9:17–44(a) (West 2018). In rejecting the need for parity in this scenario, the Appellate Division did not find the infertile husband in 44(a) similarly situated to A.L.S. here. *In re T.J.S.*, 16 A.3d 386, 398 (N.J. 2011). The panel stated that "the surrogate mother whose parental rights are deemed worthy of protection … stand in the way of the infertile wife's claim to automatic motherhood." *In re Parentage of T.J.S.*, 16 A.3d at 395–96.

Contrary to the Appellate Division's holding, the gestational carrier in this case does not wish to stand in the way of A.L.S.'s claims to motherhood. *In re*

T.J.S., 16 A.3d 386, 389 (N.J. 2011). The gestational carrier has not been coerced into giving up her child by payment as was a concern in *Baby M.*

A.F. has joined in the petition and certified that she wishes to relinquish the parental rights foisted on her by the Parentage Act. *In re T.J.S.*, 16 A.3d 386, 389 (N.J. 2011). If this court faces a case of a gestational carrier that may in the future object to the intended mother's parental rights at a later date, we will need to grapple with those facts. However, the general rights accorded to gestational carriers are not at issue in the case before us, as there is no objecting surrogate in this case. Additionally, the seventy-two-hour waiting period is meant to ensure effective consent and a gestational carrier can always object within that time period.

A legal scheme that treats differently those who should be treated alike violates the equal-protection guarantee of Article I, Paragraph 1 of the New Jersey Constitution. The Appellate Division held that our state Constitution's equal-protection guarantee did not require that an infertile wife be afforded the same benefits conferred on the infertile husband under the Artificial Insemination Statute. N.J. Stat. Ann. § 9:17–44 (West 2018); *In re Parentage of T.J.S.*, 16 A.3d at 395–99. The panel reasoned that A.L.S. was not similarly situated to the infertile man because of "the introduction of a birth mother whom the law cloaks with superior protection." *Id.* The panel felt that the existence of a gestational carrier was enough to differentiate the infertile husband who used a sperm donor but earned automatic parental rights under the Artificial Insemination Statute from A.L.S.'s situation. N.J. Stat. Ann. § 9:17–44 (West 2018); *In re Parentage of T.J.S.*, 16 A.3d at 395–99.The panel's reasoning would be compelling if A.F. was attempting to assert a parental right. However, she was not.

It is important to analyze whether this gender distinction between infertile husbands and infertile wives is "based on real physiological differences," in which case it would be afforded more protection; or whether it is "based on archaic, invidious stereotypes about men and women," in which case it would be afforded less protection. *See State v. Vogt*, 775 A.2d 551, 557–58 (N.J. Super. App. Div. 2001) (recognizing that "[t]he Equal Protection Clause . . . does not demand that things that are different in fact be treated the same in law, nor that a state pretend that there are no physiological differences between men and women").

The Parentage Act is intended to ensure that "all children and parents have equal rights with respect to each other and to provide a procedure to establish parentage in disputed cases." Sponsor's Statement, Statement to S. Bill No. 888 (Jan. 19, 1982); *see also* S. Judiciary Comm. Statement to S. Bill No. 888 (June 21, 1982); *R.A.C. v. P.J.S., Jr.*, 927 A.2d 97, 104 (N.J. 2007). The

Parentage Act allows an action to be brought against any person – including a mother – "for the purpose of determining the existence . . . of the parent and child relationship." N.J. Stat. Ann. § 9:17–45(a) (West 1998). Seeking adequate child support from fathers was a primary concern of the Parentage Act. *R.A.C. v. P.J.S., Jr.*, 927 A.2d at 104. *See also Fazilat v. Feldstein*, 848 A.2d at 765–66 (holding that the New Jersey Parentage Act helps families deal with the problems posed by fathers who seek to avoid paying child support). Specifically, the Parentage Act, by delineating how to establish parentage, guarantees that children will receive the financial support that is rightfully due from their parents. *R.A.C. v. P.J.S.*, Jr., 927 A.2d at 104. It is important to understand the nature of the right that is at stake – the right of an infertile wife to be considered a natural parent no different than an infertile husband – and that this right is being impinged upon by requiring an infertile woman to adopt a child conceived with help from a gestational carrier when an infertile man who gets help from a sperm donor is automatically named the child's parent without having to go through the adoption procedure.

1 Nature of the Affected Right

The right at issue here is the right an infertile married man has, by state statute, to be named the natural father of a non-genetically related child conceived by assisted reproduction. An infertile married woman who uses assisted reproduction is entitled to "equality of treatment relative to comparable" infertile married men. *Lewis v. Harris*, 908 A.2d 196, 215 (N.J. 2006).

The Artificial Insemination Statute confers parentage upon an infertile man who has no genetic connection to the child. Thus, this man enjoys the rights and responsibilities of parenthood without having to go through the slow, costly, and sometimes uncertain process of adoption. N.J. Stat. Ann. § 9:17–44 (West 2018). An infertile wife, like A.L.S., has no such benefit. Instead, she must go through the time-consuming, expensive adoption process. *In re T.J.S.*, 16 A.3d 386 (N.J. 2011). This not only disadvantages the woman but also the child. The benefits conferred on the infertile husband are passed on to his child, who receives the promise of financial support, rights of inheritance, and myriad other statutory protections. Other benefits include life insurance, worker's compensation, and social security benefits. *In re Adoption of Baby T.*, 709 A.2d 1381, 1385–86 (N.J. Super. Ct. App. Div. 1998); *see also In re Adoption of Child by J.M.G.*, 632 A.2d 550, 552 (N.J. Super. Ct. Ch. Div. 1993).

The child in this case, whose gestational carrier relinquished her parental rights seventy-two hours after his birth, is left legally motherless, and is disadvantaged in ways that the child of the infertile husband is not. *Lewis v. Harris*, 908 A.2d at 216–17. Thus, the nature of the right – the right of an infertile wife to be considered a natural parent no different than an infertile husband – is substantial.

2 How the State Intrudes upon This Right

This right is significantly burdened by the failure of the Parentage Act to treat infertile wives equally. Requiring adoption is more than a mere inconvenience. Not only is adoption expensive and time-consuming, but when an intended parent is required to adopt, she has no certainty that she will actually be legally recognized by the state as a parent. John Robertson, *Gay and Lesbian Access to Assisted Reproductive Technology*, 55 CASE W. RES. L. REV. 323, 350 (2004). Furthermore, she will have to retain a lawyer, pay court fees and related expenses, and may suffer from emotional anxiety for the months it will take to obtain the state's approval. Anthony J. Vecchio, *Current Issue in Public Policy: The Unequal Application of New Jersey's Artificial Insemination Act*, 5 RUTGERS J.L. & PUB. POL'Y 594, 608 (2008) ("[T]he adoption process in New Jersey can be time consuming and costly").

A married infertile male who used assisted reproduction will begin enjoying the benefits of parenthood immediately. In contrast, a similarly situated married infertile woman will not. Even more significantly, the child will not have the benefit of the woman as her mother. In this case, T.D.S. will be legally motherless from the time that A.F. relinquishes her maternal rights, seventy-two hours after birth, until A.L.S.'s adoption proceeding is successful, which can take several months. N.J. Stat. Ann. § 9:3–41(e) (West 1994). This is a significant intrusion on her right of parenthood and is analogous to the uphill battle to the right to parent faced by many unmarried fathers, who must establish not only a biological connection to a child but also a relationship; married fathers need not establish either. Prior to *Stanley v. Illinois*, 405 U.S. 645, 648–50 (1972), states often denied parentage rights to unwed fathers. Even after *Stanley*, unmarried fathers often were not recognized as parents. For example, in *Nguyen v. INS*, 533 U.S. 53, 63 (2001), the U.S. Supreme Court found no equal protection violation, in part because "[f]athers and mothers are not similarly situated with regard to the proof of biological parenthood … Given the proof of motherhood that is inherent in birth itself, it is unremarkable that Congress did not require the same affirmative steps of mothers." *Id.* at 64. Additionally, parentage determinations often consider the best interests of the child. Here, having T.D.S. potentially motherless for several months seems to completely ignore T.D.S.'s well-being or best interests.

3 The Public Need for the Restriction

The disparate treatment here of an infertile woman and an infertile man is not based on physiological differences. The lower courts point to the presence of a gestational surrogate as a difference in this case. To be sure, if A.F. was disputing A.L.S.'s claim of maternity and seeking it herself, this would be a different case. In surrogacy arrangements, there is a need to protect gestational surrogates' rights and autonomy. *See* Seema Mohapatra, *Stateless Babies & Adoption Scams: A Bioethical Analysis of International Commercial Surrogacy*, 30 Berkeley J. Int'l L. 412, 415–17 (2012). Specifically, some have argued that gestation itself may be sufficient for a biological claim for parenthood, even if there is not a genetic connection to the baby.[6] However, that is not the issue in this case as A.F. has repeatedly requested that A.L.S.'s name, and not hers, be placed on the baby's birth certificate.

Rather, establishing fathers' parentage is presumed to ensure a child's financial support because of archaic stereotypes that fathers are the dominant income-earners and without legal parentage there is no legal duty for fathers to provide support to their child. However, today, both parents, regardless of gender, often financially support the child, and if the parents' relationship ends, both are legally obligated to financially support a child. In fact, requiring an intended mother unrelated to a child to undergo the expense, hassle, and uncertainty of an adoption proceeding deprives the child of a legal mother who can provide both financial and emotional support. This does not seem tied to a legitimate state interest.

In fact, this actually thwarts the purpose of the Parentage Act, ensuring a child's financial support. *See Robinson*, 890 A.2d 1036, 1041–42 (N.J. Super. Ct. Ch. Div. 2005) (ruling that public policy establishes that interest of child is paramount and that benefits from having two legal parents include economic security, right to support, and right to inherit by intestacy). Denying the infertile wife and her intended child the same benefits and privileges given to her male counterpart and his intended child bears no substantial relationship to a legitimate governmental purpose and abridges her right to the equal protection of the laws. The Appellate Division acknowledged "the intrinsic societal worth, emotional appeal, and compelling logic of granting [the intended mother]

[6] There is a need to protect gestational surrogates' decision-making ability and power in situations where intended parents may have more clout and deeper pockets. Many legislatures have ensured protection for gestational surrogates by enacting legislation that requires that intended parents pay for a gestational surrogate's own attorney when negotiating a contract. Jennifer S. Hendricks, *Essentially a Mother*, 13 Wm. & Mary J. Women & L. 429, 477 (2007).

parenthood to the child." *In re Parentage of T.J.S.*, 16 A.3d at 396. Until the legislature enacts a law governing gestational surrogacy, courts must intercede to apply the commonsense reading of state statutes governing parentage in novel situations. Requiring an intended mother to petition to adopt her own non-genetically related child when an intended father does not have the same responsibility does not serve any legitimate state purpose.

Whenever possible, New Jersey courts attempt to construe a statute in a way that preserves its validity. This court has noted that "the overriding judicial function is to determine legislative intent and this prevails over the plain language of the statute." *Roig v. Kelsey*, 641 A.2d 248, 256–57 (N.J. 1994). We held in *Wollen v. Borough of Fort Lee* that "it is not the words, but the internal sense of the statute which governs." 142 A.3d 881, 886–87 (N.J. 1958). In *State v. Hill*, this court noted that we "would (expand or contract statutory language) if we believed that there were any genuine need to perform 'judicial surgery' on this statute." 714 A.2d 311, 313–14 (N.J. 1998).[7] This is precisely such a case: "Where a literal interpretation would create a manifestly absurd result, contrary to public policy, the spirit of the law should control." *Perrelli v. Pastorelle*, 20 A.3d 354, 358–59 (N.J. 2006). Accordingly, "when a 'literal interpretation of individual statutory terms or provisions' would lead to results 'inconsistent with the overall purpose of the statute,' that interpretation should be rejected." *Id.*

Reading this provision of the Artificial Insemination Statute broadly to apply to assisted reproduction including gestational surrogacy will serve the statute's purpose in ensuring financial support of the child. To be sure, to do otherwise would mean that T.D.S. would be motherless for the time it takes for A.L.S. to be approved as an adoptive parent. If T.J.S dies within seventy-two hours of T.D.S.'s birth, A.F., the surrogate, would be the legal parent of T.D.S. in contravention of her intention. Then, if A.F. relinquishes her rights, T.D.S. would be parentless. Similarly, if T.J.S dies after seventy-two hours of T.D.S.'s birth but before the adoption, T.D.S. would be motherless. If A.L.S. dies before she is able to adopt T.D.S., T.D.S. will be deprived of any death benefits that may be accorded to A.L.S.'s children. Both women and men should have the benefit that the statute on its face only affords to men. It is important for the legislature to act to update the Parentage Act to reflect the

[7] *See also Roig v. Kelsey*, 641 A.2d 248 (N.J. 1994); *Petrozzino v. Monroe Calculating Mach. Co., Inc.*, 222 A.2d 73, 73–74 (N.J. 1966) (looking beyond plain language of statute to find that child of working mother was entitled to equal presumption of dependency as other children of deceased claimants even though statute was not gender neutral); *see also* Stewart G. Pollock, *The Art of Judging*, 71 N.Y.U. L. REV. 591, 599 (June 1996) (describing process by which courts expand and contract statutory language when they believe it consistent with legislative intent).

realities of parenthood today. It is in the state's interest to ensure that all parties involved in parentage are protected. The Parentage Act primarily protects individuals who have genetic ties to their child. However, intent and care are just as important in determining who is a parent, and we encourage the legislature to amend the Parentage Act to reflect this. Many families raise children that they are not genetically related to, outside of the traditional adoption paradigm. Same-sex couples and others who are not able to be genetically related to their child are no less parents and they should not have to resort to adoption if their intent is to parent. Thus, we invite the legislature to update the Parentage Act to use gender-neutral terminology to afford same-sex parents the same protections as opposite-sex parents. In the meantime, we urge lower courts in New Jersey to allow pre-birth orders as A.L.S. and T.J.S. properly requested here with the consent of their gestational carrier A.F. Although the need for the seventy-two-hour window is not clear in cases of surrogacy, as mentioned earlier, until the legislature acts, any pre-birth orders for birth certificates should reflect this time period to comport with current, although imprecise law, in this arena.

As noted, earlier, this case does not require us to make a moral or public policy judgment about gestational surrogacy. Rather, we are required to decide the issue before us – that of equal treatment of an infertile married woman and an infertile married man utilizing assisted reproduction to have a child. The state's interest in a two-parent family is advanced, not impaired, by promoting equality of treatment in the circumstances of this case. *In re Marriage of Buzzanca*, 72 Cal.Rptr.2d 280, 289 (Cal. Ct. App. 1998) ("It would be lunatic for the Legislature to declare that establishing paternity is a compelling state interest yet conclude that establishing maternity is not"). The arbitrary gender classification in this case cannot masquerade as a legitimate public need.

In reality, not allowing A.L.S. to be named as a legal mother on the birth certificate is contrary to the public interest and undermines the goals of the Parentage Act. Until he or she is adopted by the intended mother, a child will be deprived of the many benefits "of having two legal parents." *In re Parentage of Child of Robinson*, 890 A.2d at 1037.

IV CONCLUSION

Here, New Jersey has bestowed upon an infertile husband and his intended child conceived via assisted reproduction the right to be a legal parent, via the Artificial Insemination Statute. Thus, the Parentage Act must afford a similarly situated infertile wife and her intended child the same right. Just as the

Department allows an infertile husband's name to be placed on the birth certificate of his non-genetic child through artificial insemination, the Department must allow the name of A.L.S. to be placed on the birth certificate of her intended child after the surrogate's knowing and voluntary relinquishment of her parental rights. Any other decision unfairly disadvantages not just the infertile wife, but also her intended child. The unequal dispensation of benefits and privileges to an infertile married woman, A.L.S., on the basis of her sex abridges her right to the equal protection of the laws in violation of Article I, Paragraph 1 of the New Jersey Constitution.

For that reason, we reverse the judgment of the Appellate Division and remand to the lower court to enter the name of A.L.S. as the mother of the T.D.S. without the need to resort to an adoption proceeding.

15

Commentary on *Matter of* A-B-

NATALIE NANASI

INTRODUCTION

For the nearly four decades since international refugee protections were codified in U.S. law, uncertainty has existed regarding whether survivors of intimate partner violence comprise a "particular social group" ("PSG") that entitles them to asylum protection in the United States.[1] Litigation in the first domestic-violence-based asylum case to reach the Board of Immigration Appeals ("BIA"), *Matter of* R-A-,[2] dragged on for fourteen years without resulting in precedent. Thereafter, in a move that would astonish strict adherents of civil procedure, advocates seeking asylum for clients who had endured intimate partner abuse would cite a *brief* authored by the Department of Homeland Security in another domestic violence asylum case, *Matter of L-R-*, in support of their arguments.[3] Then, in 2014, the BIA issued a decision in *Matter of* A-R-C-G- that definitively established the right to asylum for survivors of intimate partner violence.[4] The Board granted relief to Ms. C-G- based on her membership in the particular social group of "married women in Guatemala who are unable to leave their relationship."

The certainty provided by *Matter of* A-R-C-G- was, however, short-lived. In June of 2018, Attorney General Jeff Sessions issued a decision in *Matter of*

[1] In order to be eligible for asylum, an applicant must demonstrate that she has faced or fears future persecution on account of one of five grounds enumerated in the refugee definition – race, religion, nationality, membership in a particular social group or political opinion. INA § 208(b)(1)(B)(i).

[2] *In re R-A-*, 22 I. & N. Dec. 906 (B.I.A. 1999), *vacated*, 22 I. & N. Dec. 906 (Att'y Gen. 2001), *remanded*, 23 I. & N. Dec. 694 (Att'y Gen. 2005), *stay lifted*, 24 I. & N. Dec. 629 (Att'y Gen. 2008).

[3] Department of Homeland Security's Supplemental Brief, *In re L-R-*, [redacted] (B.I.A. Apr. 13, 2009), http://cgrs.uchastings.edu/sites/default/files/Matter_of_LR_DHS_Brief_4_13_2009.pdf

[4] 26 I. & N. Dec. 388 (B.I.A. 2014).

A-B-, a case that not only overrules *Matter of* A-R-C-G-, but makes the sweeping assertion that claims "pertaining to domestic violence ... perpetrated by non-governmental actors will not qualify for asylum."[5] In reaching his decision, Sessions relies on antiquated notions of family violence as a "private" matter and ignores the cultural context of male privilege and misogyny that allows men to abuse with impunity.

In contrast, Professor Suzan Pritchett's feminist judgment envisions a Department of Justice that possesses a nuanced approach to domestic violence. It utilizes international perspectives to understand the issues that underlie the disparate treatment of survivors of intimate partner violence, including the reinforcement of male privilege in law, culture, and society and the lack of sufficient resources to adequately address domestic abuse. The feminist judgment in *Matter of* A-B- not only affirms the right to asylum for survivors, but uses the case as a vehicle to overturn harmful case law governing PSGs in asylum law more generally, returning to formulations that take both international law and lives of survivors into account.

THE ATTORNEY GENERAL'S OPINION IN *MATTER OF A-B-*

Attorney General Jeff Sessions referred *Matter of* A-B- to himself in March of 2018,[6] with the stated goal of seeking to answer the question of "whether, and under what circumstances, being a victim of private criminal activity constitutes a cognizable 'particular social group' for purposes of an application for asylum."[7] Three months later, in an opinion rife with dicta, Sessions overruled *Matter of* A-R-C-G- and generally cast doubt on the viability of asylum claims based on domestic violence.[8]

5 27 I. & N. Dec. 316, 320 (B.I.A. 2018).

6 The manner in which *Matter of A-B-* reached the Attorney General's desk is a matter of some controversy. The case was originally heard by an Immigration Judge (IJ) in Charlotte, North Carolina, who denied Ms. A-B-'s claim. The BIA reversed on appeal and remanded the case to the IJ for approval. However, the IJ did not do as instructed in the appellate court's order and instead attempted to recertify the case to the Board. At some point thereafter, the Attorney General learned of the decision (through unknown means) and certified the case to himself. Although Attorneys General have the legal authority to review decisions by the BIA, 8 C.F.R. 1003.1(h)(1)(i), Sessions exercised this authority significantly more frequently than his predecessors. In his twenty-one-month tenure at the Department of Justice, he certified to himself as many cases as Attorneys General Lynch and Holder combined during the Obama administration. Jeffrey Chase, *The A.G.'s Certifying of BIA Decisions*, JEFFREYSCHASE.COM (Mar. 29, 2018), https://www.jeffreyschase.com/blog/2018/3/29/the-ags-certifying-of-bia-decisions

7 27 I. & N. Dec. 227 (A.G. 2018).

8 27 I. & N. Dec. 316 (A.G. 2018).

Analyzing the PSG recognized by the Board of Immigration Appeals in *Matter of A-R-C-G-*, the Attorney General first restates existing law, which requires a PSG to possess "social distinction," or "evidence showing that society in general perceives, considers, or recognizes persons sharing the particular characteristic to be a group."[9] Sessions then states that the group "married women in Guatemala who are unable to leave their relationship" lacks the requisite social distinction because "there is significant room for doubt that Guatemalan society views these women, as horrible as their personal circumstances may be, as members of a distinct group in society, rather than each as a victim of a particular abuser in highly individualized circumstances."[10] He goes on to reject the BIA's finding of nexus[11] in *Matter of A-R-C-G-*, based on his view that Ms. C-G-'s husband "attacked her because of his preexisting personal relationship with the victim,"[12] a finding that justifies and reinforces his conception of intimate partner abuse as "private violence."[13]

Sessions also deviates from the BIA's prior holdings regarding "state action," the requirement that persecution be perpetrated either by the government or a nonstate actor that the government is unable or unwilling to control. He states, "the fact that the local police have not acted on a particular report of an individual crime does not necessarily mean that the government is unwilling or unable to control crime, any more than it would in the United States."[14] Sessions then, without providing a citation or rationale for his departure from longstanding and established precedent, creates a new, heightened standard for state action, demanding that an applicant "show more than the government's difficulty controlling private behavior" but instead that the government either condoned or "demonstrated a complete helplessness to protect" her from persecution.[15] Ultimately, he concludes that "the mere fact that a country may have problems effectively policing certain crimes – such as domestic violence or

[9] *In re W-G-R-*, 26 I. & N. Dec. 208, 217 (B.I.A. 2014); *see also In re M-E-V-G-*, 26 I. & N. Dec. 227, 228 (B.I.A. 2014).

[10] *Matter of A-B-* at 336.

[11] The refugee definition requires an applicant to demonstrate a nexus between the persecution suffered and a protected characteristic. 8 U.S.C. § 1101(a)(42)(A) (2012); Immigration and Nationality Act § 101(a)(42)(A). In other words, to obtain asylum in the United States, one must show that the harm suffered was "on account of" that person's race, religion, nationality, membership in a particular social group, or political opinion. *Id.*

[12] *Matter of A-B-* at 339.

[13] *Id.* at 319.

[14] *Id.* at 337.

[15] *Id.*

gang violence – or that certain populations are more likely to be victims of crime, cannot itself establish an asylum claim."[16]

THE FEMINIST JUDGMENT

Professor Pritchett, writing as Attorney General Pritchett, takes a wholly different approach from Attorney General Sessions. Although she humbly states that her opinion seeks only "to bring clarity to the jurisprudence of gender-based asylum claims," it in fact does much more. She preserves the core holding of *Matter of A-R-C-G-* that grants asylum to those who have experienced intimate partner violence but also uses the decision to expand and clarify, rather than restrict, eligibility for survivors.

Pritchett's opinion begins by placing *Matter of A-R-C-G-* in an international and comparative context. Because U.S. asylum law was enacted in response to a treaty obligation, in the aftermath of human rights violations perpetrated by state actors in World War II, one must understand the historical framework of the Refugee Convention before undertaking an analysis of the asylum provisions in the Immigration and Nationality Act.

The feminist judgment highlights the public/private distinction that originated in international law, wherein, for example, a violation such as rape that occurs in the public sphere of "politics, government and the state" is considered a human rights violation, unlike a rape that occurs in the privacy of one's home or within one's family.[17] As a result of this dichotomy, in asylum law, the persecution faced by survivors of intimate partner violence is subordinated to the harms suffered by political dissidents, despite the fact that the violence each group endures (e.g., torture, rape, physical abuse) is often identical. Pritchett's opinion thus rightly surfaces the gendered nature of this distinction and challenges the rationale behind distinguishing between public and private violence, noting that intimate partner abuse is "a powerful tool of oppression" that is inflicted on account of power imbalances and subordination in both the private and public spheres.

The most significant portion of Pritchett's opinion is her analysis of "particular social group," the ground routinely utilized by survivors of intimate partner abuse to seek asylum. The feminist judgment departs from Sessions's opinion in two major ways. First, it directs a return to the original particular social group definition articulated by the Board (in the 1987 case *Matter of*

[16] *Id.* at 320.

[17] Hilary Charlesworth, *Feminist Methods in International Law*, 93 AM. J. INT'L L. 379, 382 (1999).

Acosta): individuals who share "a common, immutable characteristic" that either cannot be changed or is so fundamental to the individuals' identities or consciences that they should not be required to change it.[18] In doing so, the feminist judgment overrules a post-*Acosta* line of cases that require particular social groups to possess "social distinction"[19] and be sufficiently "particular,"[20] requirements that Pritchett argues run counter to international standards and both disproportionately and adversely impact women seeking legal protection in the United States.

With a return to *Acosta*'s more equitable particular social group definition, the opinion asserts, again based on established international and domestic law, that gender alone would be the most appropriate PSG for individuals seeking asylum based on intimate partner violence. A gender-only PSG, according to Pritchett, avoids many of the problems presented by the "unable to leave" formulations advanced in prior cases, namely that they are both over- and underinclusive, failing to provide protection to those who do not present as weak or passive victims lacking in agency but also denying relief to those who do not fit its otherwise narrow parameters.

Pritchett next turns to "nexus" and unambiguously asserts that domestic violence is perpetrated because of the victim's gender. Unlike Sessions, she does not focus on the perpetrator's personal failings, such as a "violent and jealous nature," to justify abusive behavior. Instead, taking into account the nuanced and complex social and cultural dynamic in which domestic violence is perpetrated, Pritchett's opinion recognizes that domestic abuse is rooted in broad-based, and often state-sanctioned, violence against women.

Lastly, Professor Pritchett uses *Matter of A-B-* as a vehicle to clarify the state action requirement in asylum claims. Taking a holistic view of the refugee definition, she draws from existing asylum jurisprudence to create a new test to determine whether the government is "unwilling or unable" to control a private actor, namely, whether the government has taken "measures that reduce the risk of persecution to below the well-founded fear … threshold." The feminist judgment recognizes the futility of seeking government protection in countries where laws prohibiting domestic violence are ineffective and

[18] *In re Acosta*, 19 I. & N. Dec. 211, 212 (B.I.A. 1985), *overruled in part on other grounds by In re Mogharrabi*, 19 I. & N. Dec. 439 (B.I.A. 1987).

[19] *See infra* note 9.

[20] The BIA has defined particularity as "whether the proposed group can accurately be described in a manner sufficiently distinct that the group would be recognized, in the society in question, as a discrete class of persons." *In re S-E-G-*, 24 I. & N. Dec. 579, 584 (B.I.A. 2008); *see also In re A-M-E & J-G-U-*, 24 I. & N. Dec. 69, 73 (B.I.A. 2007).

unenforced, and in doing so, acknowledges that when it comes to violence against women, state inaction is a form of complicity.

THE REWRITTEN OPINION'S RETURN TO FAIRNESS AND GENDER EQUITY

Professor Pritchett's opinion is heavily grounded in both context and women's lived experiences, which gives it both its strength and its feminist perspective.[21] Her analysis stems from understanding intimate partner violence in various frameworks, including: historical, political (i.e., the notion that domestic abuse results from and perpetuates both male privilege and female subordination), the cultural and social conditions in survivors' countries of origin, and the actual experiences of survivors who bravely rise up against their abusers but must also often navigate the complex asylum system alone. Feminist ideals manifest in many aspects of the opinion, but given space constraints, I will address here only its meaningful contributions to the two most significant elements of the refugee definition raised in Professor Pritchett's opinion: particular social group and nexus.

A Return to *Matter of Acosta*'s Formulation of Particular Social Group

As noted above, a series of decisions after *Matter of Acosta* developed onerous requirements for viable particular social groups. Although facially neutral, demanding "social distinction" and "particularity" has an adverse impact on the asylum petitions of women seeking protection from intimate partner violence.[22]

The addition of these new elements adds subjectivity to the asylum analysis that complicates claims and leads to inconsistent decisions from decision-makers who may not understand the sociocultural dynamics of domestic abuse, especially in the home countries of some applicants, where conditions may vary significantly from those in the United States. For example, a U.S.

[21] *See* Katharine T. Bartlett, *Feminist Legal Methods*, 103 HARV. L. REV. 829, 851 (1990) (describing "feminist practical reasoning" as that which determines "what must be done, and why and how it should be done … on the basis of the intricacies of each specific factual context"). Professor Bartlett also notes that feminist decision-making recognizes that "actual circumstances" can "yield insights into … difficult problems" that abstract concepts alone cannot. *Id.*

[22] In fact, the standard is arguably not even facially neutral, for as Pritchett notes, the heightened requirements of social distinction and particularity do not apply to any of the other four grounds for asylum.

Immigration Judge may have difficulty understanding why single women who have left their abusive spouses would be easily identified – and even marked or targeted for future harm – in a patriarchal culture where religious mores are strongly enforced.

Such concerns are exacerbated by the fact that asylum seekers do not have the right to counsel; a significant percentage of applicants thus appear in immigration court without an attorney.[23] A *pro se* litigant faces substantial obstacles in establishing and proving membership in a post-*Acosta* particular social group. A survivor who does not speak English, has suffered significant trauma, and is unfamiliar with the U.S. legal system would likely be unable to formulate a group that would be sufficiently immutable, socially distinct, and particular. The ruling in *Matter of* W-Y-C- *&* *H-O-B-*, a case handed down a few months before *Matter of* A-B-, makes these challenges particularly detrimental.[24] In that case, the BIA held that failure to articulate a viable PSG in an initial hearing could result in the summary denial of a claim.

Lastly, the imposition of additional requirements for those seeking asylum based on particular social group are problematic because the petitioner bears the burden of proof in an asylum case, which is heard in an adversarial system and where evidentiary burdens are high. Demonstrating social distinction and particularity requires significant documentary evidence and expert testimony regarding the applicant's home country, which are difficult and expensive to obtain for any applicant, much less a survivor of domestic violence who likely faces significant financial, logistical, and psychological constraints.[25]

Pritchett's proposed return to the *Acosta* standard, through which applicants would need only prove that members of a proposed particular social group possess a "common immutable characteristic"[26] takes into account the lives of survivors. A pared down PSG definition would increase access to justice for those who have turned to the United States for protection from abusive partners but are unable to meet the unnecessarily exacting legal and evidentiary standards implemented after *Acosta*.

[23] A 2015 study found that only 37 percent of all immigrants, and 14 percent of detained immigrants, secured representation in immigration court. Ingrid V. Eagly & Steven Shafer, *A National Study of Access to Counsel in Immigration Court*, 164 U. PA. L. REV. 1 (2015).

[24] 27 I. & N. Dec. 189 (BIA 2018).

[25] *See* Joline Doedens, *The Politics of Domestic Violence-Based Asylum Claims*, 22 DUKE J. GENDER L. & POL'Y 111 (2014) (stating that asylum claims are "a very fact-intensive process that [involve] the recruitment of expert to testify on the perception of domestic violence in the applicant's country of origin, and extensive preparation of the applicant herself (or himself), to ensure that she effectively [portrays] her perception of herself as a member of the relevant social group, and that her abuser identified her as a group member as well").

[26] *In re Acosta*, 19 I. & N. at 212.

B Gender *Per Se* as a Particular Social Group Avoids Essentializing Narratives of Victimization

Professor Pritchett's opinion next holds that gender *per se* is a viable particular social group. As she notes in the feminist judgment, a PSG of gender alone is supported by international guidelines.[27] Several U.S. federal circuit courts have also accepted the formulation; immigration law scholars have deemed such a group viable as well.[28]

The feminist judgment correctly states that a particular social group of "women" would be an improvement over the "women who are unable to leave their relationship" formulation advanced in *Matter of R-A-*, *Matter of L-R-*, and *Matter of A-R-C-G-*. The more generally described group has the benefit of including survivors who demonstrated strength and agency in the face of abuse, thereby limiting reliance on essentialized narratives of victimization. A PSG of "women from Guatemala," for example, would encompass both a wife who endured years of violent abuse while family or economic circumstances prevented her escape as well as a girlfriend who regularly fought back against her abuser but determined that only flight from her home country, where police refused to act upon her numerous demands for help, could ensure her safety.

Another benefit to a gender-only particular social group is its departure from the "unable to leave" formulation that had effectively limited the use of any alternative particular social groups. During the decade-and-a-half-long legal saga of *Matter of R-A-*, the Department of Justice ("DOJ") issued a proposed rule that provided guidance on gender-based asylum claims.[29] In that rule, DOJ declined to articulate a particular social group for domestic violence claims, noting that group definitions are fact-specific and "likely will vary

[27] *See, e.g.*, U.N. High Comm'r for Refugees, *Guidelines on International Protection: Gender-Related Persecution Within the Context of Article 1A(2) of the 1951 Convention and/or Its 1967 Protocol Relating to the Status of Refugees*, § 30, U.N. Doc. HCR/GIP/02/01 (May 7, 2002) ("It follows that sex can properly be within the ambit of the social group category, with women being a clear example of a social subset defined by innate and immutable characteristics, and who are frequently treated differently than men. Their characteristics also identify them as a group in society, subjecting them to different treatment and standards in some countries" (footnote omitted)).

[28] *See generally* Bethany Lobo, *Women as a Particular Social Group: A Comparative Assessment of Gender Asylum Claims in the United States and United Kingdom*, 26 GEO. IMMIGR. L.J. 361 (2012); David L. Neal, *Women as a Social Group: Recognizing Sex-Based Persecution as Grounds for Asylum*, 20 COLUM. HUM. RTS. L. REV. 203 (1988).

[29] Asylum and Withholding Definitions, 65 Fed. Reg. 76588 (proposed Dec. 7, 2000) (to be codified at 8 C.F.R. § 208.13). Nearly two decades after its release, this proposed rule has not been finalized.

depending upon the social context in [the] country" from which the applicant seeks protection.[30] The agency stated that it was "ill-advised to try to establish a universal model for persecution claims based on domestic violence" and that a "case-by-case adjudication" was instead more appropriate.[31] Yet *Matter of R-A-*, *Matter of L-R-*, and *Matter of A-R-C-G-* all utilized the "unable to leave" PSG, making that formulation the most certain means of obtaining asylum for survivors. Utilizing Professor Pritchett's formulation, however, gender can either stand alone as the group targeted for persecution, or can be supplemented with characteristics specific to the individual applicant that led her abuser to perpetrate violence (e.g., marital status, pregnancy, opposition to his misogynistic behavior).

Ultimately, the feminist judgment's particular social group takes into account the diverse responses that women might have to abuse in the home. A gender *per se* group, as Professor Pritchett states, "allows for the accommodation of the various social, political, cultural, and geographic factors that may differentiate the experiences of survivors." A PSG of "women" emphasizes survivors' stories, as opposed to their relationship status or purported personal failings that made them "unable to leave." The group described by a single word – "women" – thus achieves numerous feminist goals relating to anti-essentialism as well as respecting the autonomy and agency of survivors.

C *Returning to a Proper Nexus Standard*

Professor Pritchett also uses her feminist judgment as an opportunity to address the issue of nexus, or the requirement that persecution be inflicted "on account of" or "in order to overcome" a protected characteristic. She unequivocally states that intimate partner violence exists because of gender, a claim meticulously substantiated with evidence from various United Nations bodies, the U.S. State Department, and others. She rightly rejects the notion that domestic violence is a "mere criminal act" in favor of a contextualized approach to intimate partner abuse that takes into account patriarchy as well as a "cross-cultural context [that] supports the understanding that women's gender and consequent subordinate status in society make them more likely to be victims of domestic and intimate partner violence." Recognizing and appreciating the critical nature of this context is a core value of feminist theory. As Professor Mary Dietz states, "context is all," and as such, "feminists have long recognized as imperative the task of seeking out, defining, and

[30] *Id.* at 76589.
[31] *Id.*

criticizing the complex reality that governs the ways we think, the values we hold, and the relationships we share."[32]

This section of Pritchett's opinion is particularly important because courts hearing asylum claims based on intimate partner violence routinely impose *ultra vires* requirements with regard to nexus that reveal a substantial gender bias. For example, in *Matter of R-A-*, the BIA ascribed the abuser's "unchecked violence" to "the inherent meanness of his personality."[33] Both Sessions and the Immigration Judge fixated on the personal failings of Ms. A-B-'s abuser, his "violent and jealous nature," and his "selfish and criminal demands for sex."

These approaches are not exceptional. Judges in domestic violence cases often hold "that the abuse occurred because the abuser was a 'despicable person,' because of his 'inherent meanness,' because of his alcohol abuse, because of his jealousy, or because of other 'personal' or 'criminal' reasons."[34] However, in more traditional asylum claims, such as those "in which the applicant is fleeing a repressive dictatorship, immigration judges ... do not stop to ask whether the dictator is a 'despicable person'" or otherwise inquire about the personal characteristics or failings that led to his violence.[35] This disparity exemplifies the issues Professor Pritchett's opinion raises regarding the public-private distinction and asylum claims involving nonstate actors. As such, the feminist judgement's focus on nexus works to correct a gender imbalance in the adjudication of asylum claims by requiring of survivors of intimate partner violence only what is asked of all other asylum seekers.

CONCLUSION

The Attorney General's decision in *Matter of A-B-* was part of a coordinated attack on asylum seekers that occurred in the summer of 2018. The opinion was issued not long after the Department of Justice announced a "zero tolerance" policy that criminalized anyone trying to enter the United States without authorization and as the administration forcibly separated children from parents detained pursuant to that policy.[36] Professor Pritchett's feminist

[32] Mary G. Dietz, *Context Is All: Feminism and Theories of Citizenship*, 116 Daedalus 1 (1987).

[33] *In re R-A-*, 22 I. & N. at 926.

[34] Anjum Gupta, *Dead Silent: Heuristics, Silent Motives, and Asylum*, 48 Colum. Hum. Rts. L. Rev. 1, 3 (2016).

[35] *Id.*

[36] United States Department of Justice, *Attorney General Announces Zero-Tolerance Policy for Criminal Illegal Entry* (Apr. 6, 2018), https://www.justice.gov/opa/pr/attorney-general-announces-zero-tolerance-policy-criminal-illegal-entry

judgment is therefore especially relevant and timely, as gender-based asylum, and refugee protections for vulnerable populations more generally, are currently under siege. Sessions's opinion in *Matter of A-B-* upends not only domestic violence-based asylum law, but protections for survivors of other related so-called "private" harms such as sexual abuse, female genital mutilation, forced marriage, and violence against LGBTQ individuals. Unlike Attorney General Sessions, whose archaic understanding of gender-based violence as a private matter turns the clock back to a time when the United States ignored and tolerated violence against women, Attorney General Pritchett's feminist judgment recognizes that the personal is political, and, in doing so, restores both protection and gender equity to asylum jurisprudence.

MATTER OF A-B-, 27 I&N DEC. 316 (A.G. 2018)

OPINION OF ATTORNEY GENERAL, PRITCHETT
JUNE 11, 2018

On March 7, 2018, I directed the Board of Immigration Appeals ("Board") to refer for my review its decision in this matter. *See* 8 C.F.R. § 1003.1(h)(1)(i). *Matter of A-B-*, 27 I&N Dec. 227 (A.G. 2018). Specifically, I sought briefing on the following questions: (1) whether domestic violence can rise to the level of persecution; (2) whether gender *per se* can constitute a particular social group (PSG); (3) whether there is a nexus between gender and domestic violence; and (4) whether, and under what circumstances, an applicant can demonstrate that the government is unable or unwilling to control domestic violence inflicted by intimate partners for purposes of an application for asylum or withholding of removal.

For reasons set forth in the accompanying opinion, I vacate in part and clarify in part the Board's previous decision in *Matter of A-R-C-G-*, 25 I&N Dec. 338 (BIA 2014), and remand the case at hand to the immigration judge for further proceedings. The basic framework for asylum law is well-established. 8 U.S.C. §§ 1101(a)(42)(A), 1158(b)(1)(a), (b)(i). In order to establish a claim for asylum, an applicant must meet her burden of proving that she suffered harm rising to the level of persecution. *See INS v. Stevic*, 467 U.S. 407 (1984). In addition, she must establish that the harm she suffered was on account of one of five protected grounds (race, religion, nationality, membership in a particular social group, or political opinion). 8 U.S.C. §§ 1101(a)(42)(A), 1158(b)(1)(a), (b)(i). When the protected ground asserted is particular social group, the applicant must identify a particular social group and establish her membership within it. *See, e.g., Niang v. Gonzales*, 422 F.3d 1187, 1199 (loth Cir. 2005). Finally, when the persecutor is a private actor rather than a governmental actor, the applicant must establish that the government is unable or unwilling to control the private actor or protect the victim of persecution. *See, e.g., Paloka v. Holder*, 762 F.3d 191, 195 (2d Cir. 2014).

More specifically, in the domestic violence context, when a victim flees her country because of that harm and requests asylum in the United States, she must establish that the domestic violence she experienced and/or fears in the future is sufficiently severe to rise to the level of persecution. In addition, if she claims that her persecutor inflicted domestic violence on account of her membership in a particular social group, she must clearly delineate the boundaries of her particular social group and establish a nexus between her membership in the group and the domestic violence she suffered. Finally, when the persecution is inflicted at the hands of an intimate partner, the applicant must demonstrate that the government was unable or unwilling to control the perpetrator and provide her with sufficient protection from domestic violence.

In *Matter of* A-R-C-G-, 25 I&N Dec. 338 (BIA 2014), the Board had an opportunity to bring clarity and guidance to its jurisprudence related to gender-based violence as a form of persecution qualifying victims for asylum. However, it failed to do so when it found that "married women in Guatemala who are unable to leave their relationship" can constitute a particular social group that forms the basis of a claim for asylum or withholding of removal under section 208(a) of the Immigration and Nationality Act. *Id.* Because the Board in *Matter of* A-R-C-G- failed to specifically identify domestic violence as a form of persecution, hold that gender alone constitutes a viable particular social group, establish the connection between domestic violence and gender, and provide guidance on the "unable or unwilling to control" standard, I overrule that case and any other Board precedent to the extent those decisions are inconsistent with the legal conclusions set forth in this opinion.

OPINION

The Immigration and Nationality Act ("INA") authorizes a grant of asylum to applicants who are able to establish that they meet the definition of a refugee. INA § 101(a)(42) defines a refugee as

> any person who is outside any country of such person's nationality ... and who is unable or unwilling to return to, and is unable or unwilling to avail himself or herself of the protection of, that country because of persecution or a well-founded fear of persecution on account of race, religion, nationality, membership in a particular social group, or political opinion.

Notably, nothing in this definition speaks to gender-based violence generally or to domestic violence more specifically. Moreover, there is little guidance related to the definition of particular social group and when, if ever, women can constitute a particular social group for recognition under the refugee definition.

In understanding these omissions, a brief history of the refugee definition is instructive. The definition of a refugee in the INA mirrors that in the Convention and Protocol Related to the Status of Refugees (hereinafter Refugee Convention). *See* Convention Relating to the Status of Refugees, art. 1(A)(2), 189 U.N.T.S. 150 (July 28, 1951).[1] The Refugee Convention emerged in a post-World War II landscape in which member states of the United Nations directed their attention toward international rules that regulated the public sphere and the relationship between government, the individual, and the market. *See, e.g.*, Rebecca Cook, THE HUMAN RIGHTS OF WOMEN: NATIONAL AND INTERNATIONAL PERSPECTIVES 12 (1994). For the drafters of the Convention, the archetypal refugee in need of protection was the political protestor in the public square speaking out against his oppressor – the state. Seen in another context, the refugee was an individual attempting to practice his religion in the public sphere of the temple under an oppressive governmental regime. As such, the Refugee Convention by definition provides protections to those fleeing persecution on account the freedoms traditionally expressed in the public sphere: race, nationality, religion, political opinion, and membership in a particular social group. *See* Optional Protocol Art. 1.2.

Conversely, victims of domestic violence tend to experience their persecution in the private sphere of the home at the hands of intimate partners and other family members. The drafters of the Refugee Convention failed to specifically address the harms primarily directed at women in the private sphere when they chose to omit gender from the list of protected grounds or

[1] The United States is not a signatory to the Convention itself, but acceded to the United Nations Protocol Relating to the Status of Refugees on Jan. 31, 1967, [1968] 19 U.S.T. 6223, T.I.A.S. No. 6577 [hereinafter Optional Protocol], including Article 1.2 of the Protocol, which defines a "refugee" as an individual who

> owing to a well-founded fear of being persecuted for reasons of race, religion, nationality, membership of a particular social group or political opinion, is outside the country of his nationality and is unable or, owing to such fear, is unwilling to avail himself of the protection of that country; or who, not having a nationality and being outside the country of his former habitual residence, is unable or, owing to such fear, is unwilling to return to it.

Id.

enumerate gender-based violence as a basis for asylum. Feminist international legal scholars have noted that this omission is largely consistent with the public/private dichotomy that characterizes much of international law. *See* CHRISTINE CHARLESWORTH & HILARY CHINKIN, THE BOUNDARIES OF INTERNATIONAL LAW 232 (2000). Harms that take place in the public sphere at the nation-state level are the object of regulation and concern under international law. Private harms, those most often directed at women, are insulated from the purview of transnational concern. *Id.*

As previously noted, domestic asylum law has adopted the refugee definition from the Refugee Convention. *See* INA § 101(a)(42) (defining refugee as "any person who is outside any country of such person's nationality or, in the case of a person having no nationality, is outside any country in which such person last habitually resided, and who is unable or unwilling to return to, and is unable or unwilling to avail himself or herself of the protection of, that country because of persecution or a well-founded fear of persecution on account of race, religion, nationality, membership in a particular social group, or political opinion"). In the absence of a gender-specific enumerated ground of persecution, it has fallen to the courts to interpret the refugee definition and apply it in gender-based violence contexts.

Out of the five protected grounds identified by the refugee definition, the "particular social group" category has proven to be the most flexible in accommodating claims of gender-based violence. In the seminal BIA decision, *Matter of Acosta*, the Board defined the contours of a particular social group and made an explicit reference to sex, describing a particular social group as:

> A group of persons all of whom share a common, immutable characteristic [that] … might be an innate one such as *sex*, color, or kinship ties or … a share past experience such as former military leadership or land ownership … [T]he common characteristic … must be one that the members of the group either cannot change, or should not be required to change because it is fundamental to their individual identities or consciences.
>
> 19 I&N Dec. 211, 233 (BIA 1985) (emphasis added).

Now known as the "immutable characteristic" or *Acosta* test, the Board first applied it to a gender-based asylum claim in *Matter of Kasinga*, 21 I&N Dec. 357 (BIA 1996). In that case, the Respondent was subjected to forced marriage and threatened with female circumcision. She claimed a fear of persecution on account of her membership in the particular social group of "[y]oung women of the Tchamba-Kunsuntu Tribe who have not had FGM, as practiced by the tribe, and who oppose the practice." *Id.* at 365. The Board held that the Respondent had established that the gender-based harm she feared rose to the level of persecution, that she was the member of a cognizable particular social group based on gender and other characteristics, and that there was a nexus between the harm suffered and the applicant's particular social group. *Id.*

Following *Kasinga*, the Board encountered the specific question of domestic violence as the basis for asylum in the case of *Matter of* R-A-, 22 I&N Dec. 906 (BIA 1999). The Respondent in that case, Rody Alvarado, was a Guatemalan woman who had suffered severe domestic violence at the hands of her spouse. She argued that she experienced past persecution and had a well-founded fear of future persecution based on her membership in the particular social group of "Guatemalan women who have been involved intimately with Guatemalan male companions, who believe that women are to live under male domination." *Id.* at 911. The Board rejected her claim, finding that the harm she suffered was not on account of a cognizable social group. *Id.* at 917–23.

The Board's decision in *Matter of* R-A- triggered a complicated procedural response, including proposed Department of Justice regulations regarding gender-based asylum claims, several interventions and certifications from sitting Attorneys General, and ultimately a stipulation by the Department of Homeland Security to a grant of asylum without the issuance of a precedential opinion.[2] Following *Matter of* R-A-, the Board had another opportunity to provide a precedential decision related to domestic violence as basis for asylum in the case of *Matter of L-R-*. In that case, the Department of Homeland Security submitted briefing in which they conceded that (1) Mexican women in domestic relationships who are unable to leave; or (2) Mexican women who are viewed as property by virtue of their position in a domestic relationship met the Board's "social visibility" and "particularity" requirements in particular social group cases. *See* DEPARTMENT OF HOMELAND SECURITY SUPPLEMENTAL BRIEFING IN *MATTER OF L-R-*, at https://cgrs.uchastings.edu/. While the Board failed to issue a precedential

[2] In 2001, Attorney General (AG) Janet Reno vacated *Matter of* R-A-, and remanded to the BIA to decide the case when the proposed DOJ regulations are finalized. Without final regulations in place, AG John Ashcroft certified *Matter of* R-A- to himself in 2004. In 2005, AG John Ashcroft remanded the case to BIA, instructing the Board to decide the case when asylum regulations were finalized. Finally, in 2008, AG Michael Mukasey certified R-A- to himself, and remanded to the BIA to decide the case pursuant to relevant precedent. Once remanded to the BIA, the parties jointly requested that the case be sent back to the immigration court to update the record, where the Department of Homeland Security then stipulated to a grant of asylum. For details on this process, *see* Karen Musalo, *A Short History of Gender Asylum in the United States Resistance and Ambivalence May Very Slowly Be Inching Towards Recognition of Women's Claims*, 29 REFUGEE SURVEY Q. 46 (2010).

decision in *Matter of L-R-*, instead remanding to the immigration court for additional fact-finding, the Department's proposed social group formations became the *de facto* law of gender-based violence asylum claims.

Finally, in *Matter of* A-R-C-G-, the Board addressed the specific question of whether domestic violence can serve as a viable basis for asylum. 26 I&N Dec. 388 (BIA 2014). The Board affirmed prior cases, which established that in order to constitute a particular social group for purposes of asylum, the social group must be immutable, particular, and socially distinct. 26 I&N Dec. at 392 (citing *Matter of* M-E-V-G-, 26 I&N Dec. 227 (BIA 2014) and *Matter of* W-G-R-, 26 I&N Dec. 208 (BIA 2014)). The Board held that "married women in Guatemala who are unable to leave their relationship" can constitute a particular social group that forms the basis of a claim for asylum or withholding of removal under section 208(a) of the Immigration and Nationality Act. *Id.*

Since *Matter of* A-R-C-G-, confusion regarding the nexus between domestic violence and a protected ground has prevailed in immigration courts and in the federal Courts of Appeal. For example, while many courts have cited to A-R-C-G- favorably, *see, e.g., Peres-Rabanales v. Sessions*, 881 F.3d 61 (1st Cir. 2018); *Guzman-Alvarez v. Sessions*, 701 F. App'x 54 (2d Cir. 2017); *Gaitan-Bernal v. Sessions*, 695 F. App'x 224 (9th Cir. 2017); *Marikasi v. Lynch*, 840 F.3d 281 (6th Cir. 2016), some have appeared to call into question the validity of asylum claims based on interfamilial harm. *See Velasquez v. Sessions*, 866 F. 3d 188 (4th Cir. 2017). As stated by the Department of Homeland Security in its brief in this matter, "Where the victim knows the persecutor personally, the natural conclusion is that the harm was perpetrated for private reasons, separate and apart from any protected ground. Thus, establishing persecution based on a protected ground can be extremely difficult where the persecutor is a friend or family member." Brief for the Department of Homeland Security, *Matter of* A-B- (AG Apr. 20, 2018).

It is with this complex procedural and jurisprudential history in mind that I certified the case at hand for my review. I provide this history to illustrate the need for clarification of how gender-based asylum claims and domestic violence claims specifically should be adjudicated before the courts. My intention is for my opinion to bring clarity to the jurisprudence of gender-based asylum claims and conclusively answer the question of whether victims of domestic violence can, on a case by case basis, meet the definition of a refugee.

For reasons stated below, I find that *Matter of* A-R-C-G- failed to appropriately address the universe of questions that arise when considering domestic violence asylum claims. Specifically, *Matter of* A-R-C-G- left open the question of whether domestic violence can rise to the level of persecution. In addition, the Board failed to acknowledge that international and comparative law standards are binding on the Board in determining how to formulate a particular social group. By layering on the requirements of "particularity" and "social distinction," the Board erred in straying from the *Acosta* "immutability" standard with respect to particular social group formation.

I now overturn *Matter of A-R-C-G-* to the extent that it reaffirmed the Board's holdings in *Matter of M-E-V-G- and W-G-R-* and required that particular social groups be defined with particularity and social distinction. The proper test for a particular social group is the *Acosta* "immutability" standard. Thus, cases of gender-based violence, gender *per se* is a cognizable social group. In addition, I hold that when the persecutor is a non-state actor, as is the case in the majority of domestic violence-based asylum claims, the proper standard for determining whether the government is "unable or unwilling to control" the persecutor is whether a State takes measures that reduce the risk of persecution to below the well-founded fear, i.e. a one in ten chance,[3] threshold. For these reasons, I vacate the Board's decision and remand for further proceedings before the immigration judge consistent with this opinion.

I

This case centers on the claim of Ms. A-B-, a native and citizen of El Salvador, who fled to the United States to escape persecution at the hands of her spouse. Ms. A-B- married her spouse in El Salvador when she was in her early twenties, and, shortly after their marriage, the relationship became characterized by domestic violence. The domestic violence was physical, sexual, and emotional, taking the forms of physical violence, rape, and death threats – some even during Ms. A-B-'s pregnancies. Ms. A-B-'s spouse also beat their children in front of her. In addition to the violence, Ms. A-B-'s husband forced her to abandon her pursuit of formal education and employment. Isolated in her home, Ms. A-B- endured ridicule, false accusations of infidelity, and humiliation over the fifteen-year course of her marriage. In short, Ms. A-B- daily lived in fear for her life.

Ms. A-B- made repeated requests to Salvadoran law enforcement authorities to protect her from her husband's violence. On two occasions, she was able to obtain restraining orders, only to find that Salvadoran authorities were unwilling to enforce the orders when her husband abused and threatened her. Upon realizing that the police would not provide protection, she moved to a town

[3] *INS v. Cardoza-Fonseca*, 480 U.S. 421, 440 (1987).

two hours away from her home only for her husband to find her there and continue to abuse her. In addition, she sought and obtained a divorce despite her husband's attempts to take custody of the children, which further escalated the violence. Ms. A-B-'s then ex-husband and his police officer brother confronted her and told her that the divorce was meaningless and that her life was in danger. Even after the divorce, the threats from Ms. A-B-'s former spouse continued. He enlisted the help of his friends in the community to send the message that he intended to kill her. One week prior to her departure from El Salvador, Ms. A-B-'s ex-husband again violently assaulted her. Fearing for her life, she made the decision to leave El Salvador and seek safety in the United States.

Once in the United States, Ms. A-B- claimed asylum on the basis of the domestic violence she had suffered. Shortly after her entry into the country, an asylum officer found that she had a credible fear of persecution in the form of domestic violence and referred her case to the Charlotte, North Carolina Immigration Court. There, after a hearing, the Immigration Judge denied her claim for asylum and withholding of removal finding Ms. A-B- not credible based on omissions and discrepancies in her testimony. *Matter of A-B-*, Immigration Judge Decision, Dec. 1, 2015. In addition, the Immigration Judge found that notwithstanding her lack of credibility, Ms. A-B- failed to establish that she had suffered persecution on account of her membership in a particular social group. Rather, the Immigration Judge found that the harm suffered was caused by the "violent and criminal tendencies" of the abusive spouse. *Id.*

On appeal to the Board, a three-member panel reversed the Immigration Judge's decision. *Matter of A-B-*, BIA Interim Decision 2016. Specifically, the Board overturned the negative credibility finding, holding that the few minor omissions in Ms. A-B-'s testimony were reasonable in light of the trauma and severe domestic violence she had endured in El Salvador. *Id.* In addition, the Board found that Ms. A-B- had formulated a viable social group similar to that affirmed by the Board in *Matter of A-R-C-G-* and that she had suffered persecution in the form of domestic violence on account of her membership in that particular social group. *Id.* Concluding that she had met her burden of proving her eligibility for asylum, the Board remanded the case to the Immigration Judge to grant asylum after the completion of required background checks. *Id.*

Upon remand, Ms. A-B- cleared the Department of Homeland Security's background checks. However, the Immigration Judge refused to grant asylum in the case. Noting the Fourth Circuit's decision in *Velasquez v. Sessions*, 866 F.3d 188 (4th Cir. 2017), he stated that he believed *Matter of A-R-C-G-* "may not be legally valid" and certified and administratively returned the case to the

Board for its reconsideration. Pursuant to 8 C.F.R. § 1003.1(h)(1)(i), I directed the Board to refer this matter to me for my review and to submit briefs on the questions noted above. *Matter of A-B-*, 27 I&N Dec. at 227.

II

As a threshold matter, the harm experienced by an applicant for asylum must rise to the level of persecution. INA § 101(a)(42). Persecution is not defined in the INA or by regulation. However, over time, courts have considered myriad harms presented by asylum claims to paint broad contours of what is and is not persecution. Courts generally agree that persecution "must rise above mere harassment," and can include "detention, arrest, interrogation, prosecution, imprisonment, illegal searches, confiscation of property, surveillance, beatings, or torture," or behavior that threatens the same, and "non-life-threatening behavior such as torture and economic deprivation if the resulting conditions are sufficiently severe." *Orellana-Arias v. Sessions*, 865 F.3d 476, 487 (7th Cir. 2017) (citing *Velasquez-Banegas v. Lynch*, 846 F.3d 258, 270–71 (7th Cir. 2017)). However, "generalized conditions of hardship which affect entire populations do not rise to the level of persecution." *Id.*

In *Matter of A-R-C-G-*, the Department of Homeland Security stipulated that the respondent suffered mistreatment rising to the level of past persecution. In *Matter of A-B-*, the Immigration Judge did not make a specific finding with respect to whether the harm Ms. A-B- suffered was sufficiently severe to rise to the level of persecution. However, the facts of the case clearly establish that the harm Ms. A-B- suffered does rise to the level of persecution. Like many victims of domestic violence, the harms Ms. A-B- suffered were both physical and psychological. Physically, she was severely beaten and raped on multiple occasions. Psychologically, Ms. A-B-'s husband threatened to kill her while holding weapons and on one occasion while she was pregnant, threatened to hang her from the ceiling by a rope. The psychological abuse also took the forms of isolation from family and formal employment, humiliation and accusations of infidelity, and beating their children.

The harm suffered by Ms. A-B- and the harm suffered by so many victims of domestic violence constitutes persecution. Courts routinely find that rape and physical beatings rises to the level of persecution. *See, e.g.*, *Lazo-Majano v. INS*, 813 F.2d 1432 (9th Cir.1987); *Matter of S-A-*, 22 I. & N. Dec. 1328 (BIA 2000). When the harm is psychological without accompanying physical violence, persecution can still be found. *See, e.g.*, *Mashiri v. Ashcroft*, 383 F.3d 1112, 1120 (9th Cir. 2004); *Makhoul v. Ashcroft*, 387 F.3d 75, 80 (1st Cir. 2004); *Boykov v. I.N.S.*, 109 F.3d 413, 416 (7th Cir. 1997); *Li Wu Lin v. I.N.S.*, 238

F.3d 239, 244 (3d Cir. 2001). The psychological harm that characterizes domestic violence can be deadly. Women who experience domestic violence often suffer from posttraumatic stress syndrome, depression, and anxiety. OFFICE ON WOMEN'S HEALTH, EFFECTS OF DOMESTIC VIOLENCE, https://www.womenshealth.gov/relationships-and-safety/effects-violence-against-women. Moreover, survivors of domestic violence are twice as likely to attempt suicide multiple times. AMERICAN PSYCHOLOGICAL ASSOCIATION, SUICIDE AND INTIMATE PARTNER VIOLENCE, http://www.apa.org/monitor/2014/11/suicide-violence.aspx.

Accordingly, because domestic violence can take the form of severe physical violence or psychological trauma that results in suffering, harm, and, potentially, death, it can rise to the level of persecution. Courts making the fact-specific determination of whether a particular applicant's experience of domestic violence rises to the level of persecution must take into account not only physical violence, but also the severity of the psychological effects intimate partner violence has on its victims. In addition, all domestic violence must be viewed under a "totality of the circumstances" standard in determining whether it rises to the level of persecution. *See, e.g., Karki v. Holder*, 715 F.3d 792, 805 (10th Cir. 2013) (noting that, "[w]hile threats alone are insufficient to constitute persecution, threats should be considered in assessing the cumulative impact of all of the mistreatment a petitioner suffered"). I therefore hold that domestic violence can rise to the level of persecution.

III

I now turn to the question of particular social group (or a PSG) and the appropriate formulation of social group in domestic violence cases. Here, the Respondent claims that she is eligible for asylum because she suffered persecution on account of her membership in the particular social group of "El Salvadoran women who are unable to leave their domestic relationships where they have children in common with their partners." This social group formulation mirrors the social group that the Board had previously found acceptable in *Matter of A-R-C-G-* ("married women in Guatemala who are unable to leave their relationship"). 26 I. & N. Dec. at 392. In that decision, the Board held that a particular social group must meet not only the immutability requirement established by *Matter of Acosta*, but also that it must be defined with particularity and social distinction. *Id.* (citing *Matter of M-E-V-G-*, 26 I&N Dec. 227 (BIA 2014) and *Matter of W-G-R-*, 26 I&N Dec. 20

(BIA 2014)). Accordingly, the Board formulated a social group defined in terms of gender, nationality, and relationship mobility.

The imputation of particularity and social distinction to the social group test, *Matter of* M-E-V-G-, 26 I&N Dec. 227 and *Matter of* W-G-R-, 26 I&N Dec. 20, lacks a sound legal basis in domestic or international law. To this extent, I specifically overturn *Matter of* M-E-V-G- and *Matter of* W-G-R- and return the particular social group test to the *Matter of Acosta* immutability standard. Under *Matter of Acosta*, I find that gender is an immutable characteristic, which, without further qualifiers, can constitute a particular social group. Holding that gender *per se* can serve as a PSG for victims of domestic violence overcomes the gendered consequences, described below, of the Board's findings in *Matter of* A-R-C-G- and aligns U.S. asylum law with international legal standards.

A

In *Matter of Acosta*, the Board of Immigration Appeals established that, for purposes of asylum, a particular social group is one comprised of "persons all of whom share a common, immutable characteristic, *i.e.*, a characteristic that either is beyond the power of the individual members of the group to change or is so fundamental to their identities or consciences that it ought not be required to be changed." 19 I. & N. Dec. 211, 212 (BIA 1985). In subsequent decisions, the BIA added the requirements that particular social groups also be "particular" and "socially distinct." *Matter of* M-E-V-G-, 26 I&N Dec. 227 (BIA 2014) and *Matter of* W-G-R-, 26 I&N Dec. 20 (BIA 2014). The Board defined the "particularity" requirement to be "whether the proposed group can accurately be described in a manner sufficiently distinct that the group would be recognized, in the society in question, as a discrete class of persons." *Matter of* S-E-G-, 25 I&N Dec. at 584. To meet the particularity requirement, a group must not be "too amorphous . . . to create a benchmark for determining group membership." *Id.* The Board similarly described social visibility to mean "social distinction" – not ocular visibility, but rather whether the PSG is "perceived by society as a group" or "whether the PSG is recognized within society as a distinct entity." *Matter of* M-E-V-G-, 26 I&N Dec. at 240–41.

As noted by the Respondent in her brief in this proceeding, I agree that the added requirements of particularity and social visibility to the *Acosta* immutability standard represent "an unacknowledged and unexplained departure from twenty years of precedent." Respondent's Brief at 28. Furthermore, these added PSG requirements have resulted in arbitrary and capricious decision-making at the immigration judge level, *id.*, which, as described below, has disproportionately affected women. Accordingly, I overrule the Board's previous decisions that require that a cognizable particular social group must meet the requirements of particularity and social distinction in addition to immutability. *Matter of M-E-V-G-*, 26 I&N Dec. 227 (BIA 2014) and *Matter of W-G-R-*, 26 I&N Dec. 20 (BIA 2014).

My decision to overrule Board PSG precedent is supported by the multiple gendered consequences that flow from a rigid application of the particularity and social visibility requirements. First, requirements of particularity and social distinction result in narrow and elaborate social group formations such as the one identified in this case: "El Salvadoran women who are unable to leave their domestic relationships where they have children in common with their partners." Requiring such elaborate social group formulations in an attempt to meet the particularity and social distinction requirements complicates the asylum application process. In 2017, over 20 percent of women were unrepresented by counsel in their asylum claims. *See* TRAC IMMIGRATION, ASYLUM REPRESENTATION RATES HAVE FALLEN AMID RISING DENIAL RATES, http://trac.syr.edu/immigration/reports/491/. Without representation, female victims of domestic violence have struggled to formulate viable PSGs. *See* Brief of *Amicus Curiae* the National Immigration Justice Center in *Matter of A-R-C-G-*, 26 I&N Dec. 388 (BIA 2014). Moreover, as the present case illustrates, immigration judges lack clarity and consistency in their applications of the particularity and social distinction tests. Rather than clear-cut legal principles, the particularity and social distinction requirements leave open the door to subjective and inconsistent interpretations by decision-makers who lack a contextualized understanding of the social and cultural dynamics of domestic violence. *See* Brief of *Amici Curiae* the Harvard Immigration and Refugee Clinical Program, the American Immigration Lawyers Association, Human Rights First, and Kids in Need of Defense in *Matter of A-B-*, [hereinafter AILA *et al.* amicus brief]; *see also* Gabriela Corrales, *Justice Delayed Is Justice Denied: The Real Significance of Matter of A-R-C-G-*, 26 BERKELEY LA RAZA L.J. 70, 79 (2016).

Second, as previously discussed, *supra*, because of the evolution of international refugee law and its design to protect harms primarily occurring in the "public sphere," gender is not an enumerated Convention ground. Instead, most claims relating to women and gender-based violence have fallen under the nebulous, catch-all "particular social group" ground. However, as noted by the Respondent in her brief, the requirements of particularity and social visibility are inconsistent with what is required to prove the other grounds for asylum (race, religion, nationality, political opinion). Thus, a double standard emerges wherein individuals (here, female victims of domestic violence) making a PSG claim must take the extra step of establishing particularity and social visibility whereas victims of persecution on account of race, religion, nationality, and political opinion do not have to do the same. *See Acosta*, 19 I&N Dec. at 233.

Accordingly, because the additional requirements of particularity and social visibility have gendered consequences that undermine the principles of fair treatment, equality, and nondiscrimination within our asylum regime, I overturn *Matter of M-E-V-G-*, 26 I&N Dec. 227 (BIA 2014) and *Matter of W-G-R-*, 26 I&N Dec. 20 (BIA 2014). The test for a cognizable particular social group is that the group must be "a group of persons, all of whom share a common, immutable characteristic, i.e., a characteristic that either is beyond the power of the individual members of the group to change or is so fundamental to their identities or consciences that it ought not be required to change." *Matter of Acosta*, 19 I. & N. Dec. at 212. As such, *Matter of Acosta* shall control in establishing the criteria for a viable particular social group for purposes of asylum.

B

Having overruled the Board's precedent with respect to particularity and social visibility, I now hold that victims of domestic violence can establish that they faced past persecution on account of their membership in the particular social group of "women." In finding that gender *per se* is a viable PSG for purposes of asylum, this holding returns PSG jurisprudence to the *Matter of Acosta* standard, addresses the problems inherent in the PSG formulations in *Matter of A-R-C-G-* and *Matter of A-B-*, and brings U.S. asylum law into compliance with international and comparative standards.

As previously noted, *Matter of Acosta* established that sex is an innate characteristic that could define a particular social group. 19 I&N Dec. at 233. Consistent with this holding, federal appellate courts across the country have found that particular social groups based on gender alone are a sufficient basis for an asylum claim. *See* Briefs of *Amici Curiae* citing *Fatin v. INS*, 12 F.3d 1233, 1240 (3rd Cir. 1993) (satisfying the *Acosta* requirement "to the extent that . . . [she] suggest[ed] that she would be persecuted . . . simply because she is a woman"); *Mohammed v. Gonzales*, 400 F.3d 785, 797 (9th Cir. 2005) ("the recognition that girls or women of a particular clan or nationality (or even in some circumstances females in general) may constitute a social group is simply a logical application . . . [of the conclusion that] a 'particular social group' is one united by . . . an innate characteristic"); *Niang v. Gonzales*, 422 F.3d 1187, 1199–200 (applying the Acosta definition and finding that female members of a tribe qualified as a PSG); *Hassan v. Gonzales*, 484 F.3d 513, 513 (8th Cir. 2007) ("Somali women" are a viable social group based on the applicant's "possession of the immutable trait of being female").

In addition to returning PSG jurisprudence to the *Acosta* standard, recognizing gender as a *per se* social group overcomes many of the problems identified in previous gender-based violence PSG formulations. For example, the majority in *A-R-C-G-* held that "married women in Guatemala who are unable to leave their relationship" constitutes a cognizable PSG. In attempting to mirror the *A-R-C-G-* formulation, the Respondent here in *Matter of A-B-* similarly claimed asylum on account of her membership in the particular social group of "El Salvadoran women who are unable to leave their domestic relationships where they have children in common." These formulaic and unwieldy social group formulations that include qualifiers beyond gender have been detrimental to victims of domestic violence attempting to claim asylum.

First, the groups as formulated are overinclusive in that they require all claimants of asylum who have suffered domestic violence to be described as "victims" trapped and unable to leave their relationships. *See* Natalie Nanasi, *Domestic Violence Asylum and the Perpetuation of the Victimization Narrative*, 78 Ohio St. L.G. 733 (2017). In requiring that victims of domestic violence be "unable to leave" the relationship in order to fall under the PSG as defined, women who have exercised agency and escaped the relationship in their home countries will not be recognized as worthy of protection. *Id.* The social group also fails to reflect the many complicated dynamics that characterize domestic violence relationships, such as the propensity for victims to leave only to return to their abusers after reassurances of reform and safety in the future.

Second, the group as formulated is underinclusive and fails to provide protection to the many individuals whose relationships cannot be described by *A-R-C-G-* formulations. For example, what about women who are in intimate relationships but are not married or do not have children with their partner? What about women who are able to physically separate from their spouse but the spouse will not recognize the separation or acknowledge that the woman has the power to end the relationship? What about women in same-sex relationship or those for whom religion or other cultural factors are substantial deterrents to leaving a relationship? *See* Blaine Bookey, *Gender-Based Asylum Post-*Matter of A-R-C-G-*: Evolving Standards and Fair Application of the Law*, 22 SW J. Int'l L. 1 (2016). Importantly, rigid PSG formulations required by *Matter of A-R-C-G-* and its subsequent jurisprudence have often served to reinforce the heteronormative stereotypes and sexism underlying domestic violence.

By recognizing gender as a social group *per se*, the law will better reflect the lived reality for victims of domestic violence. Defining the social group in terms of gender alone allows for the accommodation of the various social, political, cultural, and geographic factors that may differentiate the experiences of survivors of domestic violence. Individuals who have experienced domestic violence who fall under the particular social group of "women" can include those who have exercised agency to escape the abuse, those who have reached out to family or the state for protection from the abuse, and those for whom religion or other sociocultural norms play a factor in determining whether or not to leave the relationship. Women who proceed in their applications for asylum *pro se* must only answer the question of whether she "belongs to a group whose members share a characteristic which they cannot change or should not be expected to change." Brief of *Amicus Curiae* the National Immigration Justice Center in *Matter of* A-R-C-G-, 26 I&N Dec. 388 (BIA 2014) at 7. Notably, expanding the social group to reflect gender as the defining characteristics draws attention to the fact that women experience domestic violence vis-à-vis their position as women in society.

In addition to overcoming the challenges of the *Matter of* A-R-C-G- formulation, holding that gender *per se* constitutes a viable social group brings U.S. asylum law into line with international obligations. The United States became a signatory to the Refugee Convention and its Optional Protocol in 1968. *See* UNHCR, *States Parties to the 1951 Convention relating to the Status of Refugees and the 1967 Protocol* (June 2014). The purpose of the Refugee Act of 1981 was to bring the United States into compliance with its obligations under the Refugee Convention. *Brief for Immigration Law Professors as* Amici Curiae, *Matter of* A-B-, at 32. Therefore, interpretations of the Refugee Act should be consistent with the spirit and intent of the 1951 Refugee Convention, i.e. to protect those who have faced past persecution or are fleeing persecution on account of, among other grounds, their membership in a particular social group.

Requiring victims of domestic violence to articulate a particular social group beyond their gender runs counter to well-established international norms. Courts in various comparative jurisdictions have found that domestic violence may constitute persecution on account of membership in a particular social group of women under the Refugee Convention. *See* Brief of *Amicus Curiae* UN High Commissioner for Refugees in Support of Respondents *in Matter of* A-R-C-G-, 26 I&N Dec. 388 (BIA 2014) at 9 [hereinafter UNHCR Amicus Brief]. These decisions have recognized that domestic violence is inflicted because of a woman's gender, and, as such, there is a nexus between the PSG and the persecution. *Id.* Specifically, courts in Canada and the United Kingdom both accept gender alone as the basis for a PSG because it meets the *Acosta* immutable characteristic definition – the accepted criteria for a cognizable PSG under the Refugee Convention. *See* Melanie Randall, *Particularized Social Groups and Categorical Imperatives in Refugee Law*, 23 AM. U. J. GENDER SOC. POL'Y & L. 520 (2014).

Moreover, the United Nations High Commissioner for Refugees (UNHCR), the U.N. agency tasked with overseeing the implementation of the Refugee Convention, has issued guidance with respect to how signatory states should interpret gender-based persecution under the PSG ground. In particular, the UNCHR has stated that "sex can properly be within the ambit of the social group category, with women being a clear example of a social subset defined by innate and immutable characteristics, and who are frequently treated differently to men." UNHCR, *Guidelines on International Protection: "Membership of a Particular Social Group" within the Context of Article 1A(2) of the 1951 Convention and/or Its 1967 Protocol Relating to the Status of Refugees*, para. 12, HCR/GIP/02/02 (May 7, 2002). *See also INS v. Cardoza-Fonseca*, 480 U.S. 421, 439 n. 22 (UNHCR Handbook and Guidelines provide "significant guidance" to domestic applications of the refugee Convention). As the UNHCR itself has stated, "[i]n UNHCR's view, the particular social group applicable in domestic violence cases may be defined by gender alone under the protected characteristic approach." UNHCR Amicus Brief at 15. Thus, international and comparative law establishes that gender alone can constitute a cognizable particular social group for the basis of an asylum claim.

In its brief, the Department of Homeland Security warns that a PSG defined on the basis of gender alone will open the floodgates to all asylum claims of women who have experienced harm in their country of origin. *Department's Brief* at 21–22. However, the "floodgates" concern is misplaced and finds no support in case law. *See cases cited by Amici*, including *N.L.A. v. Holder*, 744 F.3d 425, 438 (7th Cir. 2014) (noting "it would be antithetical to asylum law to deny refuge to a group of persecuted individuals who have valid claims merely because too many have valid claims"); *Perdomo v. Holder*, 611 F.3d 662, 669 (9th Cir. 2010) (recognizing "size and breadth of a group alone does not preclude a group from qualifying as such a social group"). *See also*, Karen Musalo, *Protecting Victims of Gendered Persecution: Fear of Floodgates or Call to (Principled) Action?*, 14 VA. J. SOC. POL'Y & L. 119, 132 (2007). As the 10th Circuit Court of Appeals has stated:

> There may be understandable concern in using gender as a group-defining characteristic. One may be reluctant to permit, for example, half a nation's residents to obtain asylum on the ground that women are persecuted there. But the focus with respect to such claims should be not on whether either gender constitutes a social group (which both certainly do) but on whether the members of that group are sufficiently likely to be persecuted that one could say that they are persecuted "on account of" their membership.
>
> Niang, 422 F.3d at 1199–200.

In addition, the canon of *ejusdem generis* should guide the interpretation of particular social group. According to that canon, courts should interpret particular social group consistently with all other similar categories enumerated in the refugee definition (i.e., race, religion, nationality, and political opinion). As noted by amici, "it makes no sense to shun gender as a qualifying characteristic because it sweeps too broadly when other categories that indisputably fit the refugee definition have the same expansive reach." AILA *et al.* amicus brief at 4–5.

Finally, an applicant for asylum faces other evidentiary, statutory, and discretionary hurdles beyond proving that she is the member of a cognizable social group. Women who are victims of domestic violence must also show that the harm they experienced rises to the level of persecution, that they were persecuted because of their gender, and that the government was unable or unwilling to provide protection. Applicants must also establish that they are deserving of asylum as a matter of discretion. These additional criteria serve as counterarguments to the floodgates concern. *See* Corrales, *supra*, at 86; AILA *et al.* amicus brief at 41.

In conclusion, I overturn *Matter of* M-E-V-G- and *Matter of* W-G-R- to the extent those decisions required particularity and social visibility in establishing a particular social group for a viable asylum claim. Rather, I find that, consistent with the Board's holding in *Matter of Acosta*, in order to establish membership in a particular social group an applicant for asylum need only show that her membership in a group is defined by an innate, immutable characteristic. Gender is one such immutable characteristic.

With respect to victims of domestic violence, I find that "women" constitutes a viable particular social group for purposes of asylum. In doing so, I overrule the PSG formulations proposed by *Matter of* A-R-C-G- and the Respondent in this case. The social group formulation in *Matter of* A-R-C-G- posed a number of problems for victims of domestic violence attempting to assert an asylum claim, including being over- and under-inclusive, complicating the application process for *pro se* applicants, and failing to reflect the diversity of sociocultural contexts that shape women's experience of domestic violence. Moreover, in finding that women *per se* can constitute a particular social group for purposes of domestic violence, I realign PSG jurisprudence with our international obligations under the Refugee Convention.

While the Department of Homeland Security cautions against the floodgates that will open upon a recognition of gender *per se* as a PSG, I find no merit to this claim. All other protected grounds of asylum pose the same floodgate concerns but have not been subjected to any limiting criteria. All applicants for asylum must meet their burden of establishing that they experienced harm rising to the level of persecution on account of one of the protected grounds. These evidentiary burdens serve as limiting factors to asylum eligibility. Accordingly, I remand this case to the Immigration Judge to determine whether the Respondent in this case established that she was a member in the particular social group of "women."

IV

Under 8 U.S.C. § 1158(b)(1)(B)(i), "To establish that the applicant is a refugee within the meaning of such section, the applicant must establish that race, religion, nationality, membership in a particular social group, or political opinion was or will be at least *one central reason* for persecuting the applicant." In the instant case, the Immigration Judge found that the Respondent failed to establish that her spouse persecuted her on account of her membership in a protected group. Instead, he found that the abuse "was related to his violent and jealous nature, and frequent intoxication from alcohol," and was "intended to intimidate and threaten her to comply his own selfish and criminal demands for sex." Immigration Judge decision at 13. This finding of the Immigration Judge was clearly in error. Domestic violence rather than an isolated criminal act, is systematically perpetrated on account of a victim's gender such that there is a nexus between the harm suffered and a protected ground.

The Respondent's experience as the victim of domestic violence at the hands of a male partner is shared by women around the world. The World Health Organization estimates that about one in three women worldwide has experienced either physical and/or sexual intimate partner violence or non-partner sexual violence in her lifetime. WHO, *Violence against Women*, http://www.who.int/news-room/fact-sheets/detail/violence-against-women. The U.S. Department of State has noted that in countries across the globe, domestic violence is a human rights problem that impacts women disproportionately.[4] In many communities, gender-based violence is considered socially acceptable and regularly underreported or unaddressed by government officials. *See generally* U.S. State Department, Human Rights Reports, https://www.state.gov/j/drl/rls/hrrpt/. By viewing the problem of domestic violence in a cross-cultural context, it becomes clear that gender is the shared characteristic that unites victims across the world. As experts have noted, "[b]eing female, in short, is the strongest risk factor for whether an individual will become a victim of partner violence." *Expert Declaration of Nancy Lemon*, filed before the Immigration Court in *Matter of A-R-C-G-*, 26 I&N Dec. 388 (BIA 2014). This, in turn, is compelling evidence that gender is a motivating factor for perpetrators of domestic violence.

Systemic subordination and oppression allow domestic violence against women to perpetuate. *See* CATHARINE MACKINNON, ARE WOMEN HUMAN (2007). Radhika Coomaraswamy, the former United Nations Special Rapporteur on Violence against Women, has noted that,

> at its most complex, domestic violence exists as a powerful tool of oppression. Violence against women in general, and domestic violence in particular, serve as essential components in societies which oppress women, since violence against women not only derives from but also sustains the dominant gender stereotypes and is used to control women in the one space traditionally dominated by women, the home.
>
> Report of the Special Rapporteur on violence against women, its causes and consequences, § 27, E/CN.4/1996/53 (Feb. 5, 1996), http://hrlibrary.umn.edu/commission/thematic52/53-wom.htm.

While women around the world share the experience of domestic violence, cultural expectations and patterns can shape the dynamics of domestic violence in specific geographical contexts. For example, in the Respondent's home country of El Salvador, high levels of domestic violence are accompanied by excessive rates of femicides, i.e. the systematic murder of women. El Instituto de Medicina Legal, registró 468 feminicidios en 2017, http://www.observatorioseguridadciudadanadelasmujeres.org/documentos/fem_2018-02-09_01.pdf. These human rights problems are juxtaposed against a cultural context in which women lack financial and political power in the public sphere and decision-making power within the home. *A Salvadoran Law to Achieve Equality between Men and Women*, UN WOMEN (Dec. 2, 2011), http://www.unwomen.org/en/news/stories/2011/12/a-salvadoran-law-to-achieve-

[4] The State Department's Gender Guidelines for Overseas Refugee Processing explicitly recognize that domestic violence is inflicted on account of gender and can form the basis for an asylum claim. *See* U.S. Department of State, Human Rights Reports for 2018, https://www.state.gov/reports/2018-country-reports-on-human-rights-practices/

equality-between-men-and-women. A community's embrace of traditional, gendered roles for men and women – particularly in the family and in marriage – can exacerbate the level of violence against women in a country or region. Moreover, religion and religious beliefs can impact a woman's ability to avail herself of divorce or leave the relationship.

When taken as a whole, the cross-cultural context supports the understanding that women's gender and consequent subordinate status in society make them more likely to be victims of domestic and intimate partner violence. Going forward, I instruct the Board and immigration courts to recognize the systemic nature of domestic violence and reject arguments that attempt to frame gender-based violence merely as characteristic of dysfunctional relationships or isolated acts of interfamilial criminal activity. A clear nexus exists between the particular social group of women and the harm of domestic violence.

In addition to the nexus issue, the Board has previously left open the important question of what type of evidence is needed for a victim of domestic violence to establish that her persecution was motivated on account of her membership in a gender-based particular social group. Nexus can be proven by direct or circumstantial evidence. *Elias-Zacarias*, 502 U.S. 478, 483–84. Direct evidence of the persecutor's motive might be statements that the perpetrator believed his partner to be his property or that he could inflict violence on the applicant with impunity. The status of women in the culture and society in question, the cultural expectation of gender performance, and proper gender roles, and the level of equality women experience in society would provide circumstantial evidence of a persecutor's motives. *See Brief for Tahirih Justice Center, The Asian Pacific Institute on Gender-Based Violence, ASISTA Immigration Assistance, and Cases de Esperanza as Amici Curiae in Support of Respondent, Matter of A-B-*.

Here, the Respondent provided both direct and circumstantial evidence to establish that she was persecuted on account of her gender. She testified that her husband sought to exert power over her and repeatedly expressed his belief that she was "his woman" who existed to serve him. *See* Supp. Decl. § 37. When the Respondent challenged gendered norms by refusing to have sex with her spouse and threatening to leave the relationship, the violence escalated. *Id.* §§ 29, 37. Moreover, the Respondent provided detailed information about the high rates of violence against women in El Salvador, the subordination of women in all areas of Salvadoran society, and the cultural acceptance of intrafamilial violence. *See* Respondent's exhibits. Together, these pieces of evidence satisfied the nexus element for asylum.

Finally, I hold that nexus can also be established if the state fails to protect a victim of persecution on account of a protected ground. For example, although an applicant for asylum may not be able to prove through direct or circumstantial evidence that her intimate partner abused her on account of her gender, she may be able to establish that the government was unable or unwilling to protect her because of her gender. As such "she may be able to establish a valid claim for refugee status: the harm visited upon her by her husband is based on the State's unwillingness to protect her for reasons of a Convention ground." *See* UNHCR, *Guidelines on International Protection*, § 21.

In this case, A-B- also established her nexus to her particular social group by introducing evidence that the police were entirely ineffective in protecting her from domestic violence *because of* her gender. She made multiple calls to police without resolution of the violence. On one occasion, she was required to hand-deliver an order of protection to her abuser. Supp. Decl. §§ 26, 28. Once in place, the police refused to enforce the order. *Id.* On another occasion, the police advised Ms. A-B- to leave the relationship because they lacked the capacity to protect her. *Id.* § 33. The actions of the police reflect a larger societal belief that domestic violence is a family matter, not a serious crime warranting law enforcement intervention. As such, this evidence also establishes that the state was unwilling to adequately protect Ms. A-B- because she was a woman in a patriarchal culture that devalues women's dignity and worth. For the foregoing reasons, the immigration judge erred when he concluded that nexus was not established.

V

The final question I certified relating to this decision is whether, and under what circumstances, an applicant can demonstrate that the government is unable or unwilling to control domestic violence inflicted by intimate partners for purposes of an application for asylum or withholding of removal. This question is especially relevant for domestic violence asylum claims because, in almost all cases, the perpetrator is a spouse, intimate partner, or family member rather than a governmental actor.

Under *Matter of Acosta*, in order to qualify for asylum, the harm must be inflicted by the government or a nonstate actor the government is unable or unwilling to control. 19 I&N Dec. at 222. Courts have routinely found that harms inflicted by private actors can constitute persecution if the applicant for asylum can establish that the government is unable or unwilling to control the private actor. *See all Brief for Immigration Law Professors as* Amici Curiae, *Matter of* A-B- (citing relevant cases). Therefore, the answer to whether a private actor can inflict persecution on account of a protected ground is a resounding "yes."

The more specific question then is under what circumstances can an applicant prove that a government is unable or unwilling to control persecution. Alternatively stated, what type of evidence will establish inability or unwillingness to control? First, courts must be willing to consider law enforcement failure to respond, a lack of law enforcement resources, corruption or impunity, and a "societal pervasiveness of the persecution" as evidence establishing a government's inability or unwillingness to control domestic violence. *See id.* at 19 (and all cases cited therein). These types of evidence will continue to be probative of a government's responsiveness to domestic violence.

However, an additional inquiry will help to illuminate whether an asylum applicant has met her burden of proving domestic violence persecution by a private actor. Decision-makers should ask whether a state has taken sufficient measures that reduce the risk of persecution to below the well-founded fear threshold. *See* Brief of Respondent in *Matter of* A-R-C-G-, 26 I&N Dec. 388; *see also* Deborah E. Anker, Law of Asylum in the United States (2011). Such a test allows applicants to present information about actual police response, but also to acknowledge that, in many cases, reaching out for government protection would be futile. Women should not be penalized or held accountable when they failed to contact law enforcement because such contact would be unlikely to reduce their risk of persecution and, in fact, may even increase the risk. *See* Elizabeth A. Schneider, Cheryl Hanna, et al., Domestic Violence and the Law: Theory and Practice (2012).

In sum, persecution committed by nonstate actors, such as perpetrators of domestic violence, can constitute the basis for a claim for asylum. An applicant for asylum need not prove government acquiescence in the harm, nor must she reach out to law enforcement if doing so would increase the risk of violence or be futile. In order to meet the evidentiary showing of "inability or unwillingness" on the part of the government to control the persecution, an applicant for asylum must only show that the government has failed to take sufficient measures to reduce the risk of persecution to below the well-founded fear threshold. On remand, I direct the Board to apply this standard to the facts of the Respondent's case.

VI

Despite the prevalence of domestic violence as a human rights violation directed primarily at women, the Board has long grappled with the issue of domestic violence as a basis for asylum. Since *Matter of R-A-* first raised significant domestic violence-related questions, the Board has struggled to establish a clear basis or issue guidance on the contours of an asylum claim based on domestic violence. While *Matter of A-R-C-G-* provided some direction to victims of domestic violence, the decision also raised more questions than answers. The Immigration Judge's decision in *Matter of A-B-* is emblematic of the confusion that remained.

I have used this decision to address four important issues related to domestic violence claims. First, with respect to whether domestic violence can rise to the level of persecution, I have held that domestic violence can be so severe that it constitutes the type of suffering and harm associated with persecution. Second, I have explicitly overruled *Matter of A-R-C-G-*, and by association *Matter of M-E-V-G- and W-G-R-*, to the extent that those decisions required social groups to be defined with particularity and social visibility. Instead, I have held that gender *per se* can constitute a particular social without further qualifiers. In the case of domestic violence, "women" can be a cognizable social group for purposes of an asylum claim.

Third, I have explored the issue of whether there is a nexus between gender and domestic violence. High rates of domestic violence are closely tied to the level of women's subordination in society, and men abuse women because they believe them to be property and because they know they can do so with impunity. Accordingly, this opinion establishes that the global phenomena of patriarchy and women's oppression is *prima facie* evidence that perpetrators of domestic violence abuse women *on account of* their gender.

Finally, I have found that gender-based violence committed at the hands of private actors can constitute persecution. The relevant inquiry is under what circumstances an applicant will be able to establish that the government was unable or unwilling to protect her. I have held that probative evidence of a government's inability or unwillingness to protect will include failure to respond, failure to meaningfully enforce the laws, a lack of law enforcement resources, and a culture of impunity for perpetrators of domestic violence. Moreover, I have instructed decision-makers to inquire into whether a state has taken sufficient measures that reduce the risk of persecution to below the well-founded fear threshold in answering the private persecutor question.

In conclusion, my hope is that today's decision provides constructive guidance to decision-makers considering claims of asylum based on domestic violence. In a world where one in three women will experience gender-based violence in her lifetime, it is imperative that decision-makers understand how our asylum regime must expand to accommodate harm particular to women and specifically those who seek safety from domestic violence within our borders. I remand this case to the BIA to apply the standards established herein to the Respondent's application for asylum.

16

Commentary on *Sessions v. Morales-Santana*

CYNTHIA GODSOE

INTRODUCTION

The *Sessions v. Morales-Santana* decision was groundbreaking in prohibiting discrimination against nonmarital fathers. Perhaps because of the highly politicized immigration context, however, the decision was somewhat retrograde in its remedy. Tracy Thomas's rewritten opinion adheres closely to the liberal feminist model of Justice Ginsburg's original, but opts for the more just remedy of leveling up in terms of access to American citizenship. It also raises questions about the interaction between legislative and judicial power, the intertwined relationships of gender and race and marriage and parenthood, as well as the complex tradeoffs between equality and justice.

These questions are particularly timely as I write this commentary in the summer of 2018. For months, President Trump's administration has engaged in a new immigration policy, separating children from their parents at the border in a largely fruitless attempt to deter people from seeking refugee status or otherwise entering the country.[1] The policy has been widely criticized as inhumane and illegal.[2] Fathers have featured in some news stories,[3] but the

[1] *See* Joanna Walters, *Judge Orders US to Reunite Families Separated at Border within 30 Days*, GUARDIAN (June 27, 2018), https://www.theguardian.com/us-news/2018/jun/27/us-immigration-must-reunite-families-separated-at-border-federal-judge-rules

[2] *See, e.g.*, Jena McGregor, *CEOs Are Calling the Separation of Children and Families at the Border "Inhumane" and "Tragic,"* WASH. POST (June 20, 2018), https://www.washingtonpost.com/news/on-leadership/wp/2018/06/20/ceos-are-calling-the-separation-of-children-and-families-at-the-border-inhumane-and-tragic/?noredirect=on&utm_term=.e7dc21f1cd26; Sasha Ingber, *Faith Leaders Oppose Trump's Immigration Policy of Separating Children from Parents*, NAT'L PUB. RADIO (June 16, 2018), https://www.npr.org/2018/06/16/620651574/faith-leaders-oppose-trumps-immigration-policy-of-separating-children-from-paren

[3] *See, e.g.*, Michelle Mark, *A Migrant Father Separated from His Wife and Child at the US-Mexico Border Had a Breakdown at a Texas Jail and Took His Own Life*, BUS. INSIDER (June 18, 2018), https://www.businessinsider.com/migrant-father-suicide-family-separation-trump-zero-

vast majority of media and public discourse has concerned mothers torn from their children, and "the horrific 'Sophie's Choice' for a mom" that this policy presents.[4] This reflects the "stickiness" of gendered stereotypes about parenthood that simultaneously make the Morales-Santana opinion so important, while also revealing how much work remains to be done.[5]

ORIGINAL OPINION

Sessions v. Morales-Santana illustrates the robust use of immigration law to shape normative views of the American family structure, with attendant gendered roles. The respondent, Luis Ramon Morales-Santana, was born in the Dominican Republic to an American father and Dominican mother, who were not married. (They married shortly after they arrived in the United States, however). Morales-Santana challenged the provisions in the Immigration and Nationality Act (INA) which govern granting U.S. citizenship from American parents to children born abroad. Unmarried couples are treated differently, and must meet a residency requirement to pass on citizenship to their foreign-born children. The statutory scheme at the time required that nonmarital fathers live in the United States for ten years prior to the child's birth, at least five of which must be when they are fourteen years or older. Mothers, in contrast, only had to reside in the United States for one year prior to a child's birth.[6] Morales-Santana's father had lived in the United States for almost ten years prior to his son's birth, missing the residency requirement by a mere twenty days.[7] Morales-Santana himself, who moved to the United States at age thirteen and had lived there "most of his life," faced deportation.[8]

tolerance-border-policy-2018-6. The government's failure to track the number of children and families means we do not know how many of the parents are men and how many women.

4 *See, e.g.*, Caitlin Dickerson, *Hundreds of Immigrant Children Have Been Taken from Parents at U.S. Border*, N.Y. TIMES (Apr. 20, 2018) (quoting an advocate who is referencing the famous novel and movie in which a Jewish woman during World War II is forced to choose which of her two children will survive). Even in early twentieth-century immigration policy, the government balked at separating mothers from their children out of concern that "much distress and possible criticism" would accrue. Kristin A. Collins, *Equality, Sovereignty, and the Family in Morales-Santana*, 131 HARV. L. REV. 170, 185 (2017).

5 *See* Cynthia Godsoe, *Marriage Equality and the "New" Maternalism*, 6 CAL. L. REV. CIRCUIT 145, 146 (2015).

6 8 U.S.C. § 1401(a)(7) (1958); 8 USC § 1409(a)–(c) (1958). American citizens married to noncitizens had a five-year waiting period for their children born abroad.

7 *Sessions*, 582 U.S. at 1. Congress amended the statutory scheme during the pendency of the case to impose a five-year residency period on unwed fathers, maintaining the one-year exception for unwed mothers.

8 *Id.* at 4.

Authored by Justice Ginsburg, the opinion reflects her rights-based approach to sex-based equal protection and breaks new ground by recognizing the longstanding discrimination against a largely overlooked group – nonmarital fathers.[9] Ginsburg began the opinion by noting that the INA provisions at issue "date from an era [1958] when the law books of our Nation were rife with overbroad generalizations about the way men and women are."[10] The distinction between unwed fathers and mothers was based on outdated views of marriage as a patriarchal institution and single or unwed parenthood as solely the province of women. Immigration law perpetuated these stereotypes by according only husbands the power to pass citizenship to a spouse or child, and, for children born outside of marriage, positing the mother as "the child's natural and sole guardian" and the unwed father as "car[ing] little about, indeed [a] stranger to" his child.[11] Section 1409 was intended to ensure that foreign-born children would be sufficiently Americanized to become U.S. citizens; American mothers as the primary caregivers would "counteract the influence of the alien parent," while unwed fathers were unlikely to do so because they "would care little about, and have scant contact with, their nonmarital children."[12] Accordingly, a lengthy residency requirement was necessary to weed out those (presumed few) unwed fathers who were involved with their children and thus could legitimately pass on citizenship.

Ginsburg's opinion situated gender-based parenthood roles within the larger context of "overbroad generalizations about the different talents, capacities, or preferences of males and females."[13] Citing earlier cases discriminating against unwed fathers, Justice Ginsburg opined that such laws not only "disserve men who exercise responsibility for raising their children" but also perpetuate discrimination against women based on maternalist expectations.[14] In one of the strongest parts of the opinion, Justice Ginsburg teased out the complex connection between people's lived experiences and gender stereotypes. Pointing to data that unwed fathers are increasingly involved in their children's lives, she also clarified that even gender-based legislative distinctions "with statistical support" may not survive scrutiny if the categorizations

9 *See, e.g.*, Cary Franklin, *Biological Warfare: Constitutional Conflict over "Inherent Differences" between the Sexes*, Sup. Ct. Rev. 1, 8 (2018) (noting that "the Court has resisted [finding an equal protection violation in a case involving unmarried fathers] since the advent of sex-based equal protection law nearly half a century ago").

10 582 U.S. at 7.

11 *Id.* at 10–12, 18.

12 *Id.* at 12.

13 *Id.* at 13 (quoting *United States v. Virginia*, 518 U.S. 515, 533 (1996)).

14 *Id.* at 14.

are overly broad or could be more impartially drawn.[15] Such is the case here, given the "stunningly anachronistic" norms underlying the vastly discrepant residency requirements for unwed mothers versus fathers.[16] Accordingly, the Court found the INA provisions at issue violate the Equal Protection Clause.[17]

The Court lamented, however, that it was "not equipped to grant the relief Morales-Santana seeks," the extension of the shorter one-year residence clause to unwed fathers.[18] An equal protection violation can be remedied either by extending the benefit to all or withdrawing it from the privileged group.[19] While acknowledging the preferred remedy is to extend, or "level up," the majority concluded that they could not do so because of the legislative intent demonstrating Congressional preference for a longer residency requirement.[20] The Court supported its reasoning by noting the broad power Congress has to regulate immigration. It also remarked that a one-year rule for both female and male unwed parents would be shorter than the residency requirement for an American parent married to a foreign citizen, deeming it "irrational" to prioritize nonmarriage over marriage, and remarking that "[d]isadvantageous treatment of marital children in comparison to nonmarital children is scarcely a purpose one can sensibly attribute to Congress."[21] The Court closed the exception and applied the five-year rule of general residency to all unwed parents regardless of gender.[22]

The opinion is thus a mixed bag. Novel in its recognition of the outdated stereotypes disadvantaging nonmarital fathers, its reasoning nonetheless further entrenches, or at least does not question, the primacy of the marital family and the vulnerability of nonmarital children.[23] In doing so, it overlooks the increasing class and racial divides between the married and the unmarried. Finally, in imposing the longer waiting period, the decision denies citizenship to many children of American parents.

[15] *Id.* at 14 n. 13.

[16] *Id.* at 14.

[17] The opinion has no dissent. A short concurrence by Justice Clarence Thomas, joined by Justice Alito, states that because the Court's remedy precludes the respondent from granting relief, a ruling on the constitutionality of the INA is unnecessary. 137 S.Ct. 1678, 1701 (2017) (Thomas, J., concurring). Justice Ginsburg responds discussing the harm from systemic discrimination even where an individual litigant cannot achieve relief. 582 U.S. at 23 n. 21.

[18] 582 U.S. at 23.

[19] *Id.* at 24.

[20] *Id.* at 26.

[21] *Id.* at 26.

[22] *Id.* at 27–28.

[23] Numerous scholars, including myself, have critiqued this aspect of the Court's reasoning in *Obergefell. See, e.g.*, Melissa Murray, Obergefell v. Hodges *and Nonmarriage Inequality*, 104 CAL. L. REV. 1207 (2016); Cynthia Godsoe, *Perfect Plaintiffs*, 125 YALE L. J. FORUM 136 (2015).

THE FEMINIST JUDGMENT

Justice Tracy Thomas's rewritten majority opinion agrees with the original opinion that the INA violates equal protection by relying on gendered stereotypes about parents. It also adheres closely to Ginsburg's liberal feminist framework, although, as some scholars have recently pointed out, Ginsburg's vision of equality is nuanced and evades easy categorization.[24] Thomas likewise is concerned about structural gender inequality beyond individual rights. Moreover, Thomas adds to the original opinion with a deeper discussion of parenthood stereotypes, as well as with the ways immigration law has been informed by ethnic and racial animus to oppress particularly those with intersectional identities. Her opinion departs from the original in its proposed remedy.

LEVELING UP OR DOWN?

Thomas calls for a remedy that extends the benefit to all unmarried parents – fathers as well as mothers. Arguing that the remedy is inextricably tied to overcoming discrimination, Thomas writes that selecting the correct relief "is about the operative substantive constitutional norms that must be effectuated by an appropriate remedy." The original opinion acknowledges leveling up as the presumption. Thomas argues here for an even more robust presumption, with extremely rare exceptions "where there is an undue burden to the defendant based on important governmental interests or equitable concerns." In making this argument, Thomas draws on past race and sex equality cases, as well as international law, noting that courts within the European Court of Justice system are required to extend, rather than nullify, any benefit.

Leveling down brings both expressive and practical costs. As Thomas describes, it "dilutes the normative value of equality . . . reduc[ing it] to formal sameness, denying benefit or opportunity, and thus leaving the continued social and legal consequences of past discriminatory harm." Leveling down offers the Hobson's choice of denying the benefit to a group versus denying it to everyone, thus providing a significant disincentive for plaintiffs to bring

[24] At risk of oversimplifying, liberal feminism focuses on individual rights and treating men and women the same to achieve gender equality. *See* Martha Chamallas, Introduction to Feminist Legal Theory 17 (2d ed. 2003). Complicating the vision of Justice Ginsburg as a pure liberal feminist, *see, e.g.*, Neil S. Siegel & Reva B. Siegel, *Struck by Stereotype: Ruth Bader Ginsburg on Pregnancy Discrimination as Sex Discrimination*, 59 Duke L.J. 771, 774–75, 790 (2010) ("calling into question certain feminist characterizations of her as a proponent of formal equality" and noting her opposition to traditional sex stereotypes because their role as "part of a system of social roles and understandings that anchored women's inequality").

discrimination lawsuits. The Court noted this in the most prominent leveling-down decision before *Morales-Santana*, *Palmer v. Thompson*.[25] There, plaintiffs challenged whites-only pools run by the City of Jackson Mississippi. The Court found race discrimination, but allowed Jackson to close all its public pools, rather than open integrated pools. It did so while acknowledging the "high … price of protest" and "further animosity from [the] white community" this decision engendered.[26] Thomas points out that this risk undermines "the private attorney general policy of the civil rights statutes[,]" rendering them less effective. Thomas argues that the case at hand is not like *Palmer*, with its high costs to the government to maintain public pools, and suggests that this case is more like *Califano v. Westcott*.[27] There, the Court struck down a federal law granting welfare benefits to children of unemployed fathers but not mothers. In deciding to extend the benefits to all low-income children, the Court replaced the term "father" with the gender-neutral "parent."[28] Such a similar correction, Thomas opines, is necessary here because the same equitable considerations apply, including the need for meaningful, individualized relief for those affected. In this case, the burdens on nonmarital fathers and their children militate strongly toward a briefer residency period for immigration.

There are also, however, costs to a shorter waiting period. The government's primary stated goal is to ensure that those born abroad who become citizens have a strong connection to the United States. In this way, they preserve the valuable asset of birthright citizenship (as opposed to naturalization) for the most "worthy" and do not expend as many resources, such as public education, healthcare, and other social benefits. The government undoubtedly has both the responsibility and the power to regulate immigration. Indeed, this plenary power is so sweeping that scholars have described it as "unfettered" by judicial review[29] and a virtually "constitution-free zone."[30] Nonetheless, there are some limitations,[31] especially for birthright citizenship (even when via a parent). Moreover, as Thomas points out, courts have generally not leveled

[25] *Palmer v. Thompson*, 403 U.S. 217 (1971).

[26] *Id.* at 235.

[27] *Califano v. Westcott*, 443 U.S. 76, 92–93 (1979).

[28] *Id.* at 92–93.

[29] Susan Bibler Coutin et al., *Routine Exceptionality: The Plenary Power Doctrine, Immigrants, and the Indigenous under U.S. Law*, 4 U.C. Irvine L. Rev. 97, 106 (2011).

[30] Garrett Epps, *Testing Federal Power over Immigration*, Atlantic (Oct. 24, 2016), https://www.theatlantic.com/politics/archive/2016/10/testing-federal-power-over-immigration/505232/

[31] *See* Catherine Y. Kim, *Plenary Power in the Modern Administrative State*, 96 N.C. L. Rev. 77, 88 (2017) (noting courts' declining deference on immigration issues, as evidenced by the U.S. Supreme Court vacating an immigration decision "roughly every other year" since 2009).

down unless the legislative intent was "identifiable … [as evidenced by] express, post-decision action" by the government.

Significantly, the INA framework at issue in this case was designed in large part to exclude children and adults from certain countries and to perpetuate class-based and gendered familial structures.[32] Extending these lengthy waiting periods to even more potential citizens, now the children of nonmarital mothers as well as fathers, perpetuates the racially biased American immigration policies of the 1950s and earlier.

Scholars and advocates have noted the use of family restrictions in immigration to exclude people of certain races or ethnicities, beginning most explicitly with the Chinese, but also extending to numerous other groups. As Kristin Collins describes it, the "two vectors – gender-traditional conceptions of the parent-child relationship and racial nativism – have shaped American immigration and citizenship law" to this day.[33] The ten-year waiting period for certain families with one non-American parent was first enacted in 1940 and aimed to bar children from getting citizenship whose "national character had been shaped by a foreign husband-father," and in particular to keep out immigrants from Mexico and China.[34] This connection between gendered parental roles and fear of the racial reach of derivative citizenship has continued to drive immigration policy until now, including the different rules for nonmarital fathers and mothers at issue in this case.[35]

DIFFERING VISIONS OF EQUALITY

In arguing for leveling up, Thomas asks the bigger question of what equality means. This means looking beyond the "parallelism of equal treatment"

[32] *See* Collins, *supra* note 4. Again, this historic framework has been revitalized under the Trump administration, including a ban on all visitors from certain Muslim countries, and the President himself expressing a desire to exclude immigrants from "shithole" countries. Josh Dawsey, *Trump Derides Protections for Immigrants from "Shithole" Countries*, Wash. Post (Jan. 12, 2018), https://www.washingtonpost.com/politics/trump-attacks-protections-for-immigrants-from-shithole-countries-in-oval-office-meeting/2018/01/11/bfc0725c-f711-11e7-91af-31ac729add94_story.html?noredirect=on&utm_term=.6262eec3c96a

[33] *See* Collins, *supra* note 4, at 173.

[34] *Id.* at 187; *see also* Brief of the ACLU, NYCLU et al., as Amicus Curiae, *Lynch v. Morales-Santana*, 137 S. Ct. 1678 (2017) (No. 15-1191), https://www.aclu.org/legal-document/sessions-v-morales-santana-amicus-brief ("The most plausible explanation for the disparate residency requirements is that Congress was legislating based on stereotypical assumptions regarding maternal responsibility and paternal irresponsibility for children born outside of marriage, as well as furthering racially nativist immigration policies").

[35] Brief of Professors of History, Political Science, and Law as Amicus Curiae, *Lynch v. Morales-Santana*, 137 S. Ct. 1678 (2017) (No. 15-1191).

characteristic of liberal feminism. Thomas is particularly influenced by Deborah Brake's concept of "equal concern."[36] The broader and more flexible reading of equality that Brake and Thomas envision suggests that the law "should strive to improve the situation of the disadvantaged group rather than take away benefits from the favored group."[37] In short, leveling down is at odds with the underlying principles of equality law.

Going beyond whether to level up or down, the discussion of equality could extend to a more nuanced remedy, or even to different rules governing mothers and fathers. Historically, these provisions were driven not only by the racialized immigration policies described above, but also as part of a broader maternalist platform of the era. I have previously argued that maternalist policies can be seen as rooted in a private/public sphere ideology restricting women's (and men's) choices.[38] Another way to view the devaluation of women's caregiving, as cultural or difference feminists have, is to suggest that women *are* natural caregivers and that the problem is not this division of labor so much as society's failure to adequately value caregiving because it has been associated with the "feminine."[39] Feminist scholars, most prominently Professor Martha Fineman, have argued for refocusing family law, and state benefits to families, on caregiving – specifically in the archetypal figure of "the Mother" – and decoupling state benefits from the "sexual family" of marriage.[40]

Women's greater engagement in parenting, both by convention and as an empirical matter, coupled perhaps with their economic disadvantages, might merit special rules facilitating the transmission of citizenship to their children.[41] As one commentator described it, "it's also possible that the exception for unwed mothers was motivated by the desire to allow them to return to the U.S. more easily, perhaps on the assumption that they would need support

[36] Deborah L. Brake, *When Equality Leaves Everyone Worse Off: The Problem of Leveling Down in Equality Law*, 46 Wm. & Mary L. Rev. 513 (2004).

[37] *See* Godsoe, *supra* note 5, at 154.

[38] *Id.*

[39] *See* Robin West, Caring for Justice 4 (NYU Press, 1997) ("The failure of our political and legal institutions to *either* protect and nurture the connections [including primarily children and parents] … is reflected in and amplified by – and partly explained by … the failure of modern legal theory to consider the [female] 'connected individual'").

[40] *See generally* Martha Albertson Fineman, The Neutered Mother, the Sexual Family and Other Twentieth Century Tragedies (1995) (encouraging dependent relationships, not marriage, as the basis for state regulation).

[41] Many of the children born outside of marriage live with single mothers. In numerous Latin American and African countries, close to 40 percent of children live with mothers only and 4 percent with fathers. Joseph Chamie, *Out-of-Wedlock Births Rise Worldwide*, Yale Global Online (Mar. 16, 2017), https://yaleglobal.yale.edu/content/out-wedlock-births-rise-worldwide [https://perma.cc/KC4A-V9QV].

from U.S.-based families more than married mothers or unwed fathers."[42] Insisting on formal equality may in fact harm unmarried women and their children "in the name of making [them] equal to men."[43]

Even if it were Congress's motive to help nonmarital mothers, however, there are significant costs to further entrenching gendered caregiving roles – to men, women, and to the larger goal of gender equality. Perhaps a better place to draw the line is at marriage, rather than sex, and, counter to what Justice Ginsburg suggested, to benefit nonmarital instead of marital parents. In recent decades, an increasing number of children are born outside of marriage. This is particularly so for certain countries, including the United States (about 40 percent), and numerous Latin American countries such as Brazil, Jamaica, Mexico, and Colombia, where over 60 percent of children are born outside of marriage.[44] This is a significant change; in 1964, most of these countries had less than 10 percent of out-of-wedlock births. What has changed less is the state-accorded and economic privileges that marriage "confers". In the United States, the data is clear that unmarried parents, and by extension their children, are economically very disadvantaged compared to married parents.[45] First, marriage is increasingly limited to higher-income people.[46] Second, married parents have greater household incomes, more assets, including often owning their homes, and other financial advantages often linked to state benefits.[47] These factors are creating an intergenerational cycle wherein children born outside of marriage are at greater risk for poverty and early, nonmarital parenthood themselves.[48] This class-based marriage differential,

42 Noah Feldman, *Ginsburg's Surprisingly Retro Feminism*, Bloomberg (June 19, 2017, 3:39 PM), https://www.bloomberg.com/view/articles/2017-06-14/ginsburg-s-surprisingly-retro-feminism [https://perma.cc/8XC4-6TGC].

43 Bridget Crawford, *Is Ginsburg's Decision in* Sessions v. Morales-Santana *Good for Women?*, Feminist L. Professors Blog (June 12, 2017), http://www.feministlawprofessors.com/2017/06/is-ginsburgs-decision-in-sessions-v-morales-santana-good-for-women

44 Chamie, *supra* note 44 (using 2014 data).

45 This is true whether the children live with two unmarried parents or a single parent.

46 June Carbone & Naomi Cahn, Marriage Markets: How Inequality is Remaking the American Family (2014) (persuasively arguing that "marriage [is] a defining element in the class divide remaking America"). Anthropologist Kathryn Edin has described this dynamic of lower-income women prioritizing children before marriage in some detail. *See* Kathryn Edin & Maria Kefalas, Promises I Can Keep: Why Poor Women Put Motherhood before Marriage (U.C. Press, 1st ed. 2007).

47 Lindsey Cook, *For Richer, Not Poorer: Marriage and the Growing Class Divide*, U.S. News (Oct. 26, 2015), https://www.usnews.com/news/blogs/data-mine/2015/10/26/marriage-and-the-growing-class-divide ("Marriage has immense economic benefits that the rich continue to reap but that the poor don't accumulate in a time when income inequality already is skyrocketing").

48 *Id.* To be clear, most children raised by single parents thrive, but single-parent families do have fewer resources due to the ongoing linkage of state benefits to marriage.

compounded by the lack of a social safety net for parents, is recreating a caste system in the United States – economics doing what the now unconstitutional illegitimacy rules used to.[49]

CONCLUSION

Thomas's reimagined opinion shows that courts must not only find liability for discrimination, but must also craft the right remedy in order to give their decisions "teeth." Only in this fashion can the oppressive gender-based stereotypes, like those infusing the INA provisions at issue here, begin to be dismantled.

In the original decision, equality appears to clash with justice. Perhaps other values would best support parents – men and women, married and unmarried – to care for their children and help them thrive as productive and healthy future citizens. Dignity might do better. While dignity has played a central role in recent jurisprudence on adult intimacy,[50] it has not figured in children's rights or protection of parenting choices, particularly by low-income and unmarried people.[51] Focusing on dignity could mean a state system wherein every child and parent had access to healthcare, childcare, and reasonable access to citizenship. Indeed, more state support for families and more shared parenting are among Justice Ginsburg's wishes were she Queen: "[I would] give men encouragement and incentives to share more evenly with women the joys, responsibilities, worries, upsets and sometimes tedium of raising children . . . [and I] would make quality daycare available from infancy on."[52] This dream was perhaps curtailed in *Morales-Santana* both by Justice Ginsburg's deference to legislative intent and the rigid nature of equal protection jurisprudence. A feminist reimagining could go beyond.

49 *Levy v. Louisiana*, 391 U.S. 68 (1968) (holding that a distinction based upon illegitimacy violated the Equal Protection clause).

50 *Obergefell v. Hodges*, 576 U.S. __, 135 S.Ct. 2584, 2603 (2015) ("In addition these liberties extend to certain personal choices central to individual dignity and autonomy, including intimate choices that define personal identity and beliefs . . . The [appellants] ask for equal dignity in the eyes of the law. The Constitution grants them that right").

51 Commentators have criticized American law for providing parents with virtual ownership rights over their children. *See* Barbara Bennett Woodhouse, *Who Owns The Child? Meyer and Pierce and the Child as Property*, 33 Wm. & Mary L. Rev. 995, 997 (1992).

52 Ruth Bader Ginsburg, *Some Thoughts on the 1980's Debate over Special versus Equal Treatment of Women*, 4 L. & Inequality 143, 146 (1986).

SESSIONS v. MORALES-SANTANA, 137 S. CT. 1678 (2017)

JUSTICE THOMAS DELIVERED THE OPINION OF THE COURT

The U.S. immigration laws allow children born abroad to one American citizen parent and one foreign parent to claim derivative U.S. citizenship. Immigration and Nationality Act ("INA"), 8 U.S.C. § 1401. The law conditions such derivative citizenship on the parent's prior physical presence in the United States for a time prior to the child's birth. 8 U.S.C. § 1401(a)(7) (1958 ed.); 8 U.S.C. § 1401(g) (2012 ed.). Under the 1952 version of the Act, which was in effect when respondent Luis Ramon Morales-Santana was born in 1962 in the Dominican Republic to an unwed citizen father, the law required that his father have been present in the United States for periods of time totaling ten years prior to his birth, at least five of which were after the age of fourteen. 8 U.S.C. § 601(g) (1940 ed.). The law was subsequently changed and currently requires five years of pre-birth presence of the father, two of which must be after age fourteen. 8 U.S.C. § 1401(g) (2012 ed.). Morales-Santana's father lived in Puerto Rico, a U.S. territory, until twenty days short of his nineteenth birthday, narrowly missing the requirement of five years' physical presence after age fourteen in order to confer U.S. citizenship. However, had it been his mother, rather than his father, who was the U.S. citizen, Morales-Santana would have obtained citizenship. The citizenship law distinguished children of unwed mothers from unwed fathers, requiring the mother's U.S. presence for only a continuous period of one year prior to the birth. 8 U.S.C. § 1409(c). Thus, the law imposes more onerous criteria for unwed fathers to pass on citizenship to their children than mothers.

Respondent Luis Ramon Morales-Santana moved to the United States at age thirteen with his parents, then married, and has resided in this country most of his life.[1] Now facing deportation, he asserts U.S. citizenship at birth based on the citizenship of his biological father, Jose Morales, who accepted parental responsibility and included Morales-Santana in his household. Deportation proceedings began in 2000 based on Morales-Santana's 1995

[1] Under current law, the Child Citizenship Act of 2000, a person in Morales-Santana's position would have obtained automatic citizenship. The law provides that foreign-born children of one U.S. parent who reside in the United States prior to the age of eighteen in the legal and physical custody of that parent automatically acquire citizenship. 8 U.S.C. § 1431(a). This law, however, was not retroactive and thus did not apply to respondent here.

conviction for burglary and attempted murder under New York state law. He contested his deportation on grounds of his citizenship as "the son of an American citizen." Brief for the Petitioner at 7. An immigration judge rejected Morales-Santana's claim to citizenship derived from the U.S. citizenship of his father, and ordered Morales-Santana's removal to the Dominican Republic. After moving to reopen the proceedings, Morales-Santana then challenged his denial of citizenship under the prior presence rule on the basis of the gender discrimination against his father[2] in violation of the Fifth Amendment's guarantee of equal protection.[3]

The Second Circuit found that the citizenship law's distinction on the basis of gender was unconstitutional. *Morales-Santana v. Lynch*, 804 F.3d 520, 527–35 (2015). It remedied that discrimination by extending the benefit of the one-year rule to all unwed parents, essentially substituting the gendered statutory term "mother" with the gender-neutral term "parent." The government challenges the ruling on the merits, and further argues that in the case of invalidity, the appropriate remedy is to nullify the shorter time rule for all parents. We disagree. The constitutional right to equal protection demands more, and thus we affirm the decision below both as to right and remedy.

I GENDERED ASSUMPTIONS OF PARENTS IN IMMIGRATION LAW

History reveals what lurks behind the gender-based distinctions of the Nationality Acts of 1940 and 1952. During this era, two once habitual, but now untenable, assumptions pervaded our nation's citizenship laws and underpinned

[2] Morales-Santana has third-party standing to vindicate his father's right to equal protection of the law because of his "close relationship with the person who possess[es] the right." *Kowalski v. Tesmer*, 543 U.S. 125, 130 (2004); *Powers v. Ohio*, 499 U.S. 400, 411 (1991). Jose Morales's failure to assert a claim in his own right "stems from disability," not "disinterest," for Jose died in 1976, many years before the current controversy arose. *See Miller v. Albright*, 523 U.S. 420, 450 (1998) (O'Connor, J., concurring). Morales-Santana is thus the "obvious claimant" and the "best available proponent" of his father's right to equal protection. *See Craig v. Boren*, 429 U.S. 190, 197 (1976); *Singleton v. Wulff*, 428 U.S. 106 (1976).

[3] This case involves federal, not state, legislation, and thus the applicable equality guarantee is not the Fourteenth Amendment's explicit Equal Protection Clause, but the implicit guarantee of equality found in the Fifth Amendment's Due Process Clause. *See Weinberger v. Wiesenfeld*, 420 U.S. 636, 638 n. 2 (1975). As we held, "while the Fifth Amendment contains no equal protection clause, it does forbid discrimination that is so unjustifiable as to be violative of due process. This Court's approach to Fifth Amendment equal protection claims has always been precisely the same as to equal protection claims under the Fourteen Amendment." *Id.*

judicial and administrative rulings. First, that in marriage, the husband is dominant and the wife subordinate. And second, that the unwed mother is the natural and sole guardian of a nonmarital child.

Under the once entrenched principle of male dominance in marriage, the husband controlled both wife and child. "Dominance of the husband," this Court observed in 1915, "is an ancient principle of our jurisprudence." *Mackenzie v. Hare*, 239 U.S. 299, 311 (1915); *see generally*, Brief for Professors of History et al., as Amici Curiae, 4–15. Through the early twentieth century, a male citizen automatically conferred U.S. citizenship on his alien wife. Act of Feb. 10, 1855, ch. 71 § 2; *see Kelly v. Owen*, 7 Wall. 496, 498 (1869); CYNTHIA BREDBENNER, A NATIONALITY OF HER OWN: WOMEN, MARRIAGE, AND THE LAW OF CITIZENSHIP, 15–16, 20–21 (1998). A female citizen, however, was incapable of conferring citizenship on her husband; indeed, she was subject to expatriation if she married an alien. *Mackenzie v. Hare*, 239 U.S. 299, 311 (1915); *see* BREDBENNER, *supra*, at 58–61; LINDA KERBER, NO CONSTITUTIONAL RIGHT TO BE LADIES: WOMEN AND THE OBLIGATIONS OF CITIZENSHIP 36 (1998); Brief for Professors of History, *supra*, at 5–6. And from 1790 until 1934, the foreign-born child of a married couple gained U.S. citizenship only through the father.

For unwed parents, the father-controls tradition never held sway. Instead, the mother was regarded as the child's natural and sole guardian. At common law, the mother, and only the mother, was "bound to maintain [a nonmarital child] as its natural guardian." 2 J. KENT, COMMENTARIES ON AMERICAN LAW 215–16 (8th ed. 1854); *see Tuan Anh Nguyen v. INS*, 533 U.S. 53, 91–92 (2001) (O'Connor, J., dissenting). Because under this law of domestic relations, only unwed mothers, and not fathers, were legal custodians of an illegitimate child, in 1912, the State Department's administrative practice was to permit unwed mothers to pass citizenship to their children, despite the absence of any statutory authority for the practice. *See* Hearings on H.R. 6127 before the House Committee on Immigration and Naturalization, 76th Cong., 1st Sess., 43, 431 (1940); 39 Op. Atty. Gen. 397, 397–98 (1939); 39 Op. Atty. Gen. 290, 291 (1939); *see also* Kristin Collins, *Illegitimate Borders:* Jus Sanguinis *Citizenship and the Legal Construction of Family, Race, and Nation*, 123 YALE L.J. 2134, 2199–205 (2014).

Congress was guided by these historical patriarchal norms of gendered parenting in its legislation on nationality. Until 1940, a married citizen father whose child was born abroad transmitted his citizenship to that child if the father had resided in the United States for *any period of time* prior to the child's birth. *See Rogers v. Bellei*, 401 U.S. 815, 823–25 (1971) (discussing the Act of 1790). This was consistent with patriarchal norms of domestic relations law recognizing the father as master of the house, wife, and children.[4] These family norms descended from the English law of coverture by which the legal identity of the wife was "covered" or subsumed into the identity of her husband upon marriage. In 1934, after active campaigning by feminists, Congress granted citizen mothers, both married and unmarried, the statutory right to confer citizenship on their child born abroad if the mother satisfied the same minimal prior residency requirement applicable to citizen fathers.

However, Congress was concerned about opening the citizenship floodgates to disfavored groups, namely those of Japanese, Chinese, and Mexican heritage, and so it enacted a physical presence requirement for the first time. Collins, *supra*, at 2199. To indirectly address this concern by reducing the number of persons eligible for derivative citizenship, the 1934 Act required that children of mixed citizenship parents must reside in the United States for five years from age fourteen to eighteen in order to keep that derivative citizenship. In 1940, Congress acted again to limit derivative citizenship, adopting a physical presence requirement for parents. The 1940 Act included a provision providing that all citizen fathers, married and unmarried, and married citizen mothers could transmit citizenship to their children born abroad only after satisfying an age-calibrated ten-year physical presence requirement. But the Act provided that unmarried citizen mothers could confer citizenship with any prior physical presence, later revised in the 1952 Act to be a continuous presence of one year. The justification for Section 1409's gender-based dichotomy was the mother's role as the "natural guardian" of a nonmarital child. Collins, *supra*, at 2205. The Roosevelt administration, which proposed Section 1409, explained: "[T]he mother [of a nonmarital child] stands in the place of the father [,] ... has a right to the custody and control of such a child as against the putative father[,] ... has a right to the custody and control of such a child as against the putative father, and is bound to maintain it as its natural guardian." 1940 Hearings, at 431.

Section 1409's treatment of unwed mothers as natural guardians renders gender-based residency rules understandable at the time.[5] Fearing that a

[4] This Court has since invalidated the "ancient principle" of the husband as "head and master" of the wife and family on equal protection grounds. *See Kirchberg v. Feenstra*, 450 U.S. 455, 456 (1981).

[5] The law evolved on the presumptive legal rights of parents, beginning first with the father's sole right to legal custody and control, then in the late nineteenth century to recognize the preferred custodial rights of mothers to children of "tender years" under six, and then in the modern era to establishing joint parental rights for both mothers and fathers. D. Kelly

foreign-born child could turn out "more alien than American in character," the administration believed that a citizen parent with lengthy ties to the United States would counteract the influence of the alien parent. 1940 Hearings, at 426–27. Concern about the attachment of foreign-born children to the United States explains the treatment of unwed citizen fathers, who, according to the familiar stereotype, would care little about, and have scant contact with, their nonmarital children. For unwed citizen mothers, however, there was no need for a prolonged residency prophylactic: the alien father, who might transmit foreign ways, was presumptively out of the picture. *Id.* at 431; Collins, *supra*, at 2203 (in the "nearly uniform view" of U.S. officials, "almost invariably," the mother alone "concern[ed] herself with [a nonmarital] child").

II THE RIGHT TO EQUAL PROTECTION FOR GENDER

The constitutional right to equal protection under the Fourteenth Amendment demands that we scrutinize laws that distinguish on the basis of gender. Although caretaking practices and norms may still mirror historic norms of women's disproportionate share of childcare responsibilities, those practices cannot justify the law's imposition of gender stereotypes. As we have shown, the relevant sections on nationality date from an era when the law books of our Nation were rife with overbroad generalizations about the way men and women are. *See Hoyt v. Florida*, 368 U.S. 57, 62 (1961) (women are the "center of home and family life," therefore they can be "relieved from the civic duty of jury service"); *Bradwell v. Illinois*, 83 U.S. 130 (1873): *Muller v. Oregon*, 208 U.S. 412 (1908). State laws drawing "a sharp line between the sexes" were not only common but also considered constitutionally permissible. *Goesaert v. Cleary*, 335 U.S. 464, 466 (1948) (upholding law banning women from bartending). Today, laws of this kind are not blindly accepted, but instead are subject to review under the heightened scrutiny now required of all gender-based classifications. *United States v. Virginia*, 518 U.S. 515, 531 (1996); *Mississippi Univ. for Women v. Hogan*, 458 U.S. 718, 724 (1982); *Craig v. Boren*, 429 U.S. 190 (1976). Laws granting or denying benefits "on the basis of the sex of the qualifying parent," our post-1970 decisions affirm, differentiate on the basis of gender, and therefore attract heightened scrutiny under the Constitution's equal protection guarantee. *Califano v. Westcott*, 443

WEISBERG & SUSAN FRELICH APPLETON, MODERN FAMILY LAW 668–71 (5th ed. 2013); MICHAEL GROSSBERG, GOVERNING THE HEARTH: LAW AND THE FAMILY IN NINETEENTH-CENTURY AMERICA 234–53 (1985).

U.S. 76, 874 (1979); *accord Califano v. Goldfarb*, 430 U.S. 199, 206–207 (1977); *Weinberger v. Wiesenfeld*, 420 U.S. 636, 648–53 (1975); *Frontiero v. Richardson*, 411 U.S. 677, 688–91 (1973); *Reed v. Reed*, 404 U.S. 71, 74, 76–77 (1971).

Prescribing one rule for mothers, and another for fathers, is the same type of classification we have previously declared unconstitutional in *Reed*, *Frontiero*, *Wiesenfeld*, *Goldfarb*, and *Westcott*. The citizenship law formally differentiates, providing a five-year residence rule for unmarried fathers and a one-year rule for unwed mothers.[6] Successful defense of legislation that differentiates on the basis of gender, we have reiterated, requires an "exceedingly persuasive justification." *Virginia*, 518 U.S. at 531. Under this scrutiny, the government must show that the "classification serves important governmental objectives and that the discriminatory means employed are substantially related to the achievement of those objectives." *Virginia*, 518 U.S. at 533 (quoting *Hogan*, 458 U.S. at 724); *Nguyen*, 533 U.S. at 60 (2001). Furthermore, the government "may not rely on overbroad generalizations about the different talents, capacities, or preferences of males and females." *Virginia*, 518 U.S. at 533. Moreover, the classification must serve an important governmental interest *today*, for "in interpreting the equal protection guarantee we have recognized that new insights and societal understandings can reveal unjustified inequality . . . that once passed unnoticed and unchallenged." *Obergefell v. Hodges*, 576 U.S. ___, 135 S.Ct. 2584, 2603 (2015). Here, the government has supplied no exceedingly persuasive justification for Section 1409's gender-based and gender-biased disparity. Heightened scrutiny exposes the stereotypes at the core of this parental citizenship law which does not justify the exercise of the usual plenary power of Congress to legislate for immigration.

A

For close to a half-century, this Court has viewed with suspicion laws that rely on "overbroad generalizations about the different talents, capacities, or preferences of males and females." *Virginia*, 518 U.S. at 533; *see Wiesenfeld*, 420

[6] To the extent the law's classification might be viewed as based on marital status, rather than gender, we would still apply heightened scrutiny to the law. *Zablocki v. Redhail*, 434 U.S. 374 (1978); *Stanley v. Illinois*, 405 U.S. 645 (1972). The immigration law classifies together married fathers, unmarried fathers, and married mothers for purposes of the five-year rule, and then separately classifies unmarried mothers under the one-year rule. 8 U.S.C. § 1409(a) & (c). As such, the law distinguishes on the basis of the parent's fundamental right of marriage, and thus must be subject to strict scrutiny as it unduly burdens that right. *Zablocki*, 434 U.S. at 388.

U.S. at 643. In particular, we have recognized that if a "statutory objective is to exclude or 'protect' members of one gender" in reliance on "fixed notions concerning [that gender's] roles and abilities," the "objective itself is illegitimate." *Mississippi Univ. for Women*, 458 U.S. at 725.

In accord with this eventual understanding, the Court has held that no "important [governmental] interest" is served by laws grounded, as Section 1409 is, in the obsolescing view that "unwed fathers [are] invariably less qualified and entitled than mothers" to take responsibility for nonmarital children. *Caban v. Mohammed*, 441 U.S. 380, 382 (1979). Overbroad generalizations of that order, the Court has come to comprehend, have a constraining impact, descriptive though they may be of the way many people still order their lives. Thus, and as explained in further detail below, we struck down in *Califano v. Westcott* a federal welfare benefits law that provided benefits to needy children of unemployed fathers, but not mothers. 443 U.S. 76 (1979). We unanimously held that the statute was an unconstitutional gender distinction based on a "baggage of sexual stereotypes" presuming the father was the primary breadwinner while the mother was "the center of home and family life." *Id.* at 89. Even if stereotypes frozen into legislation have "statistical support," our decisions reject measures that classify unnecessarily and over broadly by gender when more accurate and impartial lines can be drawn. *J.E.B. v. Alabama ex rel. T.B.*, 511 U.S. 127, 139 n. 11 (1994); *Department of Water and Power v. Manhart*, 435 U.S. 702 (1978); *see Craig v. Boren*, 429 U.S. 190, 198–99 (1976); *Weinberger v. Wiesenfeld*, 420 U.S. 636, 645 (1975).[7] Laws according or denying benefits in reliance on "[s]tereotypes about women's domestic roles," the Court has observed, may "creat[e] a self-fulfilling cycle of discrimination that force[s] women to continue to assume the role of primary family caregiver." *Nevada Dep't of Human Resources v. Hibbs*, 538 U.S. 721, 736 (2003). Correspondingly, such laws may disserve men who exercise responsibility for raising their children. *Id.* In light of the equal protection jurisprudence this Court has developed since 1971, Section 1409's discrete duration-of-residence requirements for unwed mothers and fathers who have accepted parental responsibility is stunningly anachronistic.

7 In fact, unwed fathers assume responsibility for their children in numbers already large and notably increasing. *See* Brief for Population and Family Scholars as Amici Curiae 3, 5–13 (documenting that nonmarital fathers are often in a parental role at the time of their child's birth and "most . . . formally acknowledge their paternity" at the hospital just after the child is born); Brief for American Civil Liberties Union et al. as Amici Curiae 22 (observing that in 2015 "fathers made up 16 percent of single parents with minor children in the United States").

B

Despite this Court's consistent rejection for the past fifty years of laws that differentiate based on gender, the gendered laws of immigration and nationality have proven largely resistant to constitutional challenge. The Court has decided cases that might suggest that the broad legislative power to address immigration and nationalization subsumes all other constitutional guarantees. To the contrary, this legislative authority, like all powers, is subject to constitutional commands including the nondiscrimination mandate of equal protection. When "what is challenged ... is whether Congress has chosen a constitutionally permissible means of implementing that power," this Court has recognized its "duty ... of which it may not shrink, to give full effect to the provisions of the Constitution." *INS v. Chadha*, 462 U.S. 919, 940–41 (1983). Yet in four prior cases we were faced with provisions of the immigration and citizenship laws that distinguish citizenship requirements on the basis of the gender of the parent, but we did not invalidate the formal sex classifications in those laws. *Fiallo v. Bell*, 430 U.S. 787 (1977) (upholding special immigration preference to alien children of unwed mothers); *Nguyen*, 533 U.S. 53 (2001) (upholding different standard of proof of legal paternity for unwed fathers); *Miller v. Albright*, 523 U.S. 420 (1998) (fractured opinion upholding different standard of legal paternity for unwed fathers); *Flores-Villar v. United States*, 564 U.S. 210 (2011) (affirming without opinion by divided 4-4 vote). These laws, however, must be "viewed not in isolation, but in the context of our Nation's long and unfortunate history of sex discrimination." *Nguyen*, 533 U.S. at 53 (O'Connor, J., dissenting). Today, we clarify that such gendered assumptions about parents no longer have any place in our immigration laws.

In *Fiallo v. Bell*, 430 U.S. 787 (1977), we neglected to apply heightened scrutiny to a gendered special preference for entry into the United States, concluding incorrectly that rational basis scrutiny was warranted because of the vast legislative power of Congress over admission or exclusion of aliens. However, it is a basic tenet of federalism that the power of the legislative branch is subject to the constitutional parameters enforced by the judicial branch. Thus, such legislative power is still subject to the constitutional commands of equal protection and must be appropriately scrutinized. In three subsequent cases addressing gendered distinctions in the laws of citizenship, rather than immigration entry, we declined to apply that rational basis standard and instead applied heightened scrutiny. *See Miller v. Albright*, 523 U.S. 420 (1998) (split opinion); *Nguyen v. INS*, 533 U.S. 53 (2011); *Flores-Villar v. United States*, 564 U.S. 210 (2011) (split opinion 4-4).

However, in *Miller*, *Nguyen*, and *Flores-Villar*, a majority of the Court did not appreciate the gender bias of the differential treatment of unwed fathers in the immigration context, which now calls into question the continued validity of those decisions. Instead, the Court accepted explanations for the gendered distinctions based on assumptions about parenting. The provision challenged in *Miller* and *Nguyen* requires unwed U.S. citizen fathers, but not mothers, to formally acknowledge parenthood of their foreign-born children in order to transmit their U.S. citizenship to those children. *See* 8 U.S.C. § 1409(a)(4) (father must formally establish legal paternity by legitimation, legal acknowledgement, or adjudication while the child is under the age of eighteen). After *Miller* produced no opinion for the Court, the Court took up the issue anew in *Nguyen*. There, the Court held that imposing a paternal acknowledgement requirement on fathers was a justifiable and easily met means of ensuring the existence of a biological parent-child relationship, which the mother establishes by giving birth. *Nguyen*, 533 U.S. at 62–63. It accepted traditional stereotypes of the "biological inevitability" of maternal care and the mother's superior "opportunity for a meaningful relationship" due to "event of birth," even where the facts belied this assumption because the mother had abandoned the child at birth and the biological father had raised the child from an early age. *Nguyen*, 533 U.S. at 65.

As we have shown, such maternalist assumptions derive from patriarchal notions of women's sole role as nurturer and are based on overbroad generalizations about parenting. As the Court of Appeals observed in this case, a man needs no more time in the United States than a woman "in order to have assimilated citizenship-related values to transmit to [his] child." *Morales-Santana*, 804 F.3d at 531. Moreover, unlike *Nguyen*'s parental-acknowledgement requirement, Section 1409(a)'s age-calibrated physical presence requirements cannot fairly be described as "minimal." 533 U.S. at 70. They are not mere administrative requirements of documentation, but rather substantive requirements of lengthy residency with implications for the father's residence, employment, and family connections. Thus, regardless of the merits and outcome of *Nguyen*, which may be suspect in light of our decision today, articulated understanding of gender bias and patriarchal assumptions of unwed fathers, its conclusions are not applicable here where there is substantial burden on the unwed father.

C

Notwithstanding Section 1409's provenance in traditional and stereotypical notions of women's maternal nature, the government asserts that the statute serves two important objectives: (1) ensuring a sufficient connection between citizen children and the United States, and (2) preventing statelessness, that is, a child's possession of no citizenship at all. It will not do to "hypothesiz[e] or invent[t]" governmental purposes for gender classifications "post hoc in response to litigation." *Virginia*, 518 U.S. at 533, 535–36. Even indulging the assumption that Congress intended Section 1409 to serve those interests, neither rationale survives heightened scrutiny.

First is the government's assertion that Section 1409's gender-based differential ensures that a child born abroad has a connection to the United States of sufficient strength to warrant conferral of citizenship at birth. The government does not contend, nor could it, that unmarried men take more time to absorb U.S. values than unmarried women do. An unwed mother, the government urges, is the child's only "legally recognized" parent at the time of childbirth. An unwed citizen father enters the scene later, as a second parent. A longer physical connection to the United States is warranted for the unwed father, the government maintains, because of the "competing national influence" of the alien mother. Congress thus aligned unmarried mothers more closely with dual married citizen parents (requiring only prior residence of any time), and aligned unmarried fathers with mixed citizen parents. *See* 8 U.S.C. § 1401(a)(3) (child born abroad to married citizen parents is citizen at birth if either parent had U.S. residence prior to the birth of the child).

Underlying this statutory design is the assumption that the alien father of a nonmarital child born abroad to a U.S. citizen mother will not accept parental responsibility. For an actual affiliation between an alien father and a nonmarital child would create the "competing national influence" that, according to the government, justifies imposing on unwed U.S. citizen fathers, but not unwed mothers, lengthy physical-presence requirements. Hardly gender neutral, that assumption conforms to the long-held view that unwed fathers care little about, and indeed are strangers to their children. Lump characterization of that kind, however, no longer passes equal protection inspection. There is no reason why unwed fathers would need more time than unwed mothers to establish their child's connection with the United States. Assumptions to the contrary, that women automatically establish this connection by giving birth or that men require time to acclimate to emotional connection to their children, are based on overbroad stereotypes of nurturing mothers and distant fathers that cannot stand. Because even if a sufficient connection is an important state interest, the gender-based means scarcely serves that end. It is overbroad by sweeping in mothers who have little connection to the United States and remain abroad after the child's birth. And it is underinclusive by omitting fathers who have lived in the United States for a lengthy time and who raise the child in this country. One cannot see in this gendered scheme the close means-end fit required to survive heightened scrutiny. *See, e.g., Wengler v. Druggists Mut. Ins. Co.*, 446 U.S. 142, 151–52 (1980); *Westcott*, 443 U.S. at 88–89.

Second, the government argues that preventing statelessness is an important governmental interest. It suggests that a child born out of wedlock abroad may be stateless if they are born inside a country that does not confer citizenship based on place of birth and neither of the parents conferred derivative citizenship. The risk, according to the government, was substantially greater for the foreign-born child of an unwed mother rather than an unwed father. But there is little reason to believe that a statelessness concern prompted the differing physical presence requirements. Nothing in the congressional hearings and reports on the 1940 and 1952 Acts refers to the problem of statelessness for children born abroad, although reducing the risk of statelessness was the express goal of other sections of the 1940 Act. The justification for Section 1409's gender-based dichotomy was not the child's plight, but rather the mother's role as the "natural guardian" of a nonmarital child.

Nor has the government shown that the risk of statelessness disproportionately applies to the children of unwed mothers. To the contrary, the risk was equal, if not greater, for unwed fathers. Experts who have studied the issue report that, at the time relevant here, in at least thirty countries, citizen mothers generally could not transmit their citizenship to nonmarital children born within the mother's country. *See* Brief for Scholars on Statelessness as Amici Curiae 13–22, A1–A15. Further, as many as forty-five countries did not permit their female citizens to assign nationality to a nonmarital child born outside the subject country with a foreign father. *Id.* at 18–21. In still other countries, they observed, there was no legislation on point, leaving the nationality of nonmarital children uncertain. *Id.* at 21–22; *see* Durward V. Sandifer, *A Comparative Study of Laws Relating to Nationality at Birth and to Loss of Nationality*, 29 AMER. J. INT'L L. 248, 256 (1935). Taking account of the foreign laws actually in force, these experts concluded, "the risk of parenting stateless children abroad was, as of [1940 and 1952], and remains today, substantial for unmarried U.S. fathers, a risk perhaps greater than that for unmarried U.S. mothers." Brief for Scholars on Statelessness as Amici Curiae, 9–10. One can hardly characterize as gender-neutral a scheme allegedly attending to the risk of statelessness for children of unwed citizen mothers, while ignoring the same if not greater risk for children of unwed citizen fathers. Indeed the United Nations' project to eliminate statelessness by 2024 concentrated on eliminating gender discrimination in citizenship and nationality laws. United Nations High Commissioner for Refugees

(UNHCR), The Campaign to End Statelessness: April 2016 Update, at 1; UNHCR, Background Note on Gender Equality, Nationality Laws and Statelessness 2016, at 1. In light of this international effort and recognition, we cannot countenance risk of statelessness as a reason to uphold, rather than strike out, differential treatment of unmarried women and men with regard to transmission of their citizenship to their children.

In sum, the government has advanced no "exceedingly persuasive" justification for Section 1409's gender-specific residency requirement. Those disparate rules, we hold, cannot withstand inspection under a Constitution that requires the government to respect the equal dignity and stature of its male and female citizens.

III THE IMPORTANCE OF MEANINGFUL RELIEF FOR GENDER DISCRIMINATION

Having found that the INA prior presence rule constitutes unconstitutional gender discrimination, we must now determine the appropriate remedy to equalize the available citizenship right consistent with equal protection. Remedies for constitutional violations operate on both general and specific levels, both structural and individual. At the broadest level, remedies serve a structural function to curtail governmental action and ensure institutional conformity with constitutional commands. *Alden v. Maine*, 527 U.S. 706 (1999); *see* Richard H. Fallon & Daniel J. Meltzer, *New Law, Non-Retroactivity, and Constitutional Remedies*, 104 HARV. L. REV. 1731, 1736 (1991). "As we have repeatedly emphasized, discrimination itself" in the different legal treatment of the sexes "perpetuat[es] archaic and stereotypic notions" incompatible with the equal treatment guarantee by the Constitution. *Heckler v. Mathews*, 465 U.S. 728 (1984). Thus, an injunctive remedy that stops the government from perpetuating the discrimination is an important aspect of responding to an equal protection violation. *Id.*

Constitutional remedies, however, must also operate on the specific level to redress the individual harm to the plaintiff. The individualized redress is a core aspect of judicially sought action, as we have held that standing for access to the courts requires a "personalized," "individualized," "particularized," and "concrete," injury that can be redressed by the court. *Lujan v. Defenders of Wildlife*, 504 U.S. 555, 557, 560 (1992). As we made clear in *United States v. Virginia*, the plaintiff's rightful position is the proper goal for an equal protection remedy. 518 U.S. 515, 547 (1996); *see also* DOUGLAS LAYCOCK, MODERN AMERICAN REMEDIES 265 (4th ed. 2010); Brief for Amici Curiae Constitutional Law, Federal Courts, Citizenship, and Remedies Scholars *1 (the fundamental remedial goal is to place the victim of the wrong, to the maximum extent possible, in the position they would have occupied but for the wrong). "A remedial decree … must closely fit the constitutional violation; it must be shaped to place persons unconstitutionally denied an opportunity or advantage in the position they would have occupied in the absence of discrimination." *Id.* This means not only that ongoing discrimination must be eliminated prospectively, but also that the remedy must "eliminate [so far as possible] the discriminatory effects of the past." *Id.* The constitutional remedy must thus provide both retrospective and prospective relief as the harm dictates. Brief of Constitutional Law and Remedies Scholars, at 12–13. Thus, in *Virginia,* we refused to accept a remedy that failed to provide individualized, retrospective relief of the specific benefit sought – admission to the Virginia Military Institute.

The structural function of constitutional remedies may be achieved here by restraining the government's ability to continue to apply a gender-differentiated physical presence rule of derivative citizenship in the future. The physical presence rule for derivative citizenship must be the same for all unmarried parents. The question becomes whether all unwed parents should be subjected to the five-year father rule, or the one-year mother rule, pending further legislative action by Congress. Our prior cases, described below, have made clear that there is a strong presumption of so-called leveling up – extending the benefit to those plaintiffs denied.[8] Dictates of equal protection and due process require that, presumptively, courts should act to extend the benefit denied to the individual plaintiff. Only in rare and exceptional circumstances would equitable concerns justify overcoming that presumption and support a withdrawal of the benefit to all.

A

Ordinarily, we have reiterated, extension rather than nullification is the proper course to remedy an equal protection violation. *Westcott,* 443 U.S. at 89. In the overwhelming majority of cases, the Court has in fact done just this, extending benefits to those statutorily denied. *See, e.g., Westcott,* 442 U.S. at 89 (unemployment benefits); *California v. Goldfarb,* 430 U.S. 199, 303–304 (1977) (survivor's benefits), *affirming,* 396 F.Supp. 308, 309 (E.D.N.Y. 1975);

[8] A similar rule governs in the European Court of Justice, consistently directing courts to extend, rather than nullify the benefit, although the legislature remains free to choose a different path. *See, e.g., The Netherlands v. FNV,* Case 71/85, ECR 1986, p. 3855, at 22 (women should enjoy same unemployment benefits as men).

Califano v. Silbowitz, 430 U.S. 924 (1977), *summarily affirming*, 397 F.Supp. 862, 871 (S.D. Fla. 1975); *Weinberger v. Wiesenfeld*, 420 U.S. 636 (1975), *affirming* 367 F. Supp. 981, 991 (N.J. 1973); *Jimenez v. Weinberger*, 417 U.S. 628, 630–31, 637–38 (1974) (disability benefits); *Department of Agriculture v. Moreno*, 413 U.S. 528, 529–30 (1973) (food stamps); *Frontiero*, 411 U.S. at 678–79 n. 2, 691 n. 25 (military spousal benefits); *United States Dep't of Agriculture v. Moreno*, 413 U.S. 528, *affirming* 345 F. Supp. 310, 315–16 (D.C. 1972).

Accordingly, in the most direct case on point, we leveled up in *Califano v. Westcott*, 443 U.S. 76 (1979). There, we struck down a federal law that provided welfare benefits to needy children when the father, but not the mother, was unemployed. *Id.* at 89. The Court agreed that the gender differential was unconstitutional gender discrimination, and then extended the welfare benefits to the children of unemployed mothers. *Id.* at 92. It rejected the government's request to rewrite the statute to apply only to "primary breadwinners" and it rejected the dissent's approach of leveling down and denying welfare benefits to all. *Id.* at 92–94. Instead, the Court essentially replaced the statutory term "father" with the gender-neutral term "parent." In *Westcott*, the Court held explicitly that extension of the benefit was the proper course in a gender-discrimination case.

To the extent dicta in a few cases forty years ago suggested otherwise, that is, that nullification and extension are equally available remedial alternatives, we clarify that extension is the preferred relief. *See Westcott*, 443 U.S. at 89 ("A court may either declare [the statute] a nullity and order that its benefits not extend to the class that the legislature intended to benefit, or it may extend the coverage of the statute to include those who are aggrieved by exclusion"); *Heckler v. Mathews*, 465 U.S. 728, 740 (1984) ("when the right invoked is that to equal treatment, the appropriate remedy is a mandate of equal treatment, a result that can be accomplished by withdrawal of benefits from the favored class as well as by extension of benefits to the excluded class"); *see also Welsh v. United States*, 398 U.S. 333, 362 (1970) (Harlan, J., concurring).

For the Constitution is not silent as to how equality is accomplished. Constitutional norms of equality and due process constrain the remedial decision, requiring a remedy that remains true to those dictates of liberty. Evan Camiker, Note, *A Norm-Based Remedial Model for Underinclusive Statutes*, 95 YALE L. J. 1185 (1986); *see also* Eric S. Fish, *Choosing Constitutional Remedies*, 63 U.C.L.A. L. REV. 322 (2016). Determining the appropriate remedy for constitutional harms is not a simple textualist exercise of reading between the statutory lines or second-guessing the legislature's intent had it known its enactment was unconstitutional. Instead, selecting constitutional remedies is about the operative substantive constitutional norms that must be effectuated by an appropriate remedy. For without an adequate remedy, legal rights become mere empty aspirations rather than operative commands. *Ex parte United States*, 257 U.S. 419, 433 (1922) (Justice Holmes stating that "[l]egal obligations that exist but cannot be enforced are ghosts that are seen in the law but are elusive to the grasp"); *see also* Tracy A. Thomas, Ubi Jus, Ibi Remedium: *The Fundamental Right to Remedy under Due Process*, 141 SAN DIEGO L. REV. 1633, 1638–39 (2004). Thus, it "is a settled and invariable principle ... that every right, when withheld, must have a remedy, and every injury its proper redress." *Marbury v. Madison*, 5 U.S. 137, 163–66 (1803) (quoting 3 WILLIAM BLACKSTONE, COMMENTARIES ON THE LAW OF ENGLAND 23 (1768)).

Accordingly, we have held that the constitutional norms of due process control the choice of remedy. The Due Process Clause and its guarantees against arbitrary denials of liberty and property require courts to award a successful plaintiff a minimally adequate remedy that provides "meaningful relief." *Reich v. Collins*, 513 U.S. 106, 109 (1994); *Harper v. Virginia Dep't of Taxation*, 509 U.S. 86, 101–102 (1993); *McKesson Corp. v. Division of Alcoholic Beverages*, 496 U.S. 18, 39 (1990). Thus, in a series of tax cases challenged under equal protection, this Court applied this due process norm to the remedial choice and required a particularized, retroactive tax refund for an unconstitutional tax. *Reich*, 513 U.S. at 108; *Harper*, 509 U.S. at 100–102; *McKesson*, 496 U.S. at 39. While the state retains flexibility in the future to choose whether to extend the discriminatory tax exemption to all or instead to nullify that benefit, it is nevertheless obligated to ensure that past discrimination is redressed with a minimally meaningful remedy. *McKesson*, 496 U.S. at 39; *Harper*, 509 U.S. at 102; *see also Grayned v. City of Rockford*, 408 U.S. 104, 107 (1972) (individual convicted of violating anti-picketing law for civil rights protest must be granted retrospective remedy extending school labor union exemption to him regardless of whether the legislature might cure the infirmity in the future by nullification of all protest exemptions); *Gebser v. Lago Vista Indep. School Dist.*, 524 U.S. 274 (1998) (courts will defer to a legislative remedy for a statutory right only as long as it provides minimally adequate relief).

In addition, the operative constitutional norm in equal protection cases of equality dictates the presumption of extension of the requested benefit. Scholars, especially feminist scholars, have explained how equality embodies much more than formal parallelism of equal treatment. *See* Deborah L. Brake, *When Equality Leaves Everyone Worse Off: The Problem of Leveling Down in Equality Law*, 46 WM. & MARY L. REV. 513 (2004). Instead, it includes a concept of "equal concern." Additionally, early American state constitutional clauses required provision of "equal benefits" of the law, focusing the right on equal extension of the benefit denied. Only leveling up furthers this constitutional norm of equality. Leveling down, to the contrary, dilutes the normative value of equality by denying the excluded benefit. Nullification reduces equality to formal sameness, denying benefit or opportunity, and thus leaving the continued social and legal consequences of past discriminatory harm. Brake, *supra*. In this way, the nullification remedy perpetuates inequality, reinforcing discriminatory biases and stereotypes and allowing discriminatory conduct to go unchecked.

Nullification of the benefit also produces significant disincentives for plaintiffs. *Palmer v. Thompson*, 403 U.S. 217, 235 (1971) (Douglas, J., dissenting). Creating a penalty or risk of litigation by denying the tangible benefit sought even to the successful plaintiff places equality plaintiffs in a double-bind. *Id.*; *see* Brake, *supra*. If they fail to sue, the discrimination continues; if they sue and win, the benefit is withdrawn, harming themselves and third parties and "engendering further animosity." *Palmer*, 403 U.S. at 235. This double-bind creates social justice incentives not to sue, and compromises the private attorney general policy of the civil rights statutes. Therefore, nullification of the requested benefit or advantage in a gender-discrimination case is presumptively disfavored.

B

The constitutional remedial presumption of extending the benefit to all, or leveling up, will rarely be overcome. As we have seen, such a presumption is critical to effectuating the constitutional norms of equality and due process. Thus, only rarely will the presumption be overcome in the exceptional case where there is an undue burden to the defendant based on important governmental interests or equitable concerns. *Westcott*, 443 U.S. at 90; *McKesson*, 496 U.S. at 44; *see also City of Los Angeles Dept. of Water and Power v. Manhart*, 435 U.S. 702, 720–23 (1978).

The government claims that the presumption is overcome here due to the legislative intent of Congress in the Immigration and Nationality Act (INA). Legislative intent maybe a relevant factor in identifying a proper remedy for an unconstitutional statute. *Califano*, 443 U.S. at 94; *Welsh v. United States*, 398 U.S. 333, 361–65 (1970) (Harlan, J., concurring); *see also Ayotte v. Planned Parenthood of Northern New Eng.*, 546 U.S. 320, 330 (2006). However, that legislative intent must be identifiable or else the Court is merely engaging in nonjudicial second-guessing of policy. Thus, cases in which we have deferred to legislative intent required express, postdecision action on the part of the government. *See Heckler v. Mathews*, 465 U.S. 728 (1984) (Congress legislated after a judicial finding to remedy an unconstitutional distinction in the Social Security law by eliminating the dual benefit for married women); *Palmer v. Thompson*, 403 U.S. 217 (1971) (following judicial decree of unconstitutionality of racially segregated swimming pools, city remedied inequality by eliminating all pools). In contrast, the evidence of intent in the INA is much more generalized: there is the typical severability clause and then a structure in which the first, general rule is the five-year rule, then followed in a subsequent provision by the one-year modification for unwed mothers. 1952 Immigration and Nationality Act § 406; 8 U.S.C. § 1409(c) & 1401(a). Neither the severability clause nor the statutory structure address the specific remedial question. More importantly, the severability clause could be read to support extension of benefit by requiring the most minimal alteration in the statute by redacting the word "mother" and replacing it with "parent," thereby extending the one-year benefit to all unwed parents. *See* Brief of Constitutional Law and Remedies Scholars, at 6–7. Accordingly, in *Califano v. Westcott*, we rejected the dissenting view that would have relied on a severability clause to deny welfare benefits to all. 443 U.S. at 94 (Powell, J., dissenting). Instead, the majority found that the notion of limited repeal through severability supported extension of benefits to all parents by replacing the statutory term father with the term parent. 443 U.S. at 92.

Moreover, legislative intent includes the policies and goals of the statute. Here, in the INA, the goal is to provide derivative citizenship to foreign-born children. Denying that right to children of unmarried mothers currently eligible for such citizenship conflicts with that clear legislative intent. *See Westcott*, 443 U.S. at 90 (nullifying welfare benefits to parents would contradict original intent of statute to provide such benefits to children). In addition, we have subjected the government's remedial intent to inquiry to verify that it does not further perpetuate discrimination. *See Palmer*, 403 U.S. at 219, 222, 224–25. Here, history and evidence suggests that Congress was motivated by racial animus against Mexican, Japanese, and Chinese people in adopting the ten-year rule for citizenship, which altered the longstanding rule since 1796 permitting derivative citizenship for any prior period of time. 1940 Hearings, 426–27; Collins, *supra*, at 2199. Such legislative intent embedded with racial animus cannot be used to support a constitutional judicial remedy.

Moreover, legislative intent is not the only consideration we have assessed in determining whether to overcome the presumption of extension of benefit for an equal protection remedy. The Court has also evaluated the equitable considerations of defendant's interests and harms to third parties in selecting the proper remedy. *Westcott*, 443 U.S. at 90. This analysis comports with our broader jurisprudence outside of the leveling down context in which such equitable considerations are relevant to balancing the proper remedial choice. The Court considers the government-defendant's interests in scrutinizing discriminatory action that burdens constitutional rights. *Virginia*, 518 U.S. 515; *Craig v. Boren*, 429 U.S. 190 (1976). We consider defendant's concerns and "special factors counseling hesitation" in deciding whether to imply remedies for constitutional harms in the *Bivens* context. *Chappell v. Wallace*, 462 U.S. 296 (1983); *Bivens v. Six Unknown Named Agents of Fed. Bureau of Narcotics*, 403 U.S. 388 (1971). And, most relevant, we routinely evaluate defendant's undue burdens from the imposition of equitable injunction relief. *eBay Inc. v. MercExchange*, L.L.C., 547 U.S. 388 (2006): *Winter v. Natural Resources Defense Council*, 555 U.S. 7 (2008). The undue hardship to the defendant outweighs the plaintiff's entitlement to injunctive relief to restore her rightful position only if the burden is disproportionately greater than the plaintiff's remedial right. *eBay*, 547 U.S. at 388; *see* TRACY A. THOMAS, DAVID I. LEVINE & DAVID JUNG, REMEDIES: PUBLIC AND PRIVATE (79–83, 6th ed. 2017). Equity thus structures the defendant's concerns as the exception, rather than determinant rule. Accordingly, this Court noted in *McKesson* that once a discriminatory law is held invalid, "the State is obligated to provide relief consistent with federal due process principles" and rarely will equitable considerations be sufficient to override the constitutional requirement of meaningful relief. 496 U.S. at 44.

Accordingly, this Court has expressly evaluated such equitable considerations in evaluating the remedial choice of extension or nullification in *Califano v. Westcott*. 443 U.S. at 90. In the sole case to directly engage with the issue presented here regarding the propriety of leveling down in a gender differential case, we held that "equitable considerations" supported the choice of leveling up by extending the welfare benefits to all unemployed parents, not just fathers. *Id*. These equitable considerations included the many children in need of such benefits and the potential hardship to these beneficiaries and other "innocent recipients" from nullification. *Id*. Beyond this, we found no need to elaborate on the "conditions under which invalidation rather than extension" exists. *Id*.

Our cases, however, have suggested the types of equitable concerns relevant to overcoming the presumption of leveling up. As in *Westcott*, "cost might prove a dispositive factor." 443 U.S. at 93; *see also Manhart*, 435 U.S. at 720–23; *Palmer v. Thompson*, 403 U.S. 217, 218 (1971). Thus, in *Heckler v. Mathews*, Congress remedied an unconstitutional gender discrimination in the Social Security law by nullifying dual spousal payments to all workers rather than extending the dual payments to men as well as women. And in *Palmer v. Thompson*, a narrow majority of the Court upheld the defendant's choice to remedy segregated swimming pools by eliminating the recreation benefit for all residents due to substantial evidence that the pools could not be operated economically. 403 U.S. at 225. However, in the context of judicial remedial choice, such costs have rarely justified nullification of the benefit. In *McKesson*, the Court rejected the defendant's contention that monetary concerns were sufficient equitable grounds to override the presumption of retrospective, individualized relief in favor of prospective uniformity only. 496 U.S. at 44. Similarly, in *Westcott*, the Court did not deviate from the remedial presumption of extension of benefits due to costs. There were undeniably potential costs from extending the unemployment benefits to all working parents rather than nullifying the benefits for all or restricting them to primary breadwinners. "The Court," it held, "is ill-equipped both to estimate the relative costs of various types of coverage, and to gauge the effect that different levels of expenditures would have upon the alleviation of human suffering." Instead, such a balance was "properly left to the democratic branches of the Government." 443 U.S. at 93.

Noneconomic burdens on the defendants' operations might also justify the rare remedial exception of leveling down. In *Winter*, the Court considered the negative impact on national security from a remedy restricting military training operations, and found that consideration sufficient alone to deny the plaintiff's requested relief. 555 U.S. at 7. Also in *American Trucking v. Smith*, concerns of retroactivity and "substantial inequitable" results which burdened the State's operations militated in favor of denying retrospective individualized relief. 496 U.S. 167, 183 (1990); *see also Wesctott*, 443 U.S. at 93 (Powell, J., dissenting) (finding that the concern about impact on other benefit programs was consideration supporting nullification). Here, the government has noted only the concern for conferring citizenship "upon untold numbers" of foreign-born children "who have never had any reason to believe they were citizens." Petitioner's Brief at 51. It does not quantify how many people this might affect and does not explain why conferring citizenship on children of U.S. citizen parents would be problematic.

Finally, harms to third parties are also relevant to the question of choosing an appropriate equitable remedy. Such harm to the public interest is part of the standard four-part test for evaluating the propriety of injunctive relief. *eBay*, 547 U.S. at 388. In *Westcott*, the potential harms to needy children by denying families unemployment benefits was a key factor in selecting the presumptive remedy of extension. 443 U.S. at 90. Nullifying all benefits in the case pending further legislative action, as recommended by the dissent in

Westcott, would have imposed hardship on 300,000 needy children Congress intended to protect. *Id.* Conversely, the absence of such harm to third parties in *Heckler* was instructive in the Court implicitly endorsing Congress's legislative choice to nullify the spousal benefit for market workers. 465 U.S. at 728.

In seeking the appropriate remedy for gender discrimination, we have applied this type of remedial calculus weighing equitable considerations in determining the proper, individualized remedy. In *City of Los Angeles Department of Water and Power v. Manhart*, 435 U.S. 702 (1978), we held that a city practice which charged women employees 15 percent more for their pension benefits because women, on average, lived longer than men, was unconstitutional. The plaintiffs sought more than prospective equal treatment of the rule, and also sought retrospective restoration of the misappropriated funds. We noted the general rule that in Title VII cases, the strong presumption is that "the injured party is to be placed, as near as may be, in the situation he would have occupied if the wrong had not been committed." *Manhart*, 435 U.S. at 719; *Albemarle Paper Co. v. Moody*, 422 U.S. 405, 418 (1975). Retrospective relief, we held, should be denied only "for reasons which, if applied generally, would not frustrate the central statutory purpose of eradicating discrimination through the economy and making persons whole for injuries suffered through past discrimination." *Manhart*, 435 U.S. at 719 (citing *Albemarle Paper*, 422 U.S. at 421). Accordingly, the Court awarded such retrospective individualized relief in a similar prior case brought by men challenging a state retirement plan that allowed women to retire five years earlier than men. Emphasizing this general presumption, the *Manhart* Court noted that "the presumption in favor of retroactive liability can seldom be overcome, but it does not make meaningless the district courts' duty to determine that such relief is appropriate." The Court went on to find, however, that the case presented the exceptional situation, where the financial costs to the private employer and the potential harm to other pension beneficiaries from diluted benefits weighed in favor of denying retrospective benefit.

Thus, the remedial question of leveling up or leveling down is also seen in the context of suits under Title VII of the Civil Rights Act of 1964 where courts have also considered undue economic and operational concerns. These cases often challenge laws prescribing terms and conditions of employment applicable to women only, such as minimum wage, premium pay, rest breaks, or lunch breaks. Most courts, perhaps mindful of the mixed motives implicated in passage of such legislation – some conceiving the laws as protecting women, others as discouraging employers from hiring women – have invalidated the provisions. In so doing, they have often taken into account the economic burdens extension of those employment benefits to men would impose on the private employers. *See, e.g.*, *Homemakers, Inc. of Los Angeles v. Division of Industrial Welfare*, 509 F.2d 20, 22–23 (9th Cir. 1974), *affirming* 356 F. Supp. 1111 (1973); *Burns v. Rohr Corp.*, 346 F. Supp. 994, 997–98 (S.D. Cal. 1972); *see also* Ruth Bader Ginsburg, *Some Thoughts on Judicial Authority to Repair Unconstitutional Legislation*, 28 CLEVE. ST. L. REV. 301, 323–24 (1979).

However, this case does not present these potential costs and burdens on third parties. The extension of citizenship to foreign-born children of unwed fathers imposes no financial costs, much less costs to private nongovernmental actors. No third parties are harmed by the grant of citizenship to the children of unwed fathers. Indeed, conversely, a harmonization of the discriminatory provisions by applying the five-year rule to all children of unwed parents directly harms those third-party foreign-born children intended to be assisted by the law. Given this impact, and in the absence of other negative equitable considerations, the usual presumption of leveling up the constitutional remedy cannot be overcome.

For all of these reasons, we conclude that the appropriate remedy in this case is to extend the one-year prior physical presence rule to unwed fathers until Congress acts to redress the gender disparity in the derivative citizenship law. This achieves structural, prospective relief by treating all unwed parents the same in the future, regardless of gender. It accomplishes individual, retrospective relief by treating this unwed father the same as an unwed mother by allowing him to similarly transmit derivative citizenship under the shorter time rule. In this way, leveling up the benefit restores the plaintiff to his rightful position in a personal, particularized, and meaningful way. For equality is more than mere lip service to formal treatment. It is a constitutional value of equal opportunity and substantively meaningful rights to equal concern for all under the law.

Index

Made in the USA
Monee, IL
13 September 2026

62976734R00252